Praise for *Landed China*

"Dillon delivers again! His detailed research and clear writing style make short work of the Chinese property market's idiosyncrasies and bureaucracy. *Landed China* is the best book in the Landed series and a must-read for anyone interested in Mainland real estate."

Stephen Chu
Founding CEO, 2011 – 2012
Hui Xian Asset Management Limited
(Manager of the Hui Xian REIT)

"Much more than a how-to guide, *Landed China* explains the history, context and drivers behind a sector that represents — directly and indirectly — a quarter of China's economy. For its clarity, useful anecdotes and sharp observations, I recommend *Landed China* not just to potential property buyers but to anybody investing or considering investing in China."

Nial Gooding, CFA
China Portfolio Manager
Eight Investment Partners

"Easy to read but packed with useful details, *Landed China* is a great reference for anyone with an interest in the Chinese real estate market. The historical and cultural background and actionable advice are especially valuable."

Victor Yeung, CFA
Managing Director, Asia Pacific Securities
LaSalle Investment Management

"*Landed China* is the perfect primer for buyers considering a home purchase in one of the world's most volatile property markets. The book brings shopping for property to life with real-world examples of what it's like for expatriates to buy in China's biggest and most exciting cities."

Alex Frew McMillan
Reuters real estate correspondent for Asia
2011 – 2012

"In *Landed China*, Christopher Dillon provides not only a crisp and succinct guide to buying property on the Mainland but also a useful summary of the development of property laws and regulations in the People's Republic. If you are thinking of purchasing a house or an apartment in China this book is indispensable."

Robert T. Grieves
Chairman & CEO
Hamilton Advisors Limited

L∆NDED
CHINA

Christopher Dillon

For the next generation of homeowners:
Alexander, Lindsey and Danielle

For more information, contact Dillon Communications Ltd., 2706 Singga Commercial Centre, 148 Connaught Road West, Hong Kong, China.

ISBN: 978-988-17147-5-6

The author and publisher have made every effort to ensure the accuracy and completeness of the information in this book but assume no responsibility for errors, inaccuracies or omissions. This book is published as a general reference and is not intended to be a substitute for professional legal, investment or tax advice. Readers should always obtain independent, professional advice before signing any legal document.

CONTENTS

Acknowledgments 7
Introduction 9

China's housing market **13**
The history of property in China 15
Market dynamics 31
Is there a bubble? 37
Demographics 41

Your new home **53**
The buying process 55
What to buy 73
Developers and development 83
Renovations 95
Risk factors 109

Finance **143**
Mortgages 145
Taxes and fees 155
Insurance 159

Cities **163**
Beijing 165
Guangzhou 181
Shanghai 199
Shenzhen 217

Resources **233**
Law 235
Useful information 247
Appendix 303

Notes 335
Index 365
About the author 379

ACKNOWLEDGMENTS

I am grateful to the following people for generously sharing their time, expertise and contacts: Stephan Bosshart, Daniel Cheng, Kitty Cheung, Mina Choi, Andy Church, Phil Davis, Janet Da Silva, Daniel Ding, Spencer Dodington, Michael Evans, Terry Finch, Jan Flohr, Adam German, Kevin Gin, Tony Gostling, Bruce Grill, Joan Gu, Peter Humphrey, Jack Jackson, Rosemarie Kriesel, Christine Lee, Dr. T. H. Lee, Alice Lei, Binke Lenhardt, Janet Leung, Lauren Li, Richard Li, Michelle Lin, Larry Lipsher, Rickie Lo, Bruce Meng, Martin Merz, Joanna Ong, Gavin Opperman, Toshi Ota, Joanna Pilarczyk, David Pitcher, Andy Rothman, Shitong Qiao, Bonnie Qiu, Paul Salo, Leo Seewald, Jennifer Shay, James Shepherd, Paul Stocker, Richard Ten, Jane Teng, Yves Therien, John Van Fleet, Song Wang, Verna Wei, Carol Wu, Marion Wu, Wen Xie, Lily Yang, Victor Yeung, William Young, Haiping Zhan, Xiang Zhou and Steffen Ongah and the team at Diseno Advertising.

Photo credits — Orange Villa: CIMIC Holdings Ltd. Author's photo: Terry Duckham / Asiapix. Ownership booklet: Andy Church. All other photos by the author.

INTRODUCTION

Landed China was written for anyone purchasing, or thinking of purchasing, property in China.

In writing *Landed*, I've left out the sales pitch. I assume that you are already interested in buying real estate in China and want practical information about the buying process, how to avoid common problems and where to find help. *Landed* includes all of that, and an explanation of China's opportunities and pitfalls.

Information asymmetry

For most people, buying real estate is a classic case of information asymmetry. You might buy one or two properties in your lifetime. When you do, you will use an agent with intimate knowledge of the local market. You will work with a lender who knows the mortgage market inside and out. And you will buy from a vendor who is aware of her property's shortcomings, including the neighbor upstairs who likes to entertain until the early hours of the morning. In short, everyone in the process knows more than you do. That puts you at a big disadvantage, especially if you are operating in a second language and with unfamiliar laws and customs. *Landed* addresses this asymmetry.

This book is also intended to help couples in which one partner is fluent in Chinese and the other is not. Often, this leaves one partner with insufficient information and places an unfair burden of translation and interpretation on the other, whose property and financial knowledge may not match his language skills.

Inside Landed

Landed opens with an overview of the Chinese property market. This section looks at the changes that have taken place since 1949, the current property bubble, the factors that drive local people to buy, and the demographic trends that will influence the market for years to come.

"Your new home" examines the process of buying a new or pre-owned home. It includes information about where and what to buy, developers and how they operate in China, how to decorate and renovate your home, and the risk factors that affect China's property market.

"Finance" explains where to find a mortgage, how insurance works and China's property tax regime.

"Cities" features chapters on China's Tier 1 cities: Beijing, Guangzhou, Shanghai and Shenzhen. Each chapter describes the factors shaping the local housing market, distinctive homes, the neighborhoods where expatriates live, and how property is bought and sold in that city. The chapters conclude with a case study about a resident or nonresident who has successfully purchased a home.

The last section, "Resources," starts with an overview of China's legal system. It includes information to help you manage everything from asbestos to zoning, and concludes with translations of a preliminary sale and purchase (S&P) agreement, an S&P agreement and a home renovation contract. Notes are included for readers who want to learn more about the topics covered in *Landed*.

A final note

Unlike most places, the Mainland's property market changes very quickly. In part, this is because China's leadership is working to deliver sustainable economic growth while preventing a large and fast-growing real estate market from overheating. These changes also reflect the nation's transition from a centrally planned economy to "socialism with Chinese characteristics."

This rapid rate of change means that *Landed* cannot be the last word on China's property market. But it will give you the background and resources to make a more informed and — I hope — more successful buying decision.

The inclusion of a company or organization in *Landed* should not be taken as a recommendation. Conversely, the omission of a company does not mean you should avoid it. Throughout the book, I use the word "home" to refer to residential dwellings, including apartments and detached houses. To avoid using "he or she" and "s/he," I alternate between male and female pronouns.

Finally, I hope you find *Landed China* helpful and look forward to including your comments and suggestions in the next edition of this book.

CHINA'S HOUSING MARKET

The history of property in China

15

Market dynamics

31

Is there a bubble?

37

Demographics

41

THE HISTORY OF PROPERTY IN CHINA

If you are thinking of buying a home on the Mainland, reading about the past can be instructive. The history of private property in China stretches back over a millennium and includes wrenching changes as well as booms and busts. These events shape attitudes toward real estate today and provide useful clues about the future.

The history of property in China can be divided into three sections: Before the establishment of the People's Republic of China in 1949; from 1949 until 1978, when China had a centrally planned economy; and the period of liberalization that began in 1978 and continues to the present day.

Before 1949

China has a long history of urban development. Cities are believed to have appeared on the North China Plain during the Shang Dynasty (1760 – 1122 BCE). By the 11th century, China had more than 3,200 cities, several of which had more than a million residents. Before the middle of the 19th century, China had more city dwellers than any other country.[1]

Early Chinese cities were primarily administrative and political centers. During the Song Dynasty (960 – 1279), China's port cities benefited from growing volumes of maritime trade. Land taxes were collected during the Han Dynasty (206 BCE – 220 CE),[2] and by the middle of the Tang Dynasty (618 – 907), cultivated land was transferable by sale or inheritance.[3]

Dian

From the Ming Dynasty (1368 – 1644), and possibly as early as the Shang Dynasty, to the Republican period (1911 – 1949), China had a system known as *dian*, where a borrower could transfer the rights to a parcel of land to a creditor as security for a loan. Dian agreements typically provided the creditor/buyer with a guaranteed usage period and stemmed from the belief that it was wrong to sell inherited land.[4] There were two forms of dian: strong and weak.

In the strong form, the right of redemption theoretically lasted forever. When the borrower/vendor died, the redemption right descended to his heirs. The redeemer had to repay only the sum the buyer had paid to the original vendor, without an adjustment for inflation or increases in land prices. Under strong dian, vendors could not waive their redemption rights, and some historians believe that the redeemer would not have had to compensate the buyer for improvements to the land.[5]

At various times, the Ming, Qing (1644 – 1911) and Republican governments relaxed the regulations surrounding dian to encourage economic growth, collect more taxes and stop the violence that often accompanied dian-related disputes. This created weak dian, which included measures allowing a vendor to sell land without redemption rights or with a limited redemption period. The 1929 Civil Code of the Republic of China, for example, set a redemption cap of 30 years from the date of the initial sale.

While dian avoided the need to sell and ultimately surrender land, it also discouraged economic development, because few buyers would improve a property with fertilizer, dikes or buildings. A sale using dian reduced the value of land to 60% – 80% of an outright sale.

Treaty ports

Local attitudes toward foreigners and the Western architecture in many Chinese cities are due, at least in part, to the treaty ports that were forcibly opened by Western powers trying to increase trade with China.

From 1760, China confined international trade to Guangzhou. Foreigners were not allowed to live in the city, except during the October – March trading season, and all business was conducted through a Chinese monopoly. European demand for tea, silk and porcelain, combined with the Chinese government's indifference to Western products, created a large trade deficit.

To correct the imbalance, the British sold opium, which was banned under local law, to Chinese customers. In 1839, the Qing court sent Lin Zexu to Guangzhou to stop the trade, which he did by destroying 20,000 chests of opium and blockading foreigners, including some who were not involved in the drug trade, in their factories.[6] The British responded by starting the Opium War, which China lost. In 1842, the two countries signed the Treaty of Nanjing, under which China ceded Hong Kong Island to the British and opened five cities — Guangzhou, Fuzhou, Ningbo, Xiamen and Shanghai — to international trade.[7] Foreigners were allowed to live in these cities, which were called treaty ports.

Shortly afterward, the French and American governments negotiated similar treaties with China. The agreements included a most-favored-nation clause, which ensured that any concession granted to one foreign power was granted to all.

In 1856, hostilities resumed and Britain seized Guangzhou. Two years later, the Treaty of Tianjin was signed, allowing foreigners to travel more freely in China and opening four new treaty ports along the Yangtze River and another six along the Pacific coast. When the Chinese government attempted to renege on the treaty, British and French troops looted the Summer Palace in Beijing. In the subsequent

Treaty of Beijing, China ceded the Kowloon Peninsula in Hong Kong to Britain and made Tianjin a treaty port.

Under the Chefoo Convention of 1876, Suzhou, Hangzhou and Chongqing were opened, as were a number of smaller ports. Many of these cities were later closed.

Shanghai became the most successful treaty port and architectural reminders of this period can be still be seen, particularly in the French Concession. However, the treaty ports and the unequal treaties that gave rise to them are reminders of an era when China was weak and dominated by foreign powers.

1949 to 1978

Before 1949, most people in China lived in privately owned homes. For the majority of the population, housing conditions were poor and overcrowding was common.

With the establishment of the People's Republic of China in 1949 and the introduction of socialism, the government took control of all assets, including housing. But this did not happen overnight. From 1949 to 1956, private housing continued to exist, but rents were controlled to prevent tenants from being exploited. In 1955, for example, more than half the people in Beijing and two-thirds of Shanghai's population lived in privately owned homes.[8]

Through the Agrarian Reform Law of 1950, 47 million hectares of farmland was confiscated from landlords and redistributed to 300 million peasants,[9] owners of small plots and landlords, all of whom now had to earn a living in the fields. This system of small-scale family farming survived until 1955, when the entire countryside was forced onto collective farms. All crops became property of the state, and anyone who resisted was branded a criminal.[10]

For many city dwellers, housing quality deteriorated during this period. The population continued to grow, stretching the available housing stock, while the central government focused on heavy industry and military production.

The Great Leap Forward (1958 – 59) was a disaster. People starved as the government built ill-conceived industrial projects, like backyard steel smelters, in an attempt to catch up with the West. Millions of people were displaced to make way for reservoirs and peasants' houses were destroyed so timber could be used as fuel.

Danwei

In the late 1950s, the central government introduced the *danwei*, or work unit, housing system. A key element in China's centrally planned economy, danwei provided employment, as well as education, healthcare and other essential services. Danwei allocated housing based on a worker's length of employment and social status.

Danwei would build entire communities, with housing adjacent to the workplace. This could be pleasant if you were a university professor, but was less enjoyable if you were assigned to a steel mill. Residents paid nominal rent, which only covered the cost of building maintenance and would later lead to housing shortages. Danwei financed housing construction from their surpluses, linking a worker's quality of life to the performance of her work unit.

By 1966, the central government had used the danwei to effectively end China's private housing market. Danwei were also a form of social control, because housing was only provided to people who were officially registered as urban residents through the *hukou* system.

There were several drawbacks to this arrangement. Work units had to provide housing, regardless of whether they had expertise in the design, construction and management of residential property, and there were few opportunities for danwei to achieve economies of scale. Corruption was not uncommon and there were inequalities, with people performing the same job in different danwei receiving varying standards of accommodations.

During this period, homes were built using standardized designs for maximum efficiency, not consumer choice, and there were few incentives for innovation. Under the slogan, "industrial production first and comfort of living second," housing blocks were built with a floor area of 32 – 34 square meters per home. These dwellings had simple doors, windows without screens and no heating or private bathrooms.

During the Cultural Revolution (1966 – 76), universities stopped taking new students, design institutes were closed and people who were considered to be intellectuals, including architects and engineers, were sent to the countryside for labor. China's heritage was diminished by the Four Olds Campaign, which aimed to rid the nation of customs, culture, habits and ideas from the past. At the end of the Cultural Revolution, there were no functioning banks or other financial institutions.[11] The number of urban centers dropped from 5,402 in 1953 to 3,600 in 1979.[12]

Landlords

Chinese investors' tendency to leave homes untenanted — and often unfinished — is rational in light of low rental yields and because it is easier to sell a vacant home. But there is also a historical context.

Under Mao Zedong, land reform started before the Communist Revolution, with a "struggle against the landlords." The landlords in question were rarely large landowners, just people who were wealthier than or resented by their neighbors. In 1947, entire families were publicly tortured and killed, including children who were called "little landlords." The Communist Party dictated that 10% of the population were landlords and in Mao: The Unknown Story, Jung Chang and Jon Halliday estimate that up to one million people were killed or driven to suicide in these campaigns.

At the end of 1947, Mao sent Kang Sheng to Shandong to conduct a second round of land reform. In one town, 120 people were beaten to death, including "landlord sympathizers." From 1950 to 1951, the reform campaign continued in parts of the country that were newly occupied by the Communists. By early 1953, the landlord class had been eliminated.[13]

During the Cultural Revolution, the vilification of China's landlords continued. The poster child for this effort was Liu Wencai (1887 – 1949), who was one of Sichuan's largest landowners and renowned for mistreating his tenant farmers. In the 1950s, Liu's mansion in Dayi County was converted into a museum, which featured a water-filled dungeon where tenants were tortured. In 1965, 114 life-size clay peasants, shown paying rent to a despotic landlord, were installed in the museum. Known as the *Rent Collection Courtyard*, the sculptures became an important piece of propaganda that was later expanded to 119 figures and replicated in Beijing.[14] Recently, Liu's reputation for cruelty has been reconsidered, and a 2012 story in *China Daily* conceded that "some historical records exaggerate the facts."[15]

1978 to the present

In the wake of the Cultural Revolution, in 1978 the central government began a series of economic reforms. A small private sector was allowed to emerge and state control over investment was relaxed. The Household Production Responsibility System was introduced, giving rural families new control over their farms.[16] Paramount leader Deng Xiaoping saw market-oriented reforms as a way to ease China's housing shortage, which had grown to one billion square meters when he came to power in 1978.

In 1980, Deng publicly proposed the reform of China's housing market. Reforms were introduced gradually, through three experiments. From

1979 to 1982, homes were sold at the cost of construction in Xian and more than 60 other cities.[17] From 1982 to 1985, four cities tried subsidized sales. Danwei employees could buy homes by paying one-third of the purchase price, with a third paid by their work unit and the balance paid by the municipal government. From 1986 to 1988, the government began selling homes at cost again, this time while raising rents to make home ownership more attractive. In 1988, this program was expanded across China.

Using the lessons learned in these experiments, in 1988 the central government introduced the National Housing Reform Plan, which articulated a policy of decreasing the state's role in the provision of housing, increasing rents and encouraging home ownership. The same year, the State Council issued the Implementation Plan for a Gradual Housing System Reform in Cities and Towns, which began the sale of public housing.[18] The plan prioritized sales over rentals in the distribution of new homes, stated that sales prices should reflect construction and land costs without subsidies and specified a 30% minimum down payment with the balance payable over 10 – 20 years.[19]

The reform process became more firmly entrenched in 1988, when the constitution was amended to recognize the private sector and allow developers to lease public land by auction, tender or negotiation.[20] Shenzhen's civic leaders were unable to wait for the reforms to become official and, on December 1, 1987, the city held China's first land auction.[21]

The Hainan bust

In 1988, the State Council made Hainan — a collection of tropical islands between Hong Kong and Vietnam that had been under the administration of Guangdong — China's 30th province. That change set the stage for the largest real estate bust in modern Chinese history.

When Hainan split from Guangdong, it became a special economic zone (SEZ), with low taxes and regulations that allowed Chinese companies to retain their foreign currency export earnings. As an SEZ, Hainan was supposed to focus on exports, but investors quickly realized that there was more money to be made in real estate. China's army and navy, national and local state-owned enterprises, and thousands of ambitious individuals from all over China flocked to Hainan to buy property. In 1990, Kumagai Gumi (Hong Kong) took out a 70-year lease on 3,000 hectares of coastline, where the company was going to build China's first free port and an industrial park. Fueled by easy credit, home prices in Hainan's capital, Haikou, jumped from 1,400 yuan per square meter in 1991 to 7,500 yuan per square meter in 1993.[22]

The boom turned to bust in 1993, when Zhu Rongji, who was then the vice-premier of the State Council and governor of the People's Bank of China, tightened the money supply to cool an overheating economy. By 1999, the losses associated with the Hainan real estate bubble were estimated at 39 billion yuan. Hainan was left with nearly 70 million square meters of unoccupied buildings and 12 million square meters of unfinished structures.[23]

In the years that followed, Hainan regained its popularity. International hotel chains, including Hilton, Marriott and Sheraton, opened in Hainan, and plans were announced to make the island, which hosts the annual Boao Forum for Asia, a global tourist destination.

In 2010, home prices in Hainan rose 48% before falling 28% in the first 11 months of 2011.[24] Wealthy investors from other parts of China returned to Hainan, where more than 80% of home sales were to nonlocal buyers. By February 2012, nearly 90% of the homes in Hainan were vacant, and the government was threatening to introduce a tax on empty dwellings.[25]

In May 2012, developer Hainan Meiyuan Real Estate was shut down with debts of 10 billion yuan. Amid allegations of bribery, land hoarding and illegal construction, the Haikou Municipal Government reclaimed more than 50 hectares of land that were obtained illegally or had sat idle for too long. Meanwhile, in July 2012 a former government official admitted to accepting 16 million yuan in kickbacks to award construction contracts in the Hainan Yangpu Economic Development Zone.

Following Deng Xiaoping's 1992 tour of Southern China, where he made speeches calling for economic openness and welcoming foreign investment, the pace of reform accelerated. Hong Kong developers rapidly increased their presence in Guangdong. By 1995, nearly half the housing in Shenzhen was being built by Hong Kong companies.

In 1994, the central government issued the Decision on Deepening Urban Housing Reform, setting a direction for the next round of reforms. It included the creation of the Economical and Comfortable Housing program, which made public housing available to low- and middle-income families while permitting wealthy people to buy commercial dwellings.[26] The Housing Provident Fund — a compulsory savings plan based on the Singaporean model — was launched to help workers finance a home. Professional property managers were allowed to run residential complexes and banks began offering mortgages to individuals and making financing available to commercial developers.[27]

In 1998, the central government issued A Notification from the State Council on Further Deepening the Reform of the Urban Housing System and Accelerating Housing Construction, which prohibited danwei from building or buying new homes for their workers, who would receive cash subsidies instead. By breaking the link between work units and housing, the government facilitated the emergence of China's state-owned enterprises. It also made real estate an engine of economic growth and helped China weather the Asian financial crisis.

The results of the reforms were dramatic. Between 1998 and 2004, residential floor space per capita increased from 18.7 to 25.0 square meters and China's home ownership rate reached 80%.[28]

In 2004, China's constitution was amended to include the right to own private property. It was the first time since 1949 that this right was protected by law.[29]

Circulars 171 and 186

On July 12, 2006, Opinions on Regulating the Entry into and the Administration of Foreign Investment in the Real Estate Market was promulgated by six organs of the central government. Known as Circular 171, this regulation introduced a one-year minimum residency period and a one-property limit for foreign individuals buying property in China. Circular 171 also contained restrictions on property purchases by foreign companies.

On November 4, 2010, the Circular on Further Regularizing the Administration of Real Estate Purchases by Foreign Entities and Individuals was issued by the Ministry of Housing and Urban-Rural Development and the State Administration of Foreign Exchange. Circular 186 tightened the documentation requirements for foreign businesses and individuals buying property in China.[30]

For more information on the circulars, see "The buying process" chapter.

In 2007, after years of controversy the Property Rights Law of the People's Republic of China was promulgated.[31] The law, which took effect on October 1, 2007, provided a framework for individual, state and collective ownership of real property and defined the rights to ownership, usage and security.

In response to a boom that started in 2005, in 2007 the central government introduced market-cooling measures that included higher mortgage rates for buyers of multiple homes, increased equity investment requirements for development projects and more stringent conditions for bank borrowing by developers. As a result, 2008 sales volumes dropped more than 10% and volumes in Shanghai were halved from year-earlier figures. Then Lehman Brothers collapsed. The government responded with a loose monetary policy and a four trillion yuan stimulus package. In late 2008, mortgage rates for people buying a first home were discounted 30%. Sales volumes in 2009 returned to 2007 levels and prices began rising again.

Reform experiments continued in 2008, when Chongqing began issuing land tickets, called *dipiao*, to peasant farmers. Dipiao let farmers auction their homes and residential land, but not their fields, to developers, who would get the right to develop an equivalent amount of land near the city center.[32] The farmer received a city hukou as well as a cash payment, and rural land was freed up for use as farmland. The program appears to have stalled, following the fall from grace of Chongqing Communist Party chief Bo Xilai.

In early 2010, the central government intervened again. It canceled the 30% discount on mortgage interest for first-time home buyers, increased the down payment requirement to 30% for first-time buyers and to 50% for buyers of second homes. People who owned two homes were prohibited from buying additional properties and restrictions were introduced at the local level.[33]

The central government also tightened financing options for developers. This gave a major boost to state-owned enterprises, which continue to enjoy easier and cheaper access to credit. See the "Developers and development" chapter for more information.

In response, smaller builders began offering new cars and other incentives to people who bought homes. Some developers, like Poly Real Estate Group, that bought land as the market peaked in 2010, kept finished homes off the market in hopes that prices would rebound.

Others, such as Greentown China Holdings, sold commercial projects to finance their residential developments.

Local vs. central government

In July 2012, Premier Wen Jiabao emphasized the government's resolve to cool the real estate market, saying, "We must unswervingly continue to implement all manner of controls in the property market to allow prices to return to reasonable levels."[34] Wen's comments highlight an ongoing conflict between the central government — which wants social stability, an orderly market, affordable housing and a "Goldilocks" economy that is neither too hot nor too cold — and local governments that are trying to generate revenues through land sales and keep local workers employed and businesses afloat.[35] Both levels of government know they must maintain enough profitable activity to sustain the developers, whose interests are more closely aligned with the local than the central government. More than 30 local governments, including Shanghai and Nanjing, have attempted to stimulate property sales through a variety of initiatives, most of which have been quashed by the central government. In July 2012, the central government sent inspection teams to 15 provinces and municipalities, including Beijing, Shanghai and Guangdong, to ensure that its regulations were being obeyed.

Conflicting goals		
Central government	**Local government**	**Developers**
Maintain social stability	Generate revenue from land sales	Increase sales
Promote balanced, stable economic growth	Deliver economic growth (and performance-based promotions for individual cadres)	Maintain profitability
Prevent the housing market from overheating	Service government and local government financing vehicle (LGFV) debt	Clear inventory backlog
Provide social housing to low-income groups	Sell land to developers for private homes, not social housing	Build high-margin private homes, not social housing

The future

Economics, demographics and government policies suggest several long-term trends for China's housing market.

First, people will continue to migrate from the countryside to China's cities. While urbanization continues, the migrants' destination will be second- and third-tier cities in the west, as the central government works to balance growth and relieve pressure on Beijing, Guangzhou, Shanghai and Shenzhen. That migration pattern will have a major impact on everything from public transit to education and healthcare.

Demographics will play an important role. China's growing population of old people will create demand for homes for elderly and nursing facilities. At the same time, affluent, single *shengnu* women and men who are unable to find brides will drive growth in one-person homes, especially well-located properties that let owners avoid China's increasingly congested roads. As incomes increase, those homes will be larger, following a trend that saw the average living space per capita among urban residents rise from 6.7 square meters in 1978 to 28 square meters in 2008.[36] See the "Demographics" chapter for more information.

Higher energy prices will encourage the development of environmentally friendly cities. Nearly 300 Chinese cities have announced plans to become "eco-cities" and 90% of the nation's prefecture-level cities have proposed low-carbon developments.[37] The eco-city movement will also benefit from the population's growing environmental awareness, the central government's policy of promoting businesses that serve the green market and the environmental measures announced in the 12th Five Year Plan (2011 – 2015).

The property taxes that were introduced on a trial basis in Chongqing and Shanghai in 2011 will spread to other cities. In 2010, local governments financed over 80% of China's public spending but collected just 45% of the nation's tax revenues.[38] As local governments run out of land to sell, they will look to property taxes to fill this shortfall.

Finally, China's growing economic power and geopolitical influence will see new conflicts and the revival of old disputes with its neighbors.

Territorial disputes

In July 2012, the central government officially established the city of Sansha on Yongxing Island, Hainan. Home to 1,000 Chinese fishermen, a dual-use military/civilian airport and not much else, Yongxing Island occupies about two square kilometers in the South China Sea, 350 kilometers from the Chinese mainland.

Yongxing Island is part of what China calls the Xisha, Zhongsha and Nansha islands, which are also known as the Paracel Islands. Parts of this resource-rich geographical formation, and the Spratly Islands, Macclesfield Bank and Scarborough Shoal, are claimed by Vietnam, the Philippines, Malaysia, Taiwan and Brunei.

According to the Xinhua News Agency, Sansha was established to "safeguard China's sovereignty and serve marine resource development."[39] In response, Vietnam and the Philippines issued official protests and the United States expressed its concern about "an uptick in confrontational rhetoric." Some analysts believe that the nations' competing claims could escalate.

There is also a long-running dispute between China and Japan over the Diaoyu Islands — known in Japan as the Senkaku Islands — which lie south of Okinawa. The dispute inflamed nationalist sentiments in both countries, after the Japanese government agreed to purchase three of the islands from the Japanese family that owns them. The seas surrounding the islands, which are also claimed by Taiwan, are rich in fish and minerals.

China is also involved in territorial disputes with Bhutan, India, Nepal, Pakistan and South Korea.

MARKET DYNAMICS

China's history, economic development and social structure have created a distinctive mind-set among local property buyers. Understanding this dynamic will help you buy, own and sell property more successfully.

Bureaucracy

Bureaucracy in China can be intensely frustrating. Government departments and businesses inflict opaque, overly complex and irrational processes on home buyers. The default answer to the most innocuous request is usually "no," managers actively avoid making decisions and competing bureaucracies issue contradictory instructions. Often, no one is to blame for a problem or situation and thus no one is responsible.

To survive in this environment, you must be persistent, patient and flexible. It also helps to cultivate and understand the power of relationships.

Buying season

Property sales in China peak in the autumn, during what is known as "Golden September and Silver October." The weeklong holiday that starts with National Day each October 1 is a particularly popular time to buy a home.

Cash

China is a cash-oriented society. This extends to real estate, where many people buy their home with cash, or make a large down payment and take out a small mortgage. Buyers do this by choice for first homes and because of government regulations for subsequent ones.

China's largest banknote has a face value of 100 yuan, and it's not unusual to see transactions carried out with shopping bags full of cash.

China's love affair with real estate

A lack of alternative investments makes real estate attractive for domestic investors.

In 2009, for example, home prices in Beijing, Shanghai, Guangzhou and Shenzhen rose by about 50%.[1] But according to J.P. Morgan, 1,000 yuan invested in bank deposits from 2001 to 2010 would have appreciated to just 1,014 yuan on an inflation-adjusted basis.[2] Deposit rates have increased recently, as higher reserve requirements have raised demand for deposits, but they are still unattractive. The returns on life insurance policies are not much better.[3]

China's bond market is illiquid and prices do not reflect actual risk levels.[4] Chinese stocks listed on domestic markets, as well as those trading in Hong Kong and New York, have been hit by numerous scandals. And domestic investors have limited opportunities to legally invest abroad.

Chinese investors have a historical affinity for gold. However, gold does not generate income and physical gold has storage and security costs.

Wealthy people have begun investing in collectables like fine wines and artwork that have experienced bubbles of their own. China's shadow banking system, which includes trust companies and underground banks that lend at loan shark-like interest rates, is another investment option. However, the shadow banking system, which some estimates value at 17 trillion yuan, is opaque, unregulated and exposed to high-risk borrowers.[5]

In comparison, real estate is attractive. Many buyers have never experienced an extended downturn and believe that property will continue to provide capital appreciation, particularly with China's rising incomes and urbanization. Property is a tangible asset that is less vulnerable to manipulation than paper investments, such as stocks and bonds, and real estate has residual value as a source of shelter. Although property taxes have been introduced on a trial basis in Shanghai and Chongqing, the carrying cost of an apartment is modest, particularly if the interior is unfinished.

Some investors see market-cooling measures as a signal to buy, believing that prices will rise when the restrictions are discontinued and pent-up demand is released.

Empty homes

Apartments and houses bought as investments are often left untenanted and with unfinished interiors. Photos of these bare-shell homes are dramatic reminders of the imbalances in China's real estate market.

Properties are left vacant because, with some exceptions, rental yields are so low that it is not worth the aggravation of having a tenant. It is also easier to sell a home that is untenanted. And until recently, there were no property taxes, minimizing the carrying cost of an empty home.

New homes are usually sold as bare shells. If the home remains empty, the investor saves money by not decorating. Furthermore, interior decorations deteriorate over time and will likely be replaced by subsequent owners.

Feng shui

Feng shui, or Chinese geomancy, is used to design, locate and orient buildings, including homes.

In 1966, feng shui was targeted in the Four Olds Campaign, which was intended to rid China of outdated customs, culture, habits and ideas. In the intervening years, prohibitions on feng shui were relaxed. Today, it enjoys a significant following in China and elsewhere.

Good (or bad) feng shui can influence a home's price and its resale value.

Home improvements

Chinese homeowners prefer to have someone else handle renovations and improvements. U.K.–based B&Q shrank its China operations from 63 stores in 2009 to 39 in 2012.[6] America's Home Depot closed its big-box outlets in China in 2012.[7]

Short-term thinking

The rapid pace of change in Chinese society, combined with an opaque legislative process and uneven enforcement, encourages a "get it while you can" attitude and short-term thinking by suppliers and business partners. As Carson Block of Muddy Waters Research observes, "Coming from the West, where everybody grew up with two cars on the driveway and multiple televisions in the house, we don't understand what desperation for money is, and how that affects people's behavior. It means they will sell you out for a dollar today, rather than trying to make two dollars in the next three years with you."[8]

In post-1949 China, customer service was rarely a priority and the country's recent economic boom has done little to improve the situation. With long lines of customers waiting to buy their products and thin profit margins, vendors have few incentives to placate unhappy clients. This is exacerbated by frontline staff who change jobs quickly and who are often not well paid or well trained. The default reaction is often to ignore a problem in the hope that it, and the person complaining about it, will go away.

Whether it is blatant ripoffs or more subtle, long-term scams like "quality fade" (see the "Risk factors" chapter), you need to protect yourself by checking everything and assuming nothing.

Built to last?

Short-term thinking also affects construction. In Imperial China, for example, homes were built for flexibility and not durability. This allowed the house to grow to accommodate births and marriages and for the estate to be divided upon the death of the parents.[9]

From the 16th century, wood imported from Thailand, the United States and other countries was a popular building material. In an environment where labor was cheap and plentiful, and where floods, earthquakes and typhoons are common, lightweight wooden houses were practical and were often safer than stone buildings.

Unlike in Europe, where houses were expensive to construct but had relatively low maintenance costs, homes in Imperial China were built inexpensively, with the expectation that money would be spent on maintenance as the home aged.

Shanghai led the way in the modernization of China's housing market. Charlie Song's home, which was built in Hongkou in the 1890s, included a flush toilet and gas heating. By the 1920s and 1930s, ferro-concrete apartment blocks were common in Shanghai, and despite the addition of conveniences like elevators and modern kitchens, construction quality was often poor. As Frank Dikötter observes in his book *Exotic Commodities: Modern Objects and Everyday Life in China*, "The cheapest materials possible were used at all levels of society, the only exception being plasterwork, which could be used to conceal poor workmanship."[10]

Wedding bills

In the West, newlyweds typically buy their first home soon after they are married. In China, young men are expected own a home before they wed, and many women refuse to consider a potential suitor who does not own a home.

China is also facing a well-publicized gender imbalance. In 2005, 120 boys were born for every 100 girls. A growing shortage of women makes it even more important for young men to own a home. One estimate suggests that between 30% and 48% of the increase in housing prices in 35 major cities from 2003 to 2009 was due to the gender imbalance.[11] For more information see the "Demographics" chapter.

IS THERE A BUBBLE?

As this book went to press, many people were debating whether China was in the middle of a real estate bubble. The answer to that question is complex and a lot is riding on it. If you include the full spectrum of related activities, real estate accounts for up to one-quarter of China's economy, shaping demand for everything from Japanese construction equipment and Chilean copper to European furniture and Chinese cement.

The argument for a bubble...

Headlines like "Shanghai New Home Prices up 273% in 7 years"[1] make a strong case for the existence of a bubble. At one point in 2010, home prices in Beijing were 22 times higher than the average annual income, putting home ownership beyond many people's reach.[2] One survey concluded that China has 64 million empty dwellings,[3] many of them in cities like Kangbashi, Inner Mongolia, which was built to accommodate 300,000 people but houses less than 10% of that number.[4] Since 2010, the central government has implemented a range of costly and unpopular measures to cool the property market, a course that the Chinese leadership was not likely to take unless it believed that a bubble was forming.

...and the case against

As economists Carmen Reinhart and Kenneth Rogoff point out in their 2008 paper, "This Time is Different: A Panoramic View of Eight Centuries of Financial Crises," the pervasive view that 'this time is different' is precisely why it usually isn't different, and catastrophe eventually strikes again.'"[5] That said, there are parts of China's experience that — if not different — are distinctive. For example, research by CLSA indicates that in 2011, one-third of all Chinese buyers paid cash for their homes, up from 24% in 2007. Furthermore, 53% of people buying a dwelling for investment purposes paid cash.[6] In addition, there is a 30% minimum down payment for first homes, with higher minimums for subsequent purchases, and the exotic mortgages that fueled the American subprime crisis are not available in China.

There is also a strong cultural bias toward repaying debt. When property prices in parts of Hong Kong fell two-thirds after the 1997 Asian financial crisis, the mortgage default rate peaked at just 1.4%.[7]

China has an overhang of empty homes, although the size of the surplus is open to debate, with some estimates placing the number at 16.6 million.[8] A large proportion of these empty homes are held as investments because there are few other options. The inflation-adjusted returns on bank deposits and bonds are negative, China's stock markets are notoriously fickle and most people cannot invest overseas. As a result, holding empty apartments is often the "least worst" choice.

There is also strong demand from end-users, with 93% of buyers planning to live in the homes they purchase.[9] McKinsey estimates that China's cities will add some 350 million inhabitants between 2005 and 2025,[10] creating a need for 10 million new homes each year. Nearly one-third of the nation's 225 million urban households don't have a private kitchen or bathroom, so there is also demand from people upgrading their homes.[11]

Luxury homes in the nation's Tier 1 cities are undeniably expensive. But China is not a homogenous market, and a villa in a gated community in Beijing is no more representative of China than a penthouse in New York's Central Park is typical of the United States.

Finally, there is little question of China reverting to a centrally planned economy. Deng Xiaoping's doctrine of "socialism with Chinese characteristics" has been affirmed by China's new leaders,[12] and accumulated surpluses give China a significant financial cushion.

But is it the right question?

In the most dire predictions, China's property bubble bursts and causes the nation's financial system to collapse. In a worst-case scenario, the global financial system fails, too.

Like the central government, this author believes the threat of a bubble is real. But if you are an end-user who plans to live in China for the medium-to-long term and have a reasonably secure job, the patience to endure the market's turbulence and a manageable debt load, you should be fine. There's still the risk of losing your job in a global recession, a developer failing to complete a home bought off the plan or the insolvency of a local government.

Based on what psychologists call availability bias, I would be more concerned about documented — yet less dramatic — threats like air pollution than a housing bubble bursting, especially if you've done your homework and bought sensibly.

In the end, I agree with Professor Gregory M. Stein of the University of Tennessee College of Law. In his 2012 paper, "Is China's Housing Market Heading Toward a US-Style Crash?," Professor Stein concluded, "Anyone who claims to have a definitive answer to this question is overly confident."[13]

Who do you trust?

Your perception of the size and severity of China's real estate bubble will be influenced by your information sources. In any market, it is unusual to hear developers, real estate agents and industry associations say anything other than "it's a great time to buy." In February 2006, the chief economist of the National Association of Realtors, David Lereah, famously published a book entitled *Why the Real Estate Boom Will not Bust and How You Can Profit From It*, just before the U.S. market collapsed.

The central government's pronouncements are more balanced, with the country's top leadership stating its unequivocal commitment to maintaining an orderly property market. China's local governments tend to be more boosterish, lacking Beijing's concern for the bigger economic picture. However, many analysts view Chinese government statistics as unreliable and subject to politically motivated manipulation. Frequently, provincial numbers do not square with national totals.

China attracts its detractors, like Jim Chanos and Marc Faber (also known as "Dr. Doom"), who are convinced that the country is on the verge of economic collapse. It also inspires more bullish sentiments. In 1993, Morgan Stanley executive Barton Biggs was famously quoted as saying that he was "tuned in, overfed and maximum bullish" on China. Today, that view is usually held by investment banks looking for business on the Mainland.

When you read comments like these, it's important to remember that the media loves extreme, provocative statements, and that people like Chanos, Faber and Biggs are investors looking at the macroeconomic picture. The state of China's economy is undeniably important, but it should be one of many factors that you consider when making a buying decision.

DEMOGRAPHICS

The real estate industry is driven by demographics. This is particularly true in China, where rapid economic development, urbanization, the one-child policy, the *hukou* household registration system and changing social values increase the impact that demographic trends have on the housing market.

Population snapshot

In the census conducted on November 1, 2010, the population of China's 31 provinces, autonomous regions and municipalities was 1.3 billion, an increase of 5.8% from 2000.

Males represented 51.3% of the total. Females were 48.7%.

China had 401.5 million households with an average size of 3.1 persons, down from 3.4 in 2000.

People aged 0 – 14 accounted for 16.6% of the total (2000: 22.9%), those aged 15 – 59 were 70.1% (2000: 66.8%) and individuals aged over 60 represented 13.2% (2000: 10.3%). Some 8.9% of China's population was over 65 (2000: 7.0%).[1]

The one-child policy

The one-child policy (OCP) is a national population-control program that is credited with preventing 400 million births since it was introduced in 1979 – 80.[2] The OCP does not apply to everyone: There are exemptions for ethnic minorities, rural families, couples who are both only children and other groups.

Ultimately, the policy may not have been necessary. Elsewhere, family sizes have fallen as women became more educated, incomes rose, access to contraception improved and people moved from the countryside to the city. China's fertility fell from 6.1 in 1950 – 1955 to 1.8 in 1995 – 2000, well below the natural replacement rate.[3] Hong Kong, which did not participate in the OCP, saw its fertility rate drop from 4.4 to 0.4 over the same period.[4] Despite China's declining population, the OCP remains in force.

The OCP has been criticized for forcing women to undergo abortions and sterilizations. In June 2012, a couple in Zhejiang were fined a record 1.3 million yuan for having a second child. The same month, a woman in Shaanxi who did not pay a 40,000 yuan fine was forced to abort a seven-month-old fetus. Three government officials were suspended following this abortion, which received international attention.[5]

The OCP has been blamed for creating a generation of "young emperors" and "young empresses." Indulged by parents and grandparents since birth, these young people did not have siblings from whom they could learn social skills.

The one-child policy also caused what is known as the 4-2-1 problem, where a single adult child supports two parents and four grandparents. The result is that many grandparents — who in the past would have been cared for by their families — live out their days in a home for the elderly. Often these homes are in a rural area, while the child lives and works in a city.

Finally, the OCP has contributed to a growing gender imbalance. Chinese families traditionally prefer sons, who can continue the family line and contribute to its wealth when they become adults. Daughters, on the other hand, join their husband's family. Given this reality, many families choose abortion or female infanticide in the hope of later having a son. In 2010, 118 boys were born for each 100 girls. These numbers will cause problems in 2030 – 2050, when many young men will be unable to find brides.

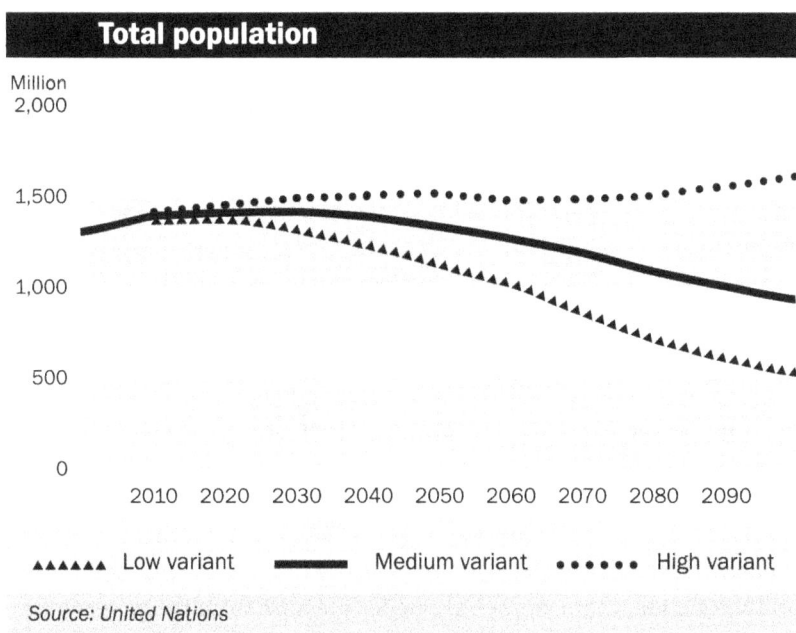

Total population

Million
2,000

1,500

1,000

500

0

2010 2020 2030 2040 2050 2060 2070 2080 2090

▲▲▲▲▲▲ Low variant   ▬▬▬ Medium variant   ●●●●●● High variant

Source: United Nations

Marriage and gender issues

As in other markets, getting married and starting a family in China is a common trigger for buying a home. China's shrinking social safety net, coupled with rising real estate prices, makes property ownership particularly important. A home is many families' largest asset.

In a 2010 survey of 32,676 Mainlanders aged 20 – 60 by the All-China Women's Federation, more than 70% of female respondents said that they would not accept a marriage proposal unless the prospective groom owned a home.[5] The same year, actress Ma Nuo sparked a national furor when she told an unemployed suitor on a reality TV show that she would "rather cry in the back of a BMW than ride a bicycle while laughing." This attitude is not uncommon.

The expectation of home ownership before marriage and the growing shortage of marriage-age women puts young men under a great deal of financial stress. It is not unusual for families to pool their funds to buy a bachelor an apartment. It has also provoked a backlash against women who are seen as gold diggers.

In August 2011, an interpretation of the Marriage Law by the Supreme People's Court changed the way that family assets are handled in divorce cases. Previously, property was divided evenly between the two parties. Now, houses and other major assets that are not explicitly registered in the names of both parties are returned to the initial owner. The court's interpretation also specified that a wife retains the sole right to decide whether to have or keep a child. However, husbands may file for a divorce on this basis.[7]

Marriage is also an issue for a group known as *shengnu* (leftover women). Over 25, single, with a university degree, money in the bank and a good job, these women are under pressure from the government, family and friends to get married. But despite China's widening gender imbalance, they are unable to find suitable mates. Shengnu are common in the Tier 1 cities that offer the best career opportunities. One estimate put the number in Beijing at over 500,000.[8]

Marriage is also a tool for people trying to buy property. Arranged marriages, where one party has money and the other has a hukou, are not uncommon. Some couples will fake a divorce to evade restrictions that treat a couple as a single entity when purchasing real estate.

Aging

China's population is aging rapidly. In the 2010 census, the country had over 119 million people over 65, and this group is expected to reach 330 million by 2050.[8] People are living longer because they are becoming wealthier and benefiting from better healthcare and nutrition.

Percentage of population 65+

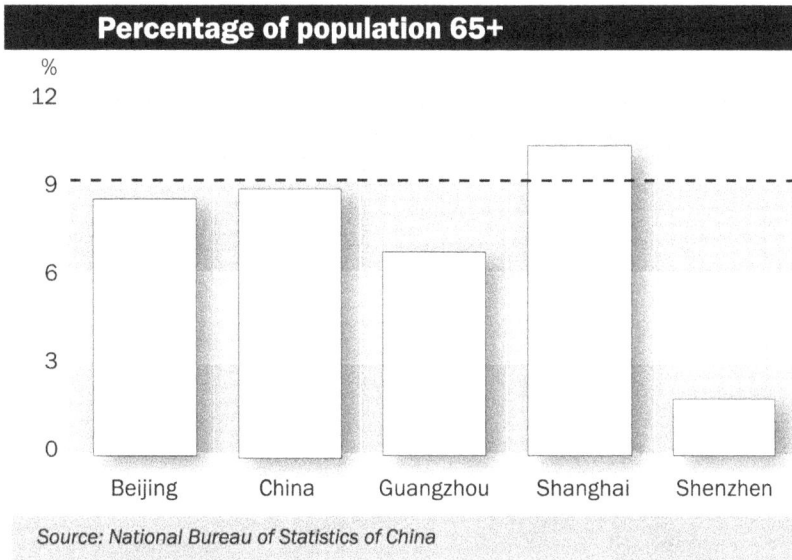

Source: National Bureau of Statistics of China

The distribution of China's elderly is not uniform. Despite its vibrant image, Shanghai has the highest proportion of over-65s among the four Tier 1 cities. Guangzhou and Shenzhen, in contrast, benefit from a steady influx of young migrants from other parts of China.

In the past, Chinese families would care for their elderly at home. But the trend toward urbanization, elderly parents living in the countryside and adult children working in the city, and smaller families makes this difficult. As a result, China faces a shortage of nursing homes. There are approximately 38,000 homes for the elderly with 2.7 million beds, enough for less than 2% of the population over 60.[10] Many facilities are of low quality, staffed by poorly trained migrant workers and lack medical facilities. According to the China Research Center on Aging, one-third of nursing homes in cities and over 40% in rural areas do not accept seniors who cannot take care of themselves.[11]

Retirement housing, which is common in the West, is rare in China, where it represents less than 0.1% of the housing stock. Reverse mortgages, which allow elderly people to use their home as security for a nonrecourse loan that is repaid when the home is sold after the borrower and his spouse die, are also rare. China CITIC Bank began offering reverse mortgages in Shenzhen in October 2011, but they have not gained widespread acceptance.[12] Elderly people also find it difficult to obtain financing to buy a home, because lenders fear they will die and default on the mortgage.

Population by age group

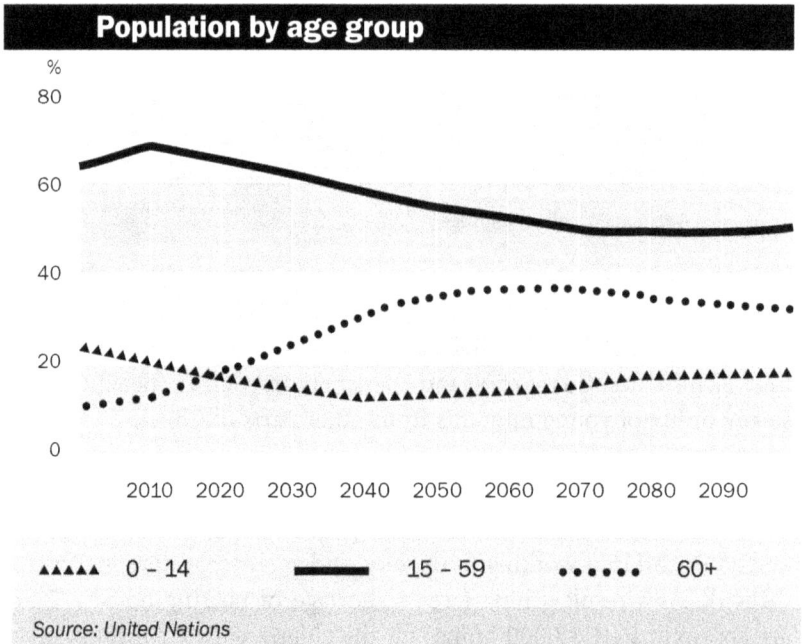

Source: United Nations

China's aging population has attracted interest from large domestic developers, such as China Vanke and China Poly Group, from Hong Kong companies like Kerry Properties and from nursing home operators from Australia and the United States. But high staffing costs, the need for additional facilities tailored to the elderly and China's looming pension shortfall can make it difficult to turn a profit.

Governments are also getting into the act. Shanghai is launching a pilot program to allow foreign investment in the elderly care sector. At the end of 2011, Shanghai had more than 600 homes for the elderly, with enough beds to accommodate just 3% of the senior population.

Urbanization

At the end of 2011 — for the first time in history — more Chinese people lived in cities than in the countryside. Management consultancy McKinsey estimates that by 2025, nearly one billion people will live in China's cities, 221 of which will have more than a million inhabitants.[13]

As members of China's emerging middle class urbanize, many trade an old home in a village for a new apartment in the city, fueling the nation's housing boom and demand for home appliances. Urbanization has also created an underclass of 160 million rural migrants who cannot become permanent residents in the cities they inhabit, limiting their economic contribution to the urbanization process.

China's 2010 census identified 221.4 million migrants (defined as people who have left the locality of their registered address for more than six months), an increase of more than 100 million from 2000.[14] Some 70% – 80%[15] of the workers in southern cities such as Shenzhen and Dongguan are migrants as are 20% – 30% of the residents of Beijing, Guangzhou and Shanghai.[16] This represents one of the largest human migrations in history, one that is running head-on into the hukou system.

♟ **The hukou system**

Introduced in 1958 to limit the movement of people between rural and urban areas, the hukou system of household registration plays a central role in Chinese people's day-to-day lives. Effectively an internal passport, the system divides households into two categories: urban and rural.

The hukou system has been relaxed since it was introduced, and it is now possible for rural people to move to cities on a temporary basis. But without an urban hukou, migrants have restricted access to social services, including education, pensions and healthcare, in their adopted city. Rural hukou holders must return to their place of registration (usually their birthplace) to register a marriage, apply for a passport and perform other official functions.

Housing is also affected by hukou status. Migrants cannot rent subsidized housing and face tough restrictions, like providing five years of tax receipts before they can buy a home in cities such as Beijing. In the late 1990s, to absorb a housing glut, Shanghai issued what were called "blue stamp hukous" to people who bought a home in the city.[17] Today, some young migrants return to their rural roots, where they can buy or build a larger home for significantly less money than in a big city and have a second child.

Parents pass their status on to their children, and an urban hukou — especially for Tier 1 cities like Beijing, Guangzhou, Shanghai or Shenzhen — is highly coveted. The black market price for a Beijing hukou was recently reported to be 270,000 yuan,[18] and people go to extreme lengths to obtain residency. In 2012, a woman who married a schizophrenic Beijing man to obtain residency rights had her marriage annulled when the court ruled that the groom was unsuitable for marriage.

It is possible to legally change from a rural to an urban hukou. The process is easiest in small cities and more difficult in medium-sized ones. It is much harder to obtain a hukou in a Tier 1 city, where the central government is actively trying to restrain population growth.

Because it denies rights to rural residents, some people have likened the hukou system to apartheid.[19] But it has provided millions of mobile, low-cost workers for China's factories. And since the migrants cannot stay in their adopted cities, China has not developed slums (although conditions in some urban villages approach this standard).

The effects of urbanization are being felt throughout the nation, as people from all walks of life move to cities in search of work, education and a better life. The central government set an urbanization goal of 51.5% in the 12th Five Year Plan (2011 − 2015), which will drive the development of everything from hospitals to sewage treatment plants. But while migrants provide the labor for China's export industries, they also create enormous demand for water, food and energy. The strain on the nation's transportation networks is especially evident during national holidays, such as the Lunar New Year, when migrants return to their hometowns.

Tier 1 cities remain prime destinations for migrants. From 2000 to 2005, Guangdong, which is home to Guangzhou and Shenzhen, was first, receiving 27% of internal migrants, Shanghai was third at 7% and Beijing was fifth with 5%.[20] To relieve the strain on these cities, the central government is encouraging decentralization and the development of the nation's interior.

Urbanization also contributes to booming demand for homes. As the Economist Intelligence Unit noted, in 2010 new residential floor space completed in China reached 1.8 billion square meters, just less than the entire housing stock of Spain.[21] To create space for these new homes, cities are growing and creating a uniquely Chinese structure, the urban village.

Urban villages

As cities expanded, neighboring rural land that was owned by village collectives was converted to urban use. The local government could convert both the village's farmland and its residential land to urban use. Or to expedite the development process, the government could convert only the farmland and leave the residential land in the hands of the village collective. These residential enclaves, which became encircled by rapidly growing cities, are known as urban villages, or *chengzhongcun*.[22]

Urban villages exist today because city governments believed it would be faster and less expensive to leave the villages alone when they acquired the farmland. However, this strategy backfired, as the value of the land in the urban villages rose along with that of the surrounding city. Ultimately, it would have been cheaper for governments to buy out the villagers at the beginning of the development process.

Urban villages are most common in southern China — Guangzhou has more than 130 — but they can also be found in Beijing, Shanghai and other cities. Individual villages house tens of thousands of people and are popular with migrant workers, who rent rooms from the villagers. In some villages, migrants outnumber villagers by a 30-to-1 ratio.

Residents of urban villages are typically younger, less educated, less likely to have an urban hukou and poorer than their peers in the adjacent city.[23] Many are first-generation migrants who are employed as laborers on construction projects and in small businesses and informal enterprises.

By providing cheap accommodations for migrant workers, an urban village supports the neighboring city's economic development. But the villages also pose problems. Structures are built using lax village construction codes and urban planning regulations are frequently ignored. Access to water, sewerage, electricity, toilets and kitchens is substandard and streets are so narrow that they are inaccessible to firetrucks.

Urban villages are frequently hotbeds of crime, including drug abuse, burglary and prostitution. For these reasons, urban villages do not make good neighbors.

YOUR NEW HOME

The buying process
55

What to buy
73

Developers and development
83

Renovations
95

Risk factors
109

THE BUYING PROCESS

Preliminaries

Start the buying process by confirming that you meet the local and national requirements for length of residency, tax payments, number of houses owned, etc. Local requirements vary by city and regulations change frequently, so ensure your information is current.

Can I buy property in China?

Foreigners' eligibility to buy property in China is limited by two circulars issued by the central government: No. 171, released on July 12, 2006, and No. 186, issued on November 4, 2010.

To buy a home, a foreign individual must have been a legal resident of China for at least one year and provide proof of residency. Working illegally while on a tourist visa and making visa runs to Hong Kong would not qualify.

Foreigners may own one home for their own use and must sign an undertaking that they don't own any other residential property in China. Foreigners are not allowed to own homes near certain government facilities, which can be a particular problem in Beijing.[1]

Foreign companies must sign an undertaking that the property is for the use of their branch or representative office in China. Foreign businesses must provide proof of incorporation.

Foreign companies and individuals buying property for other purposes, such as investment, must do so through a foreign-invested subsidiary that has been licensed to engage in the property business, also known as a foreign-invested real estate enterprise.[2]

Additional local regulations may apply. See the individual city chapters, especially Shenzen, for details.

After you have verified that you qualify, create a budget. If you are not paying cash, your overall budget will be determined by the size of your down payment. Minimum down payment requirements vary according to government policy and whether you are buying a first home or an investment property. It is prudent to buy a little less than you can afford and to assume that the current low interest rate environment will eventually end. Add 5% – 15% to the purchase price for closing costs, moving, renovations, new furniture, contingencies and other expenses.

Review real estate listings on the Internet to learn about prices in the neighborhoods that you find attractive. You will quickly discover that, for example, a new one-bedroom apartment in the city center costs the same as a 10-year-old, two-bedroom unit several subway stops away. At this point, you will need to divide your requirements — such as proximity to schools and employment, floor space and facilities like parking and swimming pools — into essential, desirable and optional.

With this information and a prioritized list of your preferences, you can create a short list of prospective neighborhoods and buildings. Learn as much about your new home and neighborhood as possible before you sign a contract. If possible, talk to residents to find out if there are problems with the neighborhood, the complex or the management company. Visit the area and building at different times of the day and on weekends and weekdays, so you can gauge levels of background noise, air pollution and traffic. In June 2012, riots broke out at one Guangzhou housing complex because residents were angry about noise from a nearby highway and airport, which they claimed exceeded national standards.[3] Both the road and the airport predated the housing complex.

Traffic congestion, as well as related issues like noise and air pollution, is an increasingly important consideration when buying a home. The number of cars on China's roads is expected to grow from 100 million at the end of 2011 to more than 200 million in 2020.

Real estate agents

China's booming housing markets have attracted a variety of real estate agencies. Homegrown, Hong Kong and international agencies are well represented, as are firms focusing on specific market segments, such as Beijing's *siheyuan*.

It is common for agents to work for and collect commission from both the buyer and the vendor. Buyers do not pay commission when they purchase a new home directly from a developer.

As in other markets, real estate agents in China often focus on single neighborhoods. Ideally, you can find an agent who combines local expertise with experience serving expatriates. This will enhance communication and help you avoid wasting time on homes that don't meet your requirements. Recommendations from friends and coworkers can be a good way to locate a competent agent.

As Lily Yang, a senior executive at a Hong Kong–owned agency in Beijing, observed, "It's very easy to be cheated. Buyers need to take charge of the process and make sure the documents are complete and authentic." Ms. Yang recommended working with a large, professional agency, because they usually have more resources and knowledge. But she also cautioned, "Remember that the agency may be ethical, but the agent may be playing tricks."

The China Institute of Real Estate Appraisers and Agents is a national regulatory body. The institute's Website includes a directory where you can check members' credentials (www.cirea.org.cn, Chinese only). Local industry associations also operate in China's Tier 1 cities (Beijing, Guangzhou, Shanghai and Shenzhen). See the "Useful information" chapter for details.

Shifting sands

A change in government policy is one of the threats outlined in the "Risk factors" chapter. So what happens when your purchase straddles a policy change? In September 2010, a Shenzhen man made a 10 million yuan down payment on a 46 million yuan home. Before the sale was completed, new rules were announced capping the number of homes that residents could own at two. The buyer and vendor agreed to cancel the sale. But the vendor believed the buyer should forfeit the down payment, while the buyer, who already owned two homes, maintained that the deposit should be refunded.

In 2011, the Nanshan district court ruled that the vendor should refund the down payment. The vendor refused, citing the Shenzhen Municipal Urban Planning, Land and Resources Commission, which stated that anyone who had made a partial or full payment before September 30, 2010, could complete the sale. As of December 2012, the vendor was appealing the case to the Shenzhen intermediate court.[4]

Price information

Accurate historical sales data are hard to get in China. Unlike Hong Kong, where it is easy to get transacted prices for a specific home, in China the numbers tend to be "broad brush" and are based on a small sample that rarely gives a true sense of the overall market. Information is available from trade associations and research firms, usually on a subscription basis, but this is of little use to an individual buyer. Often end-users must rely on agents — whose interests don't always coincide with those of the buyer — for pricing information.

Prices in China vary widely, depending on the city and the age, size and location of the dwelling. But there are some rules of thumb. In general, Tier 1 cities are more expensive than secondary and tertiary cities. Dwellings near the city center and transport facilities such as subway stations are more expensive than less convenient properties. New homes are more expensive than pre-owned ones.

When developers are liquidating inventories or the government is encouraging home purchases, you will be in a stronger position to negotiate concessions. These can include price reductions or guarantees and sweeteners, like a free parking space. If the market is hot, you'll need to act quickly when you find a suitable property. You may have to make an above-market offer or a larger down payment to seal the deal.

There is a great deal of liquidity in China and many sophisticated investors are searching for bargains. As a result, mispriced homes tend to be snapped up quickly. You will occasionally find a heavily discounted property, but there is usually an underlying flaw. For example, there are 79 developments in the suburbs of Beijing built on rural land owned by collectives.* These homes, all built since 2008, sell at a discount because they offer limited property rights.

Ultimately, you must gather as much data as you can, weigh it for accuracy and relevance and decide to buy — or not — knowing that your information is both incomplete and flawed. That's an imperfect way to make a big decision, but there are few alternatives in China.

Scams

Property is such a big part of China's economy that numerous scams have been created to evade the laws and regulations.

Some are clearly illegal. For example, in May 2012, a Beijing woman was the first person to be prosecuted in that city for selling her apartment to two different buyers. The property registration system in China's large cities makes this difficult, but not impossible, to do. The woman received a 10-year jail sentence and a 10,000 yuan fine. She had to return the money paid by one buyer, while the other buyer kept the apartment.[5]

Also in 2012, some Beijing developers were taking 5% of the purchase price as a "first" down payment and letting buyers make the balance of their down payment in installments. This is against the law, which currently requires a minimum down payment of 30%. Furthermore, banks will only process a mortgage application when the entire down payment has been made. Buyers participating in this scheme could find themselves liable for penalties if they fail to make the full down payment or do not complete the purchase.[6]

---

* A list of the illegal developments is available in Chinese from the *People's Daily* at http://finance.people.com.cn/BIG5/n/2012/0918/c70846-19038988.html.

To avoid taxes, vendors and buyers will declare a sale price that is lower than the actual price, in what is known as a "yin yang" contract. Authorities in some jurisdictions track market prices and prosecute people making false declarations, although enforcement is variable.

Ownership restrictions are based on the family unit, not the individual, so married couples will sometimes fake a divorce — but continue living together — to evade restrictions on the number of properties they can own. Or a wealthy nonresident will pretend to marry a poor local so he can buy property in a city like Beijing that has strict residency requirements. A Shenzhen woman was surprised to discover she was married to and jointly owned an apartment with a man who had forged documents to qualify for subsidized housing reserved for married couples.

Others are more unethical. For example, serviced apartments are misrepresented as residential units, despite being categorized as commercial property with a shorter land lease term. One expatriate buyer was surprised to discover that he had signed a sale and purchase agreement specifying that he would pay the 5% business tax on behalf of the vendor. He wasn't happy, but he paid the tax on the Shenzhen apartment. Caveat emptor.

Property rights and registration

In China, there is no private ownership of land. With minor exceptions, urban land is owned by the state and rural land is owned by collectives.

When you buy a home in China, you are also buying the balance of the land use rights, which start with a fixed, 70-year term for residential property. Land use rights are inheritable and let you possess, use and gain interest from the land, but not sell it.[7] Buildings are considered to be immovable property that is separate from the land.

Article 149 of the Property Code of the People's Republic of China, which took effect on October 1, 2007, states that residential land use rights will automatically be renewed upon expiry, except when it is in the public interest not to do so. However, the property code does not specify the length of the new term or the cost, if any, for renewing these rights.

The property code also covers apartment buildings. Buyers have individual ownership of their apartment and joint ownership of common areas and facilities. Owners are jointly obliged to manage, maintain and fund the upkeep of buildings and associated facilities, and an owners' association, composed of individual owners, is responsible for managing and administering the buildings and facilities. All owners become members of the association when they buy an apartment. Resolutions reached by an owners' association are binding on all owners, and a majority vote is required for major resolutions that affect the property rights of individual owners.[8]

China's property registration system is fragmented, and different systems exist in different parts of the country. Buyers of urban homes must obtain a certificate of housing ownership from the housing authority and a certificate of land use rights from the state land administration.[9] Normally, both certificates are issued by the local Real Estate Trading Center.

For many people, purchasing a new home from a reputable developer is preferable to buying a pre-owned one. While new homes lack the character of older dwellings like Beijing's siheyuan and Shanghai's lilong, they offer full land lease terms, fewer problems with squatters and multiple or absentee owners and superior construction quality. New developments are also less likely to be expropriated.

In general, new homes suffer from fewer structural defects and environmental problems, like the use of asbestos. If you are buying a pre-owned home, agents and vendors are unlikely to welcome questions about these issues. If the agent and vendor are aware of a problem, disclosing it will affect the price of the home and the viability of the transaction. If they are unaware of a problem, most would prefer to remain ignorant.

Buying a new home

1. The buyer visits the developer's office or show unit and selects an apartment.

2. The buyer signs a subscription agreement, which is equivalent to a provisional sale and purchase (S&P) agreement, and pays a deposit ranging from 20,000 yuan to 5% of the purchase price.

3. Within three to seven days of signing the subscription agreement, the buyer signs a formal S&P agreement and makes a down payment, bringing the total deposit to 30% of the purchase price. The down payment is larger if the buyer is purchasing a second or third home.

4. The buyer takes the subscription agreement to the bank, which confirms that the buyer is eligible for a loan. If the buyer qualifies for the mortgage, the bank pays funds to the developer. If the buyer doesn't qualify for a mortgage, the buyer applies for a refund of the down payment. Developers do not offer financing, but usually have relationships with banks.

5. If the buyer is not a Chinese citizen, she will need to pay a notary to have the contract notarized. Noncitizens will also need to prove — typically with a certificate from the Public Security Bureau, an employment contract, a work permit or a student visa — that they have legally resided in China for at least one year. Some cities require buyers to provide additional proof of residency, such as tax receipts. Buyers have to prove their marital status and declare that they do not already own a home in China. These documents may need to be notarized.

6. For an off the plan sale, about two years will elapse between the signing of the provisional S&P agreement and the government issuing a certificate of completion. When the certificate has been issued, the buyer can take possession.

A new villa in Wuhan

Orange Villa (www.orange-villa.com, Chinese only) is a luxury residential project in Wuhan, the capital of Hubei. Located near the Optical Valley Software Park, this development comprises 137 villas ranging from 234 to 301 square meters. Orange Villa features an international school, as well as a golf course, tennis courts and other facilities.

The villa in this example has a total floor area of 252 square meters. This includes 179 square meters on three above-ground floors and a 73-square-meter basement. The villa has three bedrooms, each with an en suite bathroom.

Homes in the Orange Villa development in Wuhan. Planned communities like this are increasingly common throughout China.

Item	Yuan
Purchase price	2,974,072
Registration, property certificates and transaction fees	1,400
Deed tax (2,974,072 yuan × 4.0%)	118,963
Stamp duty (2,974,072 yuan × 0.05%)	14,870
Agent's commission (paid by developer)	0
One-time payment to the development's maintenance fund (55 yuan × 252 square meters)	13,860
Subtotal	**3,123,165**
Less 30% down payment	(936,950)
Mortgage amount	2,186,215

Monthly cost	Yuan
Mortgage (30-year fixed rate at 6.0%)	14,086
Management fee (1.9 yuan × 252 square meters)	1,400
Total	**15,486**

Data courtesy of CIMIC

Your papers, please

If you buy a home, you may need to have documents certified so that they will be officially recognized by the Chinese government. Unfortunately, there are few standards and a document that is accepted by one bureaucrat may be rejected by another, often without an explanation.

Documents issued overseas can be particularly challenging and may need to be translated into Chinese and notarized. Chinese officials may request something — like an authenticating seal on each page of a multipage document — that the issuing government refuses to provide. There is not much you can do about this, except remain pleasant, negotiate and try not to lose your temper. Common forms of certification include:

- A notary public can witness (or notarize) a signature on a document. In some jurisdictions, notaries can make "certified true copies" of documents. Note that notaries do not certify the contents of a document.

- A consularized document is certified by an embassy or consulate, sometimes with a ribbon and a wax seal. For example, to be recognized in China an American birth certificate would be consularized by the Chinese embassy in Washington.

- An apostille authenticates a public document like a birth or marriage certificate. Apostilles are issued by the government that issued the original document and are either placed on or attached to the original document. See the Hague Conference Website (www.hcch.net) for more information.

Buying a pre-owned home

1. The buyer sets a preliminary budget and determines his requirements, including the home's size, location and facilities.

2. If a mortgage is required, the buyer researches lending rates, currencies and terms and creates a short list of lenders.

3. The buyer obtains approval in principle from the lender. Some lenders require that a provisional S&P agreement (also known as a letter of intent) be completed before they will provide approval in

principle. Approval is not binding on the bank, but it does give the buyer confidence that he will qualify for a mortgage.

4. The buyer reads online listings, views prospective homes and finds a home he likes and can afford.

5. With the agent's assistance, the buyer makes the vendor a verbal offer. When the offer is accepted, the buyer and the vendor sign a preliminary S&P agreement, which specifies all of the key transaction details, including the price, dates and amounts of subsequent payments, contract signing date and penalties for breach of contract.

6. The agent confirms the vendor's identity by checking that her name and identification card number match the name and number on the property ownership certificate.

7. The buyer pays the vendor a deposit, which ranges from as little as 10,000 yuan to as much as 20% of the purchase price. In a "hot" market or for an attractively priced property, buyers often pay a larger deposit to ensure the deal is completed. There is no escrow in China, and the deposit is usually paid in cash directly to the vendor. The deposit may also be paid to the agent, who will sign a document acknowledging receipt of the deposit and agreeing to have the vendor accept or reject the offer (and return the deposit), usually within three days.

8. The transaction is registered at the local Real Estate Trading Center, which is operated by the government. The vendor completes a Property Sale Registration Form and the buyer completes a Property Purchase Registration Form. If the property is owned by more than one person or will be bought by more than one person, the registration forms and contract must bear the names of all of the vendors or buyers.

9. In some jurisdictions, the Real Estate Trading Center issues a security code that identifies the vendor as the home's owner and the buyer

as the person purchasing the home. The security code is important and should be kept secret and secure. This process officially registers the transaction and prevents the vendor from selling the same property to more than one buyer.

10. The buyer makes a second payment to the vendor. After this payment, the buyer will have paid the vendor at least 30% of the purchase price.

11. If needed, the buyer applies for a mortgage. The bank transfers the mortgage proceeds to the vendor's bank account when the home has been registered in the buyer's name.

12. The buyer and vendor sign the S&P agreement, which is a standard form that is supplied by the government. The form cannot be changed but there are places where riders and special terms can be inserted. The form includes a section where the residents' names and hukous (residency permits) are listed. This is important because the residents need to be registered as having moved out before the buyer can move in.

13. If the buyer is not a Chinese citizen, he will need to pay a notary to have the contract notarized. Noncitizens will also need to prove — typically with a certificate from the Public Security Bureau, an employment contract, a work permit or a student visa — that he has legally resided in China for at least one year. Some cities require buyers to provide additional proof of residency, such as tax receipts. Buyers have to prove their marital status and declare that they do not already own a home in China. These documents may need to be notarized.

14. The buyer and vendor go to the Real Estate Trading Center, where the buyer pays the stamp duty, the vendor pays any outstanding taxes and the property ownership certificate is transferred into the buyer's name. This usually take several hours and the buyer and vendor must appear in person, with proof of identity, to sign the documents.

15. The buyer, vendor and agent make a final visit to the property, where the buyer checks that the property is in order and that there has

been no damage. The vendor hands over the keys and proof that the utility bills have all been paid. The utility accounts are transferred from the vendor to the buyer's name. If it is a cash transaction, the buyer gives the balance of the purchase price to the vendor. If there is a mortgage, the lender transfers the balance to the vendor's bank account.

16. A new property ownership certificate is issued in the buyer's name.

A heritage apartment in Shanghai

This 60-square-meter apartment is on the third floor of a protected historical building that was built in 1920. Located in Jing'an district in the center of Shanghai, the apartment is a six-minute walk to West Nanjing Road subway station. The unit was renovated by an American designer and offers sunshine and southern exposure. The notary fee would only apply if the apartment was purchased by a non-Chinese citizen.

Item	Yuan
Purchase price	2,600,000
Registration, property certificates and transaction fees	500
Notary fee (2,600,000 yuan × 0.25%)	6,500
Deed tax (2,600,000 yuan × 3.0%)	78,000
Agent's commission (2,600,000 yuan × 1.0%)	26,000
Stamp duty (2,600,000 yuan × 0.05%)	13,000
Subtotal	**2,724,000**
Less 30% down payment	(817,200)
Mortgage amount	**1,906,800**

Monthly cost	Yuan
Mortgage (20-year fixed rate at 6.0%)	13,661
Management fee	120
Cable TV and Internet	175
Parking fee	800
Total	**14,756**

Data courtesy of Salo Homes

Closing time

Closing times vary greatly. A cash purchase of an unmortgaged home in Beijing or Shanghai can be accomplished in as little as seven days, from payment of the initial deposit to property handover. But this is a best-case scenario, with flawless paperwork and a cooperative buyer, vendor and agent.

Transactions can take two to three months to close if they occur outside a major market, involve discharging an existing mortgage or arranging a new mortgage, or encounter other difficulties, such as missing or incomplete documents.

In a 2012 survey by the World Bank and the International Finance Corporation, China ranked 44th out of 185 economies surveyed for the speed of property registration. On average, it took 29 days, four procedures and 3.6% of the property's value in China.[10] By comparison, Hong Kong ranked 60th, taking an average of 36 days, five procedures and 3.9% of the property's value.

Warranties

There are two sets of construction warranties in China. The first is provided by the builder to the developer and is effective from the date of final acceptance. Under Article 40 of the Construction Quality Management Ordinance, which was promulgated in 2000, the minimum warranty periods for components in new homes are as follows.[11]

The second warranty is between the developer and the buyer. Under the Commercial Buildings Sale Management Regulation, which was introduced in 2001, developers are required to provide buyers with a

Component	Warranty duration
Foundations and main structural components	Reasonable life of the project
Waterproofing of the roof, bathroom and exterior walls	5 years
Heating and cooling systems	2 years
Electrical system and plumbing	2 years
Other items	As agreed between the builder and developer

warranty that starts from the transfer of ownership. The warranty must not be shorter than the warranty in the Residential Housing Quality Assurance regulations, introduced in 1998. These regulations specify a one-year warranty for interior decorations, three years for the roof and a reasonable period, usually seen as 10 years, for the main structure.[12]

Warranties are transferable. The developers interviewed for this book did not offer extended warranties.

WHAT TO BUY

Opportunities

Distressed property

Low loan-to-value ratios and Chinese buyers' tendency to pay cash mean you are unlikely to see panic selling if there is a property market correction. But there will be some values available for investors with cash, an understanding of the market and an appetite for risk.

Government offices

Since 2005, cities throughout China have seen a boom in the construction of government offices, many of which are in new development zones. Despite the growth of the private sector, government continues to play a dominant role in Chinese society and is a stable source of employment and tenants. Homes near government offices should maintain their value over the long term.

Green developments

Research in the United States suggests that environmentally friendly designs and energy-efficient equipment are becoming standard features for both buyers and tenants. John K. McIlwain at the Urban Land Institute notes that it is "still hard to show that renters will pay more for an energy-efficient apartment," but there is increasing evidence that green homes rent more quickly and experience less tenant turnover.[1]

In China, environmental awareness and pro-environmental behaviors (like sorting garbage or volunteering for environmental causes) are strongest among city dwellers who are educated, young, single, female and in leadership positions.[2] Green homes will be easier to sell or rent to people in these groups.

Heritage homes

Beautiful old homes can be found in many Chinese cities. Examples include *siheyuan* (courtyard houses) in Beijing, *qilou* (shophouses) and villas in Guangzhou and *lilong* (town houses) and art deco homes in Shanghai. These properties can be expensive to buy and, if they have not been renovated, often require significant investments of time and money. They are also at risk of expropriation. Banks will provide mortgages for these homes, if they have been maintained properly and there are no issues with multiple or missing owners. For more information, see the individual city chapters.

Infrastructure projects

Industrial parks, export processing zones and similar projects can act as economic anchors that attract investors, homeowners and tenants. Examples can be found in Qianhai, near Shenzhen, and in Guangzhou's Nansha district. These projects vary in quality, so evaluate the financial stability of the developer and the development's viability before using an infrastructure project as the basis for an investment decision.

Islands

In November 2011, a businessman from Ningbo became the first person in China to own a private island. Huang Yimin bought the rights to the uninhabited Danmenshan Island in Zhejiang for 3.4 million yuan. China has nearly 7,000 uninhabited islands, 176 of which were put up for sale in April 2011 by the State Oceanic Administration (www.soa.gov.cn, Chinese only). Sixty of the islands, the rights to which can be purchased by Chinese nationals and qualified foreign and domestic companies for 50 years, are in Guangdong.[3]

Lofts

China has an active loft scene in places such as Beijing's 798 Space, the Xinyi International Club in Guangzhou, the M50 complex and Tianzifang in Shanghai and the OCT Loft area in Shenzhen. Art galleries and studios feature prominently in these areas and some, like Beijing 798 and Tianzifang, feature distinctive architecture. Arts groups have also announced plans to convert the former Shougang steel mill in Beijing's western suburbs into a cultural complex, like 798 Space.[4]

Despite the threat of expropriation, many prime loft sites have been redeveloped. Investors interested in buying a loft should be prepared to pay cash and ensure that the site has been properly remediated.

Lofts can be found throughout China. Shanghai's M50 complex, which is located on Suzhou Creek, has become a prominent art hub.

National and local priorities

Five-year plans identify economic and development priorities at the national, provincial and city levels. The Catalog for the Guidance of Foreign Investment Industries — a list of industries where foreign investment is encouraged, restricted and prohibited that is issued by the National Development and Reform Commission — can also provide useful information, especially if you plan to sell or rent to expatriates (www.fdi.gov.cn).

Parking spaces

With prices starting at about 350,000 yuan, car park spaces are relatively inexpensive and require limited maintenance. These characteristics, coupled with the growing number of vehicles on Chinese roads, can make them an attractive source of rental income, particularly in city centers. See the building's management company for more information.

Transport hubs

China's 12th Five Year Plan (2011 – 2015) calls for the construction of 42 transport hubs. Homes nearby usually command a premium price, but exercise caution if you are buying a home that is priced based on an unbuilt transportation project. Projects funded by overextended local government financing vehicles may be delayed or canceled. But if there is an economic downturn, infrastructure spending will probably benefit from stimulus spending by the central government. See the "Risk factors" chapter for more information.

Villas

In June 2006, the Ministry of Land and Resources banned the supply of new land for the construction of luxury villas. The ministry also introduced restrictions on new low-density and large homes.[5] The prices of detached houses have soared in recent years, but the lack of new supply makes them a potentially interesting investment. Many houses that were purchased as investments have sat empty for years and will require rehabilitation and the installation of kitchens, bathrooms and other fittings.

If you are buying a villa on a golf course, ensure that the development is legal. According to one estimate, only 10 of China's 600-plus golf courses have all of the necessary approvals.[6] The government has taken over some of the illegal developments, including a 65-hectare project built by Beijing Hongfenghu Ecological Garden Co. State-owned enterprises are not immune from legal action and have been fined for building illegal villas.

Pitfalls

Bad feng shui

Many Chinese people are sensitive to *feng shui*. The location of a property in relation to water and mountains, the orientation of doors and windows and the presence of cemetery views can affect the price of a home and the value of the underlying land.[7] While you may not be concerned about feng shui, it can influence your home's resale value and your ability to attract tenants to a rental property.

Brownfield sites

Thousands of former industrial sites in Beijing and the Pearl and Yangtze river deltas have been converted to residential use. Many brownfield sites are badly contaminated with heavy metals, organic pollutants and electronic waste. See the "Risk factors" chapter for more information.

Commercial property

Following government measures to cool the residential market, many developers shifted their attention to commercial property. As a result, there is a growing glut of shopping malls — nearly 15 million square meters of new retail space was under construction in mid-2012[8] — and yields have fallen.

To circumvent residency restrictions and limits on the number of homes that people can own, some developers are selling serviced apartments and units in small office/home office developments as residences. These may be worthwhile investments, but the underlying land lease will have a 40-year term, not the 70 years granted for a conventional residential dwelling. In addition, the loan-to-value ratio will be lower and the mortgage term will be shorter than for a comparable residential unit.[9]

Foreign companies and individuals can only own commercial real estate in China through a foreign-invested enterprise such as a wholly foreign-owned entity or through a joint venture with a Chinese company.[10] For most people, these requirements make it uneconomical and impractical to own commercial real estate.

Custom-built homes

China's land use laws and land prices put custom-built homes out of reach for all but the wealthiest people.

Expropriation targets

In other markets, investors buy property in an area with redevelopment potential in the hope of selling it later at a profit. That strategy can be used in China, but expropriation payouts are usually small and there are few avenues for appeal if you are unhappy with the compensation that you are offered. Residents have also been subjected to intimidation and physical violence to "encourage" them to move. See the "Developers and development" chapter for more information.

Local governance

Local officials can ignore directives from the central government and grassroots-level corruption is an unfortunate reality. In 2010, 146,517 people in China were disciplined for corruption and 5,373 people were "transferred to judicial agencies for criminal proceedings."[11] An Internet search and discussion with local residents should be part of your due diligence before buying property in an unfamiliar area.

Finances can also be an issue. According to a June 2011 report by China's National Audit Office, 231 local governments have established 6,576 financing companies with total debts of 4.97 trillion yuan.[12] Some analysts believe that falling land sales — a key source of local government income — could limit the financing companies' ability to service this debt. While officials have downplayed the risk of local governments defaulting, there is the possibility of infrastructure projects being delayed or canceled, local service cutbacks and other austerity measures. See the "Risk factors" chapter for more information.

Noxious neighbors

You probably won't want to live next to a garbage dump or incinerator, a prison, a nuclear power plant, a chemical factory, a busy expressway, an airport or a red-light district.

Expressways and homes are often in close proximity. Noise and air pollution can be a major drawback for nearby residents.

Old homes

Homes built between 1949 and the late 1990s are usually ugly, badly built and poorly maintained. Banks are usually hesitant to provide a mortgage for these properties, so you will have to pay cash.

"Once-in-a-lifetime" deals

Property is an important asset class and China has many sophisticated investors. If you are offered a deal that seems too good to be true, there's probably a hidden catch. This includes "special" arrangements designed to circumvent government regulations.

Residential rentals

For small foreign investors, China's residential rental market is unappealing. Residential property that is not owner-occupied is considered to be commercial, which means that you will need to establish a Chinese company or form a joint venture (see above). Furthermore, rental yields are low: locals buying investment property usually leave the interior of the home unfinished because the rent doesn't justify the cost of decorating and the aggravation of dealing with a tenant. There are niche markets, however, like homes for expatriate families. See the case study in the "Shanghai" chapter.

Schools

Schools are usually considered to be desirable neighbors. This is especially true in China, where there is a reverence for education and a shortage of school places in many cities. Parents will often buy a home in a desirable school's catchment area in the hope of getting their children a better education.

However, there are downsides to living near a school. Music and outdoor exercise sessions can generate a lot of noise. It's not unusual to see cars double- and triple-parked as parents drop off and pick up their children.

In addition, when researchers from the Chinese Academy of Sciences analyzed soil samples from 10 Beijing colleges, they found the schoolyards were contaminated with DDT and other organochlorine pesticides (OCPs). The study concluded that "there existed potential exposure risk of [the] college population to OCPs."[13]

Small developers

Small builders often have difficulty obtaining project financing, and there is a greater chance that a small, privately held developer will encounter cash-flow or operational difficulties, particularly in a market correction. These companies are also more likely to disappear than to arrange an orderly restructuring when trouble strikes. See the "Developers and development" chapter for more information.

Cutting-edge architecture is not limited to China's big cities. The Youth and Children's Center is one of several futuristic buildings in Dongguan.

Themed towns

After 1949, China's leadership focused on finding the most efficient, inexpensive way to accommodate a growing population. Aesthetics and creature comforts were low priorities. Many Chinese cities still feature rows of bland, identical apartment blocks built using designs from the Soviet Union.

As market-oriented reforms were introduced and China became wealthier, more architecturally interesting buildings were erected. Shanghai's Jin Mao Tower and the CCTV Headquarters in Beijing have become icons of China's progress and success. Even smaller cities built adventuresome structures, such as Dongguan's Youth and Children's Center.

This experiment also extended to themed housing developments. Some, like the Bauhaus-inspired Anting New Town northwest of Shanghai, which was designed by Albert Speer & Partner, are visually distinctive but commercial failures. Others, like Thames Town in Songjiang, with its red phone boxes and fish and chip shop copied from Lyme Regis, Dorset, have become minor tourist attractions. The Shanghai suburbs are also home to a Spanish town near Fengcheng, a Canadian town near Fengjing, a Scandinavian town in Luodian, an Italian town in Pujiang and Santa Barbara Villa in Songjiang that is modeled on Southern California.

But China's most spectacular themed town is 30 minutes outside Huizhou, Guangzhou, where Minmetals Land built a $940 million copy of Hallstatt, an Austrian town that is also a UNESCO World Heritage Site. The project, which opened in April 2012, is a faithful replica of the entire town, right down to its 1860 Protestant Christuskirche (Church of our Lord).[14] Villas in the Chinese project sell for up to five million yuan, more than homes in the Austrian original.

DEVELOPERS AND DEVELOPMENT

Residential property developers in China are a diverse group, ranging from private businesses to state-owned enterprises (SOEs) and multinational corporations. The industry is fragmented: There are local champions and developers that operate in major cities, but no one firm dominates the market.

Driven by urbanization and rising incomes, residential developers are building single-family homes and villas, apartment blocks, gated communities incorporating golf courses and marinas and more. They are also diversifying into commercial developments and building so-called HOPSCA projects, which are mixed-use complexes that comprise hotels, offices, parks, shopping, convention facilities and apartments.

Developers often work through joint ventures, holding companies and subsidiaries that can make it difficult to determine who owns a project. Many developers are listed on stock exchanges in Hong Kong, Shanghai, Shenzhen and Singapore. A stock exchange listing, particularly an overseas one, attracts more scrutiny from regulators, ratings agencies and the media. In general, this attention results in better corporate governance. But as Lehman Brothers and Enron demonstrated, there are no guarantees.

Companies from Japan, Singapore and other countries are active in China, mainly through joint ventures or as investors in commercial projects. Foreign companies are increasingly interested in buying distressed assets in China.

For a list of developers active in Beijing, Guangzhou, Shanghai and Shenzhen, see the "Useful information" chapter.

Types of developers

Private companies

These include small businesses — China has an estimated 20,000 small and medium-sized developers — as well as industry leaders like China Vanke, which is the nation's largest listed developer.

Private companies can combine local knowledge with entrepreneurial skills to exploit opportunities that are too small or unprofitable for Hong Kong companies and SOEs. However, private companies are often hampered by a lack of scale and difficulties accessing capital.

State-owned enterprises

SOEs are former units of the central government that are now under the central government's State-owned Assets Supervision and Administration Commission (SASAC). SOEs can also be former units of provincial or local governments that are now overseen by a regional SASAC.

In the past, SOEs' government connections gave them preferential access to land. They were also noted for being bureaucratic and more focused on filling production quotas than building homes that anyone would want to buy. Today, SOEs are market-oriented corporations in which 50% or more of the shares are owned by a SASAC, which is effectively a government holding company.[1] Some SOEs, such as Sino-Ocean Land Holdings and Franshion Properties, are listed on the Stock Exchange of Hong Kong, where they are known as "red chips."

Because SOEs enjoy easy access to capital, they helped inflate China's property market. One survey of land auctions in Beijing showed that prices were 27% higher when the winning bidder was an SOE controlled by the central government.[2]

In 2010, 78 centrally owned SOEs that were not primarily involved in the real estate business were prohibited from taking out new development-related bank loans and making new investments in property. The central government is gradually forcing these SOEs out of the property business.[3] Homes built by these companies may be dumped on the market or orphaned as the SOEs return to their core businesses.

Hong Kong companies

This group includes Sun Hung Kai Properties — the world's largest residential developer by market capitalization — and smaller enterprises, such as privately held Nan Fung Group. China is an important market for Hong Kong–based developers, with some companies deriving a third of their revenues from the Mainland.

Hong Kong developers often retain an interest in their projects and rent space to tenants. This can benefit other owners because the developer will protect its rental income by providing a high standard of maintenance and property management, areas where local companies often fall short. Developers from Hong Kong usually offer international designs with superior fittings and finishes.

Developers at a glance		
Type	**Strengths**	**Weaknesses**
Hong Kong companies	Good designs, construction and property management	Less local knowledge
		Fewer political connections
	Finacially stable with low leverage	More expensive
	Understanding non-Chinese buyers	
Private Mainland companies	Market-oriented	Highly leveraged
	Nimble	Vulnerable to credit tightening
		Lack economies of scale
State-owned companies	Easy access to capital	Bureaucratic
	Better political connections	Production-oriented
	Stable	Can be subject to government interference

The development process

Developers pay local governments for the right to use land. The rights take the form of a lease, with a duration of 70 years for residential use; 50 years for industrial, technological, scientific or cultural applications; and 40 years for commercial or recreational use.[4] The state retains ownership of all urban land in China.

Land for development comes from two sources: existing urban land and rural land that has been converted to urban use. All of China's rural land is owned and managed by village collectives, which must arrange and approve the conversion before the land use rights can be sold to a developer. Compensation is paid to the collective, and farmers are only allowed to sell their land to the collective. Farmers receive a small portion of the compensation paid to the collective based on the value of their agricultural output and not the value of the land.[5] A farmer might receive 10,000 yuan per mu* for land that the municipality sells to industrial or residential users for 200,000 – 250,000 yuan per mu.[6]

In general, land use rights, along with any improvements or structures that have been built on the land, revert to the state at the end of the lease, and users are not compensated for their improvements or structures. When the lease expires, the user may apply for an extension. If an extension is granted, the user must pay the renewal fees specified by the state.[7]

However, Article 149 of the Property Code of the People's Republic of China** specifies that residential land use rights will be automatically renewed upon expiration, except when it is in the public interest not to renew.[8]

The first land auction was held in Shenzhen in 1987, so the practical aspects of renewing a lease remain largely unknown.

*   One mu equals 666.7 square meters.
** An English translation of the property code is available from www.npc.gov.cn/ englishnpc/Law/2009-02/20/content_1471118.htm.

Land auctions

Initially, developers could negotiate the purchase of land use rights from local governments or buy the rights from state-owned enterprises. The regulations were changed so that, effective September 1, 2004, all urban land use rights must be sold by public auction or tender, with the results posted on the Internet.[9]

Twenty days before the auction, the plot's location, size and any use restrictions are announced, along with a reserve price, which is determined in consultation with independent appraisers. Bidders must make a deposit, which is usually 10% of the reserve price. The deposit can be substantial, especially for large or well-located lots.

Three types of auction are used. The first is a conventional English-style auction. The second is a two-stage auction, in which participants make bids in person or online during the first section. If only one bidder remains at the end of the first stage, that bidder wins the auction. If more than one bidder remains at the end of the first stage, the second stage — an English-style auction — begins. A sealed-bid auction (also known as a tender), where the winner is determined using a formula that considers the amount of the bid as well as the bidder's credibility and social responsibility, are occasionally used in Beijing and Shanghai. In principle, the winning bidder is expected to develop the land that he has purchased.[10]

If a developer does not start work within one year of the date specified in the land use contract, it can be fined 20% of the land's acquisition price.[11] If the developer has not started work within two years, it may forfeit the right to use the land without compensation. In June 2012, the Ministry of Land and Resources amended the Measures of Idle Land Disposal to plug loopholes that allowed developers to drag out the construction process.[12]

Expropriation

Expropriation occurs when the state takes an object or rights belonging to an individual for a public purpose. Expropriation is known as eminent domain in the United States, compulsory purchase in England and resumption in Australia.

Land that will be developed or redeveloped is often expropriated and cleared before it is auctioned. Local governments compensate urban homeowners, who receive a fraction of the money that the developer pays the government. Rural residents are compensated by the village collective.

Residents frequently object to being resettled in a distant neighborhood and to the low levels of compensation they are offered. Entire villages — located on rural land adjacent to large cities — are sometimes demolished and historic urban neighborhoods, such as those in Beijing's hutongs, have been leveled. Demolition crews can arrive without warning, razing homes with the occupant's belongings still inside. Desperate residents have resorted to everything from self-immolation to riots like those that rocked Wukan, Guangdong, in 2011.[13] In May 2012, two men in Yunnan who were angry about an expropriation case tricked an innocent third man into carrying a bomb into a government office, where it detonated, killing four people and injuring 16.[14]

The absence of property taxes makes local governments dependent on land sales to fund their daily operations, and expropriation creates land that can be sold. Expropriation can also be used as punishment. In January 2011, artist Ai Weiwei's Shanghai studio was demolished in what was believed to be retribution for his political activism.[15] Governments have used the pretext of clearing illegal structures to expropriate land, even when people have lived in the homes for decades. An infrastructure project, like widening a road, can also provide a convenient excuse to take land adjacent to the project and sell it to a developer.

China's leaders are aware of these abuses and the harm they cause. In January 2011, the State Council amended the Administrative Regulations on Urban Housing Demolition and Relocation and promulgated the Regulations on Expropriation and Compensation of Housing on State-owned Land.[16] This introduced several changes and clarifications:

- Expropriation is only permitted when it is in the public interest.

- Local governments require court approval before they can demolish a home without the resident's consent.

- A resident who is unhappy with the compensation offered by a local government can take the government to court.

- Developers and demolition companies can no longer participate in the expropriation process.

- Compensation must be paid before a resident can be removed from the property.

- Residents must receive market value for the property.

In April 2012, the Supreme People's Court ruled that lower courts can reject a local government's request to demolish a home if the lower court believes the compensation offered to the resident is unfair.[17]

These changes strengthen residents' rights. But local governments do not always obey Beijing's directives and the new legislation only applies to urban land. Rural land, which represents about 80% of all expropriations, falls under the Land Administration Law of the People's Republic of China, which has not been amended.[18]

How developers work

Developers make money by acquiring land use rights when prices are low, building homes on the land and then selling finished homes when prices have risen. Successful developers anticipate the direction in which a city is growing and ensure their projects have access to infrastructure and services, such as subway lines, roads and stores. Developers also need to understand demographic trends and the market's position in the price and policy cycles. Buyers can use this information to obtain a favorable price and terms when the market is depressed and avoid purchasing a home at the top of an overheated market.

Project financing is critically important for developers. It takes several years from the time developers obtain land use rights until payment is received from the sale of a home. During this period, the developer must pay staff, subcontractors and architects, buy materials and market the project. The developer may also be buying land for future projects. Developers that cannot match expenses with revenues, or obtain bridge financing to tide them over, go bankrupt.

Financing costs and availability vary depending on whether a developer is private, listed on a stock exchange or an SOE. For example, in July 2011 state-owned enterprises arranged bank loans with an annual interest rate of 3%. Large firms listed on the Hong Kong stock exchange issued bonds with coupon rates of about 10%.[19] Small developers in Wenzhou, a city in Zhejiang famous for its entrepreneurial culture, were paying interest rates of 20% – 30% per month for short-term loans.[20]

Domestic companies' financing choices are shaped by central government policies, which can affect the sources, cost and availability of funds. The cost and availability of loans and other funds raised offshore (i.e., outside China) are affected by market sentiment.

Due diligence

This information will help you confirm that a developer is a legitimate company with the financial capacity to fulfill its contractual obligations. This is particularly important if you are buying a home off the plan or from a smaller developer.

Start by checking the developer's Website (see the list of developers in the "Useful information" chapter). Many companies have an English-language Website and a separate site or subsite for each development. This step is unlikely to highlight any problems with the project or company, but it will give you information, like the developer's name and stock ticker symbol, that you can use to search for general news on Google and Baidu, and for financial information on Reuters and Bloomberg.

A preliminary Internet search can help you identify problems — like contaminated soil or a nearby infrastructure project — that could make the home a bad investment. If the problem isn't a deal breaker, you may be able to use this information to negotiate a discount or other incentive if you decide to go ahead with the purchase.

Buying from a large, reputable developer is always a good start. But even big developers can have problems. In 2012, China Vanke was accused of installing wardrobes made from something resembling paper in Shenzhen apartments that were selling for four million yuan.*

This checklist is not exhaustive and not all of the items will apply to every developer. You will need a Chinese lawyer to obtain some of the information listed below from the State Administration for Industry and Commerce.

---

* Large developers generate more media coverage than small ones (unless they do something especially newsworthy), so they are more likely to appear in Internet searches.

Due diligence checklist

Item	Importance
Registered name	Essential for conducting a background check and ensuring that you are paying the right company. For example, are you buying from Sino Land or Sino-Ocean Land?
Registered address	Should be consistent with the size and nature of the company. Large developers aren't usually headquartered in residential apartment buildings.
Authorized signatories	Lets you check that the person signing the contract is empowered to do so. If not, the contract may be unenforceable.
Bank account	Does the company name match the name of the bank account holder? Is it a corporate account or a personal account? If the answer to either is no, you may be paying the wrong entity.
Email account	Does the salesperson's email account (name@companyname.cn) match the company's Web address (www.companyname.cn)? If not, they may not be an authorized company representative.
Scope of business	The company should be registered as a property developer.
Corporate seal	A corporate seal binds the company to a contract. Seals can be faked.
Corporate structure	Developers listed on overseas stock exchanges have higher corporate governance standards and more transparency in their reporting. Corporate structure is also important in questions of liability.
Shareholders and directors	These are the people and companies that own and operate the developer. Ensure they are not criminals or politicians who have fallen from favor.
Date of incorporation	Older is better. The number of completed projects should match the age of the company. If not, the developer may be inexperienced.

Due diligence checklist	
Item	**Importance**
Registered capital	This must be sufficient for the developer's activities. A company with registered capital of 100,000 yuan will not have enough money to build 100-villa compounds.
Debt-to-equity ratio	A lower ratio means greater financial stability.
Bond ratings	Indicate the ratings agencies' assessment of the developer's ability to meet its financial commitments.
Market capitalization	The total value of the developer's tradable shares is the market's estimation of the company's future prospects.
Profitability	Well-managed companies have a consistent record of profitability.
Completed projects	An indicator of the developer's track record. Check the number of projects the developer has completed in the city where you plan to buy.
Unfinished projects	A company with many stalled projects may be in danger of bankruptcy.
Outstanding lawsuits	Look for unpaid suppliers and unhappy customers. Note that reputable companies get sued, sometimes frivolously.
Anything odd or incongruous	Things that are unusual or don't make sense — like missing documents, broken promises, people who are never available, etc. — could be a sign that there is a problem with the transaction.

Warning signs

Watch out for the following when researching a developer. These are not necessarily deal breakers, but they can suggest trouble ahead.

Inexperience – Developing real estate is a complex process that requires management skill, money and technical expertise. New developers have a high failure rate, and you do not want to buy a home that will never be completed or deal with a company that cuts corners to avoid bankruptcy.

Diversification – Great fortunes have been made in Chinese real estate. As a result, successful companies sometimes diversify from their core business into property. Unfortunately, their initial success does not always translate into real estate. You can find yourself financing a developer's education as delays, cost overruns and other problems occur.

Local ignorance – From weather to civic politics, successful developments accommodate the local environment. A developer who is successful in a southern province can experience problems in the north.

Mission creep – A company that has successfully developed residential property begins developing commercial space. SOHO China began buying projects by these companies in 2012 at deep discounts.

RENOVATIONS

The basics

Defining your dream

Start by assembling a wish list of everything that you'd like in your new home. Think about the features and design elements you've admired in hotels, resorts, friends' homes and previous places where you have lived. Take pictures on your mobile phone. If you've always wanted a Jacuzzi, a sewing room or a home theater, then add them to your list.

If you are concerned about personal security, consider adding alarm and surveillance systems or a safe room (also known as a panic room), where your family can take shelter in a typhoon, robbery or abduction attempt.

This is also a good time to consult interior design books and magazines, like *Architectural Digest* (www.architecturaldigest.com) and *Better Homes and Gardens* (www.bhg.com). Sites like ArchDaily (www.archdaily.com) and Architizer (www.architizer.com) are also helpful. Local interior design magazines can be a source of pictorial inspiration, even if you can't read Chinese.

Design books, magazines and Websites are an inexpensive way to spur your imagination. They will also provide nonverbal ways of communicating your ideas to the designer or contractor. This can be useful if there is a gap between your Putonghua skills and the designer's English abilities. You can combine photos, magazine pages, paint chips and fabric swatches on a foam board to create palettes of colors, textures and styles. Keep your ideas organized on the cloud using Pinterest (http://pinterest.com).

The purpose of this process is to help you consider all of the possibilities. You may not act on them, but it is much easier and less expensive to make changes at this stage than when work is under way. You may also find that something that you've always dreamed of — a home spa, for example — is not that much more expensive than a conventional bathroom.

Getting help

It is possible to renovate without a designer by hiring a general contractor directly. But most people lack the experience, time, patience and network to successfully plan and execute a renovation. The added cost of an architect or designer is more than offset by their technical knowledge, problem-solving and project management skills and relationships with contractors and suppliers. It is much easier to hire a designer at the beginning of a project than to find someone to rescue a job that has encountered problems.

The designer typically offers a turnkey package that includes overall project management, obtaining all necessary approvals, specifying and sourcing construction materials and overseeing the construction team. The designer hires a general contractor, who provides the tradespeople, like electricians, painters and masons, necessary to complete the job. The designer can also recommend or specify appliances as well as the furniture, drapery and accessories needed to give your home a completed look.

A talented designer can anticipate and avoid problems. She will interpret and refine your ideas, make time- and money-saving suggestions and help you overcome any limitations that your property has, like low ceilings or narrow rooms. She can also save you time by bringing material samples to your home or office.

The cost of a renovation will be determined by several factors, including the condition of the home; the quality of the materials; whether the project involves demolition and structural changes; whether furniture and appliances are included; and the popularity of the designer.

Given the number of variables involved, budgets vary widely. The designer will typically charge you a price per square meter, with an hourly change for time spent on site. A Beijing-based decoration company that I interviewed quoted a minimum price of 3,000 yuan per square meter, with luxury homes starting at 6,000 yuan per square meter. According to one survey, a typical middle-class Chinese family spends $15,000 to fit out a bare, 1,000-square-foot apartment.[1]

Hiring a designer

Create a short list of designers who meet your criteria.

Brief them on the project and ask for a preliminary quote.

Get at least three quotes to ensure that the prices are competitive. Ensure that the quotes include comparable materials and services.

Evaluate the quotes and pick a designer.

The designer will prepare a detailed quote, with completion dates, project scope and a payment schedule. The quote may be amended as you refine your choices and negotiate schedules.

Ensure the contract includes an explanation of how the work will be completed. Normally, this is in three phases: schematic design, design development and construction documents. The contract should also specify how and where disputes will be settled and the liquidated damages that will be paid if either party fails to fulfill the contract. Have a lawyer review the contract before you sign it, especially if it is a large project and your Chinese is less than fluent. (See the "Law" chapter and the sample decoration contract in the Appendix.)

When you've settled on one company and are confident you can work with them, advise the others that they were unsuccessful.

After you have signed the contract, you will pay a deposit. You will also make payments as the project progresses.

There will be a final payment to the contractor, typically 5% of the total, that is held back for up to a year after the project is completed. This payment protects you in case there are defects in the materials or workmanship and covers the cost of fixing common, minor problems like cracks that appear in plaster as it dries.

Finding a designer

Once you have a clear idea of your needs, it's time to start shopping for a designer. Friends, coworkers and neighbors are excellent sources of information and referrals. You can find designers through trade organizations like the China Building Decoration Association (http://cbda.ccd.com.cn, Chinese only), the China Institute of Interior Design (www.ciid.com.cn, Chinese only) and the China Interior Design Network Website (www.a963.com, Chinese only). Lifestyle magazines often feature designers' projects.

Once you've located some candidates, you'll want to evaluate their suitability for your project. This is a three-part process based on chemistry, workmanship and money.

Chemistry – Your relationship with the designer will contribute to the project's overall success. Find someone with whom you can communicate, who understands your tastes and sensibilities. Trust and respect will help you overcome the challenges and setbacks that inevitably occur.

The designer should be comfortable with your level of involvement in the project. Some clients are hands-on and want to make site visits and shop for bathtubs, hardware and furnishings. Other customers prefer to leave everything up to the designer.

The designer must be reliable about keeping appointments and other commitments. Initial difficulties here can foreshadow bigger problems later on.

There's no substitute for a spending time with the designer to get a sense of her personality. Interviewing her clients, seeing her work and asking the questions outlined below will provide insights into the designer's strengths and weaknesses.

What was the designer like to work with?

Was she open to your ideas and suggestions?

Did she complete the project on schedule and on budget?
If not, why?

What did you like most (and least) about working with the designer?

Were you happy with the quality of the materials and workmanship?
If not, why?

If you had the renovation to do over again, what would you do differently?

How much did you spend?

Workmanship – You're going to spend a substantial amount of money on your renovation, so it's important that you're happy with the finished product. The easiest way to do this is to inspect an example of the designer's work. For maximum candor, this should be done while the designer is not present.

If possible, inspect a project that is several years old, so that you can see how the materials and workmanship have aged. Pay close attention to cabinetry, floors and custom woodwork. Check that the doors and shelves are hung straight and that floors and countertops are level. Look for water leaks and inspect the quality of the finishes. Ask plenty of questions, take notes, and if the owner doesn't mind, bring along a digital camera. You may see something interesting that you'll want to incorporate into your own design.

Money – Quality costs money, and good designers and contractors are usually in demand and able to charge premium prices. That said, companies price projects differently for a variety of reasons, including their current workload, the market outlook, how interesting the project is, the project's potential to generate referrals or media coverage and whether they are working on a job nearby.

Get several quotes, and pick the company that has the optimum combination of chemistry, workmanship and price. If you like the people and the workmanship, but the price seems high, ask why. The designer or contractor may be basing his price on an incorrect assumption, or there may be something that you can do to bring the price into your budget.

Naturally, you will want to get the lowest possible price. But allow the designer some profit, particularly if you have high expectations or the project is complex. Otherwise, the designer may cut corners to ensure that the job is profitable, or be slow to fix problems later on. "Things can be done cheaply, but you will pay later," notes Binke Lenhardt of Crossboundaries Architects in Beijing.

Making the project a success

There are several things that you can do to increase the chances that your project will be a success.

Conduct due diligence. Ensure the designer takes pride in her work, doesn't cut corners on materials and workmanship, and has the skills and resources to complete the project. In addition to talking to previous clients, you can hire a lawyer or an investigator to do a background check. This may seem like a lot of work, but it's nothing compared to the time and trouble needed to extricate yourself from a project gone wrong.

Have a realistic budget and timetable. You won't be happy with the results if you insist on an impossibly tight schedule, have a tiny budget or use cheap materials. Don't forget to allow for contingencies and delays.

Treat the designer well. Pay your bills, recognize that there will be unforeseen problems and make decisions in a timely fashion. This is particularly important in China, where disputes can turn ugly.

Remember that construction quality in China can be poor. Often, floors aren't level, walls aren't true and corners aren't square. While some of these issues can be overcome, others cannot and some problems will not be apparent until work starts. Usually the cost and difficulty involved mean that compromises will need to be made.

Have reasonable expectations and communicate them clearly. Your expectations may be unrealistic — or impossible — for your budget, building or schedule. Or they could be delivered with a few adjustments. But if the designer doesn't know what you want, it isn't going to happen.

⚘   Get covered. Make sure the project is covered by your homeowners' insurance, a separate rider or the designer or contractor's policy.

⚘   Stay organized. Use a filing system for the signed renovation contract, drawings, permits, insurance policies, receipts, notes, photos, instruction manuals and warranty information for appliances and catalog numbers for paints and floor coverings. Keep backup copies in the cloud, using a service like www.dropbox.com. Having this information organized will make life much easier if there is a dispute or if you need to arrange repairs or additional renovations at a later date.

China-specific considerations

In addition to the following entries, the "Law," "Risk factors" and "Useful information" chapters may be helpful when planning a renovation project.

Architects and design institutes

For minor renovations, you will not need the services of an architect. But for larger projects, particularly jobs involving structural changes, an architect's services will be essential. Hiring a foreign architect, who is likely to understand your aesthetic preferences and be comfortable operating in English, can save headaches.

However, foreign architects are required to partner with a local design institute (LDI). The scope of the foreign architect's work cannot exceed that of its LDI, which will be assigned a class, ranging from "A" through "C," based on its size and skill.[2]

After 1949, China's private architectural practices were closed and architects went to work for state-owned LDIs. The LDIs were normally tied to cities and administrative units, where they designed structures such as airports or hospitals for these bodies. Individualism and innovation were discouraged and utilitarian, functional designs became the standard. Many architects and engineers were sent to the countryside.

In the 1980s, private architectural practices re-emerged, but the LDIs continue to play a large role. When partnered with a foreign architect, the LDI verifies and chops (signs) the foreign architect's designs, all of which must be in Chinese. For clients, the LDI's involvement adds time and expense to the design and approval process.[3]

Bare-shell homes

New homes in China are usually sold as bare shells. There will be external doors and windows, but no kitchens, bathrooms, floor coverings or other fittings. This approach serves two purposes: It ensures that the buyer gets the interior design that he wants, and it makes it cheaper and easier for investors to buy and hold property as investment.

Some developers offer a decoration service for customers who buy new, bare-shell homes. One Shanghai-based developer quoted 5,000 yuan per square meter to fit out their luxury villas.

If a home has been vacant for an extended period, you may need to conduct a structural survey to determine if there has been any damage or deterioration. You'll want to replace or repair pipes, drains or wiring that is buried in the walls and floors before undertaking finishing work, like installing floors or wallpaper.

The windows of an unoccupied home may have been left open, allowing water to accumulate on the floors and mold to grow. Balcony railings may have rusted through, wooden doors and other structural elements can rot and windows may need to be replaced. Some high-end villas have passenger elevators, which must be checked carefully before they can be returned to service.

Investment properties that have been left empty often require major renovations. The doors on this villa in Dongguan have rotted away, exposing the home's interior to the elements.

New homes in China are usually sold as bare shells. This villa in Shenzhen has basic wiring but lacks interior doors, staircase railings and wall and floor coverings.

Culture and communication

If you are using Putonghua as a second language and the designer is using English as a second language, there is a good chance that subtleties and nuances will be missed. This is a particular danger with subjective things, like shades of paint. Use photos and samples, ask questions and generally over-communicate to reduce the possibility of misunderstandings. Ask the designer or architect to obtain and approve sample materials. It is also a good idea to ensure that the contract explains the work to be performed clearly and in detail.

Culture can also pose challenges. For example, it is common to "talk around" a problem in Chinese, rather than addressing it directly. Sometimes suppliers will say nothing rather than admit that they cannot meet a request. The need to save face by hiding mistakes can be more important than a business relationship, and sometimes money. Staff are unlikely to take initiative, because it is usually easier (and less dangerous) to do nothing. Furthermore, work will stop over major holidays, like the Spring Festival, which is also known as the Lunar New Year or Chinese New Year.

Patience and a sense of humor can be invaluable assets. Terry Fitch, a designer with many years experience in Shanghai notes, "Be skeptical, conduct your due diligence and don't assume anything."

Disputes

In other markets, disputes between homeowners and designers and builders are routinely resolved through exchanges of lawyers' letters and the threat of litigation. But the high cost, time and energy needed to take a case to court — coupled with the fact that the parties usually have a good idea of how a judge or arbitrator will rule on a given issue — means that these disputes are almost always settled out of court.

This is not the case in China, where the outcome of cases is less certain. Since you can represent yourself in court or in arbitration, litigation is relatively cheap. Chinese courts rarely award lawyer's fees to successful litigants, further reducing the costs of suing. It can be very difficult to collect a judgment in China. As Dan Harris observes in China Law Blog, "If you are going to sue in China, you must be prepared to participate in the litigation for the long haul."[4] Litigation should be viewed as a last resort.

When disputes happen, a designer will sometimes abandon a job. Other companies are usually (and understandably) reluctant to step in and finish the work, adding to the cost and time required to complete the project. This situation can be extremely stressful for a homeowner, who is left with a mortgage to pay, a dwelling she can't occupy and rapidly escalating costs.

In China, commercial disputes can turn ugly. Threats, physical violence and kidnappings occur, and expatriates have been stranded in China after their passport has been confiscated by the authorities. Sometimes, the "least worst" option is to pay to make a problem go away, even if you are in the right.

If your renovation contract includes an arbitration clause, the China International and Economic Trade Arbitration Commission (www. cietac.org) or the Beijing Arbitration Commission (www.bjac.org.cn) are international and well-regarded arbitration venues.

Heritage properties

This category can be subdivided into homes that are formally registered as heritage properties and those that are not. With registered homes, there are limits on the scope and nature of renovations that you can undertake.

For example, in 2003 Shanghai promulgated Preservation Regulations of Historic and Cultural Districts and Historic Buildings of Shanghai City, which was China's first local law protecting heritage structures.[5] There are also renovation restrictions on some *siheyuan* in Beijing.

If the property is unregistered, the scope of the renovations will be determined by your taste, budget and whether you are looking to create a faithful restoration of an original design or to simply modernize the home.

If you are renovating a heritage property of either type, it makes sense to work with an architect or designer with experience in this type of home.

Kitchens

Specialist kitchen contractors operate in cities throughout China. In a renovation or fitting-out project, the general contractor will install the surrounding infrastructure — lights, wiring and plumbing, as well as the floor, wall coverings and ceilings — and leave the counters, cupboards and appliances to a kitchen specialist.

Kitchen specialists use a "system" approach, where drawers, storage racks and countertops are sourced from a single manufacturer and installed as an integrated package. Many of these systems are from the U.S. or Europe, but an increasing proportion of the materials is manufactured in China.

The systems usually include built-in lighting; self-closing drawers with easy-to-clean plastic liners; storage units that make effective use of corners and other dead space; wipe-clean, laminated cupboard door panels that are designed to withstand the temperature and humidity that accompanies cooking; and molded countertops made from Corian™ and other synthetic materials. Kitchen specialists add value by making the most efficient use of the available space and ensuring the kitchen has functional ergonomics, with countertops of a workable height and depth, and adequate lighting. Specialists can also supply — and build around — appliances such as dishwashers, ovens, refrigerators and refrigerated wine cabinets.

Tradespeople

In general, tradespeople in China are poorly trained, badly paid and transitory, because many are migrant laborers. Construction is perceived to be a low-status occupation and few skilled workers, such as masons, welders and plumbers, are certified. As a result, there is little incentive for people to take pride in their work.[6]

Projects can also run into trouble because tradespeople are unfamiliar with the products or materials they are installing. For example, few Chinese construction workers have a dishwasher or wine cellar at home. Problems can also occur when workers do not share your standards for details like doors being hung squarely, finishes matching, etc. Hiring a designer or project manager who has a strong relationship with — and the ability to motivate — tradespeople can be money well spent.

Despite government efforts to eliminate corruption, it remains common in China's construction industry. Bribes are sought for approvals and for expediting work, and it is not unusual for contractors to offer discounts for work done on a cash basis. These activities are illegal, and in the wake of tragedies like the 2010 fire that killed 58 people and injured 71 in Shanghai, the authorities are intent on punishing offenders.[7]

This siheyuan in Beijing includes original buildings and infill housing that was added to accommodate the city's growing population. Electricity and telecommunications were added later.

RISK FACTORS

The following risks are national in nature. For city-specific risks, see the chapters for Beijing, Guangzhou, Shanghai and Shenzhen.

Air pollution

Industrialization, economic growth and rising rates of automobile ownership have contributed to China's increasingly bad air quality, which can be exacerbated by climatic conditions. Governments at all levels have made air pollution a priority, but if you have respiratory problems or small children, you should think carefully about where you live.

The central government monitors air pollution in 113 Chinese cities. Air quality is categorized as surpassing, within or below the standards. In the first half of 2011, no cities were included in the first category, Shanghai and 67 other cities were in the second group and Beijing and 44 other cities were in the third category.

In November 2011, the Ministry of Environmental Protection said it was considering standards that would include PM2.5, which are particles smaller than 2.5 microns that cause haze and damage people's lungs.[1]

Asbestos

A naturally occurring family of minerals prized for its tensile strength and resistance to heat, electricity and chemicals, asbestos has been known in China since the Zhou Dynasty (1046 − 256 BCE), when asbestos cloth was mentioned in dynastic records.

Today, China is the world's largest user and second largest producer of asbestos.[2] The country has more than 100 working mines, most of which are in Sichuan, Qinghai, Liaoning, Gansu, Jilin and Heibei. Almost all the asbestos mined in China is chrysotile.[3]

Companies manufacturing asbestos-based products employ over a million people in China.[4] Asbestos is used in the shipbuilding, petrochemical and pharmaceutical industries and in the manufacture of electrical equipment and automotive components. In Chinese buildings, asbestos can be found in flooring, joint compound, ceiling tiles, roofing, wallboard and other applications.

In Beijing, the use of building materials containing asbestos was banned, but asbestos-based products are used in other parts of the country. Chinese national standard GB50574-2010, which took effect on June 1, 2011, banned the use of asbestos in siding and wallboard.[5]

Inhaling asbestos fibers causes lung cancer, mesothelioma, asbestosis and other diseases. The World Health Organization notes that, "There is no evidence for a threshold for the carcinogenic effect of asbestos and that increased cancer risks have been observed in populations exposed to very low levels."

Most people become ill from asbestos through occupational exposure. Otherwise, building materials pose the greatest risk. Asbestos in ceiling tiles and other building materials is generally regarded as posing a low risk, unless the materials are cut or broken and asbestos fibers are released into the air. This can occur during renovations, demolition projects and earthquakes. Ship breaking is another source of airborne asbestos fibers, and researchers have observed that cigarette smokers who are exposed to asbestos are more likely to develop lung cancer.[6]

Bankruptcy and default

The property market slowdown that began in 2011 left many participants in a financially vulnerable condition. Before the downturn, property agencies expanded quickly, while individuals and companies speculated aggressively. Developers bought land at inflated prices, took on high levels of debt and structured deals using optimistic projections.

There are signs that the market is correcting. For example, in November 2011 Centaline Property Agency — China's largest broker — closed 60 offices and laid off 1,000 staff in Shenzhen,[7] with local and international agencies in other cities reporting similar retrenchments. The following month, in a four billion yuan transaction, SOHO China acquired a 50% stake in a Shanghai commercial development from a group that included Greentown China Holdings. Before the sale, Greentown's debt-to-equity ratio (a measure of financial leverage) exceeded 250%. In April 2012, Hangzhou Glory Real Estate was the first of several small and medium-sized developers to fail.[8]

Large, well-established developers, especially state-owned enterprises, are generally safer than small, private ones. Companies listed on the Stock Exchange of Hong Kong typically have debt-to-equity ratios of about 75%, making them less vulnerable to interest rate increases, credit tightening and economic slowdowns. Hong Kong– and Singapore-listed developers have a higher standard of corporate governance than unlisted companies or ones listed in Shanghai or Shenzhen. Small developers have been forced to borrow, at interest rates of 20% – 30% per month,[9] from trust companies and underground banks because they cannot obtain bank loans or issue bonds. Ratings agency Standard & Poor's notes that smaller developers with operations concentrated in specific cities and projects are vulnerable to policy risk.[10]

Property agencies are also suffering as developers delay their commission payments in an effort to preserve cash. Contractors and material suppliers are also being forced to wait for payment. As a result, it's important to work with businesses that have the resources to honor their obligations, especially if you are buying a home off the plan. While China does have consumer protection laws, a deposit paid to a developer who goes bankrupt or disappears could take years to recover.

Or you could be the only owner in a complex that is not being maintained, or a compound that doesn't get completed.

Finally, people can behave irrationally in extreme circumstances. A firm with an excellent reputation could be teetering on the brink of insolvency, with management hoping that your contract or a change in government policy could be enough to rescue them. And an otherwise honest person who is about to lose his job may behave unethically.

Black swans

As Nassim Nicholas Taleb explains in his book, black swan events are rare, have a profound impact and are predictable only with the benefit of hindsight.[11] The September 11, 2001, terrorist attacks are one example. The severe acute respiratory syndrome (SARS) outbreak that began in Guangdong in 2002 and killed more than 900 people worldwide is another.

Black swans are — by definition — impossible to predict, but they are worth considering. It's a good idea not to assume that tomorrow will be a repeat of today. It's also sensible to include some flexibility in your plans and financial projections, so you can handle black swans as well as predictable events like interest rate increases and market corrections. Betting everything on one transaction is rarely a good idea, especially in an emerging market like China.

Counterfeits

Counterfeit goods represent 15% – 20% of the branded products available in China.[12] Movies, computer software and designer clothes are the most visible examples, but food, aircraft parts and medicine are also faked, as are home appliances and building materials. Counterfeits may not work or fail shortly after they are installed. They may also incorporate defective or dangerous materials, like radioactive metal or toxic chemicals, that pose a health and safety hazard.

The quality of counterfeits ranges from laughable — like the 700 iPhone-branded gas stoves discovered in Wuhan in February 2012 — to indistinguishable from the original, such as items made on a "fourth shift." This occurs when a company manufacturing under license to a brand owner makes products that are sold on the black market and not declared to the brand owner.

To avoid counterfeit goods, use reputable suppliers and vendors. Be suspicious of products that are heavily discounted, that come without packaging or have flawed packaging, such as misspelled brand names and odd colors. It is also a good idea to check for certification marks from UL, TUV and other testing companies. As U.S. President Ronald Reagan was fond of saying, "trust, but verify."

Crime and corruption

China ranked 75th out of 183 countries in Transparency International's Corruption Perceptions Index 2011. In Jones Lang Lasalle's Global Real Estate Transparency Index 2010, China's Tier 1 cities ranked 45th out of 81 markets surveyed with a rating of "semitransparent."

China has the full spectrum of real estate crime. Bribery is not uncommon, and people have been caught impersonating company representatives; setting up companies — complete with bank accounts, fake offices, websites, business cards and supporting documents — with names that are very similar to legitimate companies; and selling properties that they don't own. The seals used to "sign" a document can be forged, and it is not always clear whether the person using the seal has been authorized to do so.

To protect yourself, don't take anything for granted. Work with reputable companies and beware of offers that seem too good to be true. Do a Google and Baidu search for contractors, real estate agents and other suppliers and ask them for references. Check the agent's license number against the registry on the China Institute of Real Estate Appraisers and Agents Website (www.cirea.org.cn, Chinese only). Examine the national directory maintained by the Supreme People's Procuratorate (www.spp. gov.cn, Chinese only) to see if your counterparty has been convicted of bribery (the directory is not online). You can also hire a Chinese law firm to inspect the State Administration for Industry and Commerce file on the company. See the "Developers and development" chapter for a due diligence checklist.

Death

Chinese people avoid things associated with death, including funeral homes, cemeteries, crematoria and the number four, which is a homophone for death. Homes near cemeteries and those with graveyard views are unpopular, as are dwellings where an unnatural death, such as a suicide or murder, has taken place. The resale and rental values of these properties are reduced because they are believed to be inhabited by ghosts. The value of apartments adjacent to a murder or suicide scene can also be affected.[13]

Even if you are unconcerned about ghosts, a haunted property can be difficult to resell. Some entrepreneurs have bought these homes and rented them to non-Chinese tenants, who are often less sensitive to the spirit world.

During the Qingming (tomb sweeping) Festival, which is held on April 4, 5 or 6 each year, cemeteries attract huge numbers of people. Traffic jams and fires caused by burning incense are common.

About nine million people die each year in China. To encourage the efficient use of land, the government promotes cremation, with 48% of funerals using this option in 2011. The Chinese emphasis on filial piety makes the funeral business very lucrative. It has also engendered numerous scams, including ones based on investments in cemetery plots, which can be more expensive than apartments on a square-meter basis. In Beijing, prices for a half-square-meter plot start at 70,000 yuan. Buying a cemetery plot does not convey ownership rights, just the ability to use the space for 20 years.[14]

Divorce

China's divorce rate is rising. In 2010, 2.7 million couples split, up from 1.2 million in 2000 and 800,000 in 1990. The divorce rates in Beijing and Shanghai are reportedly growing at more than 30% per year. With property representing such a large proportion of most families' wealth, a home can play a large role in a divorce.

Under an August 2011 interpretation of the Marriage Law by the Supreme People's Court, parents who buy a home for their child get the property back in the event of a divorce. The interpretation also stated that the person who made the down payment on a property, and whose name is on the title, retains sole ownership if there is a divorce. Mortgage payments made by both partners are treated as joint property and are shared evenly when the property is sold.[15]

Protect yourself by ensuring the property is registered in your name, even if you are told that this is "inconvenient." Without your name on the title, you will have a much harder time proving your interest in the property in the event of a divorce. You risk having the home sold without your authorization.

If you are a foreigner divorcing a Chinese national in China, you will need the services of a Chinese divorce lawyer. You may also need a divorce lawyer in your home country.

Ann Lee, a Chinese-licensed divorce lawyer in Shanghai, writes the Divorce in China blog (http://blog.sina.com.cn/divorceinchina), which may be a useful source of information for people involved in a divorce.

Earthquakes

Earthquakes present several threats to people and property, including embankments collapsing and liquefaction of reclaimed land, damage to buildings and other structures caused by earthquakes and subsequent fires, the release of hazardous materials such as asbestos into the environment and tsunami-related destruction. After a major earthquake, buildings may be uninhabitable; transportation, utilities and other key infrastructure may fail; and essential services may be interrupted.

The deadliest earthquake in history occurred in China on January 23, 1556, when a magnitude 8.0 temblor near Huaxian, Shaanxi, killed more than 830,000 people. More recently, on July 7, 1976, a 7.5 quake struck Tangshan, Heibei, resulting in an official death toll of 242,769. It was the third most lethal quake in history and caused damage in Beijing, more than 150 kilometers away.[16] The 7.9 quake that killed more than 69,195 people in Wenchuan, Sichuan, on May 12, 2008, was felt in Shanghai and Beijing and as far south as Hong Kong.

While the country's high population density contributed to the death toll in these quakes, there is no question that China is located in a seismic hot zone. According to the Global Seismic Hazard Assessment Program — a research project conducted between 1992 and 1998 and endorsed by the United Nations — Guangzhou, Shanghai and Shenzhen are located in low-risk areas, while Beijing is listed as being in a moderate-risk zone.[17] However, a 2008 study by the China Earthquake Administration found 130 fault lines in 21 large cities, including Beijing, Shanghai and Guangzhou. Eighty of the fault lines are believed to be inactive.[18]

Older buildings, which were erected using less strict standards, are more vulnerable to earthquake damage than newer structures. Reclaimed land in cities such as Shenzhen and Shanghai is also vulnerable.[19] In 2012, a report by Canadian environmental group Probe International estimated that 98.6% of 130 dams being built in Western China are located in moderate to high seismic hazard zones. The report claims that these dams are vulnerable to earthquakes and could actually induce earthquakes.[20]

China's building standards, including those for seismic resistance, are developed by the China Academy of Building Research (www.cabr. com.cn). An English version of the current standard, GB50011-2010, can be purchased from Code of China (www.codeofchina.com).

After the 2008 Sichuan earthquake, China's seismic standards were tightened. An updated seismic zone map was scheduled to be published in 2012. The map was to be accompanied by regulations making it mandatory for new buildings throughout China to be earthquake resistant.[21]

Economic slowdown

Between 1990 and 2010, China's gross domestic product grew at an average annual rate of 10.5%[22] and whether it's a gentle slowdown, a recession or a hard landing, China's growth will moderate. Slowing to a more sustainable rate will be beneficial, but it will come with costs as individuals, companies and governments — many of which have grown accustomed to a high-growth environment — adjust to new realities. For investors with cash, patience and a willingness to do research, the adjustment period will offer numerous opportunities.

Electricity shortages

Industrialization, urbanization and an expanding middle class have all contributed to electricity shortages in China. While numerous hydroelectric, nuclear, wind, gas and coal-powered generating facilities are being built, shortages persist.

China's electricity industry is hampered by several factors, including a mismatch between the location of its energy sources and users. About three-quarters of China's electricity is generated from coal, but the nation's coalfields are mainly in the north, and the largest consumers are in coastal provinces in the east and south. China also lacks an effective national distribution grid, and caps on retail electricity prices discourage investment in new capacity and encourage waste. Finally, persistent droughts have limited hydroelectric generation, which represents about one-fifth of China's electricity supply.[23]

There was a shortfall of 30 – 40 gigawatts in 2011. Electricity shortages are most acute during the summer, when demand for air conditioning peaks. This can cause rolling blackouts that affect industrial, commercial and residential users. Shortages can also increase China's already bad air pollution, as factories and other industrial users turn to diesel generators to meet demand. Moreover, the shortages mean that China has little flexibility to deal with natural disasters, equipment failures or other threats to the nation's generation and distribution systems.

You can help by using energy-efficient appliances and turning them off when they are not needed. An uninterruptable power supply will protect your computer from blackouts and brownouts.

Epidemics and pandemics

As the 2002 SARS outbreak demonstrated, epidemics can kill people and create economic chaos. A 2012 survey by the Chinese Center for Disease Control and Prevention showed that China has the highest annual number of cases of multidrug-resistant tuberculosis in the world.[24] Furthermore, global outbreaks of influenza in 1918, 1947 – 58 and 1968 – 69 killed more than 50 million people, and some scientists believe that we are overdue for a new pandemic. See the World Health Organization's Website (www.who.int) for more information.

Expropriation

In China, expropriation follows two patterns. In the first, rural land is taken from farmers by local officials, who rezone the land for urban use. In the second, urban land is taken by city governments. In both cases, structures are usually demolished and governments make large profits selling the land to developers, who build residential and commercial complexes on it.

In urban and rural expropriation, there have been instances of involvement by triads and of collusion between corrupt government officials and developers. To encourage residents to leave, people have been beaten, received death threats and had their power and water disconnected. One apartment complex in Shenzhen was inundated with thousands of scorpions.[25] Adjacent homes are sometimes demolished, leaving a single "nail house" sticking up in the middle of a construction site.

How can you protect yourself from expropriation? Living in a new development, preferably with affluent, politically connected neighbors, will give you some relief. But Huaxiang World Famous Garden, a five-year-old development in Beijing's Fengtai district that was popular with upper middle class people, was expropriated in the fall of 2011.[26]

Homes with heritage value are sometimes protected. But the *siheyuan* (courtyard home) in Beizongbu *hutong* where architect Liang Sicheng and his wife Lin Huiyin lived in the 1930s was demolished over the 2012 Lunar New Year holiday by a developer who claimed to be preserving the site. Ironically, Liang was famous for his research into Chinese architecture and advocacy for the preservation of historic buildings.[27]

For more information about expropriation, see the "Developers and development" chapter.

Fire
The blaze that killed 58 people in a 28-story building in Shanghai's Jing'an district in November 2010 illustrates some of the fire safety threats that are common in China. The fire was started by unlicensed welders, who accidentally ignited scaffolding and nylon safety

netting that surrounded the building. Illegal subcontracting, limited supervision, the use of polyurethane insulation that did not meet flame-retardant standards and firefighters' inability to reach the top floors of the building all contributed to the fatalities.[28]

In older neighborhoods, narrow streets and alleys can make it difficult for firefighters to reach burning buildings. Wood-frame shops and houses, which often have illegal modifications to the gas pipes or electrical system, are also at risk. China's large number of smokers and growing population of elderly people add to the fire hazards.

Celebratory fireworks are another concern. Across the country, almost 6,000 fires were reported in the first 32 hours of the Lunar New Year that began on February 3, 2011.[29] Pyrotechnics were also responsible for a blaze that killed one person and did over 160 million yuan in damage to the Television Cultural Center in Beijing in February 2009.

To protect yourself, buy a home built by a reputable developer that is more likely to use quality materials and comply with building standards. In general, new homes are built to a higher standard than old ones. A competent management company will ensure fire alarms and escape lighting systems are regularly tested and properly maintained and that emergency exits are not locked or blocked by rubbish. Install smoke alarms in your home and test them regularly, and buy a fire extinguisher and take part in regular fire drills.

Floods

In May 2010, torrential rains in Guangzhou killed six people and at least 77 died in Beijing in July 2012 when the capital was hit by the worst storm in 60 years. The economic losses from the Beijing floods were estimated at more than 10 billion yuan and over 65,000 people had to be evacuated from their homes.[30]

Many cities have invested in high-visibility infrastructure projects and neglected less glamorous things like sewers. The problem is compounded by the cities' rapid expansion and the age of the sewer systems, some which date to imperial times.

There is not much that an individual homeowner can do about this, aside from ensuring that your new home is not located in a flood zone.

Infrastructure projects

China is in the middle of the largest building boom in history. Highways, bridges, dams, power plants, rail lines, ports and airports are being built throughout the country. These projects can benefit nearby homeowners when, for example, a new subway line improves access to the city center or a new research park attracts workers and stimulates demand for housing.

Infrastructure projects can also reduce the value of your home and your quality of life. In the short term, you could face an increase in noise, traffic and dust. Subway line construction has caused cave-ins, damaged the foundations of nearby buildings and released poison gas.[31] Your home may be expropriated — 100,000 people will be relocated to make way for the reservoir for the Three Gorges Dam. You could also find yourself living downwind from the 2,000-tonne-per-day garbage incinerator that is planned for Guangzhou's Panyu district[32] or under the flightpath of Beijing's new airport. With nine runways and a 30 billion yuan price tag, the airport is expected to be the world's busiest when it opens in Daxing district in 2017.[33] China's 12th Five Year Plan (2011 – 2015) calls for the construction of 82 new airports and the expansion of 101 existing facilities.

As a result of China's rapid urbanization and economic development, many infrastructure projects are considered essential. To prevent local opposition, governments have been accused of obscuring planning and environmental impact assessment (EIA) notices. But protesters successfully stopped the construction of a molybdenum-copper alloy plant in Sichuan in 2012, a paraxylene plant in Xiamen in 2009, an oil refinery in the Nansha district of Guangzhou in 2009 and the extension of the maglev train line from Shanghai to Hangzhou in 2011.

Project cancellations are not always positive. They can leave you without infrastructure or services that may have been factored into your home's purchase price. For example, in August 2011 the central government suspended work on all new rail lines after a high-speed rail crash killed 40 people. By May 2012, 70% – 80% of China's subway projects had been postponed as city governments ran short of cash, following a slowdown in land sales.[34]

Unfortunately, there isn't much you can do to stop or avoid infrastructure projects. As with expropriation, new housing complexes with wealthy residents are less likely to be targeted for redevelopment than older, poorer neighborhoods. But there are no guarantees. Paying attention to your local media will minimize the likelihood that you will be blindsided by a new project. Finally, it pays to get involved in your community. Research by Daniel Aldrich at Purdue University suggests that once technical factors have been eliminated, communities with a strong civil society, like farmers' and fishermen's cooperatives, are less likely to have controversial facilities built in their backyards.[35]

Legal compliance

In China, there is a gap between the letter of the law and what people and businesses (both foreign and domestic) do every day. This disconnect requires you to make sometimes difficult decisions.

Complying fully with the law will cost you time and money. You may be ridiculed by family and friends. But you will find it easier to sleep at night. If you contravene the law, however, you run the risk of fines, jail, deportation and blackmail. Breaking the law can also limit your ability to seek legal redress when things go wrong. If you are not a Chinese citizen, the risk is increased because you are an easy target for a bureaucrat looking to make an example of someone. If you are

American or British, you may also be prosecuted under the Foreign Corrupt Practices Act of 1977 or the Bribery Act 2010, respectively.

At the risk of stating the obvious, I recommend that you obey the law. But if you choose not to, ensure you are fully aware of the risks. Ultimately, this is a decision that only you can make, based on your values, risk tolerance and priorities.

Local government debt

An audit ordered by Premier Wen Jiabao showed that, at the end of 2010, the governments of Chinese provinces, cities, counties and townships had borrowed a total of 10.7 trillion yuan. The loans were taken out through 6,576 companies, called local government financing vehicles (LGFVs), which were formed to circumvent a ban on local governments issuing bonds or borrowing directly from banks. The audit concluded that over eight billion yuan in loans were overdue and more than 35 billion yuan had been used for unauthorized purposes, such as stock market investments.[36]

The central government has stated that the risks from the financing vehicles are "manageable."[37] But some analysts believe the number of LGFVs, the value of their outstanding loans and the proportion of those loans that are nonperforming are greater than official estimates. Local governments' reliance on land sales as a source of cash and use of land as collateral, coupled with falling land prices and central government initiatives to cool China's property market, have heightened these concerns. In addition, the cost of education, health and social housing programs is being shifted from the central government to local governments.

In October 2011, the central government announced that it would let the governments of Shanghai, Shenzhen, Guangdong and Zhejiang issue bonds. This is the first time local governments have been allowed to issue bonds, a move that may help to alleviate some of the funding crunch, which is expected to peak by June 2013.[38]

Widespread loan defaults by local governments could cause instability in China's banking system, although this would be offset by China's foreign currency reserves, which stood at $3.3 trillion at the end of March 2012. A more likely scenario would be local cutbacks on social spending and public works, potentially resulting in higher levels of unemployment, unfinished projects and social unrest.

Neighbors

The Beijing, Guangzhou, Shanghai and Shenzhen property markets are large, liquid and anonymous. That makes these cities attractive to investors in smaller centers who are looking to diversify their portfolios.

As a developer in Shanghai explained, "There are three kinds of neighbors: Shanghainese, foreigners and people from outside the city. You have to watch out for the last group, who are inclined to be noisy, to drink a lot and to have rough friends, especially if they are nouveau riche. This can be a problem, even in a very nice development."

Tens of thousands of investor-owned apartments sit vacant, because low rental yields make them uneconomical to rent out. Most of these units are empty shells, without bathrooms, kitchens or wall and floor coverings. Policy changes or price adjustments that result in these units being tenanted or purchased by end-users could turn your peaceful home into a construction site and increase demand for shared facilities, like swimming pools and parking spaces.

Nuclear accidents

China's rapid economic development has created immense demand for electricity. Nuclear power is expected to meet a growing proportion of this demand, with net capacity rising from 11.9 gigawatts (GWe) in 2012[39] to 60 – 70 GWe in 2020 and as much as 300 GWe by 2032.[40] China has 15 operating nuclear reactors: seven in Qinshan, Zheijiang, about 350 kilometers from Shanghai; two in Daya Bay, Shenzhen; four in Ling Ao, Shenzhen; and two in Lianyungang, Jiangsu, about 400 kilometers from Shanghai and halfway between Shanghai and Beijing. There is also an experimental fast reactor in Beijing.

Twenty-five nuclear power plants are under construction and another 27 are planned, mainly in coastal areas.[41] After the Fukushima disaster, China suspended approvals of new reactors and undertook a review of all nuclear projects. The review noted that, among other problems, "Some civil reactors and fuel-cycle facilities did not meet new earthquake standards," but the shortcomings were being rectified.[42] The suspension was lifted in March 2012.

To date, the most severe nuclear incident recorded in China was a level 2 on the International Nuclear Event Scale.[43] Fukushima Daiichi 1 – 3 and Chernobyl were level 7 events.

In the NTI Nuclear Materials Security Index (www.ntiindex.org), an international survey conducted by the Nuclear Threat Initiative and the Economist Intelligence Unit, China ranked 27th among 32 countries with nuclear materials. The index rated China as above average in its control and accounting procedures, response capabilities and on-site physical protection. China was below average in terms of nuclear security and materials transparency, sites and transportation, pervasiveness of corruption and physical security during transport.[44]

Policy risk

Governments play a central role in China's real estate market, from setting interest rates to expropriating land, approving development plans and regulating sale prices. Because real estate is a popular store of wealth, maintaining an orderly market (and defusing the 180,000 mass incidents, many of which are related to real estate, that occur each year) is a top priority. Unfortunately, what is beneficial for society as a whole is not always good for individuals, especially foreign buyers. Policy changes can limit your ability to buy, finance, own, sell or enjoy your property.

When it comes to real estate, policy risks are difficult for an individual buyer to manage or hedge. Furthermore, the nature of China's media and regulatory environments means that you will get little warning that a change is coming and will have few avenues to appeal if you don't like a new policy. It would be sensible to assume that your Chinese property is an illiquid investment and ensure that it represents a manageable proportion of your total portfolio.

Sample policy risks include:

- Restrictions on the number of properties you can purchase, like those introduced in Beijing in 2010.

- Residency requirements for home buyers, like those introduced in Shanghai in 2011.

- Foreign exchange or capital controls that stop you from repatriating the proceeds of a sale.

- Business restrictions, like those introduced by the National Development and Reform Commission and the Ministry of Commerce in 2012 that banned foreigners from investing in the management and construction of villas.

- Changes to lending rules or banks' reserve requirements that reduce the availability of credit.

- Amendments to the **hukou** system that change a city's population mix.

- Construction of social housing or a waste treatment facility near your home.

- Expropriation of your home or a nearby property.

Changes to city boundaries. In the spring and summer of 2012, for example, thousands of residents of Chongqing's Wansheng district rioted to protest plans to merge Wansheng with a poorer county.

The introduction of property taxes, like those tested in Chongqing and Shanghai in 2011.

Price caps like those introduced on new homes in Zhongshan and Zhuhai, Guangdong, in 2011.

Intergovernmental conflict. For example, portions of a new residential complex near Hefei, Anhui, were ordered demolished after an overpass for the Beijing – Fuzhou high-speed rail line was built above the apartment blocks.

Economic development policy, like the drive to boost investment in western provinces and discourage low-value-added, labor-intensive and polluting industries in coastal provinces that were included in the 12th Five Year Plan.

Deregulation of the investment market. If the central government makes it easier for individuals to invest abroad or deregulates the domestic market, housing could become less attractive as an asset class, resulting in lower resale prices.

Geopolitical events that affect the relationship between China and the government of your home country. See the territorial disputes section in "The history of property in China" chapter for examples.

Price reductions

Property prices in China have been declining since the central government began its second round of market-cooling measures in

2010. While new buyers welcome lower prices, people who bought near the top of the market do not.

In October 2011, Longfor Properties and China Overseas Holdings were hit by protests when they cut prices by up to 25% for homes in Shanghai.[45] Sino-Ocean Land and Greenland Group have also been targeted by angry buyers. There has been little public sympathy for the protestors, called *fangnao*, who use violence to try to renegotiate or repudiate contracts for off-the-plan apartment purchases.[46]

There are concerns that cuts will tempt buyers to postpone purchases and wait for prices to bottom out. In the meantime, credit tightening by the central government has made it difficult for developers to obtain financing. As a result, developers are resorting to increasingly desperate measures to sell finished homes, including price guarantees, car giveaways and other gimmicks.

Widespread price cuts pose several risks. Buyers may find themselves in negative equity and prices of pre-owned homes could also be hit. A full-blown price war will push marginal developers into bankruptcy, leaving buyers with half-finished apartments and down payments in legal limbo.

Quality control

The collapse of a building in Shanghai's Lotus Riverside development is one of the most spectacular examples of the problems with construction quality in China. On June 27, 2009, a 13-story apartment block in the complex, located in Minhang district, fell over. The building, which was developed by Shanghai-listed Meidu Holding (www.chinameidu.com, Chinese only),[47] was unoccupied at the time of the accident, and one person died. The accident was caused by the excavation of an underground garage on one side of the building, a 10-meter-high pile of soil on the other, and the use of hollow pilings.

A subsequent inspection showed the remaining 10 buildings in the complex, which was taken over by China Vanke, to be safe.[48]

What former Premier Zhu Rongji called "tofu construction" affects more than just residential buildings. Substandard materials, workmanship and inspection processes were implicated in the deaths of more than 4,700 children after schools collapsed in the May 2008 Sichuan earthquake.[49]

In August 2012, the Ministry of Railways announced that 12 major rail lines would be rebuilt or overhauled after serious quality problems were discovered. In some cases, workers used as little as 60% of the cement required to make concrete, leaving structures that did not meet their design specifications.[50]

Quality control in China's building trades suffers because many laborers are migrant workers, who receive little supervision, training, pay or respect. Builders try to finish projects as quickly and cheaply as possible, and workers are discouraged from pointing out problems. Many developers experienced cash shortages after the central government's 2010 market-cooling measures, adding another incentive to cut corners. There is a shortage of construction inspectors — Shanghai has only 946 and plans to double that number — and bribery is not uncommon.[51]

There is also the phenomenon that supply chain specialist Paul Midler calls "quality fade," which occurs when a manufacturer slowly and secretly reduces the quality of a product to boost profit margins. Initial samples will meet the required standard, but over time the quality drops until the product, such as steel rebar, is so far from its specifications that the building collapses. This is a particular problem with items that are difficult or impossible for laypeople to check, like cement.

Unfortunately, even luxury buildings with international management companies are not immune from these problems. While the buildings are unlikely to fall down, leaking windows, clogged drains and similar annoyances are common.

If you are shopping for a new home, buy from a well-known, reputable developer. If you are buying a used home, do a careful inspection and ask your neighbors if they have had problems. A knowledgeable, trustworthy agent can help you avoid buildings and developers with a reputation for problems.

Secrecy

In recent years, China has become a more open society. The domestic media has become aggressive in investigating criminal activities. Through Sina Weibo (www.weibo.com, Chinese only), the local equivalent of Twitter, citizen journalists can quickly bring a story to national attention. Cable television networks, such as CNN and BBC, as well as business news services like Bloomberg and CNBC, are available in residential complexes and hotels that are popular with foreigners.

However, information is far less free on the Mainland than in neighboring Hong Kong, much less Britain or the United States. Internet access is filtered through "the great firewall of China," which blocks searches for forbidden subjects. Weibo's 200 million users must contend with a list of banned topics, which is updated regularly to reflect government sensitivities, and pressure on Weibo's owner, Sina Corporation, to stop the spread of "harmful" information. Tencent Holdings' popular QQ instant messaging service is also censored. Social media sites like Facebook are prohibited, though some people use proxies and virtual private networks (VPNs) to evade these restrictions. The Websites of The New York Times and Bloomberg have been blocked after they ran stories about sensitive topics, while Weibo accounts, including that of the U.S. Consulate in Shanghai, have been suspended. In May 2012, satellite TV network Al Jazeera closed its English-language Beijing bureau after Chinese officials refused to renew the visa and press credentials of correspondent Melissa Chan.

The government controls information through the Law on Guarding State Secrets. In addition to traditionally sensitive areas, such as national defense and diplomacy, the law covers science, technology and social and economic development. As Doreen Weisenhaus notes in her book Hong Kong Media Law, information that has been reported in domestic newspapers, such as the national divorce rate, can be deemed a state secret, and the authorities can retroactively classify information as secret.[52]

Secrecy also affects maps, which are mainly for military and government users, not individuals. Even in nonsensitive parts of China, topographical maps are classified and unavailable.[53]

China ranks 174th among the 179 countries in Reporters Without Borders' 2011 – 2012 Press Freedom Index, and the domestic media remains a tool of government policy. News blackouts of events that might cause civil unrest or reflect poorly on the government — such as the July 23, 2011, high-speed rail crash that killed 40 people near Wenzhou, Zhejiang — are common. Environmental reports are frequently censored. Meanwhile, confidential uncensored reports are produced and circulated to senior cadres.[54]

Government offices, state-owned enterprises and companies frequently ignore media inquiries or provide limited amounts of information. This fuels speculation on Weibo and in the media and encourages a sense of paranoia among the general public that facilitates the spread of rumors.

The Central Propaganda Department (http://cpc.people.com.cn) issues directives on how housing and real estate-related topics — including prices, accidents and natural disasters, the demolition of buildings, expropriation, suicides, self-immolation and demonstrations and the hukou household registration system — are reported in the domestic media.[55]

In this environment, it can be difficult to research your purchase. Augmenting media reports with information from friends, family, colleagues and neighbors can help you fill in the gaps, especially if you balance this data with first-hand research and a healthy degree of skepticism.

Sick building syndrome

Sick building syndrome (SBS) is a group of nonspecific symptoms that includes headaches; coughing; irritation of the eyes, nose, throat or skin; dizziness; nausea; difficulty concentrating; and fatigue. There is no standard clinical definition for SBS, but people suffering from this condition usually feel better shortly after they leave the building.

A definitive cause for SBS has not been identified, but it is associated with indoor air pollution, particularly from the volatile organic compounds (VOCs) in adhesives, furniture, wall coverings, paint, flooring, wood products, solvents and cleaning solutions, pesticides and other products. Polluted outdoor air that is drawn into a building can also contribute to SBS.

Because VOCs are used in construction materials, SBS is common in new and newly renovated homes, especially dwellings that have been sealed to increase their energy efficiency. SBS has also been linked to biological contaminants such as mold, bacteria, viruses and pollen and is exacerbated by inadequate ventilation and poor building maintenance.

Children are more susceptible to SBS and other forms of environmental chemical exposure than adults. Homemakers and other people who spend a great deal of time at home are also at risk. Psychosocial factors such as stress and anxiety can play a role in SBS, and some researchers have questioned whether SBS (and related conditions such as multiple chemical sensitivity and idiopathic environmental intolerance) is a panic attack triggered by exposure to "chemical" smells.

China has numerous standards relating to indoor air quality (IAQ), including codes for the levels of formaldehyde, benzene, toluene, VOCs, ammonia and radon in residential buildings (GB50325-2010), formaldehyde emissions from wood-based panels and finishing products (GB18580-2001) and harmful substances in adhesives in indoor decorating materials (GB18583-2008). There is a growing awareness of the importance of IAQ, and cities such as Shenzhen have announced plans to strengthen their inspection programs to ensure that newly completed buildings meet IAQ standards.

Despite these efforts, sick building syndrome is a problem in China. New homes are sold as bare shells, and buyers move in shortly after workers have finished decorating. Contractors use substandard materials and employ untrained migrant workers, and supervision can be lax. Building managers block or disable ventilation systems to save electricity.

The outdoor air quality in parts of China is contaminated with industrial emissions and automobile exhaust. One study estimated that the lifetime cancer risks from exposure to indoor concentrations of carcinogenic VOCs in China were about 10 times higher than those in Japan.[56]

You can reduce your SBS risk by purchasing a home built and decorated by reputable companies, using materials that meet domestic and international standards. Buying a home located away from busy roads and industrial facilities and ensuring that you have adequate ventilation will also help.

There have been reports of companies offering fraudulent IAQ testing services to sell homeowners "air improvement" services. Legitimate companies will have a metrology accreditation stamp from the State Administration of Quality Supervision, Inspection and Quarantine.[57]

Airborne chemicals can be removed via physisorption with activated charcoal, porous ceramics and natural fibers; by chemisorption using organic and inorganic compounds; and through decomposition using photocatalysts, negative ions and other techniques. Commercial products, such as electronic air cleaners and passive air cleaning boards that use manganese dioxide to convert formaldehyde into water and carbon dioxide, are also available, as are colorimetric detectors that indicate the presence of formaldehyde.

Social housing

The central government is making social housing — apartments that can be purchased or rented by low-income earners — a priority. Five million social housing completions and seven million starts were targeted for 2012, with a goal of 36 million completions between 2011 and 2015.

Local governments will provide most of the money for these homes, adding an estimated two trillion yuan to their already large debt load.[58] Furthermore, local governments derive much of their revenues from land sales, and prices have been falling with the cooling property market.

Local governments are scrambling to meet Beijing's social housing targets. As a result, holes in the ground are being counted as construction starts and already planned developments, including towers in luxury complexes, are being reclassified as social housing.

For buyers, this presents three risks. First, the cost of building social housing could impair local governments' ability to deliver services. Second, in a worst-case scenario, the added expense could make governments default on their bank loans, destabilizing China's financial system. Finally, the construction of social housing nearby may reduce your home's resale value.

Soil pollution

After 1949, land in China could not be bought or sold and had no cash value. As a result, there was no economic incentive to build factories in remote areas and many polluting facilities were built on the outskirts of cities. As recently as 2011, the Shougang Group had a steel mill in Beijing's Shijingshan district, just 17 kilometers from Tiananmen Square.[59]

As the real estate market was liberalized and the pace of urbanization increased, cities expanded into suburban areas and factories began to leave. Between 2001 and 2009, 98,000 industrial enterprises moved from locations that included Guangzhou and the future site of Shanghai Expo 2010. In Beijing, 200 factories are being moved from inside the Fourth Ring Road.

Central locations made these brownfield sites desirable places to build homes. But many sites were badly polluted with heavy metals, including arsenic, cadmium, chromium, lead and mercury; electronic waste, such as flame retardants and heavy metals; organic chemicals like benzene, hydrocarbons and solvents; and persistent organic pollutants, including polychlorinated biphenyls (PCBs) and pesticides like DDT. On some lots, the contamination exceeded the legal limit by a hundred times, penetrated the soil to a depth of 10 meters or more and leached into the groundwater.[60]

In 2006, the government began a three-year, one billion yuan program to investigate soil pollution in grain-producing and industrial areas. The survey was completed, but the findings were never disclosed, fueling speculation that, as one report put it, the pollution was "so severe that the government does not want to release the information."[61]

China's brownfield situation is compounded by the lack of a national soil pollution law. There is no requirement that land be investigated for contamination[62] and many offending factories were state-owned enterprises, where managers kept few records and had little appreciation for the environmental consequences of dumping chemical waste.

In China's cities, soil and roadside dust commonly contain elevated levels of cadmium, copper, lead, zinc, chromium and nickel. These heavy metals come from vehicle exhaust and industrial sources and can be inhaled, ingested or absorbed through skin contact. In rural areas, these contaminants come mainly from mines, sewage sludge, pesticides and fertilizers, and can enter the food chain.[63]

The health effects of chemical contamination can take years to become apparent. But sometimes they are immediate. On April 28, 2004, three workers building the Songjiazhuang Subway Station in Beijing were hospitalized after they drilled into a pocket of poisonous gas left over from a pesticide plant that operated there 30 years earlier. The site was subsequently remediated, but the incident raised awareness of the seriousness and proximity of the contamination.[64]

Problems have occurred with homes built on brownfield sites. In 2010, residents of a development built by China Vanke in Beijing's Songjiazhuang district complained of bad smells. A chemical plant and a paint factory had operated on the site, which was remediated in 2007 – 08.[65] In 2009, the ground beneath the 2,400-apartment Yangtze Pearl development in Wuhan was found to be badly contaminated.[66] For 60 years, Wuhan Jiu'an Pharmaceuticals and Wuhan Yangtze Chemicals had plants on the site. While the Wuhan and Beijing homes were built for low-income buyers, regular housing was also built on brownfield sites.[67]

As with other risk factors, buying from a reputable developer is a good place to start. With a brand to protect, they are less likely to build on a contaminated site and have an incentive to treat you properly if there is a problem. Next, do some research to find out if your prospective home is on a brownfield site. Talk to elderly people who might remember a dismantled factory; read newspapers; and visit local libraries, universities, historical societies and museums. The municipal archives can also be helpful, although you may need a letter of introduction to access their material.

Subsidence

Subsidence affects more than 79,000 square kilometers of land and 50 cities — including Beijing, Guangzhou, Shanghai and Shenzhen — and is mainly caused by depletion of underground water sources.[68] In Shanghai, which has sunk 2.6 meters since 1921, the problem is exacerbated by the city's dense network of skyscrapers. The central government has initiated a program to resolve this situation, which is made worse by chronic water shortages in many parts of China, by 2020.[69]

Subsidence can generate large bills for homeowners, as foundations are reinforced and cracks are repaired. In extreme cases, buildings have collapsed or been made uninhabitable. Subsidence is also a major expense for cities like Shanghai, which spend billions of yuan every year replenishing underground aquifers. These costs, and those associated with damaged roads, bridges and railways, will ultimately be borne by taxpayers.

Termites

Over 400 types of termites have been identified in China, including the Formosan subterranean termite, *Coptotermes formosanus* (Shiraki), which is also known as the super termite. A mature C formosanus colony can include several million insects, consume over 400 grams of wood per day and severely damage a building within months.[70]

South and Southeastern China are prone to termite infestations, as are older buildings in Shanghai. The United Nations Environmental Program estimates that up to 80% of the buildings in Guangdong may be infested and that the cost of termite infestations in China exceeds $1 billion annually.[71]

In 2009, China banned the production, sale, use, import and export of Mirex, an effective termiticide that is also a persistent organic pollutant and a suspected carcinogen. As a result of the ban, and the lack of an effective replacement for Mirex, China's termite problem is believed to be worsening.[72]

Traffic

China's roads are among the most dangerous on earth. Officially, traffic accidents are the nation's seventh-leading cause of death, killing more than 100,000 people annually.[73] However, researchers comparing the official number of traffic deaths, which is compiled from police data, with death certificates completed by physicians, believe the real number may be as high as 250,000.[74]

Inexperience is a key problem. There are more than 100 million cars on China's roads — a figure that is expected to double by 2020[75] — and the average motorist has less than five years' experience.[76] Drunk driving was only criminalized in 2011 and many drivers treat road signs and speed limits as suggestions. The rapid expansion of China's road network, coupled with complex and sometimes nonstandard intersections and interchanges, only adds to the confusion.

In addition, road noise and traffic jams on China's increasingly congested roads add to stress levels. Vehicle emissions — including diesel exhaust, which the World Health Organization classified as a carcinogen in 2012 — are a major contributor to both air and soil pollution.[77]

Given the above, living near your workplace and limiting your exposure to China's roads will benefit your physical and mental health.

Water pollution

China has a nationwide water pollution problem. Forty percent of the nation's surface water is suitable only for agricultural or industrial use,[78] and tests in 200 cities by the Ministry of Land and Resources showed the underground water quality from 40.3% of the monitored sites was "bad" and another 14.7% was "extremely bad."[79] More than a quarter of 4,000 urban water treatment facilities tested by the government in 2009 failed to meet national standards. The results of the survey were not made public and treatment facilities in rural areas are suspected to be even worse.[80]

Water pollution comes from numerous sources. China currently treats just 57% of its sewage and 10% – 20% of the sludge from its sewage treatment plants.[81] Contamination from industrial waste, chemicals and heavy metals is common, as are accidents. In November 2005, for example, an explosion at the Jilin Chemical Industrial plant released 100 tonnes of benzene and other chemicals into the Songhua River, which supplies drinking water for Harbin.[82] Twenty tonnes of cadmium was dumped into the Liujiang River in Liuzhou, Guangxi, in January 2012.[83] Benzene and cadmium are known carcinogens.

China is the world's largest consumer of chemical fertilizers and pesticides, which leach from farmers' fields into the nation's groundwater. The volume of livestock waste is estimated to be more than four times that of industrial organic pollutants.

The central government announced plans to spend 500 billion yuan on nearly 6,000 projects to prevent and control water pollution between 2011 and 2015.[84] It also introduced new drinking water quality standards, effective July 2012. But Professor Wang Zhansheng of Tsinghua University's School of Environment believes it may be "eight or nine years" before people can drink water straight from the tap.[85]

While China works to fix these issues, using a water filter — or buying bottled water from a reputable supplier and using it for cooking and drinking — would seem prudent, particularly if you have small children or invalids at home.

China uses a six-grade classification scheme for water, where grade I is the best. Grades I through III can be used for drinking. Grade IV is for industrial applications and for recreational use where there is no direct human contact. Grade V can be used for agricultural and landscaping purposes. Grade VI cannot be used for irrigation.

Xenophobia

In 2012, xenophobia in China appeared to be increasing, sparked by video footage of a drunken British man assaulting a woman on a Beijing street and an altercation between a Chinese woman and a Russian cellist on a train, both of which circulated widely on the Internet. These incidents prompted a widely publicized on-air tirade against foreigners by CCTV presenter Yang Rui. Some people compared these events to the Boxer Rebellion of 1899 – 1901, in which Christian missionaries were attacked and foreign residents of Beijing were taken hostage. In 2012, there were nationwide protests directed at Japanese interests in China, sparked by the conflict over the Diaoyu Islands, which are known in Japan as the Senkaku Islands.

As China assumes an increasingly prominent role on the world stage, there will be more conflicts between China and other countries. Given the immobility of real estate, the relatively small number of foreigners in China and their visibility, xenophobia is a good reason to practice your Putonghua and maintain cordial relationships with your neighbors.

Zoning

The combination of an ancient civilization, urbanization and growing wealth means that China's cities are expanding in unpredictable ways. There is no precedent for China's urban development and there is no handbook for the nation's urban planners. As a result, the zoning assumptions that you might make in another country, for example, about what might be built next to your new home, may not hold true in China.

FINANCE

Mortgages

145

Taxes and fees

155

Insurance

159

MORTGAGES

China's mortgage market

China's mortgage market has come a long way in a short time. After the Cultural Revolution (1966 – 76), China had virtually no functioning financial institutions.[1] But by the end of June 2012, outstanding real estate loans from major domestic and foreign-funded lenders totaled 11.3 trillion yuan. Of this amount, mortgages were 6.9 trillion yuan, real estate development loans were 2.9 trillion yuan and land development loans were 803.7 billion yuan.[2] By comparison, at the end of June 2012, outstanding mortgages in the United States (including loans for homes, farms and nonresidential property) totaled $13.2 trillion, or more than seven times the size of China's balance.[3]

Between 50% and 70% of buyers in Beijing, Guangzhou and Shanghai take out mortgages, borrowing an average of 50% of the purchase price. Buyers in secondary and tertiary cities are more likely to pay cash for their homes.[4]

Interest rates

Mortgage rates for yuan-denominated loans are set by the People's Bank of China (PBOC). As of July 6, 2012, benchmark rates were 6.55% for loans of more than five years, 6.40% for three to five years, 6.15% for one to three years, 6.00% for six months to one year and 5.60% for less than six months.[5]

Banks may discount to a maximum of 30% or charge a premium on these rates, depending on a borrower's creditworthiness, market conditions and the number of homes she owns.[6] As part of the PBOC's differentiated credit strategy, discounted rates are often available to first-time home buyers.[7]

Under current regulations, buyers must make a 30% minimum down payment to purchase their first home. The idea of a "first home" is potentially confusing, because it can be cumulative. After you have purchased one home using a mortgage — regardless of whether you have kept it or sold it — you are no longer a first-time home buyer. Second homes require a 60% minimum down payment and buyers must pay at least 1.1 times the benchmark lending rate.[8] Mortgages are not available for third homes.

In addition to changing interest rates, the central government can increase or decrease the amount of mortgage money available by raising or lowering the banks' reserve requirement ratio (RRR). When the RRR is increased, banks must keep more cash on hand; conversely, when it is lowered, banks can lend that money to borrowers.

Rules and regulations

According to the China Banking Regulatory Commission's guidelines, banks should have face-to-face interviews with mortgage applicants, visit the borrower's home when appropriate, have the mortgage contract signed in person and provide the funds to the borrower in a timely fashion when the contract has been executed. The commission also notes that lenders should not make false promises, commission intermediaries to sign and collect loan contracts or make arbitrary charges. Lenders are also expected to "firmly implement" the central government's market adjustment policies.[9]

Local vs. international lenders

When you apply for a mortgage, you can choose a regional lender like Singapore's DBS or Hong Kong's Bank of East Asia; a multinational like HSBC or Standard Chartered Bank; or a local lender, such as the

Agricultural Bank of China or the Bank of China. See the "Useful information" chapter for more information.

The local banks' biggest advantage is scale. A June 2012 Bloomberg story noted that foreign banks accounted for just 1.7% of the outstanding loans in China and had fewer than 400 branches. China's five largest state-owned banks had more than 66,000 domestic branches.[10] The domestic banks' large retail network can be an advantage if you need to visit a bank branch.

What international and regional banks lack in scale, they make up for in service. Foreign lenders offer English-language application forms and information and English-speaking counter staff. International lenders have a greater customer-service orientation and may be able to link your banking activities in another market with those in China.

International banks also offer foreign currency mortgages. For example, in addition to yuan-denominated mortgages, Standard Chartered Bank offers loans in Hong Kong, Singapore and U.S. dollars. HSBC and DBS offer mortgages in yuan and in Hong Kong and U.S. dollars.

If you buy a new home, you may find that the developer has a relationship with a bank, which may be funding the project. The relationship between the bank and developer will not get you a better deal on the mortgage, but it may result in a faster approval process. Being a premium-level bank customer can result in some savings.

Applying for a mortgage

While policies vary according to the bank, the following will help you understand the system in China:

> If you are not a Chinese citizen, you must have lived legally in China for one year before you can qualify for a mortgage.

- Banks will lend to customers between the ages of 18 and 70, with some banks specifying a minimum age of 21 and a maximum of 60.

- Loan amounts range from 300,000 yuan to 10 million yuan. Loans above 10 million yuan are available but are treated as special cases. Mortgages at the lower end of this scale are unattractive to lenders because the cost of processing and servicing a small loan is nearly the same as handling a large one, but small loans are less profitable.

- Regional and international lenders look most favorably on new apartments and villas and on pre-owned homes that are less than 15 years old. Homes in Beijing, Guangzhou, Shanghai and Shenzhen are preferred.

- The tenor (repayment period) for a mortgage runs from five to 30 years.

- Many banks will provide approval in principal for a mortgage after the buyer has signed a preliminary sale and purchase (S&P) agreement or a subscription agreement. Approval in principal is not binding on the bank.

- Mortgage applications can be approved in as little as two working days. This assumes that all of the borrower's documents are in order and there is nothing unusual about the transaction.

- Processing, from application to draw-down, typically takes between one and two months. It can take up to six months in extreme cases.

- Standard Chartered Bank and HSBC offer straight-line and reducing-balance payment options.

- Foreign banks often offer incentives, like free property insurance, legal advice and property valuation services, with their mortgages.

Documents

To apply for a mortgage, you will need to provide originals and copies of the following:

- Proof of your identity, such as a passport or ID card

- A resident's booklet, if you are a Chinese citizen

- Proof of residency, such as a utility bill

- A marriage certificate, if applicable

- Employees need proof of income, such as their last tax bill, a letter from their employer confirming their salary and employment history, and/or three months of bank records showing salary deposits.

- Self-employed people need proof of business ownership, bank statements for the past six months, their last tax bill, and/or latest profit-and-loss statement.

- Preliminary S&P agreement, subscription agreement or S&P agreement for the property

The application process

- The borrower signs a preliminary S&P agreement, a subscription agreement or an S&P agreement for the property and makes the necessary down payment.

- The borrower completes the bank's application form.

- The borrower gathers originals and copies of the documents listed above.

- The borrower submits the documents to the bank.

- The bank reviews the documents, values the property and processes the application.

- The bank approves the application.

- The bank arranges insurance on the property.

- The mortgage is notarized (if necessary) and the contract is signed.

- The mortgage is registered as a lien against the property.

- The bank releases the funds borrowed through the mortgage.

- The borrower begins repaying the mortgage.

- The borrower makes the final payment and the mortgage is discharged.

Getting approved

Stephan Bosshart, managing director at Standard Chartered Bank in Shanghai, explained that his organization uses the five Cs to assess mortgage applications. While banks will approach this slightly differently, the core concepts are used by all lenders.

Character — The applicant's credit history, including credit card ownership and repayment history

Capacity — The applicant's ability to repay the mortgage, including salary, income and employment stability and outstanding debt

Capital — The size of the applicant's down payment and net worth

根据《中华人民共和国宪法》及其它有关法律的规定，为保护房地产权利人的合法权益，对权利人申请登记的土地使用权和土地上建筑物、附着物的所有权，经调查审定，确认合法，现准予登记，发给此证。

注 意 事 项

（一）本《房地产证》记载的土地使用权及土地上建筑物、附着物的所有权，经深圳市人民政府和土地发机关圭章后生效，受国家法律保护，任何单位或个人不得侵犯。

（二）房地产权利人必须遵守国家法律、法规和政府有关房地产管理的各项规定。

（三）房地产权转移、变更或抵押的，必须按照规定程序申请办理有关登记。

（四）本证不得涂改，凡擅自涂改的，一律无效，并追究有关人员的责任。

深圳市人民政府办公厅监制

When your mortgage has been approved, you will have a new home and a property certificate like this one.

Collateral — The age, location, value, quality and overall marketability of the property

Conditions — The bank's credit policy in light of external economic circumstances

Other sources of funds

Overseas remittances

China's foreign exchange market is managed by the State Administration of Foreign Exchange (SAFE). Expatriates are permitted to convert a maximum of $50,000 in foreign currency per year into yuan. It is possible to apply to SAFE for an exemption to this limit.

To repatriate funds from the sale of a property in China, you will need a certificate from the local tax bureau showing that all relevant taxes have been paid. After obtaining the tax certificate, you apply for SAFE's approval and then apply to a bank for the fund transfer. To accomplish these steps, you will need the buyer and vendor's identification, copies of the S&P agreements showing that you bought and then sold the property, a copy of the property title, registration documents showing that title has been transferred to the new owner, a copy of the inward fund transfer documents (if applicable) and various application forms.[11]

The Housing Provident Fund

Introduced in Shanghai in 1991 and then nationwide in 1994, the Housing Provident Fund (HPF) is a compulsory saving program that is modeled on Singapore's Central Provident Fund. Employers and employees contribute a percentage of the employee's salary to an HPF account, which the employee can use to buy a home and for related expenses, such as renovations. Employees can also obtain low interest loans from the fund with local limits on the size and type of property that qualifies.[12]

The HPF was originally established for public-sector employees, but was expanded to all employees in 2005. Participation and contribution rates vary across the country, as does enforcement. By 2008, the fund was valued at 2 trillion yuan.[13]

Foreigners with permanent residency in China may contribute to the HPF in the city where they are employed and use the fund in the same manner as Chinese employees.[14]

Grants and subsidies

Grants and subsidies may be available through your city or employer. Since 2010, for example, Shenzhen has made grants of nearly 50 million yuan to over 14,000 professionals in more than 100 local enterprises. In December 2012, Shenzhen announced 1 billion yuan in new subsidies.[15]

Reverse mortgages

Reverse mortgages were introduced in Shenzhen in 2011. These agreements allow a homeowner who is over 55 and who owns two or more dwellings to mortgage one home and receive monthly payments of up to 20,000 yuan for 10 years. Newspaper reports note that China CITIC Bank did not receive any applications in the first 12 months that reverse mortgages were available. Uncertainty surrounding the 70-year residential land lease was cited as one reason for the lack of interest.[16]

The shadow banking system

China has an active shadow banking system. However, interest rates are punishingly high and it would be difficult for a nonlocal borrower to access these funds.

Credit reporting

The PBOC operates the National Credit Information Database, which collects information about businesses and individuals. For consumers, the database includes the person's name, current and previous residential addresses, identity card number, date of birth and employment history, if available. Credit data includes accounts and outstanding balances at banks and lenders, credit cards, mortgages, car and other consumer loans. The database includes negative information about late repayments and defaults, if any.[17] Prior consent must be obtained from the person whose data is being collected, and consumers have the right to inspect their files, correct erroneous information, make official complaints and seek judicial relief.[18]

Banks are required to regularly report credit data about business and individual borrowers to the PBOC. Banks can access the database when processing applications for loans, mortgages, credit cards and other credit facilities. Banks also use the data to manage post-approval risk management of their loan portfolios. With files on 600 million people in 2008, it is the world's largest credit information database.[19]

In addition to the National Credit Information Database, there are databases operated by private companies. Credit bureaus are prohibited from gathering and reporting personal information that could be used to discriminate against a borrower, such as genetic data, health history, blood type, ethnicity, religion or political affiliation.[20]

TAXES AND FEES

In China, taxes are levied at the national, provincial and local levels. Taxes are a source of revenue and a tool to manage the housing market. The taxes and tax rates change frequently in line with market conditions and government policies.

Taxes

The main taxes that affect individual home buyers, owners and sellers are as follows:

Deed tax of 3% to 5% of the value of the property or land use rights. Deed tax is paid by the buyer when the property is purchased.

Business tax of 5% of the appreciation (i.e., the sale price less the acquisition price) of the property or land use rights. Business tax is paid by the vendor when the property is sold. Property held for five years or more is exempt from this tax.[1]

Business tax of 5% of the gross receipts from a rental property.

Property tax of 1.2% of the original cost of the building less a 10% – 30% deduction depending on the location, or 12% of the annual rental income. Since 2009, Chinese companies and individuals have been exempt from this annual tax, but it still applies to foreign enterprises and individuals. In 2011, property taxes were introduced on a trial basis in Shanghai and Chongqing. Property taxes are widely expected to be introduced in other cities in the future.[2]

City construction and maintenance tax and education surcharge. These taxes are calculated as a percentage of the business tax payable. The education surcharge is 3% of the business tax payable. The city construction and maintenance tax is 7% for taxpayers in cities, 5% for taxpayers in counties and townships and 1% for taxpayers in other areas. Provinces are supposed to collect a local education surcharge of 2% of the business tax payable, but not all provinces levy this tax and the rate varies.

Urban and township land use tax is levied on the total floor area. The rate for this annual tax ranges from 0.9 yuan per square meter in small cities to 30 yuan in large ones.

Farmland occupation tax is levied when nonagricultural activities take place on farmland or buildings are erected on farmland. The average rate for this annual tax is 45 yuan per square meter in Shanghai, 40 yuan in Beijing and 30 yuan in Guangdong.

Stamp duty is payable at the rate of 0.05% of the contract value for the sale of property by both the buyer and the vendor. For rental contracts, stamp duty of 0.1% of the total rental amount is payable by both the tenant and the landlord. Stamp duty of 5 yuan is payable for each land use certificate or property ownership certificate.[3]

Notary fees

If you are a not a Chinese citizen, you must pay a notary to have your signature notarized when you purchase a piece of property. This service costs 0.25% of the purchase price.

Ordinary residences

In 2005, the concept of the "ordinary residence" was introduced into China's real estate policy. The construction of ordinary residences, which are intended for working people, is supported with preferential land allocation, credit and approval policies. The regulations are based on the home's size, plot ratio, price and location. If a dwelling is deemed to be an ordinary residence, a lower deed tax applies.[4]

For example, in February 2012, the Shanghai Municipal Government raised the upper limits for prices of ordinary residences. For homes inside the Inner Ring Road, the limit rose from 2.45 million yuan to 3.3 million yuan. For those between the Inner and Outer ring roads, the limit increased from 1.6 million yuan to 2.0 million yuan. For homes outside the Outer Ring Road, the limit rose from 980,000 yuan to 1.4 million yuan.[5]

INSURANCE

China's insurance industry

International insurers were active in China until 1949. After the revolution, foreign companies were closed or left China. In October 1949, the government formed a state-owned monopoly, the People's Insurance Company of China, which is now known as PICC. In 1988, China Merchants established Ping An Insurance in Shenzhen.

Insurance is now an accepted part of Chinese life. The 12th Five Year Plan (2011 – 2015) includes a commitment to establish and improve China's insurance industry, including catastrophe insurance and reinsurance. In 2011, property insurance premiums in China exceeded 478 billion yuan.

Despite this rapid growth, China's insurance industry is still in its infancy, with penetration rates that are well below those of other countries. A 2010 paper by the World Bank estimated that 5% of the property in China — mainly owned by industrial and commercial users — was insured. About one dwelling in 100 is insured against natural hazards.

PICC Property & Casualty is China's largest non-life insurer, with more than one-third of the market in 2011, followed by Ping An Insurance. Foreign insurers have returned to China, attracted by low penetration rates and China's 1.3 billion people. However, government regulations limit foreign companies' ability to sell insurance in China. Today, foreign firms have about a 1% share of China's property and casualty market, and their operations are concentrated in Beijing, Guangzhou, Shanghai and Shenzhen.

The following forms of insurance are marketed to homeowners in China. For a list of companies selling these policies, see the "Useful information" chapter.

Fire insurance

Fire insurance covers the structure of a home against damage by earthquakes, floods, typhoons, burst pipes, landslips, subsidence and similar risks. Banks often bundle this insurance with a mortgage.

Home contents insurance

Also known as homeowner's insurance, home contents insurance covers personal possessions from losses associated with fire and theft. It also offers protection from damage during renovations.

Liability insurance

Property owner's liability insurance covers claims associated with damage to a neighbor's property or the injury or death of a third party. This insurance is recommended during renovations.

CITIES

Beijing
165

Guangzhou
181

Shanghai
199

Shenzhen
217

BEIJING

City snapshot

Population

In the 2010 census, the population of Beijing Municipality was 19.6 million, up six million from 2000. Beijing is relatively young, with people aged 65 or above accounting for 8.7% of the population, versus 8.9% nationally. Beijing includes rural counties, but 86% of its permanent residents live in urban areas. People from other parts of the country represent 36% of the total, or seven million people. According to official statistics, Beijing was home to about 91,000 foreigners in 2010.[1] Just over 1% of Beijing's population is foreign born,[2] versus 27% in London[3] and 36% in New York.[4]

Economy

As the national capital, Beijing attracts foreign and domestic companies selling to the central government, as well as firms needing government approval to operate in China. Beijing has a growing high-technology sector; is home to most of the state-owned enterprises controlled by the central government; and is a hub for transportation, culture, education and the military. In 2010, Beijing's gross domestic product was 1.37 trillion yuan,[5] larger than that of Ireland.

Geography

At 16,411 square kilometers, Beijing is about half the size of Belgium and is the third largest directly controlled municipality in China. It comprises six core districts: Chaoyang, Dongcheng, Fengtai, Haidian, Shijingshan and Xicheng; eight suburban districts: Changping, Daxing, Fangshan, Huairou, Mentougou, Pinggu, Shunyi and Tongzhou; and two counties: Miyun and Yanqing. In 2010, two districts in central Beijing — Chongwen and Xuanwu — were merged with Dongcheng and Xicheng, respectively.

Tiananmen Square and the Forbidden City sit at the heart of Beijing, which is encircled by a series of ring roads.

Social indicators

Until 2013, the central government did not release China's Gini coefficient (a common measure of income inequality).[6] However, the 2012 Hurun Wealth Report estimated that the capital is home to the largest number of wealthy people in China. Beijing has 179,000 individuals with total assets of 10 million yuan or more and 10,500 with assets exceeding 100 million yuan. Beijing was the 17th most expensive city in Mercer's 2012 international cost of living survey.

Despite significant problems with air pollution, water shortages and traffic congestion, Beijing ranked eighth out of 30 cities in the 2011 China City Life Quality Index Report prepared by the Chinese Academy of Social Sciences.

Beijing's housing market

Human habitation in Beijing dates back some 750,000 years to Peking Man, a collection of fossils discovered in nearby Zhoukoudian. Today, Beijing is a mega-city that has more in common with a small country than with most other cities.

Beijing is a magnet for talent from China and beyond. It attracts everyone from migrant workers and students to diplomats, entrepreneurs and executives employed by foreign corporations, over 15,000 of which have offices in the city.[7] These factors, coupled with China's growing economy and rising number of affluent residents, drive demand for high-quality homes.

Most people live in apartment blocks, which range from old units built from Soviet plans to ultramodern complexes that feature swimming pools, tennis courts and other amenities. The new buildings would not be out of place in London, New York or Tokyo.

In October 2003, restrictions on the neighborhoods where expatriates could live in Beijing were lifted.[8] However, many expats continue to live in the areas east of the Forbidden City and southeast of Tiananmen Square that were designated for foreigners during the late 19th and early 20th centuries. The area around Chaoyang Park, for example, is near the American, Malaysian and South Korean embassies, the Canadian International School of Beijing and the Lufthansa Center. Sanlitun and adjoining Dongzhimen are home to many embassies as well as expat-friendly bars and restaurants and a growing range of international boutiques.

As a political and administrative hub, Beijing did not develop a traditional central business district.[9] However, two commercial zones

These apartment blocks are near Tsinghua University in northwest Beijing. Standardized building designs were used throughout China to minimize construction costs.

have emerged. One is a 399-hectare area, most of which is between the Third and Fourth ring roads in Chaoyang district, east of the city center.[10] Beijing's tallest skyscraper, the 510-meter China Zun Building, is under construction here and is scheduled for completion in 2016.

The second commercial zone is Beijing Finance Street. Located to the west of Tiananmen Square, Beijing Finance Street is a 40.5-hectare mixed-use development that includes offices, hotels, retail outlets, serviced apartments and a park.[11] Apartments near the central business district and Beijing Finance Street are popular with businesspeople trying to avoid Beijing's traffic.

Education drives many expatriates' housing decisions. Most of Beijing's international schools are outside the Third Ring Road in suburbs such as Shunyi in the city's northeast. Located near Beijing Capital International Airport, Shunyi includes detached villas in gated communities. Most offer recreational facilities, landscaped grounds, efficient security and shops and restaurants.

Beijing's stock of high-quality housing (as distinct from homes provided by *danwei*, or work units) was originally built to accommodate expatriates. However, high construction and maintenance standards and clear property rights have made "foreign housing" popular with affluent local buyers.[12]

Buying property in Beijing

Agent's commission

In August 2011, the Beijing municipal government introduced limits on the commissions that agents can charge for pre-owned homes. The caps are based on a sliding scale and range from 2% for homes under five million yuan to 0.5% for homes over 50 million yuan. These are maximum rates, and discounts can sometimes be negotiated.[13]

Conservation

Beijing has a reputation for beauty, and there is a growing interest in preserving the city's architectural heritage. However, conservation efforts in Beijing and other cities are often opposed by residents who want to live in modern homes and property companies interested in redeveloping old, centrally located neighborhoods.

There is also a movement against "Qianmenization," where an old neighborhood is razed and replaced with a modern copy.[14] The phrase was derived from Qianmen district, south of the Forbidden City, which was demolished before the 2008 Olympics and rebuilt as a historic theme park, complete with international brands and neon signs. Beijing's first commercial street, Qianmen Avenue, is more than 600 years old.[15]

Property taxes

Beijing does not levy property taxes. However, the city is expected to introduce a property tax in the future. See "The buying process" chapter for more information about taxes.

Market-cooling measures

In February 2011, in a move to stem rapidly rising prices, the Beijing government announced regulations requiring people from outside Beijing to provide five consecutive years of tax receipts before they would be eligible to buy a home in the capital. The new regulations also prevent nonlocal residents from buying a second home and prohibit local residents from buying a third home.[16] These restrictions are in addition to those contained in Circular 171 and Circular 186 (see "The buying process" chapter for details).

The market-cooling measures have had an effect, with land sales in Beijing falling 38%, to 101 billion yuan, in 2011. However, in July 2012 private developer Sinobo Group won an auction for a site in Haidian district with a bid of 2.6 billion yuan. At more than 33,000 yuan per square meter, plus a commitment to allocate 16,400 square meters to social housing, it was the most expensive residential site in China.[17]

Distinctive housing

Siheyuan

For many people, *siheyuan*, the single-story courtyard homes built around the city's ancient *hutongs*, or alleys, symbolize Beijing. Typically surrounded by a plain, gray wall with a gate at the southeastern corner, most siheyuan face south. Four buildings, including accommodations for extended family and servants, are built around a central courtyard that can feature goldfish ponds, trees and gardens.[18]

Constructed from bricks and timber using designs dating from the Han Dynasty (206 BCE – 220 CE), siheyuan vary in size, depending on the wealth of the owner. Some feature multiple courtyards and ornate gates.

Siheyuan once comprised the bulk of the housing in Beijing's old city (the area now encircled by the Second Ring Road[19]) and until 1949, siheyuan could be owned by individuals. Subsequently, the state assumed control of China's urban land and Beijing's population grew rapidly. Many siheyuan were taken over during the Cultural Revolution, and newcomers moved into compounds that once held an extended family. Small buildings were haphazardly added to courtyards, leaving a warren of narrow, dark passages with poor ventilation.

While electricity is now commonplace, many siheyuan still lack plumbing, leaving residents to use communal wells and toilets. Inhabitants enjoy a strong sense of community, where neighbors know and look out for each other. The hutongs, which include schools, shops, small businesses, police stations and government offices, have individual identities, based on a commercial or occupational focus. Dengcao Hutong, for example, was named for a nearby market that sold lamp wicks.

As property market reforms were introduced and local governments were allowed to sell land use rights, interest grew in redeveloping the siheyuan. This has taken several forms, including the gentrification of existing siheyuan; replacing them with apartment blocks and commercial projects; and comprehensive renewal programs, such as the Ju'er Hutong project designed by Wu Liangyong. Modern interpretations of siheyuan can be found in developments such as Cathay View and I-House in northeast Beijing.

Redevelopment often results in residents moving to new apartment blocks in distant satellite cities. Some people see the siheyuan as substandard housing and are happy to move to more modern, anonymous accommodations. Others feel the compensation they are

Some of Beijing's traditional *siheyuan* homes have been renovated and converted into hotels. The Beijing Sihe Courtyard Hotel is in Dengcao *hutong* in Dongcheng district.

offered is too small and decide to stay in their tight-knit communities. And there are people who worry that the destruction of the siheyuan damages Beijing's social structure and heritage.

Several Beijing real estate agents specialize in renting and selling siheyuan (see the "Useful information" chapter for details). Hotels have sprung up on hutongs throughout Beijing, allowing visitors to sample life in a siheyuan before making a long-term commitment.

If you are thinking of buying a siheyuan you should know that:

- It can be difficult to arrange a mortgage. You may have to pay cash.

- Siheyuan often command a premium on top of Beijing's already high prices.

- Some siheyuan have multiple owners, each whom controls a portion of the property. The owners may not have the land license needed to complete the sale. Separately, you may need to compensate or resettle sitting tenants.

- Some siheyuan cannot be sold to foreigners or rebuilt.

- You may need to negotiate with neighbors to repair shared walls, arrange water and sewerage connections and obtain multiple construction permits and government approvals. It is not uncommon for a new owner to pay for an improvement that benefits his neighbors.

- Siheyuan built below street level can suffer from flooding.

For a taste of life in the hutongs, see Michael Meyer's book, *The Last Days of Old Beijing*.

The rat tribe

Beijing's economic success continues to attract people from other parts of China. Over one million migrant workers live in the basements of apartment buildings and in former air-raid shelters that have been subdivided into rooms or cubicles, some of which are only large enough to hold a bed.

These subterranean residents, dubbed the "rat tribe," pay 300 yuan – 700 yuan per month for their accommodations. Living conditions are grim: there is often no natural light or heat; residents share bathrooms and showers; cooking is prohibited; and fire sprinklers and other safety systems are basic.

In December 2010, the Ministry of Housing and Urban-Rural Development issued a regulation outlawing the rental of air-raid shelters, basements and partitioned rooms as residences.[20] Some of Beijing's underground residents will benefit from a national plan to build 36 million units of social housing. But this is a long-term solution and the new social housing is unlikely to be as centrally located as their underground homes. In the meantime, rising rents are forcing poorer migrant workers out of Beijing. Some 600,000 left the capital in 2011.[21]

Livability issues

Air pollution

In 2009, Beijing's air quality ranked 26th out of 30 Chinese cities. With 121 micrograms per cubic meter of PM10 (particles smaller than 10 microns that can cause heart disease, lung cancer, asthma and acute lower respiratory infections), Beijing's air quality was the 10th worst among international capital cities in a World Health Organization report.[22] Data for the WHO report was supplied by the Chinese government.

Beijing's local air pollution comes from power stations, industrial processes, vehicle exhaust and construction and road dust. Before the 2008 Olympics, thousands of old, polluting vehicles were retired, more than 5,000 city buses were retrofitted to run on compressed natural gas, over 200 polluting industries were relocated, some 16,000 coal-fired boilers were converted to natural gas and the use of natural gas for power generation was increased 15-fold.[23] In 2012, the government announced plans to close 1,200 polluting factories in Beijing by the end of 2016.

Despite these measures, Beijing's environment remains under pressure from an expanding economy and increasing numbers of residents and vehicles. The situation is made worse by the Yanshan Mountains to the west, north and northeast, which trap air pollutants; by dust storms that blow down from Mongolia and Inner Mongolia in the spring;[24] and by air masses that carry pollutants from regions to the south, including Hebei, Shandong, Shanxi and Tianjin.[25] Beijing's air quality is usually worst during the winter months.

You can get hourly updates on Beijing's PM2.5 and ozone levels via Twitter from http://twitter.com/beijingair. The data is collected from a monitoring station at the U.S. Embassy in Beijing.

Infrastructure projects

Like most of China, Beijing has been investing heavily in infrastructure projects. This spending is likely to intensify as governments use infrastructure projects to stimulate the economy.

For example, a 30 billion yuan airport in Daxing district is now under construction and is scheduled to open in 2017, while a six billion yuan maglev train line will link suburban Mentougou district and the Pingguoyuan subway station by 2013. Beijing also announced plans to invest more than 55 billion yuan on 10 subway projects between 2013 and 2015 and plans to build 660 kilometers of subway lines by 2015.[26]

Over the long term, these projects will improve the quality of life in Beijing. In the short term, however, they will add noise, dirt and traffic congestion. They also have the potential to improve or degrade individual neighborhoods, so conduct due diligence before you commit to a purchase.

Soil pollution

Two hundred factories are being moved from inside Beijing's Fourth Ring Road, leaving as much as 800 hectares of brownfield sites in their wake.[27] Many of these sites are contaminated with industrial waste, including known carcinogens. For additional information, see the "Risk factors" chapter.

Traffic

As of September 2011, five million vehicles were registered in Beijing, up 450,000 from 2010. The Beijing Municipal Commission of Transport projects the total will reach seven million by 2015.[28] This rapid growth has contributed to the city's poor air quality and to severe traffic jams. Beijing and Shenzhen were tied for second-worst place in IBM's 2011 Global Commuter Pain Survey, which polled more than 8,000 people in 20 cities. The survey covered 10 issues including commuting time, time spent in traffic and the psychological effects of traffic.

The authorities are combating these problems with investments in public transport, license plate lotteries, registration caps, road use restrictions and other measures that contributed to a 10% increase in the average rush hour speed during the first six months of 2011, to 24 kilometers per hour, from the same period in 2010. In late 2012, the municipal government announced plans to invest over four billion yuan to expand 58 roads in the city center.[29]

Despite these initiatives, Beijing's traffic is a long-term problem, fueled by rising incomes, strong consumer demand for automobiles and urban planning that is unable to keep up. Parking is another issue. In June 2011, there were just 2.5 million parking spaces for the city's five million cars.[30]

China's roads are among the deadliest on earth, due in part to the large number of inexperienced drivers. Buying a home near your workplace can reduce your traffic-related stress, exposure to exhaust fumes and the probability of being involved in an accident.

Water and related issues

Beijing has a multifaceted water problem. The city faces a severe water shortage that is exacerbated by a drought that began in 1999, a distribution system that loses 16% – 30% to leaks[31] and low retail prices for water.[32]

Supplies per person have fallen below 100 cubic meters, one-tenth the United Nations' standard for a water shortage.[33] The shortfall comes despite long-term water diversions from sources north of Beijing, the depletion of groundwater aquifers on the Beijing plain and the 500 billion yuan South-to-North Water Diversion Project, which transports water from the Yangtze River to northern China, including the capital.

Depleted water tables are also associated with soil subsidence.[34] In Beijing, there were 54 sinkhole collapses in 2007 and 94 in 2008. In 2009, the most recent year for which official statistics are available, there were 129 incidents.[35]

In addition to a water shortage, there are concerns about quality. Beijing meets China's drinking water standards, which test for 106 contaminants. But water is tested at treatment facilities — not in peoples' homes — and some residents complain about bad smells and metallic tastes, particularly in the southern part of the city.[36] As a result, most people boil tap water before drinking it, a practice endorsed by water company technician Ren Xiaochun in an August 2011 interview with *Beijing Today*.[37] Water filters and bottled water are also popular, although there have been reports of counterfeit[38] and contaminated bottled water in Beijing.[39]

The Beijing Municipal Environmental Protection Bureau publishes a monthly report on the quality of the water in the rivers, lakes and reservoirs that supply the capital (www.bjepb.gov.cn/bjhb/publish/portal0/tab376/, Chinese only).

Despite the drought, flooding is an issue in Beijing. In July 2012, 77 people died in the worst rainstorms to hit the capital in 60 years.[40] Six billion yuan of damage occurred in Fangshan district alone, where more than 8,000 homes collapsed and another 66,000 were damaged. Fifty bridges and 750 kilometers of roads were also damaged.[41]

A crowd-sourced map showing the parts of Beijing that were affected by the floods is available at http://maps.google.com/maps/ms?ie=UTF&msa=0&msid=212396812630615178145.0004c56bf3bc327e99c55, Chinese only.

A new home in Beijing

Janet De Silva and her husband Yves Therien decided to buy a home in Grand Hills after Janet accepted a transfer from Hong Kong to Beijing to head the China operations of an international financial services company.

The Canadian couple looked at two other developments — Yosemite Villas and Palm Springs — before choosing a 450-square-meter detached home in Grand Hills, which is in Chaoyang district. Completed in 2004, Grand Hills comprises 153 detached homes and is located less than seven kilometers from Beijing Capital International Airport and near the Western Academy of Beijing, the International School of Beijing and the International Montessori School of Beijing.

Modern commercial developments are changing the face of Beijing. Sanlitun SOHO is surrounded by bars, restaurants and boutiques.

Janet and Yves chose Grand Hills because it offered the right mix of scale, greenery and features. "Palm Springs and Yosemite Villas were just too big," says Janet, while Grand Hills' park-like setting and lakes made it feel like "a little sanctuary in the middle of Beijing." The development's tennis courts, pool, health club, clubhouse and mix of expatriate and local families sealed the deal.

The couple bought their home from Jinlaxin Real Estate Development Co. in April 2005 for $950,000, using a 50% mortgage from Hong Kong–based CITIC International Bank. The developer helped arrange the mortgage, which came with a discounted rate, from the bank's Beijing office. The real estate subsidiary of Yves' employer, Santa Fe Relocation Services, acted as the agent.

Like most new houses in China, the exterior and landscaping of the new home was complete but the interior was a bare shell. Janet and Yves hired an architect, who was the spouse of a family friend in Hong Kong, to handle the design and project management for a flat fee of $50,000. "The architect's creativity and design sense gave our home a modern, international feel," says Janet, who notes that they had no trouble buying international brands of sanitary ware, appliances and fittings at nearby superstores.

After Janet and Yves approved the design, the architect solicited bids from five contractors, several of whom had completed similar projects for the couple's friends. All of the contractors promised to finish the project on time.

With the architect's assistance, Janet and Yves selected a contractor, who signed a $140,000 contract that included labor and materials. The agreement also contained a penalty clause that reduced the contractor's fee by 5,650 yuan for each day the project was delayed after a 14-day buffer. "In the end, the contractor absorbed a 34-day penalty," observes Janet. "That represented a 15% discount on the overall renovation cost and covered unbudgeted items that arose during the construction."

In addition to being late, the project experienced several technical problems. "It took the contractor five attempts to correctly install a curved staircase and matching glass railing," notes Janet, "and we had a lot of trouble convincing him that the heated basement floor should not extend into the wine cellar." But the biggest problem occurred after the couple moved in. While installing the furnace, a worker poked a hole in a plastic water pipe. Instead of replacing the pipe, the worker "fixed" the hole with duct tape. When Yves turned the furnace on for the first time, the duct tape broke, flooding the basement and leaving the house without heat for three days. In hindsight, Janet thinks they should have hired a separate project manager. "But even with a project manager, as owners, you need to be very hands-on with every detail."

Janet and Yves lived in the home from October 2005 until they returned to Hong Kong in August 2007 and then used it as an income property. Janet says they had no trouble finding tenants. "We had two families bidding to lease our home and it was fully tenanted the entire time."

In April 2010, Janet and Yves sold the house to a Hong Kong man and his Mainland wife. The sale and purchase agreement, which was prepared and executed in China, was registered with the government and specified that the sale proceeds would be denominated in Hong Kong dollars and paid in Hong Kong. "We were very fortunate," says Janet. "We bought at the start of a rising market, sold with a sitting tenant and achieved a very healthy return on our investment."

GUANGZHOU

City snapshot

Population

In the 2010 census, Guangzhou's registered population was 12.7 million, an increase of 2.8 million from 2000. Permanent residents from other parts of China represented 37.5% of the total, or 4.8 million people. Guangzhou is also home to more than seven million migrant workers who do not hold local *hukou* (residency permits). People aged 65 or above accounted for 6.6% of the population versus 8.9% nationally, with males representing 52.3% of the total.[1] Over 87% of Guangzhou's permanent residents lived in urban areas. A large proportion of Guangdong's 63,000 permanent foreign residents live in Guangzhou.

Economy

Guangzhou is Southern China's manufacturing hub. Since 1957, the city has hosted the Canton Fair (officially known as the China Import and Export Fair), which was one of the nation's most important foreign-trade vehicles. Today, Guangzhou's economy is moving from polluting, labor-intensive manufacturing into high-technology and research and development. In 2011, Guangzhou's gross domestic product was 1.2 trillion yuan,[2] greater than that of New Zealand.

Geography

Located in the Pearl River Delta, Guangzhou occupies 7,434 square kilometers and is the capital of Guangdong.

The city comprises 10 districts. Yuexiu, Haizhu, Liwan and Tianhe are Guangzhou's urban core. Baiyun, Huangpu, Huadu and Panyu are suburban. Nansha and Luogang are mainly industrial. Guangzhou also includes two county-level cities: Conghua and Zengcheng. Huadu and Panyu, which were county-level cities, were amalgamated into Guangzhou in 2000. In 2005, a section of Panyu was annexed to become Nansha and the city's administrative districts were reorganized. Luogang was created, Dongshan merged into Yuexiu and Fangcun joined Liwan.

Social indicators

The 2012 Hurun Wealth Report estimated that Guangzhou was the Chinese city with the third-largest number of wealthy people, after Beijing and Shanghai. Guangzhou had 55,000 individuals with total assets of 10 million yuan or more and 4,100 with assets exceeding 100 million yuan.[3] Guangzhou was the 31st most expensive city in Mercer's 2012 international cost of living survey[4] and ranked first out of 30 cities in the 2011 China City Life Quality Index Report prepared by the Chinese Academy of Social Sciences.[5]

Guangzhou's housing market

Lacking Beijing's political clout, Shanghai's commercial elan and Shenzhen's brash newness, Guangzhou would be easy to overlook. But the city has a long, colorful history. Historian Him Mark Lai notes that a small walled town called Chuting existed on the site of modern Guangzhou as early as 887 BCE.[6]

Guangzhou is also cosmopolitan. Arab and Persian traders lived in Guangzhou during the Tang Dynasty (618 – 907). The Portuguese arrived in 1517, followed by the Dutch in 1601. In the 1700s, the Swedes, Danes, French, English and Americans traded with China through Guangzhou. That tradition continues today with Guangzhou's African population, which officially numbers 20,000 but is believed to be 10 times larger.

While the Europeans and Americans traded in cotton, tea and porcelain, their African successors deal in mobile phones and clothing.

Foreign settlements

In 1782, the Qing emperor awarded a foreign-trade monopoly to a group of Chinese merchants, called *hongs*, in Guangzhou. In return for the monopoly, the merchants were responsible for the foreigners' behavior while they were in China and for ensuring the traders paid their taxes.[7]

The hongs were allowed to build accommodations where the foreigners could live during the trading season. They constructed 13 two-story factories* on a 340-meter by 150-meter site on the Pearl River. Known in Chinese as *shisanhang*, the factories were the only place that foreigners could live and trade in China until the Treaty of Nanjing was signed and treaty ports were opened in 1842.[8]

The factories played a central role in the Opium War. In 1839, foreign traders were blockaded inside without access to food, water or servants. The factories caught fire in 1822 and 1843 and were subsequently rebuilt. After an 1856 fire, the foreign community moved to Shamien Island, which was also known as Shamian and Shameen.[9]

In 1859, Shamien was a sandbar in the Pearl River to the west of the factories. After an 18-month reclamation, the island occupied 27 hectares and was about 2 meters above the high-water mark. Britain leased the island from China, took four-fifths of the land and auctioned plots to the foreign community. The remainder of Shamien was left to the French.

Like Shanghai's French Concession, Shamien was a European neighborhood transplanted to China. The British and French built consulates and churches, merchants erected elaborate homes and a promenade was built along the southern shore. By 1873, 10 consulates had opened on Shamien and the island became popular with banks

* The factories included offices, warehouses and living quarters. In old English, a factory was an establishment where agents or merchants conducted business in a foreign country.

and trading firms. Gas lighting was installed in 1887 and electricity followed in 1892.

Shamien was connected to the mainland by two bridges, which were guarded and locked at night. Chinese people were not permitted to own property on Shamien or to visit without a pass. Racially motivated riots occurred in September 1883, during which 14 homes were looted and burned and the residents fled. On June 23, 1925, British and French marines on Shamien exchanged shots with Chinese students and military cadets on the mainland. Fifty-two people were killed and 170 were injured in the incident.[10] Shamien was subsequently under siege for 16 months.[11]

Since 1996, Shamien has been a protected cultural site and development has been restricted.[12] The island is now a popular tourist attraction that features art galleries, tea houses and hotels.

Modern Guangzhou

After 1949, Guangzhou became a center for textiles and trade. During the 1950s and 1960s, manufacturing developed in Xicun, Chigang and Nanshitou. Guangzhou benefited from the liberalization program that began in 1978, but these reforms also eroded Guangzhou's economic importance.

Guangzhou faces other challenges. Unlike Beijing and Shanghai, Guangzhou competes with nearby cities for capital and talent. Hong Kong, which is an entrepôt, and Shenzhen, which was China's first special economic zone, offer significant advantages to corporations, investors and employees. The multibillion-dollar bankruptcy of Guangdong International Trust and Investment Corporation in 1999 damaged investor confidence in Guangzhou. More recently, rising land and labor costs, coupled with policies that discourage the labor-intensive manufacturing industries that have underpinned the city's economy, have also hurt Guangzhou's fortunes.

Guangzhou's leaders are focusing on making the city more livable, with multiple urban centers, lower carbon emissions and sustainable development. The municipal government is integrating the city's transportation network with the surrounding Pearl River Delta and increasing Guangzhou's focus on service industries.

Compared to other Tier 1 cities, Guangzhou property is relatively inexpensive. Research conducted in the second quarter of 2012 by real estate consultants Knight Frank showed that Guangzhou's price-to-income ratio (the average price of a standardized new home divided by the average annual household income) was 9.2 versus 13.9 in Shanghai.[13] A home priced at 100,000 yuan per square meter in Shanghai typically sells for just 40,000 yuan per square meter in Guangzhou.[14] Shanghai's greater population density and Guangzhou's higher plot ratios, which let developers erect larger buildings, are two reasons for this gap.[15]

Guangzhou is also much cheaper than Hong Kong, and a shared language, culture and cuisine make the city a popular destination for retirees from Hong Kong. More than 10,000 elderly people from Hong Kong live in Guangzhou.

Where to live

Several Guangzhou neighborhoods are popular with professionals and managers. In 2010, 35% of the city's 20,000 expatriate residents lived in Tianhe, 22% in Yuexia and 14% in Panyu.[16]

Ersha Island in Yuexia offers some of the city's most expensive real estate. The island is also home to numerous parks, the American International School of Guangzhou, the Guangdong Museum of Art and the Xinghai Concert Hall.

Tianhe is Guangzhou's commercial hub and the site of the 103-story Guangzhou International Finance Center in Zhujiang New Town (also know as Pearl River New Town) and the 80-story CITIC Plaza, which are popular with local and multinational corporations. The Guangzhou East Railway Station, which offers direct train service to Hong Kong, is also in Tianhe. Neighborhoods along Tianhe North Road and Huanshi East Road are popular with Western expats.

Panyu is popular with families who prefer a quieter, greener environment within commuting distance of Guangzhou's central business district. Panyu includes Clifford Estates, which contains thousands of homes and was once the largest private housing estate in China.[17] Nearby services for the international community include the JCI-accredited Clifford Hospital, Clifford School and numerous stores and restaurants.

Distinctive housing

Qilou buildings

Guangzhou's qilou buildings are used for both residential and commercial purposes. Found throughout the city, qilou became popular in the 1930s and are typically three or four stories tall. Qilou combine Chinese and

Qilou buildings on Enning Road. Fast-food restaurants and boutiques occupy remodeled qilou buildings on nearby shopping streets.

Some of the *xiguan* houses along Baoyuan Road have been upgraded or converted into boutiques. Most, however, are unimproved.

Western architecture and the ground floor includes an arcade that shields pedestrians from Guangzhou's hot sun and frequent showers.[18]

Xiguan houses

Named after the area west of the ancient city wall, most *xiguan* houses are found in Liwan. Fewer than 100 of these homes remain, from a peak of more than 800 during the Qing Dynasty (1644 – 1911). Xiguan houses can be Western or Chinese in design, or combine both influences.[19] Typically constructed of gray brick, xiguan houses often feature stained glass windows and *tanglong* (horizontal round wooden bars) across the front entrance.

Western-style villas

The Dongshan area, which is now part of Yuexia, is home to many Western-style villas, including single-family dwellings and apartment blocks. These two- or three-story buildings are typically constructed of brick and often owned by overseas Chinese or their descendents.[20]

Canadian Leo Seewald bought and restored a 1930s villa that he discovered by walking around several neighborhoods. To preserve the home's character, Seewald installed custom-made Art Deco–style iron window grills and then reused their design on other parts of the house. But he also discovered a drawback to heritage properties in China: complex ownership structures. "There were people who hadn't lived in the house for years, who demanded money before they would de-register their hukou," notes Seewald. De-registration is a prerequisite to completing the purchase of a pre-owned home.

Buying property in Guangzhou

Agent's commission

For pre-owned homes, commissions in Guangzhou typically range from 0.5% to 2.5% of the purchase price and may not exceed 3%.[21] Commissions are higher on homes selling for less than 1 million yuan. Previously, buyers and sellers both paid commission. Currently, only buyers pay. Buyers do not pay commission when purchasing a home directly from a developer.

Conservation

Shamien Island has been recognized as culturally valuable and some qilou buildings, xiguan homes and Western-style villas have been renovated and preserved. But Guangzhou has a large stock of old, dilapidated buildings, many of which are being demolished and replaced with modern apartment blocks. There is growing awareness of local conservation issues, including the preservation of the Cantonese language. In January 2013, the Guangzhou Municipal Government announced the creation of a "protection list" for historical buildings and neighborhoods.

Market-cooling measures

The Guangzhou Municipal Government introduced a series of home purchasing restrictions in February 2011. Local families that own one home may buy a second but are prohibited from buying additional dwellings. Nonlocal families that do not own a home, but can produce tax or social insurance certificates proving that they have resided in Guangzhou for 12 of the past 24 months, may purchase one home, but are prohibited from buying additional homes.[22]

In March 2012, Guangzhou issued the Circular on Publication of the Opinions on Further Strengthening the Supervision of the Real Estate Market. The circular prohibited foreigners and individuals from Hong Kong, Macau and Taiwan from buying offices, shops and serviced apartments in Guangzhou.[23]

These local restrictions supplement national measures introduced in 2010 that increased the down payment requirement to 30% for first-time buyers and to 50% for buyers of second homes. Guangzhou's restrictions also supplement those in Circular 171 and Circular 186 (see "The buying process" chapter for more details about market-cooling measures).

In October 2012, Guangzhou announced unspecified measures to cap luxury home prices. Local governments in China must approve the price of new homes before they are released to the market, and Guangzhou was the first city to introduce these curbs. At the time, apartments in prime areas like Pearl River New Town were trading at more than 60,000 yuan per square meter.[24]

Property tax

Guangzhou does not levy property taxes. However, the city is expected to introduce a property tax in the future. See "The buying process" chapter for more information about taxes.

Livability issues

Air pollution

In 2009, Guanghzou's air quality ranked sixth out of 30 Chinese cities in a World Health Organization report. Guangzhou reported 70 micrograms per cubic meter of PM10s (particles smaller than 10 microns that can cause heart disease, lung cancer and asthma).[25]

Daily air quality updates are available from the Guangzhou Environmental Protection Bureau's Website (www.gzepb.gov.cn). You can get hourly updates on Guangzhou's PM2.5 levels via Twitter at http://twitter.com/Guangzhou_Air. The data is collected from a monitoring station near the U.S. Consulate on Shamien Island.

Electricity shortages

Guangzhou faces power shortages, especially during the summer months when hot weather drives demand for air conditioning. Heavy industry, not residential customers, bears the brunt of the shortages, which were estimated to be between 4 and 6.5 million kilowatts for Guangdong in 2011.

In 2012, the Guangzhou Municipal Government announced plans to build 49 natural gas-powered generating facilities throughout the city.[26] Between 2012 and 2017, the city will invest 37 billion yuan in 133 high-voltage substations, with the goal of achieving 99.989% reliability by 2015.[27]

Infrastructure projects

Guangzhou is in the middle of a building boom. For example, between 2011 and 2020, Guangzhou Metro will invest 235 billion yuan to add 313 kilometers to the city's subway system. Seven new subway lines will form part of an integrated rail network for the Pearl River Delta and expand Guangzhou's subway system to over 500 kilometers.[28]

Five new runways are planned for Baiyun International Airport, which will be linked with Guangzhou North Railway Station.[29] A feasibility study has also been undertaken for the construction of a new airport in Nansha.

Guangzhou's main landfill in Xingfeng is full and faces closure. Five new garbage incinerators will begin operation by 2015, bringing the city's daily capacity to 11,000 tonnes. Despite local opposition, the new incinerators are scheduled to open in Panyu and Huadu, supplementing an existing facility in Baiyun.[30]

Development projects

Guangzhou's topography is being reshaped with large developments, many of which include a residential component.

In 2010, for example, work began on the 123-square-kilometer Sino-Singapore Guangzhou Knowledge City. Located in Luogang, this project focuses on information technology, biotechnology, clean technologies, next-generation materials, creative industries and science and educational services.

Guangzhou International Financial Town will occupy 8 square kilometers in Tianhe. This project, which is also known as Guangzhou International Finance City, is scheduled to be built between 2013 and 2016.

Approved by the State Council in September 2012, the 803-square-kilometer Nansha New Area will host service industries and cooperative projects with Hong Kong and Macau.[31] It includes a 150-hectare consular zone with offices and an international school and hospital.

In 2011, Singapore's CapitaLand signed a memorandum of understanding to redevelop Datansha Island in Liwan. With an estimated budget of 28 billion yuan, the project will transform the 4-square-kilometer island into a "mini Singapore."[32]

Soil pollution

Guangzhou's role as a manufacturing center has left the city with a serious soil pollution problem. According to a World Bank report, 147 large industrial enterprises were closed, suspended or relocated between 2007 and 2010. Some of the resulting brownfield sites, including the former locations of the Guangzhou Nitrous Fertilizer Factory and Southern Steel Factory, have been reused for affordable housing.[33]

Research in 2012 by South China Agricultural University showed that soil and dust samples from roadsides, residential areas, parks, campus sport grounds and commercial sites in Guangzhou had high concentrations of cadmium, lead and zinc. Some 61% of the urban soil samples were "moderately to highly polluted." All of the dust samples were "highly polluted."[34]

Traffic

Guangzhou's traffic woes are fueled by urbanization, rapid growth and planning bottlenecks. Guangzhou's 14th urban master plan, which was completed in 1981, was approved by the State Council in 1984. By 1989, the city had grown beyond the limits set in the plan for 2000. The 15th master plan was completed in 1996, but it was not endorsed by the State Council until 2003.[35]

In May 2012, 2.4 million cars were registered in the city, 2.5 times more than in 2007. The gridlock caused by this growth is exacerbated by weak traffic management and a lack of parking spaces in the city core, which leads to illegal parking.[36]

In July 2012, Guangzhou announced that it would allocate its annual quota of 120,000 new car registrations through a lottery and an auction. The city is also spending billions of yuan on subways and other transportation projects with the goal of having 70% of the population use public transit.[37] During major events, Guangzhou uses the even-odd license plate system to reduce traffic congestion. From 7 A.M. until 8

P.M. on alternate days, cars are banned from city streets based on the last digit of the vehicle's license plate

Urban villages

An urban village is a residential neighborhood built on rural land that has been encircled by a growing city (see the "Demographics" chapter for more information). Urban villages are scattered throughout Guangzhou and provide inexpensive accommodations for the migrant workers who are employed by the city's factories. They have high crime levels, poor construction standards and limited facilities.

In 2010, Guangzhou had more than 130 urban villages that covered over one-fifth of the city's area and housed almost one million people.[38] In 2009, the Guangzhou authorities decided to rebuild all of the city's urban villages within a decade, but scrapped the initiative in 2011.[39] Fear of social unrest from residents, many of whom make a comfortable living renting rooms to migrant laborers, is believed to have been behind the decision to cancel the redevelopment plan.

Water and related issues

In addition to the Pearl River, which defines Guangzhou's geography, the city has more than 200 rivers and streams. Water covers 10% of Guangzhou's surface area.

Guangzhou's water supply is badly contaminated by agricultural chemicals, industrial effluent and heavy metals. In 2011, the Pearl River in Guangzhou was rated Grade IV, meaning the water is suitable for industrial use and entertainment purposes in which it does not come into contact with human skin.[40] The Dongjiang, which supplies Guangzhou and Shenzhen, is one of the world's most polluted rivers and is unsuitable for drinking six months of the year.[41] More than three-quarters of the sewage in Guangdong is discharged directly into rivers,[42] and the water supplies in Huadu and Panyu are susceptible to contamination.[43]

The main gate of Shipai Village in Tianhe. This urban village is a kilometer from TaiKoo Hui, one of Guangzhou's most exclusive shopping malls.

Guangzhou is prone to typhoons and flood zones are scattered throughout the city. A storm on May 7, 2010, killed six people and resulted in losses of more than 1 billion yuan. Underground garages were particularly badly hit.[44]

An apartment-based office in Guangzhou

For Hong Kong–based footwear manufacturers Bruce Grill and Martin Merz, the decision to buy an apartment in Guangzhou was motivated in part by the need to escape a greedy landlord. "We were his only source of income and he took every opportunity to raise our rent and make our lives miserable," notes Bruce.

The rented apartment served as a Mainland office for Bruce and Martin's company, NJB Merz, and as a showroom where they could make presentations to visiting clients. "In the beginning, we would meet American and European customers in our Hong Kong office. As China opened up, buyers would visit our Guangzhou office. Later, they'd travel to the factory. Today, the majority of our business is done over the Internet," observes Bruce.

In 1995, Martin found an 118-square-meter apartment in Tianhe that was in the final stages of construction. "We couldn't see the unit before we bought it," says Martin. "I had to bribe a security guard so that I could have a quick look around."

Bruce and Martin, who both speak Putonghua, bought the apartment in their own names from an executive working for the developer. At the time, the local government was encouraging foreign investment, so they were able to complete the purchase in Hong Kong dollars, using a contract drawn up and executed in Hong Kong. "That seemed safer than dealing with Chinese contracts," says Bruce. "And since we had already bought property in Hong Kong, we were familiar with the process."

It took a year to receive the title for the apartment, which had to be surveyed before the title could be issued. When the apartment was found to be smaller than the dimensions in the sales brochure, Bruce and Martin received a HK$50,000 ($6,410) refund to make up for the shortfall.

The apartment is zoned residential/commercial, which allows NJB Merz to use it as an office. This is important because the authorities levy large fines and shut down businesses operating from residential quarters.

Bruce and Martin's apartment is in a compound that comprises three towers and a landscaped park. But when the towers were completed, the developer unilaterally decided to replace the park with a 10-story garage. After the developer began excavating the garage's foundations, the apartment owners banded together and started legal action. Ultimately, the developer relented and the park was built according to the original plan.

But that wasn't the end of their difficulties with the developer. Each of the complex's apartments includes a large, semicircular balcony. Shortly after NJB Merz moved in, the developer told the owners that the balconies had to be enclosed at the owners' expense. The modifications had to be completed by a subsidiary of the management company — which was a subsidiary of the developer — and cost HK$4,700, but the change did add to the apartment's usable floorspace.

Bruce and Martin paid HK$800,000 in cash for the apartment, which was delivered as a bare shell, and spent another HK$80,000 on renovations. The work was handled by a contractor who Martin found through a friend's recommendation and included moving interior walls, finishing the floors and walls and buying kitchen appliances and split-type air conditioners. Two bedrooms were combined into a product showroom, but the owners retained the master bedroom and its en suite bathroom for Bruce's use. Martin bought a second apartment in the building for his personal use.

While the bedroom added to the office's utility, water leaking from the upstairs apartment into the en suite bathroom was an ongoing source of frustration. Despite repeated complaints to the management company, the leaks continued. "We didn't pay management fees for seven years," says Bruce. "But when they finally fixed the leak, we paid the full amount."

Bruce and Martin's experience highlights a difference between Western and Chinese approaches to building maintenance. In the West, minor repairs are conducted regularly and augmented with large-scale renovations every 10 to 15 years. In China, however, managers sometimes skip the maintenance and let a building get run down before conducting a wholesale renovation.

Martin recommends investigating the building's management before you buy an apartment. "Things have improved a lot in China and building managers can be as good as those in Hong Kong. But they can also be rapacious thugs, who believe they are there to manage you."

While Bruce and Martin had problems, the decision to buy has proven to be a good one. Over the past 15 years, many businesses have opened nearby and the neighborhood's transportation infrastructure has matured: A subway station is within a 10-minute walk, the Guangzhou East Railway Station is nearby and Guangzhou's Inner Ring Road links the area to the provincial highway network.

By reducing the need for hotel accommodations and eliminating the cost of office rent, Bruce estimates that they recouped their investment in less than five years. Furthermore, apartments in the building now sell for twice what Bruce and Martin paid.

And, by providing a pleasant working environment in a convenient location and a kitchen where staff lunches can be prepared, the company has reduced staff turnover, an important consideration in Guangzhou's competitive labor market.

SHANGHAI

City snapshot

Population

In the 2010 census, Shanghai's population was 23 million, an increase of 6.3 million from 2000 and 9.7 million from 1990. Permanent residents from other parts of China represented 39% of the population, or nine million people. People aged 65 or above accounted for 10.1% of the total population versus 8.9% nationally,[1] with males representing 51.5%. Some 89.5% of the city's permanent residents lived in urban areas. According to official statistics, in 2009 Shanghai was home to about 152,000 foreigners.[2]

Economy

Shanghai is China's commercial center, a global financial hub and home to one of the world's busiest ports. Culture, services, manufacturing and heavy industry play important roles in the city's economy. In 2010, Shanghai's gross domestic product was 1.69 trillion yuan,[3] greater than that of Singapore.

Geography

Located at the mouth of the Yangtze River, Shanghai is split by the Huangpu River, with the historic Bund in Puxi (literally "west of the Huangpu") and hyper-modern Pudong and the Lujiazui financial district to the east. One of China's four directly controlled municipalities, Shanghai occupies 6,341 square kilometers and is more than five times larger than Hong Kong.

Changning, Hongkou, Huangpu, Jing'an, Putuo, Xuhui, Yangpu and Zhabei districts are situated to the west of the river. The city's suburbs comprise Baoshan, Fengxian, Jiading, Jinshan, Minhang, Qingpu and Songjiang districts and Chongming County. Huangpu district merged with Nanshi and Luwan districts in 2000 and 2011, respectively. In 2009, Nanhui district merged with Pudong.

Social indicators

The 2012 Hurun Wealth Report estimated that Shanghai was the Chinese city with the second-largest number of wealthy people. Shanghai had 140,000 individuals with total assets of 10 million yuan or more and 8,200 with assets exceeding 100 million yuan.[4] Shanghai was the 16th most expensive city in Mercer's 2012 international cost of living survey.[5]

Shanghai ranked second out of 30 cities in the 2011 China City Life Quality Index Report prepared by the Chinese Academy of Social Sciences.[6] More than 38% of the public space in Shanghai is covered with greenery.

Shanghai's housing market

Artifacts recovered in Songjiang district suggest that migrants from Henan settled in Shanghai 4,000 years ago.

The city's role as a trading port began in the Song Dynasty (960 – 1279). Cotton became a popular crop in the areas around Shanghai during the Ming Dynasty (1368 – 1644), providing raw material for the textile industry. Shanghai's importance as a commercial and shipping hub grew in the late 1600s and early 1700s, when a longtime ban on oceangoing vessels was reversed and the customs office for Jiangsu was moved to Shanghai from the city of Songjiang.

Concessions and settlements

British traders began visiting Shanghai in the 1830s in search of tea and spices.[7] In 1842, the Opium War between China and Britain ended with the Treaty of Nanjing, which made Shanghai a treaty port. In 1845, the British Settlement was formally established along the Huangpu River and Suzhou Creek. The American Settlement was founded in 1848 and the French Concession was created to the south of the British Settlement the following year. In 1863, the British and American settlements were merged into what would be known as the International Settlement.[8] To the south was the walled Chinese city.

Initially, Chinese people were not allowed to live in the foreign enclaves. After the Taiping Rebellion (1850 – 64), these restrictions were relaxed. The settlements later became popular havens for Chinese businessmen fleeing civil wars and the Kuomintang.[9]

The International Settlement and the French Concession expanded several times. By 1914, the two zones had grown from an aggregate of 56 hectares to nearly 3,300 hectares, and the population had reached 640,000. Ninety-eight percent of the residents were Chinese.[10]

The Bund, which ran along the west bank of the Huangpu River on the edge of the International Settlement, became Shanghai's business hub. Property prices on the Bund reportedly rose 500 times between 1845 and 1893.[11] Today, the Bund is home to many iconic buildings, including the former Hongkong and Shanghai Bank headquarters, the Customs House and the Peace Hotel, all of which were designed in the 1920s by the architectural firm Palmer and Turner.

The Japanese population in Shanghai grew during the early 20th century and by 1915 the Japanese outnumbered the British. In 1931, Japan occupied Hongkou district and subsequently took over portions of the Chinese city and the International Settlement. The Sino-Japanese War broke out in 1937 and in 1941 Japan took control of the International Settlement, which it dissolved in 1943. The International Settlement was returned to China in 1945.

Japan occupied the French Concession from 1943 to 1945. In 1946, France returned the French Concession to China.[12] Today, the area's parks and treelined streets make it one of Shanghai's most desirable neighborhoods.

The post-war era

Between the end of WWII and the arrival of the People's Liberation Army on May 25, 1949, Shanghai endured political instability and hyperinflation. With the return of the International Settlement and French Concession to China, many foreigners left and Shanghai lost the cosmopolitan flavor that had defined the city in the 1930s.

Communism was not kind to Shanghai. The new government viewed the Shanghainese with suspicion, and worked to rid the city of capitalism as well as social evils like drugs and prostitution. It also used Shanghai's economic might to finance programs in other parts of China. From 1949 to 1984, for example, 87% of local revenues were sent to the central government.[13] Shanghai endured decades of neglect, during which the population grew but there was little investment in infrastructure.[14] Housing and municipal services were considered to be unproductive consumption.

Shanghai reborn

Shanghai's fortunes began to improve with the appointment of Jiang Zemin — a native of nearby Jiangsu — as mayor in 1985. In 1987, when Jiang became the secretary of the Shanghai Party Committee, his protege Zhu Rongji became mayor. Jiang was named Secretary General of the Communist Party of China in 1989 and Zhu was appointed vice premier in 1993 and premier in 1998. The two men formed the core of the "Shanghai clique" that gave the city a more prominent voice in the central government.

In 1990, Shanghai got another boost when the central government approved a plan to develop Pudong into a modern financial center. The central government extended many of the tax and regulatory concessions granted to special economic zones in other parts of China to Pudong and approved the creation of the Shanghai Stock Exchange. Much of the subsequent foreign investment in China went through Pudong.

Pudong's debut was not without controversy. In 1998, just 35% of its office space was occupied.[15] Today, Pudong boasts an impressive array of skyscrapers and is Shanghai's wealthiest residential district, followed by Changning and Huangpu.[16] Many of the homes in Pudong are modern towers that are popular with local buyers.

In addition to Pudong, many expatriates live in Huangpu (particularly the former Luwan), Changning, Jing'an and Xuhui. Education drives many expats' housing decisions, and most of Shanghai's international schools are in the suburbs. As a result, families often choose homes on the periphery while singles and childless couples live in the city center.

Buying property in Shanghai

Agent's commission
Both the buyer and seller pay 1% commission, and discounts can be negotiated.

Conservation
Shanghai has many historic sites, such as the remains of a Ming Dynasty wall that was built to protect the old city from Japanese pirates. As elsewhere, these sites are often a source of conflict between conservationists and developers.

Shanghai's architecture is arguably the most diverse in China. The lilong, which combined Chinese courtyards with Western terraced houses, emerged in the 1860s. Villas (known as lao yang fang) were built in the early 20th century using Beaux Arts, Tudor and Modern styles, among others. And structures ranging from churches to slaughterhouses combined Western and local influences. As architectural historian Jeffrey W. Cody observes, many of these structures survived because the government and the *danwei* (work units) that managed them found other uses for the buildings, not because of any interest in conservation.[17] This often left buildings subdivided or heavily modified, and it is not uncommon for historic structures to be demolished and reconstructed with modern features, such as elevators.[18]

Shanghai is actively protecting its architectural heritage. The process of cataloging and classifying the city's historic buildings began in 1988. In 1994, regulations were introduced allowing historic structures on the Bund to be leased for commercial purposes, thereby providing funds for preservation work. In 2003, Shanghai was the first local government to introduce a law to protect historic buildings.[19]

Currently, 144 roads and alleyways and more than 2,100 buildings have "protected" status. If you are planning to buy and renovate an old home, check with the Shanghai Municipal Government's Historical Buildings Protection Committee before making a large commitment.[20]

Market-cooling measures

In Shanghai, "local" buyers are limited to two homes. Nonlocal buyers may own one home, but only if they can provide tax receipts proving that they have lived in Shanghai for 12 months over the past two years. In 2012, the regulations were tightened to stop unmarried nonlocal people from buying homes.

To qualify as a local buyer, you must be born in Shanghai to Shanghainese parents, be a professional who has lived and paid taxes in Shanghai for seven years or marry and remain wed to a Shanghai native for 10 years.[21]

Shanghai's local restrictions supplement national measures introduced in 2010 that increased the down payment requirement to 30% for first-time buyers and to 50% for buyers of second homes and prohibited people who owned two homes from buying additional properties.[22] Shanghai's restrictions also supplement those in Circular 171 and Circular 186 (see "The buying process" chapter for more details about market-cooling measures).

The local and national restrictions have succeeded in cooling the market. In 2011, the Shanghai government recorded land sales of 152.5 billion yuan, down from 195 billion yuan in 2010. Land sales in the first eight months of 2012 were reportedly down a further 60%.[23]

Property tax

In 2011, a property tax trial began in Shanghai and Chongqing. The annual tax rate in Shanghai is 0.6%, but is reduced to 0.4% in some circumstances. The tax applies to newly purchased homes and is initially based on the property's purchase price, rather than an assessed value. Exemptions are available, and Shanghai residents are treated differently than nonresidents.[24] See the "Taxes and fees" chapter for more information.

Distinctive housing

Art Deco

The emergence of Art Deco designs in Shanghai corresponded with what historian Marie-Claire Bergère called "the golden age of Shanghai capitalism." Between 1920 and 1930, Shanghai's coastal, river and transoceanic shipping networks handled nearly half of China's external trade. There was a growing entrepreneurial class and Nanjing Road offered the most sophisticated shopping in China.

Art Deco, which took its name from the *Exposition des Arts Decoratifs et Industriels Modernes* held in Paris in 1925, was a perfect match for Shanghainese sensibilities. Art Deco, and later styles like Streamline Moderne, were clean and contemporary and incorporated industrial and transport-related motifs — such as airplane wings and ship portholes — that reflected the city's role as a business and transport hub.[25]

Despite the breakneck pace of Shanghai's development, the city has one of the world's largest collections of Art Deco buildings.[26] These include the Park Hotel and the Grand Theater, both designed by Hungarian architect László Hudec. The Park Hotel was one of the first skyscrapers to be built outside the United States and was Shanghai's tallest building for nearly 50 years.[27] Hudec designed more than 50 buildings in Shanghai, ranging from banks to private residences.[28]

Other examples of Art Deco style include the Paramount Ballroom, the Majestic Theater, the Bank of China Building and the Metropole Hotel. Art Deco has become such an important part of Shanghai's image that

Designed by Palmer and Turner, the Broadway Mansions Hotel is one of Shanghai's many Art Deco buildings. The hotel was completed in 1934 and is near the confluence of the Huangpu River and Suzhou Creek.

it is incorporated in new buildings, like the City Lights Apartments and the J.W. Marriott Hotel in Tomorrow Square.

Lilong and shikumen

First built to accommodate refugees fleeing the Taiping Rebellion and job-seeking migrants, lilong (also called *longtang*) neighborhoods typically occupy a city block. Built in the foreign concessions and other parts of the city, lilong feature town house-like homes that abut each other; an outside wall; communal courtyards; one or two main interior lanes; smaller sub-lanes; and *shikumen* or stone entrance gates.[29] Some homes have direct access to the street outside.

Lilong homes were initially constructed from wood in order to provide economical accommodations. In the late 1800s, safety concerns caused all-wood construction to be replaced with brick walls and wooden beams.[30] In the late 1910s, the New Style Lilong — which reduced the home's interior space, shrank or eliminated the courtyard and increased the number of floors — was introduced. Semidetached versions with a garden in front were built for wealthy people. The movement ended in the mid-20th century with the Apartment Lilong, a five- to seven-story block with shared facilities that was built from concrete. These eventually gave way to modern, high-rise apartment blocks.

Lilong homes were the main form of accommodation in Shanghai for many years. In 1949, lilong totaling 20 million square meters represented 69% of the city's residential housing stock.[31]

Some 80% of the lilong in Shanghai have been demolished, usually to be replaced with high-density housing.[32] Two notable exceptions are Xintiandi, which was restored and rebuilt into a shopping, dining and entertainment zone by Hong Kong's Shui On Land, and Tianzifang, a less polished neighborhood filled with cafes, bars and art galleries in the French Concession. A development similar to Xintiandi is being built in the Jianyeli neighborhood on Jianguo Road in Xuhui district.[33]

There are parallels between Shanghai's lilong and Beijing's *siheyuan*. People have mixed feelings about them because, while both offered a sense of community and history, many lack privacy and modern conveniences such as bathrooms. As in Beijing, lilong that were intended for one family were subdivided into multifamily dwellings. If you buy a lilong, you will need to find and reach a settlement with everyone who has a land use claim on the home, a potentially expensive and time-consuming task. Even if they no longer live in the home, each of the claimants must de-register their *hukou* (residency permit) before the sale can be completed.

Many of these homes need wholesale renovation, which can easily cost 70,000 yuan per square meter and require extensive negotiations with your neighbors.

Located in the French Concession, Tianzifang is home to restaurants, boutiques and art galleries. The area has also attracted creative businesses and is a popular tourist destination.

Livability issues

Air pollution

In 2009, Shanghai's air quality ranked 10th out of 30 Chinese cities in a World Health Organization report. Shanghai reported 81 micrograms per cubic meter of PM10 particles, which are smaller than 10 microns and can cause heart disease, lung cancer and asthma.[34]

The Shanghai Environmental Monitoring Center posts daily air quality updates on its Website (www.semc.gov.cn, Chinese only). Hourly updates on Shanghai's PM2.5 levels are available from http://twitter.com/cgshanghaiair. The data is collected from a monitoring station near the U.S. Consulate's office on Huai Hai Middle Road.

Electricity shortages

Shanghai Electric Power warned offices and department stores that they could face power rationing as a result of a 500- to 1,000-megawatt shortfall during the summer of 2012. Shanghai generates about two-thirds of its electricity and imports the remaining 8,900 megawatts from neighboring provinces. Environmental concerns have prevented the construction of new generating capacity, while a lack of distribution substations in Baoshan, Hongkou, Yangpu and Zhabei have left those districts vulnerable. The economic slowdown has given Shanghai Electric Power a little breathing room and only commercial users have been affected so far.[35] But the system has little spare capacity and is particularly vulnerable during the summer, when air conditioners consume 40% of the city's electricity.

Infrastructure projects

Shanghai is in the middle of a construction boom. In February 2012, for example, the city announced 95 road, water and mass-transit projects valued at more than 116 billion yuan.[36] Shanghai's subway system will grow from 425 kilometers at the beginning of 2012 to 877 kilometers by 2020.[37] A pair of two-mile–long runways are under construction at

Shanghai Pudong International Airport. Both DreamWorks and Walt Disney are building theme parks in Shanghai. The world's second-tallest building, the 632-meter Shanghai Tower, will open in Pudong in 2014. Pudong is also the site of China's largest garbage incinerator, which was completed in 2012.

These projects — and dozens more that are either under way or being planned — will change the character of their host neighborhoods. Your due diligence should include a review of the development plan for the area surrounding your new home.

Soil pollution

Like all large cities in China, Shanghai has a soil pollution problem. The Pudong Iron and Steel Company, the Nanshi Power Plant and the Jiangnan Shipyard operated on the site of Expo 2010 Shanghai, which the government remediated to remove severe heavy metal and chemical contamination.[38] A 2009 analysis, meanwhile, showed that roadside dust in Shanghai had high concentrations of copper, zinc and nickel.[39]

Traffic

Shanghai traffic is bad and getting worse. Despite new license plates costing more than 60,000 yuan, two million cars are expected to be on the city's streets by 2015,[40] up from about 1.2 million in 2005. The expansion of Shanghai's subway system should relieve some of the pressure on the city's roads.

Water and related issues

Shanghai's water woes include threats to its drinking water supply, subsidence and weather.

The United Nations named Shanghai one of six global cities facing a severe water shortage and the Shanghai Water Authority notes that almost all of the city's surface water is polluted.[41] Shanghai relies on the Yangtze and Huangpu rivers for its water, and both are affected by agricultural, human and industrial effluent.

In December 2010, the 17 billion yuan Qingcaosha Reservoir opened at the mouth of the Yangtze, which improved Shanghai's water quality. But the Yangtze is susceptible to salt tides, where seawater enters the river and makes the river water unusable; to eutrophication, where excess nutrients stimulate plant growth, such as algae blooms; and to shipping spills and accidents, like the fuel tanker that sank nearby in May 2012, closing the reservoir.

Subsidence is a longstanding problem in Shanghai. Half of modern Shanghai was under water until the seventh century and the city has sunk more than 2.5 meters over the past century.[42] When Palmer and Turner designed the Hongkong and Shanghai Bank headquarters on the Bund, they tamed the city's marshy soil by floating the building on an innovative concrete slab foundation. After the building was completed in 1923, the first step on the entrance was six feet above grade. Shortly afterward, it settled and stayed level with the sidewalk.[43]

Shanghai spends billions of yuan each year pumping water under the city to minimize the effects of subsidence, but it's not always successful. In February 2012, an eight-meter–long crack appeared in the pavement near the Shanghai Tower. The crevasse sparked considerable attention, despite reassurances from engineers that it did not threaten the tower.[44]

Shanghai's third water-related threat comes from the weather. On average, typhoons hit the city two to three times each year, usually between June and September, bringing heavy winds, rain, flooding and storm surges.[45] Shanghai is strengthening its flood defenses, upgrading its more than 523 kilometers of levees, and improving the city's drainage system. Despite these efforts, a 2012 article in Natural Hazards ranked Shanghai as most vulnerable to coastal floods among a group of nine cities that included Buenos Aires, Calcutta, Casablanca, Dhaka, Manila, Marseille, Osaka and Rotterdam.[46] The Shanghai government rejected this conclusion, noting that its flood control systems could withstand a once-in-200-year storm surge and winds of up to 133 kilometers per hour.[47]

Flood risk in Shanghai[48]	
District or county	**Flood risk***
Baoshan	◆◆
Changning	◆◆◆◆
Chongming	◆◆◆
Fengxian	◆◆
Hongkou	◆◆◆
Huangpu	◆◆◆◆
Jiading	◆◆◆
Jing'an	◆◆◆◆
Jinshan	◆◆◆
Minhang	◆◆◆◆
Pudong	◆◆◆◆
Qingpu	◆◆◆◆
Songjiang	◆◆◆◆
Xuhui	◆◆◆
Yangpu	◆◆◆
Zhabei	◆◆◆◆

* Based on total rainfall, drainage capacity and overall vulnerability. The area formerly known as Nanhui, which merged with Pudong in 2009, was rated two out of four.

A Western haven in Shanghai

"A villa lifestyle at an apartment price" for expatriate families was the vision behind Frank Adams'* decision to buy and renovate a 220-square-meter, four-bedroom town house in Shanghai's western suburbs. The 46-year-old Australian entrepreneur has lived in China for 12 years and rates his Chinese ability as a seven on a 10-point scale.

Frank bought the town house in June 2010 with the goal of generating rental returns and long-term capital gains. He paid 10.5 million yuan for the home, which was built in 1997 in a low-rise development of 200 similar units. An international bank provided a 70%, 20-year, U.S. dollar mortgage, while Frank contributed about four million yuan in cash for the down payment, closing costs and renovations.

Frank wanted a competitively priced property that had the features and a location that would appeal to the growing number of expat families living in Shanghai. After considering several centrally located apartments and suburban villas near international schools, he chose this town house in Changning district. "It's close to the Shanghai Zoo and state guest houses, which means the air quality feels significantly better than in similar locations with equivalent access," notes Frank.

With Shanghai's increasingly congested roads, access is a key concern for tenants. The home is located between the city's middle and outer ring roads and near a recently opened subway line. Shopping and restaurants are a short taxi ride away.

To find a competitively priced property, Frank asked his real estate agent — with whom he has a longstanding relationship — to look for a Western-style income property that had been vacant for some time. Frank felt this combination would let him buy a home that could be "fixed" from a vendor who would be motivated to sell. He says that identifying the right property was the toughest part of the process: It

* "Frank Adams" is a pseudonym.

Shanghai offers modern skyscrapers and historic buildings. Tomorrow Square (right) and the former Shanghai Art Museum are in Puxi, near People's Square.

took six months and two failed offers to secure his town house. The agent helped Frank negotiate terms that were acceptable to the vendor, an entrepreneur from a neighboring province. Frank estimates that this approach saved him at least 5% and possibly as much as 20%.

Because the vendor did not have a mortgage, the sale was completed within a month. In July 2010, Frank took possession and began a three-month, 350,000 yuan renovation, using his own design and choice of materials. Frank's contractor installed an underfloor heating system and replaced the ceramic tile on the ground floor, mezzanine and bathrooms with laminated wood flooring. The finishes in the home's three bathrooms were renewed, but most of the fittings and sanitary ware were retained. The contractor also replaced the compressor for the central air conditioner.

Frank saw the garage as an underutilized space and converted it into a utility area that could be used as a playroom or servants' quarters. "Most expats have drivers who take the car home at night, while locals often park their car outdoors, where it can be appreciated by the neighbors."

He made a similar adjustment to the kitchen by opening it up and enlarging it to accommodate the Western preference for socializing while preparing meals. To take full advantage of the town house's garden, Frank repaired the existing deck. All of the work was done by a contractor who had been introduced by a friend, an introduction that Frank describes as "essential." Frank had used the contractor for other projects and, unlike many renovations, the town house was finished on time and on budget.

Frank is happy with his purchase, renovations and income the home is generating. "A French executive and his family are paying rent of 28,000 yuan per month, which covers the mortgage. We have reasonable expectations for a capital gain over the medium term, and the yuan is likely to continue strengthening against our U.S. dollar mortgage, which carried a lower interest rate than one denominated in yuan."

With hindsight, Frank says he would have made more aesthetic improvements, such as upgrading the doors and doorhandles, a process that would have added 50,000 yuan to the renovation budget and another month to the schedule. It would have also taken more of Frank's time. "You should personally source as many of the components — finishes, fittings and appliances — as you can. This is time consuming, but it will save you money and ensure the quality of the finished product," he observes.

Frank says many companies in China supply good-quality, locally made components and materials or locally manufactured foreign brands. But he cautions against installing imported luxury fittings. "Unless it's for your own use, you'll rarely recover the premium you pay for these products."

SHENZHEN

City snapshot

Population

In the 2010 census, Shenzhen's permanent resident population was 10.4 million, an increase of 3.3 million from 2000.[1] At the end of 2012, 3 million people held local **hukou** (residency permits), and Shenzhen had about 3 million unregistered workers,[2] for an estimated total population of 13 million.[3] In 1979, Shenzhen's population was just 30,000.

In 2010, people aged 65 or older accounted for 1.8% of the permanent resident population, versus 8.9% nationally,[4] and men outnumbered women 54.2% to 45.8%. At the end of May 2012, 10,836 foreigners with valid work permits lived in Shenzhen, with Japanese, South Koreans and Filipinos comprising more than half of the total. If family members, Hong Kong residents working illegally in Shenzhen and illegal workers from other countries are included, the total number of foreigners in Shenzhen is much higher.[5]

Economy

China's first special economic zone, Shenzhen has one of the Mainland's two stock exchanges and one of its busiest container ports. Shenzhen's pillar industries are finance, logistics, culture and high technology. The city is home to some of the country's most successful companies, including car- and battery-maker BYD; electronics companies Huawei, ZTE and TCL; and the nation's largest largest residential real estate developer, China Vanke. In 2011, Shenzhen's gross domestic product was 1.15 trillion yuan, greater than that of Peru.

Geography

Located in the Pearl River Delta, Shenzhen is immediately adjacent to the Hong Kong Special Administrative Region. Shenzhen Municipality occupies 1,992 square kilometers[6] and comprises six districts — Luohu, Futian, Nanshan, Yantian, Bao'an and Longgang — and four new areas: Guangming, Pingshan, Longhua and Dapeng.

Social indicators

The 2012 Hurun Wealth Report estimated that Shenzhen was the Chinese city with the fifth-largest number of wealthy people. Shenzhen had 52,000 individuals with total assets of 10 million yuan or more and 3,400 with assets exceeding 100 million yuan.[7] Shenzhen was the 30th most expensive city in Mercer's 2012 international cost of living survey.[8]

Shenzhen plans to have 2,000 kilometers of cycling and hiking trails by the end of 2012 and to increase the number of parks from 824 to more than 1,000 by 2020.[9]

Shenzhen's housing market

A description of the city's housing market must start with an explanation of how Shenzhen grew from a backward fishing village to a Tier 1 city in just three decades.

Shenzhen's transformation began with a speech by paramount leader Deng Xiaoping to the Chinese Communist Party's Central Work Committee on December 13, 1978. In the speech, Deng proposed a series of reforms that would decentralize economic activity, encourage personal responsibility and competition and ultimately create a unique combination of communism and capitalism known as "socialism with Chinese characteristics."

Designed to revitalize China's economy, Deng's vision was a sharp break with the policies of Mao Zedong, who had died two years earlier. Deng's reforms were a bold experiment that had to be conducted in a favorable environment where the fallout could be contained if they failed. In this regard, Shenzhen was an inspired choice. The village was in Guangdong, which had more than 400 years of foreign-trade history. Shenzhen was also far from Beijing, but close to Hong Kong's capital, global transportation links and overseas Chinese business networks.

The reforms began with farm families, who were allotted land and allowed to sell their excess produce on the open market. Farmers used the proceeds to build new homes, starting an entrepreneurial boom.

In 1980, Shenzhen became China's first special economic zone. As an SEZ, Shenzhen offered foreign investors — many of whom were Hong Kong Chinese — inexpensive land, tax concessions, cheap labor and limited bureaucracy.

Shenzhen's early manufacturing businesses focused on low-value-added products for export, such as toys, shoes and garments. The factories attracted migrant workers from across the country, who continue to live in company dormitories and urban villages.

During this period, two events crystallized Shenzhen's role. On December 1, 1987, the city auctioned a plot of land for a residential development — the first such transaction in the history of the People's Republic of China. The following year, the auction system pioneered in Shenzhen became national policy.[10]

Five years later, Deng Xiaoping, who was then retired, visited Shenzhen on what became known as his southern tour. Deng reaffirmed China's commitment to economic reform and to the SEZs. The results were dramatic. Foreign direct investment into Shenzhen doubled, from $250 million in 1992 to $497 million in 1993. By 2007, contracted FDI surpassed $5 billion.[11]

The city's economic development was matched by a construction boom, with more than 600 major buildings erected between 1982 and 1996. By 1995, nearly half of Shenzhen's housing stock was built by Hong Kong developers,[12] and modern designs and innovations like private property management companies began to spread from Shenzhen to other parts of China.[13]

Shenzhen's boundaries have grown with its population and economy. In 1979, Shenzhen had a built-up area of about 3 square kilometers. When the Shenzhen SEZ was created in 1980, it had a total area of 327.5 square kilometers. Bao'an and Longgang counties became districts within Shenzhen Municipality in 1993. In 2010, the central government expanded the SEZ to cover all of Shenzhen Municipality, which then had a built-up area of nearly 830 square kilometers.[14]

The city's explosive growth has created a "boom-town" atmosphere. This reputation is not helped by events like a construction company dumping buckets of scorpions to intimidate residents who refused to leave a development project[15] or fistfights over property management services for a residential complex that involved hundreds of security guards.[16]

Growth has created numerous urban planning issues. Shenzhen has what may be China's largest collections of urban villages (see below) and illegal structures. In December 2011, a municipal government official estimated that the city had nearly 380,000 such structures, representing nearly half of Shenzhen's buildings. The problem extends from poor areas to exclusive developments such as Xiangmihu No. 1 Villa in Futian, where more than half of the owners have added unauthorized floors. Enforcement is often lax and an illegal floor can add tens of million of yuan to a home's value.

Even Shenzhen's decorations are a reminder that the city is a place for commerce.

Patchwork reforms that began in 1992 have created conflicting land claims. A 2012 report by Caixin revealed that 42% of the land in Shenzhen that is designated for public construction is occupied by rural residents, but only 25% of the residents have title to the land. The magazine noted that nearly half of Shenzhen's buildings only have titles issued by the county. About 75% of those titles have multiple ownership or have not followed proper transfer procedures.[17]

Where to live

Shenzhen is a large city, and despite the growth in its public transport system, traffic can be congested. As a result, it makes sense to live near your place of employment. Futian is Shenzhen's business district, and the Lok Ma Chau boundary crossing with Hong Kong is adjacent to this district. The popular Coco Park shopping center is in Futian, as are One Honeylake and Xiangmihu No. 1 Villa, which offer expensive detached homes.

Nanshan is popular with expatriates and is the site of several of Shenzhen's international schools. Shekou, which is in Nanshan, offers modern, well-equipped residential towers as well as bars, restaurants and stores selling Western goods. The Shenzhen Bay boundary crossing with Hong Kong is in Shekou.

Luohu is adjacent to the Lo Wu boundary crossing with Hong Kong. Large parts of this district are slated for redevelopment. Many of Shenzhen's new apartments are being built in Longgang and Bao'an, districts that are less popular with expatriates.

Buying property in Shenzhen

Agent's commission

In theory, the vendor and buyer both pay 1.5% agent's commission. But it is common for vendors to refuse to pay, forcing the buyer to cover the entire commission. If you insist that the vendor pay half the commission, they will typically add the commission amount to the price of the apartment. Buyers do not pay commission when purchasing a home directly from a developer.

Security guards in housing estates often act as unlicensed real estate agents.

Conservation

As a result of Shenzhen's rapid growth, conservation is unlikely to be an issue for home buyers.

Market-cooling measures

In July 2007, the Shenzhen government announced that residents of Hong Kong, Macau and Taiwan could only buy one home in Shenzhen for their own use and must sign a declaration that the home is their first in the city. Foreign residents of Shenzhen must have lived and worked legally in Shenzhen for one year before they can buy.[18] Overseas

Shenzhen's explosive growth means that the city's housing stock is new. There are numerous modern designs, including the Yi Tiange holiday apartments.

companies with a branch in Shenzhen may purchase nonresidential property in Shenzhen. See "The buying process" chapter for additional information.

Property taxes and fees

Shenzhen does not levy property taxes. However, the city is expected to introduce a property tax in the future.

Owners of property in multistory buildings pay a monthly fee to the Special Housing Maintenance Fund. In buildings without an elevator, the rate is 1.5 yuan per square meter. In buildings with an elevator, the rate is 2.5 yuan per square meter.[19] For more information, see the fund's Website www.szwxzj.com, Chinese only.

Livability issues

Air pollution

Shenzhen's air quality is benefiting from the departure of the polluting industries that played a large role in the city's economy. However, traffic-related air pollution and construction dust — which have increased during the expansion of the city's subway system and other infrastructure projects — can be bad. In 2012, sulfur dioxide accounted for 14% of Shenzhen's air pollution, while PM10s (particles less than 10 microns in size) were 42% and nitrogen dioxide was 44%.[20]

A 2013 report by the Shenzhen Center for Chronic Disease Control indicated that cancer rates among permanent residents of Shenzhen nearly tripled from 2002 to 2011 and named lung cancer as the top killer.

Shenzhen is introducing electric vehicles to combat air pollution and plans to replace more than half of the city's bus fleet with electric models by 2015.

The Shenzhen government makes hourly air pollution data, including PM2.5 readings, available on www.szhec.gov.cn, Chinese only. The Hedley Environmental Index, which is maintained by the School of Public Health at the University of Hong Kong, provides real-time data about the air quality in neighboring Hong Kong. The index uses data from several monitoring stations, including sites in Yuen Long and Tai Po, both of which are near the boundary between Hong Kong and Shenzhen (http://hedleyindex.sph.hku.hk).

Developments

Officially called the Qianhai Shenzhen-Hong Kong Modern Service Industry Cooperation Zone, Qianhai is a 15-square-kilometer area in western Shenzhen, adjacent to Hong Kong and Macau, that was approved by the State Council in June 2012. Scheduled for completion in 2020, Qianhai will offer low corporate taxes and reduced income taxes for expatriate professionals. Qianhai's economy will focus on finance, logistics, information technology and science and technology.[21] Investment commitments totaling 300 billion yuan have been announced, and a 500-meter building, 11,000 apartments, a convention center and 12 rail and subway lines are planned. Some analysts are skeptical about Qianhai, but investors have begun buying property, seeing the zone as the next Shenzhen. The month after Qianhai was approved by the State Council, homes nearby were selling for nearly double the price of those in Shenzhen.[22]

In 2012, Shenzhen authorities announced plans to invest more than 250 billion yuan over the next 10 years to upgrade Luohu into an "international consumption center." The plans include a 666-meter commercial tower, luxury hotels and shopping malls and jewelery trading and processing centers.[23]

Mission Hills Group announced a 5 billion yuan, 500,000-square-meter project in Longhua New Area that is scheduled to open at the end of 2013. Mission Hills Centreville is a HOPSCA project that will include a hotel, offices, parks, shopping, convention facilities and apartments.[24]

Other developments include 100% Design Plaza, a 500,000-square-meter business park catering to creative industries that is scheduled to open in Buji, Longgang, in 2013. A 500,000-square-meter park on a former quarry in Antuoshan, Futian, is scheduled to open in 2015. A 200,000-square-meter convention center has been proposed for a site south of Shenzhen Bao'an International Airport.

Electricity shortages

Shenzhen faces power shortages, especially during the summer months when hot weather drives demand for air conditioning. Nonresidential customers bear the brunt of the shortages, which are usually scheduled in advance. Shenzhen is home to six of China's 15 operating nuclear power stations.

Infrastructure projects

Railways play a central role in the city's infrastructure spending. The Shenzhen Municipal Development and Reform Commission estimates that between 2011 and 2018 over 240 billion yuan will be invested in the city's subway network.[25] This includes subway lines 6, 7, 8, 9 and 11, which will add 172 kilometers to the city's rail network by 2016, bringing the total to 350 kilometers. The construction of Y-shaped Line 16, which will serve the Futian Free Trade Zone, Pinghu, Longgang, and Guanlan in Longhua New Area, will start in 2015. Plans for lines 17 – 20, which add another 140 kilometers to the network, have also been announced.

Futian Station on the Guangzhou-Shenzhen-Hong Kong express line will be completed in July 2014, and will link Shenzhen with Kowloon in 14 minutes.

Shenzhen spent 6.7 billion yuan on road construction in 2012, including more than 180 kilometers of new roads, flyovers, bus stations and transportation interchanges. Major projects include the 3-kilometer Xincai Passageway, which will link the Caitian Flyover in Futian with Xinqu Boulevard in Longhua New Area when it is competed in 2014.[26]

In November 2012, Guangdong authorities approved the construction of the Shenzhen-Zhongshan Corridor, a 55-kilometer bridge and tunnel project that will span the Pearl River. Work on the 20 billion yuan project will start in 2015 and is scheduled for completion in 2021.[27]

In 2012, Shenzhen announced a plan to upgrade corroded pipes in the city's water system. The first half of the project will cost 3 billion yuan and take three to five years to complete.[28]

Population volatility

Shenzhen's rapid growth has made it a magnet for talented, ambitious people from all over China, a fact reflected in the popularity of Putonghua over Cantonese, Guangdong's native language. The large number of migrant workers and young people in Shenzhen make the city's population susceptible to political and economic shifts. It also stretches the city's transportation infrastructure to the limit during the Spring Festival, when workers return to their home villages.

In November 2012, a senior party member announced plans to increase the number of people with local hukou from the current three million to four million by 2015.[29] This should reduce the volatility of Shenzhen's population, although each new hukou holder will cost the city an estimated 6,000 yuan per year in services.

Traffic

In August 2012, 2.2 million vehicles were registered in Shenzhen. Congestion on Shenzhen's roads is exacerbated by infrastructure projects and some of the city's worst traffic can be found near Chegongmiao in Futian, where work is taking place on subway lines 7, 9 and 11.

In 2012, Shenzhen launched an online service that displays traffic conditions in real time (http://szmap.sutpc.com, Chinese only).

Urban villages

An urban village is a residential neighborhood built on rural land that has been encircled by a growing city (see the "Demographics" chapter for more information). Urban villages provide inexpensive accommodations for the migrant workers who are employed by the city's factories. They have high crime levels, poor construction standards and limited facilities.

In 2005, Shenzhen had 320 urban villages, 138 of which were in Bao'an and 91 of which were in Longgang. The urban villages had a total floor space of 10.3 million square kilometers and were home to 5.3 million people, 93% of whom were migrant workers.[30]

In January 2013, the Shenzhen Municipal Government announced that, for the first time, rural land that had been zoned for industrial use could be sold. The announcement, which was approved by the Ministry of Land and Resources, is seen as a breakthrough in the development of China's land policy.[31]

Shekou offers modern apartments, sea views and amenities for expatriates. A ferry service links Shekou to Hong Kong.

Water and related issues

Shenzhen has more than 310 rivers and streams into which more than 500 million tonnes of wastewater is dumped each year.[32] Most of the water midstream and downstream from Shenzhen is Level V or worse on China's six-level scale.[33] Level V can only be used for agricultural and landscaping purposes. Level VI cannot be used for irrigation. In addition, more than 4,100 square kilometers of inshore seawater in the Pearl River Delta is contaminated with petroleum, heavy metals and arsenic, and these substances can be found in fish and shellfish from Guangdong's waters.[34]

Municipal and provincial governments have spent billions of yuan on water-treatment facilities, and Shenzhen's water is reported to be 100% compliant with national quality standards.

As a result of Shenzhen's location and climate, the city is subject to flooding. The drainage system in the central districts of the city is built to withstand a once-in-100-year flood, but parts of Longgang and Bao'an are only capable of withstanding a once-in-50-year event. Following the storms that devastated Beijing in 2012, the Shenzhen government announced plans to upgrade the entire city so that by 2020, it could withstand a once-in-200-year flood.[35]

Trading up in Shenzhen

An aversion to white walls prompted Andy Church, a supply chain and quality management executive based in Shenzhen, to buy his first property in 2006. "Even with a promise to reinstate the apartment at the end of the lease, the landlord wouldn't let me repaint the walls," says the 40-year-old from Louisville, Kentucky, who paid 367,500 yuan in cash for a 49-square-meter unit in Phase I of City Garden 3.

In February 2009, Andy used a U.S. dollar denominated mortgage from HSBC in Shenzhen to upgrade to an 86-square-meter apartment in Phase I of the Peninsula (www.the-peninsula.cn, Chinese only) in Shekou. Located in Nanshan, the Peninsula comprises Phase I, which opened in 2006, and Phase II, which was completed in 2010. Andy picked the Peninsula because of its proximity to transport links to Hong Kong; its facilities, which include a pool, a gym and a clubhouse; the quality of the complex's maintenance and its vibrant expatriate community. "The Peninsula is a gated community, so there's very little noise," says Andy, who calls it "a little oasis in the chaos of Shenzhen."

Andy's apartment on the second floor of the complex overlooked the main gate and had excellent feng shui. While he was saving to redecorate the 1.2 million yuan unit, Andy listed it at an above-market price with the agent from China Merchants Property who had helped him buy both apartments.

In November 2009, after a lack of buyer interest, Andy asked the agent to de-list the apartment so he could begin the fit out. But the agent soon received a serious offer and, in a single day, Andy sold his second-floor apartment and bought a 100-square-meter unit on the top floor of a different building in the complex. He paid 2.2 million yuan for the new apartment, which has three bedrooms and better harbor views. The agent helped him arrange a 1.1 million yuan mortgage with China Merchants Bank, and he paid the balance in cash.

Andy says the process of obtaining a mortgage was no more difficult in China than it would have been in the United States, although banks tend to be more thorough when checking a foreign buyer's proof of income and other qualifications. The down payment requirements are also tougher. "In the States, you could typically obtain a mortgage with 5% to 10% down. In China, banks want 50% down when a foreigner buys in his own name. As a result, many of my expat friends have arranged a mortgage in the name of their Chinese spouse," explains Andy.

After signing the sale and purchase agreement at the end of October, Andy took possession of the new apartment in mid-January 2010, just before the Lunar New Year. He decided to gut the living room, kitchen and bathroom, and make minor improvements to the three bedrooms. With a budget of 300,000 yuan, the renovations took a month-long break over the New Year holidays and were completed in mid-May, about a month behind schedule. Andy moved in at the end of May 2010.

Andy hired the contractor who had renovated his first apartment to redecorate his new home. The contractor had been recommended by a friend, and Andy says the experience of completing the first project made the second one easier. "I allowed extra time, so even though the job was a month late, it wasn't a major problem," notes Andy, who included a contingency in his budget for unforeseen costs.

But there were a few hiccups. The day before he was scheduled to move in, Andy pushed the furniture aside so a technician could bolt a television to the living room wall. When he returned that evening, the TV had been installed on the wrong wall. After an 8:30 P.M. call to the neighborhood electronics shop, the technician returned to reinstall the TV. Shortly after midnight, the contractor finished patching and repainting the wall and Andy moved in the following morning.

With minor exceptions, Andy is happy with the renovations. "There are some items — like the bathroom vanity light — where I'm still looking for the right fixture. But it's a lot easier to buy a clothes dryer or a double-wide refrigerator now than when I purchased my first home in 2006."

After living in China since 2003, Andy rates his Chinese real estate vocabulary as four on a 10-point scale. "Regardless of how fluent I think I am, there's always something new to learn. I try to take things in stride and chalk them up to experience. Things happen on China's time line, not mine," he says.

RESOURCES

Law
235

Useful information
247

Appendix
303

LAW

China's distinctive legal environment has a large influence on the process of buying, owning and selling a home. While a detailed review of China's legal system is beyond the scope of this book, the following information will help you understand the ideas that underpin China's laws and how those laws work in the context of buying a home.

The development of China's legal system

China uses a civil code, which is fundamentally different from the common law used in England, Hong Kong, the United States and many other jurisdictions. And the legal system used in China today is new. For example, China's first land auction was held in Shenzhen in 1987 and the initial batch of land leases has not yet expired or been renewed.[1]

Before 1949, China's legal system was influenced by three homegrown philosophies — Confucianism, Daoism and Legalism — and by extraterritoriality, which allowed foreigners living in coastal enclaves to manage their own affairs, starting in the Qing Dynasty (1644 – 1911). These influences continue to be felt today.

Confucius (551 – 479 BCE) and Mencius (372 – 289 BCE) were responsible for the development and spread of Confucianism, which emphasizes social harmony through a clear hierarchical structure, where parents are superior to children, men outrank women and the ruler is above his subjects. Confucianism focuses on ethics and mutual obligations and puts the smooth functioning of the group ahead of individual rights.

Daoism (also known as Taoism) is a philosophy developed by Lao Zi (sixth century BCE) and Zhuang Zi (fourth century BCE) that emphasizes a passive, accepting approach to life. Daoism rejects institutions and governments and encourages its followers to accept the natural order of the universe and embrace a simple, humble and spontaneous lifestyle.

Legalism stems from the teachings of Shang Yang (390 – 338 BCE). Legalism used rewards and punishments, coupled with a strict, clear and public legal code, to maintain order. Feudal privilege was discouraged and the state took precedence over the family or clan.

These three domestic philosophies dealt mainly with criminal issues. Civil disputes were resolved through mediation or arbitration, which was often preferable to relying on a judicial system that was opaque and arbitrary. Before 1910, China did not have a legal code for dealing with civil disputes and arbitration and mediation remain popular today.[2]

Extraterritoriality sprang from the unequal treaties that foreign powers, including the United States, the United Kingdom, France and Japan, signed with China. Under this doctrine, foreigners living in places like Shanghai's French Concession, for example, were not subject to Chinese laws and were tried by a government official from France using French laws. In addition to exempting foreigners from local taxes, extraterritoriality was grossly unfair to and a source of humiliation for the Chinese people. The foreign powers formally abandoned extraterritoriality in January 1943.

When it took power in 1949, the Chinese Communist Party abolished the Kuomintang government's legal system, which was modeled on European codes. The Communist Party issued the Common Program of the Chinese People's Consultative Conference, which served as a basic law until the country's first constitution was introduced in 1954.

In formulating China's new legal system, Communist Party Chairman Mao Zedong borrowed from Confucian traditions, but replaced loyalty to the family with allegiance to the Communist Party and adopted Legalism's belief that the state was the sole arbiter of morality. Laws from the Soviet Union were adapted for local use.

In 1951, the government established the xinfang, or petitioning, system.[3] With a history that dates to the Ming Dynasty (1368 – 1644), the system allows people who believe they have been mistreated by officials to ask the government for redress at national, provincial and local xinfang offices. Xinfang is still used today, particularly in cases of expropriation, but is usually an act of desperation. One researcher estimated that just 0.2% of petitions are successful.

The Hundred Flowers Campaign, which encouraged intellectuals to criticize abuses by the Communist Party, was launched in 1956. More than half a million people who spoke out were subsequently purged in the Anti-Rightist Campaign. This was followed by the Great Leap Forward (1958 – 61), during which agricultural collectivization was introduced,[4] over 14 million hectares of farmland was lost to ill-fated industrial projects[5] and tens of millions died in a famine. During the Cultural Revolution (1966 – 76), many of China's law schools were closed, faculty were sent to labor camps, law libraries were destroyed and the legal profession effectively disappeared. Between 1949 and 1979, the number of practicing lawyers in China dropped from more than 60,000 to just 212.[6]

In 1978, China introduced the Open Door Policy, which allowed inflows of foreign capital, the establishment of joint ventures and foreign direct investment. The new policy ended China's isolation from the West and sparked a series of reforms that gave foreign companies the legal framework they needed to invest in China.

One key change was the introduction of the Civil Procedure Law in 1991. Article five of the law specifies that foreign nationals, enterprises and organizations have the same litigation rights and obligations as their

Chinese counterparts. Part four of the law contains specific instructions for handling cases involving foreign interests.[7]

In 2000, the National People's Congress (NPC) adopted the Legislative Law, which formalized the process of drafting and amending laws. The new law specified that the NPC had exclusive jurisdiction over matters relating to the expropriation of private property and taxes, among other issues. Despite tighter regulations introduced in 2011, expropriation continues to be a major source of conflict in China (see "Developers and development" chapter for more information).

China's constitution was amended in 2004 to read, "Citizens' lawful private property is inviolable." and "The State, in accordance with law, protects the rights of citizens to private property and to its inheritance."[8]

On October 1, 2007, the Property Rights Law of the People's Republic of China came into effect. The law included a requirement for registration of real property; definitions of state-owned, collective and private property; and descriptions of the legal rights associated with ownership, use and security rights.

Lawmaking in China

In July 1979, the NPC promulgated a series of organic laws that serve as a framework for drafting, amending and enforcing laws in China.

The NPC is China's highest organ of state power. It comprises about 3,000 delegates who are elected by the provinces, autonomous regions and municipalities that are under the central government's supervision. The State Council, the Supreme People's Court and the Supreme People's Procuratorate are under the NPC, which also elects the president of the People's Republic of China.

The National People's Congress appoints and supervises the NPC Standing Committee, a group of approximately 150 individuals who are responsible for interpreting and implementing China's constitution, as well as enacting, interpreting and amending the nation's laws. Numerous task forces and special committees, responsible for everything from legal reform to environmental affairs, report to the NPC Standing Committee.

The State Council, which is also known as the Central People's Government, is China's main administrative authority. The State Council supervises ministries, commissions and local governments, including bodies such as the Ministry of Housing and Urban-Rural Development, the Ministry of Land and Resources, the National Development and Reform Commission and the People's Bank of China, that shape and influence housing policy. The State Council and the bodies under it issue orders, directives and regulations that have the power of law.

China's provinces, municipalities directly under the central government and autonomous regions have a local people's congress and standing committee that reports to the National People's Congress. The local people's congresses are authorized to enact legislation relating to their area.

The Communist Party of China permeates all aspects of political and legal life in China. The country's leaders are party members, as are about one-third of China's lawyers, who must swear an oath of loyalty to the party when they are admitted to the bar or renew their practicing certificate.[9] As Richard McGregor observes in his book *The Party*, judges must remain loyal to the party, the state, the masses and the law, in that order.[10]

The hierarchy of China's laws

China's laws and regulations can be divided into several categories. As James Zimmerman explains in *China Law Deskbook*:

A **law** (fa) is enacted by the NPC or the NPC Standing Committee.

- **Regulations** (*tiaoli*) implement a law or policy and are usually issued by the State Council.

- A **regulation** (*guiding*) is issued by a lower-level agency to address a narrower issue.

- **Rules** (*guize*) or detailed rules (*xize*) are usually issued by a ministry and explain or interpret a law or regulation.

- **Methods** or **measures** (*banfa*) are rules or regulations that are more detailed and address a specific issue.

- A **judicial** or **administrative decision** (*jueding*) is for explanatory purposes.

China also has unwritten, internal (*neibu*) laws and regulations that are only for circulation within the government or the Communist Party. Neibu provide guidance for government policies on issues ranging from immigration to foreign currency controls.

Until the 1970s, many of China's laws and regulations were unwritten. But since it joined the World Trade Organization (WTO) in 2001, China has been obliged to publish any law that affects foreign investors.[11] WTO rules also specify that foreign individuals and enterprises receive treatment that is "no less favorable" than domestic individuals and businesses.

The judicial system

The Chinese court system has four levels: The Supreme People's Court (which operates on a national basis); higher people's courts (provincial); intermediate people's courts (municipal); and basic people's courts (county). Courts usually have criminal, civil, economic and administrative sections. There is a separate disciplinary system, which is managed by the Central Commission for Discipline Inspection, for the 80.3 million members of the Communist Party of China.

As its name suggests, the Supreme People's Court is China's highest court. It supervises the administration of justice by local people's courts and issues directives that guide lower courts in applying laws and administering justice. In China, there is no system of judicial precedent that requires a court to follow decisions made by higher courts, and the Supreme People's Court does not have the authority to interpret laws.

Chinese courts enjoy judicial autonomy. But the entire system is closely supervised by the National People's Congress and the NPC Standing Committee, which retain control of the legislative process.

China also has procuratorates at the national, provincial, municipal and county levels, as well as specialist military and railway procuratorates. These state organs supervise the legal system and investigate and prosecute cases of treason, counterrevolutionary activity, corruption and dereliction of duty.

Chinese court judgments are often brief and do not include the legal reasoning used to reach the verdict. Statutory provisions may be mentioned, although case law and lawyers' submissions are usually not.

Before 1997, many judges were appointed on the basis of their military or political careers, sometimes without having received formal legal training. The Supreme People's Court now supervises training and continuing education programs for the nation's judges.

It is not unusual for litigants to offer judges bribes. Nine judges in Guangdong were discovered to have taken bribes of up to 180,000 yuan from a "litigation agent" between 2003 and 2007.[12]

Lawyers

There are more than 200,000 practicing lawyers and 17,000 domestic law firms in China, as well as a growing number of foreign law firms. Chinese lawyers are supervised by the Ministry of Justice and must belong to the All China Lawyers Association, which is a national professional body (www.acla.org.cn).

In 1997, the National People's Congress promulgated the Law of the People's Republic of China on Lawyers. Prior to the introduction of this law, which was amended in 2001 and 2007, lawyers were effectively state employees and law firms were public bodies.

The law made lawyers and their firms liable for compensation in the event of malpractice; specified standards for confidentiality, conflicts of interest and bribery; prohibited the fabrication or use of false evidence; and forbade law firms from participating in businesses other than legal services and paying finder's fees to attract business. Chinese lawyers can be disciplined for divulging state secrets and for concealing important facts in a case.[13]

Domestic law firms are generally less expensive than foreign firms, and a growing number of Chinese lawyers are both bilingual and dual qualified (i.e., admitted to the bar in China and another jurisdiction).

Foreign vs. domestic lawyers

In China, foreign law firms face restrictions on the services they can provide. For example:

- Foreign firms may not practice local law, although they may advise on international law.

- Foreign firms may not employ Chinese lawyers, except as paralegals.

A Chinese lawyer employed by a foreign firm must suspend his practicing certificate.

Foreign firms may instruct local law firms on behalf of foreign clients, but they cannot form joint ventures or enter fee-sharing arrangements.[14]

Social and administrative pressure can be brought to bear on lawyers in China. As result, it can be hard to find legal representation in politically sensitive cases.

To get the best service from your lawyer, use a well-known firm with a reputation to protect. An introduction from an existing client may also be helpful. For more information about locating and hiring a lawyer in China, see the "Useful information" chapter.

Seals

Seals, which are also known as chops, have been used to validate documents since imperial times. There are strict specifications for corporate and government chops, which are set down by the State Council. Seals for Chinese organizations are round, use red ink and vary in size.

Government seals have a five-point star or China's national emblem (five stars above the Forbidden City) in the center of the circle and are 42 – 60 millimeters in diameter, with larger sizes reserved for more important bodies. The name of the government body is arranged around the star in a semicircle.[15]

Corporate seals are 30 – 45 millimeters in diameter.[16] All companies are required to have a company official seal, which has a five-point star in the center of the circle and is used on contracts, applications to open a bank account and documents submitted to the government. There is only one official seal for each company and copies are not permitted.[17]

There are also special chops, such as a legal representative's seal, which is typically used by the company's chairman or CEO for documents such as business licenses; a finance seal, which is used for bank transfers, withdrawals and other transactions; a contract seal, which is used in place of the company official seal, but only on contracts; a human resources seal, which is used for personnel matters; and a tax seal, which is used for tax invoices.[18] Seals used by foreign businesses must incorporate the official Chinese name that the business registered with the Chinese government.

Corporate seals are registered with the local Public Security Bureau and State Administration of Industry and Commerce. Seals can be forged. To verify that a corporate seal is legitimate, hire a Chinese lawyer to visit the government office in the city where the company is registered.

Businesses will "sign" a contract using their company official seal and the signature of an authorized representative. Contracts can also be validated with the application of both the contract seal and the legal representative's seal. The seal must be completely legible, and you should confirm that the person signing the contract is legally authorized to do so. Contracts that are signed but not sealed may not be recognized if there is a dispute.

Personal seals are square and 18 millimeters in size. Foreigners do not need a seal, although it can be helpful.

Contracts

In China, Chinese-language contracts take precedence over (control) contracts in other languages, unless the Chinese contract explicitly states that the foreign-language contract takes precedence. If you do not speak Chinese, a dual-language contract can provide a false sense of security. If both the English and Chinese contracts say that they control, the Chinese version will control, regardless of what the English contract says.[19] The added complexity of a dual-language contract can increase your legal costs and inject ambiguity that makes the agreement difficult to enforce.

Chinese courts will enforce contracts in languages other than Chinese, although you may have difficulty finding a local company willing to sign a contract in a language other than Chinese for the provision of goods or services inside China. If a contract will be enforced in a Chinese court (as opposed to arbitration in Hong Kong, for example) the contract should be prepared in Chinese and translated into English.

At the risk of stating the obvious, you will be held to a Chinese-language contract that you sign, even if you cannot read Chinese. And having the contract translated or explained to you by your counterparty — such as a vendor, a real estate agent or a developer's salesperson — is rarely a good idea. High-quality translations are not cheap, but they are usually much less expensive than a lawsuit.

Finally, many real estate-related contracts in China use standard forms, where there is limited — if any — scope for alterations.

USEFUL INFORMATION

This chapter features resources to help you buy and own a home in China. The entries are arranged alphabetically and include English-language content, unless noted with "CO" (Chinese only).

The domestic organizations listed below have a presence — such as an office, showroom or distributor — in Beijing, Guangzhou, Shanghai or Shenzhen. The inclusion or omission of a company should not be taken as a recommendation that you use or avoid them. Government bureaus and departments with an interest in housing and real estate are included, and technical and professional resources are available for buyers seeking detailed information. Some resources are outside China.

Web addresses are generally for the main page. On bilingual Websites, the most current information is often on the Chinese pages. Website maintenance in China can be unpredictable, and large organizations can go offline for weeks at a time.

Finally, in China things change quickly. Consider this information a starting point, not the last word.

A

Alternative investments

In addition to owning physical property, there are several ways to gain exposure to the Chinese real estate market. You can:

- Buy shares in the developers listed below. Many of these companies are listed on the Hong Kong stock exchange (www.hkex.com.hk).

- Invest in a China-focused real estate investment trust, such as the Perennial China Retail Trust (www.perennialchinaretailtrust.com) or the CapitaRetail China Trust (www.capitaretailchina.com), which are listed on the Singapore Exchange (www.sgx.com), or the Hui Xian REIT (www.huixianreit.com) and the Yuexiu REIT (www.yuexiureit.com), which are listed on the Hong Kong stock exchange.

- Buy shares in a fund that tracks Chinese real estate companies. For example, the CSI 300 Real Estate Index ETF (www.etf.db.com) and the W.I.S.E. – CSI HK Listed Mainland Real Estate Tracker (www.boci-pru.com.hk) are listed on the Hong Kong bourse.

- Purchase shares in an exchange-traded fund, such as the SPDR Dow Jones International Real Estate ETF or the SPDR Dow Jones Global Real Estate ETF (www.spdrs.com). Both are listed on the New York Stock Exchange (www.nyse.com) and have exposure to China.

- Invest in a mutual fund, such as the Fidelity International Real Estate Fund (www.fidelity.com) or the ING International Real Estate Fund (www.ingfunds.com).

Invest through a private equity fund like those operated by CDH Investments (www.cdhfund.com) or CURA Investment Management (www.curafund.com).

Invest in Chinese insurance companies. In 2010, the China Insurance Regulatory Commission allowed insurance companies to invest a portion of their assets in real estate, including commercial developments, retirement homes and social housing.

Appraisal services

China has 33,000 certified real estate appraisers and about 5,000 companies providing appraisal services. This includes everything from small homegrown firms to multinationals.

The China Appraisal Society is a national industry body and is China's representative in the International Valuation Standards Council. The society's members appraise real estate as well as other assets (www.cas.org.cn).

The China Institute of Real Estate Appraisers and Agents is a national regulatory body. The institute's Website includes a directory where you can check members' credentials (www.cirea.org.cn, CO).

The China Real Estate Valuers Association is a national professional body (www.creva.org.cn, CO). There are local associations in Beijing (www.bjgj.org.cn, CO), Guangdong (www.gdreva.org.cn, CO), Guangzhou (www.realestateappraisal.org.cn, CO) and Shanghai (www.valuer.org.cn, CO).

The Ministry of Land and Resources maintains a searchable directory of individual appraisers and companies providing appraisal services (http://credit.mlr.gov.cn, CO).

Architects, designers and contractors

ArchDaily features the work of architects from around the world (www. archdaily.com).

The Architectural Society of China is an academic organization and national professional body. The society's Website includes a directory of architects and links to provincial architectural groups and related organizations (www.chinaasc.org).

Architizer is an Internet portal that lets architects highlight their work and find clients (www.architizer.com).

The Beijing Construction Decoration Association is a trade group for contractors and decorators. The association's Website includes news about the industry as well as home improvement information (www. bcda.org.cn).

The China Building Decoration Association is a national trade group. The association's Website includes links to local bodies, news, information about policies and regulations and a directory of designers (http://cbda. ccd.com.cn, CO).

The China Construction Industry Association is a national trade organization. The association's Website includes information on a variety of housing-related issues (www.zgjzy.org, CO).

The China Institute of Interior Design (formerly the China Institute of Interior Architects) is an academic society and trade group for interior designers. The institute's Website includes a directory of designers along with samples of their work (www.ciid.com.cn, CO).

The China Interior Design Network's Website includes a directory of designers, samples of their work and other resources (www.a963.com, CO).

The Royal Institute of British Architects (www.architecture.com) and the American Institute of Architects (www.aia.org) offer booklets on how to hire and work with an architect. The British institute maintains a directory with members in China, while the American institute has a branch in Hong Kong (www.aiahk.org).

The World Architects' Website (www.world-architects.com) includes a directory of architects operating in China, with photographs of their work (www.chinese-architects.com).

The World Association of Chinese Architects is a global body for ethnic Chinese architects (www.waca.com.cn). I.M. Pei is the association's honorary founding member.

B

Business information

The Business Anti-Corruption Portal provides practical information to help small and medium-sized businesses avoid corruption. Run by the governments of Austria, Denmark, Germany, Netherlands, Norway, Sweden and the U.K., the multilingual site has information on 64 countries, including China (www.business-anti-corruption.com).

China Business Guide is a free ebook produced by the U.K. government and the China-Britain Business Council that has useful information about negotiating, contracts, corruption and managing business relationships (http://cbbc.org).

The State Administration for Industry and Commerce is responsible for industrial and commercial market supervision and law enforcement. The administration's Website includes information on advertising, antitrust, product quality and other regulations (www.saic.gov.cn).

There are local bureaus in Beijing (www.hd315.gov.cn, CO), Guangdong (www.gdgs.gov.cn, CO), Shanghai (www.sgs.gov.cn) and Shenzhen (www.szscjg.gov.cn, CO).

C

Consumer protection

The China Consumer Network's Website offers news and advice (www.ccn.com.cn, CO).

The China Consumers' Association maintains a Website that includes news as well as English translations of consumer protection laws (www.cca.org.cn). There are local consumer protection associations in Beijing (www.bj315.org, CO), Guangdong (http://gd315.gov.cn, CO), Shanghai (http://sh315.org, CO) and Shenzhen (http://sz315.org, CO).

The Ministry of Commerce operates a fraud prevention Website, where you can register complaints about businesses and services (www.12312.gov.cn, CO). There are local sites in Beijing (http://beijing.12312.gov.cn, CO), Guangdong (http://guangdong.12312.gov.cn, CO), Shanghai (http://shanghai.12312.gov.cn, CO) and Shenzhen (http://shenzhen.12312.gov.cn, CO).

The National Bureau of Corruption Prevention's Website includes information about China's anticorruption laws and policies (www.nbcp.gov.cn).

D

Developers

The organizations listed below develop residential property for sale in Beijing, Guangzhou, Shanghai and Shenzhen.

Company	Website	Stock Exchange
Agile Property Holdings	www.agile.com.cn	Hong Kong
BBMG	www.bbmg.com.cn	Hong Kong
Beijing Capital Development Holding (Group)	www.bcdh.com.cn	—
Beijing Capital Land	www.bjcapitalland.com.cn	—
Beijing Urban Construction Investment Development	www.bucid.com, CO	Shanghai
Beijing Vantone Real Estate	www.vantone.com	Shanghai
C&D Real Estate	www.cndrealty.com, CO	—
Calxon Group	www.calxon-group.com, CO	Shenzhen
Canada Land	www.canadaland.com.hk	Sydney
CapitaLand	www.capitaland.com.cn	Singapore
Century Golden Resources Group	www.grgroup.com.cn, CO	—
Chengtou Holding	www.sh600649.com	Shanghai
China Enterprise	www.cecl.com.cn, CO	Shanghai
China Merchants Group	www.cmhk.com	Multiple
China Overseas Land & Investment	www.coli.com.hk	Hong Kong
China Railway Construction	http://crcc.cn	Hong Kong
China Railway Group	www.crecg.com	Shanghai
China Resources Land	www.crland.com.hk	Hong Kong
China Vanke	www.vanke.com	Shenzhen

Company	Website	Stock Exchange
Cifi Group	www.cifi.com.cn, CO	—
Coastal Greenland	www.coastal.com.cn, CO	Hong Kong
COFCO Property (Group)	www.cofco-property.cn, CO	Shenzhen
Cosmos Group	www.cosmosgroup.com.cn, CO	Shenzhen
Country Garden Holdings	www.countrygarden.com.cn	Hong Kong
Dahua Group	www.dahuahome.com, CO	—
Evergrande Real Estate Group	www.evergrande.com	Hong Kong
Fantasia Holdings	www.cnfantasia.com	Hong Kong
Fineland Group	www.fineland.com.cn	—
Franshion Properties	www.franshion.com	Hong Kong
Future Holdings	www.futureholdings.com.cn	—
Gemdale Holdings	www.gemdale.com	Shanghai
Glorious Property Holdings	www.gloriousphl.com.cn	Hong Kong
Gold Tai Yuen Group	www.goldtaiyuen.com	—
Greenland Group	www.greenlandsc.com, CO	—
Greentown China Holdings	www.greentownchina.com	Hong Kong
Guangdong Long Light (Group)	www.logan.com.cn, CO	—
Guangdong Pearl River Investment	www.gdpr.com, CO	—
Guangzhou R&F Properties	www.rfchina.com	Hong Kong
Haier Real Estate Group	www.haierhouse.com, CO	—

Company	Website	Stock Exchange
Henderson Land	www.hld.com	Hong Kong
Hengli Properties Development (Group)	www.hlgroup.com.hk	Hong Kong
Hopson Development Holdings	www.hopson.com.cn	Hong Kong
Huafa Industrial	www.cnhuafas.com, CO	Shanghai
Huayuan Property	www.hy-online.com, CO	Shanghai
Hutchison Whampoa Properties	www.hwpg.com	Hong Kong
Jinke Group	www.jinke.com	—
K. Wah International Holdings	www.kwih.com	Hong Kong
Kaisa Group Holdings	www.kaisagroup.com	Hong Kong
Kamfei Group	www.jinhuichina.com.cn, CO	—
Kerry Properties	www.kerryprops.com	Hong Kong
KWG Property Holding	www.kwgproperty.com	Hong Kong
Lai Fung Holdings	www.laifung.com	Hong Kong
Landsea	www.landsea.cn, CO	—
Lei Shing Hong	www.lsh.com	—
Longfor Properties	www.longfor.com	Hong Kong
Lujiazui Finance & Trade Zone Development	www.ljz.com.cn, CO	Shanghai
Mission Hills China	www.missionhillschina.com	—

Company	Website	Stock Exchange
Nan Fung Group	www.nanfung.com.hk	—
New World China Land	www.nwcl.com.hk	Hong Kong
NGS Real Estate	www.nfgroup.com.cn, CO	—
Palm Springs Holdings	www.palmsprings.cn	—
Poly Real Estate Group	www.polycn.com, CO	Shanghai
Raycom Real Estate Development	www.raycomchina.com, CO	—
Road King Intrastructure	www.roadking.com.hk	Hong Kong
Shanghai Forte Land	www.forte.com.cn	Hong Kong
Shanghai Industrial Development	www.sidlgroup.com, CO	Shanghai
Shanghai Industrial Holdings	www.sihl.com.hk	Hong Kong
Shanghai Jingrui Real Estate	www.jingruis.com, CO	—
Shanghai Pengxin Group	www.peng-xin.com.cn	—
Shenglong Group	www.slqiye.com, CO	—
Shenzhen Fountain	www.fountain.com.cn	Shenzhen
Shenzhen Investment	www.shenzheninvestment.com	Hong Kong
Shenzhen Overseas Chinese Town	www.octholding.com	Shenzhen
Shimao Property Holdings	www.shimaoproperty.com	Hong Kong
Shui On Construction and Materials	www.socam.com	Hong Kong

Company	Website	Stock Exchange
Sino Land	www.sino.com	Hong Kong
Sino-Ocean Land Holdings	www.sinooceanland.com	Hong Kong
SPG Land	www.spgland.com	Hong Kong
SRE Group	www.sre.com.cn	Hong Kong
Star River Group	www.star-river.com	—
Sun Hung Kai Properties	www.shkp.com	Hong Kong
Sunac China Holdings	www.sunac.com.cn	Hong Kong
Sunshine 100	www.ss100.com.cn	—
Tande	www.tande.cn, CO	Shanghai
The Wharf (Holdings)	www.wharfholdings.com	Hong Kong
Tomson Group	www.tomson.com.hk	Hong Kong
Top Spring International Holdings	www.topspring.com	Hong Kong
Tuan Sing Holdings	www.tuansing.com	Singapore
Tysan Holdings	www.tysan.com	Hong Kong
Wing Tai Properties	www.wingtaiproperties.com	Hong Kong
Xinhu Zhongbao	www.600208.net	Shanghai
Yanlord Land	www.yanlordland.com	Singapore
Yida Group	www.yidagroup.com	—
Yuexiu Property	www.yuexiuproperty.com	Hong Kong

E

Earthquakes

The China Earthquake Administration is responsible for the development of a national earthquake strategy as well as related policies, laws and industry standards (www.cea.gov.cn, CO). There are local organizations in Beijing (www.bjdzj.gov.cn, CO), Guangdong (www.gdsin.net, CO) and Shanghai (http://web.shea.gov.cn, CO).

Additional information is available from the China Earthquake Information Network's Website (www.csi.ac.cn, CO) and from a virtual earthquake museum operated by the Chinese Academy of Sciences (www.kepu.net.cn/english/quake/index.html).

The United States Geological Survey provides background on earthquakes (http://earthquake.usgs.gov).

Energy conservation

The China Association of Building Energy Efficiency is a national body for companies and individuals selling products and services related to energy management. The association's Website includes news, publications and a members' directory (www.cabee.org).

The China Clean Energy Network provides information about China's renewable energy industries, including statistics, news and policy updates (www.21ce.cc).

The China Energy Conservation Certificate is a voluntary labeling program for electrical appliances, building materials and other items that is administered by the China Quality Certification Center, which also certifies solar products (www.cqc.com.cn).

The China Energy Label is a mandatory labeling program for home appliances and other equipment that rates each product's energy efficiency (www.energylabel.gov.cn, CO). The program is run by the China National Institute of Standardization, which is responsible for the development of national energy efficiency standards (www.cnis.gov.cn).

Chinagb.net is a Website with news and information about green technologies and energy-efficient living (www.chinagb.net).

The China Green Building Network's Website includes academic research, tutorials, news and other resources (www.cngbn.com, CO).

The Chinese Renewable Energy Industries Association is a trade group that promotes clean energy. The association's Website offers news, research and policy information (www.creia.net, CO).

The Science and Technology Promotion Center's Website features news, standards, announcements and statistics (www.cstcmoc.org.cn, CO).

Environmental resources

The Center for Legal Assistance to Pollution Victims is a nongovernmental organization that is managed by environmental law professors from the China University of Political Science and Law. The center's Website includes resources for people seeking a legal solution to pollution problems (www.clapv.org).

The China Environmental Protection Union is supported by government departments, industry associations, media outlets and businesses. The union's Website includes news and information as well as a directory listing suppliers of environmental products and services (www.epun.cn, CO).

China Water Risk is a nonprofit organization that provides information about pollution, conservation and other water-related issues in China (http://chinawaterrisk.org).

The Environmental and Ecological Network is a clearinghouse for information about environmental science, ecology, environmental protection and public advocacy in China (www.eedu.org.cn, CO).

The Institute for Environment and Development is an independent body that promotes environmental protection and social development. The institute holds seminars and educational events and its Website includes a "Beijing forest park map" (www.ied.cn).

The Institute of Public and Environmental Affairs is a Beijing-based nonprofit organization that maintains a Website with databases and interactive maps of air and water pollution in China. The site also includes information about China's environmental policies, a glossary and other resources (www.ipe.org.cn).

The Ministry of Environmental Protection's Website includes environmental standards as well as information about air pollution, nuclear safety, toxic chemicals and related issues (www.zhb.gov.cn). There are offices in Beijing (www.bjepb.gov.cn, CO), Guangdong (www.gdepb.gov.cn), Shanghai (www.sepb.gov.cn) and Shenzhen (www.szhec.gov.cn, CO).

There are trade associations for companies providing indoor environmental testing services in Guangdong (www.gieha.org, CO) and Shanghai (www.jhxh.org.cn, CO).

The UK-China Eco-cities & Green Building Group is a platform for cooperation between China and the United Kingdom. The group is supported by the two countries' governments and produces bilingual research on eco-cities in China (www.ukchinagroup.org).

The United States Environmental Protection Agency (EPA) has information about indoor air quality, volatile organic compounds and other environmental issues (www.epa.gov).

F

Financing

The banks listed below operate in China, offer residential mortgages and are supervised by the China Banking Regulatory Commission (www.cbrc.gov.cn). You may be able to arrange a mortgage offshore by using property outside China as collateral.

Domestic banks

Agricultural Bank of China (www.abchina.com)

Bank of Beijing (www.bankofbeijing.com.cn)

Bank of China (www.boc.cn)

Bank of Communications (www.bankcomm.com)

Bank of Dalian (www.bankofdl.com, CO)

Bank of Hangzhou (www.hzbank.com.cn, CO)

Bank of Jiujiang (www.jjccb.com, CO)

Bank of Nanchang (www.nccbank.com.cn, CO)

Bank of Nanjing (www.njcb.com.cn)

Bank of Ningbo (www.nbcb.com.cn)

Bank of Shanghai (www.bankofshanghai.com, CO)

Bank of Tianjin (www.tccb.com.cn, CO)

Beijing Rural Commercial Bank (www.bjrcb.com)

China Bohai Bank (www.cbhb.com.cn, CO)

China CITIC Bank (http://bank.ecitic.com)

China Construction Bank (www.ccb.com)

China Everbright Bank (www.cebbank.com)

China Merchants Bank (www.cmbchina.com)

China Minsheng Banking Corp. (www.cmbc.com.cn)

Chinese Mercantile Bank (www.cmbcn.com.cn, CO)

Guangdong Development Bank (www.gdb.com.cn)

Harbin Bank (www.hrbcb.com.cn)

Hua Xia Bank (www.hxb.com.cn)

Industrial and Commercial Bank of China (www.icbc.com.cn)

Industrial Bank (www.cib.com.cn)

Jinzhou Bank (www.jinzhoubank.com, CO)

Ping An Bank (http://bank.pingan.com, CO)

Postal Savings Bank of China (www.psbc.com, CO)

Shanghai Pudong Development Bank (www.spdb.com.cn)

Shanghai Rural Commercial Bank (www.srcb.com)

Shengjing Bank (www.shengjingbank.com.cn, CO)

Shenzhen Development Bank (www.sdb.com.cn)

Xiamen International Bank (www.xib.com.cn)

Zhejiang Chouzhou Commercial Bank (www.czcb.com.cn, CO)

International banks

Bank of East Asia (www.hkbea.com.cn)

China CITIC Bank International (www.cncbinternational.com)

Citibank (www.citibank.com.cn)

Dah Sing Bank (www.dahsing.com)

DBS Bank (www.dbs.com)

First Sino Bank (www.fsbankonline.com)

Hana Bank (www.hanabank.cn)

Hang Seng Bank (www.hangseng.com.cn)

HSBC (www.hsbc.com.cn)

Metrobank (www.metrobank.com.cn)

Nanyang Commercial Bank (www.ncbchina.cn)

OCBC Bank (www.ocbc.com.cn)

Societe Generale (www.societegenerale.cn)

Standard Chartered Bank (www.standardchartered.com.cn)

United Overseas Bank (www.uobchina.com.cn, CO)

Wing Hang Bank (www.whbcn.com)

Woori Bank (http://cn.wooribank.com)

Fire

Firefighting in China is the responsibility of the Ministry of Public Security (www.mps.gov.cn). There are fire bureaus in Beijing (www.bjxfj.gov.cn, CO), Guangzhou (www.gdfire.gov.cn, CO), Shanghai (www.fire.sh.cn, CO) and Shenzhen (www.sz119.gov.cn, CO).

General information about preventing and surviving residential fires can be found at www.usfa.fema.gov.

G

Government: municipal

Information about municipal government departments and bureaus is also included in individual subject entries in this chapter.

Beijing

The Beijing Municipal Government portal can be found at www.ebeijing.gov.cn.

The Beijing Bureau of Justice's Website offers information about the capital's legal system (www.bjsf.gov.cn, CO).

The Beijing Municipal Administration of Cultural Heritage administers the city's cultural heritage and museums (http://bjww.gov.cn).

The Beijing Municipal Commission of Housing and Urban-Rural Development's Website offers useful information about policies and brokers, as well as sample sale and purchase agreements (www.bjjs.gov.cn).

The Beijing Municipal Commission of Urban Planning is responsible for the city's master plan as well as drafting related regulations and technology standards (www.bjghw.gov.cn).

The Beijing Traffic Management Bureau's Website has useful road-related news and notices (www.bjjtgl.gov.cn).

Guangzhou

The Guangzhou Municipal Government portal can be found at www.gz.gov.cn.

The Guangzhou Municipal Bureau of Culture administers the city's cultural heritage and museums (www.xwgd.gov.cn, CO).

The Guangzhou Municipal Justice Bureau's Website features legal information, including guides for real estate transactions (www.gzsfj.gov.cn, CO).

The Guangzhou Municipal Land Resources and Housing Administrative Bureau maintains a Website with procedures for buying and selling a home, a Q&A section, maps to transaction registration centers and other useful information (www.laho.gov.cn).

The Guangzhou Public Security Bureau manages the city's traffic (www.gzjd.gov.cn, CO).

Shanghai

The Shanghai Municipal Government portal can be found at www.shanghai.gov.cn.

The Shanghai Municipal Housing Support and Building Administration Bureau's Website includes title transfer procedures and directories of real estate brokers, developers, demolition contractors and exterminators (www.shfg.gov.cn, CO).

The Shanghai Municipal Administration of Cultural Heritage administers the city's cultural heritage and museums (http://wgj.sh.gov.cn, CO).

The Shanghai Municipal Bureau of Justice's Website offers information on legal topics, including how to hire notaries and lawyers (www.justice.gov.cn, CO).

The Shanghai Municipal Transport and Port Authority manages the city's traffic (www.jt.sh.cn, CO).

Shenzhen

The Shenzhen Municipal Government portal can be found at www.sz.gov.cn.

The Shenzhen Municipal Bureau of Culture, Sports and Tourism manages the city's arts and cultural heritage (www.szwtl.gov.cn, CO).

The Urban Planning, Land and Resources Commission of Shenzhen Municipality operates a Website that includes forms, statistics, official announcements and other information (www.szpl.gov.cn, CO).

Shenzhen Municipal Justice Bureau's Website has directories of lawyers and notaries in Shenzhen, a legal Q&A section and other resources (www.szsf.gov.cn, CO).

The Shenzhen Traffic Bureau manages road safety in the city (www.stc. gov.cn, CO).

Government: national

The main Website for the Government of the People's Republic of China contains statistics about China, links to government offices and departments and other useful information (http://english.gov.cn).

Information about national government departments, bureaus and commissions is also included in individual subject entries in this chapter.

Key ministries
The Ministry of Civil Affairs provides social support and disaster relief services (www.mca.gov.cn, CO).

The Ministry of Commerce is responsible for foreign trade policy, export and import regulations, foreign direct investment, consumer protection, market competition and international trade agreements (www.mofcom.gov.cn).

The Ministry of Education's Website includes lists of accredited educational institutions in China, including those authorized to enroll the children of foreign nationals (www.moe.gov.cn).

The Ministry of Environmental Protection offers daily air quality reports for major cities (www.zhb.gov.cn).

The Ministry of Finance formulates and implements policies and guidelines for China's economic development, including tax regulations. The ministry's Website includes official policies, interpretive notes and related resources (www.mof.gov.cn, CO).

The Ministry of Housing and Urban-Rural Development supervises the real estate and construction industries. The ministry's Website includes statistics as well as building standards for earthquake resistance and energy efficiency (www.mohurd.gov.cn, CO).

The Ministry of Industry and Information Technology regulates China's telecommunications and Internet infrastructure, but not content (www.miit.gov.cn, CO).

The Ministry of Justice supervises lawyers, legal advisers and notaries (www.legalinfo.gov.cn).

The Ministry of Land and Resources is responsible for planning, administering and the rational use of China's land and mineral and marine resources (www.mlr.gov.cn).

The Ministry of Public Security is responsible for policing, firefighting, immigration and border control (www.mps.gov.cn).

The Ministry of Railways' Website features information about railway construction projects as well as links to regional railway bureaus and companies (www.china-mor.gov.cn, CO).

The Ministry of Transport is responsible for road, water and air transport (www.mot.gov.cn, CO).

The Ministry of Water Resources' Website includes information about flood control and drought relief (www.mwr.gov.cn).

Other state organs

The General Administration of Quality Supervision, Inspection and Quarantine is in charge of testing, measurement, certification, accreditation and standardization (www.aqsiq.gov.cn).

The National Development and Reform Commission formulates and implements strategies for economic and social development. This includes everything from energy and food supplies to economic restructuring and large infrastructure projects. The commission's Website has information on national five-year plans and other policy initiatives (www.ndrc.gov.cn).

The People's Bank of China is the nation's central bank (www.pbc.gov.cn).

The State Administration of Cultural Heritage is responsible for antiques, archeological digs and related issues (www.sach.gov.cn).

China's foreign exchange markets are supervised by the State Administration of Foreign Exchange. The agency's Website includes statistics, news and policy information (www.safe.gov.cn).

The State-owned Assets Supervision and Administration Commission is under the State Council and is responsible for managing the state's interest in centrally (as opposed to locally) owned state-owned enterprises, such as Poly Real Estate Group (www.sasac.gov.cn).

The Supreme People's Procuratorate is responsible for investigating and prosecuting crime (www.spp.gov.cn, CO).

♟   **H**

Heritage and conservation

The Beijing Cultural Heritage Protection Center is a non-governmental organization that helps communities preserve their tangible and intangible culture (http://bjchp.org).

♟   **I**

Insurance

The companies listed below sell homeowners, mortgage and construction liability insurance. International insurers include joint ventures between foreign and local companies. Domestic insurers include Taiwanese firms and state-owned enterprises.

Domestic insurers

- Alltrust Insurance (www.alltrust.com.cn, CO)

- Anbang Property Insurance (www.ab-insurance.com, CO)

- Bank of China Insurance (www.bocins.com, CO)

- Bohai Property Insurance (www.bpic.com.cn, CO)

- Cathay Pacific Property Insurance (www.cathay-ins.com.cn, CO)

- Chang An Property and Liability Insurance (www.capli.com.cn)

China Continent Property & Casualty Insurance
(www.ccic-net.com.cn, CO)

China Huanong Property & Casualty Insurance
(www.chinahuanong.com.cn, CO)

China Life Property and Casualty Insurance (www.chinalife-p.com.cn)

China Pacific Insurance (www.cpic.com.cn)

China United Insurance (www.cic.cn, CO)

Cinda Property Insurance (www.cindapcic.com, CO)

Dahzong Insurance (www.e-dicc.com.cn, CO)

Dubon Insurance (www.dbic.com.cn, CO)

PICC (www.e-picc.com.cn, CO)

Ping An Insurance (www.pingan.com)

Sunshine Insurance (www.sinosig.com, CO)

Taiping General Insurance (www.etaiping.com, CO)

Tian An Insurance (www.tianan-insurance.com, CO)

Yingda Taihe Property Insurance (www.ydpic.com.cn)

Yong An Insurance (www.yaic.com.cn, CO)

Zheshang Property and Casualty Insurance (www.zsins.com, CO)

International insurers

- Allianz (www.allianz.cn)

- AXA (www.axa-ins.com.cn)

- Generali China Insurance (www.generali-china.cn)

- Huatai Insurance (www.ehuatai.com, CO)

- Hyundai Insurance (China)
  (www.hi-ins.com.cn, Chinese and Korean only)

- Nipponkoa Insurance
  (www.nipponkoa-cn.com, Chinese and Japanese only)

- RSA (www.rsagroup.com.cn)

- Zurich (www.zurich.com.cn)

Trade and regulatory bodies

The China Insurance Regulatory Commission is the state's supervisory body (www.circ.gov.cn, CO).

There are two industry groups, the Insurance Association of China (www.iachina.cn, CO) and the Insurance Institute of China (www.iic.org.cn, CO). Both offer information for consumers, including explanations of insurance terms and regulations.

International brands

Company	Website	Product
Armstrong	www.armstrong.cn, CO	Floor and ceiling coverings
Bang & Olufsen	www.bang-olufsen.com	Audiovisual equipment
B&Q	www.bnq.com.cn	Home improvement, do-it-yourself, appliances and furnishings
Blum	www.blum.com	Kitchens
Boffi	www.boffi.com	Kitchens and bathrooms
Bosch	www.bosch.com.cn	Appliances
Bulthaup	www.china.bulthaup.com	Kitchens
Carrier	www.carrier.com.cn	Heating, ventilation and air-conditioning systems
Cassina	www.cassina.com	Le Corbusier and Frank Lloyd Wright furniture
Crestron	www.crestronasia.com	Lighting and home automation systems
Duravit	www.duravit.cn, CO	Sanitary ware
Electrolux	www.electrolux.com	Appliances
Fisher & Paykel	www.fisherandpaykel.cn	Appliances
Fujitsu	www.fujitsu.com	Air-conditioning systems
Giorgio Armani	www.giorgioarmanistores.com	Furniture and accessories
Gaggenau	www.gaggenau.com	Kitchens and appliances
Hansgrohe	www.hansgrohe.cn, CO	Plumbing

Company	Website	Product
Herman Miller	www.hermanmiller.cn, CO	Eames and Aeron chairs
Hitachi	http://hitachi.cn, CO	Audiovisual equipment and appliances
Hunter Douglas	www.hunterdouglas.cn	Window coverings
Ikea	www.ikea.cn	Furniture and accessories
Leicht	www.leicht.com.hk	Kitchens
Leviton	www.leviton.com	Lighting and home automation systems
LG	www.lg.com	Audiovisual equipment and air-conditioning systems
Lutron	www.lutron.com	Lighting and home automation systems
Miele	www.miele.cn, CO	Appliances
Mitsubishi Electric	www.mitsubishielectric.com	Audiovisual equipment and appliances
Moen	www.moen.cn, CO	Plumbing and sanitary ware
Panasonic	http://panasonic.cn, CO	Audiovisual equipment and appliances
Philips	www.philips.com.cn, CO	Audiovisual equipment and appliances
Poggen Pohl	www.poggenpohl.com	Kitchens and appliances
Roche Bobois	www.roche-bobois. com	Home furnishings
Samsung	www.samsung.com	Audiovisual equipment and appliances

Company	Website	Product
Siemens	www.siemens.com	Appliances, lighting and home automation systems
Smeg	www.smeg.cn	Appliances
Snaidero	www.snaidero.it	Kitchens
Sony	www.sony.com.cn, CO	Audiovisual equipment
Sub-Zero/Wolf	www.subzero.com	Kitchen appliances
Toshiba	www.toshiba.com.cn, CO	Audiovisual equipment, appliances and air-conditioning systems
Toto	www.toto.com.cn	Sanitary ware
Versace	www.versace.com	Furniture and accessories
Viking	www.vikingrange.com	Appliances

L

Law

The All China Lawyers Association is the national professional body for lawyers. All lawyers in China are members of the association (www.acla.org.cn). There are local associations in Beijing (www.bmla.org.cn), Guangzhou (www.gzlawyer.org, CO), Shanghai (www.lawyers.com.cn, CO) and Shenzhen (www.szlawyers.com).

The Asian Legal Information Institute's Website offers free, searchable access to legal information from 27 countries and territories in Asia (www.asianlii.org). The site is maintained by the Australasian Legal Information Institute, which is supported by the law faculties at the University of Technology, Sydney, and the University of New South Wales.

The China International Economic and Trade Arbitration Commission (www.cietac.org) is supplemented by commissions in Beijing (www.bjac.org.cn), Guangzhou (www.gzac.org), Shanghai (www.accsh.org.cn) and Shenzhen (www.szac.org).

China Law Blog is published by Harris & Moure, a Seattle-based law firm. The site, which includes an RSS feed, covers a range of legal topics and is a useful source of China-related business information (www.chinalawblog.com).

The International Union of Notaries has a list of China-based notaries on its Website (www.uinl-international.com).

A searchable directory of international law firms operating in China can be found at www.hg.org.

Local law firms specializing in real estate include:

- The Beijing Real Estate Lawyer Network (www.lvshiwang.net, CO)

- Guangzhou China Real Estate Lawyer (www.peoplelawyer.com.cn)

- The Shanghai Real Estate Lawyer Network (www.lawyerfc.com.cn, CO)

- The Shanghai Real Estate Legal Services Center (www.shfdhelp.com, CO)

- Shenzhen Real Estate Attorneys (www.tjbaoda.cn, CO)

Mondaq provides commentary on legal, regulatory and financial topics from leading law and accounting firms. This free service lets you subscribe to updates, which can be filtered by topic and region (www.mondaq.com).

Nolo is a legal publisher specializing in do-it-yourself law in the United States. Nolo's Website includes calculators and other resources, as well as a dictionary that explains common legal concepts in plain English (www.nolo.com).

The State Council's Legislative Affairs Office maintains a searchable database of China's laws and regulations (www.chinalaw.gov.cn).

M

Maps

Online and printed maps in China are edited to obscure sensitive government and military sites and the homes of senior government officials.

The National Bureau of Surveying and Mapping operates an online service called Mapworld (www.tianditu.cn), which was launched in 2010. The bureau doesn't have map downloads, but it does offer technical information for cartographers (www.sbsm.gov.cn).

Online maps are also available from Baidu (http://map.baidu.com, CO); Nokia, which has agreements with Tencent and Sina (http://maps.nokia.com); and Sohu (www.go2map.com, CO).

Google (http://maps.google.com and http://ditu.google.cn, CO) and Microsoft (www.bing.com/maps) have applied for official licenses for their online Chinese map services.

SinoMaps Press, a state-owned company, produces national, provincial, city and thematic maps, as well as English-language editions. SinoMaps also has an online store (www.sinomaps.com).

Media

The outlets listed below publish or broadcast in English and operate Websites that are free, unless otherwise indicated. Many sites offer RSS (really simple syndication) subscriptions.

State-controlled outlets — including *China Daily, People's Daily* and the Xinhua News Agency — often publish identical versions of the same story, following instructions from the Central Propaganda Department (http://cpc.people.com.cn).

Domestic media

The *Beijing Review* bills itself as China's national English news weekly (www.bjreview.com).

Business China is an online news service published by the *21st Century Business Herald*, a Chinese-language daily headquartered in Guangzhou (http://en.21cbh.com).

Beijing-based Caixin Media publishes *Caixin — China Economics & Finance*, a monthly news magazine and Website (http://english.caixin.com). Caixin has a reputation for high-quality investigative journalism.

China Daily is the country's national English-language newspaper (www.chinadaily.com.cn).

China Economic Review (www.chinaeconomicreview.com) is a monthly magazine that covers business, finance and economics.

The China Media Project is run by the Journalism & Media Studies Center at the University of Hong Kong. The project produces summaries and background information on stories from the Chinese media, many of which are not covered elsewhere (http://cmp.hku.hk).

China Network Television is a multilingual channel operated by China Central Television that is available by satellite and the Internet (http://english.cntv.cn).

China Radio International is the country's overseas radio broadcaster. Multilingual programming is available via shortwave radio, the Internet, podcasts, local AM repeaters and satellite (http://english.cri.cn).

CNC World is a television channel operated by the Xinhua News Agency. Launched in 2010, CNC World is available via satellite, cable TV and the Internet (www.cncworld.tv).

Eastday.com is a multilingual news portal focusing on Shanghai (http://english.eastday.com).

The Economic Observer is an independent weekly distributed in major cities throughout China (www.eeo.com.cn).

Global Times is a 24-page tabloid with national distribution. It is published from Monday to Friday and is under *People's Daily* (www.globaltimes.cn).

People's Daily is the English edition of the leading Chinese newspaper. It publishes business and general news and is also available in Arabic, French, Japanese, Russian and Spanish (http://english.peopledaily.com.cn). *People's Daily* also has a real estate portal (http://house.people.com.cn, CO).

Shanghai Daily publishes seven days a week (www.shanghaidaily.com).

Shenzhen Daily is the English-language edition of the *Shenzhen News* (www.szdaily.com).

Shenzhen Standard is a free, online newspaper serving the city's expatriate community (www.shenzhen-standard.com).

The *South China Morning Post* is a daily broadsheet published in Hong Kong. The SCMP Website is available by subscription, with some free content (www.scmp.com).

Southern News produces a Website featuring English-language news from Guangdong (www.newsgd.com). Southern News also operates a real estate portal focusing on homes in Guangdong (http://house. southcn.com, CO).

The Standard is a Hong Kong–based free tabloid (www.thestandard. com.hk).

The Xinhua News Agency is China's state news agency (http://english. news.cn).

International media

The following outlets cover business and social news in China, often with a more critical perspective than China's state-controlled media.

Bloomberg is a global financial wire service that offers free news stories on its Website. Bloomberg is a good source of business and economic data (www.bloomberg.com).

The Economist is a weekly publication covering general and business news. Large sections of *The Economist*'s content are free, although full access requires a subscription. *The Economist* publishes a quarterly index of global house prices, which includes China (www.economist. com).

The *Financial Times* is a London-based, global business newspaper. The weekend edition includes a global real estate section called House

& Home. Much of the paper and its archives are free or free with registration (www.ft.com).

The New York Times and its global edition, the International Herald Tribune (www.iht.com), cover business and general events in China. Both papers report on residential real estate around the world. In March 2011, The New York Times introduced a paywall system that limits readers to 20 free articles per month (www.nytimes.com).

Reuters is a global wire service that covers general and business news. News stories and archived material are free on Reuters' Website (www. reuters.com).

The Wall Street Journal is a U.S.-based, global business newspaper (www. wsj.com). Sections of the newspaper and its archive are free, while full access requires a subscription. The Wall Street Journal also offers a blog, the China Real Time Report (http://blogs.wsj.com/chinarealtime).

Yahoo! News offers a China feed that compiles stories from wire services, including Reuters, Agence France-Presse and the Associated Press as well as other sources (http://news.yahoo.com).

Social media

Many people blog and tweet about China-related topics, ranging from general news and culture to finance and politics. Major stories will often appear in social media hours or even days before they are reported in China's official media. Many blog posts and tweets include rumors and speculation, so a degree of skepticism is helpful.

Some popular blogs include http://chinadigitaltimes.net, www. chinalawblog.com, www.danwei.com, http://shanghaiist.com, http:// sinocism.com and http://chovanec.wordpress.com. Many mainstream journalists also have Twitter accounts.

Megaprojects

A list of large infrastructure projects can be found at http://blog.sina.com.cn/s/blog_5a53af350100ao0k.html, CO.

N

Nuclear power

The China Atomic Energy Authority is the regulatory body for China's nuclear industry (www.caea.gov.cn).

The China Nuclear Energy Association is a national, non-governmental industry body (www.china-nea.cn).

Information about China's nuclear industry is available from the World Nuclear Association (www.world-nuclear.org).

P

Property management

The China Property Management Institute is a national trade body for professional property managers (www.ecpmi.org.cn, CO). The institute's Website includes property management news and standards, plus links to associated committees for building safety (www.chfwaq.com CO) and termite control (www.zgbyfz.com, CO).

There are local property management associations in Beijing (www.bpma.org.cn, CO), Guangzhou (www.gzpma.com, CO), Shanghai (www.shwy.org.cn, CO) and Shenzhen (www.szpma.org, CO).

R

Real estate agents

The agencies listed below sell residential property. In response to the central government's market-cooling measures, many agencies serving foreigners have closed their sales operations and are focusing on leasing. Agencies are also rationalizing their branch networks and redeploying staff to meet changing demand patterns.

Beijing agents specializing in siheyuan

Beijing Jing Cheng Wan Jie Real Estate (www.bjwjshy.com.cn)

Beijing Wandecheng (www.wdc.com.cn, CO)

Shun Yixing Real Estate (www.syx.cc)

Domestic agencies

Beijing Century Real Estate (www.beijingrealestates.com)

Fullhome Real Estate (www.fullhomechina.com)

Phoenix Property Agency (http://shanghai-realty.com)

Sinyi (www.sinyi.com.cn, CO)

Hong Kong agencies

The following agencies are headquartered in Hong Kong and may have English-speaking staff. Because these agencies derive income from Hong Kong–based clients, they are usually familiar with the needs of non-Mainland buyers.

- Centaline (www.centaline.com.cn, CO)

- HKP Estate Agency (www.hkpchina.com.cn, CO)

- Land Power (www.landpower.com.hk)

- Midland Realty (www.midland.com.cn, CO)

- Ricacorp (http://sh.ricacorp.com, CO)

International and franchise agencies

- CBRE (www.cbre.com)

- Century 21 (www.century21cn.com)

- Colliers International (www.colliers.com)

- DTZ (www.dtz.com)

- Knight Frank (www.knightfrank.com)

- Savills (www.savills.com)

Trade and regulatory bodies

The China Institute of Real Estate Appraisers and Agents is a national regulatory body. The institute's Website includes a directory of members' credentials (www.cirea.org.cn, CO). The institute also operates www.agents.org.cn, CO, which includes agent-related news and model contracts.

There are local agents' associations in Beijing (http://210.75.213.161/User/Bjraaa/web/, CO), Guangzhou (http://rea.laho.gov.cn, CO), Shanghai (http://www.278278.com/company/association/broker_association, CO) and Shenzhen (www.srba.net.cn, CO).

Real estate investment trusts

In February 2011, the CFA Institute published "Asia-Pacific REITs — Building Trust through Better REIT Governance." The report includes an introduction to real estate investment trusts and information about REITs in China (www.cfapubs.org).

The China Trustee Association is the trust industry's trade body (www. xtxh.net).

Use-Trust.com is an information portal for the trust business in China (www.yanglee.com, CO).

Real estate listings

China has many sites listing homes for sale throughout the country. The sites usually have separate pages for large cities and often include news, commentary and other resources.

The 21CN Real Estate Channel is operated by 21CN, a subsidiary of China Telecom (http://house.21cn.com, CO).

Amoy Housing lists pre-owned and rental properties (www.taofw.cn, CO).

Blue House Network lists rentals as well as new and pre-owned homes, shops and offices (http://lanfw.com, CO).

iHouseKing.com has listings for Guangzhou, Shanghai and Shenzhen. The Guangzhou page includes some information in English (http://ihk.cn).

Mysupa.com lists pre-owned and rental homes, parking spaces and commercial property throughout China (www.mysupa.com, CO).

NetEase lists new and pre-owned commercial and residential property as well as rentals (http://house.163.com, CO).

Pearl River Real Estate Network focuses on sales and rentals in Guangdong, Shenzhen and surrounding communities (www.zsjdc.com, CO).

Room Doctor Network operates property portals for Guangzhou (http://gz.fangdr.com, CO), Shanghai (http://sh.fangdr.com, CO) and Shenzhen (http://sz.fangdr.com, CO).

Shenzhen Real Estate Information Network focuses on sales and rentals of new and pre-owned homes and commercial property in the Shenzhen area (www.szhome.com, CO).

Sina.com offers comprehensive national listings (http://house.sina.com.cn, CO).

Sohu.com operates a real estate portal that includes residential and commercial listings and a directory of designers and other service providers (http://house.focus.cn, CO).

SouFun lists sales and rentals, new and pre-owned homes as well as commercial and industrial property (http://soufun.com, CO).

Renovations

Toolbase.org is a Website maintained by the National Association of Home Builders in the United States. While the site is written for an American audience, it has useful links and information about renovations, building and construction techniques, energy efficiency, universal design and other topics (www.toolbase.org).

Research and statistics

Domestic resources

Baidu provides information about residential developments throughout

China, including pricing data, photographs and video footage, forums and maps (http://house.baidu.com, CO).

The China Index Academy publishes a range of research on the Chinese real estate market, with English-language reports starting at $2,000 per copy (http://industry.soufun.com).

China Land and Resources Information Network offers statistics, analysis and news on land use, some of which requires a subscription (www.clr.cn, CO).

China Land Surveying and Planning Institute is a professional organization under the Ministry of Land and Resources that researches land policy and administration (www.clspi.org.cn).

ChinaLands.com features tender and auction notices, news and analysis (www.chinalands.com, CO).

China Real Estate Information's Website includes news, statistics and other resources, some of which requires a subscription (www.crei.com.cn, CO).

China Real Estate Network provides news, analysis and statistics. The Website covers sales and rentals as well as commercial and recreational property (http://house.china.com.cn, CO).

China Urban Land Price Dynamic Monitor provides statistics and analysis of valuation trends. Access to some information requires a subscription (www.landvalue.com.cn, CO).

Land China includes tender notices, statistics, analysis and news (www.landchina.com, CO).

The National Bureau of Statistics is a government body that provides data on a range of housing-related topics (www.stats.gov.cn).

Property Industry Network of China is a portal for developers and other real estate professionals. The site includes news, commentary, books and other resources (www.propertyallinone.com.cn, CO).

Real Estate Foresight offers research into China's property markets (www.realestateforesight.com).

Soufun sells land and housing transaction data on a subscription basis (http://fdc.soufun.com, CO).

View Real Estate Network has news, stock research and commentary by industry insiders (www.guandian.cn, CO).

World Union Real Estate Consultancy offers data, consultancy, sales and marketing and brokerage services (www.worldunion.com.cn, CO).

International resources

Financial institutions – Banks, brokers and related companies produce research for their clients and as a marketing tool. The research, which can be useful in understanding the property market and evaluating developers, often falls into two categories: macroeconomic analysis and reports on property developers as investment targets. You may need to be a client, or to register, to obtain the research.

- AllianceBernstein (www.alliancebernstein.com)

- Bank of China (www.boc.cn)

- Barclays Bank (www.barclays.com)

Citibank (www.citibank.com)

CLSA (www.clsa.com)

Credit Suisse (www.credit-suisse.com)

DBS Vickers (www.dbsvonline.com)

Fitch (www.fitchratings.com)

Goldman Sachs (www.gs.com)

HSBC (www.hsbc.com)

J.P. Morgan (www.jpmorgan.com)

Merrill Lynch (www.ml.com)

Moody's (www.moodys.com)

Morgan Stanley (www.ms.com)

PIMCO (http://pimco.com)

Royal Bank of Scotland (www.rbs.com)

Standard & Poor's (www.standardandpoors.com)

Standard Chartered (www.standardchartered.com)

UBS (www.ubs.com)

Institutes and others – This category includes multilateral organizations, consulting firms, industry associations and trade bodies.

The Asian Development Bank publishes research on a range of economic, social and environmental issues in China (www.adb.org).

The Economist Intelligence Unit produces a range of paid and free research, including reports on China's economy and housing market (www.eiu.com).

The Lincoln Institute of Land Policy publishes books, reports and other materials about the use, regulation and taxation of land (www.lincolninst.edu).

McKinsey & Company produces articles and research reports on a range of China-related topics (www.mckinsey.com).

The Urban Land Institute is a U.S.-based nonprofit organization that conducts research and publishes materials on real estate-related topics around the world (www.uli.org).

Wind Information provides financial data, information and software (www.wind.com.cn).

The World Bank publishes research and statistics on a range of economic, social and environmental issues in China (www.worldbank.org).

Real estate agencies – Large international real estate companies produce a great deal of English-language research material. While much of this research is written for investors and corporate end-users, it can be a good source of information about the broader market and emerging trends. Some sites require registration.

- CBRE (www.cbre.com)

Colliers International (www.colliers.com)

Cushman & Wakefield (www.cushwake.com)

DTZ (www.dtz.com)

Jones Lang Lasalle (www.joneslanglasalle.com)

Knight Frank (www.knightfrank.com)

Savills (www.savills.com)

S

Software

Architecture and design

Design software comes in three variations. First is professional computer-aided design (CAD) software, like the packages sold by Autodesk (http://autodesk.com). This software is powerful, expensive and has a steep learning curve, which may be hard to justify if you are only involved in one or two projects.

Second is consumer-oriented software from IMSI Design (www.imsidesign.com), SmartDraw (www.smartdraw.com), Punch! Software (www.punchsoftware.com) and others. Software in this category is less expensive — typically under $150 — and less sophisticated than professional products. It's also easier to learn.

Third, there is free software, like Sketchup, a versatile, three-dimensional modeling package that can be used to design anything from a single room to a city (www.trimble.com). Sketchup lets you import DWG files as well as colors and textures from JPG and PNG files. The basic version of Sketchup is a free download for computers using the Windows or Mac operating systems. A professional version of Sketchup and video tutorials are also available.

Floorplanner is a Web-based design tool that lets you create two- and three-dimensional room layouts and home designs (www.floorplanner. com). The basic program is free; a premium, paid service provides extra functionality. Ikea offers online design tools that may be useful if you are planning to use that company's furniture (www.ikea.com).

Autodesk has a free, Web-based program called Homestyler that lets you create and furnish floor plans in two and three dimensions (www.homestyler. com). Autodesk also offers a free program called DWG TrueView that lets you view, print and annotate DWG files made with their professional CAD software. DraftSight from Dassault is similar to DWG TrueView but works with Windows, Mac and Linux computers (www.3ds.com).

Decoration

The Internet is a useful source of tools for generating color schemes for your new home. Paint manufacturers such as Dow Chemical operate sites with tools to help you choose a color theme (www.paintquality. com). Intended primarily for Web designers, Colorotate includes useful tools for understanding and working with color (www.colorotate. com). Pinterest (http://pinterest.com) can be useful for inspiration and for keeping your plans organized.

Adobe's Kuler lets you build a color scheme from an image you upload to the site (http://kuler.adobe.com). Kuler uses the Adobe Swatch Exchange (ASE) format to send color information to Adobe's design products, such as Illustrator, InDesign and Photoshop. Kuler has a variety of other tools, including a color wheel, forums and searchable color themes. Colr. org (www.colr.org) and Colors Palette Generator (www.cssdrive.com/imagepalette/index.php) are similar to Kuler, but easier to use.

Colorjive lets you upload a photo of a room and virtually "paint" it (http://colorjive.com). A premium version, which allows you to store images online, is also available.

The myhomeideas blog has a calculator that lets you enter the dimensions of a room and determine how much paint you'll need to buy (www.myhomeideas.com/project-calculator). The site uses imperial measurements and includes other calculators and guides.

Home automation

Home automation systems that manage entertainment; heating, ventilating and air-conditioning; and security are becoming available as commercial products and open source projects. Some systems can be controlled with smartphones and personal and tablet computers, letting you monitor your home's front door while you are at the office or control the lighting in your living room from the sofa. Some systems also track energy usage.

Automation companies such as Crestron (www.crestron.com) and Lutron (www.lutron.com) have been joined in this market by computer hardware and software firms including Apple (www.apple.com), Google (www.google.com), Intel (www.intel.com) and a growing number of start-ups.

Social media

Facebook (www.facebook.com), LinkedIn (www.linkedin.com), Google Maps (http://maps.google.com), Twitter (http://twitter.com) and Weibo (www.weibo.com, CO) are increasingly useful for many things, including real estate. Weibo and Twitter often have more timely information than official sources, although rumors can take the place of facts. Facebook and LinkedIn let you investigate tenants, vendors and buyers. And there are are crowd-sourced Google Maps showing the locations of Beijing's flood zones as well as places in China with above-average levels of cancer and expropriation.

Note that social media sites outside China are often blocked and services inside China are subject to official censorship.

T

Tax

The Chinese Institute of Certified Public Accountants' Website has a range of tax and accounting information (www.cicpa.org.cn).

Deloitte publishes regular China newsletters and an annual China real estate investment handbook. Written mainly for developers and larger investors, the handbook contains background information on taxes, foreign investment regulations and real estate investment trusts (www.deloitte.com).

Ernst & Young publishes China Tax & Investment News and China Tax & Investment Express, which feature tax and business announcements by the Chinese government (www.ey.com).

Grant Thornton produces business guides and tax alerts for China (www.grantthornton.cn).

The Hong Kong Institute of Certified Public Accountants' Website includes information about Chinese tax issues and a list of Hong Kong accountants with offices in China (www.hkicpa.org.hk).

KPMG publishes regular China alerts (www.kpmg.com).

PricewaterhouseCoopers produces regular updates on China tax issues on its Website (www.pwccn.com). An annual tax summary for China can be downloaded from www.pwc.com.

The State Administration of Taxation's Website includes information on tax laws and treaties (www.chinatax.gov.cn). There are local tax offices in Beijing (www.tax861.gov.cn), Guangzhou (www.gzds.gov.cn), Shanghai (www.csj.sh.gov.cn) and Shenzhen (www.szgs.gov.cn, CO).

Termites

The Chinese Pest Control Association's Website can be found at www.cpca.cn, CO.

The Property Management Association of China operates a termite control board, which offers academic and practical information about termite management and a directory of exterminators (www.zgbyfz.com, CO).

The University of Florida has detailed information about different species of termites (http://entomology.ifas.ufl.edu/creatures/index.htm).

Title

The China Committee of Real Estate Title's Website includes laws, case studies, sample registration certificates and title books (www.ccret.org.cn, CO).

Translation

Google Translate lets you enter a word, a paragraph or an entire Website, which it then translates. Chinese, English and other language pairs are supported. While the site is no substitute for a professional translator, it will give you a general idea of the original text's meaning. It's fast, free and integrated with Google's Chrome browser (www.translate.google.com).

The Translators Association of China is both an academic society and a national trade body. The association's Website includes links to regional associations and to member companies (www.tac-online.org.cn).

Transportation

National

The Ministry of Transport (www.mot.gov.cn, CO) is responsible for road, water and air transport and is the parent of the Civil Aviation Administration of China (www.caac.gov.cn, CO). The administration's Website includes information about the construction of new airports and the expansion of existing facilities.

The Ministry of Railways' Website features information about railway construction projects and links to regional railway bureaus and companies (www.china-mor.gov.cn, CO).

Beijing

- Beijing Capital International Airport (www.bcia.com.cn)

- Beijing MTR (www.mtr.bj.cn)

- Beijing Subway (www.bjsubway.com)

Guangzhou

- Guangzhou Baiyun International Airport (www.baiyunairport.com, CO)

- Guangzhou Metro (www.gzmtr.com)

Shanghai

- Shanghai Airport Authority (www.shairport.com, CO)

- Shanghai Metro (www.shmetro.com, CO)

Shenzhen

Shenzhen International Airport (www.szairport.com)

Shenzhen Metro (www.szmc.net, CO)

Universal design

Buildings that incorporate universal design are aesthetically pleasing and usable by the greatest number of people possible, regardless of their age or ability.

The Center for Universal Design at North Carolina State University's College of Design has information for people who are building or renovating a home, including floor plans, checklists and design suggestions (www.ncsu.edu/ncsu/design/cud/).

A Practical Guide to Universal Home Design is available from the Iowa Program for Assistive Technology (www.uiowa.edu/infotech/universalhomedesign.htm).

Utilities

National

Electricity – China State Power Information Network is a portal for the nation's power industry (www.sp.com.cn).

The State Electricity Regulatory Commission regulates and administers the national electric power sector (www.serc.gov.cn).

State Grid Corporation of China operates a power distribution network that covers 26 provinces, autonomous regions and municipalities (www.sgcc.com.cn).

Gas – The China Gas Association is a national industry body. The association's Website includes information about gas storage and transmission facilities (www.chinagas.org.cn, CO).

Telecommunications – China has three national telecommunications companies. China Mobile (www.chinamobile.com) provides mobile telephone and Internet services, while China Telecom (www.chinatelecom.com.cn) and China Unicom (www.chinaunicom.com) offer both fixed and mobile telephone and Internet services.

The China Internet Network Information Center manages the Internet in China, including domain name registration (www.cnnic.cn).

Water – The China Urban Water Association is a national industry body. The association's Website includes a directory of members and information about urban water standards (www.cuwa.org.cn, CO).

Beijing

Beijing Electric Power is part of the State Grid Corporation of China (www.bj.sgcc.com.cn, CO).

Beijing Gas supplies city gas to the capital (www.bjgas.com, CO).

The Beijing Water Authority oversees water supply and related issues in the capital (www.bjwater.gov.cn, CO).

The Beijing Waterworks Group supplies water to the Beijing area (www.bjwatergroup.com.cn).

Guangzhou

The Guangzhou Power Supply Bureau provides electricity in Guangzhou (www.gdgz.csg.cn).

The Guangzhou Gas Group supplies city gas in Guangzhou (www.gzgas.com, CO).

Guangzhou's water supply is administered by the Guangzhou Municipal Water Authority (www.gzwater.gov.cn, CO) and delivered by Guangzhou Water Supply Co.(www.gzwatersupply.com, CO).

Shanghai

Shanghai Municipal Electric Power is part of the State Grid Corporation of China (www.sh.sgcc.com.cn, CO).

Shanghai Gas supplies city gas in Shanghai (www.shgas.com.cn).

Shanghai's water supply is administered by the Shanghai Water Authority (www.shanghaiwater.gov.cn) and delivered by North Shanghai Municipal Waterworks (www.shanghaiwater.com, CO), Shanghai Minhang Water (www.minhangwater.com, CO), Shanghai Pudong Veolia Water (www.pudongwater.com) and South Shanghai Municipal Waterworks (www.water-sh.com, CO).

Shenzhen

The Shenzhen Power Supply Bureau provides electricity in Shenzhen (www.szpower.com, CO).

Shenzhen Gas provides city gas in Shenzhen (www.szgas.com.cn, CO).

The Shenzhen Water Authority is responsible for water and related issues in Shenzhen (www.szwrb.gov.cn, CO).

The Shenzhen Water Group (www.waterchina.com) is the local water supplier.

W

Weather

The China Meteorological Administration provides forecasts, as well as radar and satellite imagery and information about droughts, earthquakes, floods and typhoons on its Website (www.cma.gov.cn). The CMA issues 14 types of weather warnings for typhoons, rain, snow, cold, wind, dust, heat, drought, lightning, hail, frost, fog, haze and icy roads. Shanghai also issues an ozone warning. Warnings are color coded, from yellow to orange to red, in order of danger. A blue warning, which is less dangerous than a yellow, is issued for typhoons.

Residents of Shenzhen and Guangzhou may find the information from the Hong Kong Observatory useful during typhoon season (www.weather.gov.hk).

Tropical Storm Risk combines the efforts of the British Meteorological Office and several insurance and reinsurance companies to map and predict the progress of storms worldwide (www.tropicalstormrisk.com). The U.S.-based Cooperative Institute for Meteorological Satellite Studies offers a similar service (http://cimss.ssec.wisc.edu/tropic2/).

APPENDIX

This appendix includes three sample contracts: A provisional sale and purchase (S&P) agreement and an S&P agreement from Shanghai and a home renovation contract from Beijing.

The contracts are included to give people who don't read Chinese an overview of typical contract terms. The contracts are synopses, not word-for-word translations. Different contracts are used in different jurisdictions and China's laws and regulations continue to evolve. Get competent legal advice before signing any contract.

Appendix I

Preliminary sale and purchase agreement for a pre-owned home

Buyer .... (Party B) agrees to the following terms and conditions and entrusts (name of agency) .... (Party C) as the broker in the purchase of real estate from the vendor .... (Party A). All parties to this agreement have the right to amend the contract before it is signed.

1. Payment terms:

Party B agrees to pay an initial deposit of .... yuan to Party C for the purchase of real estate introduced by Party C. If Party A agrees to the terms and conditions in this contract and signs the contract, Party C will immediately pass the deposit paid by Party B to Party A. The initial deposit will constitute the first down payment from Party B to Party A.

2. Property information:

If the description of the property in this contract does not conform to the property's actual status or is otherwise inadequate, all parties agree to use the contents of the ownership certificate or other relevant legal documents pertaining to this property as a benchmark. All three parties agree that no additional contracts, amendments or agreements will be signed for the basic description of the property.

2.1 Property type: ....

2.2 Location: ....
Room: .... Street number: .... Street or road: .... City: ....

2.3 Surveyed area: .... square meters

2.4 Property owner: ....

2.5 Certificate of property ownership number: ....

2.6 Interior decorations: ....

2.7 Equipment and accessories: ....

2.8 Does the property have an outstanding mortgage?: .... Yes .... No

2.9 Is the property leased to a tenant?: .... Yes .... No

3. Contract terms:

3.1 Party B and Party C agree that the total price of the real estate is
.... yuan (in figures); .... yuan (in characters).

3.2 Payment terms:

(A) Within .... days of Party A and Party B signing the sale and purchase agreement (and notarizing the agreement, if necessary), Party B agrees to make a down payment to Party A of .... yuan by cash or bank transfer. Together with the initial deposit of .... yuan these two payments shall constitute the total down payment of .... yuan.

(B) Party A agrees that Party B will pay the second installment of .... yuan by a mortgage loan. Party B agrees to complete the mortgage loan application procedure within seven days of signing this contract. This includes applying for the mortgage loan; signing the mortgage loan contract and related agreements; settling all related issues; making all necessary payments; and notarizing the mortgage loan contract, if necessary.

(C) Within .... days of Party B's mortgage loan application being approved by the lender, the deeds for the sale and purchase agreement and mortgage loan contract being issued by the notary public office and

Party A's mortgage having been discharged, Party A and Party B will go to the (location) .... Real Estate Trading Center in person or entrust Party C to handle the property transfer and mortgage registration procedure.

On the day of the loan release, Party B should settle the second installment — which is paid by the lender on behalf of Party B — with Party A.

(D) Within .... days of the lender depositing the second installment in the appointed account, Party A and Party B shall inspect the property. When the condition of the property has been confirmed to be acceptable, Party A will hand over the property to Party B. All associated bills, including water, electricity, gas, telephone, cable TV, estate management, elevator, cleaning, etc., should be paid by Party A before the handover. All bills after the handover should be settled by Party B. Party C will settle the final payment, of .... yuan, to Party A either by cash or bank transfer.

3.3 Other terms:

(A) Deposits that Party A has made to the property developer, management company or other organization for the management fund; management deposit; and installation fees for telephone, gas, cable TV, etc., are included in the sale price of the property. If there is a fee for re-registering these deposits in Party B's name, the fee will be paid by Party B.

(B) All ancillary equipment and interior decorations in the property will be transferred to Party B during the handover. The price of the equipment and decorations is included in the property purchase price.

(C) Party A will transfer the residential registration within 20 days of the property handover. If the transfer is not accomplished within this period, Party A will pay compensation to Party B of .... % of the total real estate value for every overdue day until the transfer is completed.

(D) Party A and Party B are responsible for paying the taxes and fees associated with this transaction according to the relevant laws and regulations. If the sale and purchase agreement is to be notarized, the fee will be paid by the party requesting the notarization. If the mortgage loan contract is to be notarized, the fee will be paid by Party B.

(E) If Party B's application for a mortgage loan is not approved by the lender, or the lender approves an amount less than the amount for which Party B has applied, on the date stated in section 3.2 (D), Party B will make up any shortfall by paying Party A the difference, either in cash or by bank transfer.

(F) Party A is responsible for issuing a receipt for the total purchase price to Party B.

4. Party C will report the progress of the transaction to Party B within .... days of receiving the initial payment from Party B.

4.1 During this period, if Party B cancels the offer to purchase, Party B will pay a penalty to Party C equal to 2% of the total real estate price stated in section 3.1 of this agreement.

4.2 During this period, if Party A refuses to accept any of the clauses in section 3 of this contract and this leads to the failure of this transaction, Party C will refund the initial payment to Party B without interest within two working days or at a time agreed by Party B after two working days. This clause shall not apply if Party A and Party B reach another agreement.

5. If Party A agrees to the clauses in section 3 of this contract and signs the contract, Party B agrees to make the initial deposit payment to Party A. By signing this contract, Party A acknowledges that Party C has the right to collect commissions from Party A and Party B, according to the agreements in this contract. If Party A and Party B sign this contract or another similar contract for this property, both Party A and Party B agree to pay 1% commission on the total purchase price to Party C during the contract signing.

6. If Party A agrees with the clauses in section 3 of this contract and signs the contract, Party B agrees to sign a sale and purchase agreement with Party A within .... days of Party A signing this contract. The specific contract signing date can be confirmed by Party C or through a supplemental agreement between Party A and Party B. If Party B fails to sign the sale and purchase agreement within this period, Party A may keep the initial deposit, demand a penalty of .... % of the purchase price from Party B and demand the fulfillment of this contract by Party B.

7. Party A agrees to sell the property described in section 2 to Party B via Party C, based on the clauses stated in section 3 or other terms agreed by Party A and Party B.

8. If Party B agrees to the clauses in section 3 and signs the contract, Party A agrees to sign a sale and purchase agreement with Party B within .... days of Party B signing this contract. The specific contract signing date can be confirmed by Party C or through a supplemental agreement between Party A and Party B. If Party A fails to sign the sale and purchase agreement within this period, Party A agrees to refund double the amount of the initial deposit to Party B. Party B also has the right to demand a penalty of .... % of the purchase price from Party A and demand the fulfillment of this contract by Party A.

9. If either Party A or Party B, or both Party A and Party B fail to complete this contract, and a sale and purchase agreement is not signed, the delinquent party is liable for breach of contract as described in sections 6 and 8 of this contract.

10. If Party B makes payments to Party A by bank transfer, the payments shall be made to: Account name: .... ; Bank name: .... ; Account number: ....

11. Party A, Party B and Party C agree that the addresses shown on the signature page of this contract are the addresses to which all documents shall be delivered. If the recipient refuses delivery or the address information is incorrect and this leads to the failure of the delivery, the delivering party will have been deemed to have fulfilled their obligations based on the postmark time. If any party alters their contact address, they are obliged to notify the other parties in writing, in a timely manner.

12. If a dispute occurs during the execution of this contract, Party A, Party B and Party C agree to negotiate a settlement. If negotiations are unsuccessful, all three parties agree to refer the dispute to the real estate section of the People's Court. If force majeure leads to the failure of this contract, the contract will automatically be discharged, and all three parties will be free from liability for breach of contract.

13. Party A, Party B and Party C have entered into this contract voluntarily. After this contract has been signed, no party may change the contract's contents without the agreement of the other two parties. When this contract has been signed by all three parties, Party C will have been deemed to have accomplished his duties. All three parties are expected to understand their rights, obligations and responsibilities under this contract. Any supplemental agreements to this contract agreed by all three parties shall be considered to be part of this contract. If any party breaches this contract, the other parties have the right to seek remedies according to the terms and conditions of the contract.

14. Other terms and agreements of this contract:
(Attach supplementary provisions here)

15. This contract is in triplicate and will take effect immediately upon all three parties' signatures. Each party keeps one copy of the contract.

Party A (Vendor):

Name: ....

Name of agent or representative: ....

Signature: ....

Telephone: ....

ID card #: ....

Address: ....

Date: ....

Party B (Buyer):

Name: ....

Name of agent or representative: ....

Signature: ....

Telephone: ....

ID card #: ....

Address: ....

Date: ....

Party C (Broker):

Name: ....

Signature of responsible person: ....

Telephone: ....

Broker certificate #: ....

Address: ....

Date: ....

Appendix II

Sale and purchase agreement for a pre-owned home

Contract #: ....
Vendor (Party A): ....
Buyer (Party B): ....

In accordance with the relevant laws and regulations of the People's Republic of China and the Shanghai Municipal Government, Party A and Party B voluntarily enter into this contract and agree to abide by the contract's terms in the spirit of fairness and good faith.

1. Party A and Party B, who met independently or were introduced by a real estate agent (name) .... (license number) .... (delete as appropriate), hereby agree that Party A will sell the housing and land use rights (hereinafter referred to as the real estate) described below to Party B.

(A) Title deed number: ....

(B) Location: .... Housing type: (e.g., apartment, detached house) .... Structure: (e.g., wood, concrete) .... Including parking space number: ....

(C) House floor area: ..... square meters. Land use rights area: ..... square meters.

(D) Floor plans are attached in Annex 1.

(E) The land occupied by the house is owned by the state .... or owned by a collective .... Land use rights acquired by sale .... or by transfer ....

(F) Including the equipment and decorations listed in Annex 2.

(G) Including related parties, such as tenants or mortgagees, listed in Annex 5.

Party A warrants that they have accurately described the real estate as well as the ownership status, equipment, decorations and related parties listed above. Party B acknowledges that they understand this disclosure and purchase the real estate voluntarily.

2. Party A agrees to sell the above real estate to Party B for the sum of .... yuan (in characters); .... yuan (in numerals). If the price specified in this contract is less than the minimum transfer price set by the Real Estate Trading Center, Party A and Party B agree to pay any taxes arising from the difference between the two amounts. However, Party B shall not be obliged to pay Party A the difference between the contract price and the minimum transfer price.

Party A and Party B agree on the payment terms specified in Annex 3. Party A agrees to give Party B an official receipt for the payment.

3. Party A shall transfer the real estate according to the following ....

(A) The real estate includes land use rights from: (date) .... to: (date) .... Party A agrees to transfer the real estate and land use rights and obligations to Party B.

(B) In accordance with the laws and regulations of the People's Republic of China, Party B agrees to handle the transfer of land use rights and pay the land use right transfer fee.

(C) Other: ....

4. Party A agrees to vacate the real estate on: (date) .... and notify Party B that the real estate is vacant. Party B shall have .... days from the notice date to inspect the real estate, its decoration and equipment. Party B will have been deemed to have accepted the real estate when Party B has ....

(A) Signed the housing handover book

(B) Received the keys to the real estate from Party A

5. From the date of the contract signing until acceptance of the real estate by Party B, Party A will be responsible for safeguarding the equipment and decorations listed in Annex 2. If the decorations and equipment are not delivered to Party B as specified in Annex 2, Party A shall pay Party B liquidated damages.

6. Party A and Party B agree that the transfer date of the real estate will be: .... This date shall not apply if the Real Estate Trading Center rejects the transaction in accordance with the law. The transfer will be made according to the following ....

(A) Party A and Party B shall jointly apply to transfer the property

(B) Party A shall apply to transfer the property

(C) Party B shall apply to transfer the property

(D) Party A and Party B jointly entrust (name) .... to transfer the property

If Party A delays the transfer or does not provide the necessary documents, Party B may seek relief for breach of contract.

Party A and Party B agree that after signing this contract, one or both parties shall be entitled to apply for a notice of registration at the Real Estate Trading Center.

7. Party A shall be responsible for all risks to the real estate from the signing of this contract until ....

(A) The property rights are transferred to Party B

(B) Party B has accepted the real estate

8. After this contract has been signed, Party A and Party B shall pay all government taxes and fees relating to the real estate according to the county and city regulations.

Party A shall be responsible for all unpaid management fees and water, gas, electrical and communications costs until: ....

(A) The property rights are transferred to Party B

(B) Party B has accepted the real estate

Party B shall be responsible for these costs thereafter. See Annex 4.

9. If Party B fails to pay Party A according to the contract terms, Party B shall pay Party A .... % of the overdue payment for every day that the payment is late. If the payment is more than ...... days late, Party A and Party B agree that the following remedy shall apply ....

(A) Party B shall pay Party A .... % of the overdue payment for every day that the payment is late until the date of the actual payment. The contract will continue to be valid.

(B) Party A shall have the right to notify Party B in writing and unilaterally terminate the contract. If Party B does not object within .... days of the notification, the contract shall be terminated. Party B shall pay Party A .... % of the real estate purchase price as compensation for breaching the contract.

C) Other, as specified here: ....

10. If Party A fails to transfer the real estate as specified in this contract, Party A agrees to pay Party B .... % of the real estate purchase price for every day that the delivery is later than the agreed delivery date. If, after .... days, Party A has not delivered the real estate, Party A and Party B agree that the following remedy shall apply ....

(A) For each day of delay, Party A shall pay .... % of the purchase price in liquidated damages to Party B. The contract will continue to be valid.

(B) Party B shall have the right to notify Party A in writing and unilaterally terminate the contract. If Party A does not object within .... days of the notification, the contract shall be terminated. Party A shall pay Party B .... % of the real estate purchase price as compensation for breaching the contract.

(C) Other, as specified here: ....

11. Party A and Party B agree that, so long as they do not violate the relevant laws and regulations of the People's Republic of China, the supplementary provisions and supplementary agreements shall form an inseparable part of this contract. If the supplementary provisions are inconsistent with the articles of this contract, the supplementary provisions shall prevail.

12. This contract shall take effect on: (date) ....

13. This contract is governed by the laws and regulations of the People's Republic of China. Party A and Party B agree that disputes arising from this contract shall be resolved through consultation. If it cannot be resolved by consultation, the dispute will be resolved: ....

(A) Through arbitration at the Shanghai Arbitration Commission

(B) Through the People's Court

14. There are .... copies of this contract. Party A and Party B each have .... copy. One copy will be retained by the Real Estate Trading Center, the lending bank and the notary.

Supplementary provisions 1.
(Attach supplementary provisions here)

Supplementary provisions 2.
Before signing this contract, Party A and Party B acknowledge that they are both aware of the national and local restrictions on the sale of housing. If this sale is found to be in violation of these restrictions, the Real Estate Trading Center will not register the real estate in Party B's name and will issue a notice that it has refused to process the real estate transfer. If this happens, Party A and Party B agree to the following:

1) Party A and Party B shall jointly apply to terminate this contract.

2) If Party B fails to provide truthful information and this causes economic losses to Party A, Party B agrees to compensate Party A for the corresponding loss and Party B shall bear .... yuan liability for breach of contract.

Annex 1.
(Attach floor plans for the real estate and a copy of Party A's property certificate here)

Annex 2.
Included with the real estate are the following items of equipment and/or decoration:

Equipment: ....
Decorations: ....

For the equipment and decorations listed above the following shall apply ....

(A) The equipment and decorations are included in the price agreed in this contract. Party A shall deliver the equipment and decorations to Party B when Party A transfers the real estate to Party B.

(B) The equipment and decorations listed above are not included in the price agreed in this contract. Party B shall pay Party A the sum of .... yuan in addition to the price agreed in this contract. Party A shall deliver the equipment and decorations to Party B when Party A transfers the real estate to Party B.

Annex 3.
(Attach terms of payment here)

Annex 4.
In addition to the costs specified in section 8,

(A) Party A agrees to assume the cost of ....

(B) Party B agrees to assume the cost of ....

Annex 5.
The following adults who live in the real estate agree to sell the above-mentioned home.

(Signature) ....
(Signature) ....
(Signature) ....
(Signature) ....

Details of outstanding leases: ....
Details of outstanding mortgages: ....
Details of adjacent properties: ....

Party A (Vendor):

Name: ....

Name of agent or representative: ....

Signature: ....

Telephone: ....

ID card #: ....

Address: ....

Date: ....

Party B (Buyer):

Name: ....

Name of agent or representative: ....

Signature: ....

Telephone: ....

ID card #: ....

Address: ....

Date: ....

Appendix III

Home decoration contract

Party A (Employer): ....
Party B (Contractor): ....
Contract #: ....

1. This contract is to be used only for residential renovations in Beijing.*

2. The contractor (Party B) should have a license issued by the Beijing Municipal Administration for Industry and Commerce and a construction enterprise certificate issued by the competent administrative department.

3. If the contract is between Party A and Party B, the contract shall be competed in duplicate with one copy for each party. If the contract is arranged through a design company, the contract will be completed in triplicate, with one copy each for Party A, Party B and the design company.

4. The project will be deemed to have started when the designs, engineering and technical tests have been completed, the materials and construction personnel have arrived at the project site and the deposit has been paid.

5. The project will be deemed to have been completed when the work described in the contract, including indoor air quality testing, has been completed by Party B, and Party A, Party B and the engineer have signed Schedule 4.

6. If the engineer hired by Party A has signed Schedule 4, the project will be considered to have been accepted by Party A.

---

* This is a synopsis of the standard home decoration contract prepared by the Beijing Municipal Administration for Industry and Commerce and revised in March 2012. It is included for illustration purposes only. See the "Law" chapter for information about contracts in China.

7. If the project is delayed for reasons beyond Party B's control, the project period will be extended and Party B will not be liable for breach of contract.

Attach tax stamps here:

Contract terms

Party A (Employer):
Name: ....
Name of agent or representative: ....
Telephone: ....
ID card #: ....
Address: ....

Party B (Contractor):
Name: ....
Name of legal representative: ....
Telephone: ....
Business license #: ....
Construction enterprise certificate #: ....
Address: ....
Name of designer: ....
Telephone: ....
Name of foreman: ....
Telephone: ....

This contract is for Party A's home decoration project and is subject to the Contract Law of the People's Republic of China and all other relevant laws and regulations. The contract includes the following terms:

1. Project overview

1.1 Project location: ....

1.2 Project decoration area: ....

1.3 Number of rooms: ....

1.4 Work to be completed and specifications (see attached quotation and drawings)

1.5 The contractor agrees to complete the project using the following method ....

(A) Party B provides all of the materials (see Schedule 3).

(B) Party B provides some materials and Party A provides the balance (see Schedule 2 and Schedule 3).

1.6 The project duration is .... calendar days, starting on: (date) .... and finishing on: (date) ....

1.7 Price:

(A) Contract amount: .... yuan (in characters); .... yuan (in numerals).

(B) The quote should follow the standard pricing model set by the Beijing Municipal Construction Committee and the Beijing Building Decoration Association. Both parties may agree to use higher-quality materials and workmanship at a higher price.

(C) The quotation must specify, and both parties agree on, the quality of materials and workmanship to be used in the project.

2. Project supervision

If this project is to be supervised by a third party, a separate contract should be concluded between Party A and the construction supervision company. Party A must notify Party B of the construction supervision company's name and the supervisor's name and contact details.

3. Construction drawings and pollution control calculations

3.1 The parties agree that the project will be completed using the following method ....

(A) Party A will provide all construction plans and indoor environmental pollution control pre-evaluation calculations and give them to Party B in triplicate.

(B) Party B will provide all construction plans and indoor environmental pollution control pre-evaluation calculations. Party B will give one copy to Party A.

3.2 The construction drawings and indoor environmental pollution control pre-evaluation calculations must comply with the Code for Indoor Environmental Pollution Control of Civil Building Engineering (GB50325-2001).

3.3 Both parties should acknowledge receipt of the construction plans and indoor environmental pollution control pre-evaluation calculations.

3.4 Neither party may make unauthorized copies of the construction drawings or design data for this project, transfer this data to a third party or use this data for projects outside of this contract.

4. Party A's responsibilities

4.1 Party A shall give Party B access to the project site, and the site shall be ready for work at least three days before work is to begin.

4.2 During the project, Party A shall provide free of charge water, electricity and heating in winter.

4.3 Party A is responsible for arranging all necessary permits from the property manager and paying all related costs.

4.4 Party A is responsible for ensuring that all work complies with the property manager's rules and regulations.

4.5 Party A is responsible for coordination between Party B and the residents of adjacent homes.

4.6 The following activities are prohibited:

(A) Altering the building frame or load-bearing structure

(B) Changing the size of the original doors or windows, or removing walls

(C) Adding a masonry wall more than one centimeter thick

(D) Altering the waterproofing of the kitchen or toilet floor, heating system, water heater, gas pipes or related systems and equipment

(E) Party A may not force Party B to do any of the things listed in A to D, above

4.7 For work listed in 4.6 above, Party A must submit an application to the Housing Management Department and receive the department's written approval before work begins.

4.8 If Party A remains in the home while work is taking place, Party A must cooperate with Party B to prevent fires and ensure the project site is safe.

4.9 Party A will supervise the quality of the project construction, engineering materials, concealed work and final project acceptance.

5. Party B's responsibilities

5.1 Party B will strictly adhere to the construction specifications, quality standards, safety procedures, fire safety requirements and durability and engineering specifications in this contract.

5.2 Party B will strictly adhere to all construction site management regulations, including:

(A) Following all design drawings and government approval procedures, and not altering the load-bearing structure of the building or the heating system, water heater, gas pipes or related systems and equipment.

(B) From 12 noon to 2:00 P.M. and from 6:00 P.M. to 8:00 A.M., Party B shall not hammer, chisel, plane, drill or engage in any other activity that generates noise or creates a nuisance.

(C) Party B will not cause adjacent homes to have blocked pipes, water leakage or electricity interruption. Party B will be responsible for repairing any damage caused by the decoration work.

(D) Party B will protect the building, equipment and furnishings left in the home during construction.

(E) Party B will ensure the home is clean and the sewers are not blocked.

(F) Party B will ensure the cleanliness of the construction site during the decorations and clean the site within one day after the project is complete.

5.3 Party B must explain its work procedures, specifications and prices to Party A before the contract is signed.

6. Project changes

Any changes to the engineering specifications of this contract during the construction period must be agreed by Party A and Party B. Changes are to be written in a change agreement, which will include an adjustment to the project fees and duration.

7. Material supply

Party B shall prepare a list of project materials, equipment and delivery methods and schedules.

(A) Party A shall notify Party B of the material and equipment quality, environmental standards and common acceptance and handover procedures.

(B) Party B shall notify Party A before materials and equipment are delivered to the construction site. Party A and Party B will jointly confirm that the materials and equipment meet all relevant quality and environmental standards.

(C) Building materials supplied by both parties must comply with the State Administration of Quality Supervision, Inspection and Quarantine regulations for harmful substances and include compliance reports issued by recognized professional testing organizations.

(D) If one party refuses to accept building materials, that party must pay all testing costs in advance. If the material fails the test, the cost of testing will be paid by the other party.

(E) After Party B receives and accepts the construction materials, Party B will be responsible for the custody and quality control of the materials.

8. Schedule delays

8.1 If a delay is caused by the following, Party A shall extend the contract completion date:

(A) Large-scale engineering or design changes

(B) Force majeure

(C) Party A agrees to an extension because of other circumstances

8.2 If a delay is caused by the following, Party A shall extend the contract completion date:

(A) Party A does not follow the terms of the contract

(B) Party A does not make the payments listed in the contract

(C) Party A causes other kinds of delays

8.3 If Party B cannot complete its obligations on schedule, the project delivery date shall not be extended. If rework is required to fix problems with Party B's workmanship or materials, the project delivery date will not be extended.

8.4 If materials that Party A has agreed to supply are late or defective, and this causes project delays, Party A will be responsible for those delays. If materials that Party B has agreed to supply are late or defective, and this causes project delays, Party B will be responsible for those delays.

9. Quality standards

9.1 All interior work shall be conducted strictly in accordance with the Civil Engineering Indoor Environmental Pollution Control Standard (GB50325-2001)

9.2 The construction will be performed to the following standard ....

(A) Beijing Family Room Decoration Works Quality Acceptance Standard (DBJ/TO1-43-2003)

(B) Beijing Senior Architectural Engineering Quality Acceptance Standard (DBJ/T01-27-2003)

9.3 If, upon completion of the project, there is a dispute about indoor air quality, a professional testing organization recognized by the relevant administrative departments will be hired to test the indoor air quality. The cost of the test will be paid by the applicant and ultimately borne by the responsible party.

10. Engineering acceptance

10.1 Acceptance of the project will be conducted jointly by the two parties in the following order: 1. materials acceptance, 2. concealed work acceptance, 3. final acceptance of the finished project.

10.2 Party B will notify Party A when the work has been completed. Party A will have three days to check and accept the work. If Party A is satisfied with the work, Party B is finished and Party A must pay the outstanding balance. Party A and Party B then sign the warranty, and Party B gives the engineering drawings to Party A.

10.3 Before final acceptance, Party B is responsible for protecting the safety of the project and project site.

10.4 If Party A moves into the home without completing the acceptance procedures, Party A will have been deemed to have accepted the work as satisfactory and Party B will not be responsible for any defects.

10.5 If there are minor outstanding problems when the project is completed, Party A and Party B can agree to let Party A move into the home. Party A should attach a note listing the problems to the acceptance form (Schedule 4). Party B will then be responsible for fixing these problems.

10.6 The warranty period for interior decoration is two years, under normal use conditions. The warranty period for waterproofing in the kitchen and bathroom is five years.

11. Payment

11.1 After the contract is signed, Party A agrees to pay Party B as follows:

Payment	Payment due date	Proportion payable	Amount payable
First	Three days before work starts	55%	yuan
Second	When half of the work is done	40%	yuan
Third	Final acceptance	5%	Yuan

11.2 For the purposes of the second payment, the project will be deemed to be half completed when half of the water pipes, wiring, walls, doors, windows, joinery and plaster and masonry is installed.

11.3 After the final project acceptance, Party B will submit project statements to Party A for review. If Party A does not object within two days, Party A agrees to pay Party B the balance due.

11.4 After payment has been received, Party B shall issue a written receipt to Party A.

12. Breach of contract

12.1 If a party to this contract fails to fulfill his contractual obligations and this results in a loss for the other party, the responsible party shall be liable to pay compensation, subject to the relevant laws.

12.2 If a party to this contract cannot complete the contract, he shall promptly notify the other party and bear the losses caused by the termination of the contract.

12.3 If Party A delays without good reason payment of the second or third payments listed in section 11.1 above, Party A shall pay liquidated damages of 2% of the contract amount for each late day.

12.4 If Party B delays completion of the project, Party B shall pay Party A liquidated damages of 2% of the contract amount for each late day.

12.5 Party B's responsibility for rework and repairs related to problems with the quality of the project and indoor air quality are as follows:

(A) Party B must rework or repair any defective materials or workmanship. Delays due to rework or repairs will be subject to the liquidated damages specified in section 12.4.

(B) Failure by Party B to meet the indoor air quality standards will be subject to the liquidated damages specified in section 12.4.

(C) If, after rework or repair, the indoor air quality does not meet the standard and this is the fault of Party B, Party B shall return to Party A the full contract price. If Party A is partially responsible for the noncompliance, Party B may reduce the refund by the corresponding proportion.

13. Dispute resolution

Disputes arising under this contract should be resolved by negotiation between the parties, with the assistance of consumer organizations or mediation. If this fails, the case may be taken to the .... People's Court or another body as specified in the arbitration clause.

14. Annex

14.1 This agreement will take effect after both parties have signed and affixed their seals to the contract.

14.2 After the contract is signed, the project shall not be subcontracted.

14.3 The terms of this contract may be amended if both parties agree. All changes must be made in writing.

14.4 If there are losses or an inability to perform this contract due to circumstances beyond the control of the parties, both parties should negotiate a settlement based on the principle of fairness.

14.5 If Party B is introduced to Party A by a design company, and Party B fails to perform the work in this contract according to the contract terms, Party A can recover costs from the design company. The design company can then recover those costs from Party B.

14.6 After this contract is discharged, the contract is automatically terminated.

15. Other matters agreed:

....

....

Party A (Employer):
Name: ....
Name of agent or representative: ....
Signature and chop: ....
Date: ....

Party B (Contractor):
Name: ....
Name of legal representative: ....
Signature and chop: ....
Date: ....

Decoration company:

Name: ....

Name of legal representative: ....

Signature and chop: ....

Date: ....

Telephone: ....

Schedule 1
Quotation of works

Number	Unit	Unit price	Quantity	Total	Work to be done and description of materials

Party A: (signature and chop) ....

Party B: (signature and chop) ....

Note: Add a separate page if there is not enough room on this form.

Schedule 2
Party A agrees to supply the following material and equipment on this schedule:

Number	Description	Quantity	Delivery date	Delivery location

Party A: (signature and chop) ....

Party B: (signature and chop) ....

Note: Supplied materials and equipment must be approved by the State Administration of Quality Supervision, Inspection and Quarantine.

Schedule 3

Party B agrees to supply the following material and equipment on this schedule:

Number	Description	Quantity	Delivery date	Delivery location

Party A: (signature and chop) ....

Party B: (signature and chop) ....

Note: Add a separate page if there is not enough room on this form.

Schedule 4

Project completion and acceptance: (date) ....

Project name:

Project location:

Completion	Party A	Signature and chop:
Acceptance	Engineer	Signature and chop:
Comments	Party B	Signature and chop:

Note: Completion and acceptance does not indicate that the project is free from defects. Schedule 4 must be signed by Party A and Party B and indicate what defects or issues need to be fixed or repaired.

Schedule 5
Project warranty

Party A:

Party A's
representative: Contact:

Party B:

Party B's
representative: Contact:

Project address:

Commencement date: Completion date:

Warranty period: From: (date) ....
                        To: (date) ....

Party A: (signature and chop) ....
Party B: (signature and chop) ....

Note:
1. The warranty period for interior decorations is two years, under normal use conditions. The warranty period for waterproofing in the kitchen and bathroom is five years.

2. During the warranty period, Party B shall promptly fix any problems caused by defective material or construction.

3. During the warranty period, Party B may charge for repairs caused by improper use or maintenance by Party A.

4. The warranty takes effect when it has been signed by Party A and Party B.

NOTES

Chinese names

In running text, the names of Chinese people appear in the Chinese style, with the family name followed by given names. In the "Notes" and "Acknowledgments," where Western and Chinese names appear side by side, the names appear in the Western style, with the given name followed by the family name.

Throughout the book, Chinese names are transliterated into English using the pinyin system.

Dollar figures

All dollar figures in this book are expressed in United States dollars unless otherwise indicated. As *Landed China* went to press, one U.S. dollar equaled approximately 6.2 yuan.

The history of property in China

1. Youqin Huang, "Urban Development in Contemporary China," in *China's Geography: Globalization and the Dynamics of Political, Economic and Social Change*, (Roman & Littlefield Publishers, 2006), 233.

2. Yan Xu, "No Taxation Without Representation: China's Taxation History and Its Political-legal Development," Hong Kong Law Journal, 39, no. 2 (2009): 520.

3. H.F. Schurmann, "Traditional Property Concepts in China," The Far Eastern Quarterly, 15, no. 4 (August 1956): 509.

4. Lei Chen, "The New Chinese Property Code: A Giant Step Forward?," Electronic Journal of Comparative Law, 11, no. 2 (September 2007): 19.

5. Robert Ellickson, "The Costs of Complex Land Titles: Two Examples from China," (Yale Law School, 2012), 8.

6. Henry Kissinger, *On China*, (Penguin, 2011), 46.

7. Jasper Becker, *The Chinese*, (Oxford University Press, 2002), 114.

8. Chengri Ding and Yan Song, *Emerging Land and Housing Markets in China*, (Lincoln Institute of Land Policy, 2005), 164.

9. Colin Brown and Kai Chen, "Land Reform, Household Specialisation and Rural Development in China," (University of Queensland, October 1999), 2.

10. Jung Chang and Jon Halliday, *Mao: The Unknown Story*, (Anchor, 2006), 411 – 412.

11. Carl E. Walter and Fraser J.T. Howie, *Red Capitalism: The Fragile Financial Foundation of China's Extraordinary Rise*, (Wiley, 2011), 29.

12. Becker, *The Chinese*, 93, 95.

13. "1950: The Land Reform," China.org.cn, September 15, 2009.

14. Britt Paulson, "Rent Collection Courtyard," St. Olaf College, 2004.

15. Kaihao Wang, "Surprising Discovery," *China Daily*, April 19, 2012.

16. Xun Li, Xianxiang Xu and Zhigang Li, "Land Property Rights and Urbanization in China," The China Review, 10, no. 1 (Spring 2010): 16.

17. Xinhau Liang, "The Housing Sector in China: Market Formation and Supply," (National University of Singapore, 2006), 20.

18. Lan Deng, Qingyun Shen and Lin Wang, "Housing Policy and Finance in China: A Literature Review," (U.S. Department of Housing and Urban Development, November 2009), 3.

19. Liang, "The Housing Sector in China: Market Formation and Supply," 17 – 18.

20. Jing Wu, Joseph Gyourko and Yongheng Deng, "Evaluating Conditions in Major Chinese Housing Markets," (National Bureau of Economic Research, July 2010), 6.

21. Thomas Campanella, *The Concrete Dragon: China's Urban Revolution and What It Means for the World*, (Princeton Architectural Press, 2008), 43.

22. Qian Zhao, "Hainan Moves to Cool Overheated Property Sector," *Global Times*, January 18, 2010.

23. Becker, *The Chinese*, 127.

24. Bonnie Cao, "Hainan Home Bubble Pops as Curbs Deflate Prices," Bloomberg, December 20, 2011.

25. "China's Hainan May Levy Property Vacancy Tax," Business China, February 13, 2012.

26. Deng, Shen and Wang, "Housing Policy and Finance in China: A Literature Review," 3.

27. Ding and Song, Emerging Land and Housing Markets in China, 175.

28. Deng, Shen and Wang, "Housing Policy and Finance in China: A Literature Review," 6.

29. "China Endorses Private Property," BBC, March 15, 2004.

30. Paul McKenzie, Gregory Tan and Charles Coker, "China: Measures to Cool Chinese Property Market Target Both Foreign and Local Purchasers," (Morrison & Foerster / Mondaq, January 17, 2011).

31. "The Property Rights Law of the People's Republic of China," Lehman, Lee & Xu, October 1, 2007.

32. "Migration in China: Invisible and Heavy Shackles," The Economist, May 6, 2010.

33. Ken Rhee and Chen Jie, "Anticipating the Correction of China's Housing Bubble," Urban Land, April 20, 2012.

34. Dexter Roberts, "China May Be Ready to Embrace Its Real Estate Boom," BusinessWeek, July 19, 2012.

35. Baibing Yang, "No Loosening of Housing Curbs, Gov't Reiterates," Caixin, July 20, 2012.

36. Deng, Shen and Wang, "Housing Policy and Finance in China: A Literature Review," 16.

37. "Progressing Eco-city Policies into Mainstream Practice in China," (The UK–China Eco-cities & Green Building Group, July 2012), 5.

38. "Taxing China: Pay and Play," The Economist, February 4, 2012.

39. "China Establishes Sansha City," Xinhua News Agency, July 24, 2012.

Market dynamics

1. Shujie Yao, Dan Luo and Lixia Loh, "On China's Monetary Policy and Asset Prices," (The University of Nottingham, March 2011), 3.

2. Jing Ulrich, "Have China's Property Curbs Changed Investment Behavior?," (J.P. Morgan, April 13, 2011), 2.

3. "Chinese Insurance: Where the State Does Too Little," *The Economist*, July 21, 2011.

4. Carl E. Walter and Fraser J.T. Howie, *Red Capitalism: The Fragile Financial Foundation of China's Extraordinary Rise*, (Wiley, 2011), 86.

5. Nicholas Borst, "China Shadow Banking Primer," China Economic Watch, The Peterson Institute for International Economics, November 1, 2011.

6. "Big Box Store Bites the Dust," *People's Daily*, January 27, 2011.

7. "Home Depot Closing Last 7 China Big Box Outlets," Yahoo News / AP, September 14, 2012.

8. Robert Cookson, "Here Be Dragons: Anthony Bolton," *Financial Times*, May 12, 2012.

9. Frank Dikötter, *Exotic Commodities: Modern Objects and Everyday Life in China*, (Columbia University Press, 2007), 157.

10. Ibid., 161.

11. Shang-Jin Wei, Xiaobo Zhang and Yin Liu, "Status Competition and Housing Prices," (National Bureau of Economic Research, April 2012), 1.

Is there a bubble?

1. Hong Xu, "Survey: Shanghai New Home Prices Up 253% in 7 Years," *Caixin*, September 1, 2011.

2. "Beijing Home Prices Rise to 22 Times of Income Levels: Report," *South China Morning Post*, July 19, 2010.

3. "China's Ghost Towns: New Satellite Pictures Show Massive Skyscraper Cities Which Are Still Completely Empty," *Daily Mail*, June 18, 2011.

4. Bonnie Cao, "China Housing Boom Spreads to Smaller Cities," Bloomberg, June 23, 2011.

5. Carmen Reinhart and Kenneth Rogoff, "This Time Is Different: A Panoramic View of Eight Centuries of Financial Crises," (Harvard University, April 16, 2008), 34.

6. Andy Rothman and Julia Zhu, "Food, Flats and the Party" (CLSA, May 2011), 24.

7. Ibid., 26.

8. Gus Lubin, "About Those 65 Million Vacant Homes In China...," Business Insider, June 20, 2011.

9. Bonnie Cao, "China Home Prices Fall in Record No. of Cities," BusinessWeek, June 18, 2012.

10. "Preparing for China's Urban Billion," (McKinsey Global Institute, February 2009), 13.

11. Arthur Kroeber, "Bear in a China Shop," The Brookings Institution, May 22, 2012.

12. "Vice President Stresses Socialism with Chinese Characteristics, Party Building," Xinhua News Agency, July 24, 2012.

13. Gregory M. Stein, "Is China's Housing Market Heading Toward a US-Style Crash?," (University of Tennessee College of Law, August 2012): 1.

Demographics

1. "Communique of the National Bureau of Statistics of People's Republic of China on Major Figures of the 2010 Population Census," National Bureau of Statistics of China, April 28, 2011.

2. "400 Million Births Prevented by One-child Policy," People's Daily, October 28, 2011.

3. "China, Demographic Profile, Medium Variant 1950 – 2030," United Nations, Department of Economic and Social Affairs, Population Division, June 21, 2012.

4. "China, Hong Kong Special Administrative Region, Demographic Profile, Medium Variant 1950 – 2030," United Nations, Department of Economic and Social Affairs, Population Division, June 21, 2012.

5. Pinghui Zhuang, "Officials Suspended After Forced Late-term Abortion," South China Morning Post, June 22, 2012.

6. Will Clem, "No Real Estate? She's Unlikely to Say 'I Do'," *South China Morning Post*, December 17, 2010.

7. Tze-wei Ng, "Law Exposes Unease at State of Modern Marriage," *South China Morning Post*, August 21, 2011.

8. Roseann Lake, "All the Shengnu Ladies," *Salon*, March 12, 2012.

9. "Global Health and Aging," National Institutes of Health, U.S. Department of Health & Human Services, March 27, 2012.

10. Frederik Balfour, "China No Country for Old Men as Government Battles 'Demographic Tsunami'," Bloomberg, April 1, 2012.

11. "Vast 'Empty Nests', Disabled Aging Population Challenging China's Social Network," *People's Daily*, March 2, 2011.

12. Martin Li, "Reverse Mortgages Program Rarely Used in SZ," *Shenzhen Daily*, October 23, 2012.

13. "Preparing for China's Urban Billion," (McKinsey Global Institute, February 2009), 13.

14. "Factbox: China's 2010 Census," Reuters, April 28, 2011.

15. Wing Chan Kam, "China, Internal Migration," in *The Encyclopedia of Global Migration*, (Blackwell, 2013), 1.

16. Changqing Qi, Volker Kreibich and Sabine Baumgart, "Informal Elements in Urban Growth Regulation in China – Urban Villages in Ningbo," ASIEN, 103 (April 2007): 25.

17. Jasper Becker, *The Chinese*, (Oxford University Press, 2002), 106.

18. Zaobao Lianhe, "Price of Beijing Hukou on Black Market: 270,000 RMB," *Economic Observer*, May 30, 2011.

19. Kam Wing Chan and Will Buckingham, "Is China Abolishing the Hukou System?," The China Quarterly, 195 (2008): 583.

20. Population Distribution, Urbanization, Internal Migration and Development: An International Perspective, (United Nations Department of Economic and Social Affairs, Population Division, 2011), 90.

21. "Building Rome in a Day — The Sustainability of China's Housing Boom," (The Economist Intelligence Unit, 2011), 3.

22. Li Tian, "The Chengzhongcun Land Market in China: Boon or Bane? — A Perspective on Property Rights," International Journal of Urban and Regional Research, 32, no. 2 (2008): 282.

23. Yan Song, Yves Zenou and Chengri Ding, "Let's Not Throw the Baby Out with the Bath Water: Suggestions for Redevelopment Policies of Urban Villages in China," (Lincoln Institute of Land Policy, 2006), 15.

The buying process

1. Yvonne Liu, "Limits on Foreigners' Property Purchases Go Mainland-wide," South China Morning Post, November 13, 2010.

2. Paul McKenzie, Gregory Tan and Charles Coker, "China: Measures to Cool Chinese Property Market Target Both Foreign and Local Purchasers," Morrison & Foerster / Mondaq, January 17, 2011.

3. Fiona Tam, "Three Hurt in Flat Owners' Noise Protest," South China Morning Post, June 14, 2012.

4. "Legal Dispute over Luxury House Deal," Shenzhen Daily, December 28, 2012.

5. "Woman Duped Flat Buyers," South China Morning Post, May 9, 2012.

6. Yalin Zhou, "Beijing's Credulous Home Buyers," Economic Observer, May 11, 2012.

7. Mo Zhang, "From Public to Private: The Newly Enacted Chinese Property Law and the Protection of Property Rights in China," (Temple University, January 16, 2008): 35 – 36.

8. Lei Chen, "The New Chinese Property Code: A Giant Step Forward?," Electronic Journal of Comparative Law 11, no. 2 (September 2007): 13.

9. Ibid., 8.

10. "Doing Business 2013," (The World Bank, October 23, 2012), 156.

11. "Construction Quality Management Ordinance," The People's Republic of China State Council, August 6, 2005.

12. "Housing & Home Warranty Programs World Research," (Organization for Housing Warranty Japan, September 2005), 70.

What to buy

1. John K. McIlwain, "The Rental Boost From Green Design," *Urban Land*, January 4, 2012.

2. Xiaodong Chen et al., "Effects of Attitudinal and Sociodemographic Factors on Pro-environmental Behaviour in Urban China," Environmental Conservation, (2011): 6.

3. "Govt Offers Rights to 176 Islands for Development Work," *People's Daily*, April 13, 2011.

4. Yeping Yin, "Culture Vulture," *Global Times*, June 3, 2012.

5. "China Bans Land Use for New Luxury Villas in Effort to Slow Building Boom," Sina / AP, June 1, 2006.

6. Carolynne Wheeler, "As China Swelters, Beijing Tees Off on Golfers," *The Globe and Mail*, August 17, 2011.

7. Weidong Qu and Xiaolong Liu, "Assessing the Performance of Chinese Land Lease Auctions: Evidence from Beijing," (Renmin University of China, December 31, 2011), 7.

8. "China Malls Chase Western Europe's," *South China Morning Post*, June 18, 2012.

9. Sandy Li, "Socam Banks on Year-round Luxury," *South China Morning Post*, May 23, 2012.

10. Steve Dickenson, "Foreign Ownership Of Real Estate In China / China's New Forex Rules," China Law Blog, February 21, 2007.

11. "139,621 Corruption Cases Handled in 2010," China.org.cn, June 22, 2011.

12. "China's Local Governments in $1.6 Trillion Debt," *People's Daily*, June 28, 2011.

13. Xiaofei Wang et al., "Residues of Organochlorine Pesticides in Surface Soils from College School Yards in Beijing, China," Journal of Environmental Sciences no. 20 (2008): 1090.

14. "Made in China: $962 Million Austrian Village Clone," *The Sydney Morning Herald*, June 5, 2012.

Developers and development

1. Yongheng Deng et al., "Monetary and Fiscal Stimuli, Ownership Structure, and China's Housing Market," (National Bureau of Economic Research, March 2011), 12.

2. Jing Wu, Joseph Gyourko and Yongheng Deng, "Evaluating Conditions in Major Chinese Housing Markets," (National Bureau of Economic Research, July 2010), 3.

3. "Central SOEs Exit Needs Time," *People's Daily*, February 24, 2011.

4. Wu, Gyourko and Deng, "Evaluating Conditions in Major Chinese Housing Markets," 8.

5. Lanchih Po, "Redefining Rural Collectives in China: Land Conversion and the Emergence of Rural Shareholding Co-operatives," Urban Studies Journal 45 (July 2008): 1607.

6. Fubing Su, "Land Market in China's Modernization: Regulations, Challenges, and Reforms," (East Asian Institute, National University of Singapore, December 11, 2008), 3.

7. James M. Zimmerman, *China Law Deskbook: A Legal Guide for Foreign-Invested Enterprises*, (American Bar Association, 2005), 736.

8. Mo Zhang, "From Public to Private: The Newly Enacted Chinese Property Law and the Protection of Property Rights in China," (Temple University, January 16, 2008): 36.

9. Wu, Gyourko and Deng, "Evaluating Conditions in Major Chinese Housing Markets," 8.

10. Hongbin Cai, J. Vernon Henderson and Qinghua Zhang, "China's Land Market Auctions: Evidence of Corruption," (National Bureau of Economic Research, June 2009), 5.

11. Cherry Cao, "Developers Face 20% Charge for Leaving Plots Idle," *Shanghai Daily*, June 8, 2012.

12. Ulrike Glueck, "New Measures On Disposal Of Idle State Owned Land," CMS Cameron McKenna / Mondaq, July 23, 2012.

13. Stephen Chen, "Angry Villagers Riot over Land Grab," *South China Morning Post*, September 23, 2011.

14. Mimi Lau, "'Suicide Bomber' Was an Innocent Victim," *South China Morning Post*, August 8, 2012.

15. "China Artist's Studio Demolished," BBC, January 12, 2011.

16. Yan Jun and Chen Haiting King, "Understanding the Regulations on Expropriation and Compensation of Housing on State-owned Land," King & Wood / Mondaq, February 12, 2011.

17. Yinan Zhao, "Top Court Rules on Home Demolition Rights," *China Daily*, April 10, 2012.

18. "Demolition Rule: One Arm for the Sledgehammer," *Caixin*, January 28, 2011.

19. Simon Rabinovitch, "Property Limits Lay Foundations for Division," *Financial Times*, July 19, 2011.

20. "A Not-so-hot Property," *People's Daily*, July 11, 2011.

Renovations

1. Tom Doctoroff, "What the Chinese Want," *The Wall Street Journal*, May 18, 2012.

2. Charlie Q.L. Xue, *Building a Revolution: Chinese Architecture Since 1980*, (Hong Kong University Press, 2006), 157.

3. "Client Note: Dealing with the Construction Regulatory Regime in the PRC: Practical Solutions for Foreign Investors and Contractors," (Lovells, April 2005), 6.

4. "Litigation and Arbitration in China. No Surrender. Ever.," China Law Blog, May 5, 2012.

5. Wan-Lin Tsai, "The Redevelopment and Preservation of Historic Lilong Housing in Shanghai," (University of Pennsylvania, January 1, 2008), 21.

6. Sophie Yu, "Built on Ignorance," *South China Morning Post*, July 16, 2011.

7. "26 Charged in Shanghai Fire, Blamed on Corruption," Yahoo News / AP, June 25, 2011.

Risk factors

1. "China to Widen Air Monitor Scope," Xinhua News Agency, November 11, 2011.

2. "Asbestos: 'Magic' Mineral Was Once Canada's Gold," CBC News, February 25, 2012.

3. Melody Kemp, "The Other Deadly White Dust: Russia, China, India and the Campaign to Ban Asbestos," The Asia-Pacific Journal, March 29, 2010.

4. Jim Morris and Te-Ping Chen, "China: A Ravenous Appetite for Asbestos," The Center for Public Integrity, July 21, 2010.

5. Laurie Kazan-Allen, "China Increases Asbestos Restrictions," International Ban Asbestos Secretariat, February 27, 2011.

6. Shi Xiong Cai et al., "Epidemiology of Occupational Asbestos-Related Diseases in China," Industrial Health, 39, (2001): 75 – 83.

7. Keith Bradsher, "Government Policies Contribute to Cooling of China Real Estate Boom," The New York Times, November 10, 2011.

8. Sandy Li, "Developers Fail in Guangdong, Hangzhou," South China Morning Post, April 20, 2012.

9. "A Not-so-hot Property," People's Daily, July 11, 2011.

10. "S&P: China Developers Getting Closer to Downgrade Thresholds," Reuters, March 8, 2012.

11. Nassim Nicholas Taleb, The Black Swan, (Random House, 2010).

12. Professor Daniel C.K. Chow, "Counterfeiting and China's Economic Development," 2006.

13. Yuen-ting Yeung, "The Effect of Chinese Culture on the Implicit Value of Graveyard View in Hong Kong Residential Property Market," (The University of Hong Kong, 2005), 28.

14. Likun Zuo, "Rent in Peace at China's Cemeteries," China Daily, April 2, 2011.

15. Ivan Zhai, "Home Comfort for Divorcees' Folks," South China Morning Post, August 13, 2011.

16. "Earthquakes with 50,000 or More Deaths," U.S. Geological Survey, April 14, 2011.

17. "Global Seismic Hazard Assessment Program," January 14, 2000.

18. Baijie An, "Fault Lines Found in Major Chinese Cities," Global Times, March 21, 2011.

19. Zifa Wang, Tun Lin and George Walker, "Earthquake Risk and Earthquake Catastrophe Insurance for the People's Republic of China," (Asian Development Bank, June 2009).

20. "Feverish Chinese Dam Building Could Trigger Tsunami," Probe International, April 4, 2012.

21. Huanxin Zhao, "New Buildings Reinforced for Earthquakes," *China Daily*, February 11, 2012.

22. Henry Mance, "China: Rapid Growth, Few Jobs," *Financial Times*, October 11, 2010.

23. Keith Bradsher, "China's Utilities Cut Energy Production, Defying Beijing," *The New York Times*, May 24, 2011.

24. Richard Knox, "Drug-Resistant Tuberculosis a 'Serious Epidemic' in China," NPR.org, June 6, 2012.

25. Yuanyuan Wang, "Thousands of Scorpions Found in Community," *Shenzhen Daily*, July 21, 2011.

26. Andrew Jacobs, "Harassment and Evictions Bedevil Even China's Well-Off," *The New York Times*, October 27, 2011.

27. "Chinese Developers Demolish Home of Revered Architects," *The Guardian*, January 30, 2012.

28. Dong Liu, "No Smoke Without Fire," *Global Times*, December 28, 2010.

29. "Fires Damage Chinese Cultural Sites," Yahoo News / AFP, February 8, 2011.

30. "Residents in Capital Quick to Voice Anger," *South China Morning Post*, July 24, 2012.

31. "Soil Pollution Poisons More Than Farmland," *China Daily*, March 10, 2011.

32. "Controversial Garbage Incinerator Project Delayed in South China," Xinhua News Agency, December 10, 2009.

33. "New Beijing Airport Touted as World's Busiest-media," Reuters, February 26, 2012.

34. Ning Yu et al., "City Subway Construction Decelerates in China," *Caixin*, June 1, 2012.

35. Daniel P. Aldrich, "Location, Location, Location: Selecting Sites for Controversial Facilities," The Singapore Economic Review 53, no. 1 (2008): 145 – 172.

36. Henry Sanderson, "China Auditor Finds Irregularities in $1.7 Trillion Local Government Debt," Bloomberg, June 27, 2011.

37. "China's Local Government Financing Vehicle Risks Manageable," *People's Daily*, July 12, 2011.

38. Lin Yuan, "China Banking — Local Government Financing Vehicle Loans," (Bank of China International, June 3, 2011).

39. "Nuclear Power in China," World Nuclear Association, April 30, 2012.

40. Juan Du, "Nuclear Power to Become 'Foundation' of Country's Electrical System," *China Daily*, December 7, 2011.

41. "WNA Reactor Database," World Nuclear Association, April 30, 2012.

42. "Openness Crucial to Safety at Mainland's Nuclear Power Plants," *South China Morning Post*, June 14, 2012.

43. "Nuclear Power in China."

44. "China," Nuclear Materials Security Index, April 30, 2012.

45. Qian Cao, "Home Buyers Angry as Project's Prices Lowered," *Shanghai Daily*, October 24, 2011.

46. Daniel Ren, "Homebuyers Just Want a Fair Deal," *South China Morning Post*, June 2, 2012.

47. Sky Canaves, "Shanghai Building Collapses, Nearly Intact," China Real Time Report, June 29, 2009.

48. "Report Gives All-clear to Buildings at Topple Site," Eastday.com, September 26, 2009.

49. Binbin Yang, "Why Did so Many Sichuan Schools Collapse?," Caijing.com.cn, June 17, 2008.

50. "Graft-linked Faults Require Rail Repairs," *Shenzhen Daily*, August 10, 2012.

51. Jessie Dong, "'Alarming' Shortage of Construction Inspectors," *Shanghai Daily*, February 24, 2012.

52. Doreen Weisenhaus, *Hong Kong Media Law: A Guide for Journalists and Media Professionals*, (Hong Kong University Press, 2007).

53. Peter Hessler, *Country Driving: A Chinese Road Trip*, (Harper Perennial, 2011), 127.

54. Richard McGregor, *The Party: The Secret World of China's Communist Rulers*, (Harper, 2010).

55. David Bandurski, "Press Policy 2011: One Photo Says All," China Media Project, January 17, 2011.

56. Takeshi Ohura et al., "Comparative Study on Indoor Air Quality in Japan and China: Characteristics of Residential Indoor and Outdoor VOCs," Atmospheric Environment 43, no. 40 (December 2009): 6352 – 6359.

57. "Air Quality Companies 'Lying to Customers,'" Eastday.com, August 8, 2011.

58. "Lending Hangover Looms as Wen Spurs Construction," South China Morning Post, June 3, 2011.

59. "China's Leading Steelmaker Halts Production in Capital to Cut Pollution," People's Daily, January 13, 2011.

60. Jian Xie and Fasheng Li, "Overview of the Current Situation on Brownfield Remediation and Redevelopment in China," (The World Bank, September 1, 2010), 3 – 4.

61. Inga Caldwell and Xinyu Wang, "A Hidden Problem: China's Contaminated Site Soil Pollution Crisis," (Vermont Law School, August 5, 2011), 3.

62. "Environment: China — Contaminated Land," Practical Law Company Limited, August 1, 2011.

63. Binggan Wei and Linsheng Yang, "A Review of Heavy Metal Contaminations in Urban Soils, Urban Road Dusts and Agricultural Soils from China," Microchemical Journal 94 (2010): 106.

64. Xie and Li, "Overview of the Current Situation on Brownfield Remediation and Redevelopment in China," 6.

65. "Something Stinks at Past Industrial Site," Global Times, September 9, 2010.

66. Caldwell and Wang, "A Hidden Problem: China's Contaminated Site Soil Pollution Crisis," 17.

67. Xiaodong Bao and Xinyuan Zhang, "Building on Toxic Land: China Builds Housing on Untreated Brownfield Sites Left Behind by Urban Factories and Soil Remediation Remains Rare," Chinadialogue, January 12, 2012.

68. Ximin Han, "Subsidence Found in Bao'an Estate," Shenzhen Daily, April 13, 2011.

69. Harold Thibault, "Shifting Foundations Threaten to Undermine China's Cities," The Guardian, April 3, 2012.

70. "Formosan Subterranean Termites — Fact Sheet," (BASF, April 19, 2007).

71. "Finding Alternatives to Persistent Organic Pollutants (POPs) for Termite Management," (United Nations Environmental Program, 2003).

72. Wenjun Cai, "Here's the Termite Forecast...," *Shanghai Daily*, May 11, 2011.

73. "A Leading Cause of Death and Disability in China," World Health Organization Representative Office in China, May 10, 2011.

74. Guoqing Hu, Timothy Baker and Susan Baker, "Comparing Road Traffic Mortality Rates from Police-reported Data and Death Registration Data in China," Bulletin of the World Health Organization 89 (2011): 41 – 45.

75. "Car Numbers to Double to 200m," *Shenzhen Daily*, August 3, 2012.

76. "China: Traffic Safety and Road Conditions," Bureau of Consular Affairs, U.S. Department of State, April 24, 2012.

77. James Gallagher, "Diesel Fumes Cause Cancer — WHO," BBC, June 12, 2012.

78. Peter H. Gleick, *The World's Water 2008 – 2009: The Biennial Report on Freshwater Resources*, (Island Press, 2008), 81.

79. "China's Underground Water in Poor Condition," Xinhua News Agency, May 10, 2012.

80. Jing Gong, "The Dirty Truth About Water Quality," *Caixin*, May 7, 2012.

81. Dawei Yu, "As Number of Sewage Plants Soars, Nation's Sludge Problem Mounts," *Caixin*, March 26, 2012.

82. "Water Pollution Emergencies in China: Prevention and Response," (The World Bank, June 2007), 2.

83. "Cadmium Pollution to Affect 300-km Section of River in S China: Experts," Xinhua News Agency, January 31, 2012.

84. "Gov't to Fight Water Pollution with More Funding," Xinhua News Agency, May 17, 2012.

85. Jiangtao Shi and Hanyang Wei, "Alarm at Poor Quality of Tap Water," *South China Morning Post*, July 13, 2012.

Mortgages

1. Carl E. Walter and Fraser J.T. Howie, *Red Capitalism: The Fragile Financial Foundation of China's Extraordinary Rise*, (Wiley, 2011), 29.

2. China Monetary Policy Report Quarter Two (People's Bank of China, August 2, 2012), 42.

3. "Mortgage Debt Outstanding," Board of Governors of the Federal Reserve System, United States Government, December 7, 2012.

4. Bonnie Cao and Dingmin Zhang, "China Helps First-Home Buyers as Market Cools," Bloomberg, April 25, 2012.

5. "Mortgages," Standard Chartered Bank (China) Limited, February 5, 2013.

6. Cao and Zhang, "China Helps First-Home Buyers as Market Cools."

7. Peggy Sito, "Preferential Lending Rates May Come Back," *South China Morning Post*, May 16, 2012.

8. "Notice of the CBRC General Office on Improving Housing Financial Services and Strengthening Risk Management," China Banking Regulatory Commission, March 8, 2011.

9. Ibid.

10. Jun Luo, "China Wall Hit by Global Banks With 2% Market Share," Bloomberg, June 5, 2012.

11. "Investing in Mainland China," HSBC Bank (China), 2013.

12. Qian Cao, "Limit Set in Beijing on Favorable Loans for Second Houses," *Shanghai Daily*, January 5, 2013.

13. Lan Deng, Qingyun Shen and Lin Wang, "Housing Policy and Finance in China: A Literature Review." (U.S. Department of Housing and Urban Development, November 2009), 12 − 13.

14. "Foreigners with Chinese Green Cards May Contribute to Housing Fund," Guangzhou International, January 28, 2013.

15. Ximin Han, "Subsidy Program to Benefit 200,000," *Shenzhen Daily*, December 5, 2012.

16. Martin Li, "Reverse Mortgages Program Rarely Used in SZ," *Shenzhen Daily*, October 23, 2012.

17. Guibin Zhang and Russell Smyth, "An Emerging Credit-Reporting System in China," (Monash University, 2008), 9.

18. Xiaolei Wang, "Credit Reporting System in China," (People's Bank of China, January 2008).

19. Ibid.

20. James Kwan, "Credit Bureaus in Asia," (Federal Reserve Bank of San Francisco, October 2011), 4.

Taxes and fees

1. Jing Ulrich, "Impact of China's New Property Tax and Latest Round of Tightening – Views from Shanghai," (J.P. Morgan, February 2, 2011), 2.

2. "China Alert: Shanghai and Chongqing Pioneering Property Tax on a Trial Basis," (KPMG, February 2011).

3. "China Real Estate Investment Handbook 2012," (Deloitte Touche Tohmatsu, 2012), 7.

4. Yanling Zhang, "Bringing Down Beijing's Housing Prices," *Caixin*, December 20, 2011.

5. Qian Cao, "Shanghai's Revised Criteria May Boost Buying of 'Normal' Houses," *Shanghai Daily*, February 19, 2012.

Insurance

1. "Chinese Insurance: Where the State Does Too Little," *The Economist*, July 21, 2011.

2. "Foreign Insurance Companies in China," (PwC, December 2011).

3. Dingmin Zhang, "PICC Surges in Debut as Valuation, Growth Attract Buyers," Bloomberg, December 7, 2012.

4. Jun Wang, "Catastrophe Insurance Policy for China," (The World Bank, December 2010).

5. Zhang, "PICC Surges in Debut as Valuation, Growth Attract Buyers."

Beijing

1. "Beijing's Population Tops 19.6 Mln, Migration Key Contributor to Growth," Xinhua News Agency, May 5, 2011.

2. Yuli Huang, "Capital Growing More Global as New Expats Arrive," Xinhua News Agency, October 11, 2010.

3. "Census 2001: London," Office for National Statistics, Government of the United Kingdom, May 19, 2011.

4. "The Newest New Yorkers 2000: Immigrant New York in the New Millennium," (Department of City Planning, The City of New York, October 2004), 4.

5. "Beijing, Shanghai Record Robust Economic Growth in 2010," Xinhua News Agency, February 3, 2011.

6. "China Refuses to Release Gini Coefficient," MarketWatch, January 19, 2012.

7. Peggy Sito, "Landlords Call Shots in Beijing Office Squeeze," South China Morning Post, December 7, 2011.

8. Fulong Wu and Klaire Webber, "The Rise of 'foreign gated communities' in Beijing: between economic globalization and local institutions," Cities 21, no. 3 (2004): 212.

9. Thomas Campanella, The Concrete Dragon: China's Urban Revolution and What it Means for the World, (Princeton Architectural Press, 2008), 136 – 137.

10. "Future of the Property Market in Beijing CBD East Expansion Area" (CBRE, May 2010).

11. "SWA Group Project Awarded Prestigious 2008 Urban Land Institute Global Award for Excellence," News Blaze, December 10, 2008.

12. Wu and Webber, "The Rise of 'foreign gated communities' in Beijing: between economic globalization and local institutions," 212.

13. Peggy Sito, "Ceiling on Beijing Agents' Fees to Cool Home Sales," South China Morning Post, August 31, 2011.

14. Sebastian Blanc, "Heritage Projects More Copying Than Conservation," *The China Post*, May 7, 2012.

15. "Qianmen St. to be Ready Before Olympics," *People's Daily*, May 14, 2008.

16. Sandy Li, "Beijing Imposes Stiff Rule to Fight Rising Property Prices," *South China Morning Post*, February 17, 2011.

17. Yvonne Liu, "Record Price Paid for Site in Beijing," *South China Morning Post*, July 11, 2012.

18. Keith Ray, "Hutongs and Quadrangles of Beijing," China in Focus, Winter 2001.

19. "Protection of the Old City of Beijing: Good Plans, No Follow Through," Beijing Cultural Heritage Protection Center, September 29, 2005.

20. "Exodus from Underground," *Global Times*, January 28, 2011.

21. "China Digest: Rising Rents Force Exodus," *South China Morning Post*, September 4, 2012.

22. Jiangtao Shi, "Beijing in Top 10 of Dirtiest Capitals," *South China Morning Post*, September 28, 2011.

23. "Independent Environmental Assessment: Beijing 2008 Olympic Games," (United Nations Environment Programme, 2009), 29.

24. Xiuqi Fang,"Effects of Duststorms on the Air Pollution in Beijing," Water, Air and Soil Pollution: Focus 3 (2003): 93 − 101.

25. Wentao Wang et al., "Atmospheric Particulate Matter Pollution During the 2008 Beijing Olympics," Environmental Science & Technology 43, no. 14 (July 15, 2009): 5314 − 5320.

26. Han Shih Toh, "Beijing to Pack 56b Yuan into Metro Expansion," *South China Morning Post*, August 10, 2012.

27. Jian Xie and Fasheng Li, "Overview of the Current Situation on Brownfield Remediation and Redevelopment in China," (The World Bank, September 1, 2010), 4.

28. "Beijing Plans to Charge Tolls on Some Roads," Beijing Traffic Management Bureau, September 3, 2011.

29. "China Digest: Billions to Expand Roads," *South China Morning Post*, September 6, 2012.

30. "Beijing's New Traffic Plan to Hit Car Owners," Beijing Traffic Management Bureau, July 21, 2011.

31. Mu Yang and Siow Song Teng, "China's Looming Water Crises," (East Asian Institute, National University of Singapore, June 12, 2008), 7.

32. "Beijing's Water Crisis 1949 – 2008 Olympics (2010 Update)," (Probe International, July 20, 2010).

33. "Severe Water Shortage Hits China's Capital," *People's Daily*, May 18, 2011.

34. "Report: Land Under 50-plus Cities Is Sinking," *Caixin*, February 24, 2012.

35. Zheng Cui, "Sinkholes a Growing Problem in Urban Areas, Say Experts," *Caixin*, September 3, 2012.

36. Wiefeng Liu, "Beijing Tap Water Now Safe to Drink," *China Daily*, July 3, 2007.

37. "Are You Satisfied with the Quality of Running Water?," *Beijing Today*, August 19, 2011.

38. "Report: Fake Drinking Water Hits Beijing," *The Washington Post*, July 10, 2007.

39. "Beijing Halts Sales of Tainted Bottled Water," *The Straits Times*, July 7, 2011.

40. Jing Li, "Beijing Raises Death Toll to 77 After Long Silence," *South China Morning Post*, July 27, 2012.

41. Pinghui Zhuang, "Heaviest Rain in 6 Decades Causes Chaos in Beijing," *South China Morning Post*, July 23, 2012.

Guangzhou

1. "Communique on Major Data of the Sixth National Census of 2010, Guangzhou City," Guangzhou Municipal Bureau of Statistics (in Chinese), May 16, 2011.

2. "Guangzhou," Newsgd.com, January 10, 2013.

3. "Hurun Wealth Report 2012," July 31, 2012.

4. "Worldwide Cost of Living Survey 2012 – City Ranking," Mercer, June 12, 2012.

5. "Life Quality in Beijing Worse Than Guangzhou, Shanghai: Report," *People's Daily*, June 13, 2011.

6. Him Mark Lai, "Guangzhou to Hong Kong: Geographical and Historical Notes," Him Mark Lai Digital Archive, March 31, 2008, 2.

7. Valery M. Garrett, *Heaven Is High, the Emperor Far Away*, (Oxford University Press, 2009), 76.

8. Chen Yu, "Modernizing Chinese Cities: Guangzhou from Treaty Port to Metropolis," (National University of Singapore, 2012), 2.

9. Peter Perdue, "Rise & Fall of the Canton Trade System III: Canton Trade," Massachusetts Institute of Technology – Visualizing Cultures, 2009.

10. Lai, "Guangzhou to Hong Kong: Geographical and Historical Notes," 12.

11. Garrett, *Heaven Is High, the Emperor Far Away*, 174.

12. Ibid., 177.

13. Thomas Lam, "Housing Affordability Ratio Alarming," *South China Morning Post*, August 22, 2012.

14. Ken Rhee and Chen Jie, "Anticipating the Correction of China's Housing Bubble," *Urban Land*, April 20, 2012.

15. Charlie Q.L. Xue, *Building a Revolution: Chinese Architecture Since 1980*, (Hong Kong University Press, 2006), 62.

16. "Where Do Foreigners Live in Guangzhou?," Invest Guangzhou, June 8, 2010.

17. Joe Studwell, *The China Dream: The Quest for the Last Great Untapped Market on Earth*, (Grove Press, 2003), 126.

18. "Qilou Buildings in Guangzhou," ChinaCulture.org, January 16, 2008.

19. "Canton Calling," *China Daily*, March 30, 2012.

20. "Old Villa Style Houses in Dongshan Residential Community," Life of Guangzhou, March 17, 2009.

21. "About Real Estate Agency Fees (in Chinese)," Guangdong Provincial Price Bureau, February 2, 2008.

22. "Guangzhou Curbs Home Buys," *People's Daily*, February 25, 2011.

23. Andy Yeo, "Foreigners Expressly Restricted from Investing in Non-Residential Properties in Guangzhou," Mayer Brown, March 15, 2012.

24. Paggie Leung, "Move to Limit the Pre-sale of Flats 'Will Fail'," *South China Morning Post*, October 5, 2012.

25. Jiangtao Shi, "Beijing in Top 10 of Dirtiest Capitals," *South China Morning Post*, September 28, 2011.

26. "Guangzhou Plans to Build 49 Distributed Energy Stations," Guangzhou International, August 12, 2012.

27. "Guangzhou to Build 133 New Substations in Twelfth Five-Year Plan Period," Guangzhou International, September 6, 2012.

28. "7 New Metro Lines to Be Built in Guangzhou," Guangzhou International, July 13, 2012.

29. "Guangzhou Baiyun International Airport to Build Integrated Transport Hub with Guangzhou North Railway Station," Guangzhou International, August 8, 2012.

30. Sally Wang, "Stink of Guangzhou Garbage Plan Refuses to Go Away," *South China Morning Post*, July 7, 2012.

31. "GZ Pilot Zone Approved to Boost Ties Across PRD," *Shenzhen Daily*, October 11, 2012.

32. Ivan Zhai, "Hong Kong Is Losing to Singapore as Pearl River Delta's Role Model," *South China Morning Post*, January 19, 2013.

33. Xiaodong Bao and Xinyuan Zhang, "Building on Toxic Land: China Builds Housing on Untreated Brownfield Sites Left Behind by Urban Factories and Soil Remediation Remains Rare," Chinadialogue, January 12, 2012.

34. Quan-Ying Cai et al., "Heavy Metal Contamination of Urban Soils and Dusts in Guangzhou, South China," Environmental Monitoring and Assessment 185, no. 2 (February 2013): 1095 – 1106.

35. "China: Building Institutions for Sustainable Urban Transport," (The World Bank, January 2006), 11.

36. Wang Feng and Jin An, "Traffic Demand Management in Guangzhou City for the 21st Century," (Guangzhou Transport Planning Research Institute, July 2000).

37. "Guangzhou Car Restrictions Spark Debate," English.News.cn, August 28, 2012.

38. Ivan Zhai and Mimi Lau, "Urban Villages Face the Wrecker's Ball," *South China Morning Post*, July 26, 2010.

39. "Rethink on the Rush to Demolish," *South China Morning Post*, July 2, 2011.

40. "Circular on 2011 Guangzhou Environmental Conditions Unveiled," Guangzhou International, July 20, 2012.

41. Fiona Tam, "Dongjiang Water Not Fit to Drink," *South China Morning Post*, August 22, 2012.

42. Caixiong Zheng, "Most Sewage Discharged into Rivers," *China Daily*, July 10, 2012.

43. "China Digest: Substandard Water Quality," *South China Morning Post*, September 4, 2012.

44. Zhijing Chen, "Urban Floods and Implementation Plan for UFRM Project in Guangzhou City," (Guangdong Provincial Bureau of Hydrology, 2012).

Shanghai

1. "Communique of the National Bureau of Statistics of People's Republic of China on Major Figures of the 2010 Population Census," National Bureau of Statistics of China, April 28, 2011.

2. "Resident Foreigners in Shanghai in Main Years," Shanghai Municipal Statistics Bureau, 2010.

3. "Beijing, Shanghai Record Robust Economic Growth in 2010," Xinhua News Agency, February 3, 2011.

4. "Hurun Wealth Report 2012," Hurun Research Institute, July 31, 2012.

5. "Worldwide Cost of Living Survey 2012 – City Ranking," Mercer, June 12, 2012.

6. "Life Quality in Beijing Worse Than Guangzhou, Shanghai: Report," *People's Daily*, June 13, 2011.

7. Jay Pridmore, *Shanghai: The Architecture of China's Great Urban Center*, (Abrams, 2008), 12.

8. Wan-Lin Tsai, "The Redevelopment and Preservation of Historic Lilong Housing in Shanghai," (University of Pennsylvania, 2008), 4 – 5.

9. Peter G. Rowe and Seng Kuan, editors, *Shanghai: Architecture and Urbanism for Modern China*, (Prestel Publishing, 2004), 41.

10. Marie-Claire Bergere, *Shanghai: China's Gateway to Modernity*, (Stanford University Press, 2009), 111.

11. Rowe and Kuan, *Shanghai: Architecture and Urbanism for Modern China*, 86.

12. "Foreign Concessions and Colonies," Worldstatesmen.org, 2000.

13. Rowe and Kuan, Shanghai: Architecture and Urbanism for Modern China, 54.

14. Weiping Wu, "Cultural Strategies in Shanghai: Regenerating Cosmopolitanism in an Era of Globalization," Progress in Planning 61, (2004): 159.

15. Joe Studwell, The China Dream: The Quest for the Last Great Untapped Market on Earth, (Grove Press, 2003), 172.

16. "Hurun Shanghai Wealth Report 2012," Hurun Research Institute, May 11, 2012.

17. Jeffrey W. Cody, "Preservation and Progress in China's Largest Port," Places 8, no. 1 (1992): 76.

18. Zhen Dong, "Shikumen Restoration Condemned as 'Fake'," Shanghai Daily, February 6, 2012.

19. Tsai, "The Redevelopment and Preservation of Historic Lilong Housing in Shanghai," 19 – 22.

20. "Preservation of City Historical Sites," Information Office of Shanghai Municipality, 2009.

21. Bonnie Cao, "Love Limbo in Shanghai as Singles Frozen From Home Market," Bloomberg, August 16, 2012.

22. Ken Rhee and Chen Jie, "Anticipating the Correction of China's Housing Bubble," Urban Land, April 20, 2012.

23. "Land Sales Down 22 pc," South China Morning Post, September 6, 2012.

24. "China Alert: Shanghai and Chongqing Pioneering Property Tax on a Trial Basis," (KPMG, February 2011).

25. Mike Darton, Art Deco: An Illustrated Guide to the Decorative Style 1920 – 40, (Tiger, 1990), 8.

26. Wu, "Cultural Strategies in Shanghai: Regenerating Cosmopolitanism in an Era of Globalization," 165.

27. Janos Gerle, "The Resurrection of László Hudec," Eurozine, October 18, 2010, 3.

28. Pridmore, Shanghai: The Architecture of China's Great Urban Center, 98.

29. Non Arkaraprasertkul, "Towards Modern Urban Housing: Redefining Shanghai's Lilong," Journal of Urbanism: International Research on Placemaking and Urban Sustainability 2, no. 1 (2009): 14.

30. Ibid., 17.

31. Tsai, "The Redevelopment and Preservation of Historic Lilong Housing in Shanghai," 10.

32. Theresa Cole, "Shanghai, Riding High," Financial Times, June 4, 2011.

33. Dong, "Shikumen Restoration Condemned as 'Fake'."

34. Jiangtao Shi, "Beijing in Top 10 of Dirtiest Capitals," South China Morning Post, September 28, 2011.

35. Yinbin Ni, "Summer Shutdowns as City Bids to Save Power," Shanghai Daily, April 24, 2012.

36. Zhen Dong, "Suburbs Given Priority for Infrastructure Funding," Shanghai Daily, February 25, 2012.

37. Dingding Xin, Xiaodong Wang and Yingying Shi, "Experts Fear Subway Costs Could Go Off the Rails," China Daily, July 31, 2012.

38. Inga Caldwell and Xinyu Wang, "A Hidden Problem: China's Contaminated Site Soil Pollution Crisis," (Vermont Law School, August 5, 2011).

39. Binggan Wei and Linsheng Yang, "A Review of Heavy Metal Contaminations in Urban Soils, Urban Road Dusts and Agricultural Soils from China," Microchemical Journal 94, (2010): 102.

40. "Traffic Jams Serious in Shanghai," China Daily, August 31, 2012.

41. "New Reservoir Boosts Shanghai's Water Quality," Xinhua News Agency, November 26, 2010.

42. Stephen Chen, "Cities Are Facing a Sinking Problem," South China Morning Post, March 12, 2012.

43. Pridmore, Shanghai: The Architecture of China's Great Urban Center, 39.

44. "Report: Land Under 50-plus Cities Is Sinking," Caixin, February 24, 2012.

45. "Overview of Shanghai Multi-hazard Early Warning System and the Role of Meteorological Services," March 23, 2010.

46. S.F. Balica, N.G. Wright and F. van der Meulen, "A Flood Vulnerability Index for Coastal Cities and Its Use in Assessing Climate Change Impacts," Nat Hazards, (June 16, 2012).

47. "Shanghai Official Rejects Flooding Claims," China.org.cn, August 23, 2012.

48. "Overview of Shanghai Multi-hazard Early Warning System and the Role of Meteorological Services."

Shenzhen

1. "Communique on Major Data of the Sixth National Census of 2010, Shenzhen City," Shenzhen Municipal Bureau of Statistics (in Chinese), May 12, 2011.

2. "Overview," Shenzhen Government Online, 2011.

3. "At a Glance: Population Shifts," Shenzhen Daily, January 24, 2013.

4. "Communique of the National Bureau of Statistics of People's Republic of China on Major Figures of the 2010 Population Census," National Bureau of Statistics of China, April 28, 2011.

5. Ximin Han, "Illegal Foreign Workers Caught," Shenzhen Daily, June 2012.

6. "Overview," Shenzhen Government Online, 2012.

7. "Hurun Wealth Report 2012," July 31, 2012.

8. "Worldwide Cost of Living Survey 2012 – City Ranking," Mercer, June 12, 2012.

9. Martin Li, "City to Model Singapore's Greenery," Shenzhen Daily, July 5, 2012.

10. Thomas Campanella, The Concrete Dragon: China's Urban Revolution and What It Means for the World, (Princeton Architectural Press, 2008), 43.

11. Xiangming Chen and Tomas de' Medici, "The 'Instant City' Coming of Age: China's Shenzhen Special Economic Zone in Thirty Years," (Trinity College, 2008), 14.

12. Campanella, The Concrete Dragon, 42.

13. Charlie Q.L. Xue, Building a Revolution: Chinese Architecture Since 1980, (Hong Kong University Press, 2006), 100.

14. Luxin Huang and Yongqing Xie, "The Plan-led Urban Form: A Case Study of Shenzhen," (China Academy of Urban Planning & Design, 2012), 1.

15. Yuanyuan Wang, "Thousands of Scorpions Found in Community," *Shenzhen Daily*, July 21, 2011.

16. Helen Deng, "3 Detained After Housing Spurs Brawl," *Shenzhen Daily*, July 26, 2012.

17. Xuena Li and Yanling Zhang, "Shenzhen's No Man's Land," *Caixin*, June 19, 2012.

18. "[Shenzhen] Expats Forbidden to Buy Multiple Homes," Newsgd.com, July 11, 2007.

19. Yang Zhang, "Local Banks to Manage Housing Fund," *Shenzhen Daily*, May 30, 2012.

20. Yang Zhang, "NO2 'biggest Air Polluter' in SZ," *Shenzhen Daily*, June 6, 2012.

21. "China Alert: The State Council Approves Preferential Policies for Qianhai Shenzhen-Hong Kong Modern Service Industry Cooperation Zone," (KPMG, August 2012).

22. "Property Investors Eye Qianhai Riches," *The Standard*, July 19, 2012.

23. Huifeng He, "Luohu Planners Consumed by a Risky Ambition," *South China Morning Post*, July 21, 2012.

24. Sandy Li, "Mission Hills Puts Share Float Idea on Table," *South China Morning Post*, May 7, 2012.

25. Jing Wu et al., "For Subway Projects, a Costly Ticket to Ride," *Caixin*, October 9, 2012.

26. Hao Li, "Caitian Extension to Open in 2014," *Shenzhen Daily*, May 30, 2012.

27. Huifeng He, "Link Spanning Pearl River Delta from Shenzhen to Zhongshan Approved," *South China Morning Post*, November 8, 2012.

28. Yang Zhang, "City to Spend RMB3b on Water Pipes," *Shenzhen Daily*, September 13, 2012.

29. Martin Li, "City Discloses Income Reform Ideas, Goals," *Shenzhen Daily*, November 26, 2012.

30. Li Zhang, "The Political Economy of Informal Settlements in Post-socialist China: The Case of Chengzhongcun(s)," Geoforum 42 (2011): 5.

31. Ximin Han, "City Allows Collective-land Sales," *Shenzhen Daily*, January 21, 2013.

32. Caixiong Zheng, "Most Sewage Discharged into Rivers," *China Daily*, July 10, 2012.

33. Yang Zhang, "Pollution Gets Worse in Three Shenzhen Rivers," *Shenzhen Daily*, May 24, 2012.

34. Mimi Lau, "Health Warning as Pollutants Build in Delta Fish," *South China Morning Post*, October 4, 2011.

35. Helen Deng, "SZ Plans Flood Work," *Shenzhen Daily*, July 25, 2012.

Law

1. Jing Wu, Joseph Gyourko and Yongheng Deng, "Evaluating Conditions in Major Chinese Housing Markets," (National Bureau of Economic Research, July 2010), 8.

2. James M. Zimmerman, *China Law Deskbook*, (American Bar Association, 2010), 71.

3. Keyuan Zou, "The Right to Petition in China: New Developments and Prospects," (East Asian Institute, National University of Singapore, May 10, 2006), 1.

4. Jasper Becker, *The Chinese*, (Oxford University Press, 2002), 48.

5. Chengri Ding and Yan Song, *Emerging Land and Housing Markets in China*, (Lincoln Institute of Land Policy, 2005), 107.

6. Zimmerman, *China Law Deskbook*, 52, 72.

7. "Civil Procedure Law of the People's Republic of China," Supreme People's Court, People's Republic of China, June 3, 2003.

8. "Amendment to the Constitution of the People's Republic of China (2004)," China.org.cn, February 12, 2011.

9. James M. Zimmerman, "China Law Deskbook Monthly Alerts and News," China Law Deskbook, April 1, 2012.

10. Richard McGregor, *The Party: The Secret World of China's Communist Rulers*, (Harper, 2010), 24.

11. Zimmerman, *China Law Deskbook*, 67.

12. "Antigraft Brochure Has Much to Say," *South China Morning Post*, July 14, 2012.

13. "Law of the People's Republic of China on Lawyers," Supreme People's Court, People's Republic of China, May 22, 2002.

14. "How to Practise in China," The Law Society of England and Wales, September 28, 2007.

15. "Provisions of the Management of Seals by Government Bodies (in Chinese)," State Council, Government of China, October 31, 1999.

16. "Regulations on the Use of Seals by Private Enterprises (in Chinese)," Ministry of Civil Affairs, Government of China, January 19, 2000.

17. "How to Write a Chinese Contract That Works. Part II," China Law Blog, August 10, 2012.

18. "Insight into Company Chops (Seals) in China," (PricewaterhouseCoopers, 2010).

19. "Dual Language China Contracts Double Your Chance Of Disaster," China Law Blog, October 12, 2009.

INDEX

Companies, government departments, organizations and Websites mentioned in running text are included in the index. Those listed in the "Useful information" chapter are not. "Http" and "www" are omitted from Websites in the index.

"black swans," 112

"ordinary residence," 156 – 7

"quality fade," 34, 129

"rat tribe," 173

"red chips," 84

"yin yang" contracts, 61

12th Five Year Plan (2011 – 2015), 28, 49, 76, 121, 127, 159

4-2-1 dilemma, 42

abortion, 43

accountants, 294

Administrative Regulations on Urban Housing Demolition and Relocation, 89

aging, 45, 47

Agrarian Reform Law, 18

Ai Weiwei, 88

air pollution, 39, 57, 79, 109, 118, 132, 166, 173 – 4, 190, 209, 224, 260

airports, 29, 57, 79, 103, 121, 168, 174, 177, 191, 210, 225, 296 – 7

Al Jazeera, 130

Albert Speer & Partner, 82

All China Lawyers Association, 242, 274

Anti-Rightist Campaign, 237

Anting New Town, 82

appraisal services, 249

architects, 20, 90, 96, 100, 102 − 3, 105, 107, 119, 179, 201, 204, 206, 250 − 1

Art Deco, 74, 188, 205 − 7

asbestos, 10, 62, 109 − 10, 116

auctions, land, 22, 26, 84, 86 − 8, 169, 183, 219, 235, 287

availability bias, 39

B&Q, 34, 273

Baidu, 91, 113, 277, 286 − 7

bankruptcy, 90, 93 − 4, 110 − 1, 128, 184

banks, 20, 23 − 4, 26, 32, 38, 40, 46, 63, 67 − 8, 74, 80, 84, 92, 111, 123 − 4, 126, 145 − 7, 149 − 153, 160, 179, 183, 201, 206, 211, 213, 230, 239, 244, 261 − 4, 269, 288 − 90, 305 − 8, 316

Bank of China, 147, 206, 261, 288

bare-shell homes, 33, 103 − 4, 133, 179, 196

bathrooms, 20, 38, 64, 71, 77, 96, 103, 124, 173, 196, 208, 215, 230 − 1, 273, 328, 333

Beijing, 17 − 8, 21, 27 − 8, 32, 37 − 8, 40, 44 − 5, 47 − 50, 55, 57 − 8, 60 − 2, 70, 74 − 5, 77, 81 − 2, 84, 87 − 8, 97, 100, 106, 108 − 10, 115 − 6, 119 − 21, 124 − 6, 130, 134 − 6, 139, 145, 148, 156, 160, 165 − 80, 182, 184, 208, 219, 229, 249 − 50, 252, 258, 260, 264 − 5, 270, 275 − 6, 282 − 4, 293 − 4, 296, 298, 319 − 33

Beijing Arbitration Commission, 106, 276

Beijing Building Decoration Association, 321

Beijing Municipal Administration for Industry and Commerce, 319

Beijing Municipal Commission of Housing and Urban-Rural Development, 265

Beijing Municipal Construction Committee, 321

Beijing Municipal Environmental Protection Bureau, 89

Bloomberg, 91, 130, 147, 280

bonds, 33, 38, 90, 111, 123, 129, 242

Bosshart, Stephan, 150

Bo Xilai, 26

bribery, 23, 113 − 4, 123, 195, 241

Britain, 16, 18, 34, 88, 130, 183, 201, 235, 251

brownfield sites, 77, 135 − 6, 175, 192

budgets, 56, 66, 97, 99 − 101, 107, 179, 215 − 6, 230 − 1

building codes and standards, 50, 110, 116 − 7, 120, 125, 129, 132 − 3, 193, 227, 258 − 9, 268 − 9, 322, 324, 326 − 7, 329

Bund, the, 199, 201, 204, 211

bureaucracy, 31, 219

business tax, 61, 155 − 6

cancer, 110, 133, 171, 190, 209, 224, 293

cash, 31 – 2, 38, 56, 67, 69 – 70, 73, 75, 80, 108, 117, 145 – 6, 172, 196, 213, 229 – 30

Catalog for the Guidance of Foreign Investment Industries, 76

CCTV (China Central Television), 82, 139, 279

cemeteries, 77, 114 – 5

Centaline Property Agency, 111, 284

Central Commission for Discipline Inspection, 241

Central Propaganda Department, 131, 278

Chan, Melissa, 130

China Academy of Building Research, 117

China Banking Regulatory Commission, 146, 261

China Building Decoration Association, 98, 250

China City Life Quality Index Report, 166, 182, 200

China Earthquake Administration, 116, 258

China Institute of Interior Design, 98, 250

China Institute of Real Estate Appraisers and Agents, 58, 114, 249, 284

China Interior Design Network, 98, 250

China International and Economic Trade Arbitration Commission, 106, 276

China Law Blog, 106, 276, 281

China Overseas Holdings, 128

China Vanke, 47, 84, 91, 128, 217, 253

Chinese Academy of Social Sciences, 166, 182, 200

Chinese Center for Disease Control and Prevention, 118

Chongqing, 18, 26, 28, 35, 127, 155, 205

chops (see seals)

Church, Andy, 229 – 31

Circulars 171 and 186, 25, 55, 169, 189, 205

Circular on Further Regularizing the Administration of Real Estate Purchases by Foreign Entities and Individuals, the, 25

Circular on Publication of the Opinions on Further Strengthening the Supervision of the Real Estate Market, the, 25

CITIC International Bank, 179, 263

Civil Procedure Law, 237

Clifford Estates, 186

CLSA, 38, 289

Commercial Buildings Sale Management Regulation, 71

commercial property, 27, 61, 77 – 8, 80, 83, 86, 94, 111, 119, 168 – 9, 171, 178, 185 – 6, 196, 204, 225, 248, 285 – 7

Common Program of the Chinese People's Consultative Conference, 236

Communist Party of China, 20, 26, 202, 218, 227, 236 – 7, 239 – 41

Communist Revolution, the, 15, 18, 20, 102, 134, 159, 170, 202, 236 – 7

Confucius, 235

Construction Quality Management Ordinance, 71

consumer protection agencies, 252

contractors, 90, 95 – 6, 98, 100, 102, 107 – 8, 111, 113, 133, 179 – 80, 196, 215, 230 – 1, 250, 266, 319 – 333

contracts, 24, 56, 61, 63, 67 – 8, 87, 91 – 2, 96 – 8, 102, 105 – 6, 112, 128, 146, 150, 156, 179, 195, 243 – 5, 251, 284, 303 – 33

corruption, 20, 78 – 9, 108, 113, 125, 241, 251 – 2

counterfeits, 112 – 3, 177

crime, 51, 113, 193, 227, 269

Crossboundaries Architects, 100

Cultural Revolution, the, 20 – 1, 145, 170, 237

custom-built homes, 78

danwei (work units), 19 – 20, 22, 24, 168, 204

Daoism, 235 – 6

DBS, 146 – 7, 263, 289

DDT, 81, 235

De Silva, Janet, 127 – 8, 130

death, 21, 35, 114 – 6, 119, 129, 137, 160

Decision on Deepening Urban Housing Reform, the, 24

deed tax, 65, 69, 155, 157

demographics, 28, 35 – 6, 41 – 51, 90, 165, 181, 199, 217

demolition, 88 – 9, 97, 110, 131, 266

Deng Xiaoping, 21, 24, 39, 218 – 9

design institutes, 20, 102

designers, 69, 95 – 102, 105 – 8, 250, 286, 292, 320

developers, 22 – 4, 26 – 7, 29, 40, 47, 57, 59 – 60, 62 – 3, 65, 70 – 1, 74, 77 – 8, 81 – 94, 103, 111, 119 – 20, 128 – 30, 136, 147, 169, 179, 185, 188, 195 – 6, 203, 217, 220, 222, 245, 252 – 7, 266, 288, 294, 306

dian (sales), 16

Diaoyu Islands, 29, 139

Dikötter, Frank, 35

dipiao (land tickets), 26

disputes, legal, 16, 97, 101 – 2, 105 –
6, 236, 244, 309, 315, 327, 329

distressed property, 71, 83

divorce, 44, 61, 115, 132

Divorce in China (blog), 115

Dongguan, 47, 81 – 2, 104

Dongjiang River, 193

due diligence, 78, 91 – 4, 101, 105,
114, 175, 210

dynasties (see individual entries)

earthquakes, 35, 110, 116 – 7, 125,
129, 160, 258, 268, 300

eco-cities, 28, 260

Economical and Comfortable Housing
program, 24

Economist Intelligence Unit, 49, 125,
290

electricity, 50, 71, 96, 108 – 10,
117 – 8, 120, 124, 133, 170, 184, 190,
209, 224 – 5, 258, 297 – 9, 306, 314,
323 – 4

energy conservation, 118, 132, 258 – 9,
268, 286, 293

environmental resources, 259 – 60

escrow, 67

exchange-traded funds, 248

expatriates, 58, 61, 73, 80, 106, 151,
167 – 8, 179, 185 – 6, 203, 213, 215,
222, 225, 228 – 30, 280

expropriation, 62, 74 – 5, 78, 88 – 9,
118 – 9, 121 – 2, 125 – 6, 131, 237 – 8,
293

extraterritoriality, 235 – 6

Faber, Marc, 40

fangnao (protestors), 128

farms, 18, 21, 26, 50, 86, 118, 122, 138,
145, 156, 219, 237

feng shui (geomancy), 33 – 4, 77, 229

fire, 108, 114, 116, 119 – 20, 160, 173,
183, 264, 323 – 4

Fitch, Terry, 105

floods, 35, 120 – 1, 160, 172, 177, 180,
193, 211 – 2, 229, 269, 293, 300

Forbidden City, 166 – 7, 169, 243

force majeure, 309, 326

Foreign Corrupt Practices Act of 1977, 123

Four Olds Campaign, 20, 34

France, 17, 182 – 4, 202, 236

French Concession, 18, 183, 201 – 2,
207 – 8, 236

Franshion Properties, 84, 254

gas, 35, 113, 117, 120, 174, 184, 190, 298 – 9, 306, 314, 323 – 4

gender imbalance, 36, 43 – 4

Gini coefficient, 166

Global Seismic Hazard Assessment Program, 116

gold, 32

golf courses, 64, 77, 83

Google, 91, 113, 177, 277, 293, 295

government, central, 19, 21 – 2, 24 – 9, 37, 39 – 40, 48 – 9, 55, 76, 78, 84 – 5, 90, 109, 122 – 3, 127 – 9, 134, 136, 139, 146, 165 – 6, 202, 220, 238 – 9, 267 – 9, 283

government, local, 264 – 9 (also see individual city chapters)

Great Leap Forward, the, 19, 237

Greenland Group, 128, 254

Greentown China Holdings, 27, 111, 254

Grill, Bruce, 195 – 7

Guangdong, 22, 24, 27, 49, 74, 88, 112, 123, 127, 137, 156, 181, 190, 193, 219, 226 – 7, 229, 241, 249, 252, 258, 260, 280, 286

Guangdong International Trust and Investment Corporation, 184

Guangzhou, 17, 28, 32, 45, 47 – 50, 57 – 8, 74 – 5, 82 – 3, 109, 116, 120 – 2, 124, 134, 136, 145, 148, 160, 181 – 97, 226, 247, 249, 252, 264 – 6, 275 – 6, 278, 282, 284 – 6, 294, 296, 299 – 300

Guangzhou Environmental Protection Bureau, 190

Guangzhou International Financial Town, 191

Hainan, 22 – 4, 29

Han Dynasty, 15, 170

Harris, Dan, 106

heavy metals, 77, 135, 138, 193, 210, 228

heritage properties, 69, 74, 106 – 7, 119, 169, 172, 188, 204

Him Mark Lai, 182

Home Depot, 34

Hong Kong, 17 – 8, 22 – 4, 32, 38, 42, 47, 55, 57 – 9, 70, 83 – 5, 90, 111, 116, 130, 146 – 7, 177, 179 – 80, 184 – 6, 189, 191, 195, 197, 199, 207, 217 – 22, 224, 226, 228 – 9, 235, 245, 248, 251, 253 – 7, 278, 280, 283, 294, 300

Hongkong and Shanghai Bank (HSBC), 146 – 8, 201, 211, 229, 263, 289

hongs (trading houses), 183

HOPSCA projects, 83, 225

Housing Provident Fund, 24, 152

Huangpu River, 199, 201, 206, 210

Huang Yimin, 74

Hudec, László, 206

hukou (registration system), 19, 26, 41, 44, 47 – 50, 68, 126, 131, 181, 188, 208, 217, 227

Hundred Flowers Campaign, 237

Hurun Wealth Report, 166, 182, 200, 212

hutongs (Beijing alleys), 170 – 2

IBM, 175

Implementation Plan for a Gradual Housing System Reform in Cities and Towns, the, 22

India, 30

indoor air quality, 132, 261, 319, 327, 329

infrastructure projects, 74, 79, 120 – 2, 174, 190, 209, 224, 227, 269, 282

Inner Mongolia, 37, 174

insurance, 32, 102, 148, 150, 159 – 60, 189, 249, 270 – 2

interest rates, 32, 56, 90, 112, 125, 145 – 6, 153, 215

international brands, 179, 273 – 5

International Settlement (Shanghai), 201 – 2

James Lang Lasalle, 113, 291

Japan, 29, 83, 133, 139, 201 – 3, 217, 236

Jiang Zemin, 202

J.P. Morgan, 32, 289

kitchens, 15, 38, 50, 77, 103, 107, 124, 196 – 7, 215, 230, 273 – 5, 323, 328, 333

Knight Frank, 185, 284, 291

Korea, South, 30, 167, 217

Kumagai Gumi (Hong Kong), 23

Kuomintang, 201, 236

Land Administration Law of the People's Republic of China, 89

land use rights, 61 – 2, 86 – 7, 90, 155, 171, 311 – 2

landlords, 18, 20 – 1, 156, 195, 229

lao yang fang (Western villas), 203

Law of the People's Republic of China on Lawyers, the, 242

Law on Guarding State Secrets, 130

lawyers, 91, 97, 101, 105 – 6, 115, 237, 239, 241 – 4, 266 – 8, 275 – 6

Lee, Anna, 115

Legalism, 235 – 7

Legislative Law, the, 238

Lehman Brothers, 26, 83

Lenhardt, Binke, 100

Lereah, David, 40

Liang Sicheng, 119

lilong (Shanghai homes), 62, 74, 203,
207 – 8

Liu Wencai, 21

local government financing vehicles
(LGFVs), 27, 76, 123

lofts, 75

Longfor Properties, 128, 255

Lotus Riverside (Shanghai), 128

Lunar New Year (see Spring Festival)

Macau, 189, 191, 222, 224

Macclesfield Bank, 29

Malaysia, 29, 167

Mao Zedong, 20 – 1, 219, 236

maps, 117, 131, 177, 260, 266, 277,
287, 293, 300

marriage, 35, 43 – 4, 48, 66, 115, 149

Marriage Law, the, 115

McGregor, Richard, 239

McIlwain, John, 73

McKinsey & Company, 38, 47, 290

Measures of Idle Land Disposal, 87

media, 40, 83, 91, 100, 122, 126, 130 –
1, 259, 278 – 81

Mercer, 166, 182, 200, 218

Merz, Martin, 195 – 7

Ming Dynasty, 16, 200, 203, 237

Ministry of Commerce, 126, 252, 267

Ministry of Environmental Protection, 109,
260, 268

Ministry of Housing and Urban-Rural
Development, 25, 173, 239, 268

Ministry of Justice, 242, 268

Ministry of Land and Resources, 76, 87,
138, 228, 239, 249, 268, 287

Ministry of Railways, 129, 268, 296

Minmetals Land, 82

Morgan Stanley, 40, 289

mortgages, 24, 26, 32, 38, 46, 60, 63,
65 – 70, 74, 78, 80, 106, 115, 145 – 53,
160, 172, 179, 213, 215, 229 – 30, 261,
305 – 7, 311, 317

mutual funds, 248

Nan Fung Group, 85, 256

National Association of Realtors, 40

National Audit Office, 79

National Credit Information Database,
153 – 4

National Day holiday, 31

National Development and Reform Commission, 76, 126, 239, 269

National Housing Reform Plan, 22

National People's Congress, 238 – 9, 241 – 2

National People's Congress Standing Committee, 238, 241

neibu (internal laws), 240

New York Stock Exchange, 248

noise, 56 – 7, 79, 80, 121, 138, 175, 229, 324

notaries, 63, 66, 68 – 9, 150, 156, 266 – 8, 276, 305, 307, 316

Notification from the State Council on Further Deepening the Reform of the Urban Housing System and Accelerating Housing Construction, 24

nuclear power, 79, 117, 124 – 5, 225, 260, 282

Nuclear Threat Initiative, 125

one-child policy, 41 – 2

open door policy, 237

Opinions on Regulating the Entry into and the Administration of Foreign Investment in the Real Estate Market, 25

Opium War, the, 17, 183, 201

Pakistan, 30

Palmer and Turner, 201, 206, 211

Paracel Islands, 29

parking, 56, 59, 70, 76, 124, 176, 192, 285, 311

Pearl River, 181, 183, 185, 189 – 90, 193, 226

People's Bank of China, 23, 145 – 6, 153, 239, 269

People's Liberation Army, 202

pesticides, 81, 132, 135, 138

Philippines, the, 29, 217

polychlorinated biphenyls (PCBs), 135

Preservation Regulations of Historic and Cultural Districts and Historic Buildings of Shanghai City, 106

prices, property, 22 – 3, 26 – 7, 32 – 3, 36 – 8, 43, 56, 59, 61, 76, 78, 84, 90, 111, 115, 123, 125, 127 – 8, 131, 134, 157, 169, 172, 189, 201, 280

Property Code of the People's Republic of China, 62, 86

property management companies, 85, 220, 282

Property Rights Law of the People's Republic of China, the, 25, 238

property tax, 28 – 9, 33, 88, 127, 155, 169, 189, 205, 223

Public Security Bureau, 63, 68, 244, 266

qilou (Guangzhou shophouses), 74, 186, 188

Qianhai, 74, 224 – 5

Qingcaosha Reservoir, 211

Qing Dynasty, 187, 235

Qingming Festival, 114

quality control, 35, 99 – 101, 120, 128 – 9, 180, 235

railways, 129, 136, 186, 191, 197, 226, 241, 268, 296

real estate agents, 9, 40, 57 – 9, 62, 65, 67 – 70, 113 – 4, 130, 168, 172, 179, 188, 203, 213, 215, 222, 230, 245, 249, 283 – 4, 310 – 1, 318

real estate investment trusts (REITs), 248, 285

real estate listings, 56, 67, 285 – 6

Real Estate Trading Centers, 62, 67 – 8, 306, 312 – 3, 316

reform, land, 20 – 1

Regulations on Expropriation and Compensation of Housing on State-owned Land, 89

renovations, 34, 95 – 108, 110, 152, 160, 179, 188, 196 – 7, 208, 213, 215 – 6, 230 – 1, 286, 319 – 33

Rent Collection Courtyard, the, 21

rental accommodations, 20, 22, 33, 77, 80, 85, 114, 124, 155 – 6, 173, 213, 285 – 7

Republican period, 16

research, 59, 130 – 1, 286 – 91

Residential Housing Quality Assurance Regulations, 71

residency requirements, 25, 48, 55, 61, 63, 68, 78, 126, 149

Reuters, 91, 281

reverse mortgages, 46, 153

sale and purchase (S&P) agreements, 61, 63 – 4, 66, 68, 148 – 9, 152, 180, 230, 263, 303 – 18

Sansha, 29

Santa Barbara Villa, 82

Scarborough Shoal, 29

schools, 56, 64, 80 – 1, 129, 167 – 8, 170, 177, 185 – 6, 191, 203, 213, 222, 237

seals (chops), 66, 92, 113, 243 – 4, 329

Senkaku Islands, 29, 139

severe acute respiratory syndrome (SARS), 112, 118

shadow banking system, 32, 153

Shamien Island, 183 – 4, 188, 190

Shang Dynasty, 13

Shanghai, 17 – 8, 26 – 8, 32 – 3, 35, 37, 45, 47 – 50, 62, 69 – 70, 74 – 5, 80, 82 – 3, 87 – 8, 103, 105 – 6, 108 – 9, 111, 115 – 6, 119, 122 – 30, 134, 136 – 7, 145, 148, 150, 152, 155 – 7, 160, 182 – 5, 199 – 216, 236, 247, 249, 252 – 8, 260, 264, 266, 275 – 6, 279, 281 – 6, 294, 299 – 300, 304 – 18

Shanghai Electric Power, 209, 299

Shanghai Environmental Monitoring Center, 209

Shanghai Expo 2010, 134, 210

Shanghai Stock Exchange, 83, 203, 253, 255 – 7

Shanghai Water Authority, 210, 299

shengnu women, 28, 44

Shenzhen, 22, 24, 28, 32, 45 – 9, 58 – 9, 61, 74 – 5, 83, 86, 91, 104, 111, 116, 119, 124, 132, 136, 148, 152 – 3, 159 – 60, 175, 184, 193, 217 – 31, 235, 252 – 4, 256, 260, 264, 266 – 7, 275 – 6, 279 – 80, 282, 284 – 6, 294, 297, 299 – 300

Shenzhen Stock Exchange, 83, 217, 253 – 4, 256

shikumen (Shanghai houses), 207

short-term thinking, 34 – 5

Shougang Group, 75, 134

sick building syndrome, 132 – 3

siheyuan (Beijing houses), 57, 62, 74, 106, 108, 119, 170 – 2, 208, 283

Sina Weibo, 130 – 1, 293, 146 – 7, 152

Singapore, 24, 83, 111, 191, 199, 248, 253, 257

Singapore Exchange, 83, 248, 253, 257

Sinobo Group, 169

Sino Land, 92, 257

Sino-Ocean Land Holdings, 84, 92, 257

social housing, 27, 123, 134, 170, 173, 249

software, 112, 290 – 3

SOHO China, 94, 111

soil pollution, 81, 91, 134 – 5, 138, 175, 192, 210

Song Dynasty, 15, 200

South-to-North Water Diversion Project, 176

Soviet Union, 82, 167, 237

special economic zones, 22 – 3, 184, 203, 219 – 20

Spratly Islands, 29

Spring Festival (Lunar New Year), 49, 105, 119 – 20, 227, 230

stamp duty, 65, 68 – 9, 156

Standard & Poor's, 111, 289

Standard Chartered Bank, 146 – 8, 150, 264, 289

State Administration of Foreign Exchange, 25, 151 – 2, 269

State Administration of Industry and Commerce, 244

State Administration of Quality Supervision, Inspection and Quarantine, 133, 325, 331

State Council, 22 – 4, 89, 191 – 2, 224 – 5, 238 – 41, 269, 277

State Oceanic Administration, 74

State-owned Assets Supervision and
Administration Commission (SASAC),
84, 269

state-owned enterprises (SOEs), 23 – 4,
26 – 7, 83 – 5, 87, 90, 111, 131, 135,
165, 269 – 70

Stock Exchange of Hong Kong, 83 – 4,
90, 111, 248, 253 – 7

stocks, 32 – 3, 38, 40, 83 – 4, 90 – 2,
111, 123, 203, 217, 248, 253 – 7,
288 – 90

subprime crisis, 38

subsidence, 136, 160, 176, 211 – 3

subways, 56, 59, 69, 90, 121 – 2, 135,
174, 190, 192, 197, 209 – 10, 213,
224 – 7, 296 – 7

Sun Hung Kai Properties, 85, 257

Supreme People's Court, 44, 89, 115,
238, 240 – 1

Supreme People's Procuratorate, 114,
238, 269

Taiping Rebellion, 201, 207

Taiwan, 29, 189, 222

Taleb, Nassim Nicholas, 112

Tang Dynasty, 15, 182

taxes, 15 – 6, 22 – 3, 28 – 9, 33, 48,
55, 61, 63, 65, 68 – 9, 88, 127, 136,
149, 152, 155 – 7, 169, 183, 189, 202,
204 – 5, 219, 223, 225, 236, 238, 244,
268, 290, 294, 307, 312, 314, 320

termites, 137, 295

Thailand, 35

Thames Town, 82

Therien, Yves, 177, 179 – 80

Tiananmen Square, 134, 166 – 8

Tianzifang (Shanghai), 75, 207 – 8

title, 115, 152, 195, 221, 266, 295, 311

traffic, 37, 114, 121, 137 – 8, 166, 168,
175 – 6, 192, 210, 221, 224, 227, 263,
266 – 7

translation, 9, 245, 295

Treaty of Nanjing, 17, 183, 201

treaty ports, 17 – 8, 183, 201

typhoons, 35, 95, 160, 193, 211, 300

UNESCO, 82

United Nations, 43, 46, 116, 137, 176,
210

United Nations Environmental Program,
137

United States, 29, 35, 38, 40, 47, 73, 88,
130, 145, 147, 206, 235 – 6, 258, 261,
277, 286

universal design, 286, 297

Urban Land Institute, 73, 290

urban villages, 49 – 51, 193 – 4, 219 – 20,
227

urbanization, 28, 33, 41, 45, 47, 49, 83, 117, 121, 134, 140, 192

Vietnam, 22, 29

villas, 38, 64 – 5, 77, 82, 93, 104, 188, 213, 220 – 1

volatile organic compounds, 132 – 3, 261

Walt Disney, 210

Wang Zhansheng, 139

warranties, 71, 102, 327 – 8, 333

water, 21, 49 – 50, 77, 100, 103, 119, 133, 136, 138 – 9, 166, 172, 176 – 7, 180, 183, 193, 196, 209 – 12, 226, 228 – 9, 260, 268 – 9, 296, 298 – 9, 306, 314, 323 – 4, 328

water pollution, 138 – 9, 166, 228, 260, 269

weather, 94, 190, 210 – 2, 225, 300

Weisenhaus, Doreen, 130

Wen Jiabao, 27, 123

Wenzhou, 90, 131

wine, 32, 107 – 8, 180

World Health Organization, 110, 118, 138, 173, 190, 209

World Trade Organization, 240

World War II, 202

Wu Liangyong, 171

Wuhan, 64 – 5, 113, 136

Wukan, 88

xenophobia, 139 – 40

xiguan (Guangzhou houses), 187 – 8

xinfang (petitioning), 237

Xinhua News Agency, 29, 278 – 80

Yang Rui, 139

Yangtze River, 17, 77, 176, 199, 210 – 1

Zhou Dynasty, 109

Zhu Rongji, 23, 129, 202

Zimmerman, James, 239

zoning, 140

ABOUT THE AUTHOR

Christopher Dillon is an award-winning writer and entrepreneur who has lived in Hong Kong for more than 20 years. In 2002, he bought and renovated a floor in an office building in Central. Since then, he has purchased and refurbished a luxury apartment on the west side of Hong Kong Island and transformed a derelict steam laundry into a multimedia studio. That experience inspired his first book, *Landed Hong Kong*. His second book, *Landed Japan*, was published in 2010.

www.ingramcontent.com/pod-product-compliance
Lightning Source LLC
Chambersburg PA
CBHW061119220326
41599CB00024B/4093

GUIDE

AMATEURS D'ARMES

ET

ARMURES ANCIENNES

Paris. — Imp. P.-A. Bourdier, Capiomont fils et Cᵉ, rue des Poitevins, 6.

GUIDE

DES

AMATEURS D'ARMES

ET

ARMURES ANCIENNES

PAR ORDRE CHRONOLOGIQUE

DEPUIS LES TEMPS LES PLUS RECULÉS JUSQU'A NOS JOURS

PAR

AUGUSTE DEMMIN

Auteur du Guide de l'Amateur de Faïences et Porcelaines, etc.

OUVRAGE

CONTENANT 1700 REPRODUCTIONS D'ARMES ET ARMURES, 200 MARQUES ET MONOGRAMMES
D'ARMURIERS ET DEUX TABLES, DONT UNE ANALYTIQUE.

PARIS

LIBRAIRIE DE Ve JULES RENOUARD

ÉTHIOU-PÉROU, Directeur-Gérant

ÉDITEUR DE L'HISTOIRE DES PEINTRES DE TOUTES LES ÉCOLES

6, RUE DE TOURNON, 6

1869

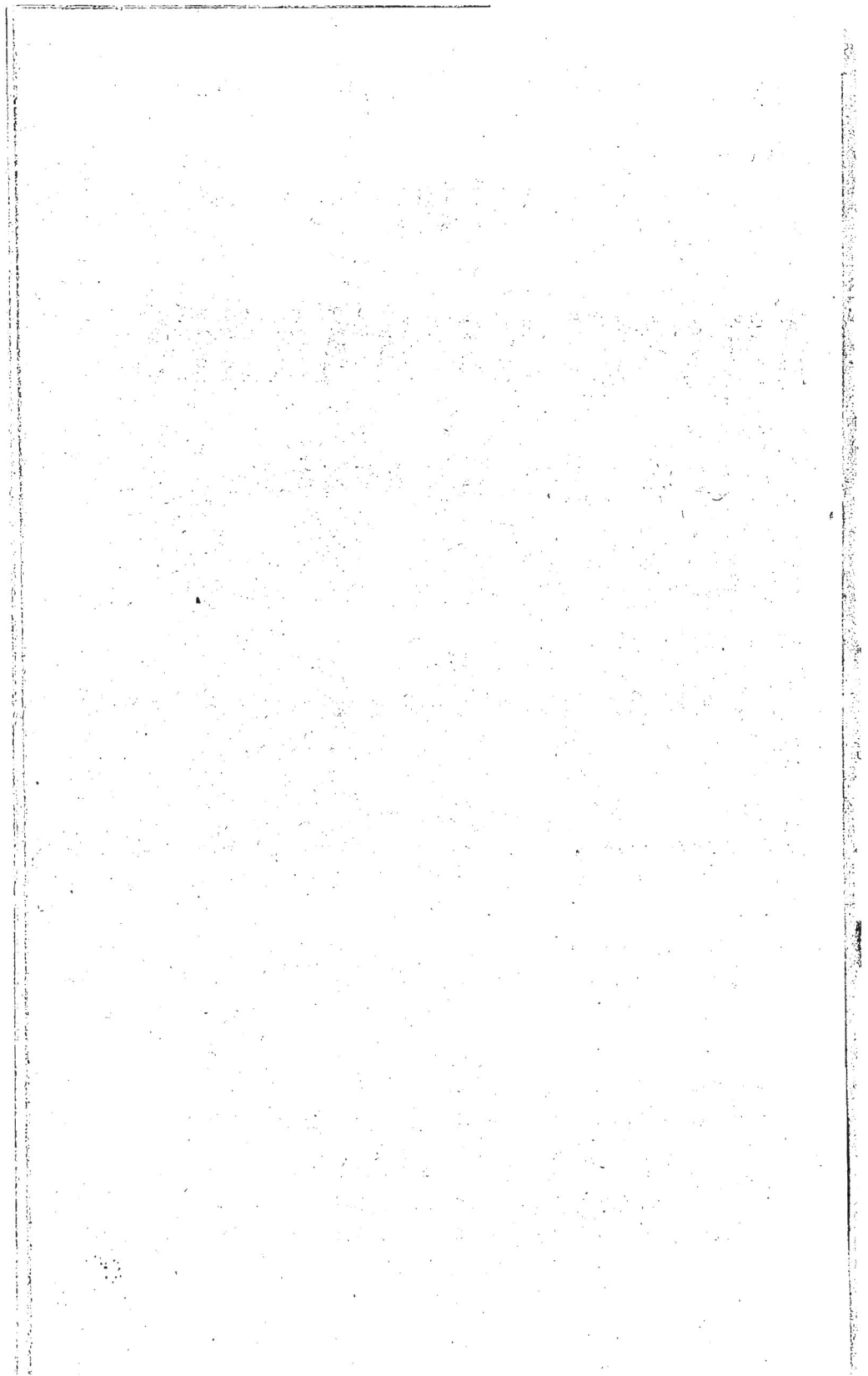

INTRODUCTION

Tout ce qui peut intéresser l'archéologue, l'historien, l'artiste, le militaire, et même le simple curieux, sur la marche progressive et sur le développement successif de l'armement des diverses nations à travers les siècles, a été condensé dans le premier chapitre de ce livre, dans l'*Histoire abrégée des armes anciennes*, dont plusieurs extraits, plus ou moins modifiés, se trouvent reproduits en tête des subdivisions, afin d'éviter au lecteur la peine de parcourir chaque fois l'histoire entière, quand il ne désire se renseigner que sur une partie.

Il aurait été inutile d'y englober aussi les développements historiques de chaque arme, qui se trouvent dans les divers chapitres spéciaux où ces armes sont décrites par ordre chronologique. C'est le système le plus rationnel pour un livre destiné à servir à la fois de guide et d'encyclopédie scientifique aux hommes du monde et aux collectionneurs ; car les quelques répétitions qui en résultent inévitablement contribueront à faciliter les études.

Un chapitre spécial décrit en outre la marche progressive de l'art de l'armurier, et donne les signes et les marques de tous les armuriers qu'on a pu réunir; un autre chapitre traite des armes et des alphabets qui ont été en usage dans les tribunaux des francs-juges.

L'ouvrage entier est divisé en six parties principales, parmi lesquelles les plus substantielles traitent des armes du moyen âge, de la Renaissance, du dix-septième et du dix-huitième siècle. L'Auteur, qui a visité durant des années tous les musées et arsenaux de l'Europe et les plus importantes collections d'amateur, a pu dessiner et recueillir assez de matières *authentiques* pour se dispenser d'avoir recours aux livres de compilation. Quant aux espèces d'armes qui n'existent plus, elles ont été étudiées dans les manuscrits, dans les miniatures et sur les monnaies du temps, et sur les monuments anciens où la sculpture a conservé les formes dont l'exactitude peut rarement être contestée.

Malgré le goût actuel si prononcé pour les recherches rétrospectives, qui a donné le jour à une véritable avalanche de traités spéciaux et locaux et à des ouvrages plus importants, aucun travail complet n'existait encore ni en France, ni ailleurs, sur l'armurerie ancienne. Y a-t-il, cependant, des connaissances plus indispensables pour l'artiste que celles qui le rendent apte à fixer à la première vue d'une épée, d'un casque, d'un bouclier ou de toute autre pièce, la nation et l'époque à laquelle l'homme qui en était armé a appartenu.

L'incertitude, sous ce rapport, a donné lieu à de bien nombreuses méprises, qui n'ont pas tardé d'acquérir le droit de bourgeoisie et de perpétuer des erreurs historiques fort regrettables. Le mauvais classement d'un grand nombre de musées et d'arsenaux a particulièrement contribué à la diffusion de ces erreurs populaires qui ont fini par se glisser dans des traités historiques, dans presque tous les guides, dans les sculptures sur les toiles et dans les peintures murales qui transforment les pinacothèques et les glyptothèques en vrais cours publics d'enseignement d'anachronismes. Plusieurs de ces collections d'armes montrent des exemplaires où les dates indiquées dépassent de centaines d'années celles des origines. C'est particulièrement dans les arsenaux et musées suisses que ces erreurs sont fréquentes. Là, il y a profusion d'épées de Charles le Téméraire, dont les formes accusent, à la première vue, la fin du seizième et même du dix-septième siècle, ainsi que des armures de ces mêmes époques, attribuées à la bataille de Sempach. Le gymnase de Morat exhibe des harnais du dix-septième siècle, « pris aux Bourguignons tués à la bataille » où, sous les murs de la ville, le terrible duc perdit, en 1476, son honneur militaire, après avoir perdu à Granson ses trésors. Une autre armure, dont la bourguignote avec son avance et ses oreillères, les cuissards écrevisses et la forme du plastron signalent également le dix-septième siècle, a été attribuée à Adrien de Bubenberg, ce vaillant chef des quinze cents Bernois qui défendirent Morat pendant dix jours, contre l'artillerie du Téméraire. A l'arsenal de Soleure, la méprise est grande encore : tous les personnages du célèbre groupe, composé d'après un dessin de Disteli, et qui doit représenter la réconciliation des confédérés à la diète de Stanz, en 1487, par l'intercession du vénérable Nicolaus Von der Vlue, sont revêtus d'armures du seizième et du dix-septième siècle.

Le fameux bouclier moderne, en fer, attribué à Philippe le Bon (1419), malgré les rondaches dont les chevaliers, sujets en relief, sont armés, et qu'une publication suisse a même fait reproduire en gravure, accompagnée d'une savante dissertation, aussi bien que le plastron de cuirasse de cavalerie française du premier empire, sur lequel un armurier peu habile a grossièrement repoussé deux emplacements pour sein de femme, y figurent encore comme précieuses reliques du moyen âge, ce dont le marchand qui les a vendus à l'arsenal, et qui habite Soleure, doit souvent rire de bon cœur, — sous cape, bien entendu.

A l'arsenal de Zurich, toutes les cuirasses à plastrons bombés des armures demi-cannelées passent pour des cuirasses de femmes, comme si la gorge de la femme se trouvait placée à la partie inférieure de la poitrine!

Même en Angleterre, pays pourtant réputé pour ses recherches archéologiques, l'arsenal de la Tour de Londres avait conservé un grand nombre d'attributions fantastiques, avant que M. John Hewett n'en eût démontré la fausseté dans un catalogue raisonné. Dans le classement de ce musée, comme dans la rédaction du catalogue de sa célèbre collection, le docteur Meyrick, qui a passé longtemps pour un puits de science en fait d'armes anciennes, avait fait des erreurs d'attributions qui dépassaient quelquefois plusieurs centaines d'années.

A l'arsenal de Madrid, les erreurs sont même telles que les dates désignées s'écartent de quatre et cinq cents années de l'époque originaire des pièces, erreurs monstrueuses qui ont même passé dans les textes qui accompagnent les reproductions publiées de ces armes. Ces méprises, on ne les rencontre pas moins dans la savante Allemagne. La collection d'Ambras, à Vienne, pour laquelle Schrenck de Notzing avait déjà publié, en 1601, une description latine, qui, traduite en allemand, par Enjelbertus Moyse van Campenhouten, fut accompagnée de nombreuses gravures plus fantastiques les unes que les autres, contient encore à l'heure qu'il est une armure de la fin du seizième siècle, attribuée dans le musée à Robert, le roi romain, mort en 1410. A l'arsenal de la même ville de Vienne, le curieux peut même se donner la satisfaction de voir s'escrimer des mannequins revêtus d'armures du commencement du dix-septième siècle, que le préposé lui désigne, sous « des Germains combattant des Romains, » comme il peut admirer au musée de Dresde une armure et un casque du dix-septième siècle attribués à Édouard VI, roi d'Angleterre, qui avait pourtant cessé déjà de régner en 1483. Ne voyait-on pas aussi au musée national bavarois, à Munich, avant que M. de Hefner-Alteneck eût été nommé directeur, un colletin ou hausse-col d'une buffleterie de la guerre de Trente ans, placée comme pièce adhérente au-dessus du précieux gamboison ou pourpoint à haut et bas de chausses du quatorzième siècle? Le musée de Cassel fait même figurer, parmi les armes antiques, un morion et un cabasset, bien rouillés il est vrai, qui proviennent de troupes *antiques* du dix-septième siècle. Au musée national de Brunswick, un semblable morion, toujours parfaitement rouillé, porte l'étiquette « douzième siècle. » On pourrait citer aussi un grand nombre de ces méprises commises par des musées français et italiens; mais arrêtons-nous là. Tous ces anachronismes ont passé dans les livres : ne voit-on pas dans un petit traité orné de gravures et publié tout ré-

cemment, à Paris même (*Armes et Armures*, par La-
combe, Hachette, 1868), un harnais de la fin du règne
de Henri IV, mort en 1610, désigné comme l'armure
de Charles le Téméraire, mort en 1477; le cabasset
figurer sous le nom de *morion;* le grand bacinet du
quatorzième siècle appelé *mezail,* mot qui comprend
simplement *la vue* et la partie frontale d'un casque;
et nommer la francisque une *arme défensive;* le long
pistolet du dix-septième siècle, *petrinal;* la hallebarde,
pertuisane; la guisarme, *fauchard;* l'esponton et la
pertuisane, *hallebardes?* etc., etc.

Le désir d'offrir des curiosités *historiques* a aussi
entraîné plusieurs musées à accepter ou à fabriquer
pour leurs objets des généalogies et des titres qui, ap-
pliqués depuis par la tradition avec une candeur naïve,
sont devenus de vrais évangiles pour les gardiens et pour
la foule parmi laquelle ils produisent et conservent des
erreurs grossières. Quand donc commencera-t-on enfin à
comprendre qu'un beau morceau de sculpture, de peinture, de ciselure, de repoussé ou de tout autre travail
artistique n'a besoin d'autre titre que celui que le con-
naisseur trouve dans l'exécution et dans *la physiono-
mie de l'époque,* manifestée par le cachet archéologique
qui a disparu avec l'art gothique, et dont l'empreinte ne
se trouve ni sur les produits de l'antiquité, ni sur les
œuvres de ses continuateurs? Les attributions si souvent
hasardées et fausses ne peuvent servir qu'à jeter du
discrédit aussi bien sur le collectionneur que sur le conservateur.

Les erreurs, si fréquentes déjà dans le classement chronologique et dans les attributions historiques des armes,
sont encore plus nombreuses quand il s'agit du fabricant

et de la nationalité. Des armuriers sans mérite et chez lesquels l'existence aurait dû avoir la longueur de la vie de Mathusalem, pour produire seulement la moitié de ce qui leur est attribué, sont prônés au détriment des véritables artistes, dont les chefs-d'œuvre figurent sous l'étiquette de l'ouvrier favorisé, le plus souvent préconisé par l'effet d'un chauvinisme indigne d'hommes occupés à jeter les jalons d'une histoire basée sur des documents plastiques, que la partialité des chroniqueurs n'a pu tronquer.

Chose triste à constater! les trouveurs archéologues ont beau remuer la poussière des siècles et passer leur existence à démontrer, *pièces en main*, toutes ces erreurs involontaires, tous ces escamotages puérils, la troupe des compilateurs continue à fabriquer des livres — avec des livres, en copiant de nouveau ce qui a été recopié déjà sans critique, de père en fils, et en écrivant sur des matières qu'elle ne connaît que par la lecture.

Tandis que les produits italiens dominent ordinairement dans les musées des céramiques et des mosaïques, comme ceux de France dans les collections d'émaux sur métaux et de pièces d'ameublement somptuaire, les arsenaux et musées d'armes anciennes sont partout composés, en majeure partie, d'œuvres allemandes. Il n'existe pas de pays où l'art de l'armure ait été aussi répandu qu'en Allemagne, ni poussé aussi loin pour la fabrication des armures à plates dont les articulations lamées y couvraient jusqu'aux jambes des coursiers. Les nombreuses capitales et résidences princières, aussi bien que les principales villes libres, ont fourni, durant le moyen âge et l'époque de la Renaissance, un vaste champ à l'artiste pour l'application de ses combinaisons d'armement de luxe dont le précieux travail lui était souvent payé au poids de l'or par de simples praticiens, tels que les Fugger et autres, riches trafiquants qui, à cette époque, savaient manier aussi bien l'épée que l'aune et le sac d'argent.

Malgré les monogrammes dont les belles arquebuses, épées, casques et cuirasses sont marqués, malgré le dessin des figures et des ornements qui indiquent l'école allemande, la plupart de ces armes continuent à figurer dans beaucoup de catalogues et de publications, sous la dénomination de produits italiens. Comme si l'Italie, la patrie des Antonio Picinino, des Andrea de Ferrare, des Ventura Cani, des Lazarino Caminazzi, des Colombo, des Badile, des Francino, des Mutto, des Berselli, des Benisolo, des Giocatane et de bien d'autres célèbres armuriers, avait besoin d'être illustrée par de la contrebande et d'être parée de plumes d'autrui.

On verra, dans le chapitre qui traite de l'*Art de l'armurier*, comment les rédacteurs de ces écrits sont peu au courant de la critique d'art et des découvertes archéologiques récentes. Pour eux, les armures faites pour les rois de France, à Munich et à Augsbourg, sont restées italiennes, comme celles exécutées par les *Peter Pah*, les *Wulff*, les *Kolmann* et les *Peter* (Pedro) de ces mêmes villes sont restées espagnoles. Ils continuent d'ignorer que Seusenhofer, d'Insbruck, avait été chargé de la confection des armes des fils de François Ier, travail magnifique qui est aussi resté sous l'étiquette italienne. Même en Allemagne, cette dépréciation de l'art national s'est infiltrée jusque dans les collections publiques ; car lorsque l'Auteur de ce livre, il n'y a pas dix ans, avait reconnu au musée de Dresde, dans plusieurs belles armures attribuées à des maîtres italiens, l'œuvre incontestable d'armuriers allemands, il ne pouvait recueillir que des haussements d'épaules et des sourires d'incrédulité. Aujourd'hui on ne le conteste plus, et on sait que ces armes ont été exécutées en partie par le même Kellermann, d'Augsbourg, à qui une seule armure fut payée 14,000 écus. La célèbre armure ornée de repoussés qui représentent les travaux d'Hercule, au musée de Dresde, est également allemande.

Que l'on compare l'armure de Henri II au Louvre avec les dessins composés par les peintres Schwarz, van Achen, Brockbergen et Jean Milich pour les ateliers de Munich, et conservés au cabinet des estampes de cette ville : on y trouvera comme sur le bouclier de la collection d'Ambras, dont la contrefaçon avait passé en France, l'exécution parfois même scrupuleuse de ces modèles publiés en reproductions photographiques, par M. de Hefner-Alteneck, qui en avait fait la découverte dans les réserves du cabinet d'estampes à Munich. C'est particulièrement la planche XVII qui a fourni la preuve la plus frappante. Pour se faire une idée de ce que les armuriers allemands ont su faire au quinzième et au seizième siècle, il faut visiter l'Arsenal impérial et la collection d'Ambras à Vienne. Les nielles et les incrustations en or et en argent (*Tauchierarbeiten* en allem.) sont même d'une solidité qui laisse bien loin en arrière celles exécutées en Espagne ; et le martelage en fer marche de pair avec celui d'Italie. Quant aux formes des armures, elles sont toujours nobles et heureuses.

L'arme à feu, encore plus que l'arme blanche et l'armure à plates, doit ses meilleurs perfectionnements aux armuriers allemands qui ont inventé le fusil à vent, en

1560 ; le canon rayé (*Buchsenlauf* en allem.), en 1440, selon d'autres en 1500 ; le fusil à rouet, en 1515 ; l'arquebuse, en 1551 ; la double détente (*Stecher* en allem.), en 1543 ; la baguette en fer, en 1698 (dont l'adoption avait contribué à faire gagner à l'armée prussienne la bataille de Mollwitz, en 1730), et depuis, en 1827, le fusil à aiguille.

Comme le caractère archéologique et en même temps spécial de la matière traitée dans ce livre pourrait facilement entraîner à des digressions stériles et à l'emploi d'un argot de métier, qui ne servent trop souvent qu'à pallier l'absence de véritables connaissances et d'études bien digérées, les notes de renvoi ont été entièrement évitées dans le chapitre historique, et des noms que chacun peut comprendre sans recherches, employés pour la désignation des objets qui se trouvent dans l'ouvrage, en français, en allemand et en anglais. L'auteur n'a cependant pu se dispenser de citer scrupuleusement les sources, — tant monuments que manuscrits et armes encore existantes, — où il a puisé, afin de fournir des moyens de contrôle et en même temps des renseignements pour les études plus spéciales.

Dès que l'édition française aura quitté les presses, deux autres, en anglais et en allemand, pour lesquelles MM. Bell et Daldy, et M. E. A. Semann ont traité, paraîtront à Londres et à Leipzig.

Avant d'entrer en matière, il sera utile de passer en revue les plus importantes collections d'armes, afin de se rendre compte, par leur formation, comment, dans l'ordre chronologique, le goût pour les armes anciennes s'est développé en Europe, à partir de la Renaissance.

Les premières réunions d'armes et d'armures comme

collections, et non pas pour servir d'armurerie d'usage, ne paraissent remonter qu'au seizième ou à la fin du quinzième siècle. On connaît par le catalogue publié par M. Leroux de Lancy, en 1848, dans la Bibliothèque des chartes, que Louis XII avait formé, en 1502, un *cabinet d'armes* à Amboise. Le célèbre musée d'armes historiques de Dresde, un des plus riches de l'Europe, doit son origine à Henri le Pieux. Auguste Ier, qui collectionna durant trente-trois ans (1553-1586), est cependant le véritable fondateur du musée actuel, composé de plus de soixante mille pièces, et particulièrement riche en épées, mais de peu d'armes et armures remontant au delà de la fin du quinzième siècle.

Le maréchal Strozzi, mort en 1558, laissa un *cabinet d'armes* qui occupa trois salles et dont Brantôme a parlé assez longuement :

« Si le Mareschal Strozzy estoit exquis en belle bibliothèque, il l'estoit bien autant en armurerie et en beau cabinet d'armes ; car il en avoit une grande salle et deux chambres, que j'ay veues autresfois à Rome, en son palais *in Burgo ;* et ses armes estoient de toutes sortes, tant à cheval qu'à pied, à la françoise, espagnole, italienne, allemande, hongroise, et à la bohémienne ; bref, de plusieurs autres nations chrestiennes ; comme aussi à la turquesque, moresque, arabesque et sauvage. Mais, ce qui estoit le plus beau à voir, c'estoient les armes, à l'antique mode, des anciens soldats et légionnaires romains. Tout cela estoit si beau, qu'on ne sçavoit que plus admirer, ou les armes, ou la curiosité du personnage qui les avoit là mises. Et, pour plus orner le tout, il y avoit un cabinet à part remply de toutes sortes d'engins de guerre, de machines, d'eschelles, de ponts, de fortifications, d'artifices et d'instruments; bref, de toutes inventions de guerre, pour offenser et deffendre; et le tout fait et représenté de bois si au naïf et au vray, qu'il n'y avoit là qu'à prendre le patron sur le naturel, et s'en servir au besoin. J'ay veu depuis tous ces cabinets à Lyon, où M. Strozzy dernier, son fils, les fit transporter, pour n'avoir esté conservez si curieusement, comme je les avois veus à Rome. Aussi je les vis là tout gastez et brouillez, dont j'en eus du deuil au cœur; et c'en est un très-grand dommage; car ils valoient beaucoup, et un roy ne les eust sceu trop achepter; mais M. Strozzy brouilla et vendit tout; ce que je lui remonstray un jour; car il laissoit telle chose pour cent escus, qui en valoit plus de mille. Et, entre autres choses rares que j'y ay remarqué, il y avoit une rondelle de coque de tortuë marine, si grande qu'elle eust couvert le plus grand homme qui fut, depuis la teste jusques aux pieds; et si dure, qu'une arquebuse l'eust mal-aisément pu percer de loin, et pourtant un peu pesante. Il y avoit aussi deux queues de chevaux marins, les plus belles, les plus longues, les plus espaisses, et les plus blanches que je vis jamais. J'auray possible esté trop long et fascheux à parler de ce cabinet d'armes; mais certes, si je m'eusse voulu amuser à en raconter des particularitez, l'on y eust trouvé du plaisir à les lire. »

La belle collection Ambras, aujourd'hui à Vienne, au Belvédère, composée uniquement de pièces de choix, a été commencée en 1570 par l'archiduc Ferdinand, comte de Tyrol, fils de l'empereur Ferdinand Ier et mari de la belle Philippine Welser d'Augsbourg, en son château d'Ambras, près de la ville d'Insbruck, où ce prince avait réuni cent cinquante armures complètes et un

grand nombre d'armes offensives et de harnais ; un cabinet de curiosités et d'objets d'art, dont le plus grand
nombre se trouve encore réuni à la collection d'armes à
Vienne, et dont une petite partie est restée à Ambras,
plus de neuf cents portraits historiques, fort peu artistiques il est vrai, une réunion de deux mille cinq cents médailles et monnaies et de plusieurs milliers d'estampes ;
une bibliothèque de quatre mille volumes imprimés et
cinq cents manuscrits, parmi lesquels on trouve toujours les trois célèbres volumes d'aquarelles, exécutés
par Gleckentohn, et contenant les reproductions exactes
des armes et armures des trois arsenaux de l'empereur
Maximilien, qui formaient alors un ensemble dont peu
de villes possédaient l'équivalent. La collection, qui n'a-
vait perdu que dix belles armures emportées par l'armée française, fut en majeure partie transportée à
Vienne, en 1806. Un premier ouvrage, contenant la reproduction et la description de ces richesses, a été publié au dix-septième siècle, en latin, par Jacob Schrenck
de Notzing, ouvrage peu sérieux, qui a été pourtant
traduit en allemand par Engelbertus Moyse de Compen-
houten. M. le baron de Sacken a publié un autre ouvrage en 1862, où il a fait reproduire les plus belles
pièces de la collection, au moyen de la photographie.
Vienne possède en outre la célèbre collection de l'*empereur à l'Arsenal d'artillerie* et celle de l'*Arsenal de
la ville*.

L'*Arsenal d'artillerie impérial à Vienne*, immenses
constructions élevées à côté de la gare du chemin de fer du
Midi, renferme une des plus riches collections d'armes de
l'Europe, provenant des cabinets d'armes des empereurs
d'Autriche. Installé dans un monument qui est certes un

des mieux réussis et des plus beaux de notre époque, et l'œuvre du conseiller Hansen, cette collection compte plus de sept cents numéros; elle est aujourd'hui sous l'intelligente direction du capitaine Querin Leitner, qui l'a parfaitement classée, et dont la publication (*Waffen-sammlung des œstreichischen Kaiserhauses im Artillerie Arsenal*, Vienne, 1868), destinée aux reproductions des pièces les plus remarquables du musée, contribuera à vulgariser le goût pour les armes anciennes.

L'*Arsenal de la ville de Vienne*, qui date de la fin du quinzième siècle, et dont la construction, moins qu'insignifiante, a été élevée vers 1732, contient peu de belles armures, mais quarante pavois ou Setzschilde de la fin du quinzième siècle et quantité d'armes de haste et de taille. On y voit aussi la tête du grand visir Moustafa, le monstre cruel à qui le Sultan avait envoyé le *cordon*, en 1684, après sa défaite sous les murs de Vienne. Les meilleures armures de ce musée, où il y a absence complète de classement et profusion d'attributions ridicules, sont affreusement barbouillées de peinture noire.

Les premières mentions d'une réunion d'armes à la *Tour de Londres* se trouvent dans un inventaire de 1547 et dans une ordonnance de 1578. Paul Hentzner, voyageur allemand, parle déjà également, en 1598, des belles armes de la Tour de Londres, quoiqu'elles composassent alors plutôt un arsenal qu'une galerie. En 1630, le véritable noyau de la collection fut commencé à Greenwich, et avec ce qui restait des pillages des guerres civiles, on forma, vers la fin du dix-septième siècle, la galerie actuelle où le docteur Meyrick dirigea plus tard le classement. Depuis 1820, les collections ont

été augmentées par des achats successifs. L'incendie de
1841 ne leur a enlevé que quelques canons, qui ont été
complétement détruits. Il n'y a pas de conservateur;
M. John Hewitt, archéologue, a pu cependant publier un
Catalogue officiel de l'Arsenal, divisé en vingt classes
où on voit figurer treize numéros pour les armes antiques, quarante pour celles de l'âge de pierre, cent vingt
pour l'âge de bronze et vingt-cinq pour l'âge de fer. Les
armes, à partir du commencement du moyen âge jusqu'à nos jours, sont au nombre de cinq mille sept cents
environ, ce qui forme une collection de plus de cinq
mille huit cents objets dont la partie orientale est particulièrement bien représentée. En outre de la collection
de la Tour, il faut encore mentionner pour l'Angleterre
la célèbre collection d'*armes de Llewelyn-Megrick*, à
Goodrich-Court (Herefordshire), une des plus complètes
de l'Europe.

L'*Arsenal de Berlin*, qui possède quelques armures
historiques des Électeurs, n'est riche ni en armes ni
en armures anciennes; composé en majeure partie de
fusils à silex et à piston, et de trophées conquis dans les
guerres que la Prusse a eu à soutenir, il occupe la belle
construction à laquelle les masques de Schluter ont
donné une célébrité européenne. On trouve en outre à
Berlin, au palais Monbijou, un certain nombre d'armes
et armures historiques, ainsi que la belle collection du
prince Charles de Prusse, collection très-riche, à laquelle manque malheureusement la place pour pouvoir
être exposée convenablement et classée par ordre chronologique.

L'origine du *Musée d'artillerie de Paris* remonte à
1788. On avait commencé une première réunion d'armes

et de machines, qui fut pillée le 14 juillet 1789. En 1795, ce musée se trouvait reconstitué au couvent des dominicains-jacobins de Saint-Thomas d'Aquin, et enrichi, en 1799, par la célèbre collection de l'arsenal de Strasbourg; en 1804, par la galerie que les ducs de Bouillon avaient jadis formée à Sedan. Pillé de nouveau en 1830, le musée perdit peu de ses trésors, dont la plus grande partie lui fut rendue après les journées de Juillet. En 1852, vingt des plus riches et des plus curieuses pièces furent extraites du Musée d'artillerie, pour être placées dans celui des souverains, au Louvre, perte qui fut en partie réparée par un décret impérial, qui fit passer au Musée d'artillerie les précieuses armes de la bibliothèque de la rue de Richelieu. Depuis lors beaucoup de dons ont été faits à cette belle collection, parmi lesquels se signalent ceux de l'empereur Napoléon III et du baron des Mazis. Aujourd'hui elle constitue la plus riche et une des mieux organisées, car l'excellent classement dû au savant conservateur, M. Penguilly-l'Haridon, laisse peu à désirer. Il y a cinquante numéros pour les armes de l'âge de la pierre, cent cinquante pour celles de l'âge de bronze, et de l'antiquité, trente pour l'âge de fer, dix-neuf cent soixante-dix pour les armes et armures du moyen âge, de la Renaissance et du dix-septième et du dix-huitième siècle, trois mille pour les armes orientales et modernes, les bouches à feu, les machines et divers autres objets; en tout, cinq mille deux cents numéros, catalogués avec soin.

Une autre vieille et importante *collection d'armes et armures* est celle des *comtes d'Erbach*, au château d'Erbach, dans la Hesse-Darmstadt, près Hoppenheim. Elle a été formée à la fin du dix-huitième et au commence-

ment du dix-neuvième siècle par le comte François, collectionneur passionné. On y trouve quatre cent soixante
armes offensives et défensives, six cent vingt armes à
feu, et quelques centaines d'armes de l'âge de la pierre,
du bronze et du fer, antiques, celtiques et germaniques, etc. M. le comte Eberhard, petit-fils du fondateur, en a rédigé lui-même le catalogue.

L'*Armeria*, *à Turin*, a été fondée par le roi Charles-
Albert, en 1833. M. le comte Vittorio Seyssel, d'Aix, en
a publié, en 1840, le catalogue, qui contient 1,554 numéros d'armes anciennes et modernes, parmi lesquelles
il y a un grand nombre d'armes défensives rares et artistiques.

Le *Musée de Sigmaringen* est, comme celui de
Munich et de Turin, une création nouvelle, car la première réunion d'objets d'art n'y remonte qu'à l'année 1842. On trouvera, dans le *Guide artistique pour
l'Allemagne*, de l'auteur, un chapitre spécial qui donne
sommairement la description des nombreuses et riches
collections que le prince de Hohenzollern a su réunir
dans sa résidence, et qui ont été encore grandement augmentées par l'achat récent de la collection de
l'intendant des beaux-arts du prince, M. le baron de
Mayenfisch. Le conseiller docteur Lehner, attaché comme
conservateur et bibliothécaire, est chargé actuellement
d'organiser les catalogues chronologiques par séries, et
de publier la reproduction des pièces les plus remarquables, au moyen de la photographie. La *collection des
armes et armures contient plus de 3,000 pièces*, parmi
lesquelles il y en a de très-précieuses, au point de vue
artistique et historique. Le bâtiment que le prince a
fait construire, dans le style gothique anglais, sur les

plans de Krüger de Dusseldorf, est harmonieux dans ses formes et digne de son contenu. Les peintures à fresque du professeur Müller, de Dusseldorff, forment déjà une œuvre d'art qui vaut le voyage à Sigmaringen, où l'amateur trouve des musées composés de toutes les branches, à l'exception de l'histoire naturelle et d'instruments de physique. M. de Hefner-Alteneck a aussi déjà publié un ouvrage sur ces musées, où l'on retrouve l'exactitude habituelle de ce dessinateur scrupuleux.

Le *Musée national bavarois*, aujourd'hui déjà un des plus riches en objets d'art gothiques et de la Renaissance, a été créé en 1853, sous le règne du roi Maximilien II. Il occupe les cinquante-neuf salles des trois étages d'un vaste bâtiment. C'est à l'activité énergique de feu le baron Aretin et aux solides connaissances du directeur actuel, M. de Hefner-Alteneck, que l'Allemagne doit la réunion rapide de tant de trésors, parmi lesquels on compte plus de *mille armes et armures anciennes*. La construction du bâtiment est défectueuse, sous tous les rapports, et le classement irrationnel. Heureusement, le nouveau directeur est occupé à rendre le classement plus propre à l'étude par un catalogue chronologique et générique. Le nombre prodigieux et la valeur artistique et historique de la plupart des objets exposés placent le *Bairische national Museum* au premier rang de ces sortes d'établissements civilisateurs.

On trouve en outre à Munich une collection d'armes anciennes à l'*Arsenal de la ville :* ce sont des pièces qui ont appartenu aux corporations. L'établissement remonte au quatorzième siècle; mais l'organisation ne date que de 1866. Tout y est groupé par ordre chronologique, afin de montrer l'armement bourgeois reconstitué pour ainsi dire par époque, dont la dernière s'arrête à la fin de la guerre de Trente ans. L'arsenal de la ville de Munich, pour lequel le conservateur, M. Kaspar Braun a publié en 1866 un catalogue-notice, contient environ en tout quatorze cents armes et armures anciennes pour hommes et pour chevaux.

Le roi de Suède, Charles XV, s'est aussi formé un cabinet *d'armes anciennes*, composé en majeure partie de la collection Soldinska, de Nuremberg, acquises vers 1856. Il y a plus de mille numéros, parmi lesquels on remarque beaucoup d'armes orientales et bon nombre d'armes occidentales du seizième et du dix-septième siècle. Une série de reproductions de cette belle collection a été publiée chez Lahure, à Paris.

Le cabinet d'armes de l'empereur Napoléon III, composé depuis peu d'années seulement, et qui se trouve installé au château de Pierrefonds, est déjà un des plus riches, particulièrement en belles armures allemandes de tournois des meilleures époques. Selon le catalogue publié par M. O. Penguilly-l'Haridon, il contient cinq cent vingt-cinq armes et armures anciennes et quatre machines de guerre antiques, dont deux *balistes* euthytone ou oxybèle, faussement appelées catapultes, destinées à lancer des flèches, reconstruites d'après les désignations de Hiéron et de Philon, auteurs grecs, qui vivaient à l'époque des successeurs d'Alexandre, et celles de Vitruve, que l'on suppose avoir vécu sous le règne d'Auguste. Les deux autres sont des *catapultes* palitones également reconstituées d'après les descriptions de Hiéron. Ces quatre machines de guerre ont été transportées depuis quelque temps au musée de Saint-Germain. Des reproductions photographiques de la collection, par Chevalier, ont été publiées en 1867 par Claye, mais ne se trouvent point dans le commerce.

Une autre belle collection d'armes et d'armures anciennes, de création récente, est celle de M. le *sénateur comte de Nieuwerkerke*, installée au Louvre, dans les appartements qu'il y occupe. Ce cabinet, entièrement formé de pièces de choix, compte déjà plus de trois cent trente numéros que M. de Beaumont s'occupe de cataloguer, ouvrage qui sera illustré d'eaux fortes.

On peut encore signaler, pour la France, le *Musée de Chartres*, qui possède une bonne collection d'armes anciennes, parmi lesquelles le harnais attribué à Philippe IV, le Bel (1285-1314), où le bacinet seul indique le temps, car la cotte de mailles, dont une partie est moderne, se rapporte à plusieurs époques.

Pour l'étude des armes en pierre et en bronze, primitives et antiques, ce sont les *musées de Mayence*, de *Copenhague*, de *Schwerin*, de *Sigmaringen* et de *Saint-Germain*, et la collection ethnographique *Cristy à Londres* qui offrent le plus de ressources.

Tous les amateurs connaissent les musées d'armes de *Madrid* et de *Tzarskoe-Selo à Saint-Pétersbourg*, dont les morceaux les plus remarquables ont été publiés en reproductions lithographiques et photographiques; mais personne n'a encore donné de notices concernant leur formation et celle des musées de *Venise* et de *Malte*.

Quant aux *arsenaux des cantons suisses*, qui remontent aux premières guerres, mais qui contiennent peu de choses dont l'origine soit antérieure à la fin du quinzième siècle, il n'y a que ceux de Genève, de Soleure, de Lucerne et de Berne qui possèdent ce qu'on peut appeler une collection d'armes anciennes; Morat, Zurich,

Bâle et Liesthal sont moins richement dotées sous ce rapport, et les autres capitales cantonales n'ont presque plus rien de leurs armures et armes offensives.

La Hollande ne possède pas de *musée d'armes anciennes* et n'a rien non plus dans ses arsenaux; les collections particulières sont rares : on n'en peut mentionner que celle de M. le baron de Bogaert van Heeswyk, à son château près Bois-le-Duc, et de feu Kruseman, peintre, qui appartient aujourd'hui à la Société archéologique d'Amsterdam.

Quant à la collection d'armes anciennes de *Bruxelles*, elle est assez nombreuse et se trouve installée au musée. de la *porte de Hall*.

En outre des musées de premier ordre qui ont été cités, il existe encore bon nombre de collections fort importantes, en grande partie mentionnées à côté des pièces reproduites dans le courant de cet ouvrage, et si on compte les cabinets en formation, on peut admettre que le goût pour les armes égale presque celui qui s'est manifesté si universellement pour la céramique.

HISTOIRE ABRÉGÉE

DES ARMES ANCIENNES

Partout, aussi bien chez les peuples primitifs que chez les nations civilisées, la question de l'armement a été d'une grande importance. Dès son origine, l'homme, exposé sur la terre sans moyens de défense, a dû imaginer des engins pour repousser les attaques de ses effrayants copossesseurs, à qui, en les privant de la raison, la force créatrice avait accordé, comme compensation, des défenses naturelles. L'arme, inventée pour la destruction, est devenue le plus puissant moyen de civilisation et sa garantie ; le perfectionnement de ces instruments meurtriers a constamment suppléé au nombre et fait triompher en définitive la raison, car, dans les temps modernes, le conquérant le plus avide même contribue à la civilisation, puisqu'il est toujours suivi par les pionniers de la culture matérielle et intellectuelle. La poudre à canon a dû ouvrir la voie à l'imprimerie, et supprimer les haltes et les reculades du progrès, en suppléant à la faiblesse des minorités policées vis-à-vis des masses barbares. L'esprit avait trouvé le moyen de résister à la brute et de la vaincre. S'il faut déplorer la guerre, on ne doit pas regretter le perfectionnement constant des armes qui, tout en la rendant plus meurtrière à des moments donnés, l'abrége en la rendant en définitive moins funeste à l'humanité.

Même chez les peuples plus arriérés, le perfectionnement de l'armement ne peut rien avoir de redoutable pour la marche progressive de la société, puisque tous les progrès sont solidaires, et dès que la culture intellectuelle gagne du terrain dans n'importe quelle branche, les mauvaises chances de guerre injuste et les craintes pour le règne de la force brutale diminuent.

Des premières civilisations connues, de celles de l'Inde et de l'Amérique, c'est cette dernière, perdue et presque ignorée, qui a laissé la plus ancienne trace d'une arme défensive perfectionnée dans sa forme. C'est le casque dont est coiffée la figure d'un bas-relief de Palanqué, de ces ruines de la ville de Culhuacan qui remonte peut-être à trois mille cinq cents ans, et qui avait une circonférence de plus de trente kilomètres.

Pour se rendre un compte exact de la marche progressive de la fabrication des armes chez les différents peuples, et des transitions et affiliations qui se remarquent dans les formes de tous ces produits, on doit les classer en quatre séries distinctes : Armes des époques antéhistoriques de l'âge de la pierre brute ou taillée par éclats et de la pierre polie; — Armes de l'âge dit du bronze, catégorie où entrent aussi bien les produits des anciens que ceux des Scandinaves, des Germains, des Bretons, des Celtes, des Gaulois et autres; — Armes premières de l'âge dit du fer, qui comprend l'époque mérovingienne et celle des règnes de quelques rois carlovingiens, c'est-à-dire de la fin de l'antiquité et de la première période du moyen âge; — et enfin les Armes du moyen âge, de la Renaissance et du dix-septième et du dix-huitième siècle.

L'établissement d'un âge du bronze ne signifie pas que le

fer était inconnu à cette période; il indique seulement que
l'usage en était peu répandu, et que presque tous les outils
et toutes les armes, même tranchantes, étaient en bronze
chez la plupart des peuples. Les lingots de fer en forme de coin
ou de pioche et les quelques autres objets en fer forgé, conservés les uns et les autres au musée Assyrien du Louvre,
et encore bien plus le fragment de cotte de mailles assyrien en *acier*, du musée Britannique, démontrent qu'au
dixième siècle avant Jésus-Christ, les Assyriens connaissaient parfaitement ce métal aussi bien que les Égyptiens.
Trente passages dans l'*Iliade* et dans l'*Odyssée*, où le fer est
souvent désigné sous l'épithète du métal « difficile à travailler, » démontrent que les Grecs le connaissaient également. Du reste, le bronze, mélange de métaux (appelé dans
le dictionnaire de Grimm très-improprement *messing*, laiton), dont l'équivalent n'existe pas dans la nature et que
l'homme a dû se former d'un composé qui varie selon les
pays et l'époque, — tantôt cuivre et étain, tantôt cuivre,
étain, plomb, *spisglas*, etc., — a pour condition la connaissance de la fusion mélangée, puisque si le cuivre pur peut
être ouvré directement au moyen du martelage, le bronze
doit être soumis à l'action du coulage. La préparation
du fer ne demande qu'un degré supérieur de chaleur de
l'oxygène et sa séparation du carbone pour être martelé, —
moyens que les Cafres même, qui se servent d'outres pour
faire passer l'oxygène dans leurs fournaises, n'ignorent pas.
Le bronze, au lieu de précéder, a dû nécessairement suivre
l'emploi du fer, qui pouvait être ouvré sans fusion complète.

La terre, le bois, la peau de l'animal et la pierre, répandus
sur tout le globe, ont dû être nécessairement les premières
matières que l'homme a employées à la confection de ses
ustensiles et de ses armes. L'emploi de la pierre pour la
fabrication de ces dernières remonte partout à l'enfance des
peuples, et ce sont encore ces mêmes créations naïves qui
composent l'armement du sauvage. Il y a même des pays,

où, malgré la connaissance de la préparation et de l'emploi des métaux pour d'autres usages, on a continué longtemps à se servir exclusivement de la pierre pour la fabrication des armes offensives. Telle était l'Amérique avant sa découverte définitive. Le silex, la calcédoine, la serpentine et particulièrement la fragile obsidienne noire, dans laquelle l'Inca se taillait aussi ses miroirs, y étaient employés pour faire les lames des lances, des épées et des flèches, les haches de guerre et les couteaux, car le cuivre ou le bronze n'y servait qu'à la confection des outils.

En Europe les armes en pierre remontent à la plus haute antiquité, et elles contribuent à démontrer que l'homme a déjà existé durant la troisième époque géologique, puisque l'image du mastodonte ou mammouth, gravée sur de la corne trouvée dans le Périgord, et de nombreux ossements d'ours de caverne, mêlés avec des haches en silex, recueillis dans des terrains plutoniques, ont dû apporter de nouveaux documents. Quand ces gravures auront été examinées au microscope, afin de s'assurer de toute absence de fraude, on pourra discuter l'hypothèse. Il ne suffit cependant pas que ces armes et ces ossements soient recueillis dans des terrains *alluviens-diluviens* qui peuvent avoir été soumis à des perturbations, comme cela est démontré par les *dépôts-meubles*, ainsi nommés parce qu'ils sont composés d'objets appartenant à différentes époques.

Le *diluvium* (Alpin) non remué ne contient aucune matière organique à l'état d'*ossine*, substance qui caractérise l'*os non fossile*, de sorte que toute alluvion contenant le moindre *os avec ossine* est postérieur à la grande perturbation terrestre, appelée déluge.

Beaucoup d'armes et outils en pierres façonnées offrent aussi un signe sûr pour reconnaître qu'ils ne remontent pas au delà du déluge : c'est qu'ils sont fabriqués avec des *galets* où tout indique qu'ils ont été *roulés avant d'être façonnés.*

Il serait impossible d'établir la priorité d'un peuple sur

un autre, pour la fabrication première de ces armes, puisqu'on en a rencontré partout. Il s'est trouvé en France des
armes en silex taillées par éclats, mêlées avec des os de
rennes et des *os fossiles*, les uns et les autres parfois sculp-
tés par la main de l'homme et adaptés comme manches
à la pierre qui forme toujours le tranchant, et dont la fabrication sans instruments de métal ni acides corrosifs ne s'explique que par la facilité avec laquelle le silex, fraîchement
sorti des carrières et avant d'avoir subi l'influence de l'air,
se prête à la division par éclats. Des démarcations exactes
entre les soi-disant âges de la pierre brute, de la pierre
polie et même du bronze, peuvent être établies avec aussi
peu de certitude que tout ce qui touche aux époques plus
ou moins antéhistoriques. On a trouvé les deux et même
les trois produits entremêlés, ce qui indique des époques
de transition. Les fouilles opérées au cimetière germanique
à Hallstatt près Ischl, en Autriche, ont fourni des armes et
des instruments en pierre, en bronze, en fer, dont quelques-
uns sont même moitié bronze et moitié fer, le tout confondu
dans les mêmes tombeaux, dont plus de mille ont été visités.
Les rebuts de cuisine (*Kiokkenmoeding*) du Danemark aussi
bien que les objets recueillis dans les palaffites des habitations lacustres de la Suisse, de la Savoie et du duché de
Bade, quoique tous trouvés dans des terrains alluviens,
peuvent cependant être attribués avec certitude à l'âge de la
pierre pure où les armes et ustensiles ne montrent aucune
trace de métal, tandis que les palaffites découverts près
Noceto, à Castiane, près Parme, et à Peschiera, appartiennent à l'époque qui correspond à l'âge dit du bronze.

De toutes ces armes primitives, ce sont celles trouvées
dans le Danemark (actuellement contrefaites en Allemagne),
qui montrent le plus de fini; elles paraissent indiquer, chose
fort curieuse, que la civilisation à ces époques était peut-
être plus avancée dans le nord que dans les parties centrales de l'Europe. Il faut cependant tenir compte que ces

armes ont été trouvées dans des alluvions, et qu'elles doivent être plus modernes que celles des cavernes et des terrains diluviens ou quaternaires.

Quant aux armes en pierre polie, elles sont le plus souvent en serpentine granitique, pierre peu dure quoique plus dure que la serpentine ordinaire. On en a aussi trouvé en silex, en calcédoine, en basalte, en jade et en jadaïque de différentes couleurs. La pierre jadaïque, si fréquente en Auvergne, est de la même espèce que celle utilisée jadis pour la fabrication des amulettes contre les maladies de reins, ce qui l'avait fait nommer pierre néphrétique. Les talismans ou *pierres de victoire* des sagas scandinaves n'étaient probablement pas autre chose que des serpentines. On a trouvé des petits coins, trop petits pour tout autre usage, où le passage du fil avec lequel on suspendait le talisman est indiqué par un trou. Au Nord, ces pierres sont toujours en *vert*, couleur qui paraît avoir été symbolique et sympathique aux peuples teutons, puisqu'elle se retrouve dominante plus tard dans leurs émaux et dans leurs miniatures, tandis que c'est le *bleu* qui règne dans ces mêmes productions d'origine gauloise et française. La haute antiquité paraît avoir eu encore des armes en pierre en même temps que des armes en bronze et en fer, puisque les musées de Londres et de Berlin possèdent plusieurs exemplaires assyriens et égyptiens très-anciens.

On a trouvé des armes en bronze, aussi fréquemment dans le Nord que sur les sols classiques. Peut-être ont-elles été introduites dans l'Occident par des peuples orientaux conquérants, puisque les armes de l'âge dit du bronze des différents pays se ressemblent plus entre elles que celles des autres époques, et dans les sagas scandinaves même, les conquérants traitent avec mépris les peuples encore réduits aux armes de pierre et les appellent : « les petits démons de la terre. » L'usage des armes en bronze n'a pas même complétement cessé dans les Gaules, après la conquête de César, et on peut admettre que la supériorité des armes en fer avait contribué au succès des Francs comme elle avait contribué à celui des Romains.

Si on veut se rendre apte à savoir classer chronologiquement les armes de ces époques dont les produits se ressemblent et dans lesquelles les périodes de transition sont si fréquentes, il faut étudier la construction et les dotations des différents tombeaux. Les monticules très-élevés, entourés ou surmontés de pierres plus ou moins colossales (*dolmens*), et dont les caveaux fermés ordinairement de dalles renferment des ossements non brûlés et des armes en pierre, peuvent être regardés comme des tombeaux très-anciens. La seconde catégorie se signale le plus souvent par un monticule moins élevé, par l'absence des grands blocs de pierre, par un caveau ou tombeau formé de pierres brutes de petites dimensions entassées avec peu d'art, et par *l'urne* qui indique la *crémation*. Ces sépulcres contiennent ordinairement des produits en bronze. Les tombeaux encore moins élevés, et dont la construction est presque entièrement en terre, appartiennent à la troisième période où la crémation avait de nouveau fait place à l'inhumation et où les sépulcres forment souvent des cimetières dans la direction du sud au nord.

Dès qu'il s'agit des armes antiques, il faut particulièrement rechercher les premières traces parvenues jusqu'à nous, sur les monuments hindous, assyriens et égyptiens. Depuis la fondation, au vingt-cinquième siècle avant Jésus-Christ, des villes de Ninive et de Babylone par Assur et par Nemrod, jusqu'au troisième siècle avant Jésus-Christ, au règne de Sardanapale V, il n'existe cependant pas de monuments où l'on pourrait recueillir les moindres notions sur l'armement du soldat des cinq grandes monarchies asiatiques. On ignore ainsi complétement l'équipement des armées avec lesquelles Bélus chassa, en 1992, les Arabes, et Ninus, son fils, conquit l'Arménie, la Médie et presque toute l'Asie septentrionale; et rien n'indique de quelle manière étaient confectionnées les armes brillantes en usage sous la fastueuse Sémiramis, la veuve de Ninus qui, de 1968 à 1916 étendit l'empire jusqu'à l'Indus et entassa à Babylone des richesses fabuleuses. A partir du règne de Ninyas, son fils, l'histoire même ne fournit sur la longue suite des rois successeurs de Ninyas que quelques récits sur le fameux Sardapanale, détrôné en 759.

Les bas-reliefs et moulages de bas-reliefs chaldéens, babyloniens, assyriens, médiques et persiques du Louvre, des musées Britannique, de Berlin, de Munich et de Zurich, suppléent heureusement aux documents écrits et fournissent ample matière pour l'histoire de l'armement de ces monarchies militaires, à partir du treizième jusqu'au septième siècle avant Jésus-Christ; car contrairement aux monuments hindous et égyptiens, les sujets de ces sculptures, presque toutes pourvues d'inscriptions cunéiformes, offrent, pour la plupart, des épisodes guerriers, qui permettent presque de reconstruire entièrement l'armement du soldat de ces vastes contrées durant sept siècles, où l'équipement militaire paraît y avoir éprouvé fort peu de changement, et le précieux document de Sennachérib (712-707) démontre que le soldat chaldéen était armé comme le soldat assyrien.

L'infanterie de la troupe régulière avait pour armes défensives le casque à jugulaires, quelquefois orné d'un cimier à crinière; le bouclier rond et le long pavois pour le siége; la cuirasse ou plutôt le corselet confectionné avec des lames de métal cousues sur étoffe ou peau, et aussi de véritables cottes en *mailles d'acier*, telles que le fragment du musée Britannique le démontre; ou enfin la longue tunique, probablement en buffle. Des cnémides ou jambières (tumelières) couvraient le devant de la jambe jusqu'en dessous de la rotule. Les armes offensives étaient la lance, l'épée, la fronde et l'arc. Le soldat, auxiliaire comme celui de la milice, portait ou le casque sans jugulaires ni cimier ou un simple bandeau à jugulaires, en cuir ou métal, qui ressemble à celui du guerrier franc mérovingien. Son bouclier, ordinairement de hauteur d'appui quand il était rond et de deux tiers de la hauteur de l'homme quand il était allongé, était le plus souvent carré en bas et arrondi en haut; semi-circulaire, il enveloppait presque le corps du soldat qui portait la longue tunique, et avait, comme le troupier d'élite, pour arme offensive l'épée, qui pendait du côté *gauche*, la lance, la fronde et l'arc. L'archer perse des bas-reliefs de Persépolis, l'ancienne capitale de la Perside et de toute l'ancienne monarchie perse (560), est souvent coiffé d'un casque ou bonnet d'armes qui a presque la forme de la toque de la magistrature française. Deux moulages de ces bas-reliefs, exposés au musée Britannique, montrent en outre des *casques à lames* et même à *mentonnière*, qui ressemblent grandement aux casques de la seconde partie du moyen âge chrétien.

Le cavalier assyrien, qui montait sans selle ni éperons, était coiffé d'un casque à jugulaires, mais sans cimier, et dont la forme semi-conique, dans le genre des casques dits gaulois, différait des casques portés par les hommes de pied; il avait rarement un bouclier, mais la cuirasse ou plutôt le corselet de mailles, espèce de squamata où la dossière était terminée par une sorte de tablier arrondi de mineur, qui ressemblait au garde-reins de l'armure à plates du moyen âge chrétien, et qui était comme celui-ci destiné à protéger le bas du dos. Il portait en outre une culotte d'armes fabriquée de la même manière que le corselet, et toujours la lance et l'épée.

L'archer, qui est quelquefois représenté à cheval, avait le corselet, mais rarement le casque. Comme chez le milicien, la tête n'était protégée que par le bandeau. Souvent le bas des jambes de l'archer montre des cnémides. A pied, il est vêtu de la longue tunique. Outre l'arc, les flèches et le carquois, il avait l'épée, mais pas de lance. Les Assyriens connaissaient le char de guerre qui se trouve sur plusieurs de leurs bas-reliefs du treizième siècle avant J.-C., ce que paraît infirmer l'opinion de Virgile qui attribue l'invention de ces chars à Érichthonius, roi d'Athènes, et celle de quelques auteurs qui la mettent sur le compte de Triptolème et de Trochilus. On voit aussi sur ces précieuses sculptures granitiques la catapulte et la baliste, dont l'invention appartient aux Assyriens, ce qui est attesté par les Anciens. La forme de ces machines de guerre destinées à lancer contre l'ennemi des traits et des projectiles de toute nature, pour battre en brèche les murailles des villes assiégées et atteindre de loin leurs défenseurs, diffère peu des engins grecs et romains. Quant à ce qui concerne les armes perses anciennes, on n'a pour tout guide que quelques moulages de bas-reliefs de Persépolis, exposés au Louvre et au musée Britannique parmi les bas-reliefs chaldéens, babyloniens, assyriens et médiques. L'armement défensif se rapproche là, comme il a été déjà observé, bien plus de celui de l'Europe durant le moyen âge que de l'armement asiatique. On y trouve le casque à lames superposées et à mentonnière, et peut-être à visière ou vue à pivot. Mithras, sacrifiant le taureau (monument reproduit par De la Chaussée, dans son M. Rom.), porte le casque à timbre bombé dans le genre étrusque. Cette sculpture, que l'on croit remonter à l'époque de la naissance de l'auteur de la réformation du magisme et du parsisme, époque qui flotte entre le douzième et le sixième siècle, offre peu de sûreté. Il est douteux que la forme de ce casque et encore moins celle du glaive avec lequel le dieu sacrifie, et qui rappelle la dague indienne actuelle, remonte aux anciens Perses dont la langue, le Zend, morte depuis longtemps, sert encore aux prêtres guèbres à réciter leurs prières, quoiqu'ils n'en comprennent plus le sens. Le casque perse en bronze et également bombé, de la dynastie des Sassanides (226-552), conservé au musée Britannique, rappelle même tout à fait la coupe du casque allemand à timbre bombé du dixième siècle.

Après la quatrième dynastie, celle des califes (652) jusqu'à la fin de la douzième, celle des Mongols, et autres dominateurs mahométans, l'armement prend en Perse entièrement le caractère musulman. Durant le règne de la dynastie des Sophis (1499 à 1736), les armes persanes n'ont presque pas changé de formes et se ressemblent toutes. Les miniatures d'une copie, faite au commencement du dix-septième siècle, du Schah-Nameh ou livre royal, composé par le poëte Fisdûsi, sous le règne de Mahmoud (999), et qui se trouve à la bibliothèque de Munich, montrent presque aussi les mêmes formes de casques et les mêmes armes que l'on trouve encore actuellement dans l'armement de la Perse, d'où nous est venu le cimeterre, dont le nom dérive du persan *chimichir* ou *chimchir*, arme appelée par les Allemands *seymitar*, l'*acinace* romain, l'aïeul du sabre, le *Sable* ou *Saebel* allemand, connu déjà par les Daces et de l'autre côté du Rhin, vers le quatrième siècle, et introduit dans le reste de l'Europe centrale à partir de la première croisade.

L'armement chaldéen et médique se confond avec celui des Assyriens. Le soldat de l'ancienne Babylone peuplée par les Chaldéens de la mer, dont la capitale était Teredon, paraît cependant avoir eu, à la place du casque conique, une coiffure d'armes semblable à celle représentée sur le bas-relief perside déjà mentionné, et qui a la forme d'une toque. La Médie, le plus puissant royaume parmi ceux qui se formèrent aux dépens du premier empire assyrien, pourrait être difficilement séparée, quant aux armements de ses troupes, de la Persique, d'autant plus que son premier roi Arbacès ne remonte qu'à 759 avant Jésus-Christ et que le royaume des Mèdes fut englobé déjà dans la Perse sous Cyrus, en 536. C'est à partir de cette époque que les dénominations de Mèdes, Médiques, Perses et Persiques,

furent toujours confondues et employées indistinctement
pour les habitants de ces diverses contrées, car même les
guerres persiques contre les Grecs sont nommées *guerres
médiques.*

Sans tenir compte de l'histoire fabuleuse dans laquelle
les Hindous font remonter leur origine à une antiquité
exagérée, on peut placer la première dynastie connue de
leurs rois, celle des Chandras, à l'an 3200 avant Jésus-
Christ, dynastie qui avait été probablement précédée déjà
de plusieurs civilisations aujourd'hui ignorées. Il est à regretter que les gouverneurs anglais qui se sont succédé
aux Indes n'aient pas recueilli plus des nombreuses et
grandioses ruines architecturales dont le sol est encore
couvert. Les quelques sculptures conservées aux musées
Britannique et de Kensington sont insuffisantes, et ni le
Louvre, ni le musée de Berlin, ne possèdent rien de ces
singulières ciselures, figures tordues et contournées dans le
goût des sculptures religieuses européennes de la fin du
dix-septième siècle et du commencement du dix-huitième.
Les musées ne possèdent donc aucun monument pour l'é-
tude de l'armement hindou. Les photographies exposées
au Kinsington-Museum, qui reproduisent un grand nombre
de ruines de palais, de temples, et quelques pierres mémoratives en granit sculpté, démontrent que les Hindous,
comme les Égyptiens, aimaient peu à perpétuer leurs faits
d'armes sur les édifices ; car, parmi toutes ces sculptures,
il n'y a que les quelques pierres de Beenjanuggur, les *Hunguls*, qui offrent des sujets guerriers, et encore ne remontent-
elles pas plus haut qu'à l'époque correspondante à la première moitié du moyen âge chrétien. Les personnages de
ces épisodes démontrent que l'armement hindou a peu varié pour les armes offensives, et que c'est seulement dans
les casques qu'un changement radical s'est manifesté à partir
du quatorzième et du quinzième siècle de notre ère, lorsque
le goût arabe a commencé à réagir contre ce qui l'avait

presque effacé dans ses propres produits. Quant à l'armement javanais un peu ancien, il n'y a que la belle statue
de la déesse de la guerre, au musée de Berlin, qui fournisse
quelques indications par rapport à l'*épée* qu'elle porte.

Les monuments funéraires et civils de l'Égypte, pays où
le génie de la nation était plus porté vers l'agriculture et
les sciences que vers la guerre, offrent également bien
moins de sujets militaires que les monuments assyriens.
Denon, dans ses *Voyages dans la Basse et Haute-Egypte*, a
donné, il est vrai, quelques reproductions d'armes ainsi que
M. Prisse d'Avesnes dans ses *Monuments égyptiens*, mais
c'est trop peu, même réuni aux bas-reliefs de Thèbes et
aux quelques armes en nature conservées aux musées du
Louvre, de Londres et de Berlin, pour pouvoir se faire
une idée exacte de l'armement de toute la troupe égyptienne. On y trouve un casque qui rappelle le bonnet à
grelot du bouffon du moyen âge chrétien et le casque du
hungul hindou; une cotte en écailles de bronze dont
M. Prisse d'Avesnes a donné le dessin d'après un monument
qui remonte aux Pharaons (18ᵉ dynastie, 1000 avant Jésus-
Christ) à juger par l'inscription biblique gravée sur une
de ces écailles qui mesure 20 mètres sur 35. Le bouclier,
carré en bas et arrondi en haut, est percé d'un trou à
travers lequel le soldat pouvait distinguer l'ennemi sans
se découvrir : c'est une arme qui était presque de la hauteur de l'homme. L'arc, les flèches avec leur carquois;
un *pare-coup*, instrument fort singulier qui rappelle
l'usage de la petite rondelle à crochets et les brise-épées
du moyen âge, servant, comme ceux-là, à saisir et à
rompre l'épée de l'adversaire; quelques épées ou plutôt
quelques coutelas à un seul tranchant dans le genre du
scrama-saxe mérovingien et rarement la lance à lame de
métal : voilà tout ce que l'on connaît sur l'armement de
ce pays, car l'espèce de capuchon du guerrier blessé, d'un
bas-relief de Thèbes ne permet pas de distinguer si c'est

bien là une arme défensive ou un simple vêtement. Les quelques dagues en bronze, conservées au musée égyptien du Louvre, paraissent indiquer par leurs formes l'origine grec, quoique ces armes aient été trouvées en Égypte. La cotte en peau de crocodile au musée égyptien du Belvédère de Vienne, et la dague en bronze au musée de Berlin, paraissent cependant remonter à la haute antiquité égyptienne.

L'Étrurie, la Grèce et Rome nous ont heureusement laissé assez d'armes où l'art se manifeste aussi bien dans l'ensemble de la forme que dans l'exécution des détails, et ce n'est qu'à partir des époques où ces pays florissaient que l'on peut baser l'histoire des armes sur des pièces conservées dans un grand nombre de musées.

Les armes offensives et défensives grecques au temps d'Homère (1000 ans avant Jésus-Christ), étaient toutes en bronze quoique le fer, comme on a vu, fût connu. L'armure défensive se composait de la cuirasse, plastron et dossière, chaque partie coulée ou martelée d'une seule pièce, et aussi du corselet d'écailles à imbrication; du casque, du grand bouclier convexe rond, et des cnémides ou jambières. Les armes offensives étaient : l'épée d'estoc et de taille, à lame droite, d'abord courte et large, plus tard longue, à deux tranchants, à pointe aiguë et à fourreau de forme carrée, toujours portée au côté *droit*; le *parazonium*, dague courte et large, espèce de langue de bœuf, portée du côté *gauche*; la lance de 11 à 15 pieds de longueur, à lame large, longue et aiguë, arrondie vers la douille et à arrêt saillant au milieu, servant d'arme de hast et de jet; le javelot avec son *amentum* ou lanière, sorte de longue flèche. Les Grecs n'avaient pas de cavalerie alors, ils manquaient même de terme pour désigner l'action de monter à cheval, ce qui est probablement la cause que la langue française manque de substantif pour rendre le *Reiten* des Allemands. Plus tard, 400 ans avant Jésus-Christ, les Grecs ajoutèrent à leurs corps d'armée ceux des frondeurs et des cavaliers.

L'armement étrusque, dont une partie devait précéder dans ce travail l'armement grec, montre dans la première période l'influence phénicienne, comme il montre dans la suite celle de la Grèce avec laquelle l'Etrurie, après l'émigration d'Énée, était unie par tant de liens. La troisième période est purement romaine; tout y est resté dans l'obscurité. Polybe, né en l'année 552 de la fondation de Rome, ou 202 ans avant Jésus-Christ, le premier auteur qui a décrit les armes du soldat romain, n'a parlé que de celles de son époque. Les indications laissées par ce maître et ami du second Scipion l'Africain, jointes aux faibles renseignements que fournissent quelques sculptures tombales trouvées aux bords du Rhin en Allemagne, les colonnes Trajane et Antonine et l'arc d'Orange forment à peu près tout ce qui est connu sur cette matière. Grâce aux chants dits d'Homère, on est mieux renseigné sur les armes grecques en usage au dixième siècle avant Jésus-Christ, sinon même au treizième, à l'époque du siége de Troie, que sur celles avec lesquelles le peuple-roi avait assujetti le monde. Il est fort probable que les Romains, comme les Grecs et les Étrusques, ne se servaient d'abord pour la fabrication de leurs armes offensives que du bronze; mais du temps de Polybe ce métal n'était plus employé que pour les casques, plastrons, cnémides et autres armes défensives. Lorsque la Gaule employait encore exclusivement le bronze, les armes romaines de trait, d'estoc, de taille et de hast étaient donc déjà toutes en fer et en acier.

L'armée romaine se composait de trois espèces de troupes : les *vélites*, fantassins armés à la légère, les *hastaires* ou légionnaires, et les *cavaliers*. Les premiers étaient armés de javelots minces, de deux coudées de longueur et où le fer mesurait une palme, de l'épée et d'un

4

petit bouclier léger, rond ou ovale, qui mesurait 3 pieds et s'appelait *parma*, dès que sa forme était arrondie. C'était le même bouclier dont se servaient les gladiateurs. Le casque, ordinairement à jugulaires, était sans crinière mais quelquefois garni de peau de loup. Le hastaire, protégé par un casque en fer ou en cuir, panaché de trois plumes rouges et noires, par des jambières (*ocræ*) et par un plastron ou une cuirasse (le corselet à deux épauliers), le tout en bronze, ainsi que par le grand bouclier convexe, en bois, peau et fer, de 4 pieds de long sur 2 1/2 de large, avait pour armes offensives l'épée ibérique qu'il portait comme le soldat grec, du côté *droit*, deux javelots dont l'un était le célèbre *pilum* légionnaire que nous retrouverons plus tard dans l'armement franc. Le frondeur était armé de la fronde imitée des Achéens.

Le cavalier, au temps de Polybe, prit l'équipement grec. Dépourvu, avant cette époque, d'armes défensives autres que le bouclier sexagone, rond ou ovale, en cuir de bœuf, son armement fut rendu plus propre à résister aux formidables coups des barbares. Plus tard, du temps de Trajan et de Septime-Sévère, il fut aussi doté d'une cuirasse flexible, soit de la *squamata* faite d'écailles de fer ou de bronze cousues sur toile ou sur peau, soit de la *hamata*, composée de chaînes de métal, sorte de cotte de mailles comme on en a trouvé à Avenches en Suisse, où on les conserve au musée. La colonne Trajane montre aussi beaucoup de soldats dont les cuirasses ne sont ni en mailles ni en écailles, mais confectionnées avec de longues lames en métal, semblables aux armures du moyen âge, et les bas-reliefs de ce monument prouvent que l'armée romaine était composée d'un grand nombre de corps dont l'armement variait autant que celui de nos armées modernes.

Les Romains comme les Grecs se servaient aussi de machines de guerre, outre le char faucheur, de provenance assyrienne comme beaucoup d'autres machines, et

les béliers, connus déjà à Paloe-Tyros, la vieille Tyr, fondée vers 1900 ans avant Jésus-Christ, et mentionnés dans
l'Ancien Testament, où Ézéchiel (599 ans avant Jésus-
Christ) dit (ch. xxi, v. 27) que « le roi de Babylone dis-
pose déjà les béliers contre les murs de Jérusalem. »

Parmi tous ces engins de guerre mentionnés, la baliste lançait des flèches monstres, et la catapulte ou *tormentum*, de plus gros projectiles, dont quelques-uns
avaient la forme d'un lingot pointu aux deux extrémités,
et qui portaient en Grèce quelquefois l'inscription ΔΕΞΑΙ,
(reçois), telle que la montrent plusieurs exemplaires en
plomb trouvés dans les fouilles. Les Grecs appelaient *euthytones* les catapultes à trajectoire rasante, et *antitones*
celles qui portaient en courbe.

Il y avait aussi le *tolleno*, sorte de bascule à deux paniers, qui versait les combattants dans les places assiégées. M. Rodios parle en outre, dans son ΠΕΡΙ ΠΟΛΕΜΙΚΗΣ
ΤΕΧΝΗΣ, etc. (Athènes, 1868), d'une catapulte ou plutôt
baliste portative, semblable à l'arbalète de notre moyen
âge, et dont il donne la description et le dessin d'après des
textes byzantins; mais on peut conserver des doutes si
cette espèce d'arbalète que M. Rhodios appelle *Gastrafete*,
puisque l'arbalétrier devait l'appuyer sur son ventre, remonte bien aux Grecs et aux Romains, puisque les anciens
textes n'en parlent pas.

On a vu dans l'Introduction que plusieurs de ces machines, décrites par Héron, Philon et Vitruve, et appelées
par eux *catapultes euthytones*, *catapultes oxybetes*, *catapultes palitones*, et *catapultes scorpions*, ont été reconstruites
pour la collection d'armes de l'empereur Napoléon III.
Quant au *polyspaste* ou *grue d'Archimède*, instrument qui
enlevait et brisait des vaisseaux entiers, il est resté indé-
terminé; mais on peut admettre qu'il était identique aux
crochets monstres servant à dégager la tête du bélier, dont
le blindage roulant s'appelait *tortue*. M. Rhodios a aussi

démontré, dans son intéressant ouvrage, que les Grecs, ses ancêtres, possédaient même des machines à explosion, sorte de canons à air comprimé, qui représentaient nos fusils à vent dans des dimensions colossales.

Des armes en bronze, fabriquées souvent plus ou moins sous l'influence des modèles antiques, ont été trouvées dans les tombes de presque tous ces peuples de l'Europe que les Romains appelaient barbares; mais celles de la Scandinavie continentale (Danemark et Allemagne septentrionale) sont, comme les armes danoises de l'âge de la pierre, supérieures aux armes des autres pays du Nord et peu inférieures même aux armes grecques et romaines. Les exemplaires conservés au musée de Copenhague et à celui de Londres, où elles sont rangées parmi les armes anglo-saxonnes et britanniques, prouvent avec quel art ces peuples savaient déjà travailler le métal. L'armement défensif du guerrier scandinave paraît avoir consisté *alors* uniquement dans le bouclier rond ou allongé, dans la cuirasse, dans le casque, quoique aucune arme de la dernière espèce et de cette époque ne se trouve au musée de Copenhague, et que les grands cercles de coiffure puissent faire supposer que le casque n'était porté que par les chefs, comme cela était l'usage chez les Francs et les Germains en général. Le casque en bronze à cornes, trouvé dans la Tamise et conservé au musée Britannique, parmi les armes nationales, pourrait bien être de provenance danoise aussi bien que le bouclier exposé à côté.

Pour les armes celtico-gauloises et bas-bretonnes en bronze, la question se complique encore davantage. Il serait difficile, sinon impraticable, d'établir des catégories distinctes pour celles qui ont été trouvées sur le sol de la France. Tout y est incertitude. Le *celt* même, cette hache ou plus probablement cette lame de javelot si caractéristique par sa douille droite et à anneau, a été trouvé aussi bien en Russie qu'en France et en Italie, en Angleterre qu'en Allemagne, ce qui démontre l'impossibilité d'un classement rigoureux. Le peuple celtique était partout et nulle part !

L'armement du Gaulois, qui était encore, du temps de Jules César, même pour les épées et autres armes offensives, en bronze, consistait pour la défense dans un casque conique très-pointu, tel qu'on le voit au musée de Rouen, et qui était probablement porté par les chefs seulement. L'attribution même de ce casque laisse encore des doutes, parce qu'on en a trouvé de tout pareils à Posen et dans l'Inn en Bavière, où l'arme figure au musée national de Munich sous la désignation de casque *hongrois* ou *avare*. La cuirasse était, comme chez les Romains, de deux pièces entières, telles qu'on les voit au musée d'artillerie de Paris, à celui de Saint-Germain et au Louvre. La défense était complétée par le bouclier. Les sculptures du sarcophage de la Vigna Ammendola et les bas-reliefs de l'arc d'Orange montrent ce bouclier sous deux formes différentes, l'un en ovale, l'autre carré allongé et plus large au milieu qu'aux extrémités. Les armes offensives étaient la hache de différentes formes, parmi lesquelles on a aussi l'habitude de ranger celle du celt déjà mentionnée et que je crois être une lame de javelot; l'épée d'espèces variées, soit la courte épée grecque, soit l'épée à trois tranchants et sans garde telle que la représente le bas-relief romain incrusté dans le piédestal de la *Melpomène* du Louvre. La lance, le javelot et l'arc étaient les armes de hast et de jet. L'enseigne-sanglier gauloise, qui se trouve sur un des bas-reliefs de l'arc d'Orange, montre par sa forme toute l'influence que l'armement romain avait fini par exercer sur celui des Gaulois. On en voit une au musée de Prague, elle est en bronze et a été trouvée en Bohême.

Les armes germaniques de l'âge dit du bronze, en général, laissent autant de vague que celles de la Gaule. Les nombreuses fouilles opérées au cimetière de Hallstatt en Autriche, où l'on a ouvert plus de mille tombeaux germaniques, ont encore augmenté cette incertitude, car les casques en bronze recueillis dans ces sépulcres où ils étaient déposés avec des armes en *bronze*, en *fer* et en *pierre*, ressemblent tout à fait aux casques à double crête, conservés au musée de Saint-Germain et attribués ordinairement aux Étrusques et aux Ombriens, et, par quelques-uns, aux Celtes. On retrouve, presque dans toutes les armes britanniques exposées aux musées d'Angleterre, les formes danoises, et les armes à Hallstatt étaient toujours accompagnées du celt; les courtes épées rappellent partout celle de la Grèce, dont le caractère se retrouve aussi bien sur l'épée scandinave que sur l'épée germanique, sans parler de ce que l'on appelle communément l'épée celtique, désignation dont le vague ne peut satisfaire.

Les armes de bronze de ces époques reculées, trouvées en Russie et en Hongrie, consistent presque uniquement en haches et lames de lances, parmi lesquelles plusieurs haches de la Russie se signalent par des têtes de bélier.

Les périodes que l'on est convenu de désigner fort improprement sous la domination de l'âge du fer devraient s'arrêter logiquement à la fin du cinquième siècle, après la chute de l'empire d'Occident; mais on les fait souvent descendre bien plus, même jusqu'à la fin du règne de la race carlovingienne (987), ce qui est fort commode, mais fort peu exact. L'époque qui précède le règne de la *chevalerie*, le septième et huitième siècle, devait certes être sa fin.

On a vu que le fer était connu partout et en tous temps, mais que son emploi *universel* pour la fabrication des armes défensives et offensives avait été mêlé à celui du bronze. Les Romains avaient compris de bonne heure la supériorité de l'arme offensive en fer sur celle de bronze, métal qui dès lors ne fut plus employé chez eux qu'à la confection des armes défensives. En 202 avant Jésus-

Christ, répétons-le, le soldat romain n'avait plus d'armes offensives de ce métal : on peut admettre que dans la seconde guerre punique l'arme de fer contribua pour beaucoup à la victoire des Romains sur les Carthaginois. Les quelques armes en fer trouvées dans les tombeaux gaulois, où elles étaient mêlées avec les armes ordinaires en bronze, recueillies particulièrement au cimetière de Catalauni (département de la Marne) et conservées au musée de Saint-Germain, paraissent plutôt d'origine germanique, puisqu'elles ressemblent beaucoup aux épées trouvées à Tiéfenau et à Neufchâtel en Suisse, que l'on doit attribuer aux Burgondes si renommés pour le travail du fer. L'Helvétie, rendue déserte en 450 par les massacres systématiques des Romains, fut repeuplée vers 550 par les Burgondes, dont les bandes s'étaient emparées de l'ouest, par les Allemanes qui occupaient toute la partie où l'on parle encore aujourd'hui allemand, et par les Ostrogoths établis dans le sud où règnent les langues italienne, française et romane. Les Burgondes étaient d'une race forte et de haute taille; la longue soie de ces épées indique des mains larges. Une hache et deux lames de lance en fer, trouvées près du village Onswala (Bara-Schonen) en Suisse, démontrent également par la différence de leurs formes qu'elles ont appartenu à un peuple autre que les Gaulois et les Francs, et peut-être aussi aux Burgondes.

L'armement des races germaniques en général est resté en grande partie inconnu; on sait seulement que la lance, la hache et l'épée étaient leurs armes offensives favorites, et que leurs boucliers, de 8 pieds sur 2 de grandeur, un osier treillissé et recouvert de peau, étaient peints en couleurs vives, de préférence en blanc et en rouge. Ces boucliers furent plus tard remplacés par d'autres en bois de tilleul bordés de fer; mais on a aussi trouvé des carcasses en fer des boucliers ronds à ombilic très-saillants, forme qui paraît avoir été particulièrement en faveur chez la race des

Francs. A Sigmaringen, en Bavière, dans la Hesse, en Silé-
sie, en Angleterre et en Danemark, partout ce même bouclier rond a été en usage. La hache des races germaniques
du Nord se distingue par sa forme de celle des races germaniques du Midi ; la *francisque* des conquérants de la
Gaule ne s'y trouve nulle part, c'est toujours la forme
saxonne. Le seul fragment d'une cuirasse germanique
connu de ces époques reculées est celui conservé au musée de Zurich ; il a été trouvé dans le sol occupé par les
Allemanes. C'est un travail fort curieux, composé de petites lames. Les Quades étaient probablement les seuls qui
avaient des armures en corne.

L'armement des Francs est mieux connu que celui de
toutes les autres races de leur famille, et grâce aux descriptions de quelques auteurs (Sidoine Apollinaire vers 450 de
notre ère, Procope, Agathias, Grégoire de Tours etc.),
et aux nombreuses fouilles exécutées dans les cimetières
mérovingiens, on peut presque reconstituer l'armement complet de ces rudes guerriers. Leur armure défensive, comme
celle du Germain en général, n'était composée que du bouclier, qui était petit, rond, convexe, en bois et en peau, de
50 centimètres de diamètre. On n'a pas encore trouvé ni
casque, ni cuirasse, mais on sait, par des textes, que les
chefs en étaient armés. Le simple guerrier qui avait une
partie de la tête rasée et portait, comme le Chinois, le restant de ses cheveux teint en rouge, natté et entassé au-
dessus du front, était garanti, en quelque sorte, par cette
coiffure comme par un casque. Son armement offensif était
plus complet : c'était l'épée de 80 centimètres de longueur,
mince, plate, aiguë, à double tranchant, et la longue dague ou
mieux dit coutelas ordinairement de 50 centim. de longueur,
appelé *scrama-saxe*, nom composé dont la seconde partie
veut dire couteau, tandis que scrama peut dériver de *sca-
mate*, la ligne de démarcation tracée sur le sable entre deux
combattants grecs, ou de *scrarsan* (tondre), d'où est dérivé

la *schere* (ciseaux) allemande, scrama-saxe, couteau de duel ou couteau rasant.

On a trouvé de ces couteaux, où la soie est d'une longueur démesurée. Un, au musée de Zurich, a plus de 22 centimètres, et un autre, au musée de Sigmaringen, mesure 25 centimètres. Quelques archéologues ont été portés à n'y voir qu'un instrument destiné à travailler le bois, puisque la longueur du manche indique le maniement des deux poignets. Le scrama-saxe est pourtant une arme et non pas un outil, puisqu'il a été presque toujours déposé dans les tombeaux des guerriers, à côté de leur longue spatha. La lame du scrama-saxe d'un seul tranchant et qui paraît avoir été en usage chez tous les peuples d'origine germanique, puisque le musée de Copenhague, tout aussi bien que la plupart des musées allemands et suisses, en possède, était aiguë et à dos évidé à plusieurs endroits pour en diminuer le poids. Une ceinture en cuir garnie d'agrafes en bronze supportait ces armes, que M. Penguilly-l'Haridon a fait si heureusement reconstruire pour le musée impérial d'artillerie à Paris. L'arc et la flèche n'étaient le plus souvent utilisés qu'à la chasse. L'angon ou le pilum à pointe barbue, la lance (framée) à longue lame en fer, et la hache complétaient l'armement. L'angon servait à abattre le bouclier de l'ennemi dans lequel il s'engageait profondément. Le Franc attaquait alors avec l'épée ou la francisque, cette hache caractéristique à un seul et non pas à deux tranchants, comme plusieurs auteurs compilateurs l'ont répété, qu'il avait aussi l'habitude de lancer sur le bouclier si le pilum avait manqué le but ou son effet.

L'épée de Childéric Ier (457-481), conservée au Louvre, a été mal restaurée et ne peut donner que de fausses notions. Le pommeau, qui devait se trouver au bout supérieur du fuseau, est placé à la partie inférieure où il double la garde et donne à l'épée une forme impossible. Pour étudier l'armement en France de la fin du règne mérovingien et du commencement de l'époque carlovingienne, on manque aussi bien de documents que d'armes. L'épée et les éperons attribués à Charlemagne sont presque tout ce qui existe, car le couvercle en ivoire de *l'antiphonaire* de saint Grégoire, de la fin du huitième siècle, a encore tous les caractères romains et provient très-probablement d'un diptyque; il faut descendre jusqu'au règne de Charles II le Chauve pour trouver quelques renseignements dans sa Bible illustrée, et encore ces renseignements paraissent peu sûrs, et plutôt le produit de la fantaisie de l'artiste, qu'on ne peut accepter qu'avec réserve. Le roi y est représenté sur son trône, entouré de gardes qui portent presque l'équipement romain avec les lambrequins en cuir des prétoriens, tandis qu'un bas-relief de l'église de Saint-Julien à Brioude (Haute-Loire), exécuté durant le septième ou le huitième siècle (?) montre le guerrier en cotte de mailles et en casque conique, et le manuscrit allemand de Wessobrunn à Munich, datant de 810, un casque à couvre-nuque et un bouclier à ombilic. Comment accorder le singulier accoutrement des gardes de Charles le Chauve avec le témoignage du moine de Saint-Gall, qui écrivait en témoin oculaire à la fin du neuvième siècle, que Charlemagne ainsi que ses guerriers étaient littéralement couverts de fer; que l'empereur avait un *casque de fer*, les bras armés de *lames de fer*, et les cuisses couvertes d'*écailles en fer*, le bas des jambes sous *plaques de fer*; que son cheval était armé en fer de pied en cap? Ce témoignage est confirmé par les lois mêmes du monarque qui prescrivent à ses hommes d'armes les *brassards* (*armillæ*), le casque, le bouclier et les *plaques* pour jambières (*lorica, brunica, bauga*). Malgré que le *Codex aureus evangel.* du monastère de Saint-Émeran à Ratisbonne, écrit certainement vers 870, montre aussi dans le costume de quelques hommes d'armes des réminiscences romaines, pareilles à celle de la Bible mentionnée et du *Codex aureus* de Saint-Gall, il est inadmissible que l'armement si formidable déjà sous Charlemagne ait rétrogradé à un tel point sous le règne de Charles II. Les *Leges Longobardorum* du neuvième siècle à la bibliothèque de Stuttgart paraissent confirmer ces doutes, car le roi lombard porte une longue targe germanique que l'on retrouve dans l'armement du quatorzième siècle, et le bas-relief du reliquaire du neuvième siècle au trésor de Saint-Maurice en Suisse représente le guerrier en cotte de mailles complète.

Après cela, il n'existe presque plus de trace historique ni archéologique, si ce n'est la *Martyrologie*, manuscrit conservé à la même bibliothèque, et la *Biblia sacra*, manuscrit de la Bibliothèque impériale de Paris; tous les deux du dixième siècle. On y voit déjà le chevalier allemand pourvu du même équipement militaire que le chevalier normand représenté sur la tapisserie de Bayeux, de la fin du onzième siècle ou du commencement du douzième.

La pénurie de documents sur cette matière durant la période carlovingienne (687-987) n'existe plus pour l'époque des croisades (1096-1270).

Un manuscrit anglo-saxon de la bibliothèque britannique, la *Psycomachia* et *Prudentius*, du dixième siècle, montre encore l'homme de guerre sans cotte de mailles et coiffé du casque à timbre bombé, tel que cette arme défensive est représentée dans la *Biblia sacra* déjà mentionnée, tandis qu'un autre manuscrit, anglo-saxon, l'*Aelfric*, du onzième siècle, représente le chevalier en cotte de mailles et avec un casque de forme singulière et sans nasal, quand dans la *Martyrologie*, manuscrit du dixième siècle, à la bibliothèque de Stuttgart, il porte déjà le casque conique à nasal. C'est l'*Aelfric* qui est particulièrement intéressant pour l'étude des diverses formes d'épée dont chacune porte, pour ainsi dire, sa date, pour l'archéologue qui fixera toujours avec certitude le siècle d'après la longueur et la conformation des lames et des gardes. On voit dans les illustrations de ce manuscrit des épées à pommeaux trilobées, les mêmes dont les guerriers de la *Biblia sacra* sont armés. Le chevalier allemand est cependant représenté autrement dans le *Jeremias-Apocalypsis*, manuscrit du onzième siècle, conservé à la bibliothèque de Dusseldorf, où le haubert à longues manches et les hauts et bas de chausses, le tout en mailles, sont complétés par le petit bacinet et le long bouclier convexe, carré en haut et pointu en bas; c'est l'armure qui se retrouve sur une des statues des fondateurs du dôme de Naumbourg, de la même époque, — avec la différence que le bouclier a la forme de ce qu'on est habitué en France à appeler le bouclier normand; — et on le voit encore sur la sculpture de la porte de Heimburg, en Autriche, près la frontière hongroise, exécuté là au douzième siècle. Les guerriers de la mitre de Seligenthal, en Bavière, sur laquelle le brodeur a représenté le martyre de saint Étienne et de l'archevêque Becket de Canterbury, sont coiffés de casques bombés, mais hauts comme des pains de sucre. Le bas-relief du onzième siècle, qui, à la basilique de Zurich, représente le duc Bourckhard, montre casque et épée, dont les formes rappellent les armes de la *Martyrologie* de Stuttgart. Une petite statuette en cuivre jaune du dixième siècle, de la collection de M. le comte de Nieuwerkerke, est aussi fort précieuse pour l'étude des casques, puisque le nasal du casque conique dont ce guerrier est coiffé diffère par la largeur de sa partie inférieure de ceux des autres nasals de cette époque. La tapisserie de Bayeux, exécutée peu de temps après la conquête de l'Angleterre par Guillaume le Conquérant (1066), et dont le curieux et naïf travail reproduit dans un certain détail l'équipement de l'homme de guerre, de la fin du onzième ou du commencement du douzième siècle, constitue un bon document pour l'histoire des armes normandes. Le casque conique du bas-relief de Brioude se retrouve sur les tapisseries, mais ordinairement pourvu du nasal fixe, tel qu'on le voit dans la *Martyrologie* allemande au dixième siècle.

Henri Ier (1100) et le roi d'Écosse Alexandre Ier (1107-1128) sont tous les deux représentés sur leurs sceaux, coiffés de ces mêmes casques coniques, nommés en France *normands* ; et c'est seulement vers la fin du douzième siècle que l'on voit apparaître en Angleterre le casque à timbre bombé, tel que le montre le sceau de Richard Ier, Cœur de Lion (1189-1199), tandis que ce même casque se trouve déjà en usage, en Allemagne, vers le neuvième siècle (v. manuscrit de Wessobrunn et le reliquaire de Saint-Maurice). Les peintures murales au dôme de Brunswick, exécutées sous Henri le Lion (mort en 1195), montrent cependant encore des chevaliers armés du casque conique à côté d'autres déjà coiffés du *heaume*.

Vers la fin du dixième et au commencement du onzième siècle, le chevalier portait une longue tunique, le *haubert* (de l'allem., *halsberg*, en vieil allem., *brunne*, — *brunica*) qui descendait ordinairement jusqu'au-dessus du genou, mais dont les manches s'arrêtaient d'abord au coude, et ne furent allongées que plus tard. Une sorte de capuchon, appelé *camail*, couvrait entièrement la nuque et la tête, de manière qu'une faible partie du visage restait seulement à découvert. Ce haubert, sorte de sarrau, était en peau ou en toile sur lesquelles étaient cousus de forts anneaux en fer forgé, disposés les uns à côté des autres, ou des chaînes placées soit en longueur, soit en largeur, ou des plaques de métal de genre différent, dont quelques-unes avaient la forme d'une écaille. Guillaume le Conquérant est déjà représenté sur la tapisserie de Bayeux avec des bas de chausses couverts d'anneaux, comme le haubert, mais les pieds des chevaliers y sont encore enveloppés, comme ceux des guerriers anglo-saxons, de lanières. La statue d'un des fondateurs du dôme de Haumbourg, du onzième siècle, déjà mentionnée, montre également des bas de chausses en armures de fer, ainsi que les monnaies frappées sous Henri le Lion, duc de Brunswick, mort en 1195.

Le haubert normand était alors une sorte de justau-corps avec haut et bas de chausses adhérentes et d'une seule pièce qui couvrait le corps, comme un tricot, du cou jusqu'à la rotule et jusqu'au coude. Le camail *détaché* ga-rantissait la nuque, une partie de la figure et la tête, qui était en outre couverte, chez les Normands, du casque co-nique, à long nasal, et quelquefois à couvre-nuque.

La cotte montre le plus souvent un treillissé dont les car-reaux sont garnis de très-gros anneaux cousus les uns à côté des autres ou de têtes de clou rivées; deux genres qu'il est presque impossible de ne pas confondre dans les des-sins des manuscrits. On voit même des cottes entièrement en écailles, et des brunes treillissées, sans garniture de têtes de clou ni d'anneaux. Le *Manuscrit de Veleslav*, à la bi-bliothèque du prince de Lobkowitz, à Raudnitz, paraît dé-montrer que l'armement du corps, en Bohême, n'était pas plus avancé au treizième siècle, mais on y voit déjà les chaussures à la poulaine, le chapeau en fer, le grand ba-cinet, et le petit bouclier qui se trouve également dans les miniatures du précieux manuscrit de la même époque, l'*Aneide* allemande de Henri de Valdeck, conservé à la Bi-bliothèque de Berlin. Dans ce dernier manuscrit, les cour-siers sont déjà revêtus de caparaçons treillissés et garnis de têtes de clou ou d'anneaux, et les chevaliers coiffés de *heaumes à cimier*, ce qui est rare pour cette époque. Le ma-nuscrit allemand, *Tristan et Isolde,* du treizième siècle, à la Bibliothèque de Munich, n'est pas moins curieux sous ce rapport, et les chevaliers y paraissent même déjà armés de jambières à plaques et de solerets à la poulaine.

L'armement défensif était complété chez le Normand, par le bouclier ordinairement en forme de cœur, c'est-à-dire rond en haut et pointu en bas, et d'une longueur qui dé-passait la hanche et quelquefois même l'épaule du guerrier. Le bouclier anglo-saxon était encore rond et bombé, dans le genre de celui du Franc et de la rondache du quinzième siècle. Les armes offensives consistaient dans la longue épée fort peu aiguë et à la garde en croix droite, dans la masse d'armes, dans la hache à hampe longue ou courte, et dans la lance au bas de laquelle flottait souvent un petit pavois et dont la longueur dépassait d'un tiers celle de l'homme. La fronde et l'arc étaient les armes de jet. Les casques des archers étaient ordinairement sans nasal. La véritable et bonne cotte treillissée était formée de plusieurs doubles d'étoffe rembourrée, piquée et renfermée par un treillis de bandes de cuir disposées en losanges réguliers où chaque centre et chaque angle étaient garnis d'un clou à large tête ou d'un anneau. Les cottes en écailles appelées *jazerans* (*korazims*), de cette période, sont des plus rares ou n'existent probablement plus du tout. La plus ancienne que j'aie trouvée dans les manuscrits du moyen âge, est l'espèce de jacque à imbrication, dont est revêtu un chevalier, dans le *Codex aureus* du neuvième siècle de Saint-Gall. Il ne faut cependant pas confondre ces sortes de jazerans avec ceux des époques postérieures et dont le musée de Dresde possède un exemplaire historique, qu'en 1629 le roi Sobieski a porté devant Vienne. Il paraît que les brunes en écailles imbriquées n'étaient pas rares dans le Nord, puisque des deniers de Magdebourg, de 1150 et de 1160, ainsi que plusieurs autres deniers allemands de la même époque, les montrent dans les effigies.

Toutes ces cottes peuvent être divisées en cottes *annelées*, composées d'anneaux plats cousus l'un à côté de l'autre; en cottes *rustrées*, faite d'anneaux ovales, se couvrant à moitié les uns les autres; en cottes *maclées* ou faites de pièces en losanges et en cottes à *écailles imbriquées*.

La véritable cotte de mailles que l'on croit à tort d'être venue de l'Orient et seulement à la suite des croisades, était déjà connue dans le centre et dans le nord de l'Europe, bien avant le onzième siècle; on en a trouvé à Tiefenau des fragments formés d'anneaux de cinq millimètres de diamètre, parfaitement travaillés, et qui remontent, certes, à quelques centaines d'années avant les croisades. Le poëme héroïque de *Gudrun* ne dit-il pas : « que Herwig faisait glisser sa brune dans le bouclier; » et plus loin, « que ses habits étaient couverts de la rouille de son haubert. » L'*Enigme Aldhelm*, écrit au onzième siècle, parle aussi de cette « lorica formée de métal, sans l'aide d'aucun tissu » passage qui désigne clairement la véritable cotte de mailles, ainsi qu'un autre passage du *Roman de Rou*, écrit après la conquête normande. C'est bien de cette cotte que la princesse byzantine, Anna Comnène (1083-1148), dit dans ses mémoires : « qu'elle était uniquement faite d'anneaux d'acier rivés, — qu'elle était alors inconnue à Byzance et seulement portée par les hommes du Nord. » La cotte de mailles est encore mentionnée par un moine de Noirmoutiers, qui vivait au temps de Louis le Jeune (1137-1180), et qui a donné la description des armes de Geoffroy de Normandie.

La cotte treillissée, aussi bien que le haubert à anneaux et à chaînes, à l'épreuve de la flèche, mais peu résistant aux armes de hast, particulièrement à la lance, et bien trop lourds, furent abandonnés peu à peu, de manière qu'au commencement du treizième siècle, les chevaliers aisés portaient presque tous déjà la cotte de mailles, également insuffisante contre les chocs et que l'art du tréfileur, trouvé en 1306 par Rodolphe de Nuremberg, devait mettre au quatorzième siècle à la portée des hommes d'armes les moins fortunés. Les anneaux forgés, confectionnés d'abord pièce par pièce et chacun d'eux rivés avaient rendu, durant plusieurs siècles, le prix des cottes de mailles trop élevé pour en permettre l'usage à la petite chevalerie et aux simples hommes d'armes. A la bataille de Bouvines (1214) le perfectionnement dans l'armement était bien plus avancé déjà : chausses hautes et basses, cottes, camails et brassards, étaient tout en mailles reliées entre elles avec un tel soin que le poignard, la perfide *miséricorde* et le

Panzerbrecher ne pouvaient même plus pénétrer nulle part, et que pour tuer l'ennemi renversé il fallait l'assommer.

Durant tout le règne de Saint-Louis (1226-1270), l'armure complète de mailles était universellement portée en France et en Italie par les gentilshommes aisés. Simple, sans envers ni doublure, elle se passait comme une chemise et on la mettait par-dessus un vêtement en cuir ou en étoffe piquée : le *gamboison* ou *gambeson*, qui était aussi, la plupart du temps, la seule armure défensive des gens de pied en France, où l'armement des troupiers roturiers a été, durant le moyen âge, en retard, car les villes n'avaient pas l'indépendance ni la richesse des grandes villes flamandes, allemandes et italiennes pour pouvoir se constituer des corps de citadins régulièrement armés. Le gamboison se retrouve encore au seizième siècle, où il était ordinairement en toile brodée d'œillets. L'armure à plates ou en plaques d'abord en cuir, et plus tard en acier, remonte, contrairement à l'opinion répandue, bien plus haut en Allemagne qu'en Italie où elle apparaît seulement au quatorzième siècle, tandis que des manuscrits allemands du treizième siècle montrent déjà le chevalier dans cette nouvelle armure et coiffé du *heaume*.

Par-dessus la cotte le chevalier portait souvent une sorte de sarrau sans manches, une cotte d'armement en étoffe légère appelée en allemand *Waffenrock*, qui descendait jusqu'au-dessus de la rotule et sur laquelle les armoiries et autres signes distinctifs étaient brodés. Cette cotte était ordinairement l'œuvre de la châtelaine. Le *grand haubert* ou *blanc haubert* (*die gonze Brünne*), l'armure complète en mailles que les chevaliers avaient seuls le droit, en France, de revêtir, et qui pesait vingt-cinq à trente livres, se composait des chausses et de la longue tunique à camail et à manches qui enveloppaient, dans la dernière période de son usage, les bras et les mains d'une sorte de fourreau d'où le pouce seul, également couvert

5.

de mailles, était détaché et sous lequel on mettait sur la poitrine une large plaque de fer. C'était alors l'armement universel de la chevalerie française. Quant aux *ailettes*, plaques attachées aux épaulières des cottes de mailles et des armures transitoires à plaques de cuir ou de corne, c'étaient des espèces d'écussons plus ou moins hauts et souvent ovales, tels que la statue en pierre de Rodolphe de Hierstein (1318) au dôme de Baal en montre un échantillon. Ces ailettes, de même que le bouclier, portaient les armoiries des chevaliers et elles n'ont été en usage que durant une cinquantaine d'années.

Le petit bacinet (du celtique *bac*), aussi nommé cervelière, qu'il ne faut pas confondre avec le grand bacinet, casque en usage du treizième au commencement du quinzième siècle, se portait aussi bien par-dessous comme par-dessus le camail qui était séparé, comme celui-ci, de la tête, par le bonnet en étoffe matelassée appelé chaperon, souvent attaché à la cervelière avec des lanières. Le tout était couvert, durant le combat et le tournoi, du heaume (de l'allemand *Helm*), vaste casque d'abord sans cimier, que le cavalier portait en chevauchant accroché à la selle. Le bouclier long, pointu en bas, arrondi en haut, complétait l'armement défensif. Plus tard on gardait même dans les tournois le grand bacinet, sous le heaume devenu encore plus vaste. Le haubergeon plus petit que le haubert n'était porté, en France, que par quelques écuyers, archers, sergents d'armes, etc.; on l'appela bientôt jacque et son usage se retrouve encore à la fin du seizième siècle. Il est très-difficile de reconnaître l'époque à laquelle appartient une ancienne cotte, puisque toutes ont été fabriquées de la même manière de mailles rivées appelées *à grains d'orge*. On peut cependant admettre que plus l'anneau est lourd plus il est ancien. La double maille dont l'existence me paraît douteuse et pour la fabrication de laquelle, en France, durant le treizième siècle, Cham-

bly (Oise), était renommé, montre toujours selon les vieux
auteurs, quatre anneaux réunis sur un seul. Beaucoup de
ces cottes de mailles simples que l'on rencontre aujour-
d'hui sont des produits de contrefaçon. L'amateur les
reconnaît au manque de rivés. Les cottes persanes et
tscherkesses se fabriquent cependant encore à anneaux
rivés comme à anneaux non rivés. Quant aux *brigantines*, si souvent confondues par les auteurs avec les korazins et même avec les hauberts, elles ne remontent pas
au delà du quinzième siècle où elles commençaient à se
répandre particulièrement en Italie. C'était alors la cotte
des archers à cheval et des gentilshommes peu riches. Il y
en avait cependant aussi où les plaques étaient recouvertes
de velours de soie; ainsi elles étaient souvent portées en
Italie, même en temps de paix par les patriciens et les nobles
riches à la place du pourpoint rembourré; elles défendaient
contre le poignard du bandit. Charles le Téméraire en portait aussi. La brigantine consistait ordinairement en petites
plaques allongées et rectangulaires, se couvrant à moitié
les unes les autres, rivées sur l'étoffe. Plusieurs musées les
ont exposées à l'envers, les écailles en dehors, ce qui est
une erreur parce que la courbe des plaquettes indiquait
que la brigantine était doublée de ces fers et portée par-
dessus le pourpoint ordinaire.

L'épée, qui durant ces différentes périodes avait conservé
la même forme de poignée à garde droite en sens rectangulaire, et la lance étaient les principales armes offensives.

Après avoir commencé, à la fin du treizième siècle, de
raccourcir le haubert et d'ajouter des jambières et des brassards en plaques de cuir bouilli, ou d'acier, un changement radical s'opéra partout dans l'armement durant le
quatorzième siècle, où l'on voit se répandre l'armure allemande plus ou moins complète en plaques d'acier, dite armure à plate (*Schïenenrüstung*). Cette armure, particulièrement lorsqu'elle est perfectionnée et bien articulée par des

lames, remonte dans le Nord à une époque plus reculée qu'en Italie et en France, où la période de transition a duré jusqu'à Philippe VI (1340) sous le règne duquel l'armure complète à plates n'existait pas encore. *Tristan et Isolde*, manuscrit allemand du treizième siècle, montre des chevaliers en armures à plates, coiffés de heaumes et montés sur des coursiers entièrement couverts d'armures, tandis que les miniatures d'un manuscrit bourguignon, une histoire romaine conservée à la Bibliothèque de l'arsenal à Paris et supposée avoir été écrite pour le duc de Bourgogne, Jean Sans-Peur (1404-1419), mais qui paraît appartenir à la fin du quinzième siècle, représentent l'armement bourguignon bien moins avancé. Ces dernières miniatures m'ont confirmé aussi ce que j'avais déjà eu l'occasion d'observer dans les arsenaux suisses : le noir domine parmi les pièces de l'armement bourguignon et sarde, tandis que les armures autrichiennes sont généralement en acier poli.

Lorsque le haubert en mailles avait été remplacé par l'armure nouvelle, le *vêtement de dessous* aussi avait été changé. Pourpoint sans manches, mais à hauts et bas de chausse adhérents, formant un accoutrement qui ressemblait beaucoup au costume d'une seule pièce des petits garçons de nos jours. Le tout était ordinairement en toile légèrement matelassée et garnie de mailles sous le plastron, aux emplacements des rotules et des creux de genoux et à la braconnière, afin de protéger le corps partout où les défauts de l'armure donnaient prise à l'épée et au petit poignard à fer triangulaire appelé en allemand *Panzerbrecher* (brise-cuirasse). Le seul exemplaire d'un tel vêtement parvenu jusqu'à nous se trouve complet et presque intact au musée national à Munich.

C'est ici la place de signaler l'erreur qui a fait admettre que la taille et la conformation des hommes du temps de la chevalerie aurait été au-dessus de celles des époques mo-

dernes; c'est juste le contraire qu'il faut admettre : à peu
d'exceptions près, les armures du quatorzième au seizième
siècle sont trop étroites pour pouvoir être portées par des
hommes bien constitués de nos jours. J'ai fait faire des expériences aux arsenaux d'Allemagne, qui ont pleinement
confirmé ce que j'avais observé déjà dans beaucoup de
collections. C'est particulièrement dans la conformation
des jambes et des mollets que la supériorité musculaire des
races actuelles se manifeste; impossible presque de faire
entrer un mollet du dix-neuvième siècle dans une armure
du moyen âge et de la Renaissance.

Durant le quinzième et le seizième siècle, les formes des
armures à plates ont subi de grandes variations : selon les
époques et les pays, ils réflètent presque toujours les
modes des costumes civils et accusent les modifications
que le changement dans la manière de combattre et l'invention des armes à feu portatives avaient rendues néces-
saires. Durant la plus grande partie du quinzième siècle,
l'armure est gothique dans toutes ses parties, et tout est
harmonieux; là, la forme de l'épée, comme celle du plastron, offre les plus beaux types de ce qui a existé en
armes. A la fin du quinzième et au commencement du seizième siècle, la forme du plastron est souvent bombée, les
passe-gardes sont devenues énormes, les tassettes articulées s'arrondissent davantage; l'armure entière perd déjà de
sa pureté de lignes et de son cachet de sévérité et de force.

L'armure cannelée, d'invention allemande, aussi nommée
maximilienne et milanaise, signale l'époque du «dernier
chevalier», car la cuirasse du temps de Henri II qui imite le
justaucorps et encore bien plus celle où le plastron imite
la bosse-polichinelle du temps des mignons, appelé *à cosse
de pois*, n'a plus rien de mâle. Bientôt l'armure tombe dans
le grotesque. Le plastron se réduit et s'aplatit, tandis que
les longs cuissards qui ont remplacé les tassettes, accen-
tuent encore davantage les hanches et transforment l'homme

en écrevisse. Enfin les bottes montantes et les housseaux
remplacent les grèves et déjà sous Henri IV, et bien plus
encore sous Louis XIV, l'armure, s'en va; en perdant sa
lourdeur elle avait déjà perdu son caractère; elle s'effacera
bientôt entièrement devant la peau tannée! En Allemagne
comme en France, durant la guerre de Trente ans, le buffletin avec son grand colletin ou hausse-col, remplaça même
la cuirasse qui n'était plus portée que par une arme spéciale.

Pour reconnaître et classer les armures, chaque pièce
sert à fixer le temps de la fabrication, par l'empreinte que
l'époque y a laissée, absolument comme sur les costumes
civils. Le casque conique, appelé en France normand, que
l'on rencontre déjà sur beaucoup de monuments du dixième
siècle; le heaume, forme anglaise, à nasal, et forme allemande, à vue, du douzième au treizième siècle ; le heaume
à cimier du treizième au quinzième siècle ; le petit bacinet
ou la cervelière, porté sous le heaume; le grand bacinet du
treizième et du quatorzième siècle; la salade du quinzième
siècle; les chapeaux en fer et les pots en tête, dont on trouve
déjà la première trace dans les manuscrits du dixième et du
onzième siècle, les nombreuses variétés des bourguignotes
du seizième siècle, avec l'armet du seizième au dix-septième
siècle (*ce dernier mot de l'armurier, en fait de casque*), ainsi
que le morion et le cabasset qui n'étaient ordinairement
portés que par les hommes de pied ; tous servent à fixer
l'époque d'une armure.

Le rôle que le bouclier a joué chez les peuples du Nord,
et particulièrement chez ceux de race germanique où il fut
même la cause de la création d'un art original et tout à fait
opposé à l'art classique, est bien plus important que chez
les Anciens. C'est aussi sur le bouclier germain qu'il faut
rechercher la première manifestation plastique de l'esprit
féodal et *l'origine des armoiries*. Quand Tacite, qui écrivait dans le premier siècle de notre ère, dit (*De moribus
Germanorum*) que les Allemands peignaient leurs boucliers

de belles couleurs et avec variations, il ne comprenait pas que ces peintures étaient en quelque sorte des hiéroglyphes qui représentaient les actions d'éclat du chef à qui le bouclier appartenait. La coutume, chez les Germains, de rappeler leurs faits d'armes par l'image sur le bouclier, était si répandue que les mots de peintre, en vieux allemand *Schilder*, et de peindre, *schildern*, dérivent même de *Schild*, bouclier. Ces actions d'éclat peintes, qui, chez ce peuple, furent reproduites sur le bouclier, soit sous la forme de l'arme à l'aide de laquelle elles avaient été accomplies, soit sous celle de l'ennemi ou du monstre vaincu, restaient durant la vie du héros son signe distinctif et constituaient ainsi les premières armoiries qui n'étaient pas d'abord héréditaires, parce que le fils n'avait aucun droit à la distinction du bouclier paternel; il devait à son tour conquérir personnellement, par un fait d'armes, le droit de peindre son bouclier et restait jusque-là, comme dit Virgile : *Parma inglorius alba.*

A partir du dixième siècle, où, en Allemagne, les tournois étaient déjà universellement répandus, l'armoirie devint bientôt commune à toute la famille, à toute la lignée, et en définitive héréditaire. C'est à partir de cette époque et bien avant les croisades que, pour rendre le contrôle de la nouvelle noblesse possible, le chevalier devait déposer à la barrière des tournois son bouclier avec son casque, qui prouvaient aux hérauts (de l'allemand *Herold*, noble crieur, d'où dérive *héraldique*) que le porteur de ces armes avait le *droit de tournoyer*. Au onzième siècle, au commencement des croisades, presque toute l'Europe avait déjà adopté ces signes distinctifs, et dès lors les armoiries et l'art héraldique n'ont plus cessé de régner parmi les peuples chrétiens et même parmi les Maures d'Espagne. C'est peu de temps après que les nobles prirent l'habitude de joindre à leurs noms ceux de leurs châteaux et de leurs terres, ce qui créa la *division* dans les armoiries de famille.

Les Normands, et plus probablement les Francs déjà, ont apporté de bonne heure en France la coutume des armoiries ; les boucliers des chevaliers normands étaient tous peints d'animaux fantastiques, etc., ce qui n'était autre chose que l'armoirie personnelle.

Le bouclier est l'arme défensive, qui a varié le plus dans ses formes. Le bouclier celtique, germain, scandinave, breton, etc., à ombilic, le bouclier germanique carré en osier treillissé des temps antémérovingiens, la rondache mérovingienne, carlovingienne et anglo-saxonne, le long bouclier peint des dixième et onzième siècles, appelé en France normand, le bouclier triangulaire de la même époque, le petit écu du douzième et du treizième siècle, le pavois allemand, le manteau d'armes, la rondache des quinzième et seizième siècles, la rondelle, la tarchette, etc., etc., se sont succédé et offrent un vaste sujet d'études.

Le gantelet aussi indique les époques. Le premier, celui du douzième et du treizième siècle, n'était d'abord qu'une espèce de sac en mailles, formé par l'extrémité de la manche du haubert. Au quatorzième siècle, on voit apparaître le véritable gantelet à doigts séparés. Le miton le remplace au quinzième siècle. Formé de lames disposées seulement dans le sens des grandes divisions de la main, on le trouve à l'armure de la Pucelle, et c'est au miton que Bayard appliqua son dicton : « Ce que gantelet gagne, gorgerin le mange. » Vers le milieu du seizième siècle, l'apparition du pistolet fit revenir au gantelet à doigts séparés.

Les chaussures en fer lamé, appelées *solerets* et *pédieux*, apparaissent partout au quatorzième siècle et dans le Nord déjà au douzième et au treizième siècle, lorsque les bas de chausse en maille furent remplacés par des *tumelières* ou plaques. La forme du soleret indique parfaitement l'époque d'une armure. D'abord *ogivale lancette*, sa pointe s'allongeait bientôt jusqu'à imiter celle de l'extravagante, chaussure *à la poulaine*. De 1420 à 1470, c'est l'*ogive tiers point;* de 1470, à 1570 le *sabot* et le *pied d'ours*, et après 1570 le *bec de canne*, qui dominent; mais les époques de transition exigent beaucoup de précaution. A la fin du dix-septième siècle, les *housseaux* et les bottes avaient entière-ment chassé les solerets et les jambières. Quant à la forme de chaussure dite à la poulaine, elle ne peut servir de guide pour le classement de l'époque d'une armure que là où l'on est sûr de sa nationalité, puisque l'adoption de cette mode a varié selon les pays. Elle a régné en France de 1360 à 1420, tandis qu'on voit déjà les chevaliers autrichiens à la bataille de Morgarten (1319) couper les longs bouts de leurs solerets après être descendus de cheval, et Henri II roi d'An-gleterre (1154-1189), cacher la difformité de son pied sous les becs des chaussures à la poulaine. C'est probablement à la Hongrie qu'il faut attribuer l'origine de cette mode.

Les armures défensives du cheval ont subi l'influence de la mode, comme celles de l'homme, car la cannelure maxi-milienne de la cuirasse se retrouve sur les bardes, le chan-frein, les flançois, la croupière et le garde-queue de la pano-plie de la monture, dont la plus ancienne que j'ai pu trouver est celle d'un denier frappé sous Henri le Lion (mort en 1195) où le cheval du duc est couvert d'un treillissé à têtes de clou que l'on rencontre tout à fait pareil dans un des des-sins de l'*Enéide* allemande de Henri de Valdeck, ma-nuscrit du treizième siècle, conservé à la bibliothèque de Berlin.

L'éperon sans molette et à col droit ne change qu'au on-zième siècle, où il commence à se relever en pente douce, tandis qu'au treizième, le col est relevé en brisure; la mo-lette (rouet à dentelure) apparaît au quatorzième siècle, elle est alors le plus souvent à huit pointes. Au quinzième siècle, le col de l'éperon s'allonge outre mesure jusque vers le seizième siècle, où la fantaisie de l'artiste le transforme et finit par le rendre enfin joujou.

La selle offre des formes très-variées, particulièrement celle des tournois. La fameuse selle allemande en bois, du treizième et du quatorzième siècle, sur laquelle le jouteur ne pouvait se tenir assis, est la plus rare.

La série des épées est longue. Elle comprend : la rapière, épée de duel et d'escrime qui ne remonte pas au delà de la première moitié du seizième siècle, où l'*escrime* moderne (de l'allemand *schirmen*) a pris naissance sous le règne de Charles-Quint ; — l'ancienne claymore, qui n'est pas du tout à corbeille comme la compilation l'a répété ; — le cimeterre et le sabre, déjà en usage chez les Daces, du temps de Trajan ; — le yatagan, le khandjar, le flissat, le koukris, offrant autant de variétés que la dague, le poignard, le stylet, le khouttar et le cris. La lance, la pique, la masse d'armes, le *Morgenstern*, la faux et le fauchard, la vouge, le marteau d'armes, le fléau, la hache d'armes, la hallebarde, la corssèque, la roncone, la pertuisane, l'esponton, la fourche de guerre et la baïonnette fournissent tous autant de sujets d'étude que la fronde, la fustibale, l'arc, l'arbalète et la sarbacane.

Les machines de guerre, telles que la baliste, la catapulte, le trébuchet, le bélier et autres, avaient été transmis par l'antiquité au moyen âge chrétien, qui en ajouta encore un nombre prodigieux de son invention, si on se rapporte aux manuscrits de cette époque, et aux auteurs de la Renaissance.

Il faut cependant se méfier de l'existence réelle de toutes les machines extravagantes qui ornent ces publications et ces manuscrits ; fort peu ont réellement existé et la plupart sont restés en projet. Quant aux petits barils et aux flèches incendiaires, lancées au moyen des balistes, leur emploi dans les siéges est cependant aussi certain que celui des pots de chaux vive lancés par les assiégés pour aveugler l'ennemi. Léonard Fronsperg en a expliqué l'usage dans son *Kriegsbuch* publié en 1573, et le musée de Zurich en possède même des exemplaires trouvés sous les décombres d'un vieux château.

Il est à observer qu'à partir du quatorzième siècle jusqu'à la fin du quinzième, les chevaliers, particulièrement en France, avaient adopté l'habitude répandue aussi en Angleterre, en Allemagne et en Italie, de descendre de cheval pour combattre à pied, tel que cela eut lieu à la bataille de Crécy, en 1346. C'est à cette dérogation aux coutumes traditionnelles de la chevalerie que l'on doit le genre d'armures particulièrement adopté sous Charles VII (1445) dont le musée impérial d'artillerie possède les deux plus beaux exemplaires, provenant de la collection d'Ambras, mais qui me paraissent n'avoir jamais servi et tout à fait impropres à l'usage. Je pense que l'homme ne peut se mouvoir dans des armures à doubles articulations; — il serait fort intéressant pour l'histoire des armes que la direction du musée veuille bien faire faire quelques essais sous ce rapport.

Dès la fin du douzième siècle, lors de l'institution des tournois *réglés* ou *réguliers*, le besoin se fit sentir de mieux garantir la tête contre les formidables chocs de la lourde lance, espèce de tronc d'arbre, fixée plus tard à la cuirasse, comme dans un étau, par l'arrêt dit foucre. Le heaume, l'énorme casque qui devait alors couvrir à la fois le camail et le bacinet et dont les plus anciens conservés sont d'origine anglaise, fut bientôt fixé à l'armure au moyen de vis et de chaînes.

On place ordinairement l'introduction des tournois dans les coutumes de la chevalerie, vers le douzième siècle, tandis que les tournois *organisés*, mais non pas tout à fait *réglés* d'après des statuts, remontent cependant bien plus haut. On en connaît déjà qui ont eu lieu en Allemagne au neuvième siècle, ce qui explique que la fabrication des armures était si perfectionnée dans ce pays. L'histoire a enregistré à peu près cent quatre-vingts tournois réguliers, sans compter un grand nombre de petites *passes d'armes*. Les plus impor-

tants à partir du neuvième siècle jusqu'à la fin du douzième, presque tous tenus en Allemagne, sont : en 811,
celui de Barcelone, à l'occasion du couronnement du comte
Linofre; en 842, à Strasbourg, sous Charles le Chauve; en
925, à Ratisbonne, sous Henri l'Oiseleur; en 932, à Magdebourg, sous le même; en 938, a Spire, sous Otto Ier; en
942, à Rothenbourg, sous Conrad de Franconie; en 948, à
Constance, sous Louis de Souabe; en 968, à Mersebourg sur
la Sala; en 996, à Brunswick; en 1019, à Trèves, sous
Conrad Ier; en 1029, également à Trèves; en 1042, à Halle,
sous Henri III; en 1080, à Augsbourg, sous Hermann de
Souabe; en 1118 et en 1119, à Goettingue; en 1148, à Liége
sous Théodore de Hollande, où assistaient quatorze princes
et ducs, quatre-vingt-onze comtes, quatre-vingt-quatre barons, cent trente-trois chevaliers et trois cents autres nobles;
en 1165, à Zurich, sous le duc Welf de Bavière; en 1174,
à Beaucaire, sous Henri d'Angleterre; en 1234, à Corbie,
en Picardie, où Floris IV, comte de Hollande, fut tué.

Les tournois étaient souvent si meurtriers qu'il arriva
que soixante personnes périrent dans une seule passe d'armes. Malgré l'anathème lancé au neuvième siècle par le
pape Eugène, contre ces jeux homicides, ils se répandaient
de plus en plus, et lorsque, au retour des premières croisades, l'usage des armoiries héréditaires avait été universellement admis, l'adoption d'un code héraldique et très-
compliqué et l'introduction d'un règlement sévère impri-
mèrent même à ces exercices militaires un caractère
éminemment chevaleresque qui, en Provence, approchait
du lyrisme. C'est dans ces tournois qu'en temps de paix
furent créés autant sinon plus de chevaliers qu'à la guerre
sur les champs de bataille, et c'est durant ces fêtes somp-
tueuses que la plupart des alliances nobiliaires furent
formées. Passant la plupart de son temps à chasser autour
du château fort, perché ordinairement sur des rochers et au
milieu d'impénétrables forêts, le jeune hobereau ne trouvait

guère d'autres occasions que celles que lui offraient les
tournois, pour rencontrer les filles nobles et patriciennes
qui y étalaient leurs charmes, parées d'*affiquets* et vêtues
d'étoffes si éclatantes que les barrières grossières et les tri-
bunes ne paraissaient contenir que des corbeilles de fleurs.
Lorsque « la plus belle des belles, » — la reine du jour, —
distribuait les prix aux vainqueurs et que les jeunes femmes
et les jeunes filles se trouvaient debout, les regards des chevaliers parcouraient les rangs pour choisir leur danseuse
qui souvent devenait leur femme. C'est aussi pour ces fêtes
que beaucoup de nobles se ruinèrent, car le désir d'éclip-
ser des rivaux par la richesse de l'armure et du harnache-
ment du coursier, les poussait souvent sous la dépendance
du bonnet jaune.

On a l'habitude de diviser les tournois en trois genres
tout à fait tranchés : le tournoi proprement dit, le *Rennen*
allemand, la joute, le *Stechen* allemand et la passe d'armes,
ou combat à pied, le *Fusstournir* allemand, divisions qui,
en Allemagne, ont été même subdivisées en dix-huit
espèces. Tout cela est trop absolu et contraire aux mœurs
du moyen âge, où durant ces réjouissances les limites
étaient bien moins rigoureusement respectées que par les
faiseurs de livres du seizième siècle dont l'imagination n'a
pas été moins fertile dans l'invention des machines de
guerre.

L'armure de joute que quelques auteurs croient avoir été
plus légère que celle destinée à la guerre, était au contraire bien plus pesante. Toutes ces belles armures en acier
poli qui se signalent par leurs lignes sévères et pures, par
leurs formidables proportions et par une lourdeur extraordinaire, un homme aurait-il pu en supporter le poids au
delà d'une heure sans succomber ? La passe d'armes et la
joute (combat à cheval avec la lance) étaient sans cesse
confondues dans les tournois où l'on continuait souvent le
combat à pied et avec la même armure, après avoir été

6.

désarçonné et jeté par terre; les armures spéciales pour combattre à pied sont bien rares, et les dessins du temps (quinzième siècle) conservés au musée Maximilien à Augsbourg démontrent, que même dans les tournois où on se battait à la massette en bois (*Kolbentournièr*) ni le *casque à grille*, ni la massette n'étaient exclusivement employés puisqu'on voit dans la mêlée des chevaliers coiffés du heaume habituel et armés d'épées attachées avec des chaînes aux plastrons, tandis que d'autres se servent de la massette en bois moins dangereuse.

L'armement gothique, d'origine germanique, s'est répandu rapidement partout où l'esprit chevaleresque s'était développé. On le retrouve en Angleterre, en France, en Espagne et même sur le sol classique de l'Italie, mais partout il a subi des modifications selon les mœurs et le goût des nations. En Italie l'armement est toujours resté sans style propre et défectueux, quoique très-artistique dans le dessin et dans les détails de l'exécution des ornements. Les artistes y étaient trop tenus sous l'influence des réminiscences antiques pour pouvoir sortir du style païen et s'assimiler le style entièrement nouveau qui exigea une grande sobriété et un oubli complet du passé. Les exigences de la défense créées par le changement de la manière nouvelle de guerroyer leur échappaient également. L'invasion arabe en Espagne a été plutôt une cause d'impulsion et de perfectionnement pour l'armurerie de ce pays que de décadence, comme quelques auteurs le croient à tort, car le déclin qui s'est manifesté dans la fabrication des armes espagnoles ne se fait sentir qu'après l'expulsion des Maures de Grenade (1492), et si pour quelques spécialités le revirement qui ramena les artistes espagnols au caractère de simplicité et au grand style du gothique fut momentanément favorable, cette période ne fut que de fort courte durée, puisque la décadence devint complète sous l'influence de l'école italienne et particulièrement sous le

règne de Charles-Quint. La peinture seule sut se débar-
rasser plus tard de cette influence étrangère mal digérée et
créer des chefs-d'œuvre où tout respire l'originalité et la
puissance. Quant aux armes orientales de notre ère, elles
ont peu varié de forme depuis bien des siècles ; elles sont
presque restées telles que les peuples de l'Orient les ma-
niaient dans l'antiquité ; les manuscrits, particulièrement
un, conservé à la bibliothèque de Munich, la copie illustrée du Schah-Hameh ou livre royal composé par le
poëte Fisdüsi, sous le règne de Mahmoud des Ghaznévides
(999 ans après Jésus-Christ), montrent que l'armement
persan aussi était déjà au seizième siècle ce qu'il est encore
aujourd'hui.

Le changement dans l'armement chinois et japonais a
été bien moins sensible, car si le costume a éprouvé un
changement qui se manifeste à des époques qui sont éloi-
gnées l'une de l'autre de trois à quatre cents ans, la forme
des armes est presque restée stationnaire. Les sabres, fourches de guerre, piques, épées, et même les cuirasses et
casques au Musée d'Artillerie à Paris, provenant de la dernière guerre, paraissent copiés sur les armes remontant à
plusieurs siècles, conservées à la Tour de Londres ou ailleurs.

Les machines de guerre, l'*artillerie* des anciens, ont été
transmises, comme il a été déjà dit ailleurs, par les Romains au moyen âge, qui les a peu modifiées, car on voit
dans les miniatures de l'époque que la construction en
était presque la même. L'existence réelle de ces engins a
été de nouveau affirmée par des débris de balistes trouvés
sous les décombres du château de Russikon, en Suisse,
détruit par le feu au treizième siècle, débris qui, avec
quantité de lames de grosses flèches, sont conservés au
Cabinet des Antiques, de Zurich. On retrouve dans les dessins avec lesquels Zeitblom a orné, au quinzième siècle, un
manuscrit qui appartient à la bibliothèque du prince de

Waldburg-Wolfegg, la catapulte ou *tormentum* des Latins, — l'onagre français, — mais d'une construction différente et semblable à celle que donne le *Recueil d'anciens poëtes français* de la Bibliothèque impériale, à Paris. Les archives de Mons, de l'année 1406, parlent aussi de ces engins, mais nulle part on ne trouve de traces d'un polyspaste. Outre ces machines à trajection, le moyen âge en a imaginé quantité d'autres qui servaient aux siéges et à la défense des camps, telles qu'on les voit dans les aquarelles qui reproduisent les armes amoncelées dans les trois arsenaux de l'empereur Maximilien, et qui furent exécutées, vers 1505, par Nicolas Glokenthon. Deux recueils de dessins du commencement du quinzième siècle, conservés, comme les précédents, dans la collection d'Ambras, montrent même des appareils de plongeurs qui paraissent très-semblables à ceux de la réinvention nouvelle. Il faut cependant se méfier, répétons-le, de l'existence réelle de toutes ces formes extravagantes qui ornent les publications et les manuscrits des époques de la fin du moyen âge et de la renaissance, où l'imagination fertile a créé autant d'armes pour la destruction des hommes que celles de nos jours, restées en *projets*.

Si on passe aux armes de trait à main, on trouve d'abord, comme partout, dans l'antiquité, la fronde, la fustibale et l'arc.

L'arbalète, que M. Rodios a cru reconnaître sous la *Gastrafete* des Grecs, me paraît être une invention de l'Europe centrale et remonter tout au plus au dixième siècle, car la princesse Anna Comnène (1083-1148), comment aurait-elle ignoré l'existence de cette arme, que M. Rodios a ainsi reconstruite d'après des textes byzantins? La princesse dit pourtant que : « la *tzagara* est un arc que nous ne connaissions pas, etc. »

La fronde et sa sœur la fustibale, cette fronde attachée à une hampe, se sont conservées même au seizième siècle, où elles servaient à lancer des boulets enflammés et des grenades, comme le démontrent les dessins déjà mentionnés de Glockenthon.

L'arc n'avait guère été en usage, chez les peuples de race germanique, qu'à la chasse; Francs, Saxons, Allemanes, Burgondes, Angles, Cattes, Chérusques, Marcomands et autres le détestaient à la guerre comme puéril et perfide, et préféraient, même comme arme de jet et de trait, la hache et l'anjon.

Sur la tapisserie de Bayeux, Normands et Anglo-Saxons sont armés d'arcs, et on doit admettre qu'à la bataille d'Hastings, les uns et les autres en ont fait fortement usage. Mais les Allemands ont continué, jusqu'à l'apparition de l'arbalète, de faire peu de cas des armes de trait. L'arc du Normand était petit, d'un mètre à peu près, tandis que plus tard celui des archers anglais, si réputés à partir du treizième siècle, mesurait presque deux mètres et variait selon la grandeur de l'homme, à laquelle il devait correspondre exactement, puisqu'il devait avoir la longueur de la distance qui se trouve entre les deux extrémités des doigts du milieu. L'archer anglais avait fini par acquérir une habileté extraordinaire au tir de la flèche; il pouvait en expédier douze dans une minute en manquant rarement son but.

L'arc italien, le plus souvent en acier, n'avait qu'un mètre et demi de longueur, comme l'arc allemand. La flèche anglaise mesurait 90 centimètres.

Au douzième siècle, l'archer portait deux étuis, l'un, le carquois, le *couin;* ce vieux *Guiver* anglais contenant les flèches (du *Flitz*, allemand), qui, selon les chroniques de Saint-Denis, étaient alors nommées *pilles* et *sayettes;* l'autre, l'*archais*, qui était destiné à l'arc. Les pointes des flèches variaient de formes, dont plusieurs étaient semblables à celles des *carrels* ou *carreaux* d'arbalètes, c'est-à-dire carrées, à deux, trois, même à quatre pointes, et aussi à

barbes, comme les pointes des flèches antiques. Il y avait
en outre des pointes tire-bouchons, des pointes pétales et
des pointes *luna;* ces dernières, en forme de croissant,
servaient à couper les jarrets des hommes et des chevaux.

L'arbalète, désignée par Anna Comnène sous le nom de
tzagra, est aussi mentionnée par Guillaume de Tyr, du
temps de la première croisade (1098). Sous Louis VI, le
Gros (1108-1137), elle était déjà très-répandue en France,
et un canon du second concile de Latran, tenu en 1139,
en défend l'usage — entre chrétiens, bien entendu, tandis
qu'il autorise de continuer d'en frapper les infidèles et
les mécréants! En Angleterre, Richard Cœur de Lion
(1189-1190), fit cependant entrer des arbalétriers dans ses
troupes, malgré le bref d'Innocent III. Philippe-Auguste
(1180-1233) aussi créa en France les premières compagnies d'arbalétriers à pied et à cheval, dont l'importance
devint telle que leur chef portait le titre de grand maître
d'arbalétriers, charge qui était la première dans l'armée,
après celle de maréchal de France, et qui ne fut réunie
qu'en 1515 à celle du grand maître de l'artillerie.

La charte de Théobald, comte de Champagne, de l'année 1220, dit : « Chacuns de la commune de Vitré aura
XX livres, aura *aubeleste* en son ostel et *quarriaux,* etc. »
On trouve également une mention sur les arbalétriers dans
la chronique de Saint-Denis. Les premières arbalètes reproduites dans les peintures du temps sont celles d'un manuscrit anglo-saxon du onzième siècle au musée Britannique, et aussi des fresques exécutées au dôme de Brunsvick
sous Henri le Lion, mort en 1195, et à la chapelle de Saint-
Jean, à Gand, au treizième siècle. On sait que Boles-
laus, duc de Schweidnitz, introduisit dans ses États, déjà
en 1286, le *tir à l'arbalète,* établi peu de temps après à
Nuremberg et à Augsbourg. — En France, où Charles VII
avait fait planter dans tous les cimetières de la Normandie
des ifs pour la fabrication de cette arme, son usage avait

entièrement remplacé celui de l'arc, que les Anglais ont
conservé jusqu'à la fin du règne de la reine Élisabeth
(1558-1603), où les archers étaient tous armés de brigantines et de casques. L'arc leur conserva longtemps une supériorité de tir sur l'armée française, où l'arbalétrier pouvait à peine répondre par trois traits de carreaux contre
douze traits de flèches. En outre, la pluie détendait la
corde de l'arbalète, et lui ôtait sa force, tandis que la corde
de l'arc pouvait facilement être mise à l'abri de l'humidité.
La perte de la bataille de Crécy (1346) fut en partie le
résultat de cet inconvénient, parce qu'aux traits sûrs des
archers anglais, les arbalétriers français pouvaient à peine
riposter, et lorsque, en 1356, après la nouvelle défaite à
Poitiers, l'infériorité relative de l'arbalète se fut de nouveau montrée, on créa en France des corps d'archers dont
l'habileté fut bientôt telle, que la noblesse en prit ombrage
et les fit dissoudre. En 1627, au siége de la Rochelle, on
trouva même encore des archers anglais mercenaires, à
la solde de Richelieu, qui y figurent à l'attaque de l'île
de Ré.

L'arbalète, qui était aussi devenue une arme favorite des
Allemands, qui la perfectionnèrent de différentes manières, cessa d'être en usage en France au dix-septième
siècle, où les corps d'arbalétriers furent définitivement
supprimés. Les arbalètes des compagnies à cheval étaient
plus légères que celles des hommes à pied, et se tendaient
au moyen d'un simple levier, appelé *pied-de-biche;* le *cric
à manivelle,* appelé *cranequin,* qui servait à monter l'arme
de l'infanterie, fit donner à ces arbalétriers le nom de *cranequeniers.* Le chroniqueur Monstrelet (1390-1453) les appelle cependant *petaudiers* et *bibaudiers.*

Il y a sept espèces distinctes de ces armes, ce sont :

L'arbalète à pied de biche, arme propre à la cavalerie ;
L'arbalète à cric à manivelle, appelée arbalète à *crane-*

quin, accessoire qui fit donner aux arbalétriers à pied, comme il vient d'être dit, le nom de *cranequeniers*;

L'arbalète à moufle, aussi nommée *à tour* et de *passot*, très-propre aux siéges et aux tirs de cible. C'est de cette arbalète que les arbalétriers génois étaient armés à la bataille d'Azincourt (1420);

L'arbalète allemande ou *à rouet d'engrenage dans l'arbrier*;

L'arbalète à galet, du seizième siècle, qui tire son nom des petits cailloux ronds qu'elle lançait, aussi bien que des balles de plomb et de terre cuite à la place des carreaux-flèches. Les Allemands l'appelaient *balestre* dès qu'elle était d'un calibre un peu grand.

L'arbalète à baguette, arme lourde et sans force, du temps de Louis XIV.

Et enfin, *l'arbalète-chinoise*, pourvue d'un tiroir qui glisse sur l'arbrier, au moyen d'un levier à poignée, et qui fournit vingt fois une flèche nouvelle, comme un fusil à répétition fournit ses charges.

Les projectiles lancés par les arbalètes, à l'exception des arbalètes à galets, s'appelaient *carrels* ou *carreaux*, dont le nom leur venait de la forme du fer qui garnissait la pointe, ordinairement carrée. Le *vireton* était un carreau empenné de plumes, ou de lames de bois ou de cuir inclinées sur l'axe pour imprimer au trait un mouvement de rotation. Le carreau assommant appelé *matras* était terminé par un disque rond qui tuait en assommant, trait de chasse plutôt que de guerre. On s'en servait contre le gibier dont on voulait conserver la dépouille intacte et sans taches de sang.

Quand on arrive *aux armes à feu*, dont l'usage en Europe ne remonte pas au delà du quatorzième siècle, la question se complique.

La poudre à canon, connue déjà des Chinois durant des siècles avant qu'elle ne fût répandue chez nous, où elle avait été regardée pendant longtemps comme l'invention des moines Constantin Amalzen ou Schwarz (1280-1320), d'un couvent de Fribourg en Brisgau, paraît aussi avoir été connue des peuples celtiques et de tous les anciens. Les palafittes ou habitations lacustres en Suisse, qui, grâce aux travaux du docteur Keller, ont été pour ainsi dire reconstruites, contiennent quelquefois des boules incendiaires dont la composition pourrait bien être celle de la poudre à canon. La dénomination de *Shet-à-gene* (*centueur*), et d'*agenaster* (armes à feu?) des livres sacrés indiens, ainsi que les engins au moyen desquels, selon Dion Cassius, Caligula imitait le tonnerre et le feu du ciel, peuvent également autoriser d'admettre l'existence d'une poudre explosive de guerre que Vossius (*Liber observationum*), croit reconnaître dans une description de Jules l'Africain qui vivait l'an 215 de notre ère.

La *Falarique* des Romains, usitée aussi au moyen âge, cette espèce de flèche incendiaire que Grégoire de Tours croit d'origine celtique, n'était probablement pas autre chose qu'une préparation de matières semblables à celles employées à la fabrication de la poudre à canon.

Les trois sortes de feu grégeois que le grec Callinicus avait appris à composer chez les Arabes et dont il communiqua le secret à Constantinus Pogonatus, pendant le siége de Constantinople, comprenaient une espèce qui paraît avoir été semblable à la poudre actuelle. *Les armes à feu*, dont selon Hagiacus les Arabes se servaient en 690 devant la Mecque, peuvent encore faire supposer que l'Islamisme n'a pas seulement été répandu à son apparition au moyen du sabre, mais aussi par la poudre à canon, dont le secret était probablement venu de l'Inde, car les Arabes appellent le salpêtre *Thely-Sini*, ce qui veut dire neige indienne ou chinoise, comme les Persans l'appellent *Nemek-T'schini*, sel indien ou chinois. Les embrasures pour canons, ménagées dans le mur de la Chine, construit deux cents ans avant notre ère, ne fournissent-elles pas encore une preuve que les Chinois connaissaient déjà l'artillerie à cette époque? Le *Liber ignium ad comburendos hostes* de Marcus Græcus (846 ans après Jésus-Christ) donne déjà clairement la recette pour composer la poudre et prouve que l'auteur connaissait même la raquette ; cette recette contient, entre autres, six parties de salpêtre, deux de soufre et deux de charbon. En 1232, l'emploi régulier de la poudre à canon dans la guerre entre les Tartares et les Chinois, ainsi qu'au siége de Séville, en 1247, est attesté, et la composition de cette poudre, aussi bien que celle de la raquette, donnée dans *De Mirabilibus mundi* de l'évêque Albertus Magnus de Ratisbonne (1280), permet de fixer des dates certaines.

Jusqu'au commencement du quatorzième siècle, ce que l'on appelait armes à feu paraît uniquement avoir servi, en Europe, à mettre le feu dans les places assiégées et à incendier les machines des assiégeants, mais non pas à lancer des projectiles en pierre, en plomb ou en fer ; et ce n'est qu'à partir de cette époque que l'histoire de l'artillerie ou des armes à feu en général, commence.

Avant l'emploi de la poudre à canon, le succès de la guerre résultait autant de la force musculaire des troupes employées que de la conception stratégique de leurs chefs et de la *furia* des combattants ; car le capitaine avait beau manœuvrer, la fin décisive résultait toujours d'une lutte corps à corps, luttes acharnées, épouvantables, dont les guerres modernes, malgré leurs formidables moyens de destruction, n'offrent point d'exemple.

Dès que l'emploi de l'artillerie eut changé la base de la guerre, les batailles changèrent entièrement de caractère. On ne débutait plus par des attaques où, après quelques traits de flèches ou de carels, les combattants, l'arme blanche à la main, se ruaient de suite les uns sur les autres. On commençait à se décimer de loin au moyen de corps

projetés par des forces explosives et mécaniques, et ce n'est
qu'à la fin de l'action, quand il s'agissait de rester ou de
se rendre maître d'une localité de la possession de laquelle
dépendait le gain de la bataille, qu'une lutte à l'arme
blanche était nécessaire pour décider de la journée. La
poudre à canon, dont le *grenage* était connu dès 1452, on
ne peut assez le répéter, a, aussi bien que l'imprimerie,
puissamment aidé à sauvegarder la civilisation actuelle du
sort des civilisations perdues.

Pour procéder avec système, il faut diviser les armes
à feu en deux parties principales, dont l'une comprend
toutes les armes à feu de gros calibre (canons, etc.), l'autre
les armes à feu portatives.

Il est rationnel d'admettre, avec la tradition, que l'idée
de se servir, au moyen âge, de la poudre pour projeter des
corps par un gros tuyau de métal, est venu à l'homme par
un accident. En écrasant dans le mortier des mixtions de
salpêtre, de soufre et de charbon, il s'est vu rejeter, lui et
son pilon, par l'explosion amenée par le pilage : *c'est avec
ce même mortier domestique, qu'il doit avoir formé sa
première bouche à feu*, en pratiquant un petit trou à
l'extrémité inférieure, pour pouvoir y mettre le feu sans
danger pour lui-même. Le *mortier* doit donc être regardé
comme la première forme de l'arme à feu européenne. Peu
de temps après l'apparition de cette arme, on confectionna
déjà des pierriers ou mortiers, au moyen de barres de
fer forgées, réunies entre elles, comme les douves d'un
tonneau, par des cerceaux, genre de bouches à feu dont
l'arsenal de Vienne possède la plus monstrueuse (1 m. 10 c.
de diamètre sur 2 m. 50 c. de longueur.) Le premier *canon* proprement dit (nom qui dérive de l'allemand : *Kanne*
ou *Canne*, pot, canette), ordinairement désigné sous le
nom de *bombarde* également en fer forgé, était encore un
mortier, mais *ouvert aux deux extrémités*. On y introduisait
la charge à l'extrémité inférieure (la culasse), et on fer-

mait cette ouverture avec des coins en métal ou même en bois, d'une seule ou de plusieurs pièces, que l'on enfonçait à coups de maillet ; c'est ce mode, le plus ancien dans la construction du canon que l'on retrouve encore en Allemagne au seizième siècle, mais perfectionné. Il fut suivi par celui de la *charge à la boîte mobile* (canon qui était composé dès lors de la *volée* et de la *chambre à feu*, et s'appelait *veuglaire*, de l'allemand *Vogler* oiseleur) et enfin du mode *de la charge par la volée* (bouche).

En se rapportant aux textes et aux dessins plus ou moins fantaisistes des auteurs du quinzième et du seizième siècle, on devrait placer l'apparition de la *bombarde ou canon ouvert aux deux extrémités*, après le *veuglaire*, *canon composé de deux parties et se chargeant par la boîte mobile dite chambre ;* les pièces qui existent, et dont l'origine et l'époque de fabrication sont connues, démontrent cependant que le veuglaire est plus moderne que la bombarde.

Les canons en fonte ont succédé aux canons en fer forgé.

La première mention de ces nouvelles armes à feu, ou mieux dit à poudre, qui, pendant bien longtemps encore, ne purent entièrement supplanter les vieilles machines de guerre, dont l'usage dans les siéges s'est continué jusqu'à la fin du moyen âge, remonte à l'an 1301, où la ville d'Amberg, en Allemagne, avait fait confectionner une *grande bouche à feu*, et où Brescia avait été accablé sous un *feu d'arquebuses* (?). En 1313, la ville de Gand avait aussi déjà des *pierriers*, et c'est peut-être des Flandres qu'Édouard III fit venir ces nouvelles armes pour s'en servir, en 1227, contre les Écossais.

En 1325, la république de Florence accorde aux *prieurs*, aux *gonfaloniers* et aux *douze bons hommes* (magistrats municipaux) le droit de nommer deux officiers chargés de faire fabriquer des boulets de fer et des canons de métal pour la défense des châteaux et des villages appartenant à la république.

Peu d'années après, en 1328, l'ordre teutonique, tout au nord de l'Europe, disposait déjà de *grands canons*, dont il fit usage dans ses guerres en Prusse et en Lithuanie. C'est à cette époque que toutes les villes libres d'Allemagne commençaient aussi à se pourvoir d'artillerie.

L'histoire constate qu'en France, aux siéges du Puy-Guillem et de Cambrai, par Édouard III, en 1339, le canon a déjà joué son rôle, comme à la bataille de Crécy, en 1346, où les Anglais se servirent de canons, dont les reproductions existent en dessins.

Si on se rapporte à un passage de *De remediis utriusque fortunæ*, de Pétrarque (1382), il existait alors en Italie des canons en bois. J'ignore si les petits canons en bois, formés de douves épaisses recouvertes de cuir, qui se trouvent à l'arsenal de Gênes, remontent à cette époque ou s'ils appartiennent à l'époque des canons en cuir suédois de la guerre de Trente ans.

En 1428, les Anglais firent jouer, devant Orléans, quinze bouches à feu *se chargeant par la culasse*.

Lorsque la charge par la volée eut remplacé celles par la culasse et par la boîte mobile, on introduisit d'abord la munition au moyen d'une chargette en cuivre, qui se trouve encore représentée dans l'ouvrage de Fronsberg, du seizième siècle, et dont l'arsenal de Soleure possède un exemplaire. Entre la charge de poudre et le boulet (d'abord en pierre, appelé *pierre* tout court) se plaçait la bourre, qui était en bois. Le feu fut d'abord mis à la pièce au moyen d'un charbon ardent ou d'un fer rougi; ce n'est que plus tard que l'on se servit de la mèche attachée à une hampe. Les mantelets ou blindes mobiles en bois (*Schirmdaecher*), qui s'abaissaient pendant que l'on chargeait les canons, servaient à mettre à l'abri le canonnier ou *constable*, et son aide, le *servant*. C'est à Tournay, en 1346, qu'un nommé Piers fit le premier essai avec des projectiles longs et pointus, qui peuvent être regardés comme les précurseurs des

7.

boulets coniques actuels, et c'est l'artillerie du duc de Brunswick qui, selon la Chronique thuringeoise de Rothe, employa, en 1365, les premiers boulets en plomb, nouveau genre de projectiles que quelques industriels allemands expédièrent peu de temps après, avec un grand nombre de canons en fer, aux Vénitiens, qui s'en servirent avec succès au siége de Claudia-Fossa.

Vers 1400, le boulet en fer remplaça le boulet en plomb. Un manuscrit du quinzième siècle, conservé à la collection d'Ambras, à Vienne, contient des dessins où, entre autres, on voit le canonnier occupé à charger sa pièce, par la culasse, de *boulets rougis au feu*. Ce même manuscrit, ainsi qu'un autre de la collection Hauslaub, à Vienne, montre aussi de quelle manière on se servait du *petit baril incendiaire* dans les siéges de cette époque.

En Suisse, l'introduction de l'arme à feu date de plus tard ; Bâle fit fondre ses premiers canons en 1371, Berne en 1413.

En 1372 déjà, à la bataille de Rhodes, des vaisseaux français tiraient des *caronades*.

Quant à l'emploi du bronze pour la fonte des bouches à feu et à l'emploi des boulets creux en plomb et en fer, il n'en est question qu'en 1378, à propos de trente pièces coulées à Augsbourg par le fondeur Aarau.

La fonte de canon de bronze en Italie ne remonte que vers 1470.

Les *tourillons* ou goujons, qui supportent le poids du canon, le tiennent en équilibre, empêchent son recul sur l'affût et rendent le *heurtoir* superflu, apparaissaient également déjà en Allemagne vers le milieu du quinzième siècle, sans qu'on sache qui, le premier, a introduit cette amélioration, dont la découverte surpasse en importance tout ce qui avait été réalisé à cette époque dans l'artillerie ; elle permettait de donner un pointage sûr et facile dans le sens vertical.

L'artillerie du *Téméraire* n'avait pas de tourillons comme on le croit; en se basant sur des documents peu authentiques. Les pièces prises à Morat (1476), conservées au musée d'artillerie de Paris et au gymnase de Morat aussi bien que celles prises à Grandson et à Nancy et conservées à Lausanne et à Neuville, n'ont point de tourillons.

Le canon fut introduit en Russie en 1389; et les *Taborins*, les vengeurs de Hus se servaient déjà d'obusiers en 1434.

D'abord immobiles et ordinairement posées sur des poutres ou dans des boîtes (*affûts fixes*), ces bouches à feu furent pourvues, vers 1492, d'*affûts mobiles* qui permettaient de diriger le tir en tout sens. La *scala librorum*, mesure de calibre, inventée en 1440 par Hartmann, de Nuremberg, fut introduite dans toute l'Allemagne, où le célèbre fondeur de Charles-Quint, Georges Lofler, à Augsbourg, répandit aussi l'*unité* des quatre calibres (de 6, de 12, de 24 et de 40). C'est à cette époque que l'on voit apparaître le *boulet en fonte*, qui devait apporter une révolution dans l'artillerie.

Quant aux *mines à poudre*, qui furent précédées, au moyen âge, par les *mines à brûlots*, on admet ordinairement que leur premier emploi a eu lieu en 1503 à Naples, assiégée par le général espagnol Gonzalve de Cordoue, quoique Vannoccio Biringuccio l'attribue à l'ingénieur italien Francisco di Giorgio.

Les bouches à feu, fixées d'abord sur des poutres et des boîtes en charpente, furent bientôt placées sur des affûts à roues, et dotées peu à peu d'engrenages et d'avant-trains. Vers la fin du quatorzième siècle, on commençait à pourvoir l'ancien chariot hérissé de lances, et destiné à la défense des camps, de petits canons encastrés dans du bois, chariots qui prirent alors le nom de *ribaudequins* (*ribaud*, aide-artilleur); ils continuaient à servir contre les surprises de la cavalerie. Ces engins, ordinairement placés sur deux roues, se retrouvent encore dans les dessins de Nicolas Glokenthon, exécutés en 1505, d'après les pièces existantes alors dans les arsenaux de l'empereur Maximilien.

Il est très-difficile, sinon tout à fait impraticable, de
classer exactement toutes les espèces de bouches à feu selon les noms en usage à cette époque, où souvent la même
espèce d'armes était désignée de différentes manières, dans
chaque grande ville. Il y avait des serpentines (*Rothschlangen*, en allem.), couleuvrines (*Feldschlangen*), demi-
couleuvrines, faucons (*Falkaunen* ou *Falkhahne*), et fauconneaux (*Falconette*). Il y avait aussi des mortiers (*Mœrser*, ou
Bœller ou *Roller*, en allem.), qui étaient transportés, comme
les pierriers, sur des chariots. Passe-volants, basilics, spirales, bombardes, veuglaires et pierriers sont encore de ces
désignations vagues dont on se servait en France. L'*orgue
à serpentins* (*Orgelgeschütz*, en allemand), et le *serpentin revolver*, arme composée d'un grand nombre de canons de petit calibre et se chargeant ou par la volée ou
par la culasse, avait ses âmes engagées jusqu'à la volée
dans une monture de charpente ou de métal; on les tirait
par rangée ou tous à la fois. En allemand, ils portaient
aussi le nom d'orgue de mort (*Todtenorgel*), ce qui fait
dire à Weigel (1698) à propos de l'arsenal de Nuremberg :
« qu'il y avait des orgues de trente-trois tuyaux, sur lesquels la mort jouait la danse. » Une des plus anciennes
armes de ce genre, des premières années du quinzième
siècle, se trouve au musée de Sigmaringen. Elle se
charge par la volée et est composée de petits canons en
fer forgé, grossièrement montés dans une sorte de tronc
d'arbre, qui est rendu transportable par deux roues primitives sans rais ni jantes. Un autre orgue de *danse macabre*, dessiné vers 1505, dans les arsenaux de l'empereur
Maximilien, par Nicolaus Glockenthon, a quarante canons
de forme carrée, parfaitement réunis entre eux et montés
sur un affût à hautes roues de pièce de campagne. Un troisième exemplaire du dix-septième siècle, de quarante-deux

canons, montés de manière à former un triangle et fournis-
sant six décharges successives, est conservé au musée de
Soleure. Il paraît, d'après les *Etudes sur l'artillerie* par
l'empereur Napoléon III, publiées en 1846, qu'il a existé
de ces orgues qui tiraient jusqu'à cent quarante coups à la
fois. Quant aux *grenades*, leur première apparition remonte
à 1536, tandis que l'emploi des *pétards*, dont l'invention
est attribuée aux Hongrois, ne date que de 1579.

Les Suédois avaient, dans la guerre de Trente ans, des
canons en cuir doublés d'un tuyau de laiton ou de cuivre
jaune. Ces canons, dont quelques exemplaires se trouvent
dans les arsenaux de Berlin et de Hambourg ainsi que dans
le musée d'artillerie de Paris et dans la collection d'armes
du roi de Suède, ont 2 mètres de longueur. Le tube intérieur, en cuivre mince, est entièrement ficelé d'une grande
corde qui sépare le fourreau de cuir du tube de laiton.
Ces bouches à feu n'avaient qu'une portée médiocre et ne
purent supporter que le quart d'une charge ordinaire. elles
furent supprimées après la bataille de Leipsig, où elles
étaient tellement échauffées qu'elles se déchargeaient spon-
tanément. On les remplaça par l'artillerie appelée alors, par
les hommes du métier, *suédoise*, arme qui différait, sur
plusieurs points, de celle de l'armée impériale autrichienne, et qui avait été proposée par le comte de Hamilton. L'arsenal de Zurich possède un autre genre de canons,
fort semblables à ces bouches à feu suédoises en cuir.
Comme celles-là, ce canon est formé d'un tuyau de cuivre
jaune, mais qui est plaqué tout autour, entre le fourreau
extérieur de cuir et le tuyau intérieur de cuivre, d'une
épaisse couche de chaux, et entouré en outre de plusieurs
cerceaux en fer forgé. Cette arme, très-propre, à cause de
sa légèreté, à être transportée à dos d'homme, dans un
pays aussi montagneux que la Suisse, est à tourillons
comme les canons suédois, et pourvue d'un couvre-platine
à charnière; elle a 2 mètres 30 centimètres de longueur.

La rayure du canon des armes portatives, inventées en Allemagne vers la fin du quinzième siècle, avait été aussi appliquée, un peu plus tard, aux canons de gros calibre, comme le démontrent le canon allemand rayé du seizième siècle, au musée de La Haye; le canon en fer à treize rayures, daté de 1661, à l'arsenal de Berlin, et le canon en fer forgé à huit raies, daté de 1694, conservé à Nuremberg. On ne s'est sérieusement occupé de la rayure du gros canon qu'après que l'Anglais Benjamin Rubens, membre de la Société royale de Londres, né en 1707, l'eut soumise à une étude mathématique. Depuis, l'artillerie moderne a été pour ainsi dire renouvelée par les travaux de Paixhans, publiés en 1822, par ceux d'Armstrong, et par les progrès extraordinaires que M. Krupp a fait faire à la fabrication des canons en acier fondu, dont il a exposé, en 1867, un modèle qui pesait cinquante mille kilogrammes et se chargeait, par la culasse, d'un projectile également en acier fondu, de cinq cent cinquante kilogrammes.

Les armes à feu portatives se confondaient en Europe, dans les premiers temps de l'emploi de la poudre, avec les pièces de l'artillerie de gros calibre. On ne rencontre de traces *d'armes à main* que vers le milieu du quatorzième siècle, et il paraît que les Flamands en avaient introduit chez eux l'usage avant qu'il ne fût répandu ailleurs. La ville de Liége avait déjà fait plusieurs essais pour la fabrication des *petits canons à main*, de ces armes portatives appelées, par les Allemands, *Knallbüchsen*, adoptés à Pérouse, en 1364, à Padoue, en 1386, et en Suisse en 1392, canons que l'on voit figurer en 1382 à la bataille de Rosbecq, en 1383 au siége de Trosky en Lithuanie, et que les archives de Bologne de 1399, appellent *sclopo*, d'où dérive *sclopeto* et *escopette*.

À Arras, en 1414, ce petit canon à main servait déjà à lancer des *balles de plomb*, comme au siége de Bonifacio en Corse (1420), où ces balles perçaient les armures. En 1429 et en 1430, la nouvelle arme commençait à servir au tir de cible, à Augsbourg et à Nuremberg, et à partir du quinzième siècle, à la cavalerie, comme le démontre l'expression de *Eques scoppetarius*, employée par Paulus Sanctinus.

Les modifications apportées continuellement dans la fabrication des différentes espèces d'armes portatives inventées depuis l'apparition du canon à main, ont donné le jour à de plus nombreuses dénominations encore que celles imaginées pour les armes à feu de gros calibre. En les classant rigoureusement selon leur mécanisme, on peut cependant les réduire à treize espèces distinctes, ce sont :

Le canon à main du milieu du quatorzième siècle, arme grossière en fer forgé, attachée sur une pièce de bois brute et impropre à l'épaulement; son trou de lumière, d'abord placé *au-dessus du canon*, est quelquefois pourvu d'un couvre-lumière à pivot ou à charnière, et destiné à préserver de l'humidité. Quelque temps après son apparition, le trou fut placé *du côté droit du canon*. Cette arme primitive se retrouve encore dans les aquarelles déjà mentionnées, que Glockenthon a exécutées vers 1505, d'après les pièces existantes alors dans les arsenaux de l'empereur Maximilien; on y voit quatre de ces petits canons attachés aux quatre angles d'une planchette et que l'arquebusier fait partir au moyen d'une mèche détachée. Ce canon à main était souvent deservi par deux hommes. De petite dimension et destiné à l'usage du cavalier, le canon à main était appelé en français *pétrinal* du vieux mot espagnol *pedernal* (pièce à feu), ou peut-être de ce qu'on l'appuyait, en déchargeant, contre la cuirasse.

Le canon à main à épauler de la fin du quatorzième siècle; il se distingue du précédent par une sorte de crosse grossièrement façonnée. Le trou de sa lumière est ordinairement *à droite du canon*. Toutes ces armes sont à mèche détachée.

Le canon à main à serpentin ou à dragon *sans détente ni*

gâchette, inventé vers 1424. La mèche était dès lors attachée à l'arme même, où elle était portée par le serpentin. Mieux fabriqué, on appelait ce canon à mains : *couleuvrine à main* et aussi *pétrinal* ou *poitrinal* dès qu'il avait une crosse pour pouvoir être appuyé sur la cuirasse.

Le canon à main à serpentin, sans détente, mais à gâchette, qui permettait déjà un tir plus sûr par l'épaulement.

La haquebuse (du mot allemand *Hack-Busse* ou canon à crochet) *à serpentin, à détente et à gâchette*, de la seconde moitié du quinzième siècle. C'est l'arme déjà perfectionnée et l'aïeule de nos fusils modernes : son canon avait environ un mètre de longueur.

La double haquebuse (*Doppelhacken* en allemand), arme à feu à double crochet ou serpentin. Elle servait ordinairement à la défense des remparts et avait de 1 mètre à 2 mètres de longeur. La platine se distingue de celle de l'haquebuse simple en ce qu'elle avait *deux serpentins* qui s'abattaient en sens opposés. Elle était souvent supportée par un pied garni au bout de pointes de fer ou de roues qui s'appelait *fourquine*. Toutes ces armes n'avaient encore ni visière, ni point de mire, et projetaient des balles en fer, en plomb ou en fer recouvert de plomb.

L'arquebuse à rouet ou *arquebuse allemande* (*Deutsche* ou *Radschlosbüchse* en allemand), inventée en 1515, à Nuremberg. Elle se signale par sa platine à *rouet* qui est ordinairement composée de dix pièces et n'a plus rien de commun avec les armes à mèche remplacée par la *pyrite sulfureuse* ou *pyrite jaune*, dite aussi *martiale* et *marcassite*, que l'on trouve en cubes d'un jaune d'or très-brillant. C'est cette même combinaison naturelle de soufre et de métal dont les patrouilles militaires romaines ne manquaient jamais d'emporter avec elles afin de se procurer rapidement du feu. Frottée par le rouet, la pyrite mettait le feu à la lumière.

La nouvelle arme n'a cependant jamais pu remplacer entièrement la haquebuse à mèche dont le mécanisme était bien plus simple, bien plus solide et bien plus sûr : durant l'action la pyrite sulfureuse, très-fragile, se cassait facilement.

Le musée de Dresde possède un petit canon à main de 28 centimètres de longueur et d'un calibre de 12 centimètres, du commencement du seizième siècle, qui paraît avoir précédé l'invention du rouet et en avoir donné la première conception. Une râpe fait jaillir des étincelles par son frottement contre de la pyrite sulfureuse, dès qu'on la retire de la platine. L'ignorance y vit pendant longtemps *la première arme à feu, inventée par* Berthold Schwarz (1290-1320), moine allemand, à qui l'on avait aussi attribué l'invention de la poudre. Le troupeau des compilateurs continue toujours d'appeler ce canon à mains, *Moenchsbüchse* (haquebuse de moine) et de le désigner comme la première arme à feu !

Le mousquet, dont la construction et le mécanisme sont les mêmes que ceux de l'arquebuse, est également, ou à mèche, ou à rouet, et il ne diffère de l'arquebuse que par son calibre ; la charge et le projectile ont le double de volume. Beaucoup plus pesant, il nécessitait l'emploi d'une fourche à appui, nommée *fourquine,* comme celle de la *double haquebuse.* Le mousquet français, en 1694, était ordinairement, selon Saint-Remy, du calibre de vingt balles de plomb à la livre ; il avait 3 pieds 8 pouces de canon, et, avec son fût ou monture, 5 pieds.

L'arquebuse ou le mousquet *à canon rayé* et à *balles forcées* par le maillet. Le canon rayé inventé en Allemagne, selon les uns, à Leipzig, en 1498, selon d'autres à Vienne, par Gaspar Zollner, ne fut adopté dans l'armée française, qu'en 1793 : c'était la carabine de Versailles.

L'arquebuse ou le mousquet à chenapan, dont le nom corrompu, de l'allemand *Schnapphahn*, coq qui happe,

indique l'origine de son invention qui remonte à la seconde
moitié du seizième siècle, puisque l'on connaît la mention
d'un payement fait en 1588 par le chambellan de Norwich
en Angleterre à l'arquebusier Henri Radoc, pour avoir
changé, à un pistolet, la platine à rouet en batterie à chenapan. Le nom de chenapan fut bientôt donné en France
aux bandits armés de cette nouvelle arquebuse. On y appelait aussi bien chenapans les miquelets des Pyrénées,
enrégimentés sous Louis XIII, que les barbets des Alpes,
ces derniers débris des malheureux Vaudois, forcés par l'in-
tolérance religieuse à se faire maraudeurs et contrebandiers.
La batterie à chenapan, qui fonctionnait toujours encore
au moyen de la pyrite sulfureuse, peut être regardée
comme le précurseur de la batterie française à silex qui en
est le dérivé. Presque toutes les armes orientales et particulièrement les fusils turcs, à partir de cette époque,
sont à chenapan.

Le fusil à batterie française à silex, selon toute probabilité inventé en France, vers 1640. Ce fusil est aussi nommé
fusil-mousquet, dès qu'il est à baïonnette *à douille* dont
l'invention est attribuée à tort au général anglais Mackay,
en 1691, et qui fut introduit dans l'armée française par
Vauban. La douille permettait de tirer en conservant la
baïonnette sur le canon. D'abord à manche, elle devait être
fixée dans le canon même au moment de l'attaque à l'arme
blanche, ce qui offrait de grands inconvénients.

Quelques auteurs italiens ont voulu attribuer à leur
pays l'invention du fusil, parce que son nom paraît venir
du *focile* italien, qui dérive du latin *focus*, feu ; mais comme
le mot fusil apparaît déjà en France, dans des ordonnances
de chasse de l'année 1515, c'est-à-dire près de cent cinquante ans avant le remplacement du rouet par la batterie à
silex, on doit admettre que le nom de fusil était alors applicable aux arquebuses des anciens systèmes. Il a été dit
plus haut, que l'invention de la douille de la baïonnette

est attribuée *à tort* au général anglais Mackay en 1691. M. Culemann, à Hanovre, possède une arquebuse à rouet de la fin du seizième siècle, où une longue baïonnette, dont la lame qui sert en même temps de grattoir de canon, est à douille.

Le changement que la platine de l'arme à feu subit par l'invention de la batterie à silex était important, mais ni subit ni radical, puisqu'il avait été précédé de la platine à chenapan qui avait déjà le *chien* et la *batterie*. Dans la batterie française, la pyrite était remplacée par le silex qui, serré dans les mâchoires du chien, était choqué avec force contre la pièce d'acier de la *batterie*, dès que le doigt lâchait la *détente* en s'appuyant sur la *gâchette*, et faisait jaillir des étincelles qui enflammaient la poudre du *bassinet* là où débouche *le trou de la lumière*.

Vauban imagina aussi un fusil à *double feu*, d'après l'arquebuse à double feu à serpentin et à rouet, pour que, dans le cas où viendrait à rater la batterie, un serpentin à mèche pût mettre le feu à l'amorce. L'ancien mousquet à mèche ne fut définitivement remplacé dans l'armée française par le nouveau fusil à batterie que vers 1700.

Le prince Léopold Ier, d'Anhalt-Dessau, l'organisateur de l'infanterie prussienne, introduisit en 1698 la *baguette en fer* dans l'armement de ses troupes, et cette amélioration contribua, en 1741, au gain de la bataille de Molwitz.

La *cartouche*, c'est-à-dire la charge de l'arme à feu renfermée toute composée dans un seul étui, paraît avoir été mise en usage, pour la première fois, en Espagne, vers 1569 : elle ne fut adoptée en France qu'en 1644, en même temps que la *giberne* inventée par Gustave-Adolphe, vers 1630.

La *carabine* est une arme à canon rayé ordinairement plus court et destinée à la cavalerie, mais on appelle aussi carabine les armes à feu de chasse et de guerre pourvues de canons rayés.

Le *mousquet-tonnerre* ou mousquet tromblon (*Streu-büchse* en allemand), avait le canon large et la volée en trompette; il lançait 10 à 12 balles à la fois.

Le *pistolet*, ce diminutif de l'arquebuse et du fusil dont le nom dérive probablement de *pistallo*, pommeau, garniture, en italien, et non pas de *Pistoia*, ville, paraît être originaire de Perugia où, en 1364 déjà, on a fabriqué de ces *canons à main* de la largeur d'*une palme*.

Le *coup de poing*, appelé en allemand *Tercerole*, est un petit pistolet de poche, probablement d'origine italienne.

Le *fusil à percussion* ou *à piston*, dont l'invention est attribuée à tort au capitaine anglais Fergusson, commandant d'un régiment hessois dans la guerre d'Amérique (1775-1783) ne date que de 1807, où son véritable inventeur, l'armurier écossais Forsith, prit un *brevet pour le fusil à percussion*. Les premières recherches chimiques concernant les composés de matières détonantes (*ammoniures*, *fulminants*), qu'il ne faut pas confondre avec les *fulminates*, paraissent dues à Pierre Bouldure, en 1699. Nicolas Lemery continua ces recherches en 1712. Bayon, pharmacien des armées sous Louis XV, paraît avoir fait connaître, en 1764, le *fulminate de mercure*, sel composé de carbone, d'azote, d'oxygène et de mercure, dont l'invention est attribuée à tort à Howard, qui, en 1800, composa la *première poudre explosive* de fulminate de mercure et de salpêtre, composition propre à remplacer la poudre d'amorce dans les armes à feu. Liebig et Gay-Lussac ont fait en 1824 les analyses des fulminates, et c'est à Fourcroy, à Vauquelin et à Berthollet que l'on doit, entre 1785 et 1787, la découverte des sels fulminants d'ammoniures d'or, d'argent et de platine, ainsi que le muriate oxygène de chlorate de potasse.

En 1808, l'armurier Pauly, qui avait modifié le fusil de Forsith, l'introduisit en France. On peut encore citer le fusil à percussion de l'Anglais Joseph Eggs, parce qu'il amena ce même arquebusier à l'invention de la *capsule* ou amorce, petit cylindre en cuivre, ouvert d'un côté et rempli de fulminate. En 1826, M. Delvigne trouva la méthode de forcer la balle dans le canon rayé de la carabine, sans l'emploi du maillet, et de manière à éviter les inconvénients des systèmes essayés avant lui.

Le *Stecher*, piqueur, fort improprement nommé en français *double détente*, mécanisme ingénieux destiné à rendre presque insensible le mouvement produit en lâchant la détente ordinaire, et qu'un armurier de Munich avait inventé en 1543, ne constitue pas un système de plus, mais seulement une amélioration qui peut être adaptée à la plupart des carabines, et dont presque toutes les anciennes armes allemandes de précision, du seizième au dix-huitième siècle, sont dotées.

On a vu que la platine à rouet a été de tout temps fort peu en usage à la guerre; mais son adoption pour les armes de luxe et de chasse était universelle, et elle n'a cédé la place qu'à la percussion.

L'arquebuse et le mousquet à mèche et à rouet sont deux genres, il faut le répéter, qui ne diffèrent l'un de l'autre ni par le mécanisme ni par la forme, mais seulement par le calibre; C'étaient les armes des corps de troupes constitués. Les *arquebusiers* étaient pourvus de *grosses poires à poudre*, de *pulvérins*, à l'usage de l'amorce, de plusieurs mètres de mèches et d'un *sac de balles*. Les *mousquetaires* avaient, outre le *coussin* et l'*épée*, un baudrier garni de capsules en bois, dit *Pulvermassen*, en allem., un pulvérin, un sac à balles, des mèches et un couvre-mèche, ustensile en cuivre inventé par les Hollandais, et qui était presque identique avec le *couvre-mèche des grenadiers*, au dix-huitième siècle.

L'origine des armes à feu portatives se *chargeant par la culasse*, celles à *plusieurs canons*, et même des *armes à revolvers tournants*, remonte au commencement du seizième et même à la fin du quinzième; elles paraissent d'ori-

8.

gine allemande. Le Musée d'Artillerie de Paris possède une
arquebuse allemande à rouet du seizième siècle, se chargeant par la culasse au moyen d'un tonnerre mobile, et
une autre, également du seizième siècle, où le canon coupé
se charge au moyen d'un dé mobile, système qui a été repris dans les temps modernes.

L'*amussette du maréchal de Saxe* (1696-1750), au musée
d'Artillerie de Paris, se charge également par la culasse.
On trouve encore de ces armes à la Tour de Londres, aux
musées de Sigmaringen, de Dresde et à l'arsenal impérial
de Vienne. Le musée de Sigmaringen possède une arquebuse allemande, du seizième siècle, à revolver tournant de
sept coups, et un fusil allemand du dix-huitième, qui
est à quatre coups. Le musée d'Artillerie de Paris conserve une de ces armes dont la platine est encore à mèche.
En France, dans les temps modernes, ce sont Pauly en
1808, Leroy en 1813, et plus récemment Lepage, Gastine-
Renette et Lefaucheux, qui ont imaginé divers systèmes
de fusil à percussion se chargeant par la culasse; celui
de Lefaucheux seul est resté en application pour la plupart des armes de chasse, après que Grévelot eut introduit une si notable amélioration dans la fabrication des
capsules.

Le *fusil-revolver* ou *à répétition non-tournant*, ou mieux
dit *à coulisse*, c'est-à-dire l'arme dont le canon reçoit plusieurs charges se plaçant les unes sur les autres, et que l'on
peut faire partir successivement, n'est pas non plus d'invention moderne. Le musée de Sigmaringen possède un ancien fusil de ce genre; il est à coulisse et tire successivement six coups.

Depuis que l'Amérique a commencé à confectionner des
cartouches métalliques, le fusil à répétition a reparu dans
ce pays, où Spencer et Winchester ont imaginé des systèmes différents.

Le *pistolet-revolver* ou à répétition, remis en usage en

1815 par l'armurier Lenormand, à Paris, qui confectionna une de ces armes à cinq coups, fut bientôt suivi du revolver Devisme, à sept coups, et du revolver Hermann, à Liége; du pistolet Mariette à vingt-quatre coups, et enfin, en 1835, du revolver Colt, le meilleur de tous, et dont le système est celui de ces armes actuelles.

Après la description ou la mention de ces divers systèmes d'armes à feu, il ne reste qu'à parler du célèbre fusil à aiguille et se chargeant par la culasse. L'inventeur, Jean-Nicolas Dreyse, né en 1787, à Sœmmerda, près d'Erfurth, fabriqua le premier fusil à aiguille en 1827, après dix-sept ans de recherches, et obtint en 1828 un brevet de huit ans pour son *aiguille-ressort* et sa cartouche fulminante. Ce fusil, dont le premier modèle définitif fut adopté en Prusse vers 1841, a eu bien des changement à subir depuis son invention : ce n'est qu'en 1836 que le chargement par la culasse a été adopté dans la fabrication de cette arme. Depuis, chaque peuple a produit son fusil à aiguille et tâché d'inventer une arme même supérieure à celle qui avait donné de si terribles résultats dans la dernière guerre. Il est difficile de dire à laquelle de ces améliorations on peut décerner la palme.

Les résultats d'un tir comparé, qui a eu lieu, le 5 septembre 1868, à l'école de tir de Spandau, avec les modèles de fusils à aiguille adoptés par les diverses armées, sont, selon le rapport officiel, les suivants. Le fusil à aiguille prussien peut tirer, par minute, 12 coups, le chassepot 11, le fusil Snider (Angleterre) 10, le Romington (Danemarck) 14, le Peabody (Suisse) 13, le fusil Wœnzl (Autriche) 10, le fusil Werndl (même État) 12, et le fusil à répétition d'Henri Winchester (Amérique du Nord) 19. Sous le rapport des *touchés*, le modèle Henri Winchester est à placer en dernière ligne, il n'a, sur 19 coups, que 11 *touchés*.

II

ARMES DES ÉPOQUES ANTÉHISTORIQUES

DE L'AGE DE LA PIERRE

ARMES EN PIERRES TAILLÉES PAR ÉCLATS.
ARMES EN PIERRES POLIES.

ARMES EN PIERRES TAILLÉES PAR ÉCLATS

Il est certain, comme je l'ai déjà fait observer, que la terre, le bois, la peau de l'animal et particulièrement la *pierre*, répandue sur tout le globe, ont dû être nécessairement les matières premières que l'homme a employées à la confection de ses outils et de ses armes ; c'est donc par ces productions primitives qu'une histoire universelle de l'armement des peuples doit commencer. Il serait superflu de répéter ici tout ce qui a été déjà dit à ce sujet dans le précédent chapitre, aux premières pages ; il a été démontré que les armes en pierres *taillées par éclats* ont partout précédé celles en *pierres polies* dont la fabrication demandait déjà des procédés moins primitifs. Il existe aussi de ces armes qui ne sont ni dans l'état brut des premières, ni dans le poli fini des secondes, *lissées* mais non pas polies : elles appartiennent à des époques de transition qui varient naturellement de dates selon les pays. On a essayé, en France, de renfermer rigoureusement ces produits en trois classes : celle de la première apparition, celle de l'existence du renne en France et celle des dolmens ; mais comme les époques, dans la marche progressive de la civilisation, diffèrent quelquefois grandement, même chez les peuples d'une même origine ou d'une même race, ce classement laisse à désirer.

Les armes en pierre trouvées dans le Périgord avec des ossements dans une caverne, et dont quelques-unes portent des gravures représentant l'image du mastodonte, pourraient ajouter quelques preuves de l'existence de l'homme durant la troisième époque géologique, mais il faudrait auparavant soumettre ces gravures à des expériences microscopiques, afin de s'assurer de l'absence de toute fraude. Il ne suffit pas du reste que ces armes et ces ossements soient recueillis dans des terrains *alluviens-diluviens* qui peuvent avoir éprouvé des perturbations, comme cela est démontré par les *dépôts-meubles*, ainsi appelés parce qu'ils sont composés d'objets appartenant à différentes époques. Le *diluvium* (alpin) non remué ne contient aucune matière organique à l'état d'*ossine*, substance qui caractérise l'*os non fossile*, de sorte que toute alluvion contenant le moindre *os avec ossine* est postérieure à la grande perturbation terrestre appelée déluge.

Beaucoup d'armes et outils en pierres façonnées offrent aussi un signe sûr pour reconnaître qu'elles ne remontent pas au delà du déluge : c'est qu'ils sont fabriqués avec des *galets* où tout indique que ces pierres, prises dans des terrains situés dans l'intérieur de notre continent, ont été *roulées avant d'être façonnées*. La fabrication des armes en pierre, sans instrument de métal ni acides corrosifs, ne s'explique que par la facilité avec laquelle le silex, fraîchement sorti des carrières et avant d'avoir subi l'influence de l'air, se prête à la division par éclats.

1. Pointe de flèche babylonienne en silex de 6 cent., du règne de Nemrod, du fondateur de Babylone. — Musée de Berlin.

2. Couteau égyptien en silex de 10 cent. — Musée de Berlin.

3. Couteau égyptien en silex de 15 cent. — Musée de Berlin.

4. Lame de lance égyptienne en silex de 15 cent. Une quantité d'éclats en silex destinés à la fabrication des armes et outils a été aussi trouvée à Sarabut El Khaden. — Musée britannique.

5. Hache germanique en basalte de 18 cent., trouvée près Lintz (Autriche). — Musée de Sigmaringen.

6. Coin en serpentine de 16 cent., trouvé près Lintz (Autriche). — Musée de Sigmaringen.

7. Lame de lance (ou ciseau) germanique en silex de 18 cent.; trouvée à Balingen. — Musée de Sigmaringen.

8. Hache germanique en silex de 12 cent., trouvée à Rügen, île de la Baltique. — Musée de Berlin.

9. Couteau germanique en silex de 12 cent. — Musée de Berlin.

10. Pointe de lance germanique.

11. Hache à double croissant en pierre lissée, fabrication de l'époque transitoire entre la pierre taillée par éclats et la pierre polie; elle a 14 cent. de longueur et a été trouvée à Lunebourg.— Musée de la ville de Hanovre.

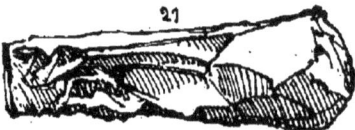

12. Hache celtico-gauloise en silex jaune et appelée Pain de beurre. Elle a 25 cent. de longueur et a été trouvée à Pressigny-le-Grand (Indre-et-Loire). V. *le Moniteur*, journal universel de l'Empire, du 18 mai 1865. — Col. de l'auteur.

13. Couteau celtico-gaulois en silex jaune de 12 cent., même provenance que n° 12. — Col. de l'auteur.

14. Couteau celtico-gaulois en silex jaune, de 7 1/2 cent. même provenance que n° 12 et 13. — Col. de l'auteur.

15. Poignard helvétique en silex de 12 cent., trouvé près Stavayé dans le lac de Neufchatel. — Musée de Fribourg.

16. Pointe de flèche britannique en silex de 6 cent. Elle peut remonter à une époque qui précède celle de la venue des Phéniciens. — Col. Llewelyn-Meyrick à Godrich-Court.

17. Pointe de flèche irlandaise à barbes, en silex blanchâtre de 14 cent. — Col. Cristy à Londres.

18. Coin ou hache britannique en silex blanchâtre de 14 cent. Elle a été trouvée à Cisburg-Camp près Sussex. — Col. Cristy à Londres.

19. Poignard ibérique ou hispanique en silex de 14 cent., trouvé à Gilbraltar. — Col. Cristy à Londres.

20. Couteau bohème en silex de 14 cent. — Musée de Prague.

21. Hache danoise en silex de 27 cent., (en danois Kiler of Flint). — Musée de Copenhague.

22. Hache danoise bien façonnée, en silex de 14 cent. (En danois *Kiler of Flint*). — Musée de Copenhague.

23. Lame ou pointe de lance danoise en silex de 18 cent. Cette arme (*Lansespits of Flint*), est pointue comme une arme en acier. Musée de Copenhague.

24. Lame de lance danoise en silex de 22 cent., moins aiguë que la précédente : elle dénote cependant la même habileté d'ouvriers. — Musée de Copenhague.

25. Poignard danois en silex de 29 cent. (*Dolk of Flint*), travaillé d'une manière admirable. — Musée de Copenhague.

26. Poignard danois à manche à pommeau en silex de 34 cent., merveille de travail. — Musée de Copenhague.

27. Sabre-hachette danois en silex de 38 cent., très-beau travail. — Musée de Copenhague.

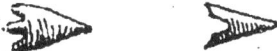

28. Deux pointes de flèches danoises à barbes et pointe en silex de 3 cent. (*Pilespidser of Flint* en danois). — Musée de Copenhague.

29. Longue pointe de flèche danoise sans barbes, en silex de 18 cent. — Musée de Copenhague.

ARMES EN PIERRES POLIES

Pour que le Danemark ait produit ces belles armes en pierre taillée par éclats, dont la finesse de travail surpasse ordinairement celle des armes en pierre polie de la seconde époque des autres pays, on peut admettre que les phases de sa civilisation ne correspondent pas à celles des peuples germaniques et gaulois, et qu'il a encore travaillé la pierre à une époque où beaucoup de ses voisins se servaient déjà du bronze. Les terrains *alluviens* où de grandes quantités de ces belles armes ont été trouvées dans des *Kiokkenmœdinge* ou rebuts de cuisine, paraissent indiquer que la fabrication de ces armes est postérieure aux armes des palaffites suisses, badoises et savoisiennes, qui n'ont fourni aucun objet en métal, et qu'elle ne remonte pas probablement au delà des palaffites de Noveto, de Castiane et de Pieschera, qui datent de l'âge du bronze.

Même en tenant compte de la marche plus ou moins rapide de la civilisation dans chaque pays, on arrive du reste difficilement à pouvoir fixer la priorité d'un peuple sur un autre dans la fabrication de ces armes primitives; là où tout est plongé dans l'obscurité historique, et où de nouvelles fouilles renversent périodiquement ce que des fouilles précédentes ont établi, on ne peut raisonner que par hypothèses. En Angleterre aussi, ces armes ont été trouvées uniquement dans des terrains alluviens ; mais les haches en silex brut ou taillé par éclats, de la collection Cristy à Londres, mentionnées dans le chapitre précédent, pourraient bien remonter au delà de la quatrième époque

9

géologique. Comme les armes modernes des peuples sauvages ne doivent pas entrer dans le cadre de cet ouvrage,
celles en pierre ont dû en être écartées aussi, même les anciennes, puisque la fabrication actuelle des sauvages est
restée ce qu'elle était dans les siècles passés. L'auteur a cru
utile cependant de faire une exception pour le Mexique,
puisque les armes qu'il a fait reproduire ne se fabriquent
plus.

Des démarcations exactes entre les époques où les
peuples se servaient d'armes en pierre brute et celles où
ces armes étaient déjà polies ou en bronze, peuvent difficilement être établies, parce qu'on a trouvé ces deux et
même ces trois produits confondus.

Les fouilles opérées au cimetière de Hallstadt ont même
fourni la preuve que le fer aussi était connu en Allemagne,
lorsque la pierre et le bronze servaient encore pour la
fabrication de la plupart des armes tranchantes. On trouvera dans le chapitre qui traite des produits de l'époque
dite l'âge du fer, des dessins qui reproduisent les pointes
d'ajonc en fer, recueillies dans les tombes de Hallstadt à
côté des armes en pierre et en bronze.

30. Coin, amulette ou talisman germanique, en serpentine, 4 cent. — Col. de l'auteur.

31. Hache germanique, serpentine, 22 cent., trouvée à Gonsenheim près Mayence. — Col. Cristy à Londres.

32. Hache germanique double, pierre de touche verdâtre, 15 cent., trouvée à Hildesheim. — Col. Cristy à Londres.

33. Hache-marteau germanique, granit, 15 cent., trouvée en Mecklembourg. — Col. Cristy à Londres.

34. Hache-marteau germanique, serpentine, 15 cent., trouvée à Kaufbeuren. — Mus. national bavarois à Munich.

35. Hache germanique, serpentine, 15 cent., trouvée à Enns près Lintz avec des armes en bronze et en fer. — Museum Francisco-Carolinum à Lintz.

36. Fragment de hache germanique, serpentine, 19 cent., trouvé avec des armes en bronze et en fer dans les tombeaux de Hallstatt. — Musée des Antiques à Vienne.

37. Hache double britannique, basalte, 11 cent. — Col. Cristy à Londres.

38. Grande hache celtico-gauloise, en jade, 38 cent. — Mus. de Vannes.

89. Petite hachette celtico-gauloise, en serpentine granitique, 8 cent., trouvée dans le Nivernais. — Col. de l'auteur.

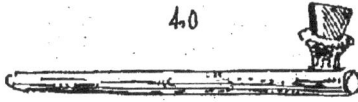

40. Hache celtico-suisse, serpentine montée en corne de cerf et à manche de bois, trouvée dans un palaffite suisse. — Musée de Zurich.

41. Hache celtico-suisse, serpentine montée sur un long manche en bois, trouvée à Rotenhausen. — Musée de Zurich.

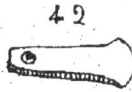

42. Hache danoise, basalte de 13 cent. — Musée de Copenhague.

43. Marteau d'armes danois, basalte de 12 cent. — Musée de Copenhague.

44. Hache danoise à deux tranchants, basalte de 21 cent. — Musée de Copenhague.

45. Hache danoise à deux tranchants, basalte de 12 cent. — Musée de Copenhague.

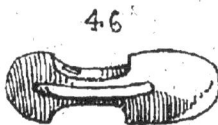

46. Hache danoise à deux tranchants, en basalte de 21 cent.

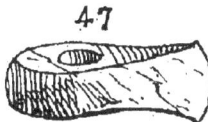

47. Hache danoise à un seul tranchant appelée *Niolner*, en basalte de 22 cent., trouvée dans un tombeau sur la côte d'Écosse. C'est le Niolner qui est l'attribut du dieu scandinave Thor ; il en est fait souvent mention dans les Sagas. — Col. Llewelyn-Meyrick.

48. Hache ibérique ou hispanique en basalte de 18 cent. — Col. Cristy à Londres.

49. Débris de hache hongroise en basalte de 18 cent. — Col. Cristy à Londres.

50. Marteau d'armes russe en pierre noire de 28 cent. — Musée de Saint-Pétersbourg. — Moulage au musée de Saint-Germain.

51. Épée mexicaine du quinzième siècle, en bois de fer garni de dix tranchants en obsidienne[1] noire. Cette arme a 60 cent. de longueur.

52. Épée mexicaine de 1 m. 20 cent. de longueur, en bois de fer et obsidienne noire. — Musée de Berlin.

53. Lame de lance mexicaine du quinzième siècle, en obsidienne noire montée sur hampe de bois.

1. L'obsidienne est un produit volcanique d'une couleur noirâtre tirant sur le vert, matière émailleuse, susceptible d'un poli fin, dans laquelle les Incas (Péruviens) se taillaient aussi leurs miroirs et les prêtres de Huitzilopochtli des ornements. L'obsidienne n'est cependant pas la seule pierre utilisée par les anciens Américains pour la fabrication de leurs armes tranchantes; ils employaient aussi le silex, la calcédoine et la serpentine.

9.

III

ARMES ANTIQUES DES AGES DU BRONZE
ET DU FER

ARMES HINDOUES; ARMES AMÉRICAINES;
ARMES CHALDÉENNES, BABYLONIENNES, ASSYRIENNES,
MÉDIQUES ET PERSES OU PERSIQUES;
ARMES ÉGYPTIENNES; ARMES GRECQUES ET ÉTRUSQUES;
ARMES ROMAINES, SAMNITES, ETC.

Les transformations d'armement chez les anciens, y
compris celles des cinq grandes monarchies assyriennes,
qui paraissent plutôt avoir communiqué le mode de la fabrication de leurs armes à l'Égypte et à la Grèce, que de
l'avoir emprunté d'elles, ont été développées dans le
chapitre historique, pages 29 à 39. On a vu que le fer
aussi bien que le bronze étaient employés indistinctement,
même dans la plus haute antiquité, pour la fabrication des
armes, et que l'établissement d'un véritable âge du bronze
et du fer est inadmissible. Si ces divisions ont été conservées dans le chapitre qui traite des armes du nord, c'est par
crainte de porter, par un classement plus rationnel, le
trouble dans les habitudes; mais l'auteur n'a agi ainsi qu'a-
près avoir pris ses réserves et expliqué comment il faut en-
tendre ces dénominations de convention. Peu d'armes et
armures, et peu de documents hindous, américains, assyriens et égyptiens sont parvenus jusqu'à nous; il a fallu
étudier l'histoire de l'équipement militaire de ces pays,
presque uniquement sur leurs monuments. Les musées sont

plus riches en armes grecques et romaines, qui permettent de suivre la transformation de l'armement sur la terre classique, durant un certain nombre de siècles. Les armes américaines ont été placées à la suite des armes hindoues, parce que tout porte à croire que les civilisations perdues de la vieille Amérique ont précédé même celles d'une grande partie de l'Inde et probablement celles des pays classiques.

Les céramiques américaines anciennes, parmi lesquelles on peut compter quelques produits palanquéens et mitlaiques, démontrent, même dans leur état de déclin artistique, à quelle hauteur avaient été élevés chez ces peuples, dont l'ombre même ne s'est pas reflétée sur les pages de l'histoire, le culte de la pureté des lignes et l'ornementation qui se retrouvent dans l'art égyptien, assyrien et grec. Le Louvre possède une de ces anciennes poteries d'outre-mer, où le dessin rappelle le décor des vases étrusques et la mythologie classique ; c'est un Hercule terrassant son antagoniste, et on connaît un grand nombre de céramiques américaines où les *grecques* indiquent également une priorité. Plus l'origine de ces produits est éloignée, plus ils se rapprochent par leur perfectionnement de l'art grec, de sorte que les moins anciens sont toujours les moins artistiques, ce qui autorise à conclure à l'existence d'une vieille civilisation déclinée dont l'époque florissante peut remonter à deux et même à trois mille ans avant J.-C.

ARMES HINDOUES.

Rien n'a été encore trouvé de ce qui concerne les armes des anciennes civilisations dont l'histoire remonte à l'an 3,000 avant J.-C. Les quelques figures ci-contre indiquent que l'armement hindou a peu varié, et que le casque seul accuse un changement radical qui paraît s'être manifesté à partir du quatorzième et du quinzième siècle de notre ère.

1. Guerriers hindous d'après les pierres granitiques mémoratives de Beenjanugar dont le musée de Kensington possède des reproductions photographiées. Ces monuments datent probablement d'une époque qui correspond à notre moyen âge [1].

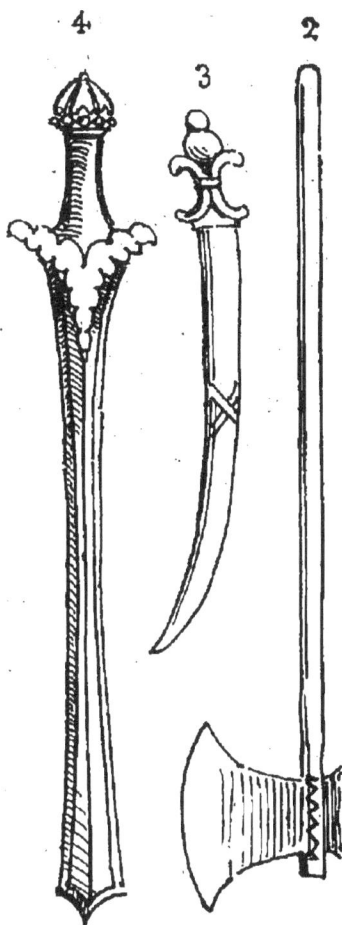

2. Hache d'armes hindoue d'après une sculpture indienne de la ville de Saitron en Rujpootana (1,100 ans de notre ère). — Musée de Kensington.

3. Sabre hindou d'après un bas-relief de Beenjanugar et du monument Hussoman.

4. Épée javanaise d'après la statue de la déesse de la guerre au musée de Berlin.

[1]. On remarquera que l'épée est placée du côté droit ; elle se trouve au côté gauche chez les Assyriens et les modernes, tandis que les Grecs et les Romains la portaient du côté droit. La gravure de ce bas-relief, imitée d'après la photographie, se trouve en sens inverse, de manière que les combattants ont à tort l'arme offensive à la main gauche.

ARMES AMÉRICAINES

J'ai fait observer, dans le chapitre historique, que les peuples de l'Amérique ne se sont jamais servis ni du bronze ni du fer pour la fabrication de leurs armes offensives, et que les conquérants européens y ont encore trouvé le règne de la pierre pure pour tout ce qui était arme tranchante. Quant à celles destinées à la défense, on en a fabriqué en bronze, en or, en nacre de perle, en corne, en bois et en peau, et on a trouvé les traces de différentes armes dont l'origine se perd dans la plus haute antiquité. Tel est le casque reproduit plus loin d'après un bas-relief en stuc des ruines de Palanqué, de ces ruines de la ville de Culhuacan[1], dont la circonférence était de trente kilomètres, ville située dans l'État de la Chiapa, partie septentrionale de l'Amérique, où l'on doit placer le berceau de la plus ancienne civilisation américaine disparue, qui pourrait bien être contemporaine, sinon antérieure à la civilisation hindoue. Le casque du bas-relief de Hochicalco est moins ancien, mais appartient toujours à une respectable antiquité où le cheval, introduit plus tard par des navigateurs, était encore inconnu. Comme les armes américaines de l'époque qui correspond au moyen âge chrétien sont insignifiantes et peu nombreuses, elles ont été placées à la fin du chapitre des armes en pierres polies, et non pas là où sont traitées les armes d'une provenance antérieure à l'époque mérovingienne. Ces armes américaines, comme on l'a vu, sont ordinairement en bois garnies de tranchants d'obsidienne.

1. Palanqué, ou mieux Culhuacan, ou Huehuetlapatl'an, n'a été découvert qu'en 1787, par Antonio del Rio et José Alonzo Calderon.

1. *Casque américain*, dessiné d'après un bas-relief de Palanqué. La figure de ce bas-relief mentionnée dans l'ouvrage de M. de Waldeck est représentée assise et la jambe gauche pliée sous le corps, tel qu'on voit souvent représenté le dieu Bouddha ou le Fo des Chinois.

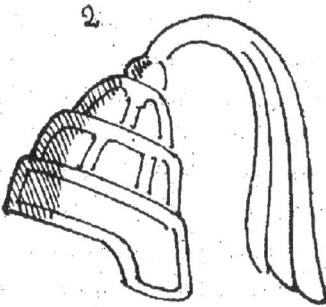

2. *Casque mexicain*, dessiné d'après un bas-relief de haute antiquité, de Hochicalco, province de Quemaraca, au Mexique.

3. *Deux casques mexicains*, reproduits d'après un manuscrit mexicain du commencement du quinzième siècle de notre ère, propriété de M. de Waldeck et qui décrit la conquête d'Ascapusala.

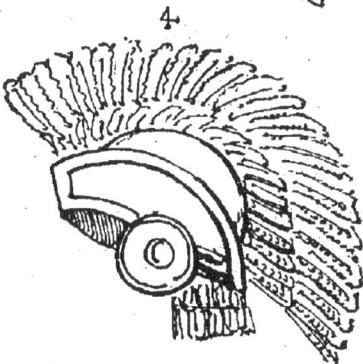

4. *Casque mexicain* en or massif garni de plumes, du quinzième siècle. Il faisait partie d'une armure royale détruite à Mexico dans un incendie.

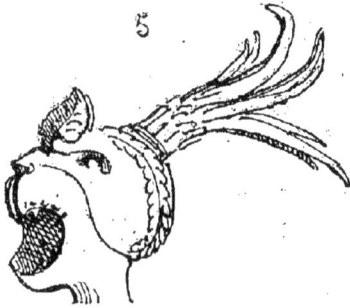

5. Casque mexicain en cuir, bois, peau de léopard et plumes, du quinzième siècle. — Reproduit d'après un manuscrit de cette époque.

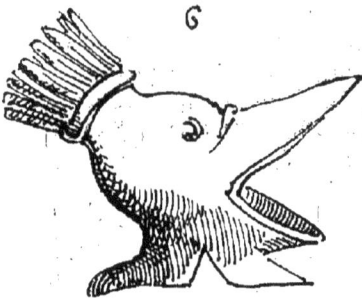

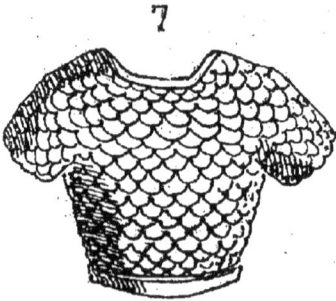

6. Casque mexicain en bois, peau et plumes, du quinzième siècle. — Reproduit d'après un manuscrit de cette époque.

7. Cuirasse mexicaine en écaille (Jazeran ou Korazin) de nacre de perles, du quinzième siècle. Cette belle arme défensive a fait partie d'une armure royale dont le casque, reproduit à la page précédente, sous le n° 4, était en or massif. Cette cuirasse a été également détruite, à Mexico, par un incendie.

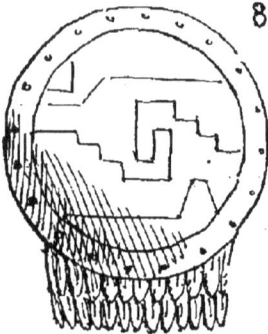

8. Bouclier, rondache mexicaine, de 60 cent. de diamètre, en or et argent, et garni de plumes à sa partie inférieure. Il faisait partie de la même armure royale du quinzième siècle détruite à Mexico. On n'a encore pu expliquer ce que les ornements hiéroglyphiques signifiaient.

9.

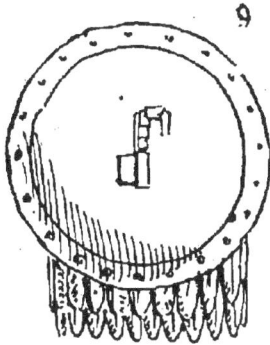

9. Bouclier, rondache mexicaine, de 60 cent. de diamètre, entièrement en cuir orné de l'hiéroglyphe par lequel on désignait chez les anciens Mexicains le chiffre *cent*, qui indique ici que ce bouclier a appartenu à un centurion ou capitaine qui commandait à cent hommes.

10

10. Enseigne ou étendard mexicain en or, du quinzième siècle, de 30 cent. de longueur et surmonté d'une *chapouline* ou sauterelle.

11

11. Enseigne mexicaine du quinzième siècle, en or, surmontée de la tête d'un aigle en grandeur naturelle.

Voir, pour les armes offensives américaines en bois et en obsidienne, la fin du chapitre qui traite des armes en pierre polie.

ARMES ASSYRIENNES, ETC.

L'histoire de l'armement des cinq monarchies que l'on a l'habitude de nommer toutes assyriennes, a été donnée pages 29 à 34. On a vu que le *fer* aussi bien que le bronze étaient déjà employés dans ces contrées au onzième siècle avant Jésus-Christ, comme les lingots et les quelques ustensiles en fer conservés au Louvre et le fragment de cotte de mailles en *acier* au musée britannique le démontrent.

---

1. Archer assyrien-babylonien en cotte d'armes, avec jambières et bandeau, à la place du casque. Bas-relief du septième siècle avant Jésus-Christ. — Musée du Louvre.

2. Homme de pied de l'armée assyrienne, armé de la cotte, d'un casque à cimier, d'une rondache et de la lance. On y remarque aussi des jambières. Bas-relief de Ninive du règne de Sardanapale V. — Septième siècle avant Jésus-Christ.

3. Sodat assyrien sans jambières, chassant le gibier. — Bas-relief de Khorsabad du règne de Sargon. — Musée britannique.

10

4. *Homme de pied de l'armée assyrienne* du temps de Sennachérib (712-707 av. J.-C.), d'après un bas-relief au musée britannique. La forme du casque conique se rapproche de celle du casque samnite (voir le chapitre des armes romaines et samnites); la cotte et les hauts-de-chausses paraissent en mailles; le bouclier est rond, à hauteur d'appui et très-convexe.

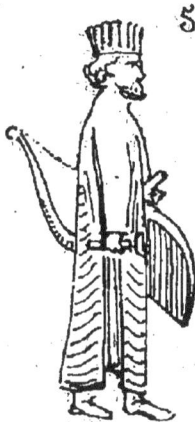

5. *Archer persique* d'après un bas-relief de Persépolis, l'ancienne capitale de la Perside et de toute la monarchie persane (560 av. J.-C.). La longue cotte, probablement en buffle, descend jusqu'à la cheville. La coiffure n'a rien d'un casque mais pourtant les caractères d'un travail en métal. L'archer porte l'épée du côté gauche tandis que les Grecs et les Romains la portent du côté droit.

6. *Guerrier persique* d'après un bas-relief de Persépolis dont le moulage se trouve au musée britannique. Le bouclier à hauteur d'appui est extrêmement bombé ou semi-circulaire, le casque à oreillères et couvre-nuque, et d'une seule pièce, diffère entièrement des autres casques assyriens que l'on connaît par les bas-reliefs.

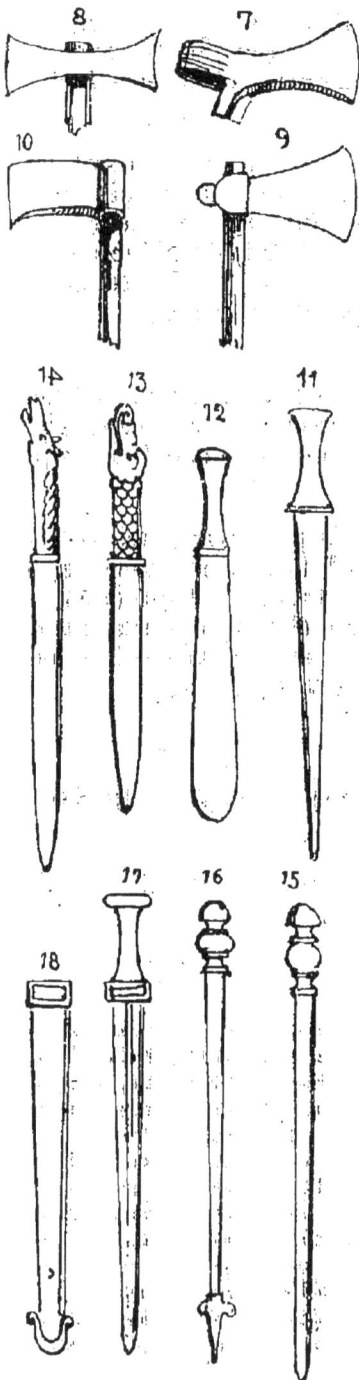

7. Hache assyrienne en bronze de 19 cent., trouvée à Babylone. — Musée britannique.

8. Hache assyrienne double, probablement en fer, d'après un bas-relief (Kogunïjk).

9. Hache assyrienne, simple, probablement en fer, d'après un bas-relief (Kogunïjk).

10. Hache assyrienne simple dont étaient aussi garnis les carquois des guerriers combattants sur des chars. D'après un moulage de bas-relief, au Louvre.

11. Dague babylonienne en bronze. — Musée britannique.

12. Dague assyrienne en bronze. — Musée du Louvre et musée de Berlin.

13. Poignard assyrien à tête d'hippopotame, en bronze probablement, d'après le bas-relief de Nemrod du dixième siècle avant Jésus-Christ. — Musée du Louvre.

14. Dague assyrienne en bronze. — Musée de Berlin.

15. Épée assyrienne en bronze d'après des bas-reliefs de Khorsabad, du règne du roi Sargon, du treizième siècle avant Jésus-Christ.

16. Épée assyrienne. Bas-relief du règne de Sardanapale, du dixième siècle. Palais de Ninive. — Musée de Berlin et au Louvre.

17 et 18. Épée persique avec son fourreau d'après un groupe antique : *Mithras* sacrifiant un taureau[1] (M. Rom. par De la Chaussée). C'est presque l'*Akinace* antique.

1. *Mithras*, le fils de la montagne Ulbordi, de la mythologie perse, dont le

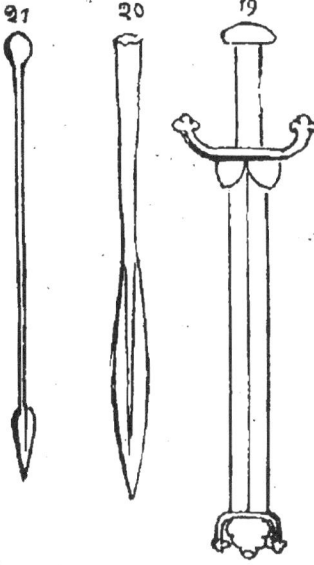

19. Épée persique. — Moulage d'un bas-relief de Persépolis. — Musée britannique et au Louvre.

20. Lame de lance assyrienne. — Bas-relief du palais de Ninive; du septième siècle avant Jésus-Christ, du règne de Sardanapale V. — Musée britannique et au Louvre.

21. Lance assyrienne. La hampe a la longueur de l'homme et un contre-poids au bout. Bas-relief.

22. Harpé assyrienne. — Bas-relief. Une arme pareille en fer a été trouvée à Pæstum en Lucanie, elle est conservée au mu-d'artillerie de Paris.—Voir aussi les armes romaines.

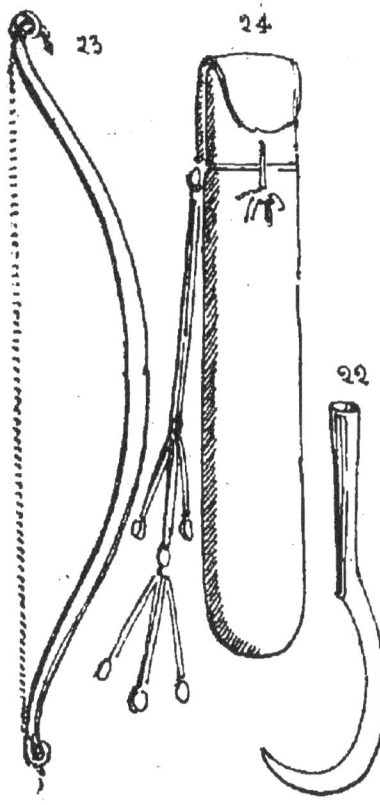

23. Arc médique. — Bas-relief.

24. Carquois médique. — Bas-relief.

Zend-Avesta, ces débris des *nooks* de Zoroastre, enseigne les détails. L'époque de la naissance de Zoroastre, le créateur du magisme, ou plutôt le réformateur du parsisme, flotte entre le treizième et le onzième siècle avant Jésus-Christ. Le Mithras d'après lequel ces armes ont été copiées, appartient probablement à la période où les anciens Parsis ou Parses parlaient encore le zend, langue morte dans laquelle les prêtres guèbres récitent encore aujourd'hui leurs prières, mais dont aucun d'eux ne comprend plus le sens.

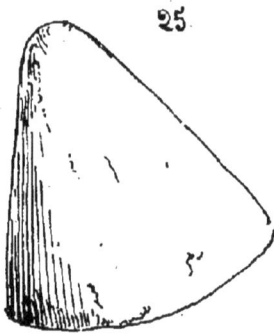

25. Casque assyrien en bronze dont l'authenticité est constatée. — Musée britannique. La forme conique de ce casque se retrouve au moyen âge chrétien, particulièrement chez les Normands. — Voir aussi, au chapitre des armes romaines, le casque samnite.

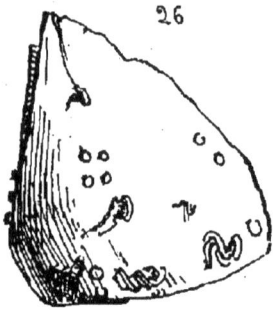

26. Casque assyrien en *fer* provenant de Kogunyk. Cette pièce très-précieuse pour l'histoire des armes démontre l'emploi du fer à l'époque appelée l'âge du bronze des anciens. — Musée britannique. Un casque tout semblable, mais en bronze et attribué aux Germains, fait partie de la collection Klemm à Dresde.

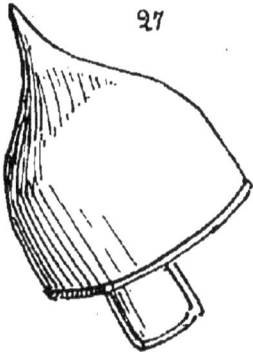

27. Casque probablement en bronze de cavaliers assyriens, dessiné d'après un bas-relief de Ninive, du palais de Sardanapale V, du septième siècle avant Jésus-Christ. — Musée du Louvre. Ce casque est intéressant par ses oreillères.

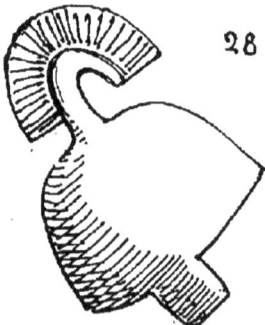

28. Casque probablement en bronze, d'homme de pied assyrien d'après un bas-relief de Ninive du palais de Sardanapale V, du septième siècle avant Jésus-Christ. — Musée du Louvre.

10.

29. Bandeau sans fond et à jugulaires ou oreillères, probablement en métal sinon en cuir garni de métal, coiffure d'archer assyrien qui protégeait le dessus de la tête et rappelle la coiffure du guerrier franc. — Bas-reliefs aux musées britannique, du Louvre et de Berlin.

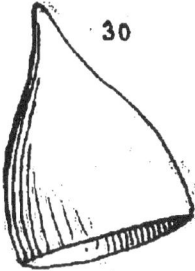

30. Casque sans jugulaires, probablement en bronze, porté par les archers et les auxiliaires assyriens. D'après un bas-relief du dixième siècle avant Jésus-Christ. — Musée du Louvre.

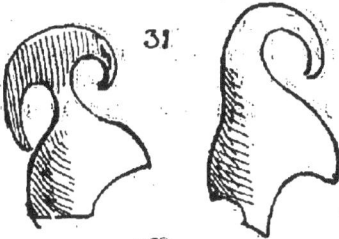

31. Deux casques assyriens probablement en bronze, d'après des bas-reliefs. La seconde forme à cimier à deux pointes a été imitée par les Grecs et paraît provenir de l'ancienne civilisation américaine.

32. Cimier en bronze de casque assyrien. — Musée britannique.

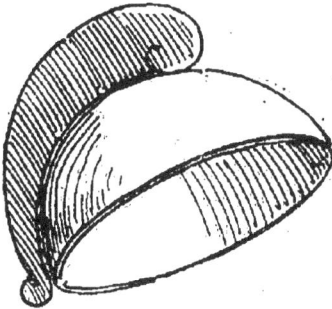

33. Casque persique d'après un groupe représentant *Mithras sacrifiant un taureau* (V. la note pages 111 et 112.)

34. Casque ou coiffure de guerre, d'un chef perse, d'après un bas-relief au musée britannique. Cette coiffure, qui paraît également en métal, a probablement servi à la guerre.

35. Casque ou coiffure d'archer persique, d'après un bas-relief de Persépolis (560 av. J.-C.?) dont le moulage se trouve au musée britannique. Même observation que pour le n° précédent.

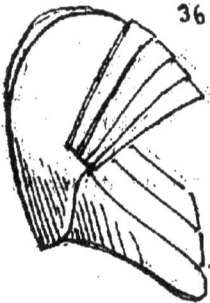

36. Casque perse à lames articulées, probablement en bronze, d'après un bas-relief persique dont le moulage se trouve au musée britannique (560 av. J.-C.). Cette arme est très-intéressante en ce qu'elle fait pressentir le casque lamé de la renaissance européenne du seizième siècle.

37. Casque persique à oreillères et à couvre-nuque, d'après un bas-relief dont les moulages sont au Louvre et au musée britannique (Même observation que pour le n° précédent).

38. Casque persique du règne de la dynastie des Sassanides (226-652 apr. J.-C.). Cette arme de bronze se trouve au musée britannique.

39. Bouclier babylonien de hauteur d'appui, probablement en bronze. — Musée britannique.

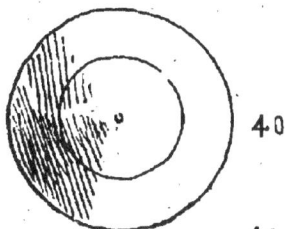

40. Bouclier assyrien. — Bas-relief. Il paraît de forme convexe, comme le n° précédent.

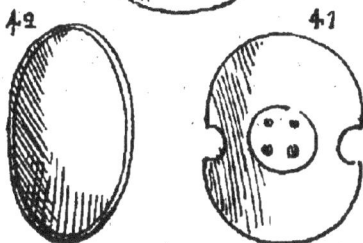

41. Bouclier persique à visière. Bas-relief.

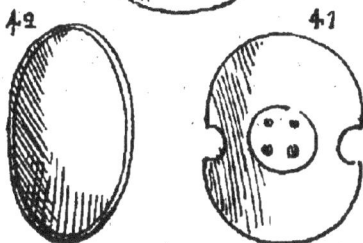

42. Bouclier persique d'après la mosaïque de Pompéi qui représente la bataille entre Darius et Alexandre. — Musée de Naples.

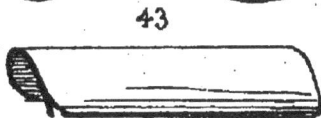

43. Pavois assyrien à hauteur d'épaule. — Bas-relief du second empire assyrien ou du septième siècle avant Jésus-Christ, du règne de Sadanapale V. — Louvre.

44. Pavois assyrien à hauteur d'appui, d'après un bas-relief qui représente le siége d'une citée par Asshur-Izir-Pal. — Musée britannique.

45. Cotte d'armes de la cavalerie assyrienne, probablement en lames de métal cousues sur peau. Elle est à couvre-reins, et reproduite d'après des bas-reliefs au musée britannique, où on trouve aussi un fragment en nature d'une véritable cotte de mailles assyrienne en *acier trempé* provenant de Babylone.

ARMES ÉGYPTIENNES.

Malgré la connaissance que l'on a de l'histoire de l'É-
gypte, qui remonte au commencement des vingt-six dynasties, c'est-à-dire au règne de Ménès, le premier roi (2450
avant Jésus-Christ), époque où ce pays formait, comme
sous la dix-huitième dynastie, plusieurs États distincts
dont chacun avait son prince indépendant, les documents
sur l'armement du soldat manquent presque entièrement.
Les dix-sept premières dynasties, à partir de Ménès jusqu'à Mœris (2450-1990), qui comptaient en tout 330 rois
qui régnaient simultanément dans Thèbes, This, Éléphan-
tine, Héraclée, Diospolis, Xois et Tanis, ainsi que la dix-
huitième dynastie, connue sous le nom de règne des
Pharaons (Mœris, Uchoreus, le fondateur de Memphis; Osy-
mandias, Ramsès, Aménophis etc.), n'ont laissé d'autres
documents que quelques rares bas-reliefs.

Nous avons déjà fait observer dans le chapitre historique,
que les monuments funéraires et civils de l'Égypte, pays
où le génie de la nation était plus porté vers l'agriculture
et les sciences que vers la guerre, offrent aussi moins de
sujets militaires que les monuments assyriens. On a vu que
Denon, dans ses *Voyages dans la haute et basse Égypte*, a
laissé, il est vrai, quelques dessins d'armes défensives et
offensives; mais c'est trop peu de chose, même réuni aux
bas-reliefs de Thèbes, pour pouvoir se former une idée
exacte de l'armement complet des soldats égyptiens.

Les quelques outils et armes égyptiens *en fer* conservés
aux musées du Louvre, de Berlin et de Londres, et qui
remontent certes à la plus haute antiquité, ne peuvent pas

-laisser de doute que ce métal était employé en Égypte, comme dans l'Assyrie, simultanément avec le bronze. Tout ce qui a été trouvé en armes offensives datant de l'âge de la pierre consiste, comme on a vu au chapitre où sont traitées ces armes, en quelques pointes de flèche, quelques couteaux et lames de lance en silex, taillés par éclats, conservés aux musées de Berlin et de Londres. Les lames de flèches ont été trouvées à Babylone même et ne peuvent pas remonter au delà de la fondation de cette ville. Outre cela, il y a encore au musée britannique quelques éclats de silex, destinés à la fabrication des armes tranchantes qui ont été trouvées à Sarabut-el-Khadon.

La pièce la plus intéressante pour la reconstitution de l'armement égyptien est la cotte imbriquée que M. Prisse d'Avennes a reproduite dans son ouvrage, puisqu'elle permet de fixer une date à cause de l'inscription biblique gravée sur une des écailles de bronze. Plusieurs des armes offensives, reproduites par le même archéologue, ont de si étranges formes que l'on ne sait expliquer leur emploi.

1. Combattant égyptien d'après des peintures murales de Thèbes. Les coiffures sont d'une forme étrange, et les armes offensives ne consistent qu'en lances et flèches.

2. Soldats égyptiens d'après des bas-reliefs de Thèbes. Outre le bouclier à visière, ces hommes paraissent uniquement armés du *shop* ou *khop*. (V. plus loin le n° 19.)

3. Cotte d'armes égyptienne en mailles, d'après l'ouvrage de Denon. Parmi les dessins de M. Prisse d'Avennes, on remarque la reproduction d'une cotte d'armes égyptienne en écailles de bronze dont chacune a 20 millimètres sur 35 de grandeur. Parmi ces écailles, celle qui porte une inscription biblique permet de reporter la date de la fabrication aux règnes des Pharaons.

4. Cotte d'armes égyptienne en peau de crocodile. — Musée égyptien du Belvédère à Vienne.

5. Bouclier égyptien, à visière, d'après Denon. Le bas-relief de Thèbes, déjà mentionné, montre un semblable bouclier, mais de forme ovale.

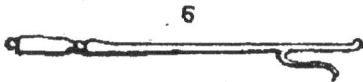

6. Brise-épée, reproduit d'après l'ouvrage de Denon.

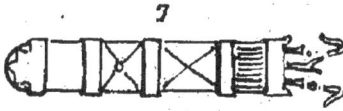

7. Carquois égyptien.   id.

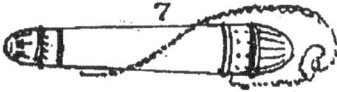

8. Hache égyptienne.   id.

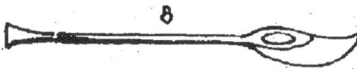

9. Épée égyptienne.   id.

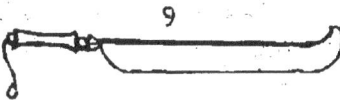

10. Cimeterre égyptien.   id.

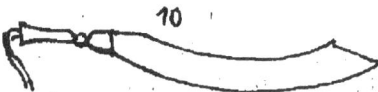

11. Dard égyptien.   id.

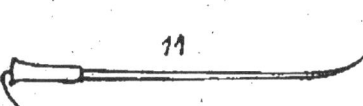

12. Fustiballe égyptien.   id.

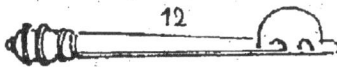

13. Arme inconnue.   id.

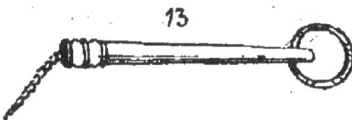

14. Arme inconnue.   id.

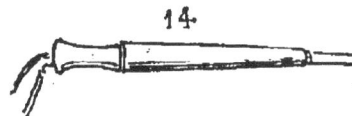

15. Hache, d'après des bas-reliefs de Thèbes.

16. Fléau ou scorpion.   id.

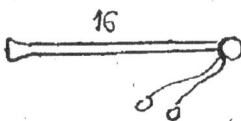

La grandeur de ces armes n'a pu être indiquée, mais elles paraissent avoir une longueur de 60 à 65 cent.

Elles étaient probablement en bronze et en fer.

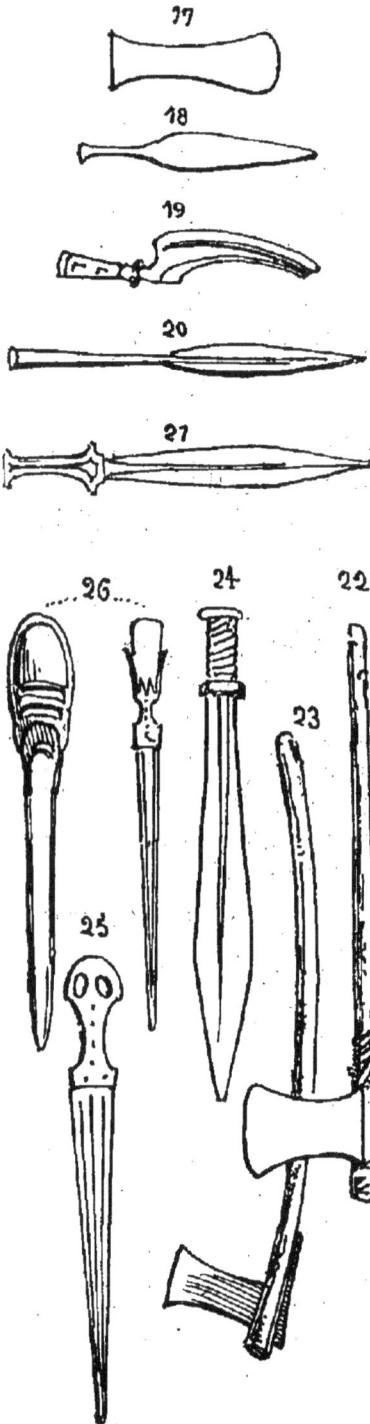

17. Coin ou hache égyptienne en bronze, 10 cent. — Musée de Berlin.

18. Couteau ou lame de lance égyptienne, en fer, 15 cent. — Musée de Berlin.

19. Shop ou Khop, arme égyptienne, en fer, 15 cent. — Musée de Berlin. On la voit aussi, un peu plus grande, sur le *Seti Messeptah*, à *Vanguishing*, *Tahennu* (?) de la dix-huitième dynastie (1990 av. J.-C.), au musée britannique.

20. Lame de lance égyptienne en bronze, 26 cent. — Louvre.

21. Poignard égyptien en bronze, 26 cent. — Musée britannique. La poignée est plaquée sur un fond de bois.

22. Hachette égyptienne en bronze de 12 cent, attachée avec des lanières sur un manche en bois de 38 cent. — Musée britannique.

23. Hachette égyptienne en bronze de 11 cent., montée sur un manche en bois de 40 cent. — Louvre.

24. Dague en bronze de 34 cent. — Louvre. Cette arme a cependant le caractère grec.

25. Poignard égyptien en bronze de 28 cent., trouvé à Thèbes et reproduit dans l'ouvrage de M. Prisse d'Avennes. La poignée est en corne.

26. Poignard égyptien en bronze de 30 cent., avec son fourreau. — Musée de Berlin. Le manche est en ivoire garni de têtes de clous en bronze doré.

11

ARMES GRECQUES ET ÉTRUSQUES

Pour éviter des recherches, on trouvera résumé de nouveau ici ce qui a été dit déjà dans le chapitre historique sur l'armement grec et étrusque.

Les armes offensives et défensives grecques au temps d'Homère (10e siècle av. Jésus-Christ) étaient la plupart en bronze et quelques-unes, pour la défense, en cuir, quoique *le fer* fût parfaitement connu en Grèce comme en Assyrie et en Égypte. L'armure défensive se composait de la *cuirasse* (plastron et dossier, chacun d'une seule pièce ou coquille), du *casque*, du grand bouclier rond convexe et des *cnémides* (jambières ou bottes défensives)[1].

Les armes offensives étaient : l'*épée* d'estoc et de taille à lame droite, plus ou moins longue, à deux tranchants, à pointe aiguë et à fourreau de forme carrée, qui se portaient au côté droit; la *lance*, de 11 à 15 pieds, à pointe large, longue et aiguë, arrondie vers la douille et à arrêt en

---

1. Les différentes *chaussures* grecques, c'est-à-dire les vêtements du pied, étaient la *sandale*, portée par les hommes; le *persique*, porté par les femmes et particulièrement par les courtisanes; la *crépide*, la chaussure ferrée des philosophes et des soldats, qui ne couvrait pas tout le pied, et la *garbatine*, la chaussure du paysan. Il y avait en outre le *cothurne* et le *brodequin*. Le premier était la chaussure des acteurs tragiques, pour paraître plus grands quand ils représentaient des héros. Des ligatures attachées à des semelles, ordinairement en liége, allaient en se rétrécissant ainsi que dans les patins de nos jours, et passaient entre l'orteil, etc. C'était aussi la chaussure des rois et des gens opulents. Le *brodequin* était particulièrement propre aux acteurs comiques : c'était une sorte de bottine lacée sur le devant et remontant ordinairement au-dessus de la cheville. Une Diane antique, au musée Pio Clementino, et nombre d'autres statues antiques sont chaussées de brodequins.

biseau saillant au milieu, servant d'arme de hast[1] et de jet ; le *javelot* avec son *amentum* (courroie fixée au centre de gravité du javelot), sorte de longue flèche que le combattant lançait avec la main et que l'on retrouve chez les Romains et les Germains ; l'*arc* et les *flèches*.

Les Grecs n'avaient pas de cavalerie d'abord et manquaient même de terme pour désigner l'action de monter à cheval, pour laquelle en français aussi n'existe pas de verbe propre, puisque chevaucher, veut plutôt dire : *flâner à cheval*.

Plus tard, 400 ans avant Jésus-Christ, ils ajoutèrent à leurs corps d'armées ceux des frondeurs et des cavaliers.

Quant aux armes étrusques, elles peuvent être subdivisées en trois catégories : celles fabriquées sous l'influence phénicienne (armes asiatiques), et qui paraissent même antérieures à la civilisation grecque; celles qui datent de l'époque de la fin de la guerre de Troie, et qui sont tout à fait identiques aux armes grecques; et enfin celles qui ne remontent qu'à l'époque latine, peu de temps avant la conquête de l'Étrurie par les Romains.

Les armes grecques ont dû être confondues avec les armes étrusques, dont il n'existe presque plus rien de la première période; les classer séparément aurait été impraticable.

---

1. Hast, qui désigne l'emmanchement sur une longue hampe, indique ici le maniement, le *stoss* (choc—coup) allemand.

1

1. Grecs combattants, reproduits d'après un vase peint, du musée du Louvre. Les guerriers sont armés de casques, de cuirasses et du bouclier, mais n'ont point de cnémides. La lance et l'épée constituent les armes offensives.

2

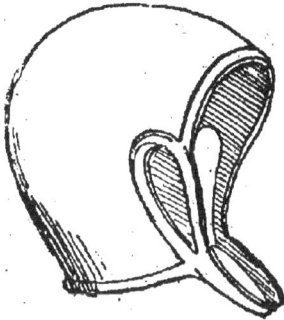

2. Casque grec, dit *kataitix*, probablement en cuir et du huitième siècle avant Jésus-Christ, reproduit d'après un bronze, une statuette de Diomède. Ce casque est sans crête, mais à jugulaires, et paraît bien indiquer la forme primitive.

3

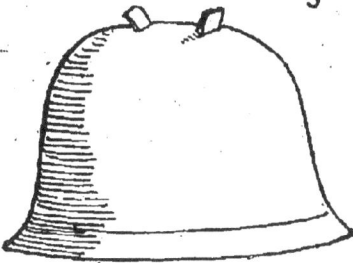

3. Casque étrusque en bronze attribué à la première période. — C. 1. Musée d'artillerie de Paris. On a cependant trouvé un semblable casque dans le cimetière germanique de Hallstatt, dont les tombeaux remontent seulement au commencement de notre ère.

4

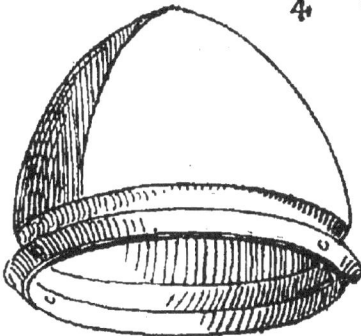

4. Casque étrusque en bronze, conservé au Louvre. On l'attribue également aux temps archaïques. De semblables exemplaires se trouvent encore au musée d'artillerie de Paris (C. 2), aux musées de Berlin, de Turin (N° 340), et de Mayence (N° 380), et à la Tour de Londres $\left(\frac{1}{7}\right)$.

5. Casque en bronze, du musée de Saint-Germain, attribué aux Ombriens[1]. Un pareil exemplaire, trouvé dans les tombeaux germaniques de Hallstatt, est conservé au cabinet des antiques à Vienne, et un autre, trouvé à Steingaden en Bavière, au musée d'Augsbourg.

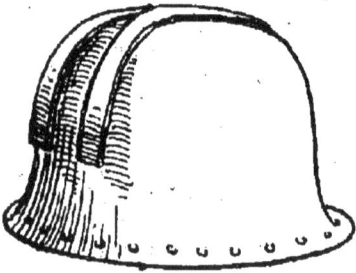

6. Casque étrusque en bronze à grandes antennes. — Exemplaires au musée d'artillerie de Paris (C. 12), à celui de Mayence et au cabinet de médailles de Paris. Le musée du Louvre possède une arme semblable en or. Les antennes (du latin *ante*, devant, et *fixus*, fixe) sont des cornes. Le nom antennes dérive de la forme qui ressemble à celle des antennes de navire.

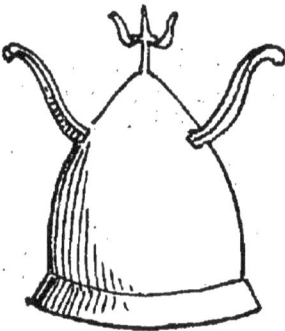

7. Casque étrusque archaïque en bronze. — Musée britannique. On y remarque une visière figurée qui rappelle les visières mobiles des casques du moyen âge chrétien.

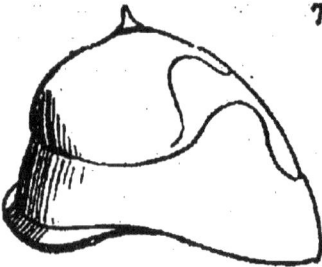

8. Casque grec en bronze avec inscriptions. — Musée britannique.

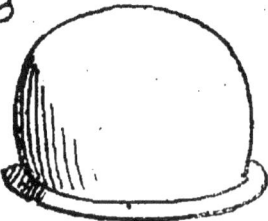

1. Les Ombriens ou Ombri étaient de race gauloise, alliés, de 311 à 307 avant Jésus-Christ, aux Étrusques. Contrairement à l'opinion de quelques historiens modernes, je pense que ce peuple était moins ancien que le peuple étrusque.

9

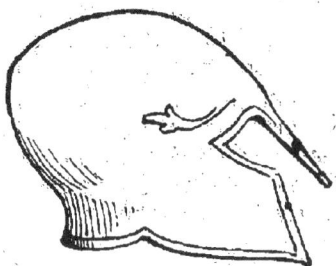

9. Casque grec d'*hoplite* [1] en bronze, d'après une statue de l'époque. De pareils exemplaires aux arsenaux de Turin (N° 341), de Berlin, de Mayence, de Goodrich-Court et au musée d'artillerie de Paris. Un casque semblable au musée britannique est pourvu d'une inscription grecque. Les salades vénitiennes du quinzième siècle affectent la forme de cette arme. Un casque tout pareil au dessin a été aussi trouvé à Steingaden, près Hohenschwanga, en Bavière; il est conservé au musée d'Augsbourg.

10

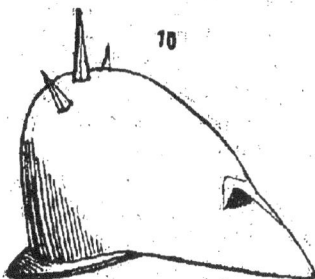

10. Casque grec en bronze. — N° 342 à l'arsenal de Turin.

11

11. Casque grec en bronze. — N° 3176 au musée de Mayence. C'est un morceau admirable. Le repoussé représente deux taureaux combattant. Il est surmonté d'antennes et d'un porte-cimier.

12

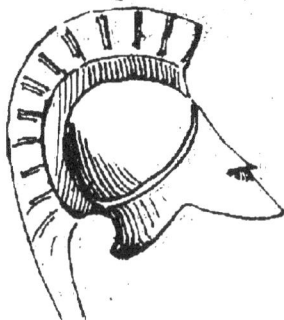

12. Casque grec, d'après un vase peint dit étrusque, au Louvre. C'est le casque grec classique par excellence, que l'on retrouve dans un grand nombre de sculptures, et dont aucun exemplaire n'est parvenu jusqu'à nous.

1. Soldat de la troupe régulière parfaitement armé, du grec *hoplon*, arme défensive.

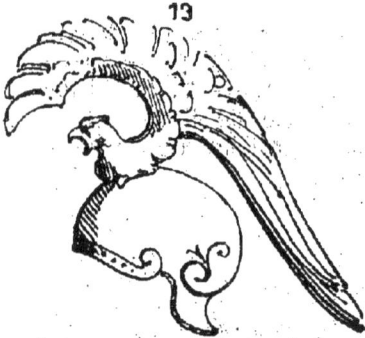

13. Casque grec, d'après les peintures d'un vase dit étrusque, au musée du Louvre ; il est d'une forme rare et très-artistique. Le porte-cimier, qui représente une espèce d'aigle, paraît garni de crins.

14. Casque grec, d'après une statue antique. Le cimier est garni de crins coupés en brosse, et le timbre offre de riches ornements en repoussé.

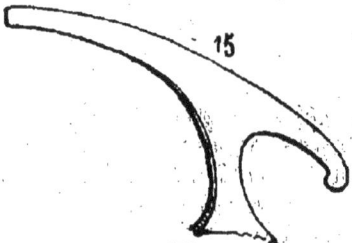

15. Cimier de casque grec, en bronze, trouvé dans un tombeau. — C. 13, au musée d'artillerie à Paris. Voir comme rapprochement le cimier assyrien, n° 32.

16. Casque grec à couvre-nuque, en bronze. — C. 6, au musée d'artillerie à Paris. Ce casque paraît avoir appartenu à un cavalier de l'époque de la décadence.

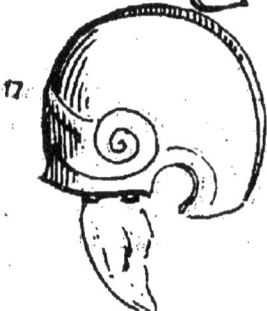

17. Casque grec à jugulaires, en bronze. — C. 8, au musée d'artillerie à Paris.

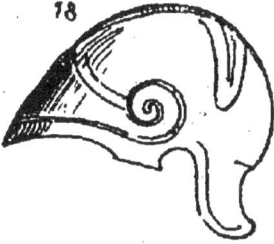

18. Casque grec de cavalier à couvre-nuque et porte-panache, en bronze. — C. 1, au musée d'artillerie de Paris. C'est un casque de l'époque de la décadence.

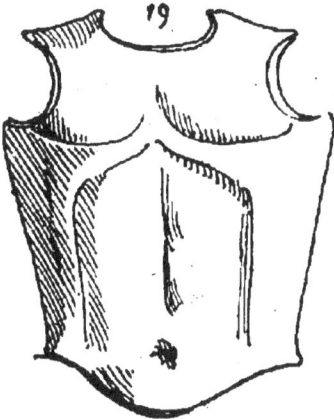

19. Plastron de cuirasse étrusque en bronze, d'une seule coquille, offrant en relief les divisions du corps humain. Il provient d'un tombeau étrusque et se trouve au musée de Carlsruhe. Le musée d'artillerie de Paris en possède le moulage. — C. 17.

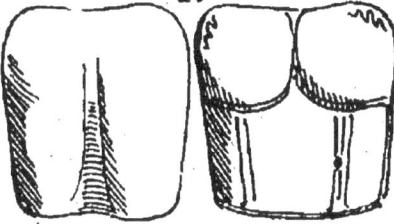

20. Cuirasse grecque complète (plastron et dossier) en bronze, trouvée dans un tombeau aux environs de Naples. — C. 13, musée d'artillerie de Paris.

21. Brassard grec en bronze, de la collection de M. de Bonstetten, près Berne, en Suisse.

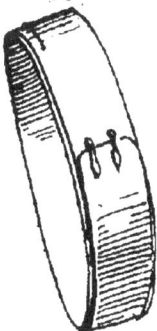
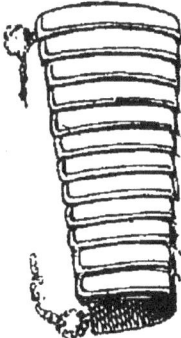

22. Ceinture grecque en bronze, de soldat (hoplite) et de gladiateur, de 30 cent. de diamètre; elle est garnie d'agrafes. — C. 15, musée d'artillerie de Paris, et 372 au musée de Mayence.

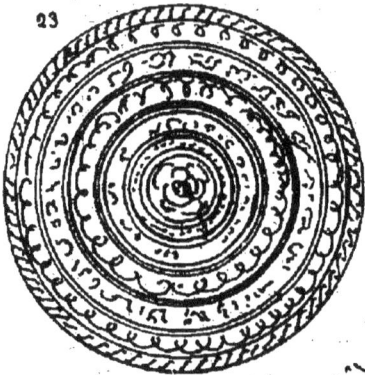

23

23. Bouclier étrusque de 86 cent. de diamètre, trouvé dans un tombeau. Les ornements repoussés et ciselés qui remplissent les cercles sont d'un travail remarquable; leur caractère est asiatique-phénicien, il indique que l'arme appartient à la première période étrusque. Le moulage de ce bouclier, appartenant au musée britannique, se trouve sous le n° C. 9, au musée d'artillerie de Paris.

23

24. Bouclier étrusque en bronze, de 40 cent. de diamètre, représenté du côté intérieur; il provient d'un tombeau et se trouve au musée de Mayence. Le musée d'artillerie de Paris en possède le moulage sous le n° C. 10.

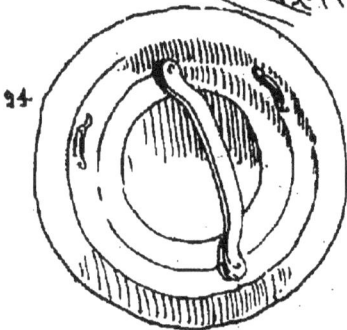

24

25. Umbelic (*umbo*) de bouclier grec[1]. Il mesure 25 cent. et a été trouvé dans les environs de Mayence, ville où il est conservé. Le musée d'artillerie de Paris en possède le moulage sous le n° C. 22.

25

1. Le bouclier grec avait deux poignées (*énarmes*), attachées l'une au centre pour passer le bras, l'autre près du bord, destinée à la main. Il était en outre pourvu de la *guige*, courroie destinée à le suspendre sur le dos.

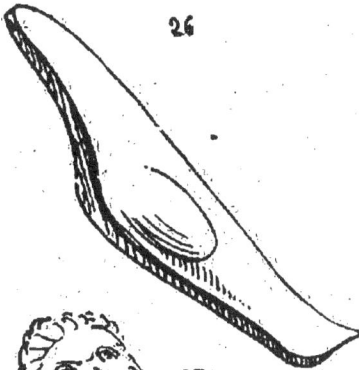

26. Cnémide ou jambière en bronze, de cavalier grec, 45 c. — C. 22, musée d'artillerie à Paris. On remarquera que l'arrière-jambe était sans-défense.

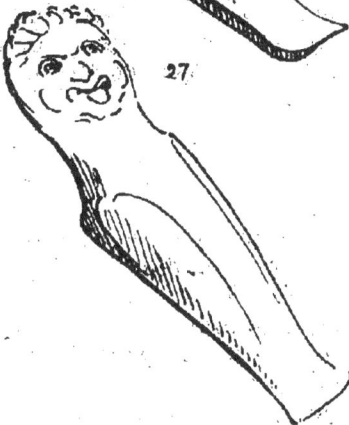

27. Cnémide en bronze, de cavalier étrusque, 50 cent. On l'a trouvée dans un tombeau. — Musée de Carlsruhe. Le musée de Mayence en possède un semblable, et le musée d'artillerie de Paris, un moulage sous le numéro C'. 16. Les genouillères fixes représentent des têtes de lion. L'arrière-jambe n'était point protégée.

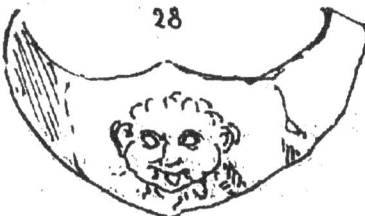

28. Bardes étrusques, en bronze, de poitrail de cheval. — Musées de Carlsruhe, de Mayence, et moulage, n° C'. 15, au musée d'artillerie de Paris.

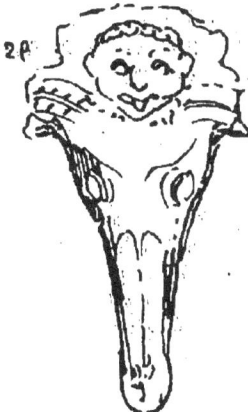

29. Chanfrein étrusque (plaque frontale de cheval) en bronze. — Musées de Carlsruhe, de Mayence, et moulage, n° C'. 18, au musée d'artillerie de Paris. Les n°s 27, 28 et 29 paraissent avoir appartenu à la même armure d'homme et de cheval.

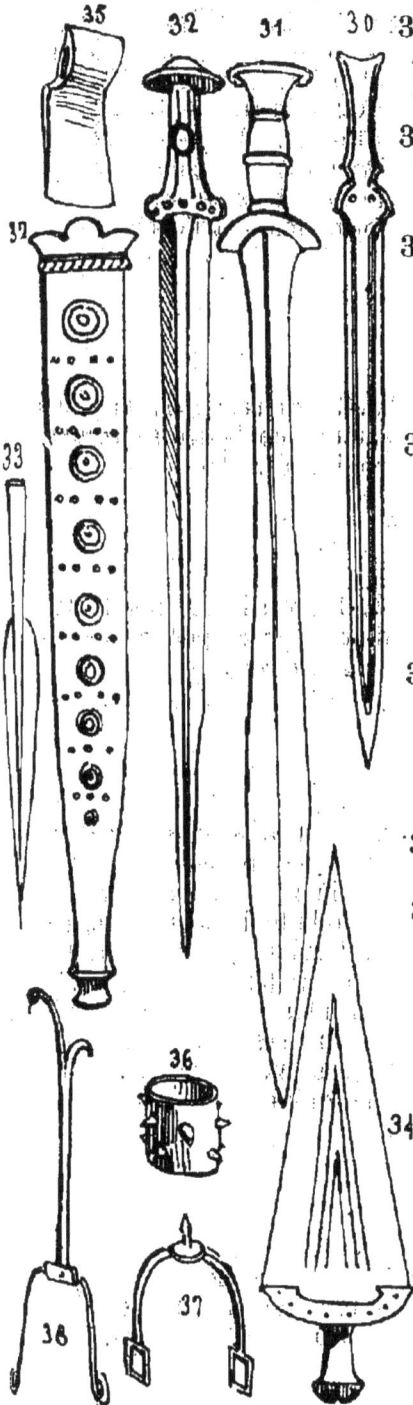

30. Épée grecque en bronze, 47 cent. — N° 348, musée de Mayence.

31. Épée grecque en bronze, 78 cent. — C'. 18, musée d'artillerie de Paris.

32. Épée grecque dite gallo-grecque, 60 cent., avec son fourreau, également en bronze, trouvée dans l'arrondissement d'Uzès. — B'. 19, musée d'artillerie de Paris.

33. Lame de flèche en bronze, probablement grecque, trouvée dans une tourbière d'Abbeville (Somme). — B'. 23, musée d'artillerie de Paris. Le musée de Mayence possède une lame pareille sous le n° 349.

34. Dague antique en bronze appelée *parazonium*, commune aux Grecs et aux Romains ; elle a 42 cent. de longueur. — Musée d'artillerie de Paris.

35. Hache grecque (?) en bronze. — Musée de Berlin.

36. Tête de massue d'armes grecque ou étrusque, à pointes hérissées, trouvée dans l'ancien royaume de Naples. — Musées de Berlin, de Saint-Germain, et musée d'artillerie de Paris.

37. Éperon grec en bronze, trouvé dans l'ancien royaume de Naples. — Musée d'artillerie de Paris.

38. — Éperon antique en bronze, probablement grec. — Musée d'artillerie de Paris.

39. Hoplite, soldat régulier, armé du bouclier en forme de trèfle, d'après le traité de M. Rodios, ΠΟΛΕΜΙΚΗΣ ΤΕΧΝΗΣ, etc., Athènes, 1868. — Ce soldat est intéressant à cause du casque forme étrusque et du bouclier forme feuille trilobée.

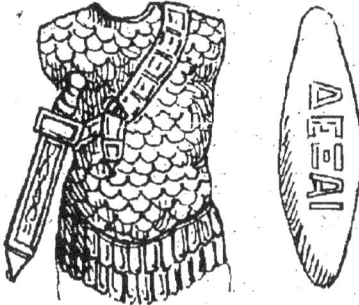

40. Cotte en écailles. On y remarquera que l'épée se trouve du côté droit.

41. Projectile en plomb de catapulte grec, portant le mot ΔΕΞΑΙ, reçois.

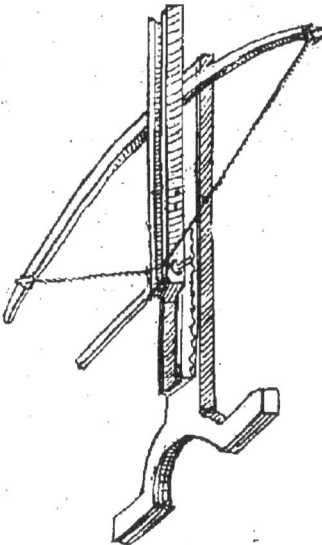

42. Gastrafète ou baliste à main, arme portative semblable aux arbalètes de notre moyen âge, reproduite d'après l'ouvrage de M. Rodios, qui l'a reconstruite selon des textes byzantins. Il est cependant fort douteux qu'une telle baliste portative, ou arbalète, ait existé chez les Grecs de l'antiquité.

43. Bélier avec sa blinde roulante, appelé *tortue* d'après l'ouvrage de M. Rodios.

ARMES ROMAINES, SAMNITES ET DACES

EN BRONZE ET EN FER.

Comme au chapitre précédent, qui traite de l'armement grec, on trouve ici le résumé sur l'armement romain qui, aux premières époques a été probablement le même que celui de l'Étrurie, pays où il s'était constitué sous la double influence phénicienne et grecque.

Polybe, né en l'année 552 de la fondation de Rome ou 202 ans avant Jésus-Christ (presque trois cents ans après la conquête de l'Étrurie par les Romains), le plus ancien auteur qui ait décrit les armes défensives et offensives romaines, n'a parlé que de celles de son époque. La description donnée par ce contemporain de Scipion l'Africain, jointe aux faibles renseignements qui ont été fournis par les quelques sculptures tombales trouvées aux bords du Rhin en Allemagne, et par les colonnes de Trajan et d'Antonin, forment à peu près tout ce qui est connu sur cette matière.

Grâce aux chants, dits d'Homère, on est mieux renseigné sur les armes en usage en Grèce, au dixième siècle avant Jésus-Christ, sinon même au treizième, époque du siège de Troie, que sur celles avec lesquelles le peuple-roi a conquis le monde.

Il est fort probable que les Romains, comme les Grecs et les Étrusques, ne se servaient d'abord pour la fabrication de toutes leurs armes que du bronze; mais, du temps de Polybe, le bronze n'était plus en usage chez eux

12

que pour les casques, plastrons et autres armes défensives, les armes offensives de trait, d'estoc, de taille et de hast, étaient toutes déjà en fer ou garnies de fer, lorsque la Gaule se servait toujours du bronze.

L'armée romaine était composée de trois espèces de troupes : les *vélites*, fantassins armés à la légère, les *hastaires*, fantassins légionnaires, et les cavaliers. Les premiers étaient armés de sept javelots minces dont la longueur était de *deux coudées*, et dont le fer mesurait *une palme*, de l'épée et d'un petit bouclier rond ou ovale et très-léger, qui, étant rond, avait 3 pieds et s'appelait *parma*[1].

Le casque, ordinairement à jugulaires, était sans cimier ni crinière, mais quelquefois garni de peau de loup.

Le hastaire était protégé par un casque en fer ou en cuir panaché de trois plumes rouge et noir, par des jambières ou bottines (*ocreæ*)[2] et par un plastron ou une cuirasse composée du corselet[3] et des deux épauliers, le tout en bronze, ainsi que par le grand bouclier ou pavois appelé *scutum* qui était ordinairement convexe et rectangulaire, en bois, en peau et en fer, de 4 pieds de long sur 2 1/2 de large et pourvu de ses énarmes[4]. Ce soldat avait pour armes offensives l'épée ibérique en fer, qu'il portait toujours au côté droit, comme le Grec, tandis que l'Assyrien, l'Hindou, l'ancien Américain ainsi que le Persan et l'Égyptien, la portaient comme les modernes au côté gauche. Le hastaire avait en outre deux javelots dont l'un

[1]. C'est le même dont étaient aussi armés les gladiateurs.

[2]. Les Romains avaient, comme les Grecs, des chaussures variées. La *solea*, ou sandale, qui consistait dans une semelle de cuir ou de bois ajustée par des lanières ; le *calceus*, ou bottine civile ; la *calige*, une chaussure de soldat ; l'*ocrea* susmentionnée, et la *solea lignea*, ou le sabot des pauvres. La botte (du celtique *bot*, pied) leur était inconnue comme à tous les autres peuples anciens.

[3]. Formé de lames de métal cousues sur un fond de peau ou de lin, il se fermait par derrière au moyen d'agrafes.

[4]. Du temps de Jules l'Africain, le bouclier n'était pourvu que d'un seul énarme en métal.

était le fameux *pilum* légionnaire, que l'on retrouve plus tard dans l'armement franc. Le frondeur romain était armé de la fronde d'Achaée imitée des Achéens.

Le cavalier avait pris du temps de Polybe l'équipement grec. Dépourvu avant cette époque d'armes défensives autres que le bouclier hexagone, rond ou ovale, en cuir de bœuf, son armement était devenu plus propre à résister aux coups des barbares. Plus tard, au temps des Trajan et de Septime-Sévère, il fut aussi doté d'une cuirasse flexible, soit de la *squamata* faite d'écailles de fer ou de bronze cousues sur de la toile ou de la peau, soit de la *hamates* composée de chaînes de métal, espèce de cotte de mailles. La colonne Trajane montre aussi beaucoup de soldats dont les cuirasses ne sont ni en écailles ni en mailles, mais confectionnées de longues lames en métal semblables aux armures du moyen âge, et les bas-reliefs de ce monument prouvent que l'armée romaine était composée d'un grand nombre de corps dont l'armement variait autant que celui de nos armées modernes.

L'armure du centurion paraît avoir été plus soignée que celle des simples hastaires-légionnaires. Son corselet était à épaulières adhérentes et couvrait les hanches. On le voit aussi souvent orné de nombreuses phalères en argent, décorations ou récompenses militaires de l'époque, que l'on trouve reproduites à la page suivante.

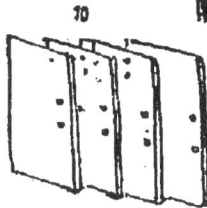

1. Soldat romain, vélite ou plutôt auxiliaire, d'après une pierre tombale trouvée dans le Rhin, et conservée au musée de Mayence; le moulage est au musée d'artillerie de Paris. Ce soldat est armé de deux longs javelots de la hauteur de l'homme, de l'épée portée au côté droit, et d'un *parazonium*, ou petite épée portée au côté gauche. Pour toute armure défensive, il n'a que le petit tablier de courroies plaquées de métal.

2. Soldat romain de la troupe régulière (hastaire), vu de dos. Il est reproduit d'après les bas-reliefs de la colonne Trajane, érigée par Trajan trois ans avant sa mort, en 114 après Jésus-Christ, et qui représente particulièrement ses exploits dans les guerres contre les Daces (103-106), qui se sont terminées par la conquête de la Dacie-Trajane (Moldavie, Valachie, Transylvanie, et le nord-est de la Hongrie). La cuirasse est *lamée*.

3. Le même, vu de face.

4. Cavalier romain, d'après la colonne Trajane. Il porte la *squamata*, ou jacque composée de chaînes de métal, sorte de cotte de mailles; le bouclier ovale, le casque à anneau et à jugulaires, et l'épée du côté droit.

5. Buste d'un légionnaire romain, d'après la colonne Trajane. Il porte le casque à cimier.

6. Tête d'un hastaire d'une autre légion, d'après la colonne Trajane.

7. Tête d'un hastaire d'une autre légion,   Id.

8. Tête d'un hastaire d'une autre légion,   Id.

9. Cuirasse d'un centurion romain, de 56 cent. de hauteur, ornée de neuf *phalères* en argent (récompenses militaires), appartenant au roi Guillaume Ier de Prusse. Le musée d'artillerie à Paris en possède le moulage. Le centurion de la légion de Varus détruite par les Germains, représenté sur une pierre tumulaire, conservée au musée de Mayence, est armé de la même cuirasse.

10. Écailles en bronze d'une *squamata*, ou cuirasse romaine à écailles, dessinées d'après celles que l'on a trouvées à Avenche en Suisse, l'ancienne capitale de la Suisse romaine, l'*Aventicum*, connu du temps de Jules César et embelli par Flavius Vespasien. Ces débris se trouvent au musée d'Avenche même. L'auteur conserve dans sa collection plusieurs autres débris d'armes romaines en bronze provenant de ces mêmes fouilles d'Aventicum.

11. Casque romain en bronze, de 24/22 cent., déterré au champ de bataille de Cannes (536 av. J. C.) et donné par le supérieur d'un couvent d'Augustins au pape Ganganelli. Cette arme se trouve actuellement, *on ne sait comment*, au château d'Erbach, en Hesse-Darmstadt. Le n° 379 au musée de Mayence et n° D. 1 au musée d'artillerie à Paris sont des casques tout semblables.

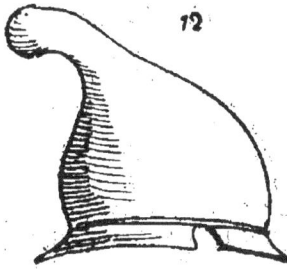

12. Casque samnite en bronze, trouvé à Isernia, dans l'ancien Samnium. Cette arme, qui fait partie de la collection Erbach, remonte probablement à la seconde guerre samnite (327-324 av. J.-C.). Un casque japonais doré, dont la forme est semblable, fait partie du musée d'artillerie de Paris.

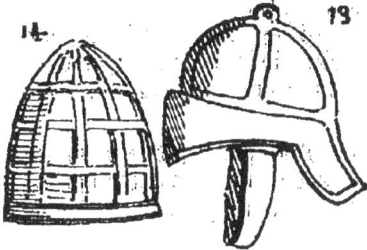

13 et 14. Deux casques romains d'après la colonne Trajane. Le n° 14 ressemble au casque reproduit d'après la colonne de Théodose, au chapitre qui traite des armes de l'âge du fer.

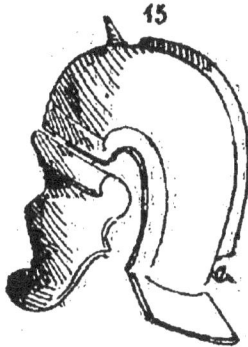

15. Casque romain, de 32 cent. de hauteur, *en fer*, garni de bronze, qui appartient au temps du Bas-Empire. — D. 29, musée d'artillerie de Paris. C'est une des plus curieuses armes de cette époque. La figure est presque entièrement protégée par une espèce de masque.

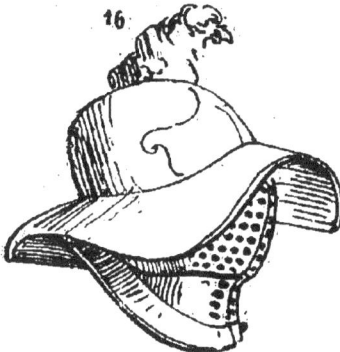

16. Casque romain de gladiateur, en bronze, provenant de la collection Portalès. — Musée de Saint-Germain. La figure est entièrement protégée par une visière immobile et criblée de trous ronds. C'est ce genre de casque que l'on retrouve au seizième siècle de notre ère.

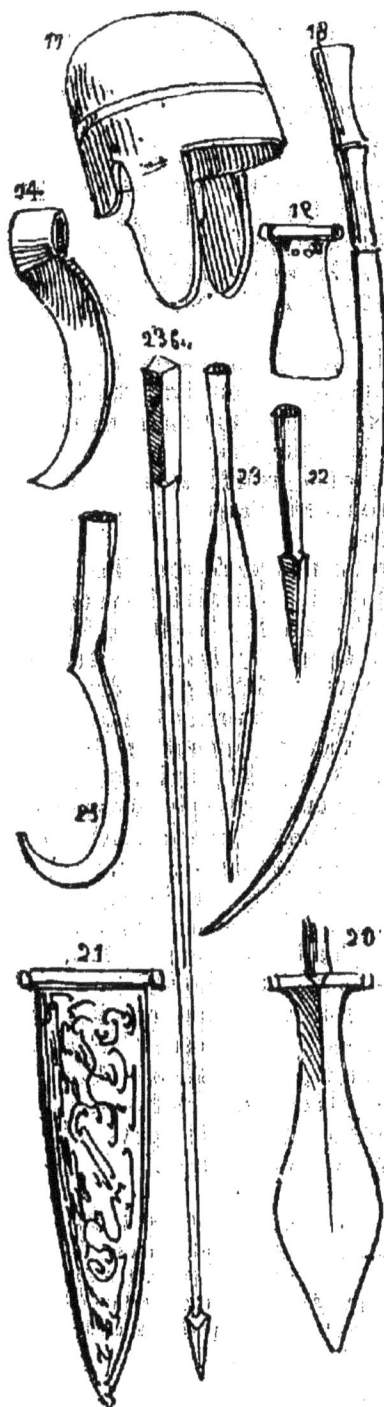

17. Casque romain trouvé à Pompéi. — Musée d'artillerie de Paris.

18. Sabre dace, d'après la colonne Trajane, érigée par Trajan trois ans avant sa mort, en 114 après Jésus-Christ. Les Daces étaient le peuple qui habitait la Moldavie, la Valachie, la Transylvanie, et le nord-est de la Hongrie. Ils combattaient tête nue et avaient pour toute défense le bouclier.

19. Hache de guerre romaine (?) en fer. — Collége Romano à Rome.

20 et 21. Épée romaine de ceinture, ou *parazonium* en fer, de 27 cent., avec son fourreau en bronze. Le moulage de cette arme, trouvée en Allemagne, fait partie, sous le D. 20, du musée d'artillerie de Paris.

22. Fer de javelot romain, 15 c. — Musée de Mayence.

23. Fer de javelot romain (?), 28 cent. — Musée de Mayence.

23 *bis*. Fer de pilum romain.

24. Harpé, hache romaine (?) en bronze, trouvée en Irlande. — $\frac{1}{167}$, Tour de Londres.

25. Harpé romaine en fer, provenant des fouilles de Pæstum, sur les côtes de la Lucanie. — C'. 2, musée d'artillerie de Paris.

Cette arme, que l'on rencontre aussi sur des sculptures assyriennes, n'est pas la harpé, le ἅρπη, ou cimeterre des Grecs, qui était une sorte de sabre pourvu d'un crochet tranchant remontant dans le taillant de la lame même, espèce de serpe avec laquelle on voit Mercure

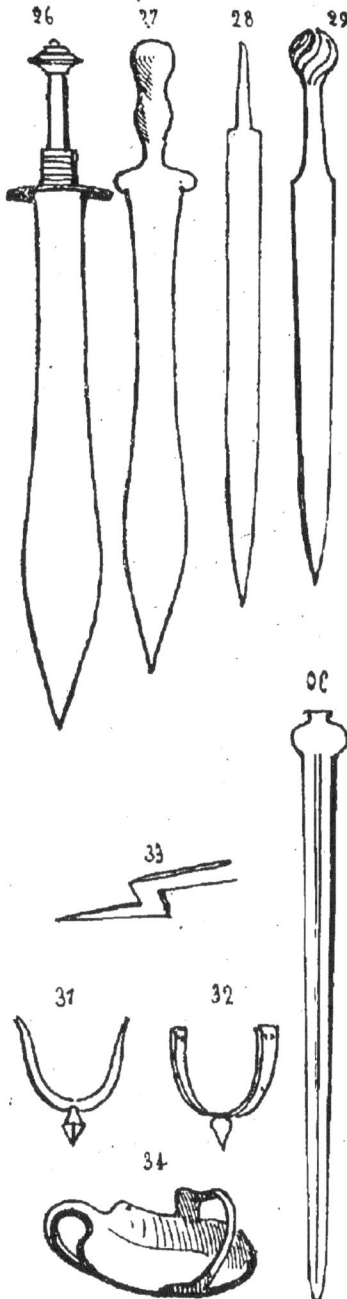

tuer Argus et Persée, trancher la tête à Méduse, et qui se trouve aussi dans la main des Traces (gladiateurs).

26. Épée romaine en fer, 66 c., poignée garnie de bronze[1]. Elle a été trouvée à Bingen. — Coll. du bourgmestre Sollen.

27. Épée romaine en fer, 64 c., trouvée à Bingen. — Coll. Sollen.

28. Épée romaine en fer, 58 c., marque d'armurier : *Sabini*. — D. 13, moulage au musée d'artillerie de Paris.

29. Épée romaine en fer, 56 c., trouvée à Bingen. — Coll. Sollen.

30. Lame d'épée romaine en fer, 48 cent., trouvée à Mayence. — D. 14, musée d'artill. de Paris.

31. Éperon romain en bronze, trouvé à Salburg, près Hombourg, par l'archiviste Habel.

32. Éperon romain en fer. — D. 43, musée d'artill. de Paris.

33. Chausse-trappe romaine en fer (*hamus ferreus*). Elle est pointue des deux côtés. — Musée d'artillerie de Paris.

34. Fer à cheval romain, que l'on fixait au canon de la jambe du cheval au moyen d'une lanière attachée au crochet du fer. — D. 12, musée d'artillerie de Paris, et aux musées d'Avenche (*Aventicum*) en Suisse et de Lintz en Autriche, pays où ces fers ont été trouvés.

1. Un fourreau, déterré à Mayence en 1848 et appartenant au musée britannique, est orné du portrait d'Auguste ainsi que d'un sujet représentant Thibenius remettant à l'empereur une statue de la Victoire.

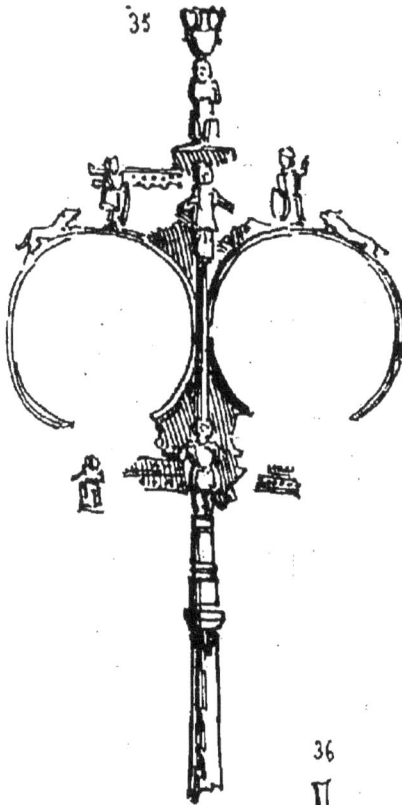

35. Signum ou enseigne romaine de cohorte, en bronze, trouvé dans l'Asie Mineure. C'est une pièce magnifique, qui est incontestablement sortie des mains d'un artiste grec. — D. 3, musée d'artillerie de Paris.

36. Poignard ou courte épée en bronze trouvé dans le palaffite de Peschiera. — Cabinet des antiques à Vienne.

37. Hache simple en bronze, trouvée dans l'ancien royaume de Naples. Sa forme indique l'arme et non pas l'outil.—B. 36, musée d'artillerie de Paris.

38. Hache simple en bronze, également trouvée dans le Néapolitain. — B. 37, musée d'artillerie de Paris. Ces deux dernières armes pourraient bien remonter à une époque plus ancienne.

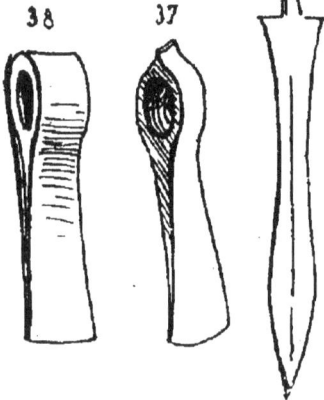

Quant aux machines de guerre dont il a été question au chapitre premier, qui traite l'histoire, il n'en existe plus aucune en nature, et les catapultes et balistes que l'on a essayé de reconstruire d'après les textes ne doivent pas figurer dans un ouvrage entièrement basé sur des documents authentiques.

IV

ARMES DE L'AGE DU BRONZE

DES PEUPLES DITS BARBARES

Les peuples celtiques, qui ont probablement aussi occupé une bonne partie de l'Europe centrale et même quelques districts du Nord, ont laissé des armes qu'il est difficile de distinguer de celles des autres races contemporaines ou peu postérieures.

Le nom de Galate ou Gaulois se trouve constamment confondu avec celui du Celte et quelquefois même avec celui du Germain. Là où tout est enveloppé d'obscurité, il serait fort hasardé d'établir des démarcations tranchées pour les armes de l'âge dit du bronze; il vaut mieux confondre les productions comme on a été constamment obligé de confondre les dénominations dès que l'on remonte aux époques antéhistoriques.

Jamais on ne pourrait classer à part les soi-disant produits celtiques; — l'élément scandinave, germain et gaulois se manifeste partout, et ceux qui ont voulu assigner aux tombeaux découverts dans ces différents pays des origines de races bien déterminées, ont été constamment contredits par de nouvelles découvertes.

L'auteur a eu soin seulement de séparer les armes des différentes provenances et de les donner par pays selon *les langues* qui y sont parlées, de manière que les armes en bronze, peut-être celtico-gauloises, — celtico-germaniques, celtico-britanniques, scandinave, etc., confondues avec les armes en bronze de notre ère, jusqu'à l'époque dite du fer, — ont été réunies et décrites par séries. Le *celt en fer* du musée national de Munich, et les haches en pierre et les longues lames de lance *en fer* semblables aux celts, trouvées avec quantité d'armes et d'objets de parure en bronze et en or, au cimetière de Hallstatt, démontrent à l'évidence que les attributions celtiques aussi bien que l'établissement rigoureux d'un âge de la pierre, du bronze et du fer, ne peuvent rien avoir d'absolu. Les fouilles exécutées dans ce cimetière où on a ouvert plus de mille tombeaux n'ont pas seulement montré que la pierre était même employée simultanément avec le bronze et le fer, mais que le fer servait déjà à la fabrication des lames et le bronze à celle des manches d'épée, tel qu'on le pratique encore de nos jours. Hallstatt est situé près d'Ischel en Autriche. Le cabinet des antiques à Vienne possède des quantités énormes d'ustensiles, d'armes et de parures, qui proviennent tous des fouilles de ce cimetière germanique dont M. Az à Linz possède également plusieurs pièces remarquables. Comme ces fouilles ont été parfaitement décrites par M. de Sacken dans son : *Grabfeld von Hallstatt*, 1868. Il est inutile de le répéter ici.

Il n'existe aucune sculpture du temps d'après laquelle le guerrier germanique pourrait être représenté dans son ensemble, et son armement a varié selon la race. Le bouclier des Germains du Nord était très-grand, lamé de cuivre et sans ombilic, tandis que les tombeaux francs de la fin de l'époque dite du fer (mérovingienne) n'ont révélé que de petits boucliers ronds à ombilics saillants, qui, chose remarquable, se retrouvent en bronze chez les Danois, parmi les objets de l'âge du bronze, et peut-être aussi chez les autres Scandinaves et les Bretons. L'époque de l'emploi du bronze à la fabrication des armes, chez les Scandinaves et les Bretons, correspond à celle du fer chez les Germains et les Gaulois. On verra dans le chapitre suivant, où sont traitées les armes de l'âge dit du fer, que la forme des haches aussi chez les Francs était différente des haches dont se servaient les Saxons.

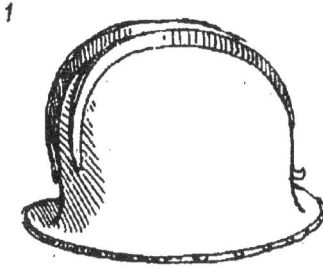

1. Casque germanique en bronze trouvé dans un des tombeaux de Hallstatt en Autriche. Ce casque à double crête ressemble beaucoup à celui du musée de Saint-Germain, attribué aux Étrusques ou aux Ombriens. — Cabinet des antiques à Vienne.

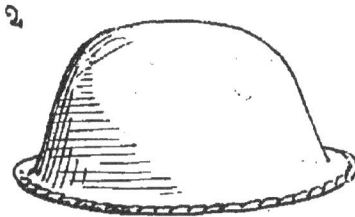

2. Casque germanique en bronze qui provient également du cimetière de Hallstatt. — Cabinet des antiques à Vienne.

Ces deux casques pourraient cependant bien provenir de l'Italie quoiqu'ils aient été trouvés en Allemagne, car la forme est étrusque.

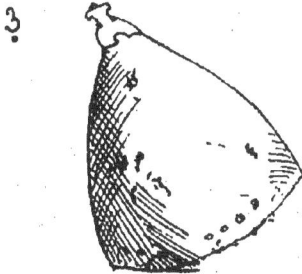

3. Casque germanique en bronze de 8 1/2 sur 9 cent. de hauteur, trouvé à Britsch près Pforten, en Saxe et conservé dans la collection Klemm à Dresde. C'est un échantillon unique et dont la forme est pareille aux casques assyriens du musée britannique.

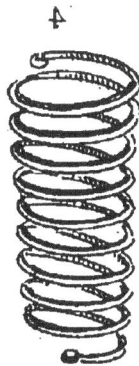

4. Brassard germanique en bronze trouvé à Winnsbach près Lintz en Autriche et conservé au musée de Lintz. De semblables brassards ont été trouvés en Danemark (V. n° 264 au musée de Copenhague).

5. Brassard germanique en bronze trouvé dans la principauté de Hohenzollern et conservé au musée de Sigmaringen. Un semblable exemplaire au musée Maximilien d'Augsbourg.

6. Fragment d'un grand bouclier germanique carré[1], en bois recouvert de bronze, trouvé dans un tombeau à Waldhausen, et publié par M. C. Rath à Tubingue. Le musée de Munich possède des fragments de cuirasse germanique dont les ornements en cuivre ressemblent à ceux de ce bouclier.

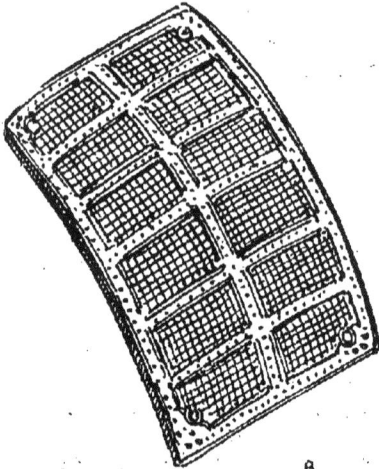

7. Bouclier germanique, id.

8. Lame ou pointe de framée germanique, de 13 cent., trouvée dans le cimetière de Hallstatt. — Col. de M. Az à Lintz.

9. Pointe de framée germanique (dite *celt*), trouvée à Stade. — Musée de Hanovre.

10. Pointe de framée germanique, de 10 cent., trouvée dans la principauté de Hohenzollern, et conservée au musée de Sigmaringen.

11. Pointe de framée germanique, de 15 cent., id.

12. Pointe de framée germanique, de 16 cent., id.

13. Six pointes de flèches germaniques, id.

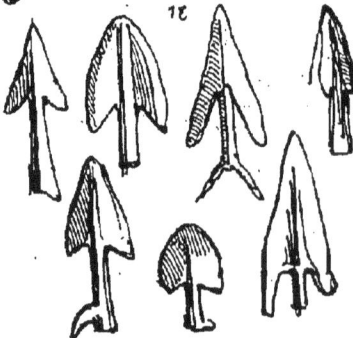

1. La dimension et la forme de ces boucliers démontrent qu'ils remontent bien avant l'influence romaine, que l'on reconnaît dans les petits boucliers francs de forme ronde, de la fin de l'époque dite l'âge du fer (mérovingienne).

13

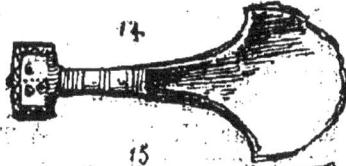

14. Hache germanique en bronze, de 25 cent., trouvée dans le Palatinat et conservée au musée national à Munich.

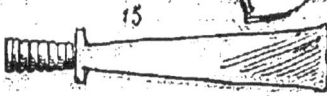

15. Lame de framée germanique en bronze, de 20 cent. Les lances abyssiniennes sont encore garnies aujourd'hui, à leurs parties *inférieures*, de ces spatules (V. le chapitre des lances).— Musée de Cassel.

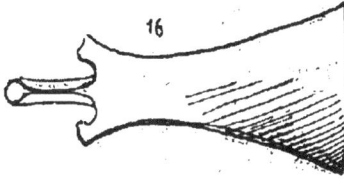

16. Lame de framée germanique. (Même observation que pour le numéro précédent.)— Musées de Cassel et d'Erbach.

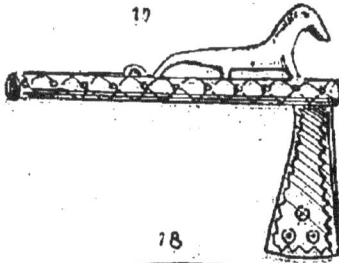

17. Hachette germanique en bronze, de 30 cent., trouvée dans le cimetière de Hallstatt. Cette pièce ressemble beaucoup plus par ses ornements aux armes danoises. — Cabinet d'antiques à Vienne.

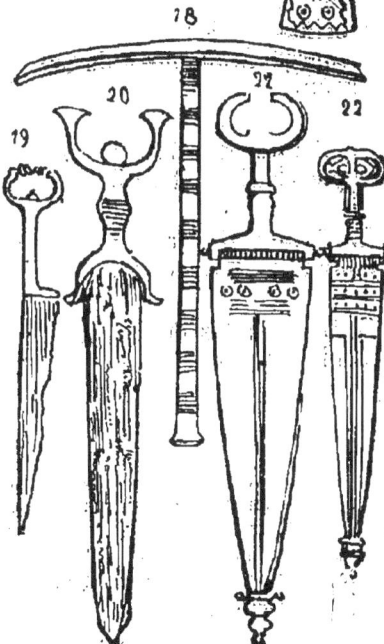

18. Marteau d'armes germanique en bronze de 40/47 cent., trouvé dans la Thuringe. Le manche est orné de 9 annneaux figurés chacun par 6 lignes gravées. Les ornements de cette pièce comme ceux du numéro précédent rappellent le travail danois. — Col. Klemm à Dresde.

19 à 22. Quatre dagues et poignards germaniques. — Musée de Sigmaringen.

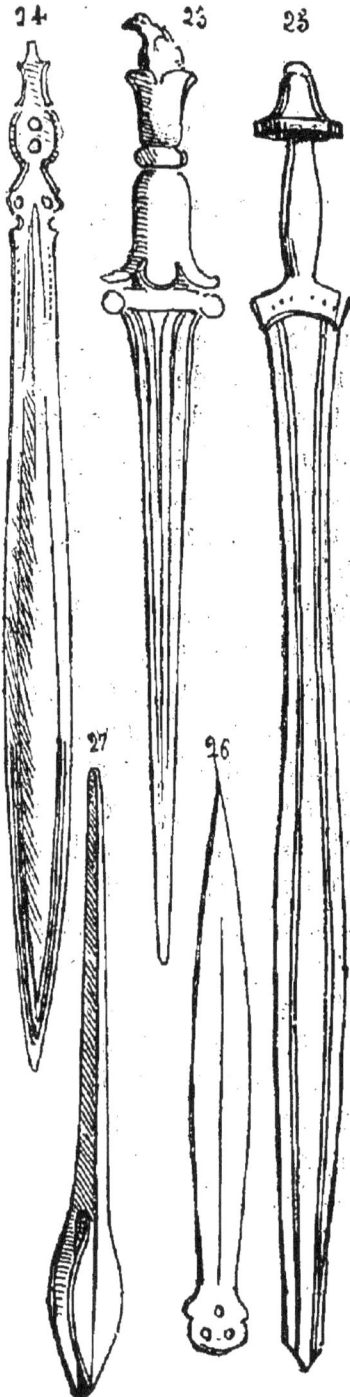

23. Épée germanique en bronze, de 55 cent. de longueur. Le pommeau représente une tête d'aigle. Cette épée est *entièrement* en métal. — Musée de Cassel.

24. Épée germanique de 66 cent. trouvée près d'Augsbourg. La soie plate et à trous pour rivets indique que la poignée était garnie d'os, de bois, de corne ou de métal. — Musée de Sigmaringen.

25. Épées germaniques en bronze, de 75 cent., à pommeau et manche en os et bronze et aussi entièrement en os, trouvées dans les tombeaux de Hallstatt. Les pointes ne sont pas aiguës. — Cabinet des antiques à Vienne.

26. Courte épée germanique en bronze. Ici la forme diffère essentiellement de celle des parazoniums grecs. — Musée de Hanovre.

27. Pointe de lance germanique en bronze, trouvée à Hallstatt. — Cabinet des antiques à Vienne.

ARMES CELTICO-GAULOISES, GAULOISES,

BAS-BRETONNES, ETC., EN BRONZE

J'ai déjà fait observer qu'un classement tranché pour les armes en bronze trouvées sur le sol de la France est impraticable. Le *celt* même, cette pointe de framée caractéristique par ses anneaux d'attache, a été trouvé partout, même en Russie. Quant aux armes gauloises du temps de César, elles étaient presque toutes encore en bronze.

Il a été dit ailleurs que si l'on veut se rendre compte pour les classer chronologiquement, des armes occidentales des époques antéhistoriques, où les produits des différents peuples se ressemblaient plus qu'à toute autre époque, et où les périodes de transition, quoique fréquentes, sont moins marquées, il faut étudier la construction et les dotations des différents tombeaux. Les monticules très-élevés, entourés ou surmontés de pierres plus ou moins colossales (dolmens) et les caveaux ordinairement clos de dalles, renfermant des ossements non brûlés et des armes en pierre, peuvent être regardés comme des tombeaux très-anciens. La seconde catégorie se signale le plus souvent par un monticule moins élevé, par l'absence de grands blocs de pierre, par un caveau ou tombeau formé de pierres brutes de petites dimensions, entassées avec peu d'art, et par l'*urne* qui indique la *crémation*. Ces sépultures contiennent ordinairement des produits de bronze, — ceux qui sont traités dans ce chapitre.

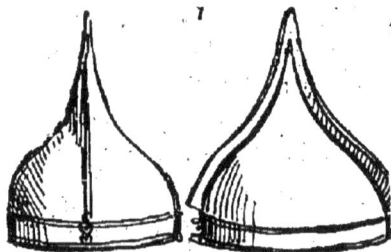

1. Casque en bronze, de 27 cent. de hauteur, attribué en France aux Gaulois. — Musée de Rouen. On a trouvé un exemplaire tout pareil à Posen et un autre en Bavière dans la rivière de l'Inn. Ce dernier casque figure au musée national de Munich comme arme hongroise ou avare.

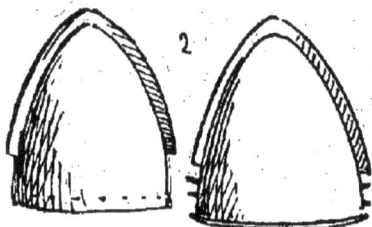

2. Deux casques en bronze, attribués, au musée de Saint-Germain, aux Gaulois. La forme est celle des casques assyriens et du casque germanique trouvé à Britsch et conservé dans la collection Klemm à Dresde.

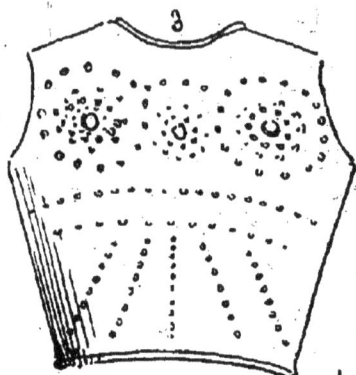

3. Cuirasse gauloise en bronze, trouvée dans un champ, près Grenoble B. 16., musée d'artillerie de Paris. Les musées du Louvre et de Saint-Germain possèdent de semblables exemplaires.

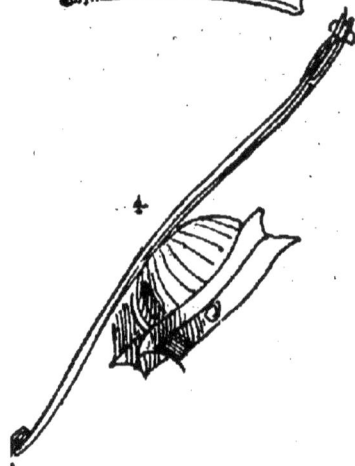

4. Carcasse d'ombilic en bronze, dont les formes se rapprochent de celles des ombilics en fer des boucliers francs; seulement on ne s'explique pas que la tringle passe au-dessus de l'ombilic, au lieu de passer au-dessous. — Musée de Saint-Germain.

13.

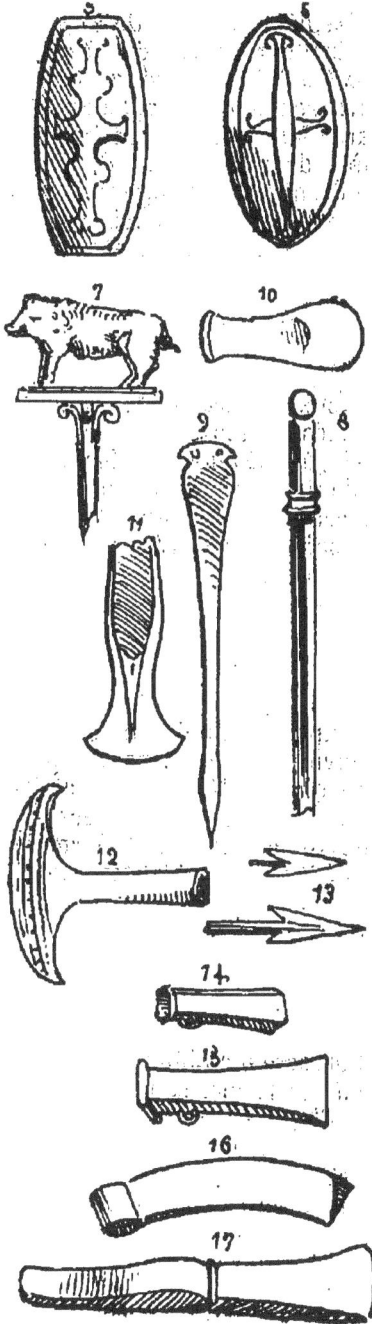

5. Bouclier gaulois, d'après la sculpture du sarcophage de la Vigna Ammandola.

6. Bouclier gaulois, d'après un bas-relief de l'arc d'Orange.

7. Signum, ou enseigne gauloise, d'après un bas-relief de l'arc d'O-range. Une enseigne en bronze toute pareille, de 13 cent. de hauteur, a été trouvée en Bohême, où elle est conservée au musée national de Prague.

8. Épée gauloise, d'après un bas-relief romain encastré dans le piédestal de la Melpomène du musée du Louvre.

9. Épée gauloise en bronze, de 45 cent., trouvée dans la Seine à Paris. — B. 7, au musée d'artillerie de Paris.

10. Pointe de lance celtico-gauloise en bronze, de 11 cent., type considéré comme un des plus anciens. — Musée d'artillerie de Paris.

11. Pointe de lance, id. — Musée d'artillerie de Paris.

12. Hache. — Louvre.

13. Pointes de flèche. — Louvre.

14. Pointe de lance dite *celt*, de 9 cent. — Col. de l'auteur.

15. Pointe de lance dite *celt*, de 15 cent. — B. 20, musée d'artillerie de Paris.

16. Hachette, de 13 cent. — B. 34, musée d'artillerie de Paris.

17. Lame de lance. — Musée du Louvre.

ARMES BRITANNIQUES EN BRONZE

Ces armes sont rares, et il est difficile de fixer avec quelque certitude leur origine et leur âge. Plusieurs exemplaires, conservées dans les musées anglais comme provenances britanniques, laissent subsister des doutes. Le casque à cornes, par exemple, aussi bien que le bouclier d'à côté, au musée britannique, et le bouclier long de la collection de Godrich-Court, pourraient bien être d'origine danoise[1].

L'époque de l'âge du bronze, en Angleterre, que la commission britannique de l'histoire du travail à l'Exposition universelle à Paris, en 1867, avait désignée comme « deuxième époque, antérieure à l'invasion romaine, » ne peut pas être limitée ainsi, parce que l'usage, d'abord général, des armes offensives en bronze n'a pas cessé sous la domination romaine et a même continué partiellement jusqu'aux époques des invasions des Saxons (ve siècle) et des Angles (vie siècle).

Si on compare les boucliers, les cors, et même les épées, les lames de lances et de haches danoises en bronze du musée de Cophenhague, avec les antiquités du même genre, exposées en Angleterre parmi les produits britanniques, on trouvera, sur la plupart, un cachet de conformité de fabrication et de goût que le hasard et l'imitation seuls ne peuvent pas avoir produit. Il est donc fort probable que beaucoup de ces armes ont été fabriquées, ou en Scandinavie même, ou dans la partie septentrionale de l'Allemagne du Nord et qu'elles furent introduites dans les îles Britanniques par les corsaires normands (*Nordmannen* ou *Nordmaenner*, ou hommes du Nord), qui n'ont cessé de ravager les côtes de ce pays, entièrement conquis par leurs descendants, en 1066.

1. On a vu dans l'introduction du chapitre qui traite des armes germaniques en bronze, que l'auteur croit que l'emploi du bronze pour la fabrication des armes correspond, en Scandinavie, à celui du fer en Germanie.

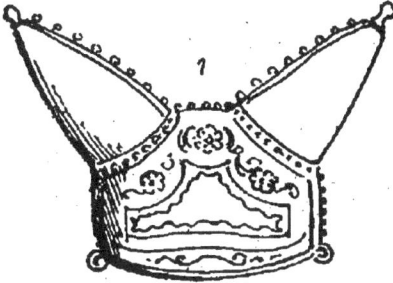

1. Casque en bronze trouvé dans la Tamise et conservé au musée britannique. Il est en repoussé, et orné de quelques incrustations en mastic colorié qui ressemble à l'émail.

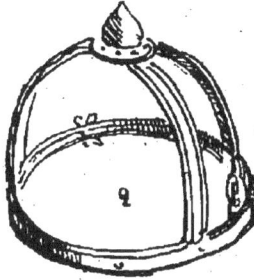

2. Carcasse de casque en bronze trouvée à Leckhampton-Hill. — Musée britannique.

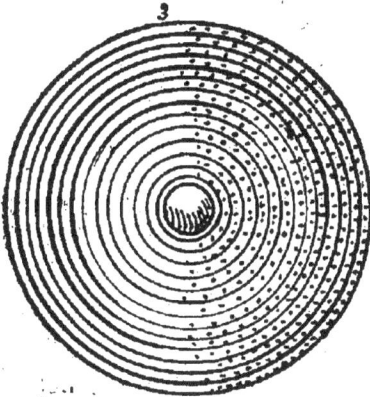

3. Bouclier en bronze. — Col. Llewelyn-Meyrick.

4. Placage en bronze doré et repoussé d'un bouclier breton dit *Ysgwgd* dont la forme rappelle le *Scutum* romain. Il a été trouvé dans la rivière de Witham. — Col. Llewelyn-Meyrick.

J'ai exposé à la page précédente ce qu'il y avait à dire concernant la conformité de goût qui existe dans la fabrication de ces armes défensives avec celles trouvées en Danemark et exposées à Copenhague. On a vu dans l'Introduction, où il est traité des armes germaniques en bronze, que l'emploi du métal fut plus tardif pour la fabrication des armes en Scandinavie qu'en Germanie et dans les Gaules.

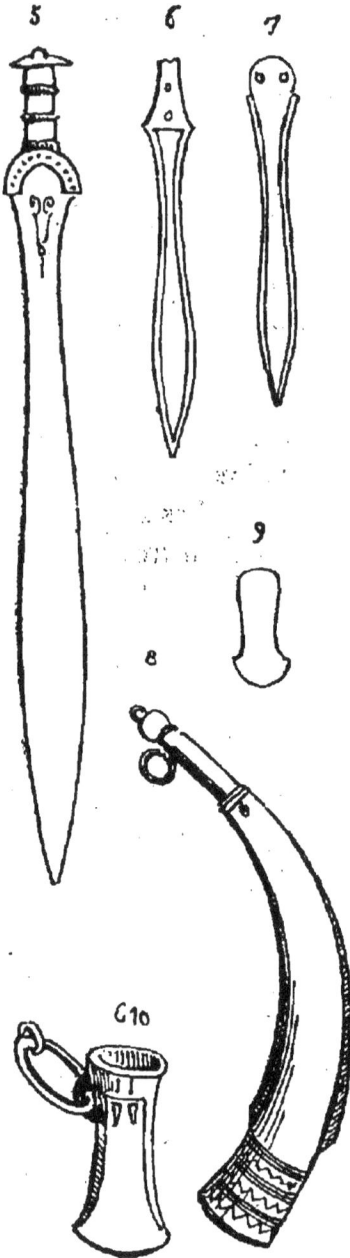

5. Épée en bronze; elle ressemble tout à fait aux armes germaniques et scandinaves et pourrait bien être danoise. — Tour de Londres, $\frac{1}{63}$. Plusieurs autres épées semblables au musée britannique.

6. Lame d'épée en bronze, nommée *Gwaew-fon.* — Col. Llewelyn-Meyrick.

7. Lame d'épée en bronze, trouvée en Irlande, id.

8. Cor de guerre irlandais, appelé *Stuic*, id.

9. Hache en bronze. — Musée britannique.

10. Lame de framée dite *celt*, en bronze, avec double anneau, id.

Les musées de Londres possèdent encore un grand nombre de lames de framées, de haches, d'épées, de dagues, de pointes de lances et de flèches dont les formes ne diffèrent en rien de celles des armes du continent de cette même époque, ce qui m'a fait hésiter à les classer dans la série des armes britanniques. (Voir les observations faites à ce sujet dans l'Introduction de ce chapitre.)

ARMES SCANDINAVES

Les armes en bronze de la Scandinavie continentale (Danemark) sont, comme celles en pierre de ce pays, supérieures aux armes des autres peuples dits barbares, et peu inférieures même à celles des Grecs et des Romains, ce qui s'explique si on admet, avec l'auteur de ce livre, que l'époque de l'emploi du bronze est postérieure en Danemark et coïncide avec celle du fer chez les Germains et les Gaulois. (V. l'observation dans l'Introduction du chapitre qui traite des armes germaniques en bronze.) Les exemplaires conservés au musée de Copenhague, dont on trouvera plus loin des reproductions, démontrent avec quel art on y savait travailler le métal. L'armement défensif du guerrier scandinave paraît avoir consisté alors uniquement dans le bouclier rond ou allongé, dans la cuirasse et dans le casque, quoique aucune arme complète de cette dernière espèce ne se trouve au musée de Copenhague [1], et que les cercles de coiffure puissent faire supposer que le casque, comme chez les Francs, n'était porté que par les chefs. On a vu dans le précédent article, qui traite des armes britanniques, un casque à cornes qui pourrait bien être d'origine danoise.

L'usage des armes en pierre et en bronze paraît s'être conservé bien plus longtemps en Scandinavie que dans le reste de l'Europe, puisque M. Worsaae s'est vu obligé de classer, dans son Catalogue illustré du musée de Copenhague, comme produits de l'époque de l'âge du fer, ce qui ailleurs appartient au moyen âge, voire au moyen âge très-avancé, puisqu'il y fait figurer même des épées du treizième et du quatorzième siècle.

1. Voir n° 1, à la page suivante, ce que l'on croit être un cimier de casque.

1. Cimier de casque (?) danois en bronze ornementé, de 22 cent. de hauteur (*Hjelmprydelse* en danois), conservé au musée de Copenhague. Ce singulier cimier a la forme d'un chandelier.

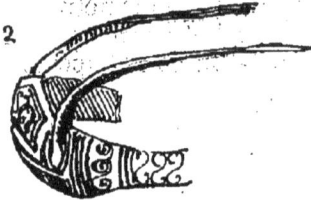

2. Coiffure bandeau, espèce de casque de 12 cent. de hauteur, en cuivre ou bronze, gravé et repoussé. — Musée de Copenhague.

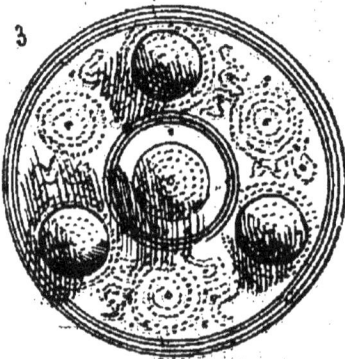

3. Bouclier danois rond en bronze (*Bronces-Kjold* en danois), de 56 cent., à ombilic central et à trois ombilics circulaires. — Musée de Copenhague.

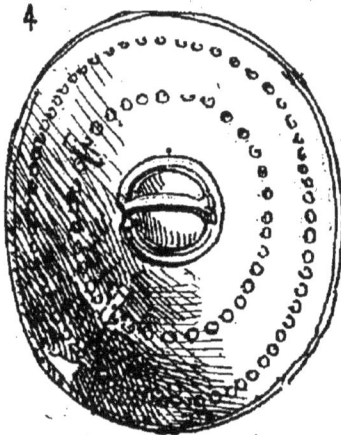

4. Bouclier danois oval en bronze de 64 cent. de longueur, vu à l'intérieur. La partie extérieure est toute semblable, et l'ombilic sert à placer la main sur l'énarme. — Musée de Copenhague.

5. Plaque d'un bouclier rond danois en bronze de 44 cent. de diamètre, à ombilic pointu et richement ornementé. — Musée de Copenhague.

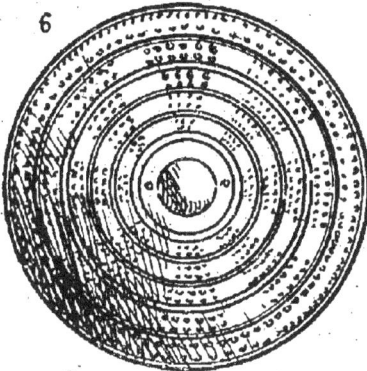

6. Bouclier danois rond en bronze de 54 cent. de diamètre, à ombilic rond et garni de têtes de clous. — Musée de Copenhague.

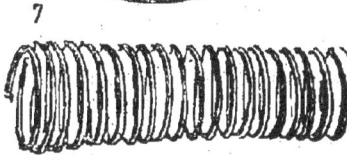

7. Brassard-ressort danois en bronze, de 30 cent. de longueur. —Musée de Copenhague.—Voir ce même genre de brassards au chapitre des armes germaniques en bronze.

8. Brassard danois en bronze, de 15 cent. de longueur. — Musée de Copenhague.

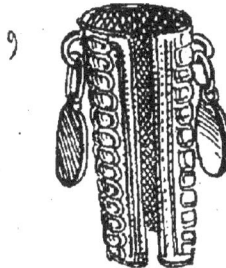

9. Brassard danois en bronze, de 18 cent. de longueur, orné de médailles. — Musée de Copenhague.

10. Lame de framée danoise en bronze, dite *celt*, de 9 cent. — Musée de Copenhague.

11. Pointe de flèche danoise en bronze, de 6 cent. — Musée de Copenhague.

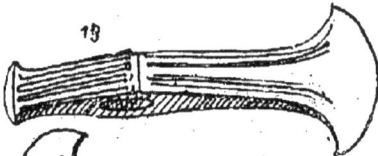

12. Pointe de flèche danoise en bronze, de 15 cent. — Musée de Copenhague.

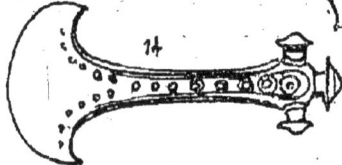

13. Hache danoise en bronze, de 16 cent. — Musée de Copenhague.

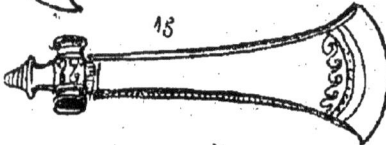

14. Hache danoise en bronze, de 24 cent. — Musée de Copenhague.

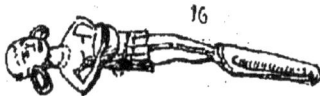

15. Hache danoise en bronze, de 44 cent. — Musée de Copenhague.

16. Couteau danois en bronze, de 16 cent. — Musée de Copenhague.

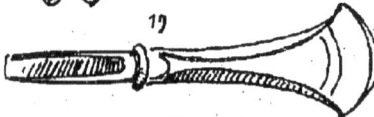

17. Lame de framée danoise en bronze, de 27 cent., avec un débris de sa hampe. — Musée de Copenhague.

18. Lame de lance danoise en bronze, de 30 cent. — Musée de Copenhague.

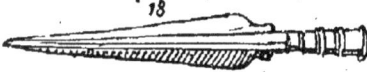

19. Dague danoise en bronze, de 36 cent. — Musée de Copenhague.

20. Dague danoise en bronze, de 21 cent. — Musée de Copenhague.

21. Poignard danois en bronze, de 10 cent. — Musée de Copenhague.

14

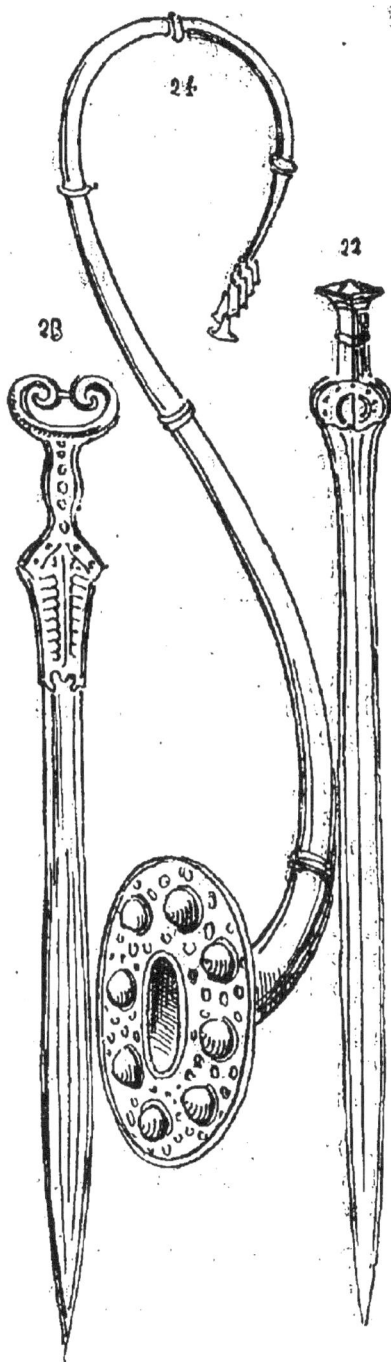

22. Épée danoise en bronze, de 90 cent. de longueur et d'un travail remarquable, tel que l'on en rencontre dans les tombeaux germaniques. — Musée de Copenhague.

23. Épée danoise en bronze, de 85 cent. de longueur. — Musée de Copenhague.

24. Cor de guerre en bronze, de 1 m. 28 cent. de longueur.—Musée de Copenhague.

Le musée de Copenhague possède de l'âge du bronze plus de deux cents objets remarquables, parmi lesquels il faut citer, en outre des pièces reproduites ici, une épée avec son fourreau en cuir, des poignards et des couteaux de formes étranges, des anneaux de coiffure et des poteries, parmi lesquelles les *urnes domestiques* sont très-précieuses pour le classement des époques, selon le mode d'inhumation et de crémation.

ARMES DE PAYS DIVERS EN BRONZE

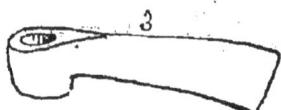

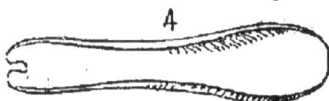

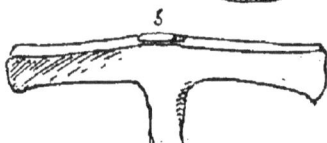

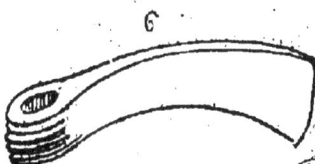

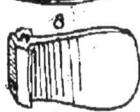

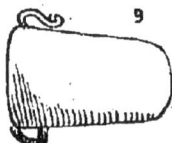

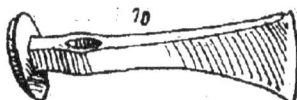

1. Lame de framée en bronze, dite *celt*, trouvée en Suisse et conservée au musée de Genève.
2. Lame de framée en bronze, trouvée en Suisse et conservée au musée de Genève.
3. Hachette suisse en bronze. — Musée de Genève.
4. Hache ou lame de lance en bronze, de 17 cent. — Musée de Lauzanne.
5. Hache en bronze trouvée à Lieli près Oberwil, non loin de Bremgarten en Suisse, et conservée au musée de Zurick.
6. Hachette en bronze trouvée en Russie. — Moulage au musée de Saint-Germain.
7. Couteau à tête de bélier en bronze, de 24 cent., trouvé en Sibérie. — Col. Klemm à Dresde.
8 et 9. Deux haches en bronze, dites *celt*, trouvées en Russie. — Col. Oziersky. — Moulages au musée de Saint-Germain.

Des fouilles faites dans les gouvernements de Minsk et de Vladimir, ainsi qu'en Sibérie, ont amené la découverte d'un grand nombre d'outils et d'armes de l'âge de la pierre brute et polie ou plutôt lissée. Beaucoup de ces exemplaires sont conservés dans la col. Oziersky, à Pétersbourg.

10. Hache en bronze trouvée en Hongrie. — Moulage au musée de Saint-Germain.
11. Pointe de lance en bronze, de 20 cent., trouvée en Bohême. — Musée national de Prague.

V

ARMES DE L'AGE DU FER

DES PEUPLES DU NORD

L'époque dite de l'âge du fer, en Angleterre, que la commission de la section britannique de l'histoire du travail à l'Exposition universelle de Paris, en 1867, avait désignée comme « troisième époque, celle de la domination romaine, » ne commence que cent ans avant l'invasion saxonne ; car la connaissance de l'arme en fer ne constitue pas son règne. L'emploi des armes offensives en bronze s'est conservé bien plus longtemps dans les îles Britanniques et dans la Scandinavie que sur le reste du continent ; c'est encore là une des causes du facile assujettissement de la Grande-Bretagne à cette époque. L'arme en fer du Romain, du Saxon, du Franc, du Burgonde et des autres races germaniques, a partout contribué aux victoires vis-à-vis des peuples encore réduits aux armes tranchantes en cuivre. Les Gaules mal armées ont été entièrement conquises par le peuple romain, qui n'a jamais réussi à réduire la Germanie, où ses légions devaient constamment éprouver des échecs.

Les périodes que l'on est convenu de comprendre sous

la dénomination générale de l'âge du fer, devraient s'arrêter logiquement à la fin du cinquième siècle, après la chute de l'Empire d'Occident; mais on les fait descendre bien plus bas, même jusqu'à la fin du règne de la race carlovingienne (987), système qui, malgré sa défectuosité, a dû être conservé en partie, afin de ne pas apporter de désordre dans la classification chronologique et aggraver les difficultés de recherches, puisque beaucoup de musées ont encore classé grand nombre d'armes appartenant déjà au moyen âge parmi les produits de l'époque dite l'âge du fer.

On a vu dans l'Introduction que le fer était connu partout et de tout temps, mais que son emploi *universel* pour la fabrication des armes défensives et offensives avait été précédé par celui du bronze. Les Romains avaient compris de bonne heure la supériorité de l'arme offensive en fer sur celle du bronze, métal qui, dès lors, ne fut plus employé chez eux qu'à la confection des armes défensives. En 202 avant Jésus-Christ, le soldat romain n'avait déjà plus d'arme offensive en bronze, et on peut admettre que, dans la seconde guerre punique, cette arme contribua pour beaucoup à la victoire des Romains sur les Carthaginois. Les quelques armes en fer trouvées dans des tombeaux gaulois, où elles étaient mêlées aux armes de bronze, telles que les exemplaires conservés au musée de Saint-Germain, et qui ont été recueillis au cimetière gaulois de Catalaunum (département de la Marne), paraissent plutôt d'origine germanique, puisqu'elles ressemblent grandement aux épées trouvées à Tiefenau et à Neufchâtel en Suisse, armes dont on trouvera plus loin le dessin, et que j'attribue aux Burgondes, si renommés pour le travail du fer. L'Hélvétie, presque rendue déserte, en 450, par les massacres systématiques des Romains, fut repeuplée, vers 550, par les Burgondes, dont les bandes s'étaient emparées de l'Ouest, par les Alemans qui occupaient toutes les parties où l'on parle encore aujourd'hui allemand, et par les Ostrogoths,

14.

établis dans le Sud, où règnent les langues italienne, française et romane.

Les Burgondes étaient une race forte, de haute taille; la longue soie de ces épées indique une main large et puissante. La hache et les deux lames de lance en fer trouvées près du village Onsvala (Bara-Schönen, etc.), en Suisse (voir le dessin plus loin), démontrent aussi par leur différence de forme qu'elles ont appartenu à un peuple autre que les Francs et probablement aussi aux Burgondes.

Les épées des Bretons étaient plus tard d'une longueur excessive, et même plus longues encore que celles des Cimbres et des Marcomans.

La forme et le caractère de la plupart des armes danoises (scandinaves), rangées au musée de Copenhague comme appartenant à la période dite de l'âge du fer, indiquent déjà le moyen âge, et rien n'autorise à les faire remonter à l'âge du fer qui doit s'arrêter à la fin du cinquième siècle, après la chute de l'Empire d'Occident (475). Comme en Angleterre, le règne du fer, en Danemark, a commencé tard, et n'a précédé que de fort peu de temps le moyen âge dont le caractère éminemment germanique a de suite laissé son empreinte sur les armes et sur les monuments.

L'armement des guerriers a peu varié dans les nombreuses branches de la grande famille germanique. C'est partout le saxe (*Sacks*) ou *Scramasax*[1], sorte de *gladius* romain à lame évidée et d'un seul tranchant, avec la longue épée, la *spata* ou l'*ensis*, si formidable, selon Guglielmus Pugliese et Hicetas Choniates, dans la main teutonique[2], qui étaient les armes offensives favorites. La grande épée souvent marquée, dans les premiers temps, du nom

---

1. Voir l'étymologie de ce mot, pages 44 et 169.

2. Les épées trouvées en Allemagne mesurent ordinairement 90 à 95 cent., et ont la lame arrondie, tandis que l'épée franque trouvée sur le sol gaulois mesure ordinairement 70 à 75 cent.; sa lame est plus aiguë.

de son propriétaire, gravé en lettres runiques, a joué un rôle important dans la vie de ces peuples chez lesquels cette arme, réputée pour sa bonne trempe, était connue par des noms propres : tels étaient le *Mimung* de Wieland ; le *Balmung* de Sigfried ; la *Durandart* ou *Durandal* de Roland ; le *Hrunting* empoisonné (Beowulf) ; le *Dainleif* de Hagen, le père de Gudrun ; le *Tryfing*, l'arme de Svafrlamis ; le *Mistelstein*, qui extermina deux mille quatre cents hommes ; les *Skeop Liusingi* et *Hwitlin-gi* de l'histoire danoise de Saro Grammaticus ; la *Joyeuse* de Charlemagne ; l'*Almace* de Turpin ; l'*Altecler* d'Olivier ; le *Chlaritel* d'Englir ; la *Preciosa* du roi Poligan ; la *Schoyeuse* d'Orange ; le *Mal* de Rother ; le *Calibarn* du roi Artus et le *Quersteinbeis* anglais de Hakon, qui, comme l'indique son nom, d'un seul coup sépara en deux l'énorme pierre meulière.

Chose curieuse à constater, chez l'homme du Nord l'épée était mâle, et chez le Méridional, femelle. C'est à cette arme, bien plus courte sous les Mérovingiens qu'au temps de la chevalerie, que l'histoire rapporte le forfait de Clotaire II qu'elle accuse d'avoir fait massacrer tous les Saxons vaincus, hommes, femmes et enfants, qui dépassaient la hauteur de son épée. Le *scramasax*, dont le nom est pourtant bien saxon, ne se rencontre presque pas dans les tombeaux saxons ni dans ceux de l'Allemagne du Nord en général. Ce sont les branches burgondes, alemanes et franques auxquelles il paraît avoir été bien plus familier.

Les haches si variées de formes, selon les races, et parmi lesquelles la *francisque* des derniers conquérants de la Gaule est une des plus réputées, étaient cependant l'arme la plus caractéristique du peuple germain ; ces haches se retrouvent aussi bien en Scandinavie que dans la Grande-Bretagne où les Saxons et les Danois en avaient introduit l'usage. Pour étudier l'armement de tous ces soi-disant barbares, on possède fort peu de documents, et encore ne se rapportent-ils qu'aux Francs. Tout ce que l'on possède en fait d'armes de la fin des règnes mérovingiens, c'est la francisque et l'épée de Childéric Ier, conservées au Louvre. L'épée et les éperons attribués à Charlemagne constituent probablement les seules armes du commencement de l'époque carlovingienne. Pour les documents écrits et peints, il faut descendre jusqu'au règne de Charles II le Chauve (840-877), pour trouver quelques renseignements dans les miniatures de la Bible de ce roi, mais qui paraissent peu exactes et plutôt le produit de l'imagination de l'artiste, puisque l'on y voit le roi représenté sur son trône, entouré de gardes, dont le costume est pour ainsi dire romain; les lambrequins de cuir et le reste montrent presque l'équipement du prétorien. Le *Codex aureus* de Saint-Gall, le *couvercle de l'Antiphonaire* de Saint-Grégoire, les *Leges Longobardorum* de la bibliothèque de Stuttgard, le *Wessebrunn* de 810 de la bibliothèque de Munich, le bas-relief à l'église de Saint-Julien à Brioude (?) et autres documents et monuments contredisent du reste l'illustrateur de la Bible.

Après cela, il n'y a plus de trace historique ni archéologique que cent ans plus tard, dans le *Martyrologe* du dixième siècle, manuscrit conservé à la bibliothèque de Stuttgard, dans lequel on trouve déjà, ainsi que sur le bas-relief du reliquaire du neuvième siècle, au trésor de Saint-Moris, le guerrier, armé comme sur les tapisseries de Bayeux, de la fin du onzième siècle.

Grâce aux descriptions de quelques auteurs (Sidoine Apollinaire, vers 450 de notre ère; Procope Agathios; Grégoire de Tours et autres), et aux fouilles exécutées dans les cimetières mérovingiens, on peut presque reconstituer l'armement du dernier conquérant des Gaules. Comme chez la plupart des autres races germaniques, l'armure défensive du Franc n'était composée que du petit bouclier rond convexe, de cinquante cent. de diamètre, en bois recouvert de peau. On n'a encore trouvé ni casque ni cuirasse, mais on sait par des textes que les chefs en étaient armés ; le simple guerrier avait une partie de la tête rasée comme le Chinois ; le restant des cheveux teints en rouge éclatant, nattés et entassés sur la partie frontale, lui formait une sorte de défense qui remplaçait le casque et qui était ordinairement entouré d'un bandeau en cuir. Son armure offensive était : l'angon ou le pilum à pointe barbue ; la lance (framée) à longue lame en fer ; la hache à un seul tranchant et appelée francisque ; l'épée et le scramasax , longue dague ou plutôt coutelas à un seul tranchant. L'arc et la flèche ne lui servaient qu'à la chasse, car l'angon et même la francisque étaient ses armes de jet. (V. pages 44 à 48.)

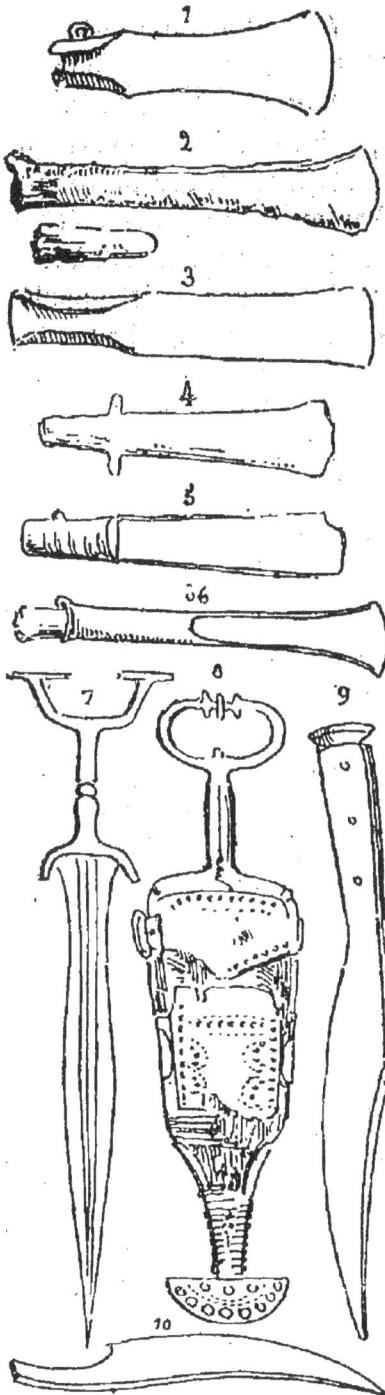

1. Lame de framée germanique en fer, dite *celt*, de 18 cent. — Musée national de Munich.

2. Lame de framée germanique à douille, en fer, de 28 cent., avec le débris de la pointe de la hampe, de 10 cent. de longueur, trouvée dans un des tombeaux du cimetière de Hallstatt, en Autriche. — Coll. Az, à Lintz.

3. Lame de framée germanique en fer, de 28 cent., id.

4. Lame de framée germanique en fer, de 28 cent., id. — Un autre exemplaire de la même provenance est au cabinet des antiques de Vienne, et un troisième, trouvé à Lunebourg, au musée de Hanovre.

5. Lame de framée germanique, à douille, en fer, de 28 cent., provenant du cimetière de Hallstatt. — Coll. Az, à Lintz.

6. Lame de framée germanique, à douille, en fer, et à anneau pareil à l'anneau des lames de lances dites *celts*. Elle mesure 36 cent., et provient du cimetière de Hallstatt. — Cabinet des antiques de Vienne.

7. Petite épée germanique, de 40 cent. de longueur, à lame de fer et manche de bronze, trouvée au cimetière de Hallstatt. — Cabinet des antiques de Vienne.

8. Poignard germanique en fer, de 36 cent., trouvé dans un tombeau de la Bavière. — Musée de Sigmaringen.

9. Couteau de guerre germanique, en fer, de 34 cent., trouvé à Ringenbach. — Musée de Sigmaringen.

10. Couteau d'armes germanique, en fer, de 28 cent. — Musée national de Munich.

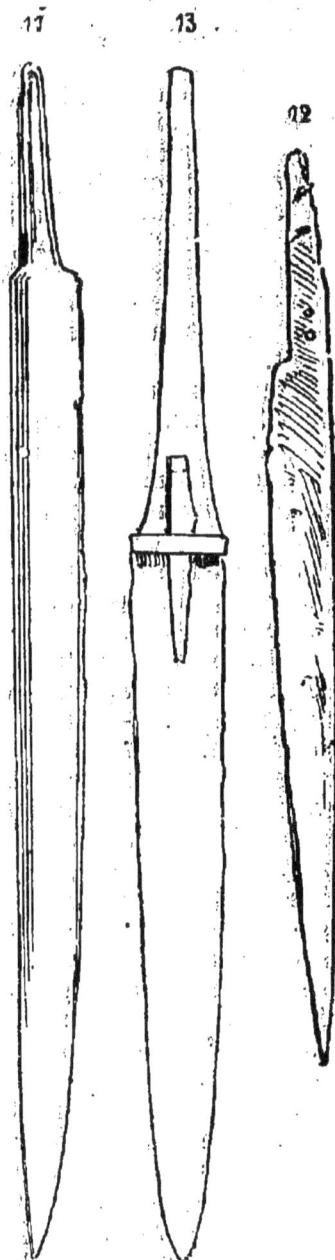

11. Dague ou semispata franque, en fer, appelée *scramasax*. Elle a un seul tranchant et des évidements produits par des rainures (*Blutrinnen*, en allemand) du côté du dos. Elle mesure 62 cent., y compris la soie, et a été trouvée près de Châlons. — N. E. 19, musée d'artillerie de Paris.

La longueur énorme des soies (manches) des scramasax trouvés en Suisse et en Allemagne (15 à 25 cent.?) a fait supposer au docteur Keller, de Zurich, que ce n'était pas là une arme, mais une hachette à deux mains pour travailler le bois. Je pense cependant que c'est bien le scramasax des Francs et autres peuplades germaniques, puisqu'on l'a souvent trouvé dans les tombeaux des guerriers à côté de la longue épée.

12. Scramasax en fer, de 46 c., trouvé en Suisse. — Coll. de l'auteur. Un de ces scramasax, provenant de Manheim, se trouve à la Tour de Londres $\left(\frac{1}{181}\right)$.

Le musée de Genève possède également une de ces armes, qui a été trouvée dans un tombeau à Bellecau (canton de Vaud). Le musée de Lauzanne en possède d'autres dont les soies (poignées) mesurent 15 cent., et paraissent indiquer la race des Burgondes. Un scramasax, du musée d'Avenches, déterré dans cette ville, pourrait remonter au troisième siècle, car c'est en 264 que les Alemans pénétrèrent dans ce pays et détruisirent Aventicum de fond en comble.

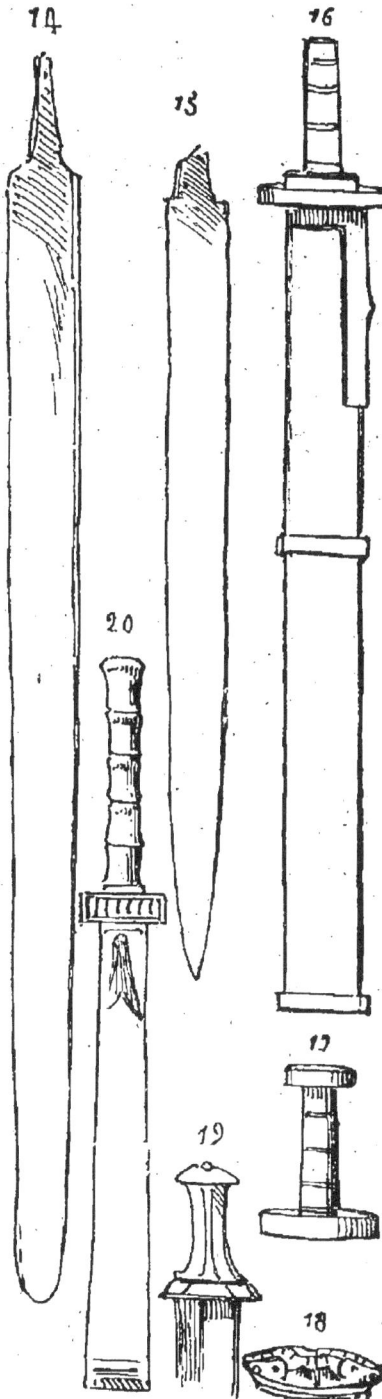

On a aussi trouvé une de ces armes à Gruningen-Windisch. Elle est conservée au musée de Zurich; sa soie mesure 22 cent. Le musée de Sigmaringen en possède une qui a été trouvée à Hohenzollern; son manche, qui mesure 25 cent., est en cuivre garni de la fusée de bois, recouvert de toiles et de lanières en cuir; la lame mesure 40 c., ce qui donne un ensemble de 65 cent.

13. Scramasax en fer, dont la lame a 38 cent. et la soie 22, trouvé à Wulflingen et conservé au musée de Sigmaringen. Cette arme se distingue des autres de son genre en ce qu'elle est pourvue, au-dessus de son fourreau, d'un petit couteau.

14. Épée germanique en fer, de 94 cent., dont la pointe de la lame est arrondie, trouvée à Langeneslingen. — Musée de Sigmaringen. — On a trouvé de pareilles épées, dont quelques-unes dépassaient la longueur d'un mètre, au cimetière de Selzen, près Nierstein, où les fouilles ont mis à découvert vingt-huit tombeaux contenant tous des squelettes, dont plusieurs étaient accompagnés, à côté de ces longues épées, de haches de formes saxonne et franque.

Le *Codex aureus* de Saint-Gall, du huitième siècle, ainsi que beaucoup de manuscrits anglo-saxons du neuvième au onzième siècle, montrent la même forme d'épées non aiguës dans leurs miniatures.

15. Épée franque de l'époque mérovingienne, de 73 cent., à

pointe aiguë, trouvée dans la Moselle. — E. 14, musée d'artillerie de Paris. Des épées semblables ont été retirées des tombeaux de Fronstetten.

16. Épée avec son fourreau, provenant du tombeau de Childéric Ier (457-481), conservée au Louvre. Il y a eu erreur dans le montage de cette arme mérovingienne. L'armurier chargé de sa restauration a doublé la garde avec le pommeau, au lieu de le poser à sa place, au bout des fusées, tel que les manuscrits et que le dessin 17 l'indiquent.

La même erreur a été commise au musée d'artillerie dans la reproduction de la spata franque. On trouve au cabinet des médailles à Paris le moulage d'une épée semblable, et probablement de la même époque, qui a 90 centimètres de longueur totale et a été trouvée sur un champ de bataille, à Pouan, département de l'Aube. La garde de cette épée ne dépasse presque pas la lame, très-large et aiguë.

17. Poignée d'épée mérovingienne, selon les manuscrits.

18. Pommeau d'une épée également attribuée à Childéric.

19. Poignée d'épée germanique trouvée à Peiting en Bavière.

20. Épée germanique ou slave, à bout carré, du sixième siècle, d'après le bas-relief d'un diptyque, qui se trouve dans le trésor de la cathédrale de Halberstadt. La longueur excessive du manche se rapproche de celle des épées burgondes trouvées en Suisse. (V. n° 21 ci-après.)

P. S. Il faut répéter ici ce qui a été déjà dit dans le chapitre historique sur l'étymologie de la singulière arme nommée *scramasax*.

Sax veut dire couteau; *scrama* peut dériver de *scamata*, la ligne de démarcation tracée sur le sable entre deux combattants grecs, ou de *scaran* (tondre), d'où est dérivé la *Schere* (ciseaux) allemande : *scramasax*, couteau de duel ou couteau rasant.

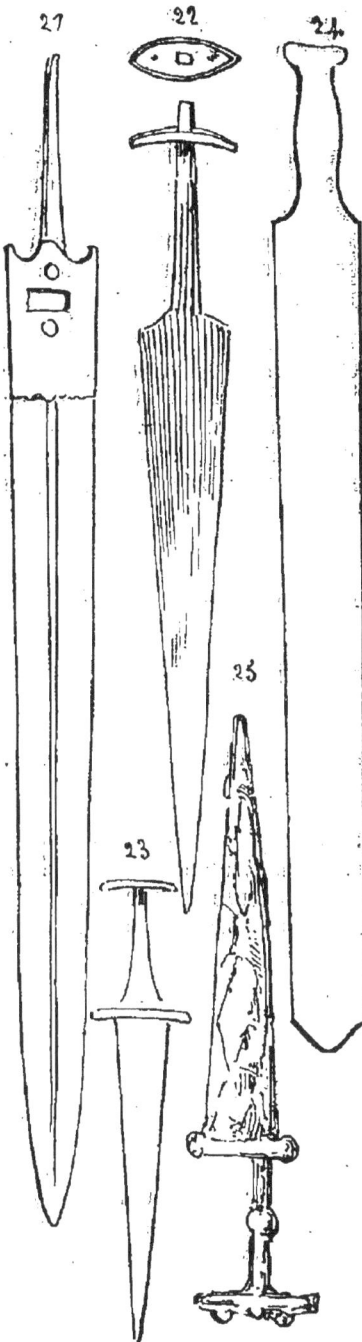

21. Épée burgonde en fer, de
98 cent. de longueur, y compris
la soie qui est très-longue, et
indique une race robuste et à
larges mains. Le musée d'artillerie de Paris possède, sous le
n° D. 42, les moulages de ces
onze épées trouvées à la Tiefenau, en Suisse, sur un champ de
bataille, et qui ont été reproduites dans l'ouvrage de Troyon,
où elles ne devraient pas figurer
parmi les armes lacustres. Le
musée de Saint-Germain possède de pareilles épées, qui ont
été trouvées dans le lac de Neufchâtel.

22. Dague germanique de l'é-
poque mérovingienne, de 42 c.,
trouvée dans un tombeau à Het-
tingen et conservée au musée
de Sigmaringen.

23. Poignard germanique de l'é-
poque mérovingienne, de 21 c.,
trouvé à Rothenlachen et conservé à Sigmaringen. Cette forme s'est continuée plus de huit
cents ans, puisqu'on la retrouve
encore au quinzième siècle.

24. Épée germanique en fer, de
85 cent. de longueur, trouvée
dans une tombe du cimetière de
Hallstatt. — Cabinet des antiques de Vienne. (Voir, pour la
forme de la pointe de la lame,
les armes de bronze.)

25. Couteau-poignard germanique, de 33 cent., de l'époque
mérovingienne, trouvé dans une
tombe près de Sigmaringen,
ville où il est conservé dans le
musée. Exemplaire rare par sa
forme, dont le semblable se
trouve au musée national de
Munich.

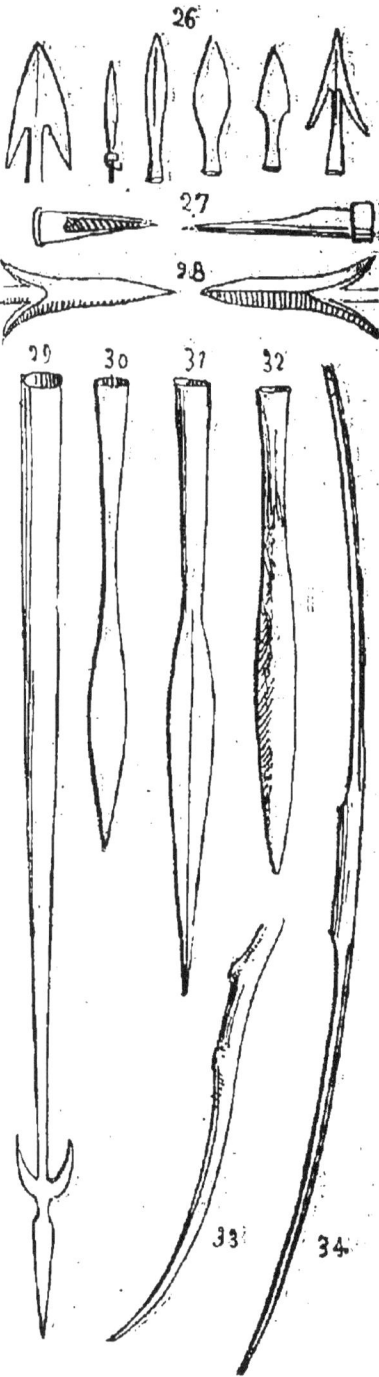

26. Six différentes pointes en fer de flèches germaniques de l'époque mérovingienne. — Musée de Sigmaringen.

27. Deux pointes de flèches empoisonnées, en grandeur naturelle. — Musée de Sigmaringen,

28. Deux pointes d'angon germaniques, trouvées dans la principauté de Hohenzollern, et conservées au musée de Sigmaringen.

29. Fer d'angon franc (mérovingien). — E. 23, musée d'artillerie de Paris.

30. Fer de framée (espèce de lance, en allemand *Pfrime* et *Frime*), de 37 cent., trouvé dans le cimetière mérovingien de Londinières. — E. 7, musée d'artillerie de Paris.

31. Fer de framée, de 39 cent., trouvé à Selzen (Hesse), dans un tombeau.

32. Fer de framée burgonde, de 34 cent., trouvé dans le village Onswala (Bara Schonen), en Suisse, et conservé au musée de Lund en Suède. — Un fer semblable, un peu plus court, a été trouvé dans le tombeau de Childéric Ier (457-487), et conservé au Louvre.

33. Débris d'arc probablement germanique (aleman?) en bois, quoique trouvé dans un palaffite de la Suisse. Cette partie mesure 1m,05, ce qui donne à l'arc complet à peu près 2m,30.

34. Arc germanique de l'époque du règne mérovingien, trouvé dans un tombeau près Lupfen. Il est en chêne, et a six pieds de longueur.

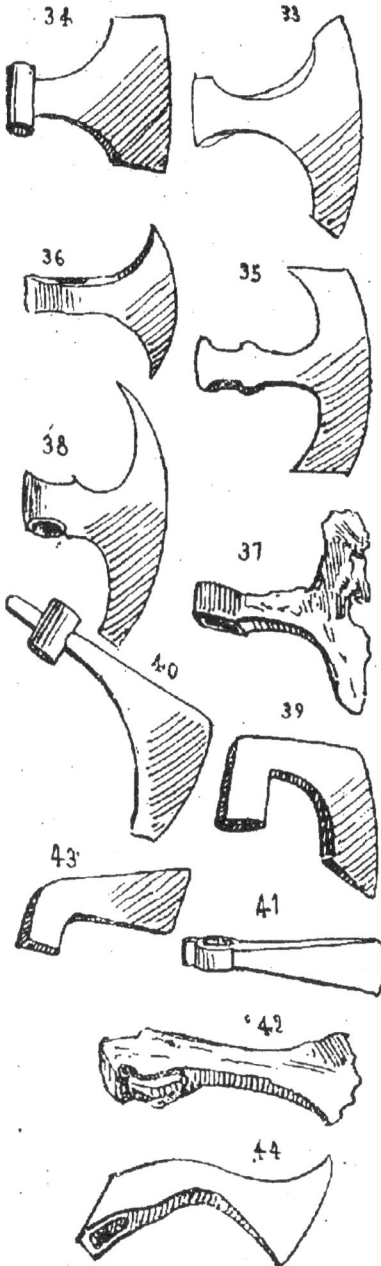

33 bis. Hache de guerre germanique, forme saxonne, trouvée dans le cimetière franc de Selzen (Hesse), où M. Lindenschmidt a visité, en 1848, vingt-huit tombeaux, fouilles dont il a publié le résultat. — Musée de Mayence.

34 bis. Hache de guerre germanique, forme saxonne, de 16 cent., trouvée dans le département de la Moselle. — E. 5, musée d'artillerie de Paris.

35. Hache de guerre germanique, forme saxonne, de 24 cent. — Musées de Saint-Germain et de Sigmaringen.

36. Hache de guerre alemane, forme saxonne, trouvée en Suisse. — Cabinet des antiques à Zurich.

37. Hache de guerre anglo-saxonne, trouvée dans la Tamise. — $\frac{1}{187}$, Tour de Londres.

38 et 39. Haches de guerre germaniques de la fin de l'époque mérovingienne. — Musée de Sigmaringen.

40. Hache de guerre germanique, de 16 cent. — Musée de Munich.

41. Hachette de guerre germanique trouvée à Schlieben en Saxe. — Coll. Klemm à Dresde.

42. Hache de guerre probablement britannique (*pol-axe*), trouvée dans la Tamise. — $\frac{1}{187}$, Tour de Londres.

43. Hache burgonde, de 22 cent., trouvée à Onswala (Bara Schonen) en Suisse. — Musée de Lund en Suède.

44. Hache franque appelée *francisque*, trouvée à Envermeu,

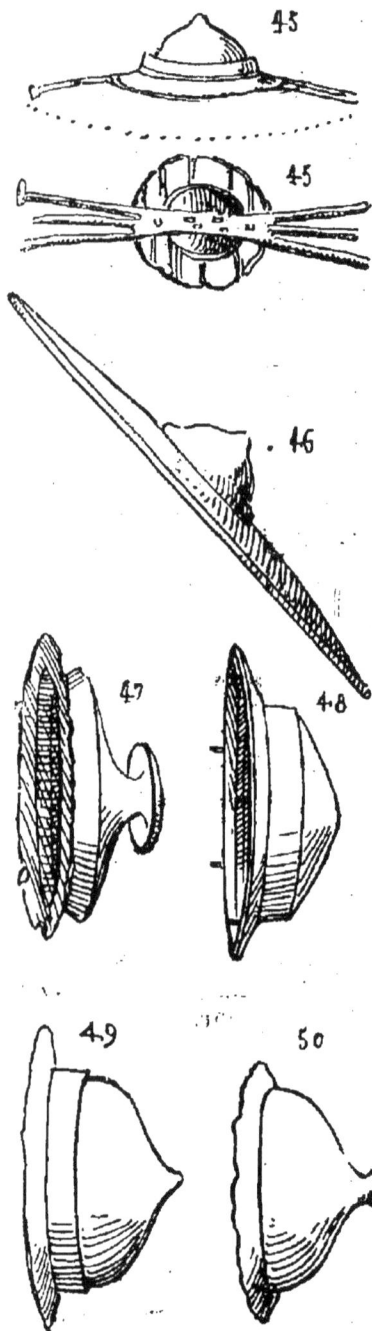

près d'Augsbourg. — Musée d'artillerie de Paris; une autre au musée d'Augsbourg; à Selzen en Hesse (musée de Mayence); dans le Hohenzollern (musée de Sigmaringen). Cette hache, dont un exemplaire se trouve au musée de la Tour de Londres, y est appelée *Taperaxe*. Le musée du Louvre possède la francisque de Childéric Ier.

45. Carcasse d'ombilic en fer d'un bouclier franc, trouvée à Tondinières et décrite par l'abbé Cochet. De pareilles carcasses de boucliers, provenant de fouilles faites dans la principauté de Hohenzollern, sont conservées au musée de Sigmaringen.

46. Bouclier franc, convexe, rond, de 50 cent. de diamètre, en bois recouvert de peau, et à ombilic en fer, de 17 cent. de diamètre. Dessiné d'après le bouclier reconstruit au musée d'artillerie à Paris.

47. Ombilic de bouclier anglo-saxon, en fer, trouvé à Lincolnshire et conservé dans la collection à Goodrich-Court. La forme des ombilics saxons s'est modifiée plus tard et a pris la forme sphérique qui se termine en pointe.

48. Ombilic germanique (franc) en fer, trouvé à Selzen (Hesse).

49. Ombilics germaniques en fer, trouvés en Bavière et conservés au musée Maximilien, à Augsbourg.

Plusieurs ombilics de cette même forme appartiennent au musée national bavarois à Munich. Ils ont été trouvés dans

15.

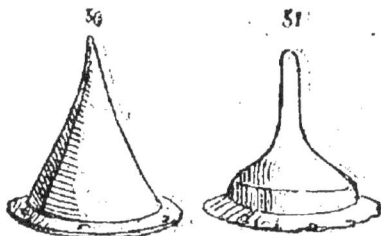

des tombeaux qui remontent au sixième siècle.

50. Ombilic en fer de bouclier anglo-saxon.

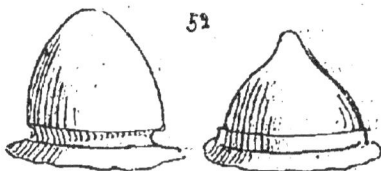

51. Ombilic en fer de bouclier germanique, trouvé à Grosch-nowitz (Oppeln) et conservé au musée de Berlin. Un semblable ombilic trouvé à Lunebourg fait partie du musée de Hanovre. — N° 492, au musée de Copenhague, même genre d'ombilic.

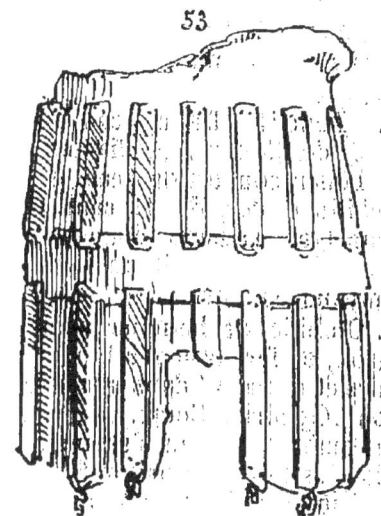

52. Ombilics germaniques en fer conservés au musée de Sigmaringen.

53. Fragment de cuirasse en fer, trouvé en Suisse et provenant probablement des Alemans qui ont envahi la Suisse au quatrième siècle. — Cabinet des antiques à Zurich. Cette précieuse pièce est composée de longues lames rivées entre elles.

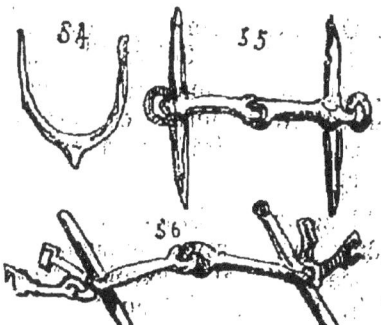

54. Éperon germanique en fer de l'époque mérovingienne. — Musée de Sigmaringen.

55. Bridon germanique (*trense*, en allemand) en fer, de l'époque mérovingienne. — Musée de Sigmaringen.

56. Bridon germanique en fer, de l'époque mérovingienne. — Musée de Sigmaringen.

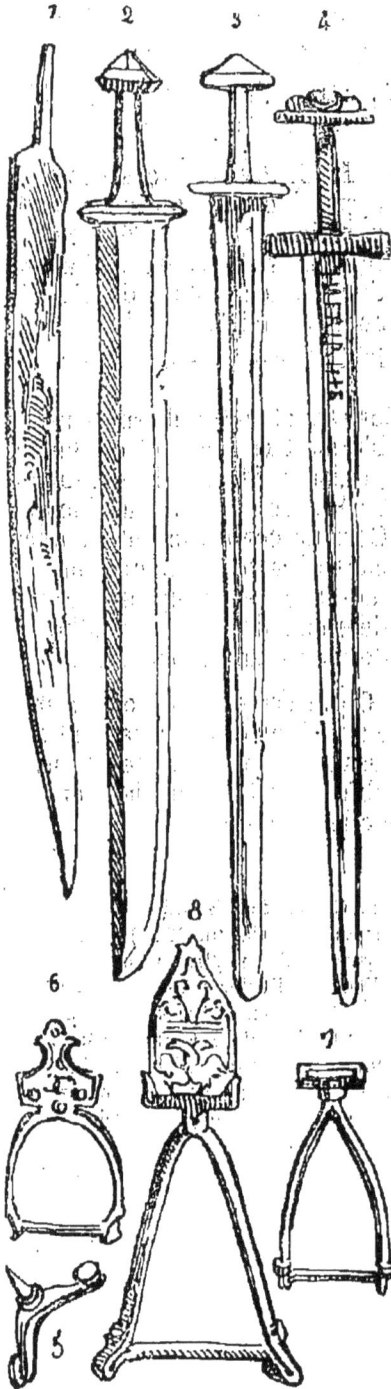

1. Épée danoise en fer d'un seul tranchant, de 90 cent. de longueur, et dont la forme est presque celle du scramasax. — 496, au musée de Copenhague.

2. Épée danoise en fer d'un seul tranchant, de 108 cent. de longueur; la poignée est semblable, par la forme de sa garde et de son pommeau, aux poignées des épées franques de l'époque mérovingienne. — N° 493, au musée de Copenhague.

3. Épée danoise en fer, de 107 c. La lame, à deux tranchants, largement évidée, n'a pas de pointe aiguë, et est presque arrondie comme celle des épées germaniques. — 494, au musée de Copenhague.

4. Épée danoise en fer, de 107 c. Le pommeau est trilobé comme ceux des épées représentées dans le manuscrit anglo-saxon *Aelfric* du onzième siècle, de la bibliothèque britannique. — Pareille épée dans la collection de M. le comte de Nieuwerkerque. Dès que le pommeau est garni de cinq lobes à la place des trois, et que les deux extrémités de la garde sont un peu inclinées vers la pointe, l'épée appartient au treizième siècle. (Voir celle du musée de Munich, au chapitre des épées du moyen âge.) L'épée de la collection Nieuwerkerque a aussi cinq lobes, mais les extrémités de sa garde ne sont pas inclinées.

5. Éperon danois en bronze. — Musée de Copenhague.

6. Étrier danois en bronze, 24 c. — Musée de Copenhague.

7. Étrier danois en bronze, in-

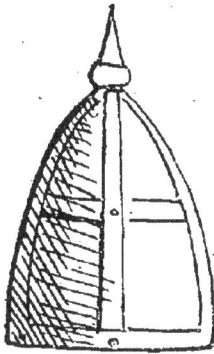

crusté d'argent, 24 cent. — Musée de Copenhague.

8. Étrier danois en bronze, 38 c. — Musée de Copenhague.

P.-S. Presque tous ces objets appartiennent au moyen âge chrétien, et ont été classés à tort dans le musée, ainsi que dans le catalogue de M. Worsaae, parmi les produits de l'époque dite de l'âge du fer.

Casque et cotte d'armes probablement en cuir et en fer, reproduits d'après la colonne de Théodose à Constantinople [1]. Comme ces armes n'ont aucun caractère romain, on peut admettre qu'elles représentent des défenses de guerriers alliés ou de mercenaires barbares.

Cette cotte n'a en effet rien de ce qui signale les armes antiques classiques, et sa forme est si singulière que l'on doit hésiter pour le classement.

1. Constantinople déjà résidence de l'empereur Constantin (330), devint, lors du partage de l'empire romain, la capitale de l'empire d'Orient; elle subit un tremblement de terre en 557 et fut prise en 1203 par les Croisés et en 1453 par les Turcs. L'empereur romain Théodose I, dit le Grand, est né en 346 et mort en 398, l'année d'où date l'empire d'Orient.

VI

ARMES DU MOYEN AGE CHRÉTIEN

DE LA RENAISSANCE

ET DES XVIIᵉ ET XVIIIᵉ SIÈCLES

L'introduction historique a montré la marche progressive qui s'est opérée dans le perfectionnement de l'arme à partir des époques les plus reculées, et si la description de l'armement des peuples de l'antiquité aussi bien que de ceux des époques antéhistoriques et des peuples barbares a dû parfois être basée sur des hypothèses, l'histoire de l'armement des deux seconds tiers du moyen âge chrétien a pu être établie sur des pièces encore existantes. A partir du dixième siècle déjà, on peut suivre pas à pas la lente transformation des armes défensives où le changement a été toujours plus sensible que pour les armes offensives de hast, de taille et d'estoc. Le haubert a régné plus de cinq cents ans, et n'a été remplacé par l'armure complète à plaques de métal qu'après avoir été suivi par l'armure de transition en cotte de mailles *en partie* à plaques de fer ou de cuir. Ce chapitre, après avoir fait passer sous les yeux du lecteur les armements complets des différentes époques, lui donnera l'histoire spéciale de chaque arme, où la reproduction de la moindre pièce, même détachée, parlera autant que le texte. Quant aux développements historiques plus généraux, le lecteur est renvoyé aux pages 47 à 72 du chapitre de l'histoire abrégée des armes anciennes.

Combattants, d'après le couvercle en ivoire de l'*Antiphonaire de saint Grégoire*, manuscrit du huitième siècle, conservé à la bibliothèque de Saint-Gall en Suisse.

Cette sculpture a encore beaucoup du caractère romain et même byzantin; elle pourrait bien provenir d'un diptyque.

La forme des boucliers n'est cependant pas romaine, et les espèces de cornes de Moïse que l'on aperçoit sur les têtes des guerriers rappellent les armes défensives de tête des peuples du Nord.

Les deux combattants ne portent pas de barbe; leur seule arme défensive est le bouclier, et leur arme offensive la courte épée et la lance. Le bouclier ne montre qu'un seul énarme.

Cavalier mérovingien d'après un bas-relief de l'église de Sain-
Julien à Brioude (Haute-Loire), attribué au huitième siècle. Ce
guerrier est recouvert du petit haubert ou de la jaque en écailles,
dits *Juzerans* et *Korazins* (V. l'explication au chapitre des cottes
d'armes et cuirasses), sans haut et bas de chausses d'armes, mais
à manches qui recouvrent les bras jusqu'au poignet. Le casque
est conique comme le casque du onzième siècle, appelé en France
normand, cependant encore dépourvu du nasal. L'espèce de
mentonnière paraît être formée par une partie du camail que l'on
voit rentrer sous le casque. Le caractère général de cet armement indique plutôt le dixième ou le onzième siècle, de sorte
que l'auteur ne le fait figurer ici qu'avec toute réserve.

1. Homme d'armes allemand du commencement du neuvième siècle, d'après une miniature du manuscrit de *Wessobrunn* de 810, conservé à la bibliothèque de Munich. Il est à remarquer que ce guerrier ne porte point de barbe, qu'il a le bouclier rond à ombilic et le casque à timbre bombé.

2. Roi lombard d'après les *Leges Longobardorum* du neuvième siècle de la bibliothèque de Stuttgard. Cette miniature est intéressante pour la forme carrée-oblongue et convexe du bouclier, forme qui se retrouve dans la longue targe allemande du quatorzième siècle. Le roi porte sa barbe en collier.

Cavalier et hommes de pied, d'après les miniatures du *Codex aureus* du huitième ou du neuvième siècle, conservées à Saint-Gall. Le cavalier et un des hommes de pied portent la barbe sous le menton et la moustache.

1. Chevalier allemand du dixième siècle, à casque conique à nasal et en grand haubert de mailles, qui se signale par ses longues manches. D'après le *Martyrologe*, manuscrit du dixième siècle à la bibliothèque de Stuttgard.

2. Chevalier en grand haubert de mailles à manches courtes et à camail, sans casque, d'après les bas-reliefs d'un reliquaire en argent repoussé, de la fin du neuvième siècle. — Trésors du couvent de Saint-Maurice dans le canton du Valais, en Suisse. Ces chevaliers ne portent point de barbe.

3. Homme d'armes du dixième siècle, d'après une statuette sur un couvercle en cuir jaune de cette époque, de la collection de M. le comte de Nieuwerkerke. Ce précieux exemplaire a 7 cent. de hauteur. Le casque conique se signale par la forme de son nasal très-large dans sa partie inférieure. L'épée est aiguë. La cotte de maille est longue, et n'a pas encore les hauts-de-chausses adhérents de l'armure normande du onzième siècle. Le bouclier long et pointu est à ombilic.

1. Hommes d'armes anglo-saxons, d'après le *Prudentius Psycho-machia*, etc., manuscrit anglo-saxon du dixième siècle, de la bibliothèque du musée britannique. Tout l'armement défensif consiste dans le bouclier rond à ombilic, et le casque à timbre rond que l'on retrouve encore dans le sceau du roi Richard Cœur de Lion (1157-1173).

2. Chevalier du dixième siècle (?), d'après un manuscrit de ce temps, la *Biblia sacra*, à la bibliothèque impériale de Paris. Cette miniature est remarquable par la forme du pommeau de l'épée, qui est trilobé, comme dans l'*Aelfric*, manuscrit anglo-saxon de la bibliothèque du musée britannique, et par le bouclier, le petit écu aussi en usage sous le règne de saint Louis (1226-1270). La même forme de selle se retrouve sur les tapisseries de Bayeux de la fin du onzième siècle.

1. Le duc de Bourchhard de Souabe (963), bas-relief dans la basilique de Zurich, en Suisse, qui a été construite vers la fin du
onzième siècle, à la place de l'église brûlée en 1078. Casque et
épée rappelant ceux du dixième siècle du *Martyrologe* déjà
mentionné de la bibliothèque de Stuttgard.

2. Homme d'armes anglo-saxon, d'après les miniatures d'un manuscrit anglo-saxon, l'*Aelfric*, de la fin du onzième siècle, de
la bibliothèque du musée britannique. Le bouclier n'a rien du
bouclier normand si long et si pointu en bas, et le casque diffère aussi entièrement de ce que l'on connaît ailleurs de ces
sortes d'armes défensives. Le pommeau de l'épée est trilobé ou
en forme de trèfle et le haubert à longues manches ne ressemble pas non plus aux hauberts normands. Ces hommes
d'armes sont représentés tous les deux sans barbe.

1. Chevalier anglo-saxon, d'après le manuscrit *l'Aelfric* du commencement du onzième siècle, mentionné à la page précédente.
Même épée à pommeau trilobé, même bouclier rond ; mais le
haubert est ici annelé, sans bas et à haut-de-chausses adhérent. Il est à remarquer que l'Anglo-Saxon est représenté avec
de la barbe.

2. Chevalier français, d'après un bas-relief du cloître de Saint-
Aubin à Angers. Il porte le casque conique à nasal, le bouclier
en forme de cœur, la framée germanique et le grand haubert
treillissé à longues manches et avec camail. Le bouclier est orné
de peintures qui représentent probablement des *armoiries per-*
sonnelles.

1. Armement allemand du onzième siècle, d'après la statue d'un des fondateurs du dôme de Naumbourg. Le casque est presque semblable à celui du *Codex aureus* de Saint-Gall. Chose singulière, la jambe gauche est sans armure. On remarque de la barbe autour du menton.

2. Chevalier allemand du onzième siècle, en haubert à longues manches, à camail et à haut et bas-de-chausses en mailles, d'après le *Jeremias apocalypsis* de la bibliothèque de Darmstadt.

1. Homme d'armes allemand de la fin du douzième siècle, d'après les broderies de la mitre du couvent de Seligenthal, à Landshut en Bavière, sur laquelle sont représentés les martyres de saint Étienne (997) et de l'archevêque Thomas Becket de Canterbury (saint-Thomas mort en 1170). — Musée national à Munich.

2. Chevalier allemand, d'après la sculpture en pierre du douzième siècle, à la porte de Heimburg en Autriche. Le haubert à longues manches collantes et à camail paraît être en lanières lamées de fer et d'une espèce inconnue. Le timbre tout à fait bombé du casque démontre bien ici la différence radicale qui existait alors entre cette arme défensive allemande et celle des Normands. Les brassards avec épaulières et cubitières qui protègent les arrière-bras, sont aussi très-caractéristiques pour l'époque. La lame de l'épée paraît être cassée dans les mains de la statue, de sorte que l'on ignore quelle en était la forme. Elle ressemble à celle du sabre dace.

1. Chevalier normand du onzième siècle, en grand haubert treillissé ou annelé, à manches, haut-de-chausses et camail adhérents. Les jambes sont entourées de lanières. Le casque conique
est à nasal et le bouclier à la hauteur de l'épaule. — Tapisserie
de Bayeux.

2. Chevalier anglo-saxon reconnaissable par son bouclier rond
à ombilic, et dont l'armement défensif ne diffère pas pour le
reste de celui du Normand. L'épée est très-longue de lame et
son pommeau simple. — Tapisserie de Bayeux.

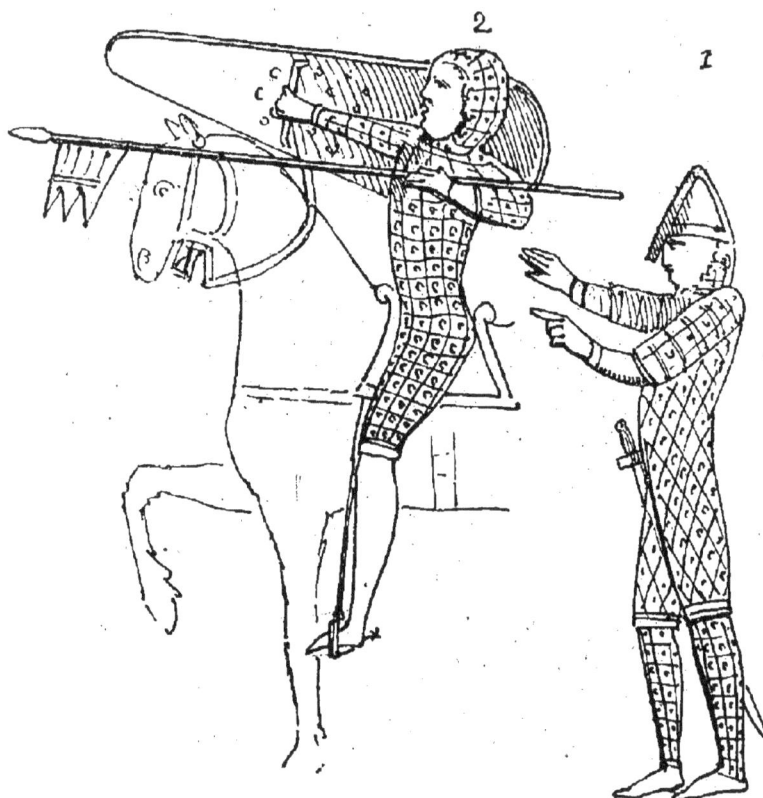

1. Chevalier normand du onzième siècle en grand haubert treillissé ou annelé, à manches, haut et bas-de-chausses et camail
adhérents. On croit que cette figure doit représenter Guillaume
le Conquérant, parce qu'elle seule a les jambes armées comme
le reste du corps. Le casque conique à nasal ne diffère pas de
ceux des autres chevaliers. — Tapisserie de Bayeux.

2. Chevalier normand combattant sans casque et seulement coiffé
du camail. — L'armement défensif est le même, mais ce cavalier est intéressant pour l'étude de la selle, du bridon et de la
banderole qui garnit la lance. — Tapisserie de Bayeux.

1. Chevalier scandinave, de la fin du onzième siècle ou du commencement du douzième, d'après la sculpture sur bois d'une porte d'église en Islande, conservée au musée de Copenhague. L'armement est remarquable par le casque conique à nasal et à couvre-nuque, et par le glaive forme sabre que le chevalier porte avec le bouclier sur l'épaule droite.

2. Le comte de Barcelone don Ramon Bérenger IV (1140) d'après un sceau. Le casque conique est à nasal, et le reste de l'armure parait consister dans un haubert avec haut et bas-de-chausses et camail adhérents, le tout en mailles. Le long bouclier est armorié sur l'un des sceaux et à cannelures sur l'autre. La lance est à banderole.

1. Louis VII le jeune (1137-1180) d'après son sceau. La cotte de mailles est à haut et bas-de-chausses, à camail, et à manches collantes. Le casque à timbre rond, sans nasal, a une croix pour cimier et le bouclier diffère grandement du bouclier normand.

2. Chevalier allemand, d'après les peintures murales au dôme de Brunswick, exécutées sous Henri le Lion, mort en 1195. L'armement est intéressant pour la cotte en écailles qui rappelle la *squamata* romaine, pour le bouclier d'une largeur extraordinaire, pour le pommeau bilobé de l'épée, et pour les anneaux de métal qui entourent les rotules.

(Voir à la page 196 l'armement de Richard Cœur de Lion (1157-1173) qui, selon l'ordre chronologique, devrait suivre ici.)

La gravure de la page précédente représente des chevaliers bohèmes ou allemands, d'après le manuscrit de *Voleslav* de Bohême, du treizième siècle, conservé à la bibliothèque du prince de Labkowitz, à Raudnitz en Bohême.

Le second groupe est précédé d'un chef dont l'armement ne diffère en rien de celui des chevaliers parmi lesquels beaucoup portent déjà le *grand bacinet*, ordinairement attribué au quatorzième siècle, et qui, garni du camail, descend sur les épaules.

Les hauberts à longues manches collantes et avec haut et bas-de-chausses sont visiblement de l'espèce appelée annelée. (V. l'explication au chapitre des cottes et cuirasses.)

Les bacinets ne paraissent pas confectionnés d'une seule pièce, à en juger par le rivet garni de têtes de clous qui partage le timbre pointu en deux moitiés.

Les épées ne sont pas encore aiguës, mais les selles déjà à dossiers élevés et les chaussures à la poulaine ou très-pointues; les chefs portent la barbe.

La pièce la plus précieuse pour l'histoire des armes défensives que l'on voit dans cette miniature, dont la finesse et la minutieuse exactitude sont remarquables, c'est le chapeau de fer à larges bords et à timbre pointu semblable à celui du bacinet. Il n'existe plus aucune de ces sortes de casques, car les chapeaux en fer du quatorzième et du quinzième siècle, que l'on rencontre dans quelques collections, n'ont pas de timbres aussi pointus.

On remarque que les deux chefs seuls portent la barbe au menton, et que les boucliers armoriés ressemblent pour leur forme au bouclier de Louis VII (1137-1180), reproduit à la page 191.

1. Armurier allemand forgeant un heaume, copié sur une miniature de l'*Énéide allemande* de Henri de Waldeck, du treizième siècle, manuscrit conservé à la bibliothèque de Berlin. La cotte que l'on voit au pied de l'enclume, inexactement copiée, paraît dans le dessin original en treillissé et garnie de têtes de clous, sinon annelée. Le heaume (*Topfhelm* en all.; *Helm* en angl.) que l'armurier forge, est à visière fixe et à timbre plat.

2. Chevalier allemand, d'après le même manuscrit. Le heaume est déjà à cimier et le bouclier en forme de cœur, le petit écu tel qu'il était universellement porté du temps de saint Louis. L'armure paraît déjà à plaques probablement en cuir, à en juger par les brassards, les cuissards, les jambières et les solerets à la poulaine, tous visiblement lamés. L'armure du cheval complète en treillissé, garnie de têtes de clous ou annelée, comme la cotte placée au pied de l'enclume du premier dessin, indique aussi un grand progrès dans l'armement. Le *Waffenrock* ou sarrau d'armes que le chevalier porte par-dessus son armure est assez grotesque avec ses longues basques, semblables à celles des redingotes dites de propriétaire de nos jours, et que l'on retrouve sur la statue hollandaise de la même époque, représentée à la page 197.

Richard Ier, Cœur de Lion (1157-1173 ¹), d'après un sceau. La cotte de mailles est à manches collantes et à camail, mais sans haut-de-chausses. Les bas-de-chausses également en mailles, s'arrêtent au genou, et le bouclier fait déjà pressentir le petit écu du treizième siècle. Le casque à timbre bombé, d'origine germanique du Nord, a remplacé le casque conique franco-normand ; mais sa forme est déjà plus élevée, et rappelle celle des casques de la broderie de Seligenthal, également de la seconde moitié du douzième siècle.

1. Ce bois qui, selon l'ordre chronologique adopté pour ce livre, devait être placé à la suite de la page 191, a dû être inséré ici pour des raisons typographiques.

1. Chevaliers allemands, ou armures à plates, à brassards et jambières à plaques et à solerets à la poulaine, lamés. Ils portent
des heaumes de joute (*Stechhelm* en all.; *tilting-helm* en angl.)
et le *Waffenrock* ou sarrau d'armes par-dessus l'armure. —
Manuscrit allemand: *Tristan et Isolde*, écrit au treizième siècle
par *Godfried de Strasbourg*, et conservé à la bibliothèque de
Berlin.

2. Statuette équestre en bronze de la fin du treizième siècle, vue
de face et de dos, de la collection de M. Six à Amsterdam. Le
chevalier hollandais en cotte de mailles à manches collantes et
à cuissards et jambières à plaques, probablement de cuir,
est d'une tournure grotesque à cause des longues basques du
sarrau d'armes et de la singulière forme de son heaume à cimier démesuré.

17.

1. Chevalier français du treizième siècle, d'après un petit haut-relief de 10 cent. en cuivre émaillé champlevé, de la collection de M. le comte de Nieuwerkerke. Il est alternativement émaillé en bleu et doré en nuances citron et orange, et date du treizième siècle. L'épée est à garde relevée aux deux bouts vers la pointe, le heaume à cimier, l'armure couverte d'un sarrau (*Waffenrock*) à basques, et le cheval caparaçonné.

2. Chevalier français du treizième siècle, d'après un émail champlevé de l'époque (chandelier), de la collection de M. le comte de Nieuwerkerke.

3. Chevalier français du quatorzième siècle, d'après la gaufrure et la ciselure d'un coffre en cuir de l'époque, de la collection de M. le comte de Nieuwerkerke ; où les inscriptions françaises en lettres gothiques indiquent une époque postérieure à 1360. La figure porte au-dessus : CHARLES. LE. GRAND. L'armure est entièrement à plates, les pédieux sont à la poulaine, et les gantelets à doigts séparés.

Chevaliers italiens du quatorzième siècle, d'après une toile imprimée à la main et au moyen de bois gravés [1], en couleurs à
l'huile, rouge et noir, appartenant à M. Odet, à Sitten. Les
chefs sont armés de heaumes, tandis que les autres cavaliers
portent le bacinet *cannelé*, dont aucun exemplaire n'existe
plus. Tous ont déjà des jambières en plaques, mais leur armure
de corps est encore le haubert, déjà abandonné en Allemagne
à cette époque.

1. M. le docteur Keller, qui en a publié le *fac-simile*, confond ce genre d'impression à la main, déjà pratiqué par les anciens Mexicains, avec la véritable
xylographie, dont l'exécution nécessite l'emploi de la presse.

Chevaliers italiens du quatorzième siècle, d'après la même toile d'où est tiré le dessin de la page précédente. Le bacinet sans cannelure est remarquable par son *avance*, espèce de visière qui ressemble aux visières des casquettes modernes, et qui paraît être le précurseur de l'avance de la bourguignote du quinzième siècle. Les majuscules gothiques, en usage de 1200 à 1360, démontrent que la toile ne peut être postérieure au quatorzième siècle.

Chevalier danois du quatorzième siècle, dont l'armure est curieuse par la braconnière et le couvre-reins en *treillissé* qui recouvrent le haubert en mailles. Le heaume est encore de la forme des *Topfhelme* allemands du treizième siècle. — Aquamanile en bronze, de 30 cent., au musée de Copenhague.

Chevalier allemand du commencement du quatorzième siècle; il
est déjà armé de jambières à plaques et de solerets à la poulaine. Le heaume est à plumet, et le bouclier plus grand que
l'écu du treizième siècle. — Manuscrit 2,576 de la bibliothèque
impériale de Vienne : *Historia sacra et profana*, etc.

1. Chevalier neufchâtelois de l'année 1372, date de l'exécution du monument funéraire au Temple-en-Haut de Neufchâtel. Il représente Rodolphe II, mort en 1196.

2. Armure d'un chevalier neufchâtelois. Elle est dessinée d'après la reproduction exacte du monument primitif du comte de Berthold, mort en 1258, époque où cette sculpture avait été exécutée. On remarque déjà des grèves ou jambières en tôle, mais le bouclier est encore le petit écu.

Chevalier espagnol de la fin du quatorzième siècle ou du commencement du quinzième, armé encore du haubert à camail et sans casque, d'après un fragment de sculpture de l'*Alhambra*. Ce bas-relief est entouré d'une inscription en lettres gothiques minuscules, dont l'usage ne remonte pas au delà de 1360.

1. Chevalier bourguignon, d'après les miniatures d'un manuscrit
à la bibliothèque de l'Arsenal à Paris, une *Histoire romaine* qui
paraît avoir été écrite pour le duc de Bourgogne Jean sans Peur
(1404-1419). On voit que l'armure consistait encore dans le
haubert en mailles et dans une espèce de salade. Le petit écu,
aussi du treizième siècle, se voit encore sur le dos du chevalier.

2. Homme d'armes tirant le petit canon à main, d'après un manuscrit du quinzième siècle.

Hommes d'armes espagnols, d'après une peinture murale exécutée, à la fin du quatorzième siècle, à la cathédrale de Mondonédo, et qui représente le massacre des Innocents.

Les épées sont déjà à pas d'âne [1] ; les bacinets à mentonnières mobiles, et la cotte en treillissé recouverte par-dessus d'une espèce de brigantine.

L'écriture sur le grand pavois d'un des soldats est encore en gothique majuscule, tandis que celle qui se trouve au-dessous du tableau est en minuscule dont l'usage ne remonte pas au delà de 1360.

Les jambes de tous ces hommes de guerre, aussi bien que les avant-bras, sont sans défenses.

Les cottes sont très-courtes et n'atteignent pas seulement le genou ; les pieds aussi sont dépourvus de solerets ou chaussures d'armes.

Tout cet armement est en définitive encore fort défectueux pour l'époque (seconde moitié ou fin du quatorzième siècle), et inférieur à l'armement anglais, français et allemand de la même période.

---

1. On désigne sous le nom de *pas d'âne* la seconde garde inférieure qui avance au devant du *talon* de la lame, du côté de la pointe. Le pas d'âne ne se rencontre ordinairement qu'à partir de la seconde moitié du seizième siècle.

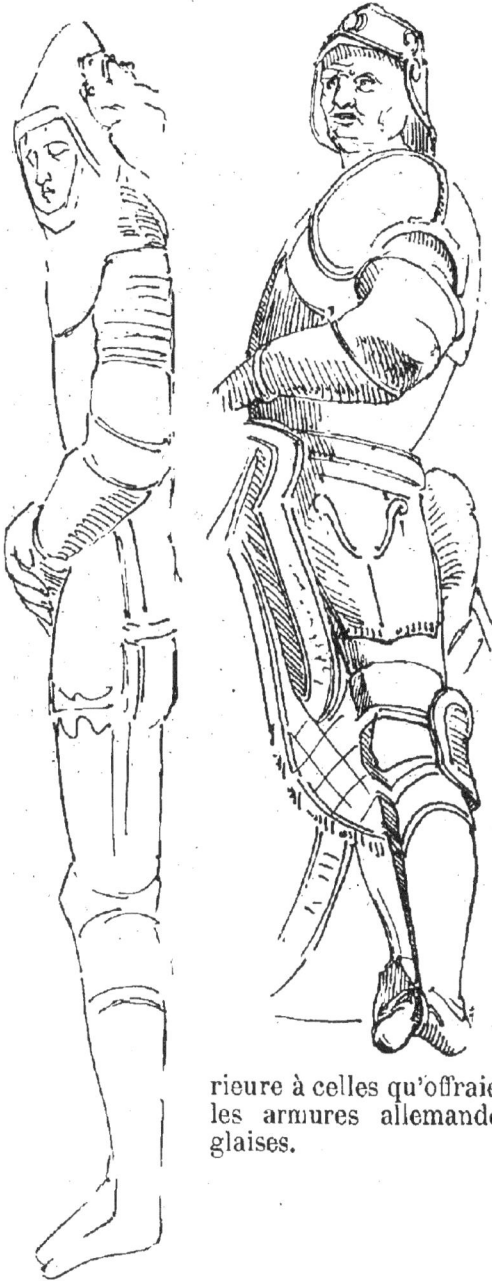

1. Armure italienne de la fin du quatorzième siècle, d'après le tombeau, à Venise, de Jacopo Cavalli, mort en 1384, dont la sculpture fut exécutée par Paolo di Jacomello de Massègne.

2. Armure italienne de la fin du quinzième siècle, d'après la statue équestre de Bartolomeo Coleoni, à Venise, exécutée en 1496, par Andrea Verrocchio et Alessandro Leopardi. Ce harnais est intéressant pour les énormes épaulières, qui ne sont reliées ni aux brassards ni au plastron ni à la dossière, pièces entre lesquelles on aperçoit la cotte de mailles sur une surface assez large. L'armure du corps, aussi bien que la salade sans visière, forme ici une défense fort défectueuse et très-inférieure à celles qu'offraient, à la même époque, les armures allemandes, françaises et anglaises.

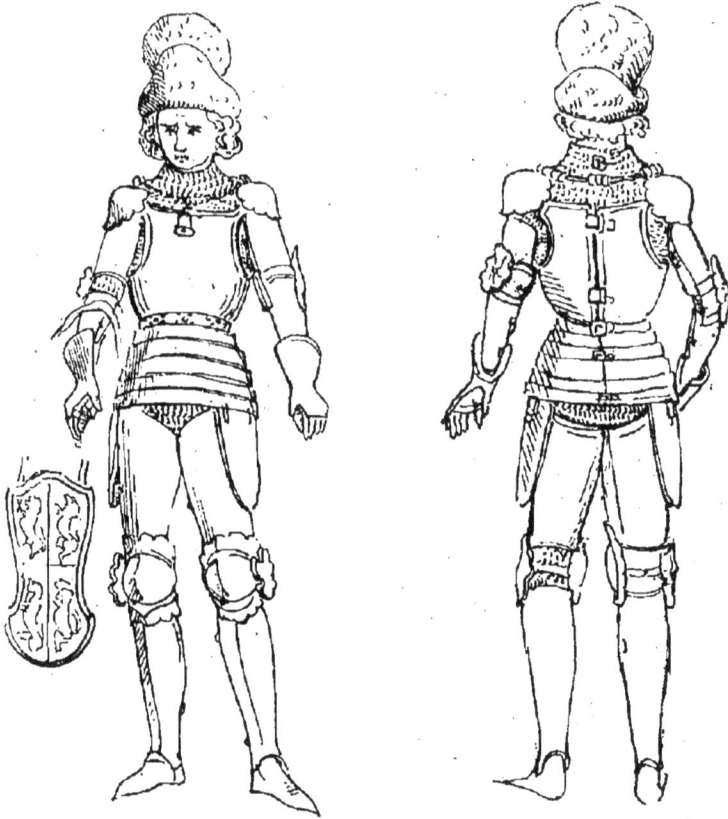

Armure hollandaise vue de dos et de face, du quinzième siècle, d'après la statuette en bronze de Guillaume VI (1404-1417), provenant des balustrades de la salle de l'ancien hôtel de ville d'Amsterdam, où siégeait le tribunal, et qui se trouve actuellement dans la collection des antiquités de cette ville. L'armure se signale par ses énormes genouillères et par la dossière composée de deux parties.

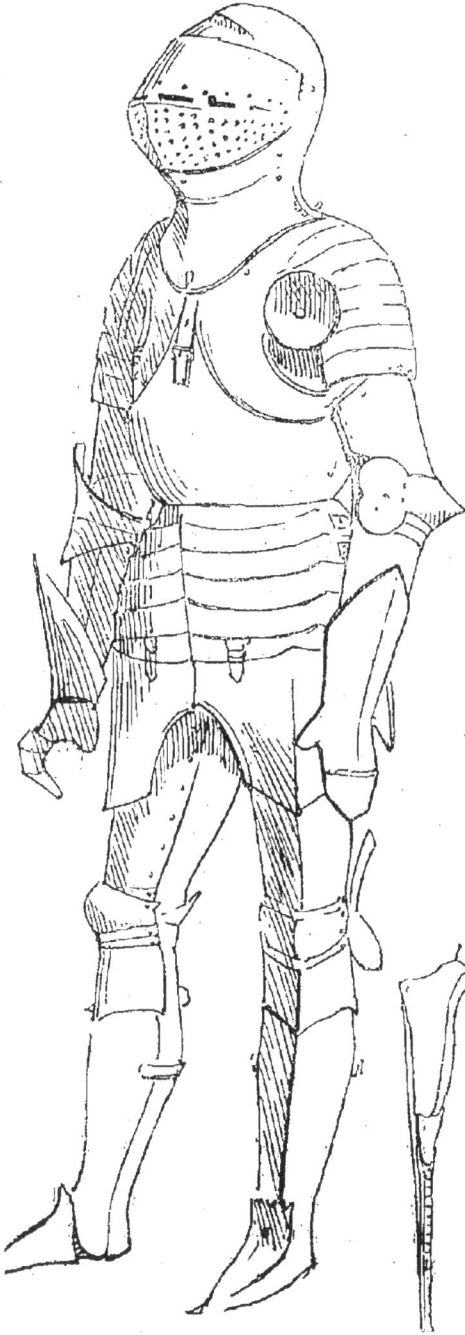

Armure gothique en acier poli, du quinzième siècle, à casque, espèce de heaume, à timbre rond et à vue à charnière ; elle est attribuée à Frédéric I, palatin du Rhin, mort en 1476. — Collection d'Ambras, à Vienne.

Une semblable armure, conservée dans la même collection, est attribuée à Frédéric le Catholique.

Ce harnais accuse à première vue le milieu du quinzième siècle, par la forme particulière de ses tassettes, de ses gantelets et des bouts de ses solerets, dont l'un se trouve dessiné à côté du pied gauche. Le casque a déjà les caractères de l'armet et paraît plus moderne que le reste de l'armure.

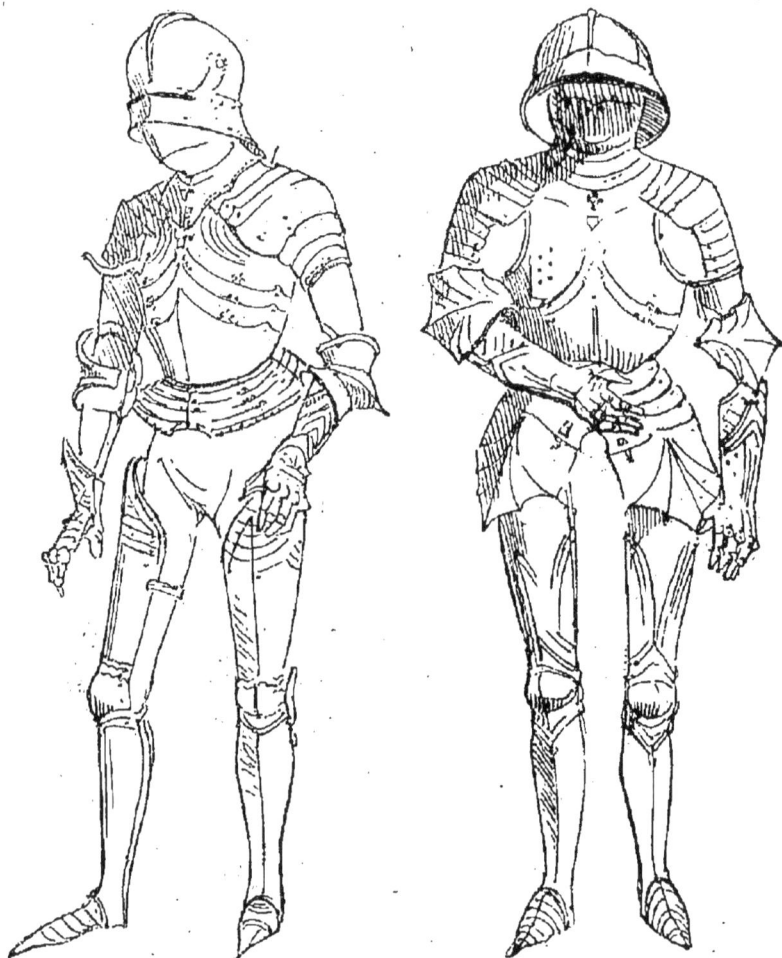

1. Armure gothique allemande du quinzième siècle, attribuée à
Sigismond de Tyrol. — Collection d'Ambras à Vienne. Cette
armure, avec sa salade, est incomplète, les tassettes manquent.

2. Belle armure gothique de la première moitié du quinzième
siècle, en acier poli. Elle fait partie du musée de Sigmaringen,
où elle est faussement attribuée au comte de Hohenzollern,
Eitel Frédéric Iᵉʳ, du treizième siècle. L'armure de la collection d'Ambras ci-dessus, attribuée à Sigismond de Tyrol, est
presque pareille à celle du musée de Sigmaringen.

Armures d'homme et de cheval attribuées à Maximilien Ier, né
en 1459, mort en 1519. Les cuissards, grèves, solerets et brassards n appartiennent pas à l'armure et sont du seizième siècle.
La salade est à visière mobile et la mentonnière lamée. —
Coll. d'Ambras. — M. le comte de Nieuwerkerque possède une
armure pour homme et cheval semblable, acquise à Nuremberg.

Armure gothique allemande de joute, de la seconde moitié du quinzième siècle, en acier poli. Elle est remarquable par ses grandes rondelles, son manteau d'armes de joute (*targe*) et son heaume. — Collection d'Ambras à Vienne. L'empereur Napoléon III possède trois armures semblables, et M. le comte de Nieuwerkerke une autre. N° G. 115, au musée d'artillerie, est une armure du même genre, des premières années du seizième siècle.

Armure allemande de joute, de la fin du quinzième siècle ou des premières années du seizième, en acier poli, et pesant 82 livres. Elle est remarquable par sa belle salade, — dont les cannelures indiquent aussi la fin du quinzième siècle, — par son grand manteau d'armes à mentonnières, pour joute, et par l'énorme faucre. — Coll. d'Ambras. Les tassettes lamées sont longues et forment pièce avec la braconnière. — N. G. 116, au musée d'artillerie à Paris, armure semblable.

Armure gothique alle-
mande de joute, de la
seconde moitié du quin-
zième siècle, en acier
poli. Elle se signale par
son heaume, son bras-
sard-gantelet de la main
gauche et son manteau-
jambière, ce dernier,
destiné à préserver le
pied gauche d'être écra-
sé contre la barrière.

Cette armure, qui est
attribuée à Maximilien I,
mort en 1493, a été faite
à Augsbourg, et se trou-
ve à l'arsenal impérial
de Vienne.

Les pièces des cubitiè-
res ont encore un carac-
tère gothique très-pro-
noncé, et les grandes
tassettes sont surmontées
d'une braconnière lamée
et en partie cannelée.

C'est une belle et gra-
cieuse armure de la bonne
époque.

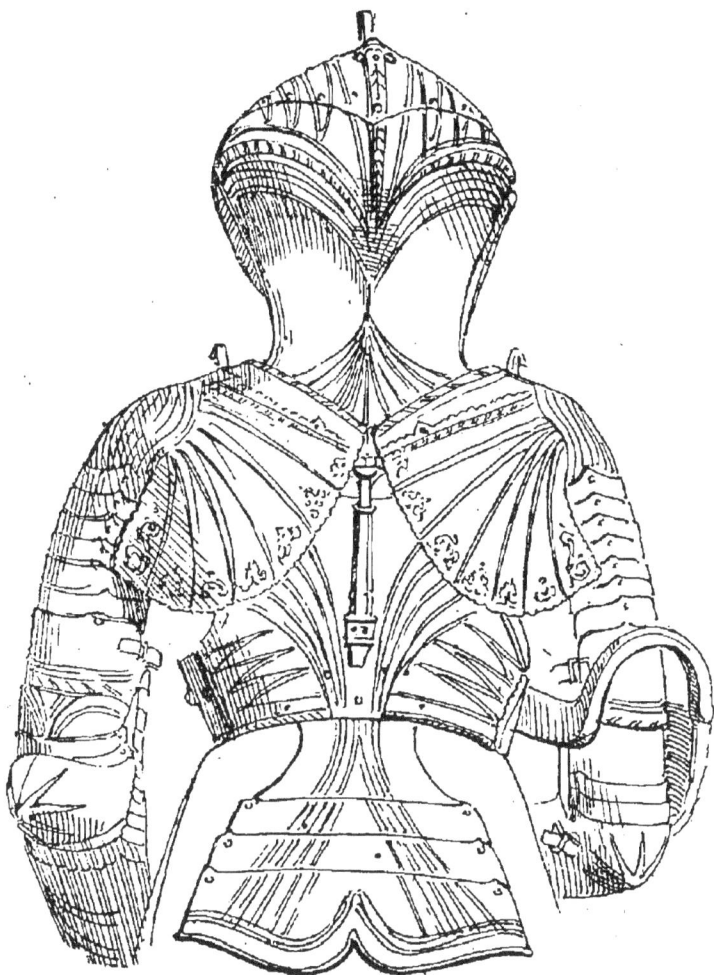

Belle armure gothique de la seconde moitié du quinzième siècle,
vue ici de dos et représentée de face à la page suivante; elle
montre le heaume de joute fixé à la dossière par une forte pièce
à charnière. Le faucre et les épaulières sont énormes; le
couvre reins est cependant défectueux, il rendait indispensable
la cotte de mailles.

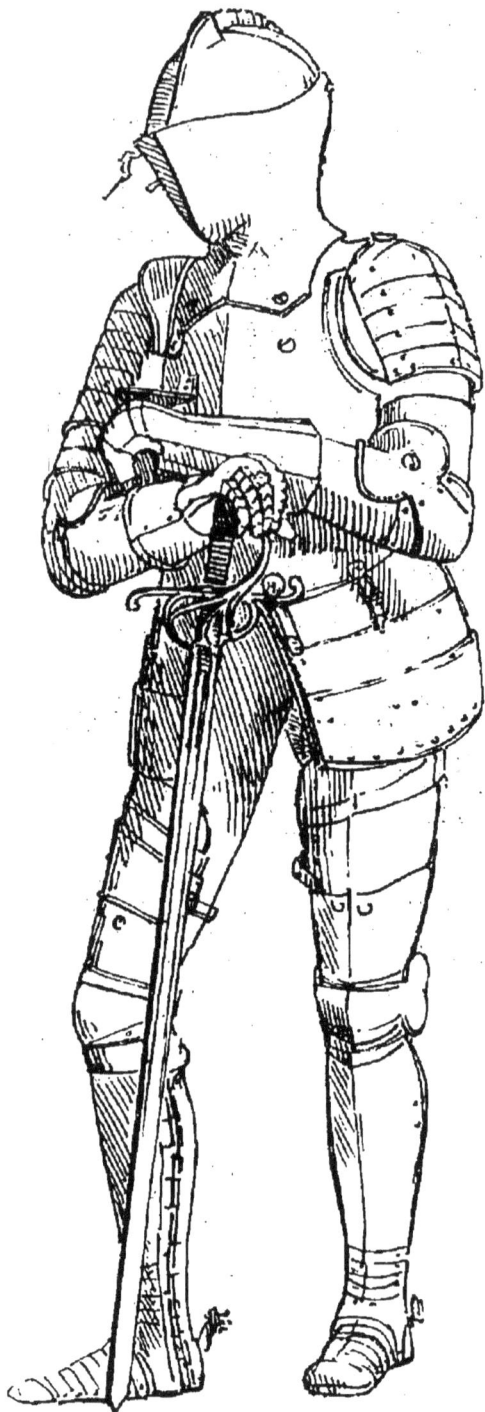

Armure allemande de la fin du quinzième ou du commencement du seizième siècle, avec haute - pièce, deux très - grandes tassettes et le plastron de la cuirasse à tabule.

L'épée est du milieu du seizième · siècle. Le casque à crête et à visière mobile se rabattant au moyen d'un pivot au-dessus du timbre n'est pas encore l'*armet* proprement dit, mais un casque de transition entre la salade et celui-ci.

Les solerets en forme de *bec-de-cane*, les cubitières et les *boucles* ou genouillères de petites dimensions, et la forme des épaulières et des gantelets indiquent parfaitement l'époque de la fabrication de cette armure. — Arsenal impérial de Vienne.

Armure cannelée alle-
mande, dite maximi-
lienne et milanaise, du
commencement du sei-
zième siècle (*Geripte
Rüstung* en allem., *fluted
armour* en angl.).
La cuirasse est bombée, le
plastron sans tabule et
les épaulières très-déve-
loppées et à passe-gardes
(*Raender* en all., *passe-
gard* en angl.).
Les cuissards et les arrière-bras sont cannelés
comme le reste de l'ar-
mure; mais les avant-
bras et les grèves sont
unis.
Les solerets en *sabots* ou
pieds d'ours, indiquent
que l'arme appartient
bien déjà au seizième
siècle.
Un tel harnais, de la collection de l'auteur, dont
la forme des solerets indique la seconde moitié du
quinzième siècle, montre
un casque où la visière
n'imite pas la face hu-
maine et permet de voir
et de respirer par douze
petites fentes. Le gante-
let est articulé seulement
pour les premières divi-
sions de la main. — Ar-
senal impérial de Vienne.

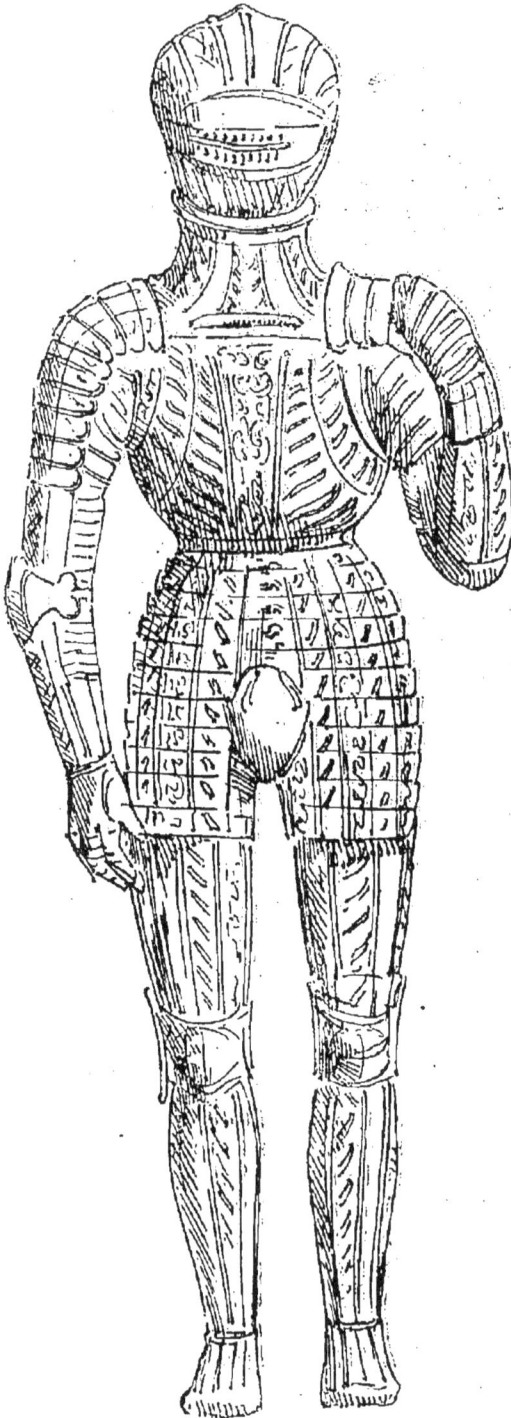

Armure allemande en acier poli et taillé à facettes, pour combattre à pied, de 1515, date de l'avénement au trône de François I, qui se trouve gravée sur le poignet droit.

Le catalogue (G. 117) désigne, comme provenant de la galerie de Sedan, cette armure qu'à Vienne on croit provenir de la collection d'Ambras. — Musée d'artillerie de Paris. — L'armure à bouillons (V. pag. suiv.) de la collection d'Ambras, ornée des mêmes taillés, provient visiblement du même atelier que celle-ci.

Ce harnais couvre le corps partout et ne laisse aucune prise; il est lamé dans toutes ses parties et ne nécessite pas l'emploi de la maille pour défendre des défauts qui n'existent pas. Il est aussi remarquable par la forme de sa brayette qui ressemble à celle dont le dessin figure sous le numéro 16, à la page 247.

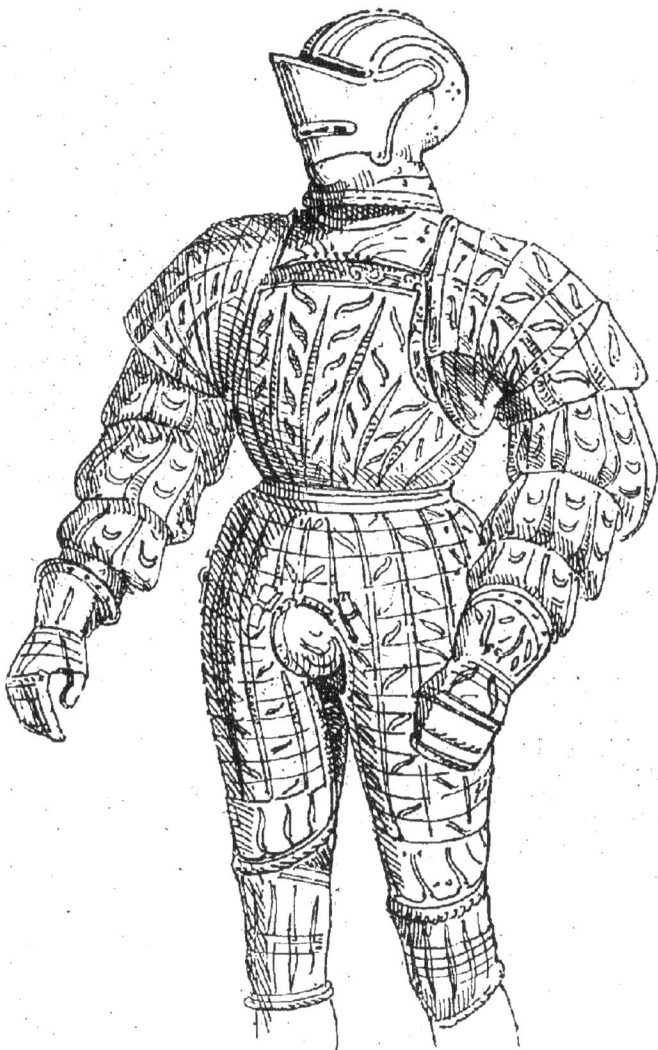

Armure allemande à bouillons, en acier taillé à facettes, de la première moitié du seizième siècle. Elle a appartenu à Guillaume de Rogendorf, un des capitaines qui défendaient Vienne en 1529 contre les Turcs, et qui est mort en 1541. Ce beau harnais, à l'exception des cuissards et des grèves, indique l'armure destinée aux combats de pied; tout y indique aussi une même origine que l'armure du musée d'artillerie de Paris, dont le dessin se trouve à la page précédente. — Coll. d'Ambras. Une armure semblable à la Tour de Londres.

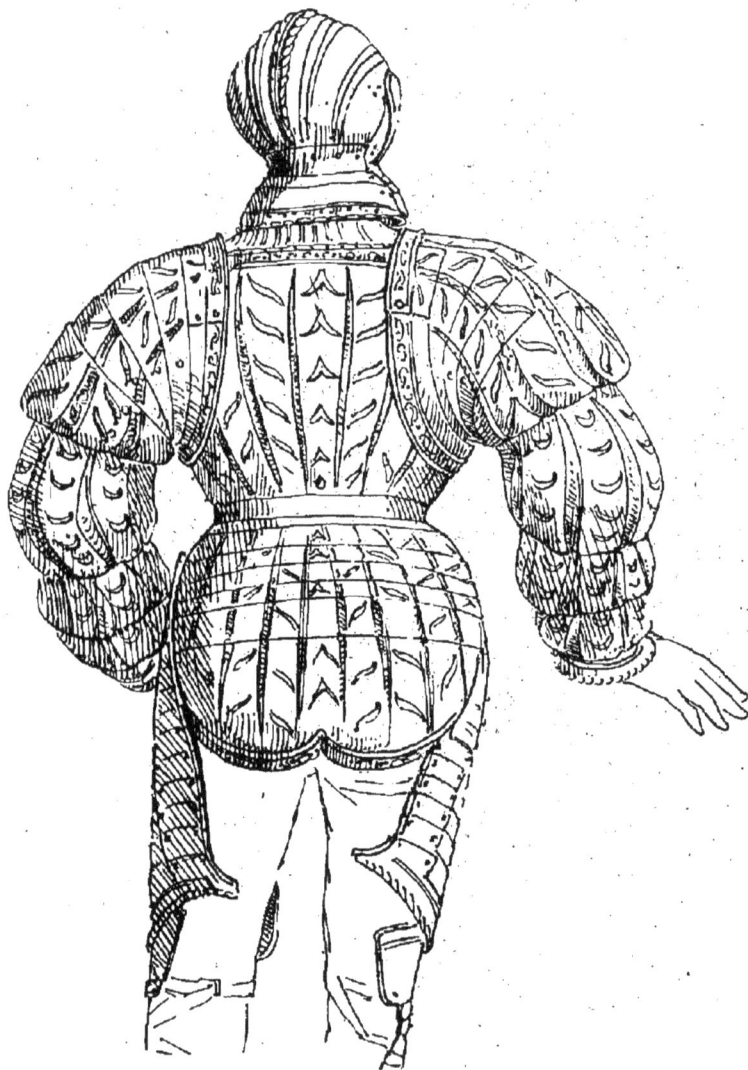

L'armure précédente, vue de dos. On remarquera que le couvre-reins lamé est tout à fait semblable à l'armure faussement désignée comme italienne du musée d'artillerie, dont le dessin a été donné à l'avant-dernière page. — Collection d'Ambras.

19.

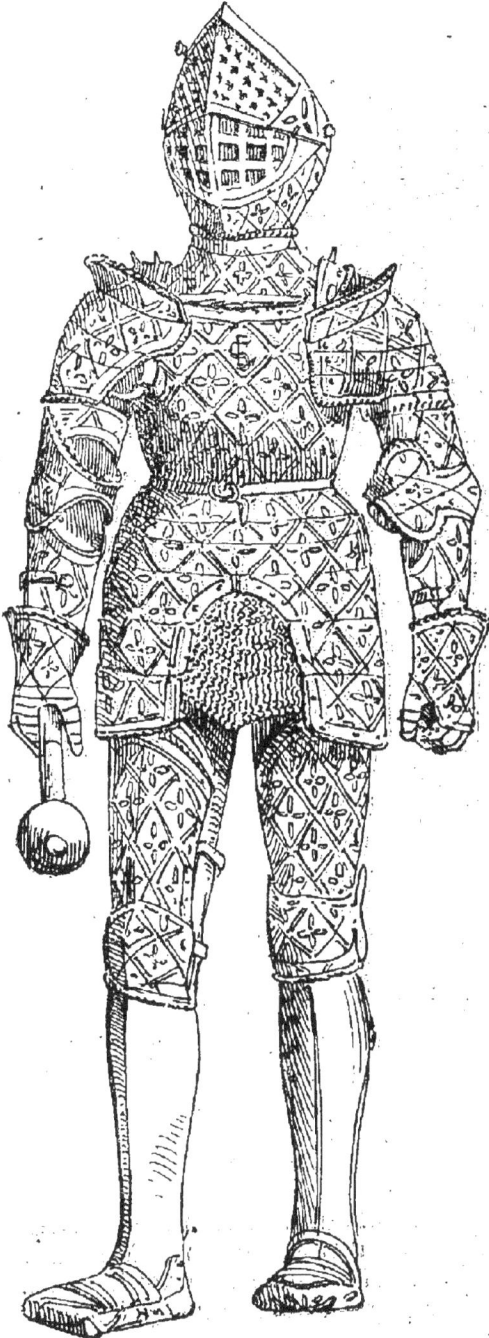

Armure allemande en acier poli et taillé à facettes, de 1526. La cuirasse est à demi bombée et porte au milieu les chiffres S. L. reunis en monogramme. Tassettes et braconnières forment pièces adhérentes, et les épaulières sont pourvues de passe-gardes. L'armet est très-remarquable par sa double visière mobile. Les solerets forme *sabot* ou *pied d'ours* et les grèves ne sont pas ornés et pourraient bien appartenir à une autre armure. Le défaut entre les tassettes et le bas de la braconnière est protégé par de la maille qui va jusqu'au couvre-reins. — Arsenal impérial de Vienne.

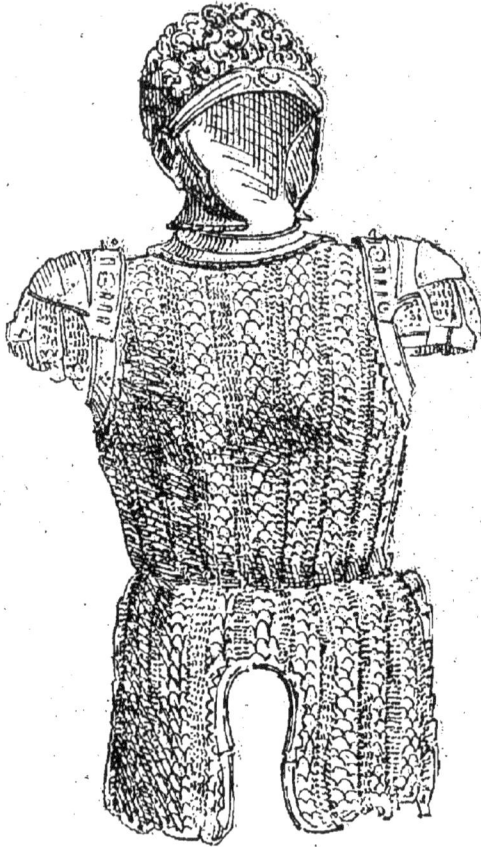

Armure italienne de la première moitié du seizième siècle, dans
le genre des brigantines, en usage en Italie au quinzième siècle. Elle est attribuée au duc d'Urbino (1538). — Col. d'Ambras à Vienne.

Armure richement damasquinée ou incrustée (*tanchirt* en allem.,
inlaid en angl.), de la seconde moitié du seizième siècle; elle
est de fabrication nurembergeoise et se trouve à l'arsenal impérial de Vienne. L'armet réuni à la cuirasse par le gorgeret
et le hausse-col, le tout fermant hermétiquement, ne laisse
aucune prise à l'épée.

Armure richement damasquinée de fabrication nurembergeoise, de la seconde moitié du seizième siècle. — Arsenal impérial de Vienne. Le bras gauche est pourvu d'un garde-bras ou grande garde de tournois ; l'armet fermant partout hermétiquement, et réuni à la cuirasse par le gorgerin et le hausse-col, ne laisse aucune prise à la pointe de l'épée.

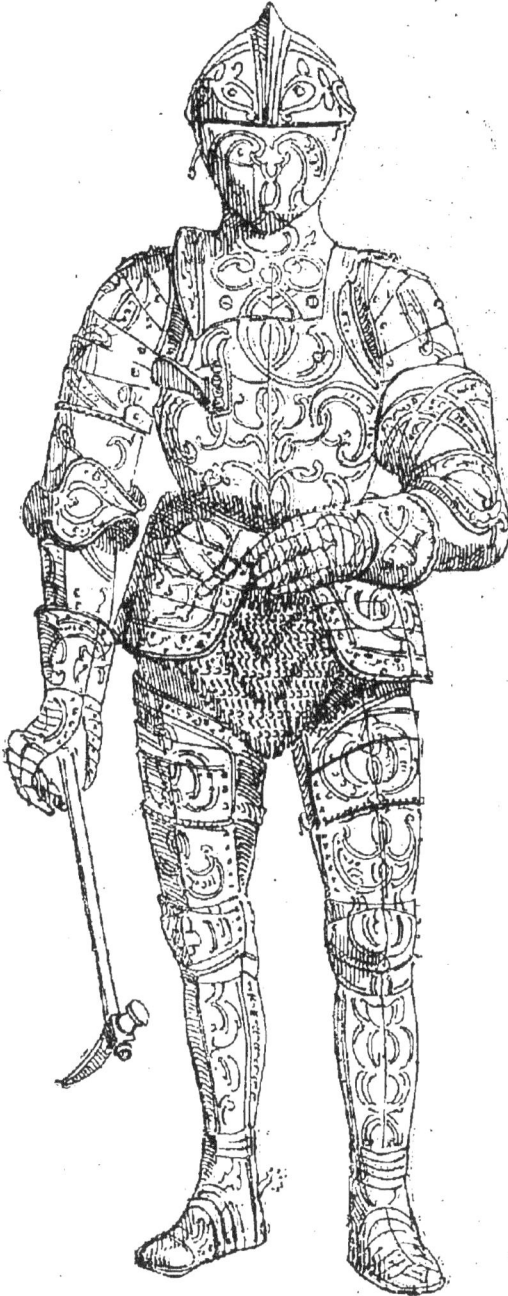

Armure allemande en acier, richement ornée de gravures et d'incrustations, de la seconde moitié du seizième siècle. La cuirasse est déjà allongée, et les tassettes, par contre, sont rapetissées. La haute-pièce (*Vorhelm* en allem., *volant piece* en angl.) est à passe-garde et vissée sur le plastron, qui montre le tabule. Les gantelets sont entièrement articulés et les cubitières peu développées.

Les tassettes et les cuissards très-courts et l'absence d'une braconnière lamée nécessitent l'addition d'une braconnière en mailles qui doit protéger le bas-ventre et une partie des cuisses. — Arsenal impérial de Vienne.

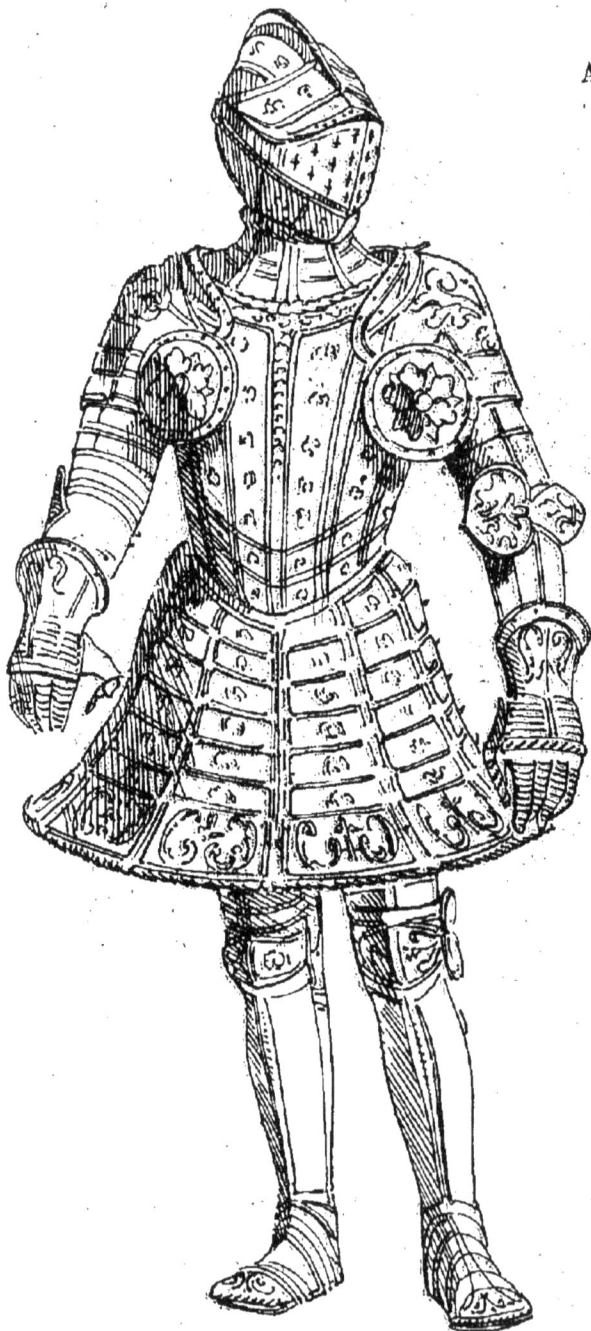

Armure allemande à tonne ou à jupon, de la seconde moitié du XVIᵉ siècle, attribuée à l'archiduc Ferdinand, comte de Tyrol. Les petits ornements gravés représentent des aigles. Cette armure devait servir pour combattre à pied, mais sa jupe pouvant être divisée, la rendait également propre à être portée à cheval. L'*armet*, la cuirasse à tabule et très-longue de taille, les grandes rondelles de plastron et la forme sabot ou pied d'ours des solerets indiquent parfaitement l'époque de la fabrication. — Collection d'Ambras.

Armure de fabrication augsbourgeoise, de là seconde moitié du seizième siècle. Elle est entièrement recouverte de riches ornements repoussés qui rappellent les dessins d'ateliers des peintres Schwarz, Van Achen, Brockberger et Milich au cabinet des estampes de Munich. — Musée d'artillerie impérial de Vienne.

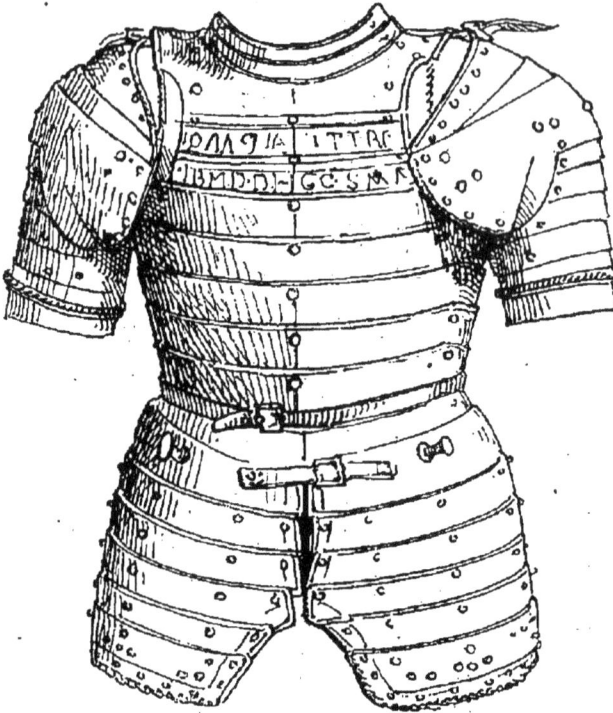

Armure allemande entièrement lamée, en acier poli, de la seconde moitié du seizième siècle. Elle porte gravé sur le plastron
le nom du chevalier à qui elle a appartenu : ADAM GALL, qui
est mort en 1574. — Arsenal impérial de Vienne.
Ce genre d'armure était plus en usage en Espagne et en Italie
qu'en Allemagne. La profusion des boutons et l'absence du faucre
la font ressembler aux harnais du dix-septième siècle où les
tassettes étaient réunies aux cuissards et formaient ce qu'on
appelait l'*écrevisse*.

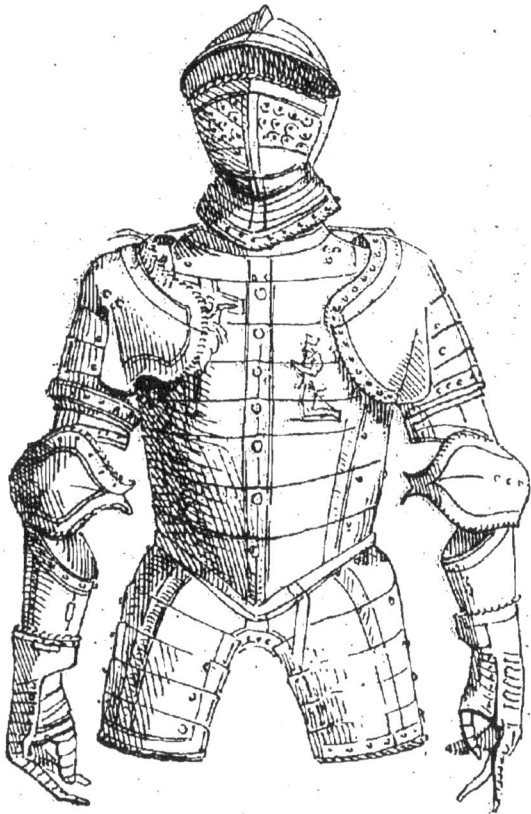

Armure espagnole lamée, attribuée au duc d'Albe, le bourreau des Pays-Bas (1508-1582). L'armet, espèce de bourguignote, laisse à désirer, puisqu'il donnait trop de prise entre la mentonnière et l'avance. On voit sur le plastron une gravure qui représente un chevalier en prières devant le crucifix. — Col. d'Ambras, à Vienne.

Même observation que pour l'armure de la page précédente.

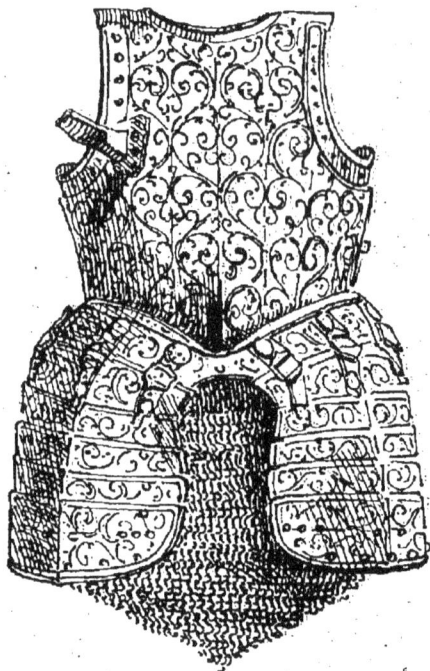

Armure italienne en acier, à incrustations d'argent, de la fin du seizième siècle, et que l'on croit avoir appartenu au duc Alexandre de Farnèse. Cette armure est d'un travail magnifique et d'une grande finesse. Le plastron est à tabule et à faucre. Le défaut entre les tassettes et l'absence de la braconnière lamée nécessitent l'emploi de la maille. — Arsenal impérial de Vienne.

Armure allemande de la fin du seizième siècle, richement repoussée (*Getrieben* en all., *embossed* en angl.), et dont le travail indique l'école de Munich ou d'Augsbourg. Elle est regardée comme ayant appartenu à l'empereur Rodolphe II (1572-1612). L'épée indique par la forme de sa garde et son pas d'âne le commencement du dix-septième siècle.

Le grand développement des épaulières et des cubitières, la forme de l'armet, les solerets *bec-de-cane* et l'absence d'une braconnière lamée, aussi bien que la forme de la cuirasse sans faucre, indiquent l'époque de la fabrication de cette belle armure. — Collection d'Ambras, à Vienne.

Armement persan complet de cavalier. L'homme est en cotte de mailles et le cheval couvert d'une armure en lames de fer réunies par des chaînettes. — D'après un manuscrit de la bibliothèque de Munich, orné de 215 magnifiques miniatures, exécutées vers 1580 à 1600. C'est la copie du *Schah-hameh* au Livre royal, poëme composé par Fisdeïsi sous le règne de Mahmoud le Gaznévide (999).

20.

Cavalier hollandais de la guerre de l'Indépendance du temps du stathoudérat de Henri-Frédéric (1625-1647), d'après un tableau de l'époque peint sur faïence par Ter Himpelen, de Delft, et qui représente le célèbre combat devant Bois-le-Duc sur la bruyère de Lekkerbeetze, entre les Hollandais commandés par le capitaine normand Bréauté et les Espagnols commandés par le lieutenant Abrahami. L'armure est encore entière et à couvre-reins; chose remarquable, on y voit déjà des fusils et des pistolets à batterie à silex. — Col. de l'auteur. Voir pour de plus amples détails, p. 634 de la troisième édition de l'*Encyclopédie céramique monogrammique* de l'auteur.

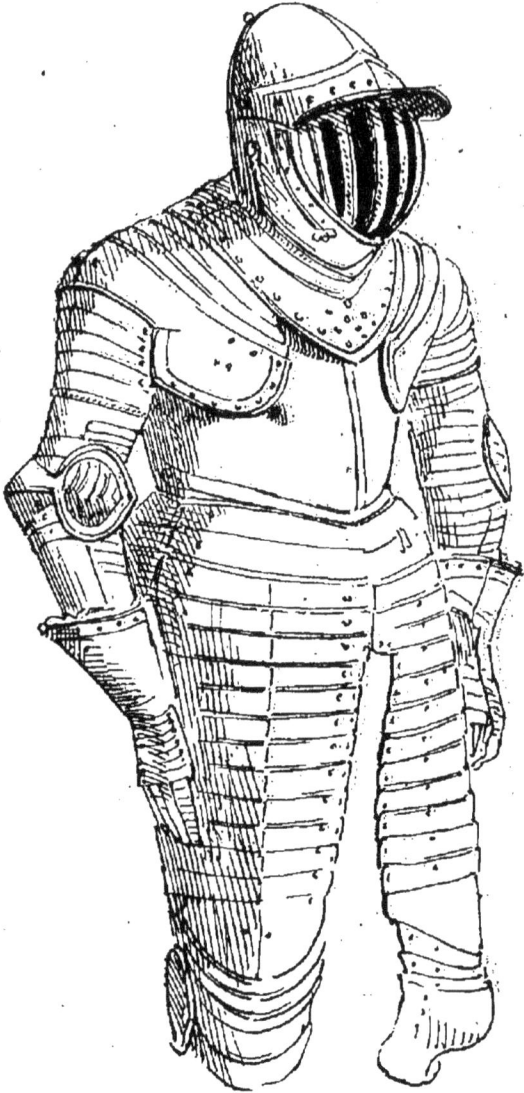

Armure allemande du dix-septième siècle, attribuée à l'archiduc Léopold, empereur en 1658; mort en 1705. — Col. d'Ambras à Vienne. Une semblable armure, au Louvre, est attribuée à Louis XIII (1610-1643), et plusieurs autres de ces armures, au musée d'artillerie de Paris, proviennent du règne de
Louis XIV (1643-1715). L'époque de la fabrication de ces harnais disgracieux se reconnaît aux énormes épaulières, au rape-
tissement du plastron et aux longues *écrevisses* qui ont remplacé la braconnière et les tassettes.

Armure hongroise de
la fin du seizième
ou du commence-
ment du dix-septième
siècle, en mailles et à
plaques. La rondache
est ornée d'une pein-
ture qui représente
une arbalète. Tout
l'armement a quelque
chose d'oriental, par-
ticulièrement les cuis-
sards et les genouil-
lères, composés de
plaquettes réunies par
des anneaux, telles
qu'elles sont en usage
en Perse. Le casque
est composé d'un tim-
bre très-bas et garni
d'un camail dont une
partie protége le front
et les joues.

L'ensemble est gra-
cieux et très-pittores-
que. — Arsenal im-
périal de Vienne.

Harnais hongrois en acier richement damasquiné, de fabrication allemande du dix-septième siècle. Il est particulièrement caractéristique par la forme du casque et du bouclier. La masse d'armes que l'on a mise dans la main droite de l'homme est une arme du seizième siècle, et n'était plus en usage à l'époque à laquelle appartient l'armure. Il paraît que cette demi-armure était portée par-dessus le buffletin qui rappelle ceux des Suédois de la guerre de Trente ans. Le sabre est de forme orientale. — Arsenal impérial de Vienne.

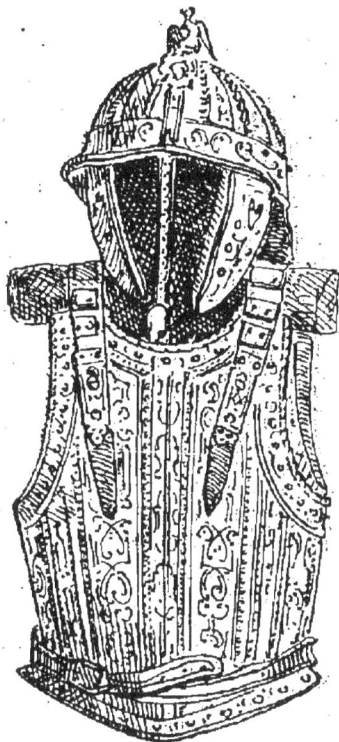

Cuirasse à plastron à tabule, et casque à nasal, à oreillères et couvre-nuque, sorte de calotte bourguignote. Armes de la fin du dix-septième ou du commencement du dix-huitième siècle, richement damasquinées et gravées. — Arsenal impérial de Vienne.

L'ARMURE DANS SES DÉTAILS

HORS LE CASQUE.

On a vu, dans le chapitre historique et dans l'introduction de celui-ci, de quelle manière l'armement s'est continuellement transformé à partir du commencement du moyen âge. L'armure à plates tout à fait perfectionnée, telle qu'elle sera détaillée ici, appartient à la fin du quinzième et au commencement du seizième siècle. Elle comprend, en dehors du casque, qui, à ces périodes, était toujours regardé comme une pièce part :

Le *colletin hausse-col* (*Halsberge* en allemand, *neck-collar* en anglais), qui supportait tout le harnais, et s'appelait en anglais au seizième siècle, dès qu'il ne formait qu'une seule pièce avec de longues épaulières, *allecret*.

Le colletin hausse-col, qu'il ne faut pas confondre avec le *gorgerin* (*Kehlstück* en allemand, *gorget* en anglais), était placé au-dessous de celui-ci, formé également de plusieurs lames.

La *cuirasse* (*Kürass* en allemand, *cuirass* en anglais). Elle était composée du *plastron* (*Brustplatte* en allemand, *breast-plate* en anglais) qui couvrait la poitrine, souvent à arétière médiate appelée *tabule* (*Graete* en allemand, *salient-ridge* en anglais), et de la *dossière* (*Rückenplatte* en allemand, *Back-plate* en anglais).

L'*arrêt* de la lance ou le *faucre* (*Rüsthacken* en allemand, *lance-rest* en anglais) qui était placé au côté gauche du plastron, et qui servait à fixer la lance.

Les *petites plaques ou lames d'aisselles* (*Kleine Schienen* en allemand, *smal-plates* en anglais).

Les *épaulières* (*Achselstücke* en allemand, *shoulder-plates* en anglais), avec ou sans *passe-gardes* (*Raender* en allemand, *pasgards* en anglais).

Les *rondelles de plastron* (*Achselhoehlscheiben* en allemand, *arms-rondels* en anglais) qui protégeaient les aisselles, et dont l'usage ne remonte pas au delà du milieu du quinzième siècle et disparaît à la fin du seizième.

La *braconnière* (*Vorderschürz* en allemand, *great brayette* en anglais), la partie de l'armure qui couvre l'abdomen. Ordinairement composée de lames d'acier, elle était terminée par les tassettes.

La *brayette*, qui imite le phallus, et que la pudeur anglaise a proscrite des armures conservées à la Tour de Londres.

Les *tassettes* (*Krebse* en allemand, *tassettes* et aussi *large tiles* en anglais) destinées à protéger le haut des cuisses, attachées avec des courroies à la braconnière. Quelques auteurs allemands nomment cependant *Krebs*, écrevisse, toute l'armure composée de lames, et *halber Krebs*, demi-écrevisse, la partie inférieure de l'armure lamée et de longs cuissards de la fin du seizième et du commencement du dix-septième siècle.

Fouchet aussi, qui écrivait vers la fin du seizième siècle, dit que les armures *entières à lames articulées* étaient nommées *écrevisses* en France ; ces mêmes armures étaient nommées en Angleterre : *a suit of splints*.

Le *garde-reins* (*Hinterschürz* en allemand, *articulated culot* en anglais), composé de lames superposées comme la braconnière.

Les *brassards* complets (*Armzeug*, aussi *Armschienen* en allemand, *brassards* en anglais) formés d'avant et d'arrière-brassards (*vor* et *hinter Armzeug* en allemand) réunis entre eux par les *cubitières* (*Meuseln* ou *Ellenbogen Kacheln* en allemand, *elbow-pieces* en anglais).

Les *cuissards* (*Dielinge, Dichlinge* ou *Schenkelschienen* en allemand, *cuissards* en anglais) qui, avant 1500, ne couvraient que le devant de la cuisse.

Les *genouillères* ou *boucles* (*Kniestücke* en allemand, *knee-cops* en anglais).

Les *grèves* ou *jambières doubles* à charnières (*Beinschienen* en allemand, *greaves* en anglais), qui, avant 1500, ne couvraient ordinairement que le devant de la jambe.

Les *solerets* ou *pédieux* (*Rüst* ou *Eisenschuhe* en allemand, *sollerets* et *goad* en anglais) *à crochet* au onzième siècle, *à la poulaine* à partir du commencement du douzième jusqu'au milieu du quatorzième, *ogivale lancette* ou *demi-poulaine* de 1350 à 1470 et de nouveau à la poulaine dans le quinzième siècle, mais aussi à *arcs tiers-points* de 1440 à 1470, à *demi-sabots* ou *demi-pieds d'ours* vers 1485, à *sabots* ou *pieds d'ours* de 1490 à 1560, et à *bec-de-cane* vers 1585.

Les *gantelets* (*Kampfhandschuhe* en allemand, *gauntlets* en anglais) à doigts séparés au quatorzième siècle (*Finger-handschuhe* ou *Gefingerte Tatze* en allemand, *articulated gauntlets* en anglais), *mouffle* ou *miton* (*Faust Handschuhe* en allemand, *inarticulated gauntlets* en anglais) au quinzième siècle, et de nouveau à doigts séparés au seizième siècle.

Les *gantelets* du dix-septième siècle, en daim et garnis d'*écailles*, s'appelaient en allemand : *Schuppenhandschuhe*, et en anglais : *Glowes armed whit scales*.

L'*épaulière-garde-bras* ou *grande garde* (*Kleiner Brust-schild* en allemand, *shoulder-gard* en anglais) en usage à partir de la fin du quinzième siècle.

L'*épaulière garde-bras à passe-gardes* (*Schulter schild mit Rand* en allemand, *shoulder-gard with passe gard* en anglais).

Le *manteau d'armes* (*Grosser Brustschild*, et aussi

Scharfrenntartsche en allemand, *tilting-breast-shild* en anglais) qui était *simple*, *à mentonnière avec ou sans vue*, *à
haute pièce*, et *à brassand*, tous en usage seulement dans
les joutes.

Le *grand cuissard de joute* (*Tournier Lenden platte* en
allemand, *great tilting-cuissard* en anglais).

La *rondelle de lance* (*Schweber Scheibe* en allemand,
Round lance-plate en anglais.

Les pièces de renfort pour le casque, que l'on trouve
toutes reproduites dans ce chapitre, étaient :

La *haute pièce* (*Vorhelm* en allemand, *volant-piece* en
anglais).

La *demi-mentonnière mobile* (*Kinnhelm* en allemand,
half mentonniere en anglais.

Et la *mentonnière mobile* (*Kinnhelm* en allemand, *great
mentonnière* en anglais).

L'armure du commencement du seizième siècle se signale
souvent par ses belles cannelures : c'est l'armure Maximilienne, aussi appelée Milanaise; celle de la seconde moitié
de ce même siècle brille quelquefois par des gravures artistiques exécutées à la pointe et à l'eau forte. Lorsque, vers
la fin du seizième siècle, l'armure avait atteint son dernier
degré de perfection, mais ne pouvait plus offrir, malgré
cela, des défenses suffisantes contre l'arme à feu, elle dé-
clina, et finit par disparaître entièrement dans la seconde
moitié du dix-septième siècle. Après que les tassettes
eurent été remplacées par les cuissards disgracieux [1], l'armure fut réduite à sa dernière transformation, où il n'y
avait plus de jambières ni de cuissards, et bientôt plus de
brassards; la cuirasse seule fut conservée à la fin, et encore
seulement pour une arme spéciale, pour les cuirassiers. Le
buffletin (*Koller* en allemand, *Buff-coat* ou *jerkir* en anglais

---

1. L'arsenal de Zurich possède des armures cannelées à plastrons bombés où
les tassettes sont déjà remplacées par ces longs cuissards ou *écrevisses* (*Krebse*).

sur lequel on portait un léger hausse-col, avait depuis remplacé l'armure dont les grèves et les solderets se trouvaient remplacés par des housseaux.

Avant d'arriver à la demi-armure, des plastrons disgracieux et reflétant les modes des pourpoints avaient été les avant-coureurs de la décadence complète de l'armure ; les plastrons imitaient la bosse polichinelle du règne de Henri III, et se signalèrent bientôt après par les formes plates du règne de Louis XIII ; ils furent enfin suivis des longues écrevisses au commencement du règne de Louis XIV.

Quant aux armures ornées de gravures à l'eau forte, genre de gravure probablement inventé par Wohlgemuth (1434-1519), sinon par son élève Durer (1471-1528), elles sont très-rares sur des armures remontant au quinzième siècle ; ce que l'on a voulu avancer sur des gravures à l'eauforte exécutées par les Arabes à partir du onzième siècle, n'a pu être confirmé par aucune pièce en nature. Quant à la gravure à la pointe, on l'a utilisée pour l'ornementation des épées à partir du second tiers du moyen âge chrétien ; mais tout ce qui remonte au delà du quinzième siècle est fort peu artistique.

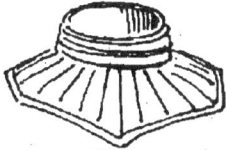

1. Colletin hausse-col (*Halsberge* en allem., *neck-collar* en angl.). Cette pièce supportait tous le harnais.

1A.   id.   id.

2. Plastron ou partie antérieure de la cuirasse (*Brustplatte* en allem., *breast-plate* en angl.). Le nom tabule désigne l'arétière mediale (*Graete* en allem., *salient-ridge* ou *tapul* en angl.), et faucre l'arrêt de la lance (*Rusthacken* en allem., *lance-rest* en angl.).

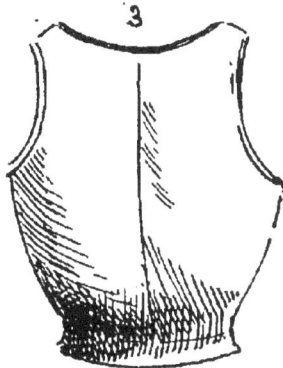

3. Dossière ou partie postérieure de la cuirasse (*Rücken plate* en allem., *bak-plate* en angl.). — Col. d'Ambras.

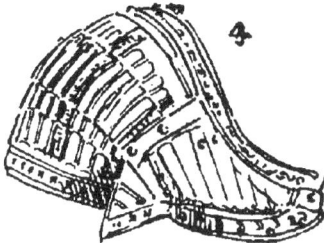

4. Epaulière (*Ackselstück* en allem., *shoulder-plate* en angl.) d'une armure cannelée de la seconde moitié du quinzième siècle. — Col. de l'auteur.

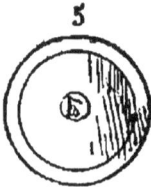

5. Rondelle de plastron (*Achsel-hœhlscheibe* en allem., *arm-rondel* en angl.) d'une armure cannelée de la fin du quinzième siècle.

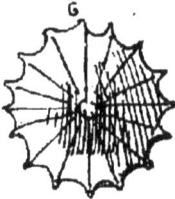

6. Rondelle de plastron d'une armure gothique du quinzième siècle.

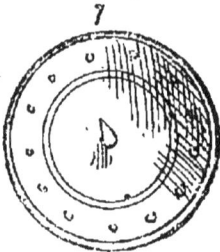

7. Rondelle de plastron plus grande que la précédente, d'une armure du milieu du seizième siècle.

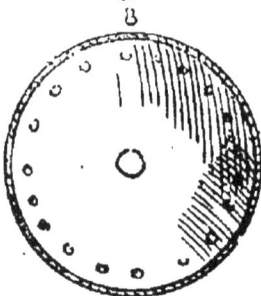

8. Rondelle de plastron de 26 cent. de diamètre, garnie de têtes de clous de cuivre d'une armure de la fin du seizième siècle, de la col. d'Ambras. Quelques armures de joute de la fin du quinzième et du commencement du seizième siècle ont cependant aussi des rondelles de cette dimension.

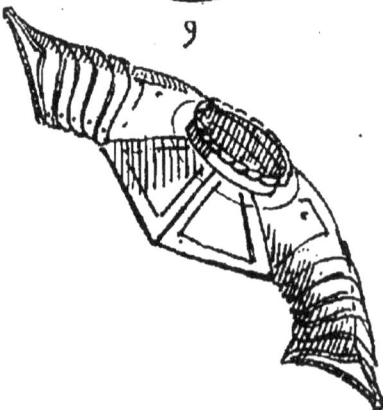

9. Hausse-col à épaulières adhérentes de la fin du seizième siècle. En Angleterre, on appelait cette pièce d'armure ainsi composée, *allcret*. De semblables épaulières hausse-col, sous le n° G. 256, au musée d'artillerie de Paris.

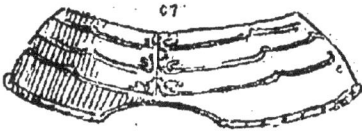

10. Braconnière (*Vorderschurz* en allem., *great-brayette* en angl.) d'une armure gothique du quinzième siècle, de l'arsenal impérial de Vienne. Cette braconnière était toujours complétée par deux grandes tassettes-tuiles qui couvraient les cuissards.

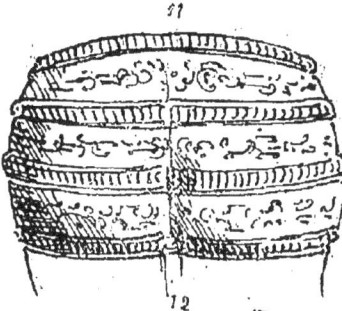

11. Braconnière d'une armure gravée et repoussée de la fin du quinzième siècle ou du commencement du seizième, pour combattre à pied. Sa forme rend les tassettes superflues.

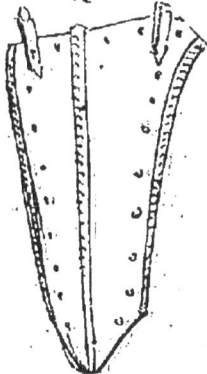

12. Tassette [1] (*Krebs* en allem., *tassette* en angl.), forme tuile, d'une armure du quinzième siècle. — Musée d'artillerie de Paris.

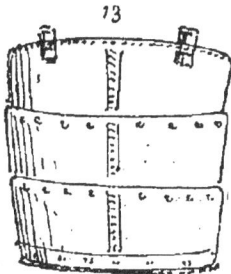

13. Petite tassette lamée du seizième siècle et de la fin du quinzième.

1. Durant le quinzième siècle, les tassettes étaient ordinairement d'une seule pièce, telle que n° 12 ; elles prirent ensuite la forme arrondie, et elles étaient ordinairement plus petites et articulées au seizième siècle.

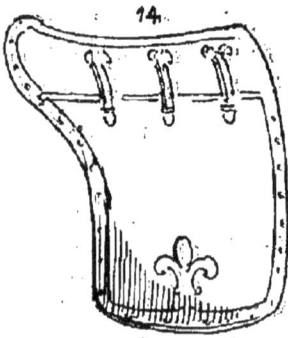

14. Tassette-braconnière d'une dimension inusitée et couvrant presque les deux cuissards comme un tablier de franc-maçon; elle fait partie d'une armure attribuée à François I (mort en 1547).

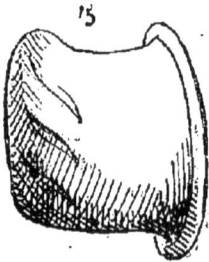

15. Brayette (*Gliedschirm* en allem., *smal-brayette à l'antique* en angl.) d'une armure du seizième siècle. Voy. p. 220.

16. Brayette d'une armure du seizième siècle. — N° G. 119, au musée d'artillerie de Paris. Voy. p. 219.

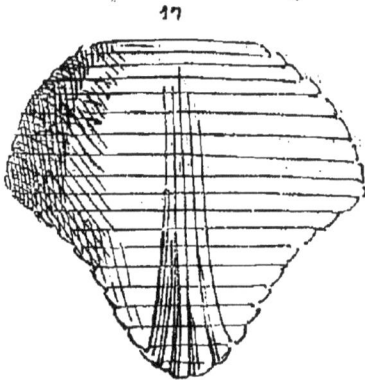

17. Garde-reins (*Hinterschurz* en allem., *articulated-culot* en angl.) d'une armure de la fin du quinzième siècle.

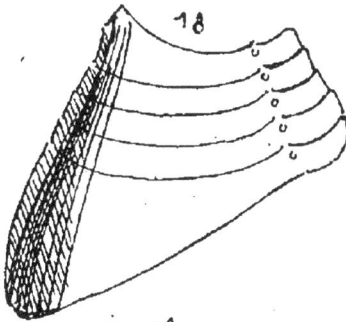

18. Garde-reins d'une armure gothique, les plus gracieuses des armures du quinzième siècle.

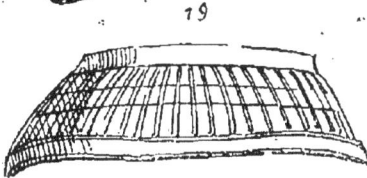

19. Garde-reins d'une armure cannelée, dite maximilienne, de la fin du quinzième ou du commencement du seizième siècle.

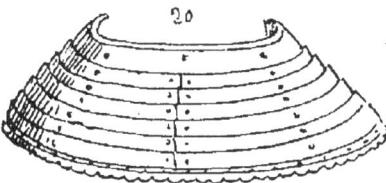

20. Deux garde-reins d'armure du dix-septième siècle. Le petit provient d'une armure du règne de Louis XIV, conservée au musée d'artillerie de Paris.

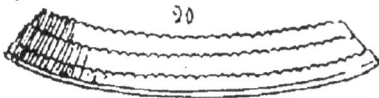

21. Brassard complet (*Ganzes Armzeug* en allem., *complete brassard* en angl.). Il est composé d'avant et d'arrière-bras (*Vor* et *Hinterarm* en allem.), et les deux parties sont réunies par la cubitière (*Meusel* ou *Ellenbogenkachel* en allem., *elbowpiece* en angl.). La forme de la cubitière a beaucoup varié. Elle est plus arrondie à la fin du quinzième siècle; quelquefois à ailerons et à lames; au seizième siècle elle est plus petite.

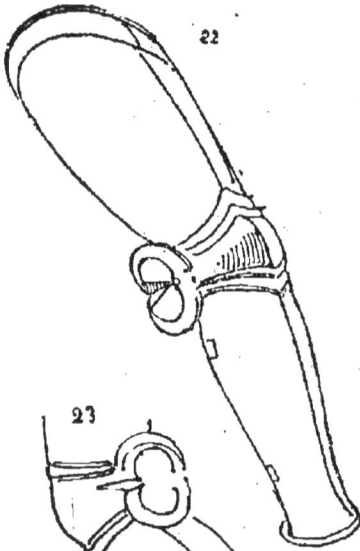

22. Cuissard (*Dieling* ou *Schen-kelschiene* en allem., *cuissard* en angl.), avec genouillère dite aussi *boucle*(*Kniestück* en allem., *knee-cop* en angl.) et grève ou jambière (*Beinschiene* en allem., *greve* en angl.). Il est double ou à charnières, ce qui indique une période postérieure à l'année 1500.

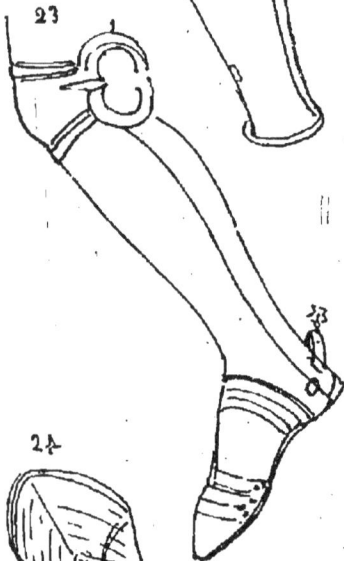

23. Grève avec soleret ou pé-dieu (*Eisenschuhe* en allem., *solleret* en angl.). Le soleret a la forme dite *bec-de-cane*, de la fin du seizième siècle.

24. Gantelet (*Kampfhandschuh* ou *gefingerte Handtatze* en all., *articulated gauntelet* en angl.). Il est à doigts séparés et appar-tient à une armure gothique du milieu du quinzième siècle.

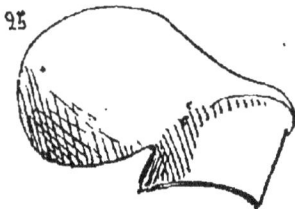

25. Épaulière, garde-bras ou grande garde (*Kleiner Schulter-schild* en allem., *shoulder-gard* en angl.), en usage dans les tournois vers la fin du quin-zième siècle.

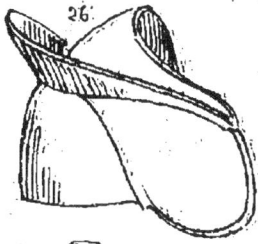

26. Épaulière , garde-bras à passe-garde (*Schulterschild mit Rand* en allem., *shoulder-gard with passe-gard* en angl.).

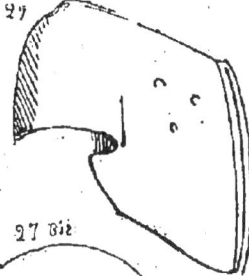

27. Grande épaulière , garde-bras ou grande garde (*Tournier-Schulterschild* en allem., *great-tilting shoulder-gard* en angl.).

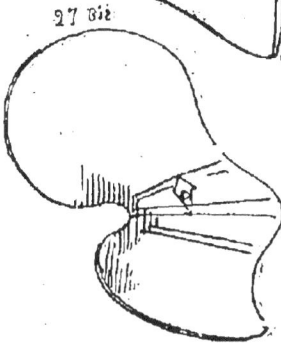

27 *bis*. Garde-bras-cubitière pour le bras gauche d'une armure allemande du commencement du seizième siècle. — G. 10, musée d'artillerie de Paris.

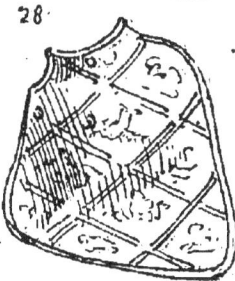

28. Manteau d'armes simple, en fer richement gravé, travail allemand d'une armure de joute, du commencement du seizième siècle. Cette pièce est appelée en allem. *Grosser Brustschild* et aussi *Scharfrenntartsche* et en angl. *tilting-breast-shild*.

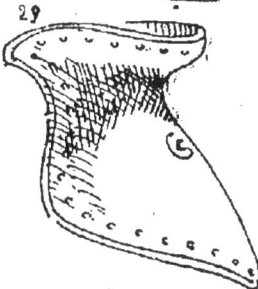

29. Manteau d'armes à mentonnière (*Grasser Brustschild mit Schembart* en all.; *tiltingbreast shild with mentonniere* en angl.), d'après le *livre de tournois* du duc Guillaume IV de Bavière (1510-1545).

30. Manteau d'armes à mentonnière avec son casque. — Même provenance que le n° 29.

31.   Id.   Id.

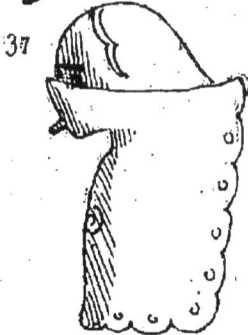

32. Manteau d'armes à mentonnière d'une armure de joute, du commencement du seizième siècle. Il est en bois épais, recouvert de toile et peint en noir. — Col. d'Ambras.

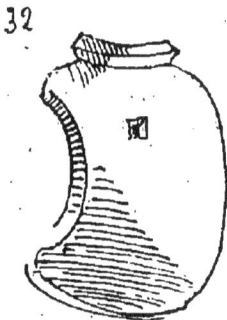

33. Manteau d'armes à mentonnière à vue. Ce renfort d'armure de joute qui couvre presque entièrement le mézail du casque et qui forme visière est plus ancien que les manteaux d'armes précédents; il a été dessiné d'après le *Triomphe de Maximilien*, gravure exécutée vers 1517.

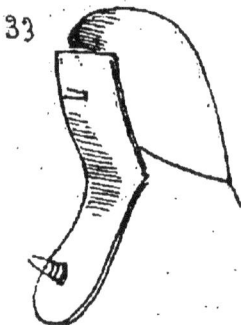

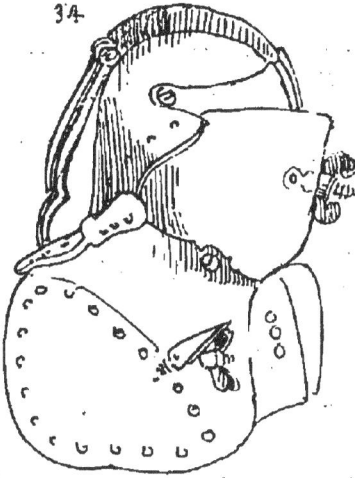

34. Grand manteau d'armes allemand avec haute pièce adhérente à vis porte-lance. Le casque déjà garanti par la haute pièce à laquelle il est vissé, est encore attaché à la dossière de la cuirasse par la *crête-échelle* appelée en allemand *Renhuth-schraube*. La vis porte-lance servait à fixer et à supporter le manteau d'armes et à suspendre les prix obtenus aux tournois et à reposer la lance. On croit aussi que le chevalier y piquait quelquefois une pomme qui devait servir de point de hast à l'adversaire. — Musée de Dresde. (G. 124, imitation, au musée d'artillerie de Paris.)

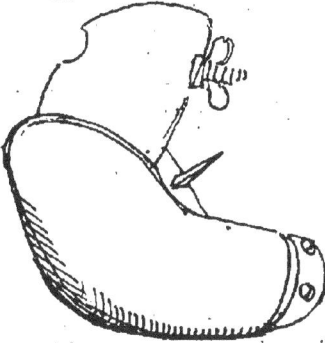

35. Id. id. sans le casque et la crête-échelle.

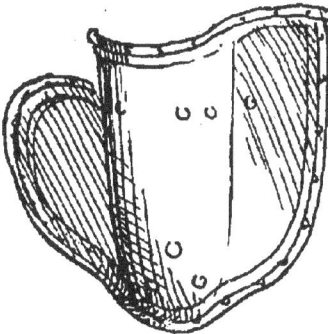

36. Grand cuissard de joute (*Tournier Lenden platte* en allem., *great tilting cuissard* en angl.), du commencement du seizième siècle, d'une armure dite maximilienne. — G. 114, musée d'artillerie de Paris.

37. Grand cuissard de joute d'une armure maximilienne du commencement du seizième siècle. — G. 115, musée d'artillerie de Paris.

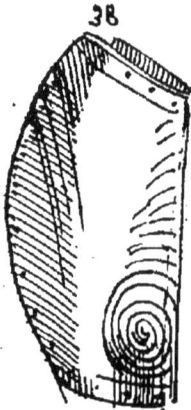

38. Jambière allemande pour tournois de la fin du quinzième siècle. On la portait par-dessus la grève de l'armure pour garantir la jambe contre les chocs de la barrière. — Arsenal impérial de Vienne.

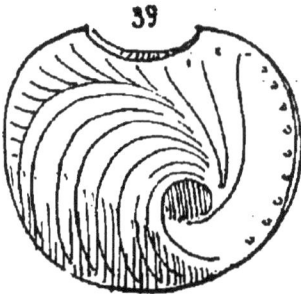

39. Grand cuissard de joute du commencement du seizième siècle. — Col. de M. le comte de Nieuwerkerke.

40. Rondelle de lance (*Schwebescheibe* en allem., *round-lance-plate* en angl.) de la fin du quinzième siècle. — Musée d'artillerie de Paris.

22

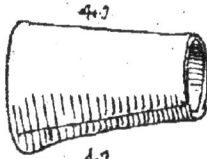

41. Rondelle de lance du seizième siècle. — Musée de Dresde.

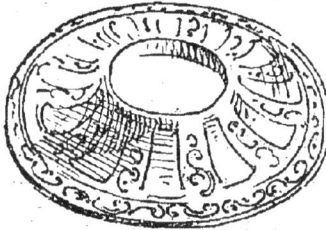

42. Rondelle de lance du seizième siècle. — Col. Llewelyn-Meyrick.

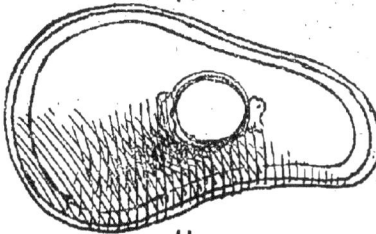

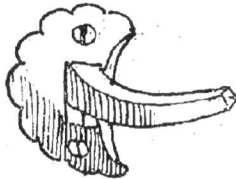

43. Rondelle de lance du seizième sièle. — Col. Llewelyn-Meyrick.

44. Faucre ou arrêt de lance (*Rüsthacken* en allem., *lance-rest* en angl.) du milieu du seizième siècle. — Musée de Dresde.

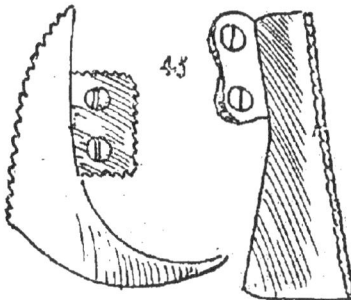

45. Deux genres de faucres de la fin du seizième siècle. — Musée de Dresde.

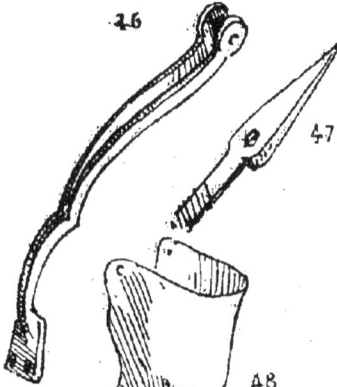

46. Crête-échelle (*Rennhuthsch-raube* en allem.). — Musée de Dresde. — Voir nº 34.

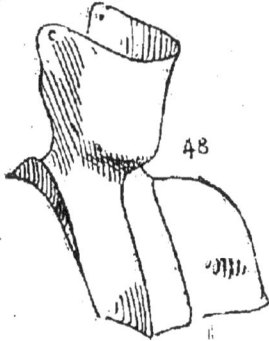

47. Vis porte-lance et porte-manteau d'armes. — Musée de Dresde. — Voir nº 34.

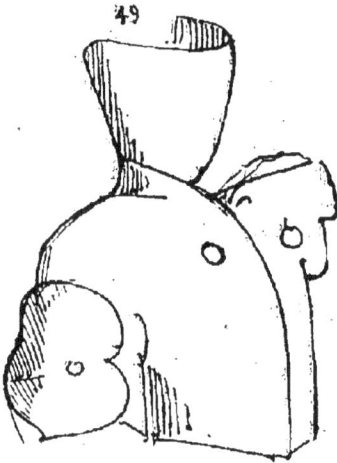

48. Haute pièce (*Vorhelm* en allem., *volant-piece* en angl.). — Musée de Dresde.

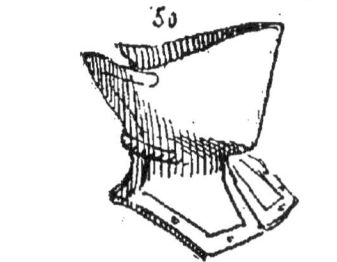

49. Haute pièce avec manteau d'armes à épaulières et cubitières d'armure de tournois, de la fin du quinzième siècle. — Col. Renné à Constance.

50. Haute mentonnière (*Grosse Barthaube* en allem., *great mentonniere* en angl.). — Col. Nieuwerkerke.

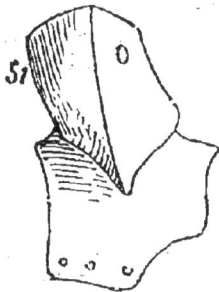

51. Haute pièce. — Col. Llewe-lyn-Meyrick.

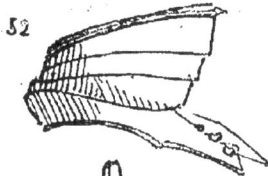

52. Mentonnière lamée à gorge-rin (*Geschobene Barthaube* en allem., *lamed mentonniere* en angl.), de travail allemand, en usage vers la fin du quinzième siècle où on la portait avec la salade. — Col. de M. le comte de Nieuwerkerke.

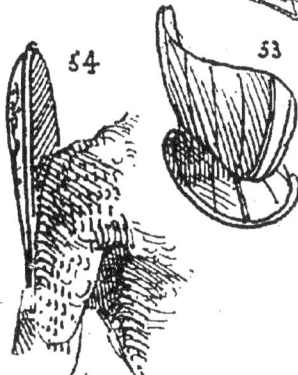

53. Demi-mentonnière (*Halbe Barthaube* en allem., *half men-tonniere* en angl.) de la fin du quinzième siècle.

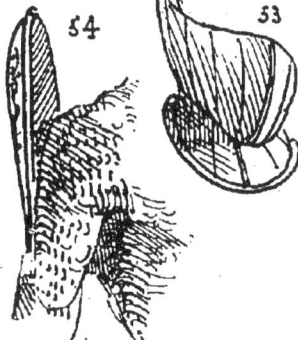

54. Ailette ou plaque armoriée qui était connue à l'époque transitoire entre la cotte d'ar-mes et l'armure à plaques de cuir, et dont l'usage a duré une trentaine d'années. On en voit sur la statue de Rodolphe de Hierstein (mort en 1318), à la cathédrale de Bâle.

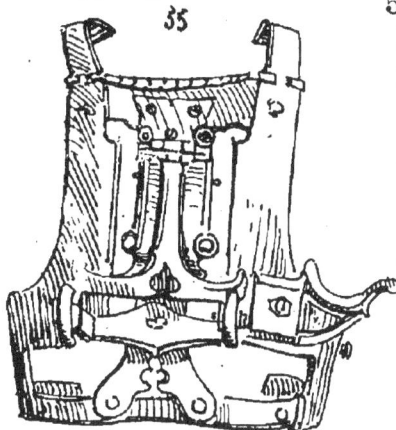

55. Plastron d'une armure de joute, allemande, de la première moitié du seizième siècle. Cette mécanique, dont il n'existe que deux exemplaires (à la col. Am-bras et au musée d'artillerie de Paris), faisait sauter en l'air les pièces de l'armure dès que l'ad-versaire atteignait avec la pointe de sa lance le milieu, désigné par un cœur percé à jour.

LE CASQUE

Le mot casque (*Helm* en allemand, *kask* et *helmed* en anglais) vient du celtique *cas*, caisse, étui, et *ked* de *cead*, tête.

On a vu quelles étaient les formes des casques antiques et des casques portés par les peuples dits barbares durant les âges du bronze et du fer, dont il n'existe plus que deux espèces : le casque à cornes, attribué au musée britannique, aux Bretons, mais qui paraît plutôt scandinave, et les casques coniques semblables aux casques assyriens de la plus haute antiquité; ils sont attribués, aux musées de Rouen et de Saint-Germain, aux Gaulois, et au musée de Munich, aux Avares. Les casques des chefs des races germaniques, dont aucun exemplaire n'a encore été trouvé, mais dont l'existence est démontrée par des textes, avaient probablement aussi la forme conique chez les peuplades méridionales de la Germanie, puisque le casque franco-normand du onzième siècle l'avait encore.

Ce dernier montre un nasal fixe (*Nasenberge* ou *Schemenbart* en allemand, *nazal* en anglais) de la largeur de plusieurs doigts, partie adhérente qui descend plus bas que le nez, dont il forme la défense. Ce casque était déjà porté par-dessus le camail (*Ringhaube* en allemand, *mail-capuchin* en anglais) dont le tissu métallique, ordinairement en chaînettes ou en mailles, était souvent une prolongation (sorte de capuchon), du haubert ou cotte d'armes.

Le casque des races de la Germanie du Nord, également à nasal fixe, était alors, selon les manuscrits, à timbre bombé, et, peu de temps après, à oreillères et à couvre-

22.

nuque mobiles tel qu'il est représenté à la page 267, sous le n° 20, d'après l'exemplaire conservé au musée d'artillerie de Paris; la forme de ce casque prenait quelquefois une hauteur démesurée, comme le démontre la broderie de Seligenthal reproduite à la page 187.

Vers la fin du douzième siècle apparaissent déjà les premiers heaumes (*Topfformhelm* en allemand, *first pothelm* en anglais) dont le musée d'artillerie à Paris possède également un exemplaire sous le n° H. I., et qui figure plus loin parmi les dessins (page 269, n° 28). C'est le casque de transition qui a encore conservé le nasal.

Le véritable heaume (*Topfhelm* en allemand, *helm* en anglais) ne remonte pas au delà de la fin du treizième siècle ou au commencement du quatorzième, et le heaume à cimier, vers la même époque, peu d'années après, car plusieurs chevaliers de l'*Énéide allemande*, de Henri de Waldeck, manuscrit du treizième siècle conservé à la bibliothèque de Berlin, sont déjà représentés avec des heaumes à cimiers de formes fantastiques. Ce heaume (mot dérivé de l'allemand *Helm*, casque) était ce gros casque, ordinairement à timbre aplati, qui, suspendu à la selle, n'était guère porté que dans les joutes et durant la bataille, car la toile imprimée, non pas au moyen d'un procédé xylographique, mais à la main, vers le milieu du quatorzième siècle, et appartenant à M. Odet, à Sitten, démontre que, même en Italie, le heaume servait aussi bien à la guerre qu'aux tournois. Il recouvrait la coiffe de mailles (camail) doublée du *bonnet* matelassé, coiffe sur laquelle le chevalier mettait encore le petit casque léger de cette époque appelé *petit bacinet*[1] ou *cervelière* (*Kleine Kesselhaube* en allemand, *smal bassinet* en anglais).

Quelquefois il avait seulement ou le camail ou le petit bacinet, mais plus souvent il portait les deux défenses

---

1. Du celtique *bac*, bateau; latin barbare, *bacinatum*.

réunies sous l'énorme heaume. Le petit bacinet était un casque pointu, de forme orientale et presque collant à la tête comme une calotte, qu'il ne faut pas confondre avec le grand bacinet du quatorzième siècle, arme défensive, d'une forme semblable, mais qui couvrait aussi les joues et la nuque, et était souvent à visière mobile qui s'ouvrait ordinairement au moyen d'une charnière du côté gauche et se rabattait quelquefois vers la pointe du timbre ; on a vu qu'un manuscrit bohémien du treizième siècle représente déjà des chevaliers coiffés de ce grand bacinet. Au quatorzième siècle, le *grand heaume* de joute (*Stechtopfhelm* en allemand, *tilting pothelm* en anglais), qui pesait 9 à 10 kilog., était bien plus en usage dans les joutes qu'à la guerre, où il était remplacé par le heaume de guerre qui ne pesait que 3 à 5 kilog., et particulièrement par le *grand bacinet* de forme ovoïde et pointue déjà mentionné (*Grosse Kesselhauhe* en allemand, *great bassinet* en anglais), sous lequel le chevalier conservait encore quelque temps la coiffe de mailles. L'usage du grand bacinet cessa complétement au commencement du quinzième siècle, où apparaît la *salade*, casque d'origine allemande, comme l'indique son nom primitif *Schale*, coupe, et que les anciens auteurs allemands appelaient *Schallern*. Cette coupe à queue ou couvre-nuque, dont quelques auteurs veulent faire dériver le nom de l'espagnol *celada*, caché, était d'abord à vue fixe, et bientôt après à visières mobiles si courtes, qu'elles ne descendaient pas au delà du bout du nez, et rendaient nécessaire la *bavière* qui devait être vissée sur la partie supérieure du plastron pour défendre le cou, le menton et la bouche.

Le *chapeau d'armes* (*Eisenhuth* en allemand, *iron-hat* en anglais), casque sans visière ni couvre-nuque, mais à bords, et le *pot-en-tête* (*Eisenkappe* en allemand, *scull cap* en anglais), qui remontent au douzième ou au treizième siècle, et se retrouvent encore au dix-septième.

Les *casques orientaux* et *russes*, etc., de ces époques, comme ceux des temps plus modernes, ont peu varié et conservé en grande partie la forme ovoïde et le nasal mobile.

La *bourguignote* (*Burgunder Helm* en allemand, *burgonet* en anglais) est un casque qui date de la fin du quinzième siècle; son timbre (*Glocke* en allemand, *bell* en anglais) est bombé et à *crête* (*Kamm* en allemand, *crest* en anglais); il se signale par son *avance* (*Augenschirm* en allemand, *helmet-shade* en anglais), ses *oreillères* (*Wangenklappen* en allemand, *cheek-pieces* en anglais) et son *couvrenuque* (*Nackenschutz* en allemand, *neck-guard* en anglais). Le président Faucher, qui écrivait vers la fin du seizième siècle, confond la bourguignote avec l'armet, quand il dit: « Ces heaumes ont mieux représenté la teste d'un homme; ils furent nommés bourguignotes, possible à cause des Bourguignons inventeurs. »

L'*armet* (*Visierhelm* en allemand, *helmet* en anglais), que le président prend ainsi pour la bourguignote, est le casque le plus perfectionné; il remonte seulement, comme l'autre, à la seconde moitié du quinzième siècle, et est encore en usage, comme la bourguignote, au milieu du dix-septième siècle. Toute sa partie antérieure était appelée *mézail;* son *timbre*, ou la partie supérieure, était bombé; la *vue*, c'est-à-dire la visière (*Visier* en allemand, *visor* en anglais), avec le nasal et le *ventail*, était mobile et se relevait vers la crête au moyen d'un pivot.

La *mentonnière* ou *bavière* (*Kinnstück* en allemand, *beaver* en anglais), destinée à défendre la partie inférieure de la figure, ainsi que le *gorgerin* ou *gorgery* (*Halsberge* en allemand, *georget* en anglais), lamés tous deux, étaient adhérents.

En outre de ces casques répandus presque partout, et qui forment, pour ainsi dire, les types des différentes époques de la chevalerie, il en existait encore une grande variété d'autres, qui étaient des armes défensives d'archers et d'hommes de pied. Ce sont, entre autres :

Le *morion* (*Morian* en allemand, *morion* en anglais), casque d'origine espagnole, dont le nom dérive de *morro*, corps rond ; il est sans visière, sans nasal, sans gorgerin et sans couvre-nuque, mais à haute crête, dont l'élévation atteint quelquefois la moitié de la hauteur du casque, et à bords relevés en pointes au-dessus du visage et au-dessus de la nuque, de manière que, vus de profil, ils forment un croissant.

Le *cabasset* (*Birnenhelm* en allemand, *pear-kask* en anglais) tire probablement son nom de sa forme, qui affecte celle du fruit à gourde, la calebasse ; sans visière, sans gorgerin, sans couvre-nuque et sans crête, mais pointu comme une poire dont la tige forme le petit bout du cimier, ce casque, comme le morion, était porté par les reîtres et par des hommes de pied, particulièrement en France et en Italie, jusqu'au milieu du dix-septième siècle. Le morion, orné d'une énorme fleur de lis repoussée, se trouve aussi dans beaucoup d'arsenaux en Allemagne, particulièrement en Autriche et en Bavière, où il provient de l'armement municipal de la fin du moyen âge. Cette fleur de lis n'a aucun rapport, là, avec les armoiries des rois de France, mais est le symbole de la Vierge dont beaucoup de corps d'arquebusiers et de hallebardiers avaient adopté l'image pour leurs drapeaux civiques.

La *bourguignote commune* (*Pickelhauhe* en allemand, *soldier-burgonet* en anglais), très-répandue en Allemagne, était le casque des *Knappen*, ou hommes d'armes au service des châtelains féodaux, et quelquefois celui des lansquenets et de la cavalerie légère.

Le *chapeau de fer* (*Eisenhuth* en allemand, *iron-hat* en anglais), qui remonte jusqu'au treizième siècle, comme le prouve le manuscrit bohème de *Voleslav*, de la bibliothèque du prince de Lobkowitz, à Raudnitz, n'avait également ni visière ni crête. Il y en a eu, au dix-septième siècle, qui affectaient la forme d'une casquette à visière, et où la visière était quelquefois traversée par un nasal mobile ; le chapeau de fer du poids de 20 livres (n° 101), que portait à la guerre Auguste le Fort (1670-1733), et qui se trouve au musée de Dresde, appartient à cette espèce, tandis que le chapeau de fer du poids de 25 livres (n° 100), que le grand électeur portait à la bataille de Fehrbellin en 1677, est à timbre rond et à large bord, comme un chapeau de berger. La coiffure des hommes de pied de la maison du roi Louis XIV (1643-1715) était le chapeau à timbre aplati et à nasal mobile (n° 114).

Le véritable *pot-en-tête* (*Eisenkappe* en allemand, *scull-cap* en anglais), espèce de calotte en fer très-épais et très-pesant, servait particulièrement, au seizième et au dix-septième siècle, dans les siéges (n° 97). Le nom de pot-en-tête est cependant aussi donné aux chapeaux de fer plus légers, et dont, entre autres, étaient armés les hommes de pied de Cromwell.

Les *calottes* et les *carcasses* en fer du dix-septième et du dix-huitième siècle servaient à garnir les fonds des chapeaux ; le musée historique du palais Monbyon, à Berlin, possède même une carcasse triangulaire qui servait à doubler les tricornes (n° 111).

Quant aux casques de formes antiques du seizième siècle, le plus souvent de travail italien, allemand ou espagnol, qui font la richesse des panoplies d'amateurs, ce sont plutôt des casques de parade que des casques de guerre et de tournois ; leur valeur archéologique est nulle, puisqu'ils datent tous de la Renaissance, et sont plutôt le produit de réminiscences antiques, où presque rien ne reflète les costumes et les mœurs de l'époque.

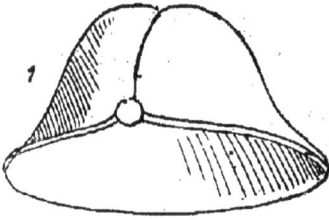

1. Casque germanique du huitième ou du neuvième siècle, en bronze ou en fer, d'après le *Codex aureus*, manuscrit de cette époque conservé à la bibliothèque de Saint-Gall.

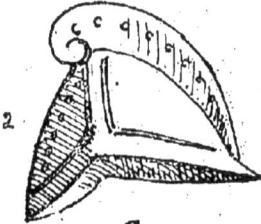

2. Casque carlovingien du neuvième siècle, en bronze ou en fer, d'après l'*Ademari-Cronicon* de la bibliothèque impériale de Paris.

3. Casque carlovingien du neuvième siècle, en bronze ou en fer, d'après la Bible de Charles le Chauve, au Louvre.

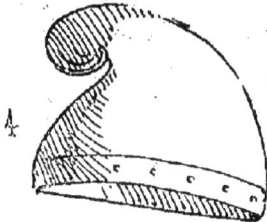

4. Casque allemand en fer du dixième siècle, d'après le *Psalterium*, manuscrit à la bibliothèque de Stuttgard. Voir cette même forme parmi les casques grecs et japonais.

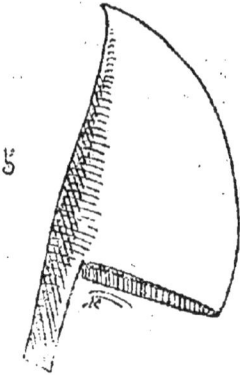

5. Casque allemand demi-conique à nasal, appelé en France casque normand, d'après le *Martyrologe*, manuscrit du dixième siècle, à la bibliothèque de Stuttgard.

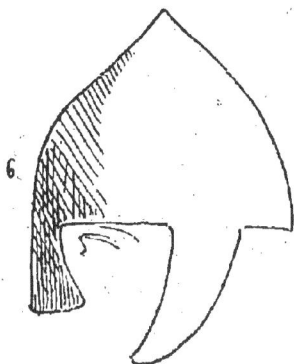

6. Casque conique à nasal élargi à sa partie inférieure, d'après une statuette du dixième siècle. — Col. de M. le comte de Nieuwerkerke.

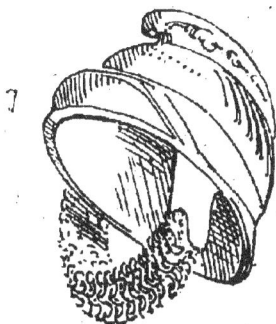

7. Casque forme antique à crête et à jugulaires, d'après un buste de grandeur naturelle en argent repoussé, du dixième siècle. — Trésor du couvent de Saint-Maurice, canton du Valais.

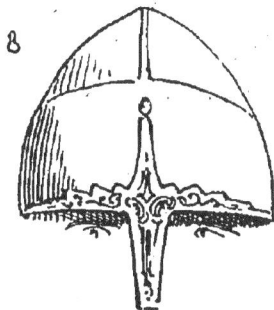

8. Casque à nasal fixe, en fer et incrusté d'argent, ayant appartenu à saint Venceslas, mort en 933. — Dôme de Prague.

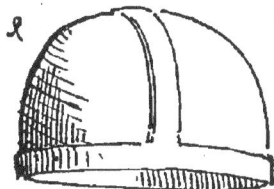

9. Casque allemand à timbre rond, en fer, d'après une miniature de la *Biblia sacra* du dixième siècle, de la bibliothèque impériale de Paris, et d'après le *Prudentius* de la même époque, au musée britannique.

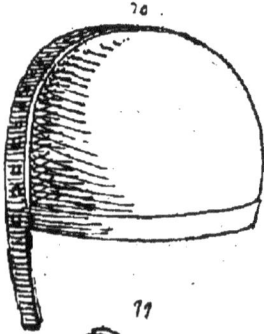

10. Casque allemand en fer à nasal fixe du onzième siècle, d'après un manuscrit de l'époque appartenant à M. de Hefner-Alteneck. Cette même forme de casque figure dans les miniatures du *Jeremias*, etc., du onzième siècle de la bibliothèque de Darmstadt.

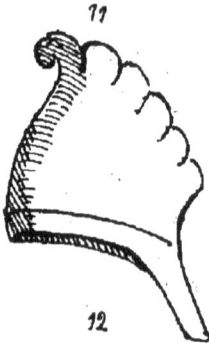

11. Casque anglo-saxon à couvre-nuque, d'après l'*Aelfric*, manuscrit du onzième siècle à la bibliothèque du musée britannique.

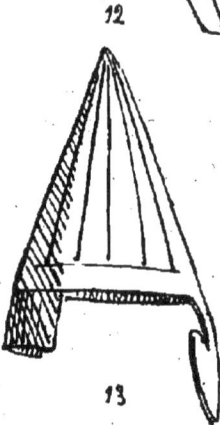

12. Casque conique normand à nasal et à couvre-nuque dont Guillaume le Conquérant est coiffé sur la tapisserie de Bayeux. Cette même forme de casque se trouve aussi dans l'*Aelfric* déjà mentionné.

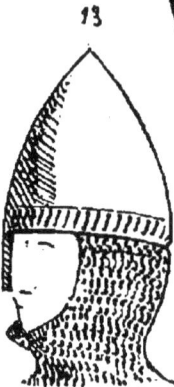

13. Casque conique allemand à nasal, d'après le bas-relief du baptistère en bronze, au dôme de Hildesheim, œuvre de saint Bernard, du onzième siècle. On retrouve cette même forme de casque dans les peintures murales du dôme de Brunswick, exécutées sous Henri le Lion, mort en 1195.

14. Casque anglo-saxon à nasal fixe, de la fin du douzième siècle, d'après une miniature du *Harlan Roll* de la bibliothèque du musée britannique.

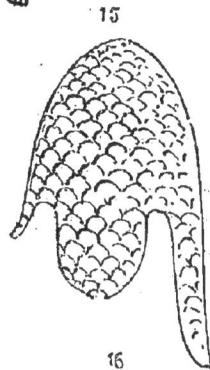

15. Casque russe, à petit nasal et long couvre-nuque en écailles de fer imbriquées, attribué à Saint-Pétersbourg, au onzième siècle.

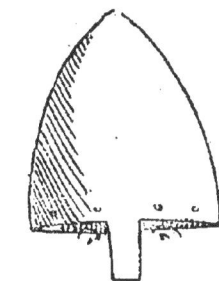

16. Casque conique en fer, à petit nasal fixe, du onzième siècle, trouvé en Moravie.—Col. d'Ambras.

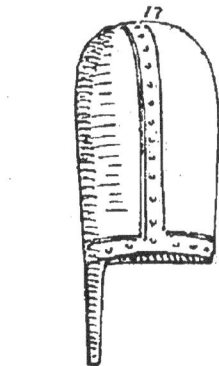

17. Casque allemand à couvre-nuque du douzième siècle, d'après les broderies de la mitre du couvent de Seligenthal. — Musée national de Munich. (Louis VII (1137-1180) et Richard Cœur de Lion (1157-1183) sont représentés sur leurs sceaux coiffés de ce même genre de casque.)

17 bis. Casque en fer du douzième siècle, attribué à Henri le Lion, duc de Brunswick, mort en 1195. Le timbre en fer est orné de six bandes et d'un cimier en cuivre doré et gravé, et d'un bandeau frontal repoussé, également en cuivre doré, dont l'ornement principal représente un lion, tel qu'il figurait dans les armes du duc. — Col. du baron de Zu-Rhein à Wurzbourg, et provenant de celle de la duchesse de Berry.

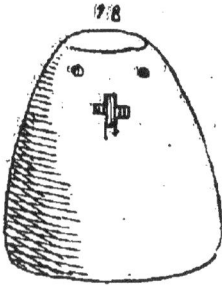

18. Casque en cuivre rouge avec croix grecque et trois trous percés à jour, de la fin du onzième siècle. Il a été trouvé dans la Saône et figure au musée d'artillerie de Paris.

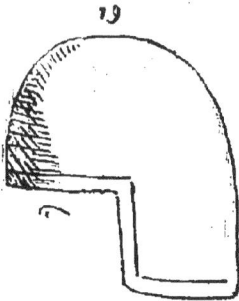

19. Casque allemand à couvre-nuque, du douzième siècle, d'après la peinture murale au dôme de Brunswick, exécutée sous Henri le Lion, mort en 1195.

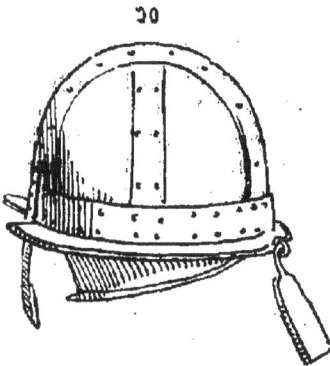

20. Casque allemand en fer, du douzième siècle, à nasal fixe, à oreillères et à couvre-nuque mobile. Il a été trouvé dans la Somme. — Musée d'artillerie de Paris.

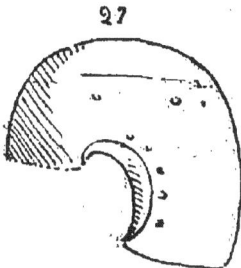

21. Casque en bronze, à couvre-nuque, probablement du douzième siècle, sinon du dixième car il a été trouvé dans la rivière du Lech, près du champ de bataille où saint Ulrich contribua à la tête de ses ouailles à la défaite d'Attila. — Musée Maximilien à Augsbourg.

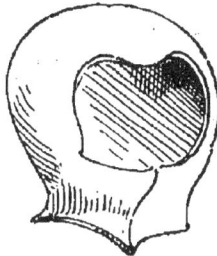

22. Casque allemand à bavière et gorgerin adhérents, et à mézail à vue ouverte, du treizième siècle, d'après le manuscrit allemand *Tristan* et *Isolde*, par Gotfried de Strasbourg. — Bibliothèque de Munich.

23. Coiffette française en mailles rivées à grains d'orge, du treizième siècle, trouvée dans un tombeau à Épernelle (Côte-d'Or). — H. 7, musée d'artillerie de Paris.

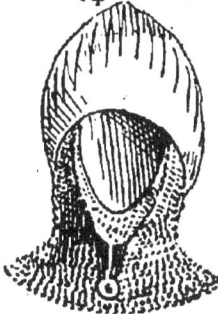

24. Petit bacinet ou cervelière allemand, du treizième siècle. Il se portait au-dessus du camail et au-dessous du heaume. — Tombeau de l'époque.

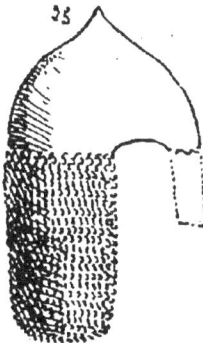

25. Petit bacinet probablement français, du treizième siècle. Il est à couvre-nuque en mailles et à nasal fixe, brisé, qui indique une dernière trace du nasal des casques du dixième et du onzième siècle. — H. 18, musée d'artillerie de Paris.

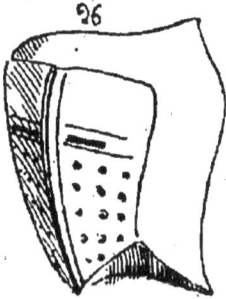

26. Heaume allemand (*Topfhelm* en allem., *helm* en angl.), du douzième siècle, d'après les peintures murales au dôme de Brunswick, exécutées sous Henri le Lion, mort en 1195.

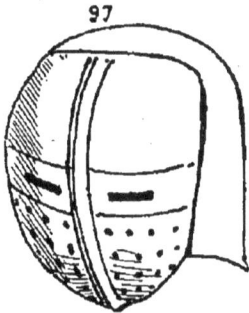

27.   Id.   id.

Ce sont les plus anciens spécimens de heaumes, de ces casques d'origine allemande, destinés à être portés par-dessus le petit bacinet, que l'auteur connaît.

28. Heaume anglais primitif, encore à nasal, de la fin du douzième siècle. Il est en fer noirci et a 42 cent. de hauteur. — H. 1. musée d'artillerie de Paris.

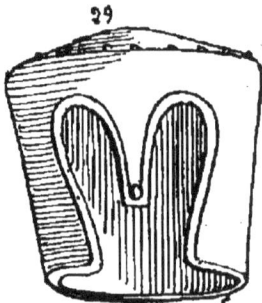

29. Heaume anglais primitif, également encore à nasal, de la fin du douzième siècle. — $\frac{4}{2}$, Tour de Londres.

23.

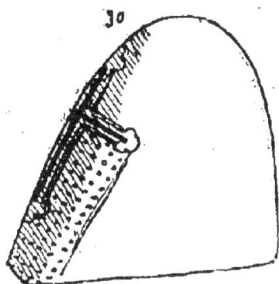

30. Heaume d'archers à pied et à cheval, du treizième siècle, d'après le *Cronicon colmariense* de 1298.

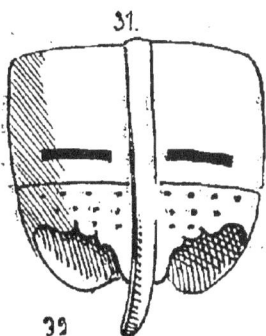

31. Heaume anglais du treizième siècle, probablement le casque nouveau dont parlent les écrivains contemporains de la bataille de Bouvines (1214). Le heaume allemand du treizième siècle des peintures murales de Brunswick est cependant bien plus perfectionné déjà. — Musée d'artillerie de Paris.

32. Heaume ou gros casque anglais, attribué dans la coll. Parham, où il est conservé, au douzième siècle, mais que l'auteur croit le produit de la contrefaçon, car la forme en est impossible et ne se trouve dans aucun manuscrit.

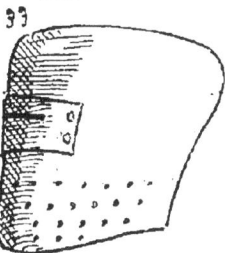

33. Heaume allemand du commencement du treizième siècle, d'après le *Tristan et Isolde* de la bibliothèque de Munich.

34. Heaume du treizième siècle, en fer, décoré de peintures polychromes. — Col. de M. le comte de Nieuwerkerke.

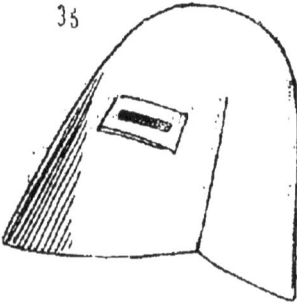

35. Heaume allemand de la fin du treizième siècle, d'après une miniature du manuscrit de *Manessis*, conservé à la bibliothèque impériale de Paris, et qui représente la mort, en 1298, d'Albrecht de Heigerloch le Minnesinger de la lignée des Hohenzollern.

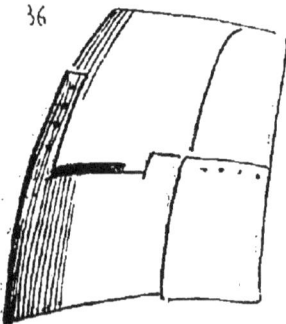

36. Heaume, conservé au musée de Prague, où il est attribué à la fin du treizième siècle. Il est en tôle excessivement mince et paraît plutôt un objet de contrefaçon.

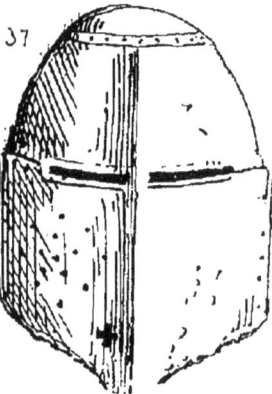

37. Heaume allemand du quatorzième siècle. Il a été trouvé, à côté des bacinets représentés plus loin, sous les décombres du château de Tannenburg, détruit au quatorzième siècle. — Le n° 570, au musée de Copenhague, est presque semblable, et un autre casque, au muséum Francisco-Carolinum à Lintz, y ressemble également.

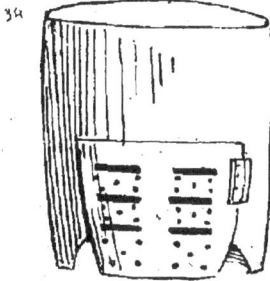

38. Heaume anglais à ventaux à charnière, du commencement du quatorzième siècle. — $\frac{4}{1}$, Tour de Londres.

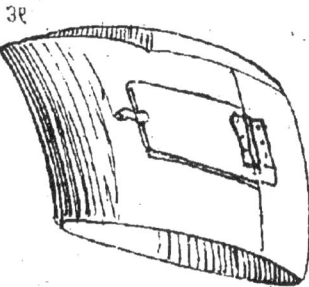

39. Heaume allemand de la fin du quatorzième siècle. — H. 5, musée d'artillerie de Paris.

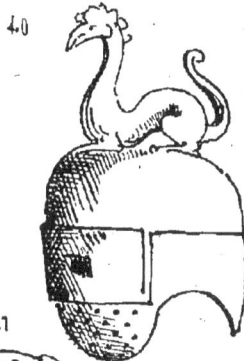

40. Heaume allemand à cimier du treizième siècle, d'après l'*Enéide allemande*, par Henri de Valdeck. — Bibliothèque de Berlin.

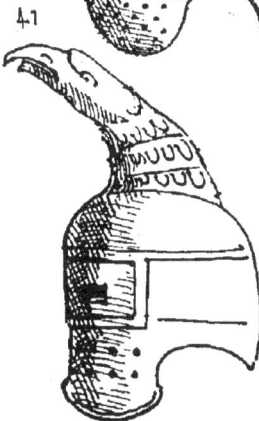

41.   Id.   id.

Ce sont les deux plus anciens heaumes à cimier que l'auteur a pu trouver. On a cru jusqu'ici que le cimier avait été adopté sur les heaumes probablement vers le milieu du quatorzième siècle et que les premières armes défensives de ce genre ne remontent qu'à la fin du treizième siècle, mais celles reproduites d'après les peintures murales du dôme de Brunswick du douzième siècle (nos 26 et 27), et les heaumes à cimier ci-dessus, infirment ces anciennes notions.

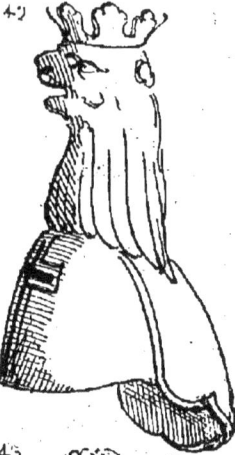

42. Grand heaume à cimier, d'après le monument funéraire du roi des Romains Gunther de Schwarzbourg, empoisonné à Francfort en 1349. — Cénotaphe, au dôme de Francfort, exécuté en pierre rouge en 1352.

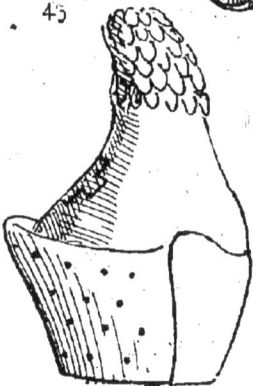

43. Grand heaume de joute (*Stechelm* en allem., *tilting helm* en angl.), en fer poli et à cimier brisé, du quatorzième siècle. La base du cimier est en écailles imbriquées et le mézail fixe. Il est probable que le cimier de ce casque n'est pas complet et qu'il y existait dans l'orgine une tête héraldique ou tout autre emblème. — H. 3, musée d'artillerie de Paris.

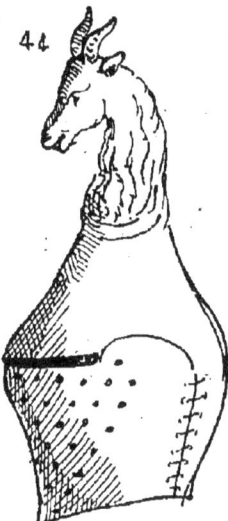

44. Grand heaume de joute anglais, en fer noirci et à cimier, du commencement du quinzième siècle. Le cimier en bois paraît moderne. — H. 4, musée d'artillerie de Paris.

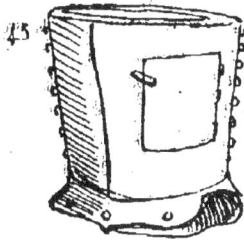

45. Grand heaume de joute allemand ou anglais, du quinzième
siècle. Il est à ventail à charnière et pourvu d'un colletin
destiné à être vissé sur la cuirasse. — Musée d'artillerie de
Paris.

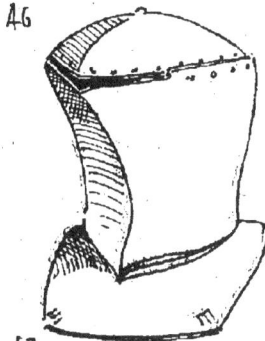

46. Grand heaume de joute anglais, de la fin du quinzième
siècle. Il est en fer poli et à
colletin. — Tour de Londres.

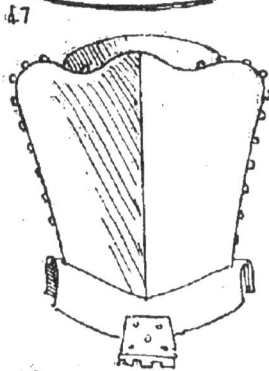

47. Grand heaume de joute allemand, de la fin du quinzième
siècle. Il est en fer poli, à colletin et semblable à l'exemplaire conservé au musée de
Munich. — H. 6, musée d'artillerie de Paris.

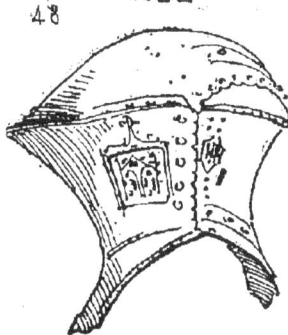

48. Grand heaume de joute, attribué à Maximilien I, mort en
1519. — Arsenal impérial de
Vienne. Un semblable casque,
trouvé à Klingenberg en Bohême, est conservé au musée de
Prague et un autre à l'arsenal
de Berlin. Cette forme s'est continuée, modifiée il est vrai, jusqu'au milieu du seizième siècle.

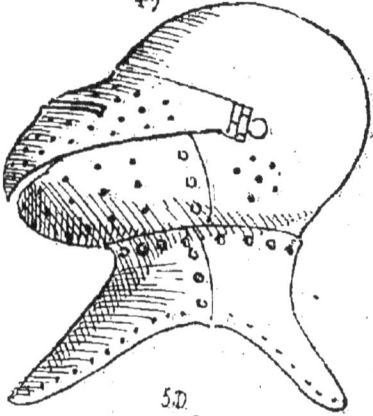

49. Heaume de guerre en fer poli, à timbre rond, vue à charnière, et dont le gorgerin-colletin est fixe, du quinzième siècle; il fait partie d'une armure complète de l'arsenal de Berne.

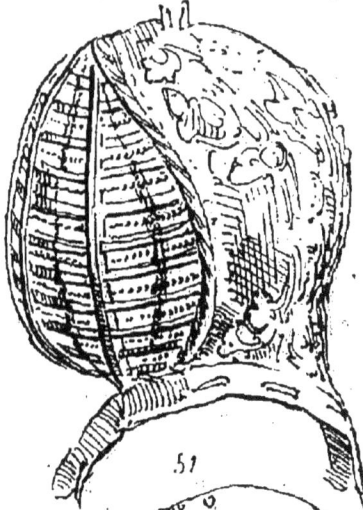

50. Heaume allemand de tournois à massettes [1] (*Kolbentournier* en allem.), de 50 cent. de hauteur, du quinzième siècle. La carcasse en fer forgé est recouverte dans sa partie postérieure d'un tissu de toile sur lequel on distingue encore les armoiries peintes des barons Spæth et quelques restants de dorure. — Musée de Sigmaringen.

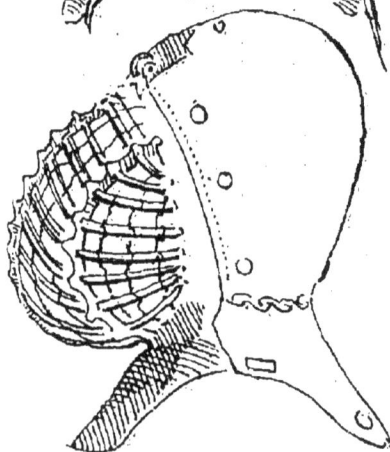

51. Heaume allemand, de tournois à massettes, du quinzième siècle. Il a appartenu au comte d'Esendorf, tué à Biberach. — Col. Sœter, au musée Maximilien à Augsbourg.

[1]. La massette et l'épée étaient employés simultanément dans ces exercices qui étaient à la fois des passes d'armes et des tournois de cavaliers.

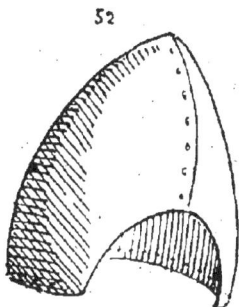

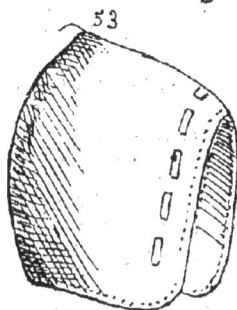

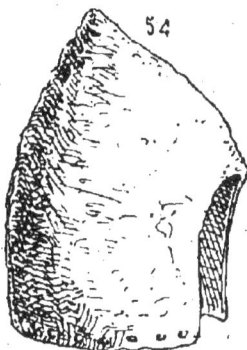

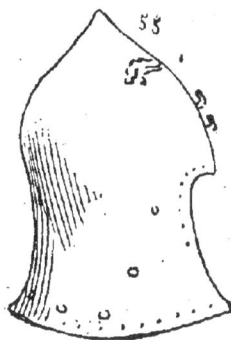

Le grand bacinet (*Grosse Kesselhaube* en allem., *great bassinet* en angl.) apparut dans la seconde moitié du treizième siècle. De forme ovoïde et pointu, il est d'abord sans visière ni nasal, mais garni de pitons pour recevoir de la maille qui remplace la visière et le couvre-nuque.

52. Bacinet bohémien, d'après le manuscrit de *Voleslav* de Bohême du treizième siècle, de la bibliothèque du prince de Lobkowitz, à Raudnitz en Bohême.

53. Bacinet allemand du treizième siècle. Il a 28 cent. sur 22 et se trouve au musée de Berlin.

54. Bacinet allemand de la fin du treizième siècle, trouvé sous les décombres du château de Tannenburg, incendié au quatorzième siècle. Il a été reproduit et décrit par M. de Hefner-Alteneck.

55. Bacinet français ou italien[1] du quatorzième siècle, garni de 12 gros pitons à trous carrés pour supporter des tringles sur lesquelles étaient enfilées les mailles. Ce casque provient de la collection du comte de Thun, à Val di Non. M. Spengel, à Munich, l'a cédé depuis à M. le comte de Nieuwerkerke.

1. Plutôt italien. La forme de ce couvre-nuque rappelle celle de la *celata veneziana* du quinzième siècle.

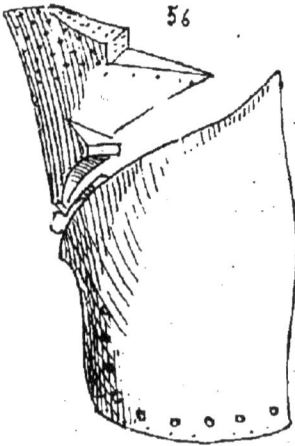

56. Grand bacinet allemand, en fer noirci, du quatorzième siècle, à mézail mobile; la vue à charnière se relève vers le timbre. Les vingt gros pitons à trous carrés servaient à supporter la tringle sur laquelle étaient enfilés les anneaux de la maille du gorgerin-couvre-nuque. — Col. de M. de Hefner-Alteneck.

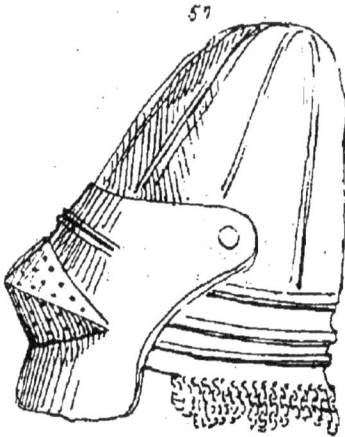

57. Grand bacinet anglais du milieu du quatorzième siècle. La visière se relève au moyen d'un pivot, comme celle des armets du seizième siècle. On y voit encore un restant du gorgerin couvre-nuque en mailles. — Château de Warwick.

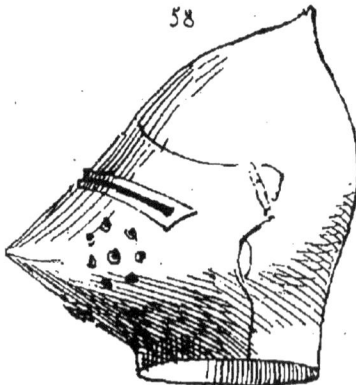

58. Grand bacinet à visière à charnière du quatorzième siècle. — Tour de Londres, musée d'artillerie de Paris et col. de M. le comte de Nieuwerkerke. Ces casques sont en acier poli; le timbre ovoïde d'une seule pièce est pointu, et la visière très-avancée laisse un grand espace pour faciliter la respiration.

24

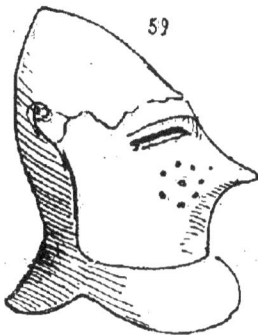

59. Grand bacinet anglais, à visière à charnière et à colletin fixe, du milieu du quatorzième siècle. — Tour de Londres et col. de M. de Renné, à Constance. Ce casque est semblable, sous certains rapports, au casque précédent.

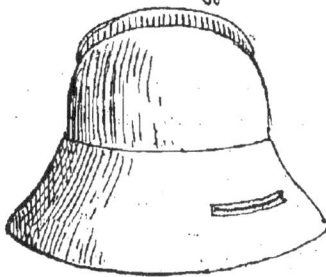

Les salades (en allemand, *Schale*, *Schallern* et *Schelern*, d'où dérive le nom français; *salade* en anglais), qui remplaçaient, au quinzième siècle, les bacinets, se signalaient particulièrement par leur couvre-nuque et avaient des ressemblances avec les chapeaux de fer. La salade se portait ordinairement avec la mentonnière qui souvent faisait pièce avec le hausse-col; elle était posée en biais, de manière que la fente ménagée pour la vue se trouvait devant les yeux.

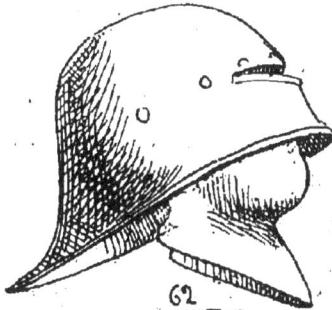

60. Salade-heaume allemande de tournois, du quatorzième siècle. Elle est à crête et à visière fixe et était portée droite. — Musée d'artillerie de Paris.

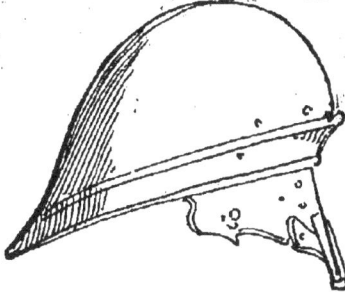

61. Salade allemande d'une seule pièce, avec sa mentonnière, du quinzième siècle. — Col. du roi de Suède, Charles XV.

62. Salade allemande à nasal, du quinzième siècle. — Col. de M. de Renné, à Constance.

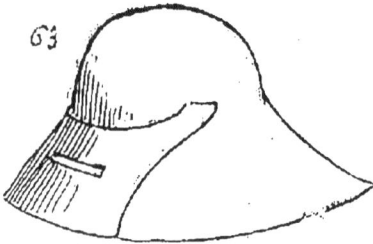

63. Salade allemande, en fer noirci à vue mobile à pivot, du quinzième siècle. Elle provient du château d'Ort, en Bavière, et a dû être portée en biais et avec mentonnière. — Tour de Londres. — Semblable pièce dans la collection Spengel, à Munich; cette dernière provient de la collection du comte de Thun, à Val di Non.

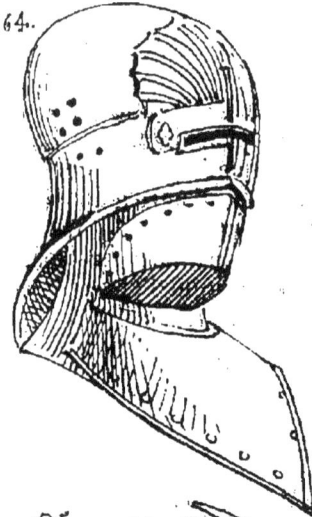

64. Salade à vue à coquille, avec mentonnière de forme étrange, carrée, et hausse-col, du quinzième siècle.

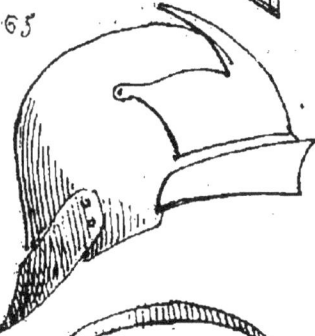

65. Salade à visière et couvre-nuque mobile, du quinzième siècle. Elle a dû être portée en biais comme la précédente. Le couvre-nuque est formé d'une pièce rapportée et peu développé. — Musée de Prague.

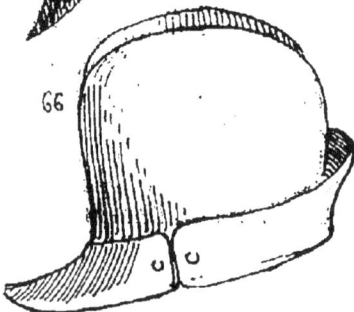

66. Salade à crête du quinzième siècle, provenant de l'île de Rhodes. Ce casque à visière figurée, et dont le couvre-nuque est une pièce rapportée, ne protégeait pas le visage et ne formait qu'une défense défectueuse. Son travail indique une origine italienne.

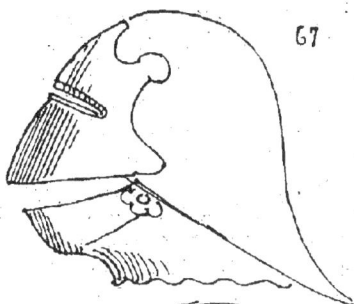

67. Salade allemande de guerre, dessinée d'après la statue du duc Guillaume le Jeune de Brunswick, sculpture exécutée en 1494. Elle est à visière fixe, à bavière mobile et à gorgerin. — Munden (Hanovre), près Cassel.

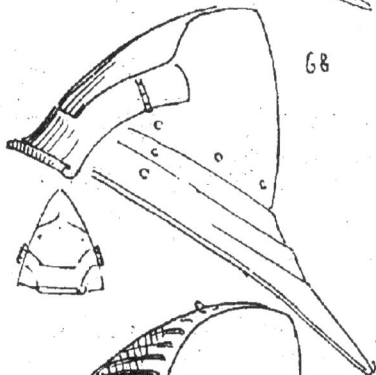

68. Salade allemande de guerre du quinzième siècle, à timbre pointu, forme très-rare et peut-être unique, visière à charnière, couvre-nuque lamé. Le petit dessin la représente de face. — Musée historique du palais Mont-bijou, à Berlin.

69. Id., avec sa mentonnière qui s'allonge en gorgerin hausse-col.

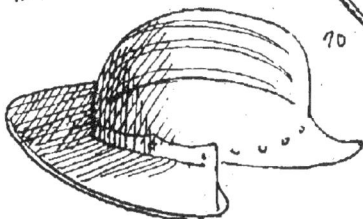

70. Salade cannelée avec avance, selon l'auteur, du seizième siècle, de l'île de Rhodes. — Musée d'artillerie de Paris, où elle est attribuée au quinzième siècle. La forme de l'avance et la cannelure doivent la faire ranger dans la première moitié du seizième siècle, où ces sortes de visières étaient très-répandues. — V. n° 125, Bourguignote.

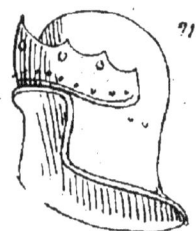

71. Salade anglaise attribuée, à la Tour de Londres où elle est conservée, au quinzième siècle, mais dont la forme singulière me paraît indiquer une contrefaçon.

72. Salade vénitienne (*celata veneziana*) à nasal, de la première moitié du quinzième siècle. — Col. Llewelyn-Meyrick, à Goodrich-Court; Renné, à Constance; Nieuwerkerke, à Paris et à la Tour de Londres.

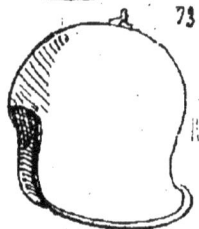

73. Salade vénitienne à cimier et sans nasal, de la seconde moitié du quinzième siècle [1]. Le couvre-nuque de ce casque est plus prononcé que celui du numéro précédent. — Col. Llewelyn-Meyrick.

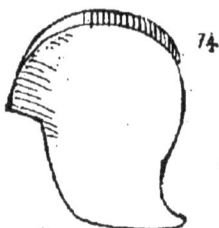

74. Salade d'archer vénitien à crête et sans nasal, de la seconde moitié du quinzième siècle. Le couvre-nuque est moins prononcé que celui du casque précédent. — H. 22, musée d'artillerie de Paris et col. de la Tour de Londres.

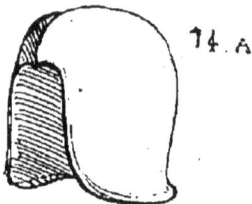

74 A. Salade italienne, de la seconde moitié du quinzième siècle, d'après les bas-reliefs en marbre blanc de l'arc de triomphe d'Alphonse V, roi d'Aragon, à Naples, qui représentent son entrée triomphale, en 1443.

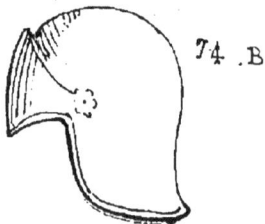

74 B. Salade italienne, à visière figurée, id, id.

1. Cette arme affecte la forme du casque grec d'hoplite (V. n° 9, page 126), dont elle paraît le dérivé, mais qui était sans couvre-nuque. La pointe sur la partie frontale qui forme une espèce de nasal, ne se retrouve plus dans les *celate veneziane* de la seconde moitié du quinzième siècle.

24.

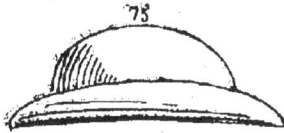

75. Chapeau d'armes en fer (*Eisenhuth* en allem., *iron hat* en angl.), du douzième siècle, d'après les peintures murales au dôme de Brunswick, exécutées sous Henri le Lion, mort en 1195.

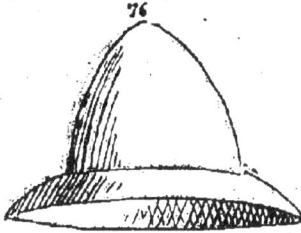

76. Chapeau d'armes en fer, d'après le manuscrit bohémien *Voleslav* du treizième siècle.

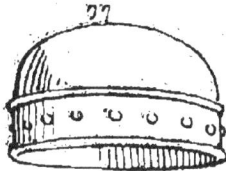

77. Calotte d'armes (*Eisenkappe* en allem., *scull-cap* en angl.), d'après l'*Enéide* allemande de Henri de Valdeck, manuscrit du treizième siècle, à la bibliothèque de Berlin.

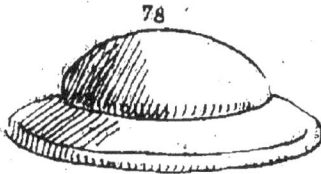

78. Chapeau d'armes en fer, d'après une miniature du manuscrit de Manessis, de la fin du treizième siècle, qui représente la mort d'Albrecht de Heigerloch le Minnesinger de la lignée des Hohenzollern. — Bibliothèque impériale de Paris.

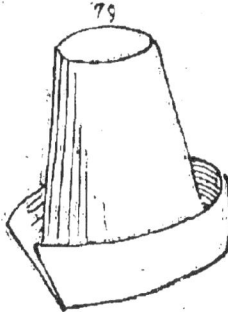

79. Chapeau d'armes en fer, de la fin du quatorzième siècle, d'après une peinture à Saint-Michel, à Schwæbisch-Hall, reproduit par M. de Hefner-Alteneck.

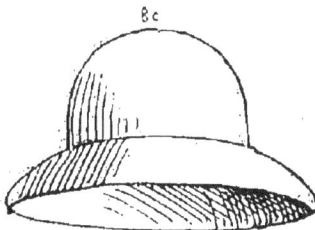

80.   Id.   id.

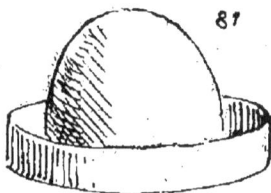

81. Chapeau d'armes en fer, de la fin du quatorzième siècle, d'après une peinture à Saint-Michel, à Schwæbisch-Hall.

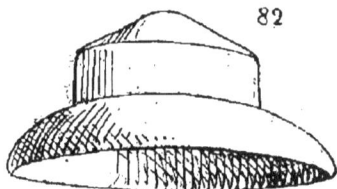

82. Chapeau d'armes en fer, d'après un manuscrit de Constance, de 1435, conservé à la bibliothèque de Prague.

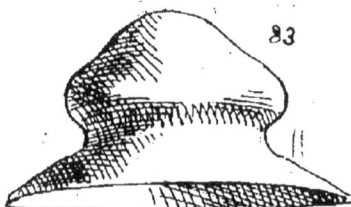

83. Chapeau d'armes en fer du quinzième siècle. — Musée de Copenhague et col. de M. de Hefner-Alteneck, à Munich.

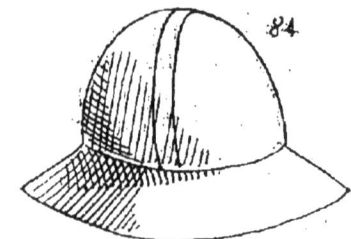

84. Chapeau d'armes en fer du quinzième siècle. — Manuscrit de la collection de M. le chevalier de Hauslaub, à Vienne.

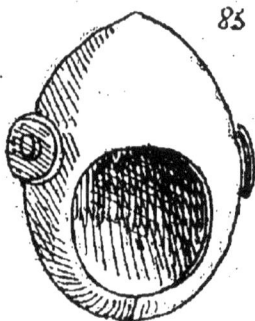

85. Pot-en-tête (*Eisenkappe* en allem., *scull-cap* en angl.) ovoïde, à mentonnière, du quatorzième et du quinzième siècle. — Manuscrit de la collection de M. le chevalier de Hauslaub, à Vienne, et peintures murales de la cathédrale de Mondonnedo, en Espagne. La forme donnée par les peintres à la partie inférieure de cette arme défensive fait supposer qu'elle devait avoir par derrière des pièces mobiles, à charnière ou à pivot, pour permettre l'entrée de la tête qu'elle entoure hermétiquement.

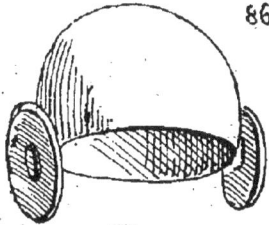

86. Calotte d'armes (*Eisenkappe* en allem., *scull-cap*, en angl.) à oreillères, d'après un manuscrit du quinzième siècle, de la collection de M. le chevalier de Hauslaub, à Vienne.

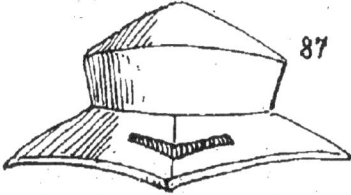

87. Chapeau d'armes-salade à visière, d'après les aquarelles de Glockenthon de 1505 qui représentent les armes des arsenaux de l'empereur Maximilien I. — Col. d'Ambras.

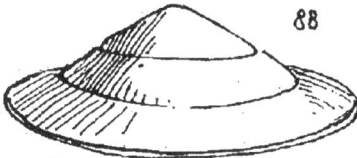

88. Chapeau d'armes, id.

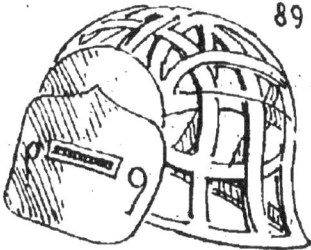

89. Pot-en-tête carcasse, id. Cette arme a probablement servi aux siéges où elle fut portée, comme le heaume, par-dessus le casque ordinaire.

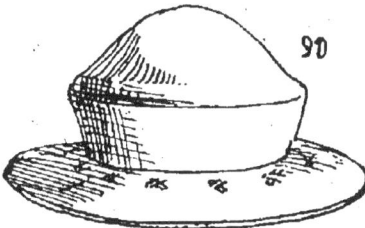

90. Chapeau d'armes allemand de la fin du quinzième siècle, d'après le moulage, au musée germanique, à Nuremberg. Sa forme est presque identique à celle du chapeau de fer n° 83, dont le dessin représente une arme de la collection de M. de Hefner-Alteneck, à Munich, et, comme celle-là, son timbre est martelé d'une seule pièce.

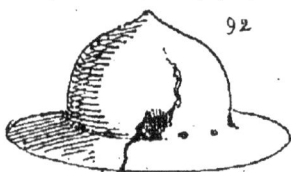

92. Chapeau d'armes du réformateur Zwingli, mort dans la bataille de Cappel, en 1531. — Arsenal de Zurich.

93. Chapeau d'armes de la fin du quinzième siècle. La rosette principale, en cuivre percé à jour, forme la croix de Bourgogne. — Coll. Renné à Constance. Semblable exemplaire, moins la croix, dans la coll. Spengel à Munich.

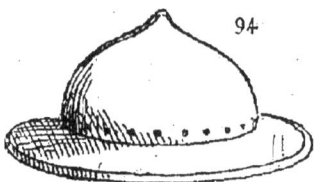

94. Chapeau d'armes, d'après le *Theuerdanck*, publié à Augsbourg au commencement du seizième siècle.

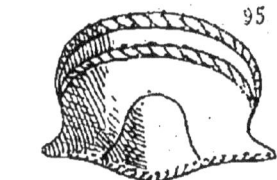

95. Chapeau d'armes allemand, du seizième siècle, surmonté de trois gros crêpes torses et pourvu d'oreillères mobiles. Ce casque est recouvert de velours rouge et servait particulièrement à la chasse. — Collections Spengel et de Hefner-Alteneck à Munich, ville dont l'arsenal possède un pareil casque encore recouvert de drap noir et jaune, qui sont les couleurs de Munich. D'autres exemplaires dans la col. d'Ambras et au château de Laxenbourg. Un semblable casque, de la coll. des Mazis, au musée d'artillerie de Paris, est attribué au roi Henri IV (1559-1610), dont il porte le chiffre et le portrait gravés. Les crêpes y sont richement ornés de trophées et autres sujets en gravé et en repoussé.

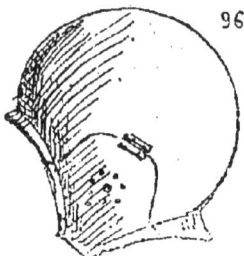

96. Pot-en-tête à oreillères, du seizième siècle. — Arsenal de Munich.

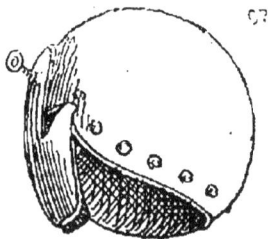

97. Pot-en-tête de siége, du dix-septième siècle. — H. 154, musée d'artillerie de Paris.

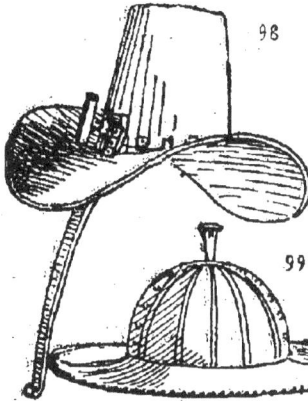

98. Chapeau d'armes en fer, de Charles Ier, roi d'Angleterre (1625-1650). Il porte la marque d'armurier : | A. B. O. | —Château de Warwick.

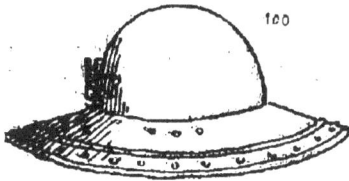

99. Chapeau d'armes en fer, du dix-septième siècle. — Col. Az à Lintz.

100. Chapeau d'armes en fer, à porte-plumet, pesant 25 livres; il mesure 30 cent. sur 40 et a appartenu au grand Électeur de Brandebourg, qui le portait à la bataille de Fehrbellin (1677). — Musée de Berlin.

101. Calotte d'armes à visière, en fer, le dessus à jour et pesant 20 livres. Elle a appartenu à Auguste II le Fort (1670-1733). — Musée de Dresde.

102. Calotte d'armes allemande en fer, à visière et à nasal, du dix-septième siècle. A couvre-nuque long en mailles; elle est extérieurement recouverte de toile grise. — Musée de Dresde.

103. Calotte d'armes du dix-septième siècle, en fer épais, et dont la partie supérieure est à jour. — Arsenal de Berlin.

104. Calotte d'armes en écailles imbriquées, d'après un dessin de Holbein, du seizième siècle. — Musée industriel à Vienne.

105. Calotte d'armes en écailles imbriquées, en acier poli, à nasal mobile, à oreillères et à couvre-nuque; le porte-plumet et plusieurs autres pièces sont en cuivre doré. Elle a été portée par Jean Sobieski, roi de Pologne, devant Vienne, en 1683. — Musée de Dresde.

106. Calotte-carcasse en fer, du dix-septième siècle. — Musée de Prague.

107. Id. Id. Id.

108. Calotte-carcasse en fer, qui garnissait intérieurement les chapeaux des carabiniers français vers 1680. — Musée d'artillerie de Paris.

109. Calotte-carcasse en fer, du dix-septième siècle, pour doublure de chapeau d'armes. — Musée de Sigmaringen.

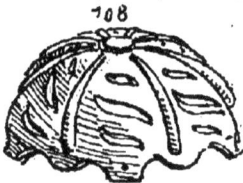

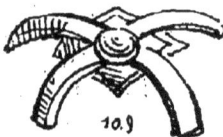

Toutes ces calottes, percées à jour, appartiennent déjà à l'époque où le casque avait été remplacé par le chapeau, dont elles formaient, comme il est dit ci-dessus, la défense intérieure.

110. Calotte en fer, allemande, pour doublure de chapeaux d'armes, du dix-septième siècle. — Arsenal impérial de Vienne.

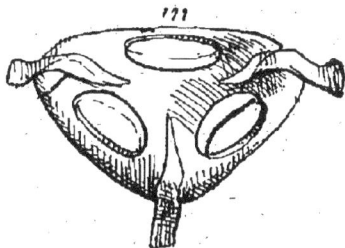

111. Carcasse pour doublure de tricorne militaire allemand, du commencement du dix-huitième siècle. — Musée historique du palais de Montbijou, à Berlin.

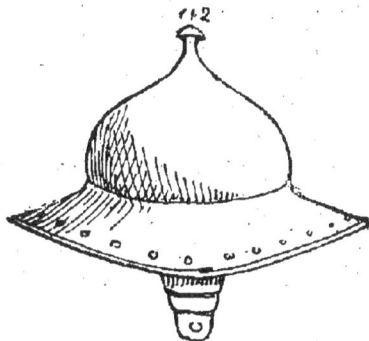

112. Chapeau d'armes, probablement italien, du dix-septième siècle. Il est en fer, à jugulaires, et orné de têtes de clous en cuivre. — Arsenal impérial de Vienne.

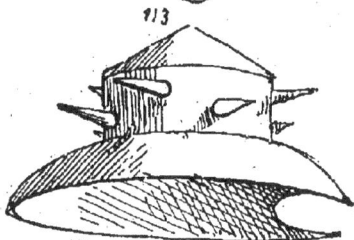

113. Chapeau d'armes allemand qui, selon l'attribution donnée à l'arsenal de la ville de Vienne, où il est conservé, servait dans les assauts des châteaux forts et des villes; où les larges bords étaient destinés à préserver la tête et les épaules des liquides bouillants dont les assiégés se servaient pour leur défense. L'auteur croit cependant que ce casque n'était porté que dans les cérémonies publiques, entrées des princes, etc.

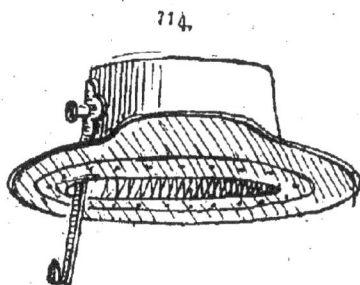

114. Chapeau de fer, à nasal, porté par les hommes de pied de la maison du roi Louis XIV (1643-1715). — H. 152, musée d'artillerie de Paris.

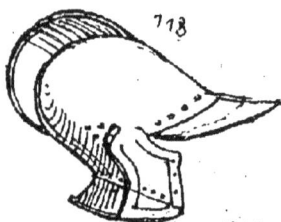

115. Bourguignote (*Burgunder Helm* en allem., *burgonet* en angl.) du seizième siècle. Cette espèce de casque se distingue par sa crête (*Kamm* en allem., *crest* en angl.), son avance (*Schirm* en allem, *schade* en angl.), ses oreillères (*Wangenklappen* en allem., *cheekpieces* en angl.), et son couvre-nuque (*Nackenschutz* en allem., *neckguard* en angl.).

116. Bourguignote du seizième siècle, avec gorgerin et mentonnière qui la font ressembler à l'armet. (Voir plus loin.) — H. 53, musée d'artillerie de Paris.

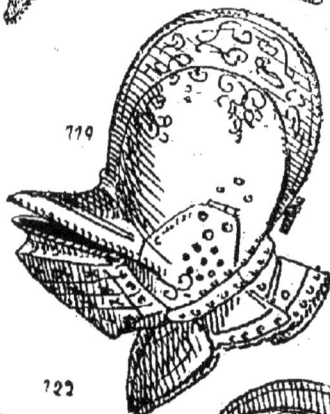

117. Bourguignote de la fin du seizième siècle. Même observation que pour le numéro précédent. — Arsenal de Soleure.

118. Bourguignote du seizième siècle, provenant de la collection du château de Laxembourg. — Arsenal impérial à Vienne.

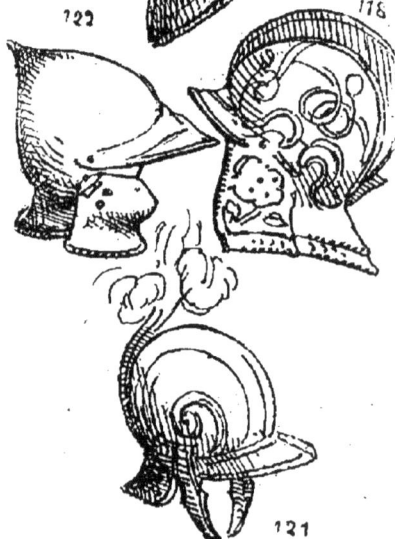

119. Bourguignote à gorgerin et mentonnière, à visière mobile, qui la font ressembler à l'armet. Beau travail allemand en fer gravé, du seizième siècle. — Collection d'Ambras.

121. Bourguignote allemande, d'après les *Descriptions des noces princières*, etc, de Wirzig, ouvrage imprimé à Vienne en 1571. — Musée industriel à Vienne.

122. Bourguignote-bacinet allemande, du seizième siècle, qui se distingue par le timbre pointu et sans crête. — Collection Az, à Lintz.

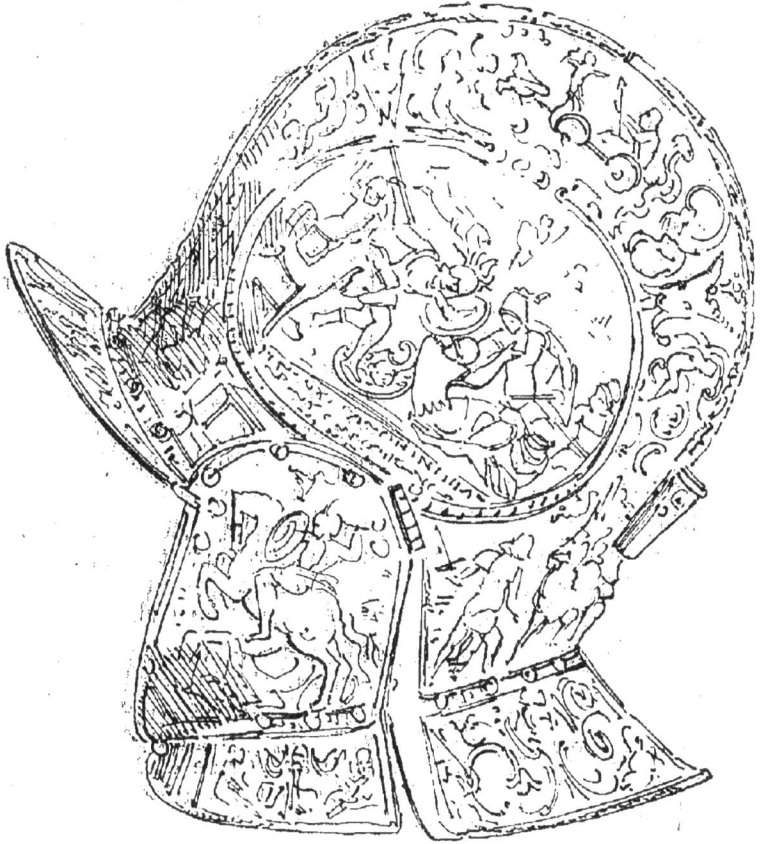

Bourguignote d'un magnifique travail italien en fer repoussé du seizième siècle, conservée à l'arsenal impérial de Vienne et provenant du château impérial de Laxembourg, près de Vienne. C'est le plus beau morceau de ce genre qui existe; il a été reproduit par la photographie d'une manière très-satisfaisante au musée industriel de Vienne.

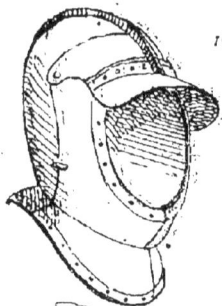

123. Bourguignote du dix-septième siècle. — Tour de Londres.

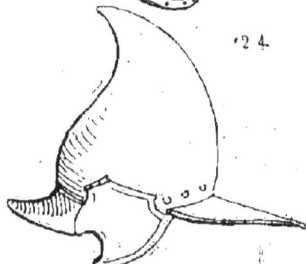

124. Bourguignote-cabasset en fer noirci, du commencement du dix-septième siècle. Elle est à avance, à oreillères et à couvre-nuque, mais sans crête; le timbre pointu a la forme du cabasset. — Arsenal de Genève.

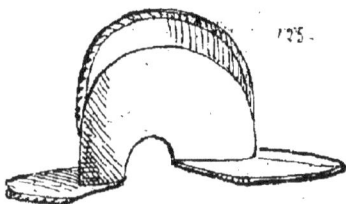

125. Bourguignote de siége, en fer très-lourd, de la fin du dix-septième siècle. L'avance et le couvre-nuque sont de forme plate. — H. 76, musée d'artillerie de Paris.

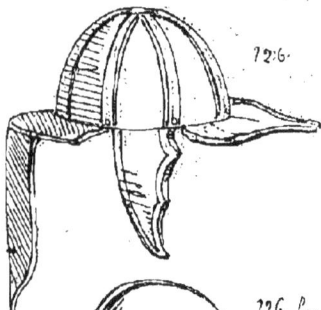

126. Bourguignote-calotte allemande, du commencement du dix-septième siècle. Elle est recouverte de velours rouge. — Musée Welf (Guelfe) à Hanovre.

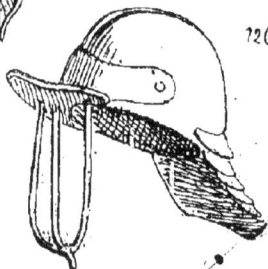

126 *bis.* Bourguignote-calotte de la fin du dix-septième siècle. Son avance est garnie d'une visière en forme de trident et le couvre-nuque est lamé. — Tour de Londres.

127

127. Bourguignote-calotte polonaise à nasal, du dix-septième
siècle. Ces casques ressemblent,
par l'espèce d'éventail qui orne
chaque côté du timbre, aux casques des cavaliers ailés (*Jazda
Skrzydlata*) de Sobieski. — Mu
sée de Dresde.

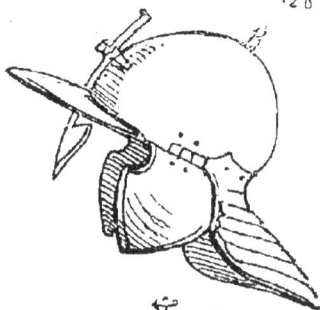

128

128. Bourguignote-calotte en fer,
à nasal mobile, à couvre-nuque
lamé, et appelé *zucchetto*, genre
de casque d'origine hongroise
connu en Hongrie sous le nom
de *dschycksc*. — Nº 366, arsenal royal de Turin.

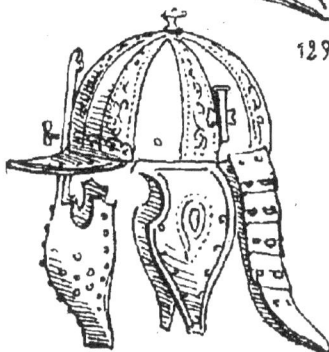

129

129. Bourguignote - calotte à
oreillères, couvre-nuque lamé
et nasal-visière, du milieu du
dix-septième siècle. Ce casque,
conservé à l'arsenal de Soleure,
y est désigné faussement comme
ayant appartenu à Vengi (1540);
il est en fer gravé et orné de
clous de cuivre.

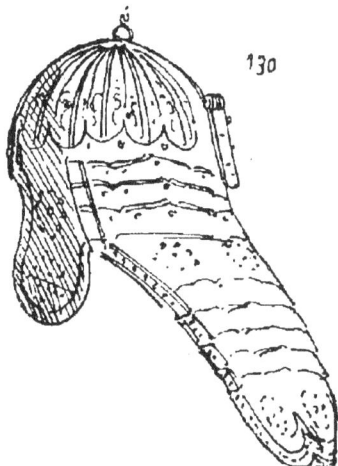

130

130. Bourguignote - calotte, à
oreillères et long couvre-nuque
lamé; elle est attribuée au comte
Charles de Tyrol, mort en 1602.
— Col. d'Ambras.

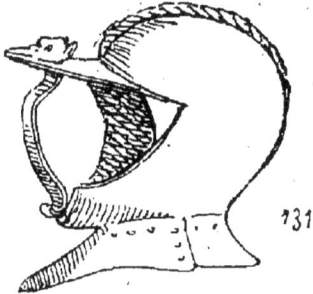

131. Bourguignote allemande du dix-septième siècle. Elle est à nasal fixe, et sa partie antérieure ressemble à celle des armets. — H. 56, musée d'artillerie de Paris.

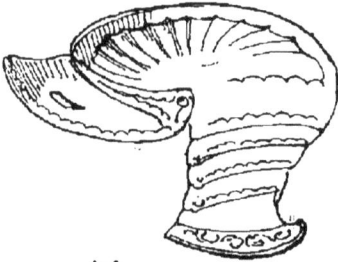

132. Bourguignote du dix-septième siècle, à couvre-nuque lamé, conservée dans la collection Llewelyn-Meyrick, où elle est attribuée au quinzième siècle. Ce casque, qui a été représenté ici vu de profil et de derrière, est remarquable par ses deux rangs d'ornements rappelant les cannelures.

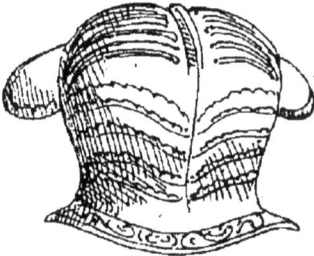

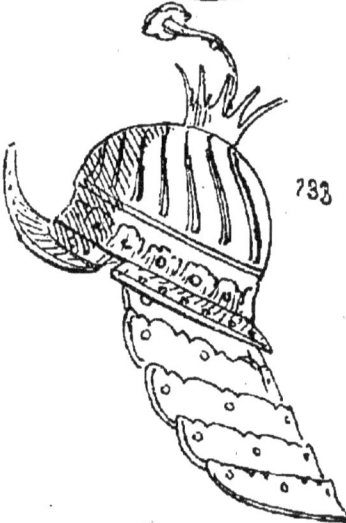

133. Bourguignote anglaise du dix-septième siècle, conservée au musée de Dresde, où elle est faussement attribuée à Édouard VI (1461-1483). Selon la tradition, elle aurait jadis fait partie de la collection d'armes de la Tour de Londres et aurait été donnée par Guillaume III à Jean-Georges Ier. L'avance, le couvre-nuque lamé et les ornements en clous dorés, aussi bien que le clinquant du cimier et du porte-plumet, indiquent à première vue la décadence du milieu du dix-septième siècle.

134. Morion (*Morian* en allem., *morion* en angl.). Ce casque italien d'homme de pied du seizième siècle, qui provient de l'arsenal de Genève, a appartenu au capitaine savoisien Chaffardin Branaulieu, tué sous les murs de Genève, ville qu'il avait voulu surprendre. L'arme est richement ornée de gravures à la pointe et d'une grande netteté. — Coll. de l'auteur.

135. Morion français d'homme de pied, de la fin du seizième siècle. Il est également couvert d'ornements gravés à la pointe. — Tour de Londres.

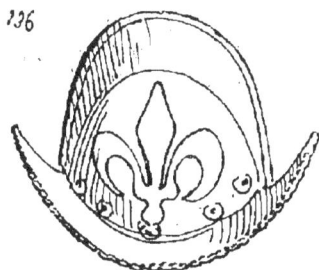

136. Morion allemand, de la fin du seizième siècle. La fleur de lis repoussée, qui orne ce casque porté par la compagnie civique de la ville de Munich, est le symbole de la Vierge et n'a point de rapport avec les armoiries des rois de France. — Arsenal de la ville de Munich et arsenal impérial à Vienne.

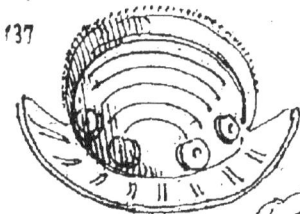

137. Morion allemand, d'après les *Descriptions des noces princières*, de Wirzig, ouvrage imprimé à Vienne en 1571. — Musée industriel à Vienne.

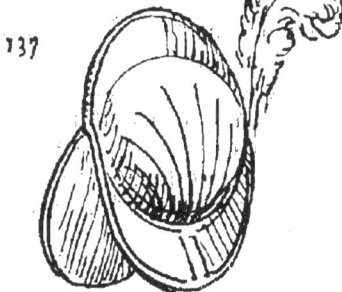

Le morion de l'armure attribuée, au Louvre, au roi de France Henri IV (1559-1610), est un peu plus haut, et ses bords moins larges sont à pans coupés. (V. p. 285, n° 95.)

137 *bis*. Id.   Id.

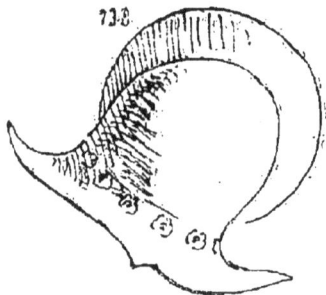

138. Morion allemand du seizième siècle. C'est une forme peu commune. — Arsenal de la ville de Munich.

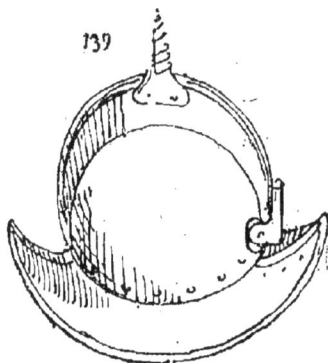

139. Morion allemand de la fin du seizième siècle, conservé au musée national à Brunswick, où il est désigné comme appartenant au douzième siècle ! La grosse vis sur la crête le fait tout à fait différer des morions ordinaires.

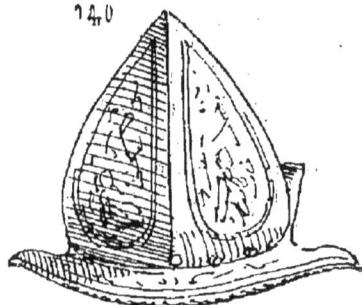

140. Cabasset (*Birnenhelm* en allem., *pear-kask* en angl.) du seizième siècle, en fer richement gravé et à porte-plumet. — Coll. de M. le comte de Nieuwerkerque.

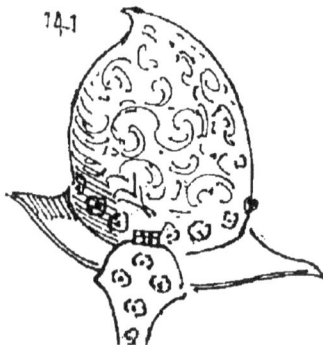

141. Cabasset allemand à oreillères, en fer gravé, du seizième siècle. Cette même forme, mais à bords différents, était très-répandue en France et en Italie. — Arsenal de la ville de Munich.

142. Cabasset italien d'homme
de pied, du seizième siècle, en
fer repoussé, ciselé et damasquiné d'or. Le sujet représente
Persée délivrant Androméde,
pièce magnifique. — H. 100,
musée d'artillerie de Paris.

143. Cabasset italien d'homme
de pied, du seizième siècle; il
est richement gravé à la pointe.
— Tour de Londres.

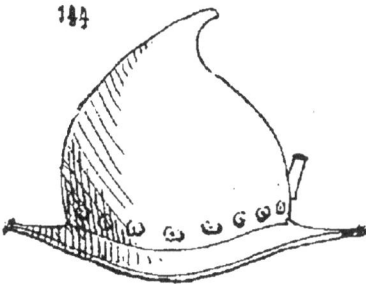

144. Cabasset allemand en fer
noirci et à porte-plumet, du
seizième siècle. Ce casque n'a
d'autres ornements que les
clous - rosettes en cuivre. —
Coll. de M. le comte de Nieuwerkerque.

145. Cabasset italien en fer repoussé, d'un très-beau travail,
du seizième siècle.

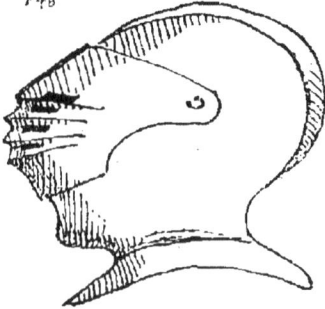

146. Armet (*Visierhelm* en allem., *helmet* en angl.) de la seconde moitié du quinzième siècle. L'armet est le casque le plus perfectionné ; il est composé du timbre surmonté de la crête, de la vue, du nasal et du ventail, dont l'ensemble se nommait mézail, et du gorgerin. — H. 28, musée d'artillerie de Paris.

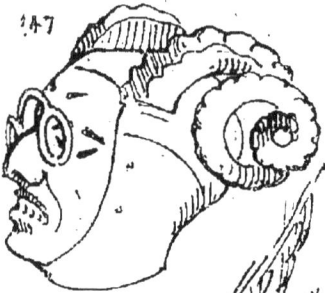

147. Armet du seizième siècle, en fer, et avec cornes naturelles de bélier ; il a fait partie de l'armure du bouffon de Henri VIII (1509-1547). — Tour de Londres.

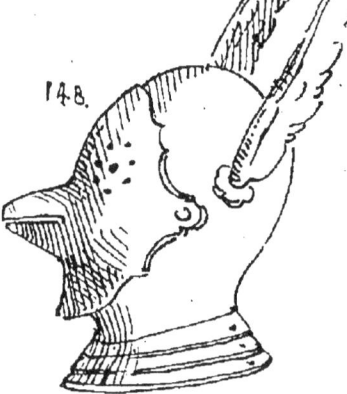

148. Armet à plumets, du seizième siècle, d'après le *Weisskunig*.

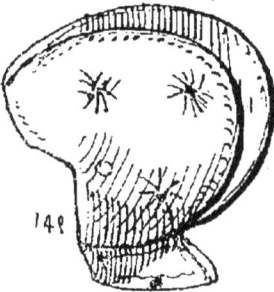

149. Armet du seizième siècle, en cuir recouvert d'ornements produits par le fer du relieur. La partie inférieure du mézail manque, ainsi que la visière. — Arsenal de Genève. C'est la seule arme de ce genre que l'auteur connaisse.

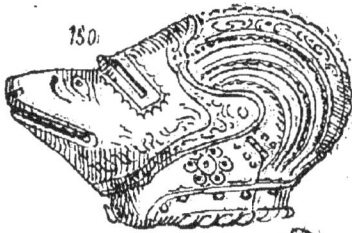

150. Armet, à timbre cannelé et à visière pivotante, d'une armure maximilienne, travail allemand de la première moitié du seizième siècle. — Arsenal impérial de Vienne. Une semblable pièce dans la collection de l'auteur.

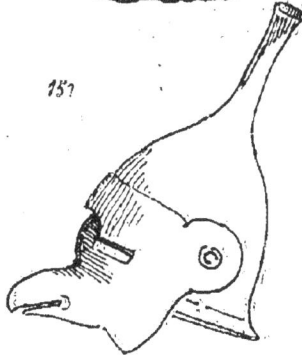

151. Armet allemand du seizième siècle, d'après le *Triomphe de Maximilien*, par Burckmayer, de 1517. La visière à pivot représente dans sa partie inférieure un bec d'aigle.

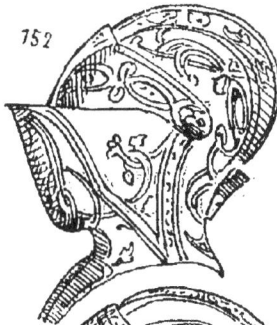

152. Armet à visière pivotante et à haute mentonnière (*Barthaube*), travail allemand de la seconde moitié du seizième siècle. Il est richement damasquiné et gravé. — Arsenal impérial de Vienne.

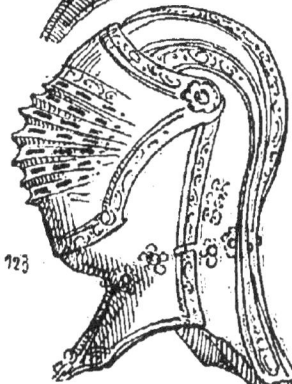

153. Armet à visière pivotante et à haute mentonnière. Travail allemand de la seconde moitié du seizième siècle. Ce casque est richement gravé à la pointe. — Arsenal impérial de Vienne.

154. Armet de la fin du seizième siècle. Le timbre repoussé représente une composition maritime et la visière est grillée. — Armeria real à Madrid.

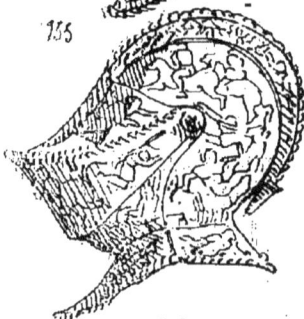

155. Armet italien de la fin du seizième siècle. Pièce richement travaillée dans toutes ses parties. — Musée d'artillerie de Paris.

156. Casque italien à l'antique, dit *caschetto*, du seizième siècle, en fer repoussé, ciselé et damasquiné. Pièce magnifique. — H. 131, musée d'artillerie de Paris.

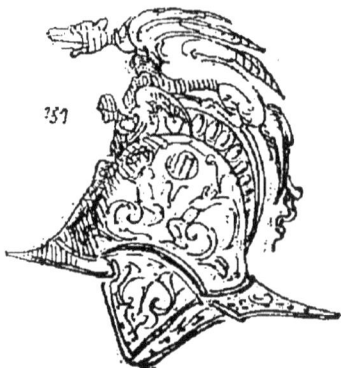

157. Casque italien dit à l'antique, mais qui a plutôt la forme de la bourguignote, du milieu du seizième siècle. D'abord conservé à la bibliothèque impériale, il fait maintenant partie du musée d'artillerie de Paris, sous le n° H., 129.

158. Casque russe (?) dit à l'antique, et dont le travail a toutes
les apparences d'une œuvre italienne. — Musée de Tsarskoe-
Selo à St-Pétersbourg.

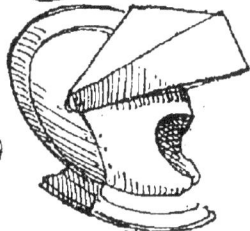

159. Armet suisse du commencement du dix-septième siècle,
en fer poli, de la compagnie de
cavalerie de la ville de Genève.
— Arsenal de Genève.

160. Armet allemand en fer poli,
de la première moitié du seizième siècle. La visière représente le visage d'un homme à
moustaches. — Coll. Llewelyn-
Meyrick.

161. Casque turc à nasal mobile,
en fer damasquiné d'or, du quinzième siècle; il a appartenu à
Bajazet II. — H. 173, musée
d'artillerie de Paris.

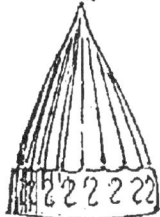

162. Casque turc du quinzième
siècle, trouvé à Rhodes. — H.
180, musée d'artillerie de Paris.

163. Casque albanais attribué
au prince Georges Castriota
Scanderberg, mort en 1467. La
tête de chèvre et les ornements
sont en cuivre.

164. Casque turc du seizième siècle, ayant appartenu au serasquier Soliman. Cette arme est à nasal, à oreillères et à couvre-nuque. — Coll. Llewelyn-Meyrick.

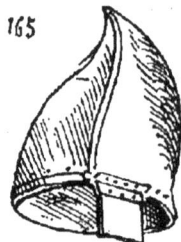

165. Casque en fer, à clous de cuivre, dont est coiffé Jean Ziska (1420), sur un tableau de la bibliothèque de Genève. On ignore si le peintre a copié ce casque d'après un dessin de l'époque ou s'il est le produit de sa fantaisie[1].

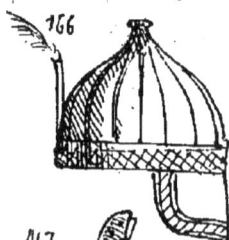

166. Casque persan, d'après un manuscrit exécuté vers 1600 : la copie du *Schah-Nameh*, ou Livre royal, poëme composé par Fisdüsi sous le règne de Mahmoud (999-1030).

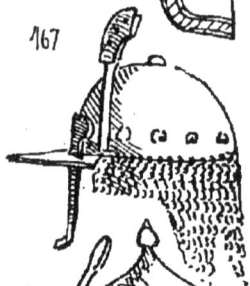

167. Casque mongol, probablement du quinzième siècle. — N° G.138, musée d'artillerie.

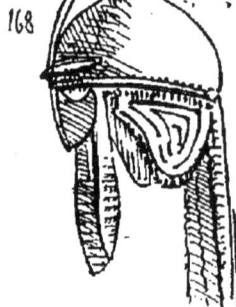

168. Casque indien de Délhy. Le nasal est mobile et le couvre-nuque composé de petites plaques.

---

1. Ziska (borgne), le chef des Hussites ou Taborites, né en 1360, mort en 1424, perdit son dernier œil en 1421. La charnière que l'on voit était destinée à cacher la cavité de son œil gauche perdu déjà avant la mort de Hus.

169. Casque mongol en fer damasquiné d'or, à nasal mobile et à couvre-nuque, trouvé sur le champ de bataille de Koulikowo (1380). — Musée Tsarskoe-Selo à Saint-Pétersbourg.

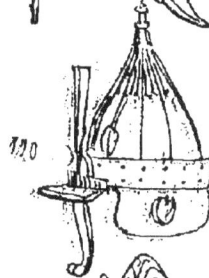

170. Casque russe à nasal mobile et à oreillères, du quinzième siècle; les riches ornements sont en cuivre doré. — H. 176, musée d'artillerie de Paris.

171. Casque russe à nasal mobile, à oreillères et à couvre-nuque très-développés. —Musée Tsarskoe-Selo à Saint-Pétersbourg.

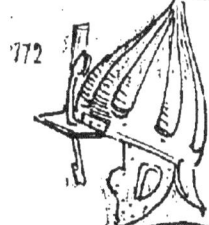

172. Casque hongrois à nasal, à oreillères et à couvre-nuque, du seizième siècle. Cette arme a appartenu à Nicolao Zrinyi, le héros qui s'est fait ensevelir sous les décombres de Sigeth[1], en 1566. — Coll. d'Ambras.

173. Casque italien, sorte de bourguignote provenant d'Ascanier Sforza Pallavicino, qui prit une part importante à la bataille navale de Lépante (1571). — Musée Tsarskoe-Selo à Saint-Pétersbourg.

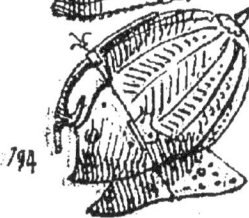

174. Casque pot-en-tête à nasal mobile, à oreillères et à couvre-nuque-gorgerin, en fer très-épais gravé, doré et orné de coquillages et têtes de clous dorés, du commencement du dix-septième siècle. La vis du nasal forme une fleur de lis. — Arsenal de Soleure.

1. Chanté par le poëte allemand Kœrner dans une tragédie célèbre.

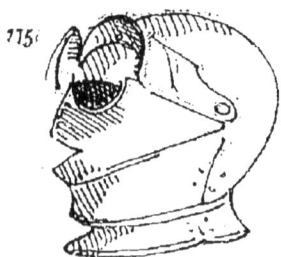

175. Armet savoisien en fer noirci, du commencement du dix-septième siècle; il a été pris sur la troupe de Branaulieu-Chaffardin, tué en 1602 sous les murs de Genève, qu'il voulait surprendre. — Arsenal de Genève et collection de l'auteur.

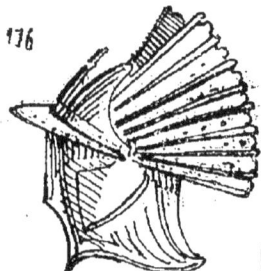

176. Casque polonais à ailettes, du dix-septième siècle, dont les troupes, sous Sobieski, appelées les cavaliers ailés (*Jazda Skrzydlata*), étaient armées. (Voir aussi nº 127, aux pages précédentes.) — Musée Tsarskoe-Selo à Saint-Pétersbourg.

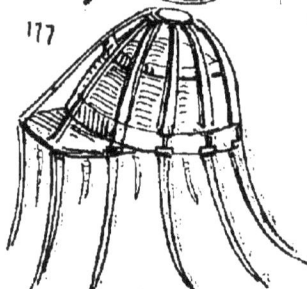

177. Casque de soldat français sous Henri IV. Il est pourvu d'une avance ou visière plate et garni tout autour de lames de fer. — Tour de Londres.

178. Casque allemand de tournois, du commencement du dix-septième siècle. Cette arme, qui est surmontée d'une crête et pourvue d'un couvre-nuque et d'une vis destinée à visser le manteau d'armes à mentonnière, a la forme de la salade du quinzième siècle. — H. 135, musée d'artillerie de Paris.

179. Armet du commencement du dix-septième siècle. Ce casque ressemble à l'armet savoisien ci-dessus (nº 175). — Tour de Londres.

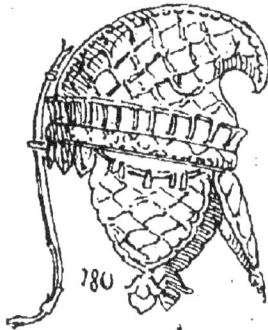

180. Casque indien à nasal mobile, à oreillères et à couvre-nuque, le tout orné de pierreries et très-richement travaillé. — Musée Tsarskoe-Selo à Saint-Pétersbourg.

181. Casque polygare (Hindoustan méridional) à nasal fixe, à oreillères et couvre-nuque-camail très-développés. — Coll. Llewelyn-Meyrick.

182. Casque mahratte (Hindoustan). Cette arme, dotée d'un long nasal mobile de forme singulière, est aussi à camail dont les parties très-développées protégent et enveloppent toute la tête; le couvre-nuque descend en forme de queue jusque sur les reins.

183. Casque mongol à avance et cimier porte-plumet. C'est une très-belle arme défensive, dont le travail consiste en riches ornements damasquinés.— Musée Tsarskoe-Selo à Saint-Pétersbourg.

184.

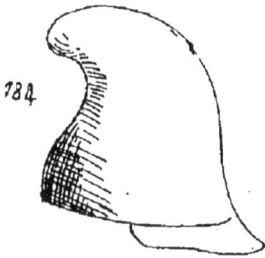

184. Casque japonais à couvre-nuque, provenant de la bibliothèque impériale. — 183, musée d'artillerie de Paris. Un casque samnite en bronze, au musée d'Erbach, ressemble beaucoup dans sa forme à cette arme. (V. p. 138.)

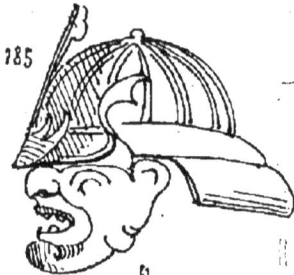

185.

185. Casque japonais en fer laqué, encore actuellement en usage. Il est à nasal fixe, à couvre-nuque, et pourvu d'un masque qui protége entièrement la figure. — G. 140, musée d'artillerie de Paris.

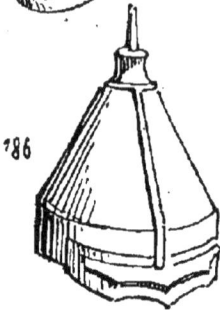

186.

186. Casque chinois conique, à avance. — Tour de Londres.

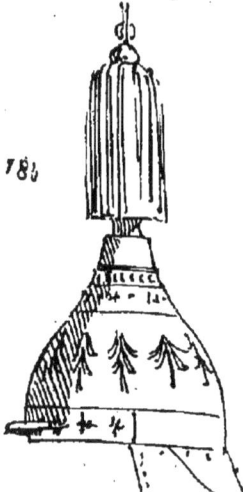

187. Casque en or et pierres précieuses, ayant appartenu à l'empereur de Chine ; cette arme a été prise à Pékin en 1860. — G. 142, musée d'artillerie de Paris.

187.

On remarque que la forme des casques japonais et chinois est restée la même durant des siècles et que ces armes n'offrent pas l'intérêt qui s'attache aux armes européennes pour l'étude du costume militaire aux différentes époques historiques.

26.

LE BOUCLIER

Cette arme défensive (dont le nom dérive du vieux allemand *Buckel*, bosse, et non pas du celtique *bwa*, couvrir, réuni au germain *leder*, cuir, étymologie de dictionnaire tirée aux cheveux) s'appelait d'abord en allemand *Scill*, aujourd'hui *Schild*, et en anglais *shield* et *buckler*.

On a vu ce qu'étaient les différents boucliers antiques, dont les formes ont peu varié.

Les boucliers les plus anciens des peuples de race germanique (Francs, Saxons, Alémans, Burgondes, etc., etc.) étaient grands, de forme carrée, fabriqués en bois, ordinairement de branches d'osier, et plaqués de bronze. Durant l'âge dit du fer ces boucliers étaient ronds, et avaient ordinairement une *bosse* en ceintre, appelée en français ombilic d'*umbo* (*Schildnahel* ou *Schildbuckel* en allemand, *shild-navel* en anglais).

Le couvercle de l'*Antiphonaire* de saint Grégoire, de la fin du huitième siècle, conservé à Saint-Gall, représente aussi des combattants armés de petits boucliers carrés et à ombilics pointus ; mais le caractère de cette sculpture montre trop de réminiscences antiques ; il pourrait bien provenir d'un dyptique.

Les *Leges Longobardorum*, manuscrit du neuvième siècle, représentent le roi avec la longue targe allemande, que l'on retrouve encore au quatorzième siècle, tandis que le *Codex aureus evangelicus* du neuvième siècle, aussi bien que le manuscrit de Wessobrunn, de la même époque, montrent de nouveau la rondache à ombilic qui se retrouve encore dans le *Prudentius* et dans le *Psalterium* du dixième siècle, des bibliothèques de Londres et de Stuttgard, ainsi que sur la tapisserie de Bayeux du onzième siècle, où le bouclier en forme de cœur allongé, et quelquefois de la hauteur d'un homme, paraît l'arme du Normand, et la rondache celle de l'Anglo-Saxon.

On voit encore dans le *Prudentius Psychomachia*, etc., du dixième siècle, de la bibliothèque du musée britannique, des guerriers anglo-saxons armés de rondaches à ombilic; mais un chevalier de la *Biblia sacra*, manuscrit attribué, à la Bibliothèque impériale de Paris, au dixième siècle, porte déjà le *petit écu*, forme de bouclier qui ne régna universellement qu'au temps de saint Louis (1226-1270).

Le duc de Bourchard, de Souabe (965), est représenté à la basilique de Zurich avec un bouclier qui rappelle ceux des Normands de la tapisserie de Bayeux, déjà mentionnée, et ce même genre de bouclier se retrouve dans les mains d'un chevalier sur le bas-relief du cloître de Saint-Aubin, à Angers, et dans celles de la statue d'un des fondateurs du dôme de Naumbourg, du onzième siècle. Le comte de Barcelone, don Ramon Bérenger IV (1140), porte sur son sceau ce même genre de bouclier, qui se retrouve aussi dans les peintures murales du dôme de Brunswick, exécutées sous Henri le Lion, mort en 1195. Ces grands boucliers étaient toujours à deux *énarmes* (*Handgriffe* en allemand), tandis que les boucliers antiques et particulièrement les grecs, n'en avaient ordinairement qu'un seul. Les longs boucliers étaient en outre pourvus de la *guige* ou *guiche* (*Hangband* en allemand), qui servait à les suspendre sur l'épaule gauche, la pointe en arrière.

Les plus anciens de ces boucliers germaniques, les grands boucliers carrés, dont aucun n'est parvenu intact jusqu'à nous, paraissent avoir été matelassés à l'intérieur, et confectionnés en bois, revêtu de cuir, le tout renforcé par une monture en fer, peinte et ornée de figures bizarres ; il a créé l'usage des *armoiries personnelles*, comme on l'a vu pages 58 à 60 au Chapitre historique. Plusieurs débris de ces boucliers se trouvent représentés au Chapitre des armes de l'âge du fer, ainsi que le petit bouclier rond des Francs.

Le *petit écu* ou le bouclier triangulaire ne paraît guère en France qu'au treizième siècle, sous le règne de saint Louis; il était alors aussi large que haut. Le bouclier dont on se servait à cette époque en Allemagne était déjà plus grand, tel qu'on peut le voir à la statue de Henri II, au monument funéraire élevé à Breslau à l'église de Saint-Vincent. Le bouclier anglais du milieu du quatorzième siècle ressemble encore au petit écu, et ne mesure que deux pieds. C'est à sa suite qu'arrive la première *rondelle* à poing, dont la grandeur ne dépasse pas 1 pied $^1/_4$ et qui s'est conservée jusqu'au seizième siècle.

Les *boucliers bourguignons* du commencement du quinzième siècle (Voir page 310, n° 13) sont ordinairement triangulaires et à hauteur d'appui. Le *pavois*, d'origine allemande, et dans lequel se retrouve la forme primitive du bouclier germanique de la plus haute antiquité, un peu ovale en haut et carré en bas, apparaît vers le quatorzième siècle. La *longue targe* en bois et en *peau* de ce même siècle se distingue facilement de la petite targe du quinzième siècle [1], qui est échancrée.

Au seizième siècle, où en Allemagne comme ailleurs le bouclier n'était presque plus en usage, on en rencontre cependant quelques-uns dont la forme imite de nouveau celle d'un cœur, mais à trois pointes en haut. C'est à cette même époque, ainsi qu'à la fin du quinzième siècle, qu'appartiennent les *manteaux d'armes*, les *rondaches*, les *rondelles* et les *targettes* à crochet, dont beaucoup montrent l'empreinte de mains d'artistes. La plupart des rondaches italiennes, ciselées et repoussées, n'étaient cependant point destinées à la guerre : c'étaient des armes de parure et de panoplies.

---

1. Targe ou targue, de l'arabe *dardy* et *tarcha*. On appelle encore aujourd'hui targe, à Toulon et à Marseille, le bouclier dont le matelot est armé dans les joutes navales.

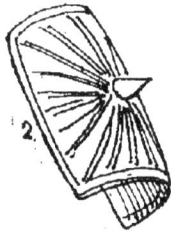

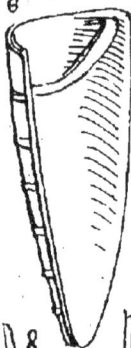

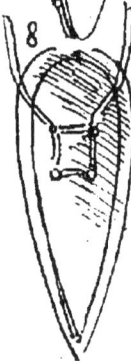

1. Bouclier (oriental?)[1], d'après la colonne Théodose (l'empereur Théodose I, dit le Grand, né en 346, est mort en 396, l'année où commençait l'empire d'Orient).

2. Bouclier carré et convexe à ombilic, d'après l'*Antiphonaire* de Saint-Gall, du huitième siècle.

3. Bouclier-rondache à ombilic (*Rundschild* en allem., *rundshield* en angl.), en usage du huitième siècle au onzième siècle, d'après le manuscrit de *Wessobrunn* de 840, de l'*Aureus evangelicus* de saint Emeran de 870, du *Codex aureus* du neuvième siècle, du *Prudentius Psychomachia* du dixième siècle, de l'*Aelfric* et de la tapisserie de Bayeux, etc.

4. Bouclier-targe lombardo-allemand du neuvième siècle, d'après les *Leges Longobardorum*.

5. Bouclier appelé en France *normand*, du dixième siècle, d'après une statuette de la collection de M. le comte de Nieuwerkerke.

6. Bouclier allemand du onzième siècle, d'après le *Jeremias Apocalypsis*.

7. Bouclier normand, d'après la tapisserie de Bayeux.

8. Le bouclier normand vu à l'envers, où sont figurés les énarmes-poignées et la guige ou guiche qui servaient à suspendre le bouclier sur l'épaule gauche.

1. Les croissants ne peuvent pas indiquer l'origine musulmane, puisque Mahomet est né seulement l'an 570 de notre ère.

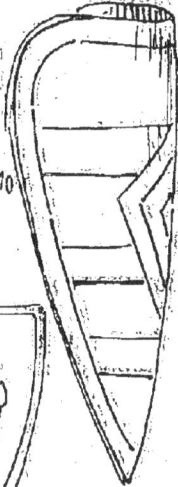

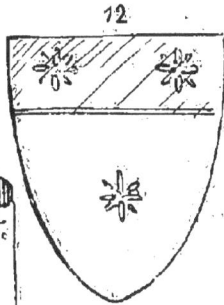

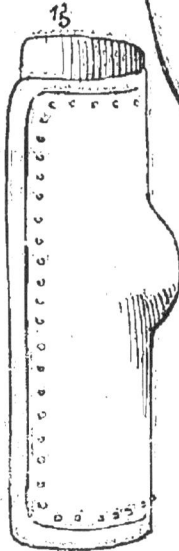

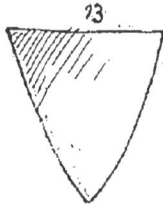

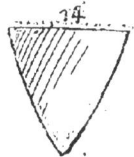

9. Petit écu allemand de 45 cent. de hauteur, du douzième siècle, d'après une monnaie à l'effigie de Henri le Lion, mort en 1195.

10. Bouclier allemand convexe, de 80 cent. à peu près, d'après les peintures murales au dôme de Brunswick, exécutées sous Henri le Lion, mort en 1195.

11. Bouclier allemand de 60 cent., d'après les peintures murales au dôme de Brunswick, exécutées sous Henri le Lion, mort en 1195.

12. Bouclier du douzième siècle, de 52 cent. sur 74, d'après une pierre tombale au couvent de Steinbach, actuellement dans la chapelle du château d'Erbach, à Erbach.

13. Bouclier triangulaire allemand, d'après le manuscrit *Tristan et Isolde* du treizième siècle. On le retrouve encore dans l'armement bourguignon du quinzième siècle, si on se rapporte au manuscrit de la bibliothèque de l'Arsenal, à Paris.

14. Petit écu en usage sous le règne de saint Louis (1226-1270).

15. Targe semi-cylindrique à ombilic rond, du treizième siècle, d'après une miniature de l'époque, au musée britannique. Cette targe sans l'ombilic se retrouve dans l'armement du quinzième siècle, comme le démontre l'exemplaire conservé au même musée. V. aussi, n° 4, targe lombarde du neuvième siècle, de la page précédente.

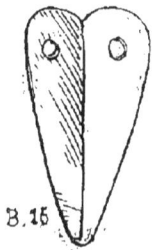

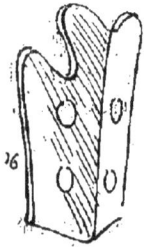

15 *bis.* Targe allemande à visières, de la fin du quatorzième
siècle, d'après un tableau à l'é-
glise de Saint-Michel, à Schwae-
bisch-Hall.

16. Targe allemande à visières,
de la fin du quatorzième siècle.
— Cathédrale de Bamberg.

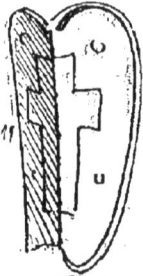

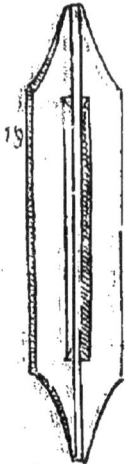

17.   Id.   id.

18. Targe espagnole de la fin du
quatorzième siècle, d'après une
peinture murale à la cathédrale
de Mondonédo, qui représente
le massacre des Innocents.

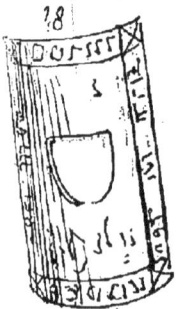

19. Bouclier allemand de la hauteur de l'homme, d'après un
combat singulier dit jugement
de Dieu, du *Codex* du maître
d'armes de Tolhofer, du quinzième siècle.

20. Bouclier espagnol, d'après
une miniature de 1480.

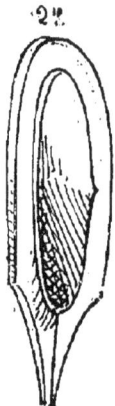

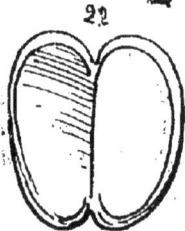

21. Bouclier, d'après une gravure sur bois du quinzième siècle. — Cabinet d'Estampes de
Munich.

22. Bouclier hispano-musulman
du quinzième siècle. — Le musée d'artillerie de Paris possède
une targe semblable en cuir.
(V. page 315, n° 45.)

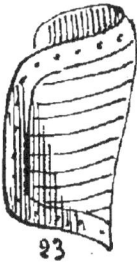 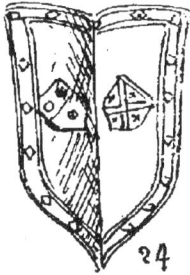

23. Bouclier allemand, d'après le *Theurdanck*, publié au commencement du seizième siècle, à Augsbourg.

24. Bouclier en acier du seizième siècle, de 58 cent. de hauteur, orné de deux écussons gravés, et tout au tour de grosses têtes de vis carrés. — Musée historique du palais Montbijou, à Berlin.

25. Pavois d'assaut allemand (*Setzschild* ou *Sturmwand* en allem.), de 126 cent. sur 188, du quinzième siècle. Il est en bois couvert de peau et peint en rouge et en jaune. Les pointes et la garniture intérieure sont en fer. — Musée de Sigmaringen.

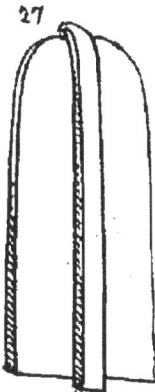 

26. Pavois d'assaut allemand, de 110 cent. sur 180, du quinzième siècle. Bois recouvert de peau. La peinture représente les armoiries de la ville de Ravensbourg en noir sur fond blanc. — Arsenal de Berlin.

27. Pavois d'assaut allemand du quinzième siècle. — I 1, musée d'artillerie de Paris.

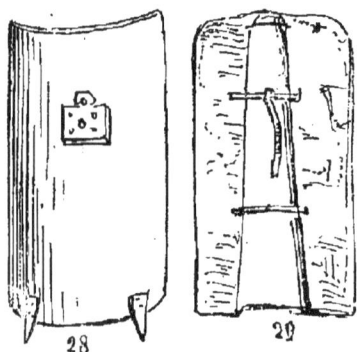

28. Pavois d'assaut suisse, de 180 cent. de hauteur, de la fin du quinzième siècle. — Arsenal de Berne.

29 et **30.** Pavois d'assaut allemand, de 65 cent. sur 112, du quinzième siècle, provenant de l'ancien arsenal d'Ens (Autriche). Le sujet peint représente saint George. — Col. Az, à Lintz. C'est une pièce précieuse pour sa belle conservation et sa bonne peinture.

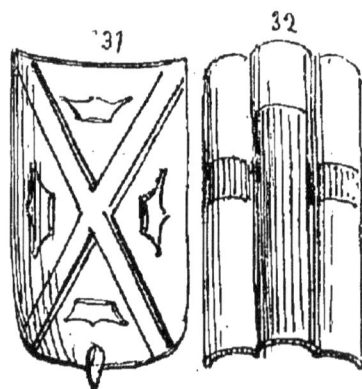

31. Targe suisse ou allemande (*Tartsche* en allem.), de 48 cent. sur 100, en bois recouvert de peau. Elle est plus petite que le pavois d'assaut, arrondie en bas, et n'a qu'une seule pointe en fer. C'était probablement le bouclier d'un archer. — Arsenal de Berne.

32. Targe allemande, trilobée, en bois recouvert de peau, du quinzième siècle. — Musée de Sigmaringen.

27

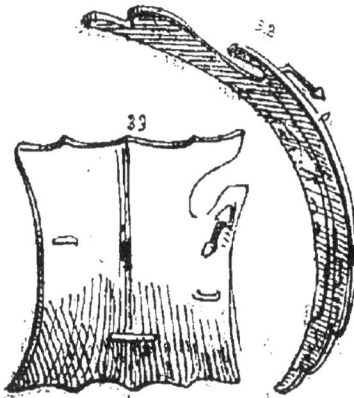

33. Targe allemande, de joute, de la fin du quinzième siècle, représentée de profil, à l'envers et de face. Elle est en bois et en peau, ornée de peintures, et a appartenu au landgrave de Thuringe. — Cathédrale de Marbourg.

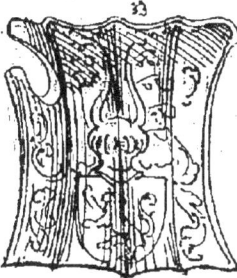

34. Targe allemande du quinzième siècle, en bois et en cuir, et ornée de peintures. — Tour de Londres.

35. Targe allemande ondulée du quinzième siècle, en bois et en cuir, de 65 cent. de grandeur. — Musée d'artillerie de Paris.

36. Targe allemande de joute du quinzième siècle, en bois et cuir, de 35 cent. sur 45. — Musée d'artillerie de Paris.

37. Targe allemande de joute du quinzième siècle, en bois et en cuir avec inscription, et décorée en polychromie d'un sujet de tournoi, remarquable au point de vue archéologique par les casques dont les chevaliers sont coiffés. — Musée d'artillerie de Paris.

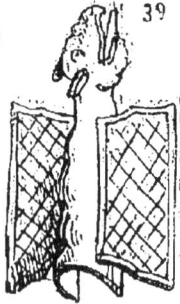

38. Targe allemande, en bois et peau, peinte et argentée, reproduite d'après les aquarelles que Glackenthon a exécutées au commencement du seizième siècle, d'après les armes et armures des arsenaux de Maximilien I. — Col. d'Ambras, à Vienne.

39. Targe toute argentée, id.

40. Targe peinte et argentée, id.

41. Targe peinte et dorée, id.

42. Petite targe convexe probablement espagnole, du seizième siècle. — Armerial de Madrid.

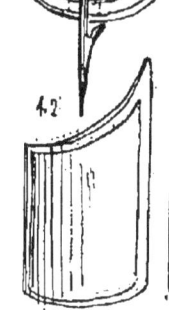

43. Targe allemande, de 80 cent. sur 90, du seizième siècle. Elle est en bois et tissu, recouvert de peintures. — Musée de Cluny.

44. Targe mauresque. — Armerial de Madrid.

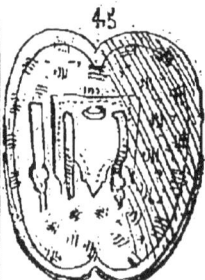

45. Targe hispano-mauresque (adarga), de la fin du seizième siècle, entièrement en cuir souple; elle mesure 75 cent. sur 95. — Musée d'artillerie de Paris. Voir aussi aux pages précédentes, n° 22.

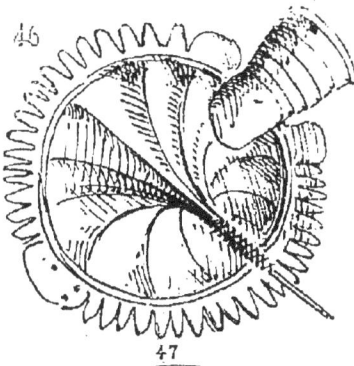

46. Rondache allemande à gantelet et à lanterne, du quinzième siècle; elle servait dans les combats nocturnes. — I. 35, musée d'artillerie de Paris. L'arsenal de Hambourg possède également une semblable rondache à lanterne, mais sans gantelet. Voir aussi, à la page 320, la rondelle n° 61.

47. Rondache italienne du quinzième siècle, en bois et en cuir, recouverte de peintures polychromes. L'arsenal de Luzerne possède 21 de ces boucliers conquis par Frischhans Theïlig de Luzerne à la bataille de Jornico (Gornis) en 1478. Le décor du bouclier reproduit ici représente les armoiries du premier duc de Milan, Jean Galeazzo Visconti, dont il montre aussi les initiales couronnées.

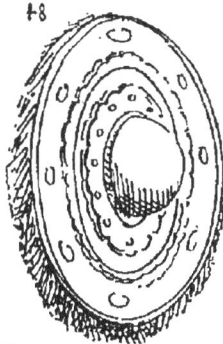

48. Rondache allemande de la fin du quinzième siècle, d'après les aquarelles de Glackenthon mentionnées plus haut. — Col. d'Ambras.

49. Rondache anglaise du commencement du seizième siècle. Ce bouclier, dont le diamètre a 45 cent., est en fer et armé d'un petit canon à main, à mèche, et se chargeant au moyen d'une boîte mobile, espèce de veuglaire. La Tour de Londres possède 25 de ces boucliers dont il est fait déjà mention dans l'inventaire dressé sous Édouard VI (1547).

50

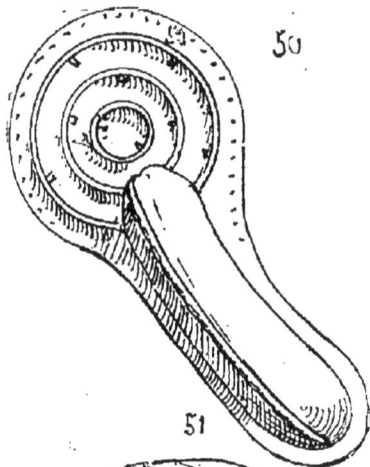

50. Rondelle, brise-épée à brassard, en fer d'une seule pièce.
— Musée d'artillerie de Paris et
arsenal impérial de Vienne.

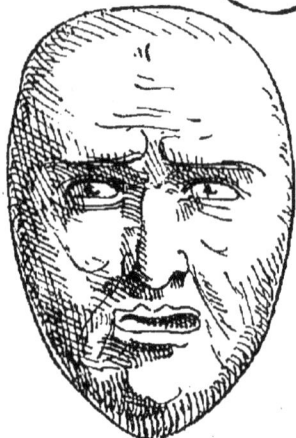

51

51. Rondache italienne du seizième siècle, qui paraît avoir
servi uniquement de parure.
Elle est d'une seule pièce et en
haut-relief repoussé. — Musée
de Turin.

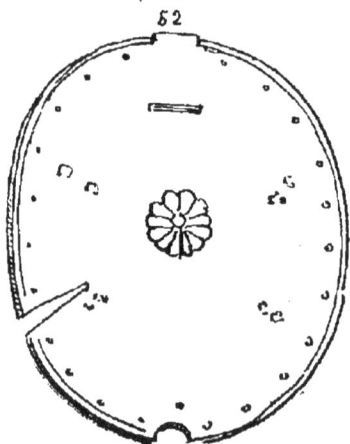

52

52. Rondache d'homme de pied
en acier noirci, de 2 pieds sur
1 1/2 de grandeur, du dix-septième siècle. Ce bouclier, qui
pèse douze livres, est à visière et
fente destinée à passer l'épée.
— Col. Llewelyn-Meyrick, à
Goodrich-Court.

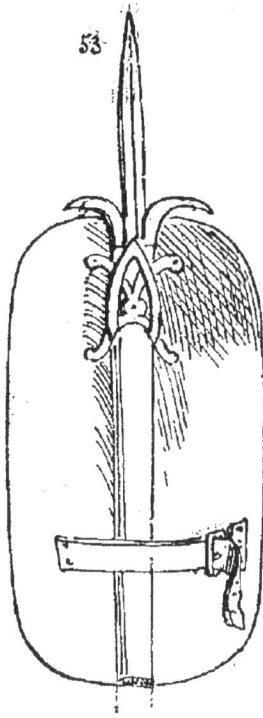

53. Bouclier italien, de 70 cent., avec épée de 50 cent. de longueur, du seizième siècle. Le dessin ci-contre le représente à l'envers. — Musée de Dresde.

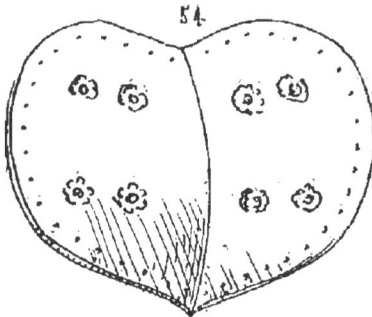

54. Bouclier allemand de 50 cent. sur 60 ; il est en fer noirci et appartient au seizième siècle. De la forme d'un cœur, sa partie centrale rentre en ligne concave. — Col. du château de Loevenburg ou Wilhelmshœhe, près Cassel.

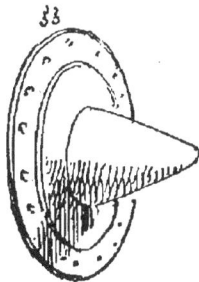

55. Rondelle à poing (*Faustschild* en allem., *fist-shild* en angl.), allemande, du quinzième siècle, d'après des gravures contemporaines, au cabinet des estampes à Munich.

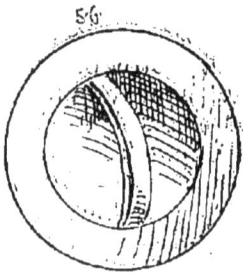

56. Rondelle à poing (*Faustschild* en allem., *fist-shild* en angl.), anglaise, du milieu du quatorzième siècle, dite *pavoisienne*, de 1 pied 1/4 de diamètre. D'après la sculpture d'un peigne de l'époque.

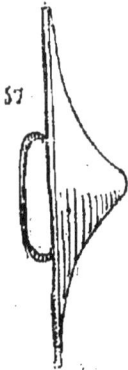

57. Rondelle à poing, allemande, de 30 cent. de diamètre, de la fin du quinzième siècle. — Arsenal de la ville de Munich.

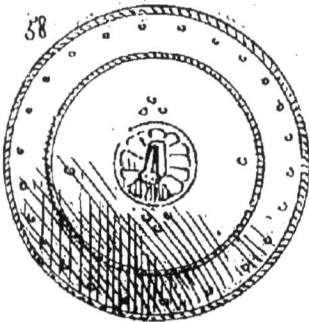

58. Rondelle à poing, à crochet brise-épée; elle mesure 27 cent. en diamètre, et appartient à la fin du quinzième siècle. — Col. Llewelyn-Meyrick.

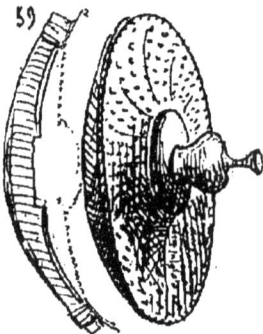

59. Rondelle à poing de 25 cent. de diamètre, en acier, du quinzième siècle. Elle est attribuée au comte de Richmond (Henri VII, roi d'Angleterre en 1485). — I. 5, musée d'artillerie de Paris.

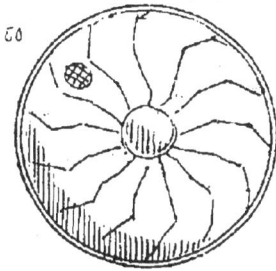

60. Rondelle à poing, turque, en fer, du seizième siècle, de 30 cent. de diamètre. Elle est marquée d'un monogramme qui représente le nom d'*Allah* (Dieu), estampille que l'on retrouve sur beaucoup d'armes provenant de l'arsenal de Mahmoud II. — Musée historique du palais de Montbijou, à Berlin. Une semblable pièce au musée Erbach, à Erbach.

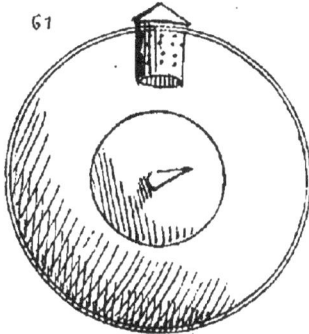

61. Rondelle à poing, allemande, en fer, de 35 cent. de diamètre. Elle est à dard et à lanterne pour les combats nocturnes. — Musée des Welfen (Guelfes) à Hanovre. (Voir, page 316, les rondaches à lanterne, n° 46, etc.

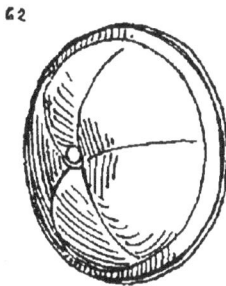

62. Rondelle à poing, allemande, du seizième siècle, d'après le *Triomphe de Maximilien*, par Burckmayer (1517).

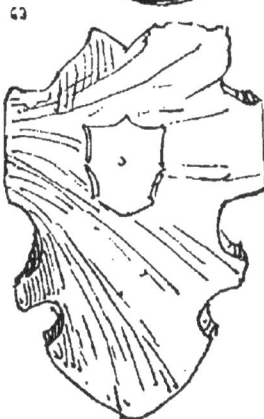

63. Rondelle à poing en corne d'élan, avec écusson en fer, seconde moitié du quinzième siècle. — I. 4, musée d'artillerie de Paris.

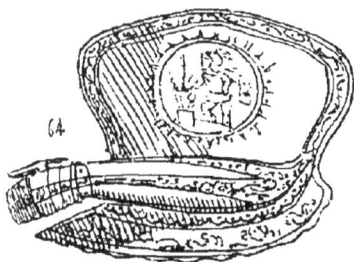

64. Targette allemande, à gantelet, de la première moitié du seizième siècle. Elle a appartenu au comte de Henneberg, et se trouve à Meiningen, en Allemagne.

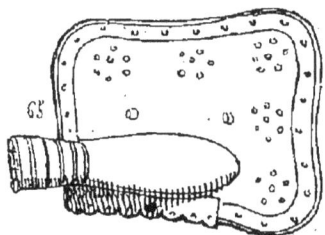

65. Targette allemande, à gantelet, du seizième siècle.—Musée de Turin.

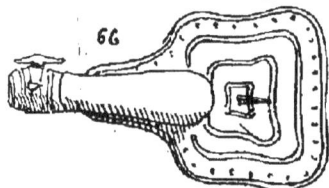

66. Targette allemande à brise-épée et à gantelet, du seizième siècle. — Musée historique du palais de Montbijou, à Berlin.

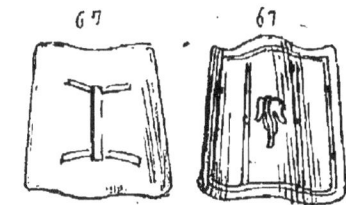

67. Targette à poing, allemande, à crochet brise-épée, de 20 c. —Col. Llewelyn-Meyrick. Cette targette a été représentée des deux côtés. Un exemplaire semblable dans la collection de M. le comte de Nieuwerkerke.

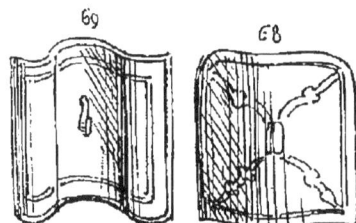

68. Targette à poing, allemande, vue à l'envers. De la fin du quinzième siècle. — Musée historique du palais de Montbijou, à Berlin.

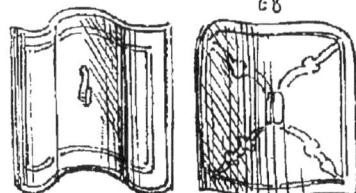

69. Targette à poing, allemande, à crochet brise-épée, de la fin du quinzième siècle. — Musée Erbach, à Erbach.

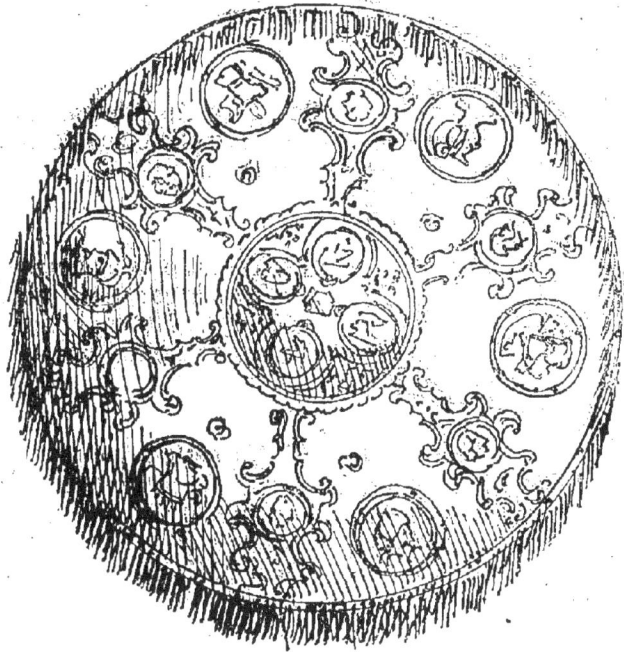

Bouclier allemand de parure du seizième siècle, de la fabrique d'Augsbourg. Il est orné de repoussés d'une grande finesse, dont les médaillons sont alternativement relevés par des trophées et des bustes admirablement dessinés. La garniture de franges qui court tout autour de ce bouclier est fixée avec des écrous, et son revers matelassé. — Col. d'Ambras, à Vienne.

Bouclier allemand de parure du seizième siècle, probablement fabriqué à Augsbourg. Les ornements de cette rondache,
d'un beau travail, indiquent, par leur caractère, les dernières
années du seizième siècle, sinon le commencement du dix-septième. Les trophées rappellent les ornements des artistes français du règne de Henri IV. — Col. d'Ambras, à Vienne.

Bouclier allemand de parure en fer repoussé, du seizième siècle,
ayant appartenu à l'empereur Charles-Quint. Cette arme
défensive, qui représente un des plus beaux morceaux de l'art
allemand de ce genre, a été plusieurs fois contrefaite et vendue
fort cher à des personnes qui n'avaient pas vu l'original. Une de
ces imitations avait passé en France, où elle a été achetée
comme une œuvre d'art italien de premier ordre par feu le
baron de Mazis. L'original, qui fait partie de la collection
d'Ambras, est cependant d'une finesse et d'un dessin qui font le
désespoir des plus habiles contrefacteurs. Ce croquis ne peut
rendre que fort imparfaitement les beautés artistiques du
chef-d'œuvre.

Il a été déjà dit ailleurs que ces sortes d'armes n'étaient pas destinées à la guerre, mais seulement aux solennités où les grands
rivalisaient alors pour l'éclat et la richesse artistique des harnais.

L'Italie fut particulièrement réputée pour ce travail durant toute
l'époque de la Renaissance, dont les artistes les plus aimés
et les plus célèbres fournissaient les compositions et exécu-
taient souvent eux-mêmes ces armes magnifiques qui brillent
dans les collections par la beauté et le fini du dessin, mais qui
ne répondent guère au but pour lequel on fabrique ordinairement des armes.

Bouclier allemand de parure en fer repoussé, du seizième siècle. Il est d'une exécution très-soignée, et le dessin peut figurer comme un type caractéristique de compositions des maîtres graveurs allemands de l'époque. — Collection d'Ambras, à Vienne.

COTTES ET CUIRASSES

Hauberts ou cottes annelées, rustrées, maclées, treillissées. — Cottes d'écailles
et de mailles. — Jaques-brigantines. — Gamboisons. — Manteaux d'évêque ou
pèlerines en mailles. — Cuirasses. — Buffletins, etc.

L'histoire de la transformation de l'armure définitive
durant le moyen âge, la renaissance, le dix-septième et le
dix-huitième siècle, a été déjà traitée dans le second chapitre de ce livre, mais il reste à déterminer ici les divers
genres de ces armures.

L'*armure-cotte* (de l'allemand *Kutte*, froc), qui a précédé
l'armure en plaques de cuir et d'acier, était appelée en
France *haubert* (de l'allemand *Halsberge*, défense du cou,
aussi nommé dans cette langue *Brünne* — *Brunica*, — et
Panzerhemd; — *hauberk* en anglais). Le *petit haubert*, qui
plus tard devint l'armure de l'écuyer et du gentilhomme
peu riche, était porté, au huitième siècle, par tous les chevaliers, comme le démontre le *Codex aureus* de Saint-Gall.
Ce haubert était une sorte de *jaque* en écailles qui ne descendait pas au-dessous des hanches, et dont les manches,
peu collantes, s'arrêtaient un peu au-dessous du coude. Le
grand ou *blanc haubert* en forme de sarrau et avec capuchon, appelé *camail*, descendait d'abord seulement jusqu'au-dessous du genou, et les manches ou brassards, peu
collants, un peu au-dessous du coude, tel que ce haubert

est représenté dans le *Martyrologe*, manuscrit du dixième siècle, à la bibliothèque de Stuttgard, et dans l'*Aelfric*, manuscrit anglo-saxon du onzième siècle, à la bibliothèque du musée britannique. Quant à l'armement du chevalier allemand du *Jeremias Apocalypsis* du onzième siècle, de la bibliothèque de Darmstadt, sa perfection est de cent cinquante ans en avance sur ce que l'on connaît de cette époque; car, selon la broderie de la mitre de Seligenthal et la tapisserie de Bayeux, toutes les deux du onzième siècle, le grand haubert, que le *Jeremias* représente déjà avec longues manches et haut et bas-de-chausses séparés, était encore, dans tous les autres pays, collant comme un tricot, avec haut-de-chausses adhérent et à manches courtes. L'armement défensif de ce chevalier allemand du *Jeremias* du onzième siècle n'apparaît en Angleterre, en France et en Espagne, qu'au douzième siècle, tel qu'il est représenté sur les sceaux de Richard Ier Cœur de Lion (1157-1173), de Louis VII le Jeune (1137-1180), et du comte de Barcelone don Ramon Bérenger IV (1140).

Le haubert ou la cotte d'armes était, avant l'emploi universel de la maille, fabriqué de bien des manières, en étoffe matelassée ou en gros cuir. L'espèce la plus ancienne était probablement le *haubert annelé* (*Beringt* en allemand, *ringed* en anglais), où la défense consistait en anneaux de métal cousus à plat l'un à côté de l'autre. La cotte ou le haubert *rustré* (*Bekettet* en allemand, *rustred* en anglais) avait, à la place des anneaux simples et ronds, des anneaux ovales et plats qui se couvraient à moitié les uns les autres.

La cotte maclée (*Beschildet* en allemand, *macled* en anglais) était recouverte de petites plaques de métal en forme de losange.

La cotte treillissée (*Benagelt* en allemand, *trelliced* en anglais) était formée de lanières en cuir disposées en treillis sur l'étoffe ou la peau ; chaque losange ou chaque carré y était garni d'une tête de clou rivée.

Le *jazeron* ou *korazin* [1] était le grand haubert *imbriqué*, c'est-à-dire armé d'écailles (*Geschuppt* en allemand, *scaled* en anglais), tel que l'était déjà, au huitième siècle, le petit haubert, et dont il a été question plus haut.

La cotte de mailles, haubert appelé en allemand *Ketten* ou *Maschenpanzerhemd*, en anglais *chain-mail hauberk*, était entièrement à mailles, ordinairement en fer, sans doublure d'étoffe ni de cuir, sans envers, formant un ensemble de tissu de métal, qui se passait comme une chemise, et dont les anneaux étaient rivés pièce par pièce, rivets qui étaient nommés *grains d'orge*.

Il existe deux espèces de ce travail : la maille simple et la maille double, pour la fabrication de laquelle *Chambly* (Oise) était renommée. La double maille, comme la simple, montre toujours chaque anneau engagé dans quatre autres.

Cette cotte de mailles remonte bien plus haut chez nous qu'au temps des Croisades, comme la routine des compilateurs continue à l'enseigner. Ce ne sont pas les croisés, qui, à leur retour de Jérusalem, l'ont introduite seulement dans leurs pays ; la cotte de mailles y était répandue bien avant le onzième siècle. La princesse byzantine Anna Comnena ne la connaissait que pour l'avoir vue sur les chevaliers venus du Nord. (Voy. ses Mémoires.)

La cotte de mailles est toujours encore portée par les Indiens, les Persans, les Chinois, les Japonais, les Mongols, les Mahrates, les Palikares, les Tcherkesses et autres peuples de civilisation arriérée. Ces cottes sont le plus souvent sans rivets, comme les cottes de la contrefaçon parisienne, mais il y a aussi des cottes persanes et tcherkesses rivées ; tout cela n'a cependant aucune valeur archéologique.

La *jaque*, espèce de haubert court qui ne descendait pas au-dessous des hanches, était fabriquée de différentes manières, comme le blanc ou grand haubert.

---

1. Nom qui dérive probablement de *Khoraçan*, pays situé au centre de la Perse.

La *brigantine* est une jaque confectionnée de petites lames de métal dans le genre des cottes maclées, et imbriquées comme les écailles; ces lames étaient rivées *au-dessous* de l'étoffe de manière que le côté extérieur, le plus souvent en velours doublé de toile, ne montre qu'une infinité de petits rivets formant de petites têtes de clous en cuivre, et que l'armature se trouve du côté du corps. La *brigantine* (*Italiænische Pauzerjacke* en allemand, *prigandine-jacket* en anglais) était particulièrement en usage en Italie durant le quinzième siècle. C'était le corselage favori de Charles le Téméraire.

Par *gamboison* ou *gambeson* on entendait l'espèce de pourpoint sans manches en peau ou en toile, piquées de manière que le tout était couvert d'œillets. Quant au *gamboison à haut et bas-de-chausses adhérents*, qui, au quatorzième siècle, se portait sous les premières armures à plates, et dont le seul exemplaire conservé se trouve au musée de Munich, il était également en peau ou en toile légèrement matelassée, et avait le plastron, la braconnière et les côtés des rotules garnis de mailles pour garantir le corps aux défauts de l'armure. Le *manteau d'évêque* ou *pèlerine de mailles*, se portait souvent par dessus une cuirasse, et était particulièrement en usage en Italie au quinzième siècle.

La *cuirasse* (de l'italien *corazza*, dérivé du latin *corium*, cuir, parce que les premières cuirasses romaines étaient probablement en cuir, — *Kürass* en allemand, *cuirass* en anglais) se compose de deux parties : du *plastron* (*pectoral-mammelière*, — en allemand, *Brustplatte*, en anglais *breast-plate*), qui sert à la défense de la poitrine; et de la *dossière* (*huméral musquin*, — en allemand, *Rückenplatte*, en anglais *back-plate*), qui protége le dos. On appelle *tabule* (*Græte* en allemand, *centre-ridge* ou *tapul*, et aussi *salient-ridge* en anglais) l'arétière qui descend au milieu du plastron.

La dossière et le plastron sont ordinairement reliés par des courroies qui passent par-dessus les épaules et le colletin. La coupe de la cuirasse fournit, comme celle des autres pièces de l'armure, une indication pour le classement. Les plastrons gothiques, aussi bien que ceux du commencement du seizième siècle, sont quelquefois pointus, bombés et demi-bombés, ils imitent généralement les costumes des époques.

On trouvera de plus amples développements sur la transformation de cette arme dans le Chapitre historique ainsi que dans celui où est traitée l'*armure complète* dans tous ses détails, et les dessins, dans celui-ci, représentent, par ordre chronologique, toutes les cuirasses qui se sont succédé jusqu'à leur suppression (1620-1660), époque où elles furent remplacées par les *buffletins* (*Koller* en allemand, *buff-coat* ou *jerkir* en anglais) ordinairement en peau d'élan, et pourvus du grand hausse-col ou colletin en fer bronzé.

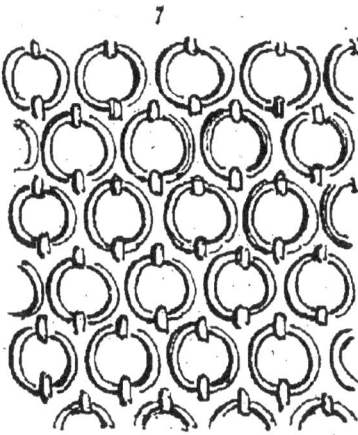

1. Spécimen de la cotte annelée (*Beringt* en allem., *ringet* en angl.), qui était composée d'anneaux plats cousus l'un à côté de l'autre sur de la toile matelassée ou sur du cuir.

Ce genre est souvent très-difficile, sinon impossible, à distinguer, sur les miniatures des manuscrits de l'espèce nommée maclée. (V. le dessin n° 4 ci-après.)

2. Spécimen de la cotte rustrée (*Beketted* en allem., *rustred* en angl.). Ici les anneaux plats sont ovales, et se couvrent à moitié les uns les autres.

Ce genre, où les anneaux ne forment pas des chaînes entrelacées, paraît dans les dessins des miniatures consister en véritables chaînes.

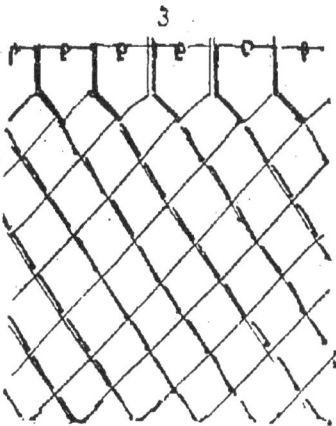

3. Spécimen de la cotte maclée (*Beschildet* en allem., *macled* en angl.). L'armure est composée de petites plaques de métal, en forme de losange, également cousues sur un fond d'étoffe ou de peau et se couvrant quelquefois à moitié.

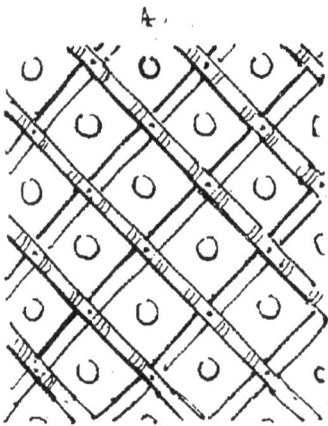

4. Spécimen de cotte treillissée (*Gegittert* et aussi *Benagelt* en allem., *trelliced* en angl.). Cette cotte, également faite de toile matelassée et de peau, est armée de lanières en cuir épais disposées en treillis; chaque losange ou chaque carré y était garni d'une tête de clou rivée.

Il est difficile de les distinguer, dans les miniatures des manuscrits, du genre annelé.

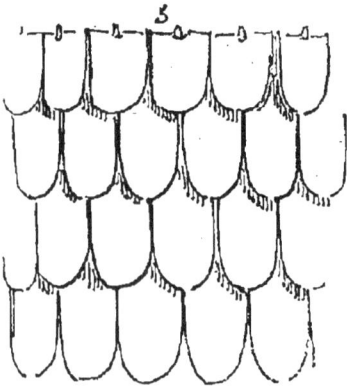

5. Spécimen de cotte écaillée ou imbriquée (*Geschuppt* en allem., *scaled* en angl.). Elle est aussi appelée jazeran et korazin. Son armure consiste en écailles de métal cousues par rangées imbriquées sur de la toile matelassée ou sur du cuir.

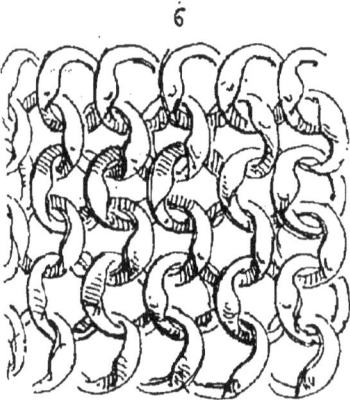

6. Spécimen de mailles à anneaux rivés, dites à grains d'orge (*Genitetes Ketten* ou *Maschengewebe* en allem., *rivet chainmail* en angl.). La cotte de mailles étant entièrement confectionnée de mailles en métal et sans envers, n'a point de doublure.

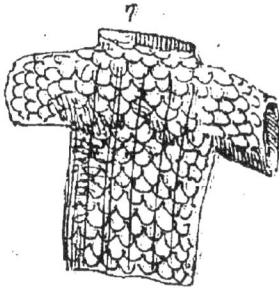

7. Petit haubert ou jaque[1], du huitième siècle (*Kleines Panzerhemd* en allem., *smal hauberk* en angl.), en écailles avec imbrication, espèce d'armure aussi connue sous le nom de cotte en jazeran ou korazin (nom qui dérive probablement de Khoraçan, pays au centre de la Perse). — *Codex aureus* du huitième siècle, de Saint-Gall.

8. Grand ou blanc haubert (*Brunne* ou *Ganzes Panzerhemd* en allem., *great hauberk* en ang.) annelé. D'après le *Martyrologe*, manuscrit du dixième siècle à la bibliothèque de Stuttgard. Il est à camail et à manches courtes adhérents.

9. Grand ou blanc haubert treillissé, normand, du onzième siècle. Il est à camail non adhérent et à manches courtes. — Tapisseries de Bayeux.

1. Des deniers de Magdebourg, de 1150 et 1160, ainsi que quelques deniers allemands plus anciens, montrent des cottes sur lesquelles on distingue parfaitement l'imbrication qui, formée d'écailles bien plus grandes, se trouve aussi sur les hauberts des chevaliers de la peinture murale du dôme de Brunswick, exécutée au onzième siècle. Le haubert imbriqué le plus ancien est celui du *Codex aureus* de Saint-Gall, du huitième au neuvième siècle, ci-dessus reproduit.

11. Haubert allemand du onzième siècle, avec camail adhérent et haut et bas-de-chausses, d'après le *Jeremias Apocalypsis*, manuscrit conservé à la bibliothèque de Darmstadt.

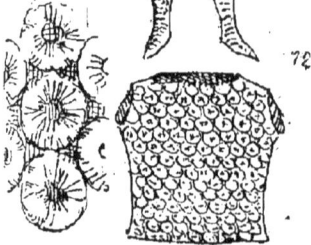

12. Gamboison ou gambeson (*Geœhrter leinener Unterpanser* en allem.), espèce de cotte ou de jaque d'armes du seizième siècle, faite de toile piquée et brodée à œillets. Le gamboison se portait ordinairement sous la cuirasse. — Musée de Cluny et col. Renné, à Constance.

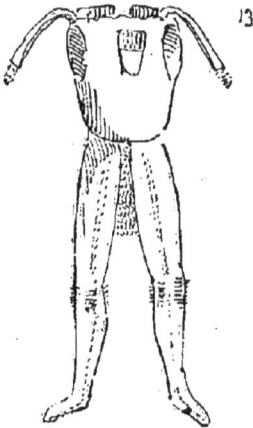

13. Gamboison du quatorzième siècle, avec haut et bas-de-chausses adhérents. Il est en toile matelassée, et garni de mailles à l'emplacement du plastron, de la braconnière et des côtés des rotules. L'unique exemplaire connu d'après lequel ce dessin est fait, se trouve au musée de Munich.

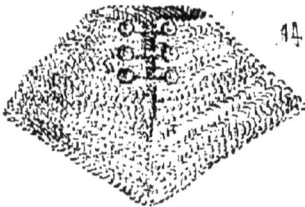

14. Pèlerine vénitienne en mailles, appelée manteau d'évêque (*Bischofs Mantel* en allem.) dont étaient armés les Doges, et qui était aussi portée en Allemagne au quinzième et au seizième siècle. — Col. Renné à Constance, exemplaire provenant du musée de Dresde.

15. Manches à gorgerin en mailles, du quinzième siècle. — Musée de Dresde.

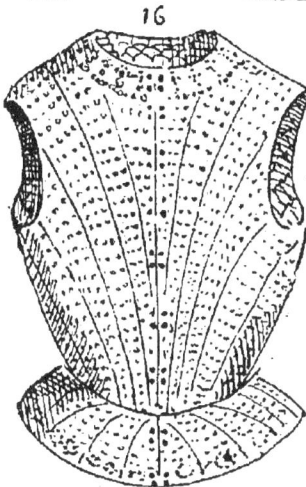

16. Brigantine (*Italienische Panzerjacke* en allem., *brigandin-jacket* en angl.) du quinzième siècle. Les écailles trilobées (n° 17) marquées de fleurs de lis sont posées en imbrication et rivées sur le pourpoint en velours dont elles composent la doublure armée. — Musée de Darmstadt.

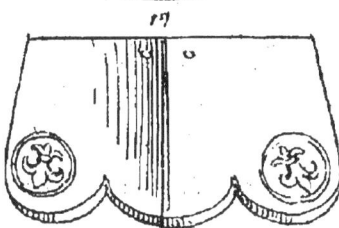

17. Ecaille trilobée, presque en grandeur naturelle, de la brigantine précédente.

18. Ecailles de brigantine avec des lions estampillés (probablement marque d'armurier), de la collection de l'auteur. Beaucoup de musées et de collections ont exposé cette arme défensive à l'envers. L'erreur provient de ce que les conservateurs ont cru que l'étoffe, le velours ou la toile, devaient être tournés du côté du corps. La courbe des écailles démontre cependant de quelle manière la brigantine était portée. L'erreur s'est glissée aux musées de Dresde, de Cluny, à la collection d'Ambras, au musée d'artillerie à Paris, etc.

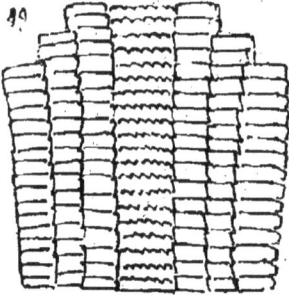

19. Plastron de brigantine du quinzième siècle, composé de petites plaques d'acier. Il est exposé au musée de Cluny à l'envers, tel qu'il est dessiné ici.

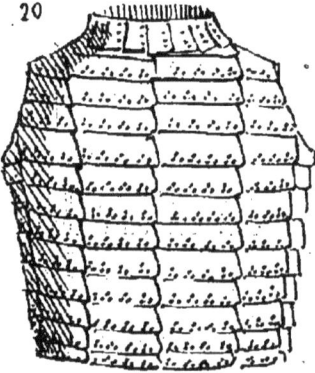

20. Brigantine du quinzième siècle, composée de petites plaques d'acier, exposée à l'envers au musée d'artillerie de Paris, sous le nº 127. — Aux musées de Sigmaringen et de Munich de semblables exemplaires.

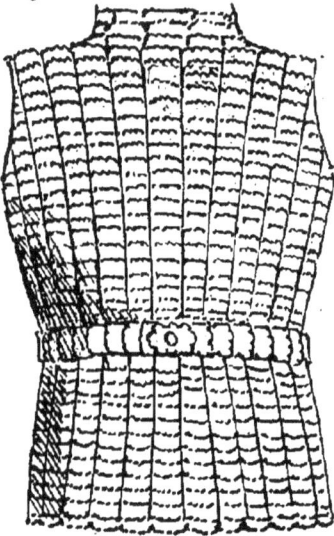

21. Brigantine du quinzième siècle, composée d'écailles trilobées et se couvrant à moitié. Cet exemplaire est remarquable par sa braconnière, qui entoure une partie des cuisses à partir des hanches. — Musée de Dresde. La collection d'Ambras possède une semblable brigantine. Les deux musées l'ont aussi exposée à l'envers.

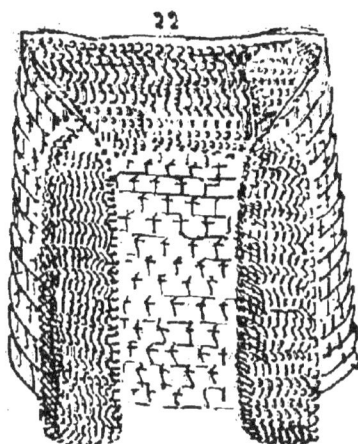

22. Jaque en plaques d'acier imbriquées avec colletin et brassards en mailles, du quinzième siècle. Les écailles de cette arme ne sont pas rivées sur étoffe, comme celles des brigantines, mais rivées entre elles ; la jaque est sans doublure d'étoffe ni de peau, comme une cotte de mailles. — Col. d'Erbach à Erbach.

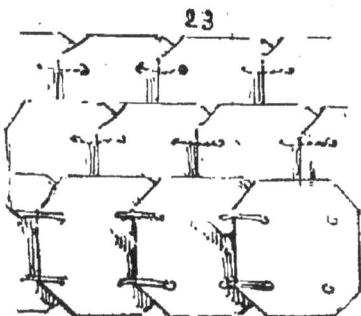

23. Ecailles de la jacque précédente, dessinées en demi-grandeur.

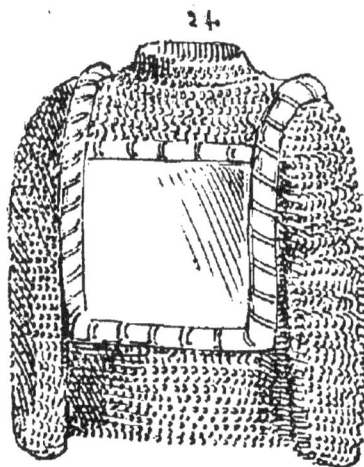

24. Cotte de mailles de Jean Ziska (mort en 1424), représentée sur un tableau ancien peint probablement d'après un dessin de l'époque et conservé à la bibliothèque de Genève. La cotte et le plastron sont en fer, mais les mailles du gorgerin et les bourrelets sont en cuivre.

25. Cotte d'armes à plaques d'acier, d'après un manuscrit persan, exécuté vers 1600. Cette copie du *Schah-Nameh* ou livre royal, poëme composé par Fisdusi, sous le règne de Mahmoud le Gaznévide (999), est ornée de 215 magnifiques miniatures, et se trouve à la bibliothèque de Munich.

26. Haubert persan en mailles à manches et haut et bas-de-chausses, reproduit d'après ce même manuscrit.

27. Ecaille d'acier poli, grandeur presque naturelle, du Jazeran, ou armure imbriquée de Sobieski (1648 ou 1696), conservée au musée de Dresde. Grand nombre de ces écailles sont ornées de croix en cuivre doré fixées au moyen de rivets. Voy. au chapitre des casques, le pot-en-tête de cette même armure.

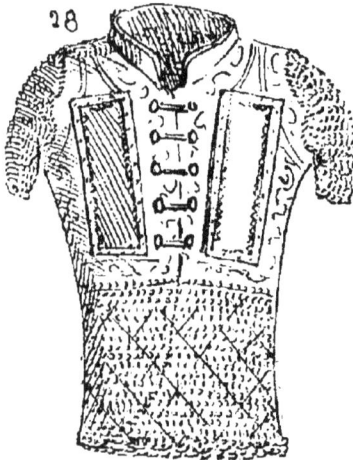

28. Cotte d'armes mongole à miroirs d'acier du commencement du dix-huitième siècle. Les mailles sont sans rivets. — G. 138, musée d'artillerie de Paris.

29. Cotte de mailles polygare.—Collection Llewelyn-Meyrick à Goodrich-Court.

Cette armure se signale par les pointes qui descendent du collier.

30. Cotte d'armes indienne. — Collection Llewelyn-Meyrick.

Le col droit paraît indiquer une origine peu ancienne.

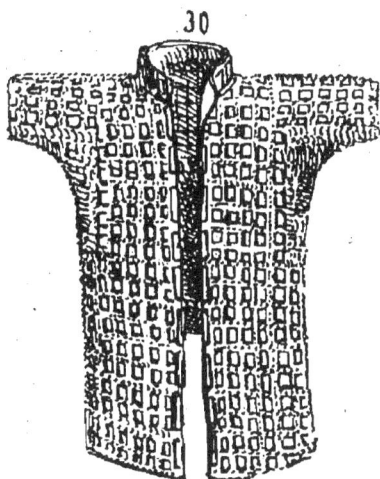

31. Cotte d'armes indienne en peau de rhinocéros[1]. Cette armure, qui est garnie de plaques damasquinées, a un caractère éminemment moderne et peu heureux. Le musée d'artillerie de Paris possède quelques cottes orientales semblables. — Collection Llewelyn-Meyrick.

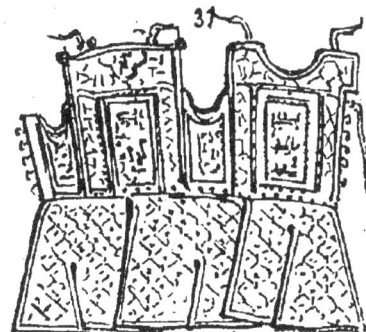

1. C'est à Mundavien, dans le golfe de Cutch, selon le catalogue Meyrick, que l'on fabrique ce genre d'armures. Les cottes, comme les boucliers ronds, sont confectionnées là avec les peaux de rhinocéros et de buffle cuites dans de l'huile.

32. Cotte de mailles sarrasine, vue de dos, du seizième siècle. Elle est doublée à sa partie postérieure d'une sorte de capuchon simple et dentelé en bas, qui sert à la fois de défense d'épaules et de camail. Cette cotte, qui se trouve au musée d'artillerie de Paris, est courte et ne dépasse que de peu les hanches.

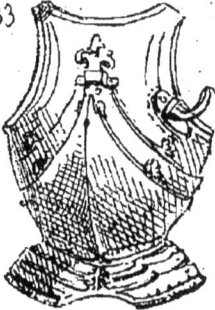

33. Cuirasse gothique à tabule (*Græte* en allem., *tapul* en angl.), et avec faucre, du quinzième siècle. — Collection d'Ambras.
C'est la plus belle forme de cuirasse.

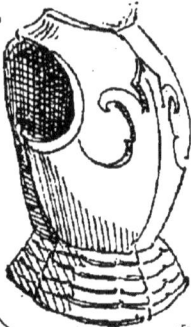

34. Cuirasse gothique du quinzième siècle, sans faucre, à dossière et à braconnière lamée. — Arsenal de Zurich.

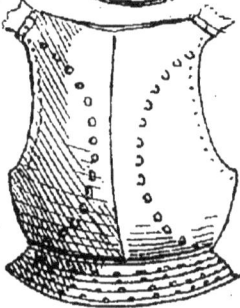

35. Cuirasse à tabule, du quinzième siècle; elle est en fer, très lourde et recouverte de velours rouge garni de têtes de clous de fer. — Musée national bavarois à Munich.

29.

36. Cuirasse gothique sans tabule, entièrement bombée et
provenant d'une armure allemande de la fin du quinzième
siècle. — Arsenaux de Maximilien Ier, d'après les dessins de
Glockenthon, exécutés en 1505.
Collection d'Ambras.

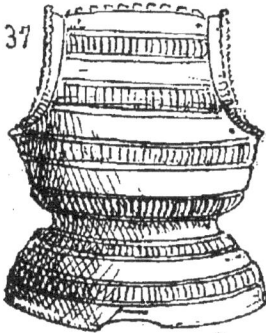

37. Cuirasse demi-bombée, sans
tabule, d'une armure allemande
de la fin du quinzième siècle, en
fer repoussé. — Collection Llewelyn-Meyrick.

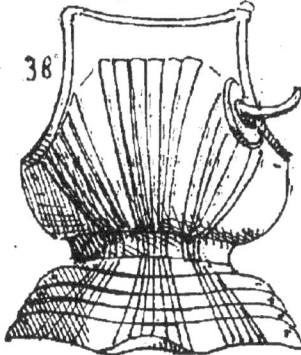

38. Cuirasse sans tabule, à faucre, demi-bombée, d'une armure
cannelée allemande de la fin du
quinzième siècle, dite armure
maximilienne, et aussi milanaise. De forme gracieuse, sa
braconnière très-grande n'est
pas terminée par des tassettes
comme cela se voit souvent dans
ces armures. Les tassettes font
pièce avec la braconnière —
Arsenal de Vienne.

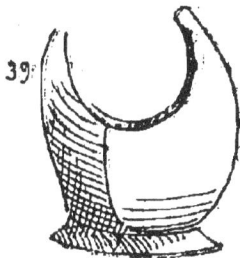

39. Cuirasse sans tabule, demi-
bombée, d'une armure allemande de la fin du quinzième
siècle et du commencement du
seizième. — G. 5, musée d'artillerie de Paris, et collection
de M. le comte de Nieuwerkerque.

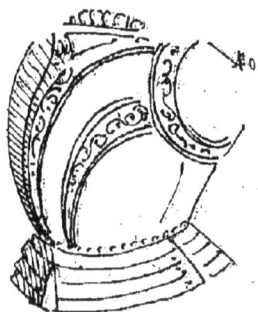

40. Cuirasse demi-bombée, à tabule et à braconnière, de la première moitié du seizième siècle, d'une armure allemande ayant appartenu au landgrave Philippe le Magnanime, mort en 1567.

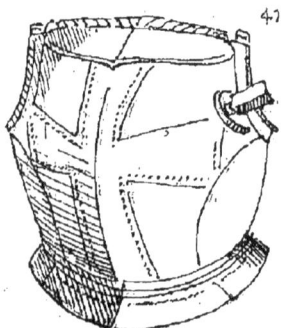

41. Cuirasse demi-bombée, à tabule et à faucre, de la première moitié du seizième siècle, d'une armure ayant appartenu à un chevalier de l'ordre de Saint-Georges. — Collection Llewelyn-Meyrick.

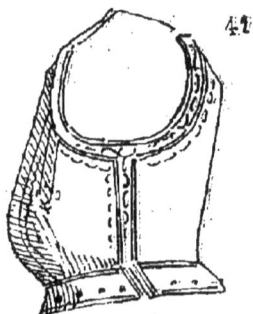

42. Cuirasse à faucre et sans tabule, d'une armure allemande du milieu du seizième siècle. — Coll. de M. le comte de Nieuwerkerque, et à l'arsenal de la ville de Vienne, où grand nombre de ces armures, provenant de la troupe civique, sont marquées du millésime de 1546.

43. Cuirasse à tabule, d'une armure de Nuremberg, de l'année 1570. — Arsenal impérial de Vienne.

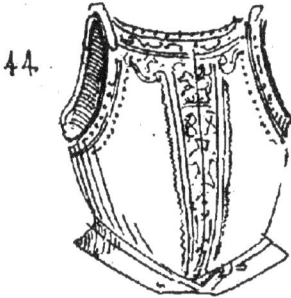

44. Cuirasse italienne à tabule et gravée, de la fin du seizième siècle [1]. — Coll. d'Ambras.

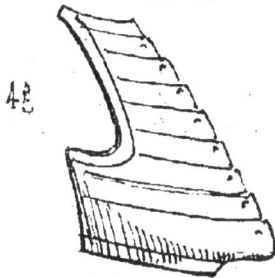

45. Cuirasse lamée et à tabule, de la forme dite cosse de pois et bosse de polichinelle (*Gaensebauch* en allem., *peascod* en angl.), de la fin du règne de Henri III (1589).

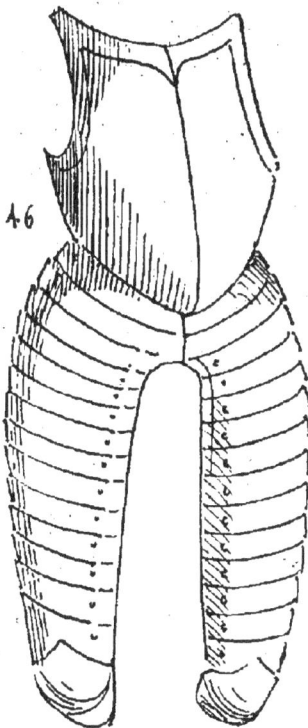

46. Cuirasse à tabule, cosse de pois, avec longs cuissards écrevisses à la place des tassettes.— Règne de Louis XIII (1610-1643).

47. Cuirasse italienne à boutons, de la fin du seizième siècle, à tabule forme cosse de pois. — Coll. de M. le comte de Nieuwerkerque, et de M. Sœter à Augsbourg.

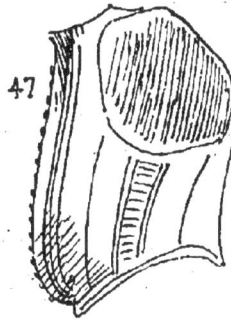

[1]. La cuirasse de l'armure attribuée, au Louvre, au roi de France Henri IV est d'une coupe semblable; sa braconnière est formée de trois larges lames.

48. Demi-armure en fer gravé, et ornée de clous dorés, de la dernière moitié du dix-septième siècle, conservée à l'arsenal de Soleure, où elle est faussement attribuée à Vengli (1550).

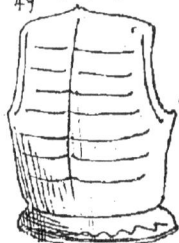

49. Cuirasse lamée d'un reître allemand, du milieu du dix-septième siècle. Quelques auteurs allemands appellent ces armures, entièrement composées de lames, *Krebse* (écrevisses).

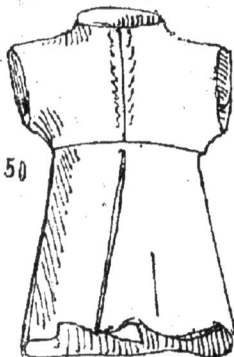

50. Buffletin en cuir d'élan (*Coller* en allem., *buff-coat* ou *jerkir* en angl.), du temps de la guerre de Trente ans et du règne de Louis XIII (1618-1640). — G. 162, musée d'artillerie de Paris. L'arsenal impérial de Vienne possède le buffletin que Gustave-Adolphe a porté à la bataille de Lutzen, où il fut tué.

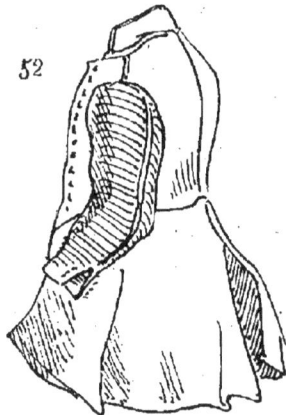

51. Colletin ou hausse-col, en acier bronzé, appartenant au buffletin n° 50.

52. Buffletin à manches, de cuirassier, de 1650.

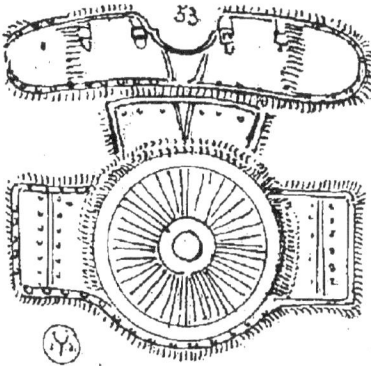

53. Cuirasse persane en cuir, probablement du seizième siècle ou du dix-septième. Cette arme, qui est damasquinée et matelassée, ressemble beaucoup aux cuirasses des janissaires ci-après mentionnées. — Coll. Llewelyn-Meyrick.

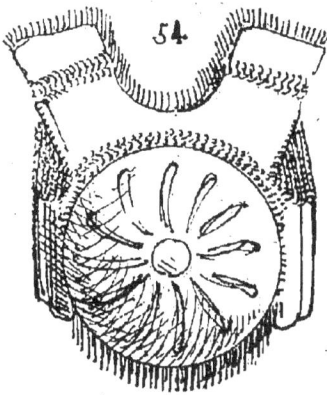

54. Cuirasse de janissaire[1], du seizième siècle. — G. 134, musée d'artillerie de Paris. Cette arme est marquée du monogramme dessiné à côté du numéro 53; c'est le chiffre par lequel les Turcs représentent le nom d'*Allah* (Dieu). (Voir l'observation faite, concernant ce signe, page 320, n° 60.)

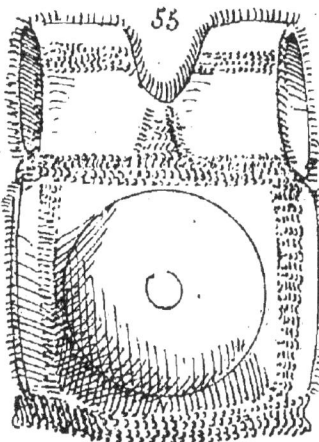

55. Cuirasse de janissaire, du dix-septième siècle. — G. 133, musée d'artillerie de Paris. Mêmes observations que pour le numéro précédent.

[1]. Les janissaires (nom qui dérive des mots turcs *ieni tcheri*, qui veulent dire nouveaux soldats), composaient la milice turque d'infanterie, créée, en 1362, par Amurat I, et dissoute et presque entièrement massacrée en 1826.

LE BRASSARD

Le brassard proprement dit (*Armschiene* en allemand, *brassard* en anglais) ne faisait pas partie de l'armement des anciens, mais on rencontre chez eux, ainsi que chez les peuples dits barbares de l'âge du bronze, le brassard tire-bouchon dont le dessin a été donné. Durant les époques de la partie du moyen âge où l'armure à plates n'était pas encore inventée, les cottes d'armes étaient souvent à manches qui formaient la défense des bras (*brassards à moufles en mailles*), et qui furent d'abord remplacées par des plaques en cuir bouilli, et, plus tard, par des plaques en acier. Il y avait des brassards simples, des brassards doubles et des brassards complets où l'armure de l'avant-bras et du haut du bras était réunie par la cubitière. Les grands brassards de tournois, de la fin du quinzième et du seizième siècle, n'existaient que pour le bras gauche, et étaient souvent à gantelet adhérent, et non articulé; on s'en servait ordinairement à la place du manteau d'armes. La forme et la grandeur des cubitières et des épaulières peuvent aider à reconnaître l'époque d'un brassard complet, qui était ordinairement à charnières et protégeait le bras dans toutes ses parties.

BRASSARDS.

1. Brassard à moufle, en mailles (*Maschen Armschutz mit Faus. thandschuh* en allem.; *brassard with mitten* ou *inarticulated gauntlet of mail* en angl.), d'une cotte d'armes.

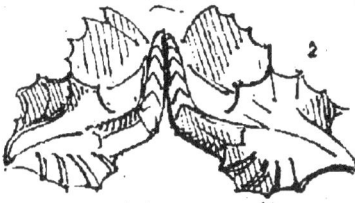

2. Brassard gothique complet, avec cubitière, haut-de-bras et gantelet, d'après un monument funéraire dans l'Oxfordshire, de 1460. Les cubitières sont d'une taille extraordinaire.

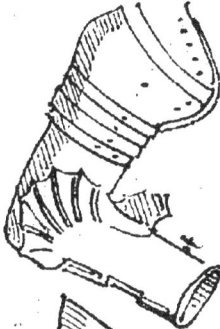

3. Brassard gothique avec cubitière et haut-de-bras, défendant l'avant et l'arrière-bras, du commencement de la seconde moitié du quinzième siècle.

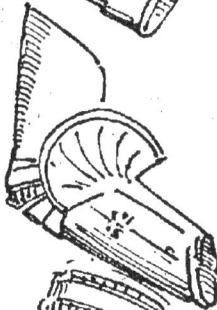

4. Id. Id.

5. Brassard complet, défendant, comme les précédents, l'avant et l'arrière-bras. Il est orné de bourrelets repoussés qui indiquent, aussi bien que la forme de la cubitière, la fin du quinzième siècle ou le commencement du seizième, car ces sortes d'armures étaient contemporaines des armures cannelées dites maximiliennes et milanaises.

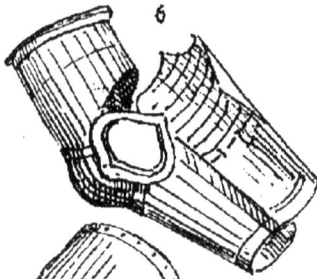

6. Brassard, avec cubitière et haut-de-bras, d'une armure cannelée dite maximilienne, de la fin du quinzième siècle ou du commencement du seizième.

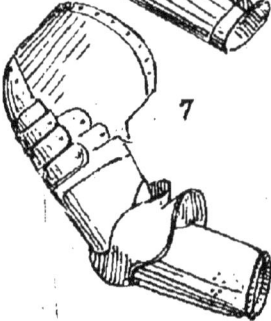

7. Brassard, avec cubitière et haut-de-bras, de la fin du seizième siècle.

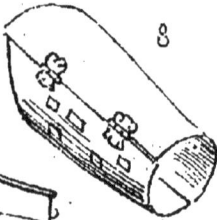

8. Brassard d'avant-bras, où la plaque de l'arrière-bras est percée de huit ouvertures carrées. — Coll. Spengel à Munich.

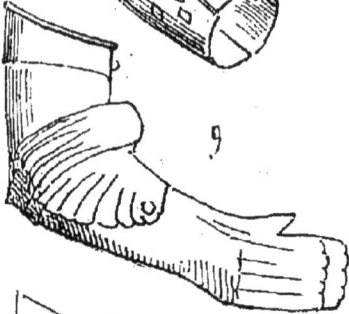

9. Brassard gothique allemand, de tournois, à gantelet inarticulé pour bras gauche, de la fin du quinzième siècle.

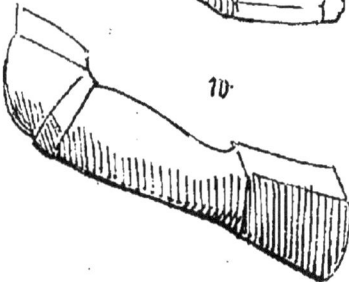

10. Brassard allemand, de tournois, à gantelet inarticulé pour bras gauche, du commencement du seizième siècle.

Tous ces brassards défendent l'avant et l'arrière-bras.

LE GANTELET

La forme du gantelet ou gant d'armes (*Kampfhandschuh* ou *Gefingerte Handtatze* en allemand, *articulated gauntlet* en anglais), qui recouvrait, outre la main, une partie de l'avant-bras, aide grandement, aussi bien que la forme du soleret ou pédieux, au classement d'une armure, car l'une et l'autre ont éprouvé de nombreux changements. Il paraît établi que l'usage du gantelet proprement dit ne remonte qu'à la fin du treizième siècle. Le *Martyrologe*, le *Prudentius Psychomachia*, la *Biblia sacra*, l'*Aelfric*, le *Jeremias Apocalypsis*, la broderie de la mitre de Seligenthal, la tapisserie de Bayeux, documents déjà mentionnés qui datent du neuvième à la fin du onzième siècle, représentent l'homme d'armes la main nue; mais le sceau de Richard Cœur de Lion (1157-1173) montre déjà la main du roi recouverte de mailles par un allongement de la manche, espèce de sac qui forme une *moufle*, où le pouce paraît quelquefois seul détaché. Un chevalier, représenté dans les illustrations de l'*Enéide allemande* de Henri de Waldeck, du treizième siècle, en heaume à cimier, et monté sur un coursier couvert d'une armure annelée ou treillissée, — a la main également encore couvert de la *moufle de mailles* ou de l'allongement des manches de sa cotte qui paraît treillissée, sinon même déjà lamée.

Le premier véritable gantelet était à *doigts séparés* et recouverts d'écailles, de lames ou d'autres imbrications en fer; le dessus de la main était protégé d'une plaque de métal ou de cuir, tel qu'elle est représentée sur la pierre tombale du roi des Romains Gunther de Schwarzbourg, exécutée en 1352 au dôme de Francfort, ville où ce prince fut empoisonné en 1349. On croit également reconnaître ce gantelet dans l'impression de la toile italienne du quatorzième siècle, de la collection de M. Odet, à Sitten. Les miniatures du manuscrit d'une histoire romaine conservées à la bibliothèque de l'Arsenal à Paris, et exécutées probablement au commencement du quinzième siècle pour le duc de Bourgogne, représentent encore tous les hommes d'armes les mains uniquement protégées par la *moufle*, sac produit par le prolongement des manches de mailles, et démontrent à quel point l'armement bourguignon était en retard.

Le *miton* ou la *moufle* (*Fausthandschuh* en allemand, *mitten* ou *inarticulated gauntlet* en anglais), gantelet où les doigts ne sont plus séparés, et qui est formé de lames d'acier disposées seulement dans le sens des grandes divisions de la main, apparaît au quinzième siècle. L'armure de Jeanne d'Arc, du catalogue de Dezest, la statuette en bronze de Guillaume VI (1404-1417), à Amsterdam, et l'armure de Frédéric Ier, palatin du Rhin, conservées à la collection d'Ambras, à Vienne, démontrent que partout le miton était en usage dans la première moitié du quinzième siècle; mais c'est au gantelet articulé qu'il faut rapporter le dicton favori de Bayard : « Ce que gantelet gagne, gorgerin le mange, » aussi bien que les dictons ordinaires de : « Prêter le gantelet et Relever le gantelet, » qui apparaissent dans la langue française au quinzième siècle.

Il existe cependant des armures gothiques de cette première partie du quinzième siècle où les gantelets sont déjà à doigts séparés, tels qu'on les voit au musée de Sigmaringen, et un grand nombre d'armures de la seconde moitié du quinzième et du commencement du seizième siècle pourvues de mitons, particulièrement les armures de joute. — Voyez les harnais de Maximilien Ier (1459-1519) à la collection d'Ambras et à l'arsenal impérial de Vienne.

C'est vers la fin du quinzième siècle, et non pas au milieu du seizième siècle, à l'époque de l'apparition du pistolet, comme la compilation le prétend, que le gantelet articulé devient déjà *général ;* presque toutes les armures cannelées sont cependant encore à gantelets inarticulés. Les gantelets à doigts séparés, où l'index a quinze, le doigt annulaire seize, et celui du milieu vingt-deux lames ou écailles, tandis que le *canon* ou le *revers,* qui protégeait le dessus de la main, est composé de trois ou quatre lames seulement, se trouvèrent alors en usage pendant quelques temps à côté du gantelet-moufle ou mitaine — qui finit peu après par disparaître. Plusieurs de ces gantelets étaient aussi pourvus d'un piton à pivot au moyen duquel la main fermée pouvait être fixée sur la poignée de l'épée ou sur celle du marteau d'armes, comme l'arsenal impérial à Vienne en possède un curieux échantillon qui fait partie de l'armure attribuée à Charles V.

Quelques-uns de ces gantelets en fer montrent aussi des saillies, sortes de têtes de clous placées à la partie supérieure et en sens opposés ; on ignore la raison d'être de ces exubérances.

Le *gantelet-brassard* de gauche pour armures de joute est une pièce de renfort qui appartient à la seconde moitié du quinzième siècle. On connaît, en outre, le *gantelet-manteau d'armes,* le *gantelet-épée* et le *gantelet pour la chasse d'ours,* tous appartenant à la seconde moitié du seizième siècle. Le dernier gantelet articulé fut bientôt remplacé par le *gant à manchettes en peau de daim,* tel qu'on le voit dans la guerre de Trente ans.

On avait cependant conservé en Angleterre, durant une partie du dix-septième siècle, des gantelets en peau garnis d'écailles (*Gloves armed with seales*), dont un exemplaire se trouve dans la collection Llewelyn-Meyrick.

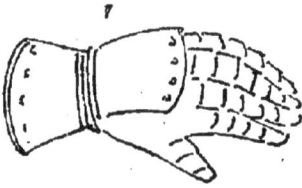

1. Gantelet articulé ou à doigts séparés (*Gefingerter Kampfhand-schuh* ou *Gefingerte Tatze* en allem., *articulated gauntlet* en angl.), d'après le monument du roi romain Gunther de Schwarzbourg érigé en 1352 au dôme de Francfort-sur-le-Mein.

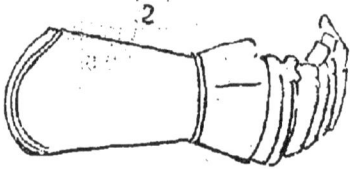

2. Gantelet dit miton et moufle (*Fausthandschuh* en allem., *inarticulated gauntlet* en angl.), du quinzième siècle. Le pouce seul est détaché.

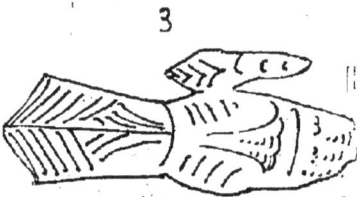

3. Gantelet dit miton, où les doigts sont figurés, de la seconde moitié du quinzième siècle.

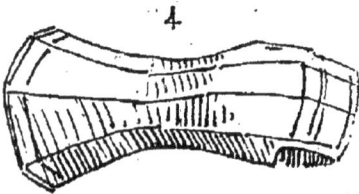

4. Gantelet-miton du seizième siècle.

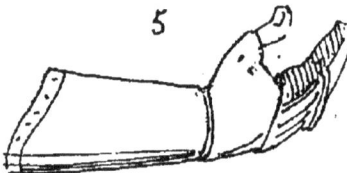

5. Id. Id. — Coll. du baron des Mazis, au musée d'artillerie à Paris.

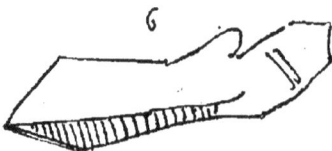

6. Gantelet gothique de la première moitié du quinzième siècle.

7. Gantelet articulé, du seizième siècle, qui se ferme au moyen d'un piton à pivot. Il fait partie d'une armure de l'arsenal impérial de Vienne.

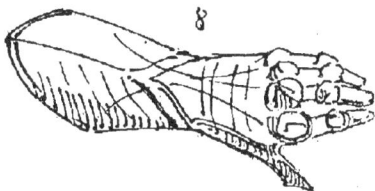

8. Gantelet articulé gothique, du milieu du quinzième siècle.

9. Gantelet-miton cannelé d'une armure maximilienne, de la seconde moitié du quinzième siècle [1]. — Coll. de l'auteur.

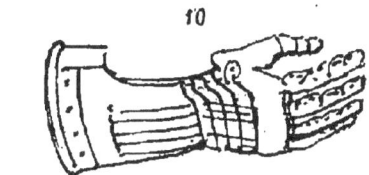

10. Gantelet articulé cannelé d'une armure maximilienne, du commencement du seizième siècle.

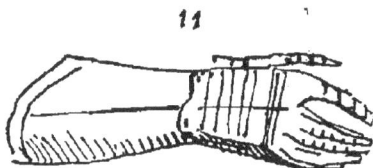

11. Gantelet de reître allemand, du commencement du dix-septième siècle.

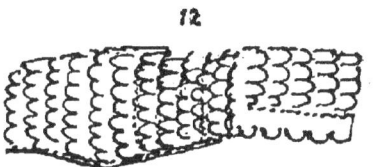

12. Gantelet anglais, du dix-septième siècle, en daim garni de lames écaillées.

1. Les armures cannelées du commencement du seizième siècle sont ordinairement à gantelets *articulés* et à *solerets-sabots* ou *pieds d'ours*. (Voy. nᵒˢ 11 et 13, au chapitre des Solerets.)

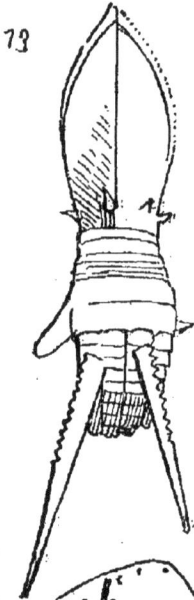

13. Gantelet du seizième siècle,
en fer, de main gauche, pour
la chasse à l'ours. Il est armé
de dards et de deux dagues den-
telées en scie. — Col. d'Ambras.

C'est une arme de fantaisie
et probablement toute locale
que l'on rencontre fort rarement.

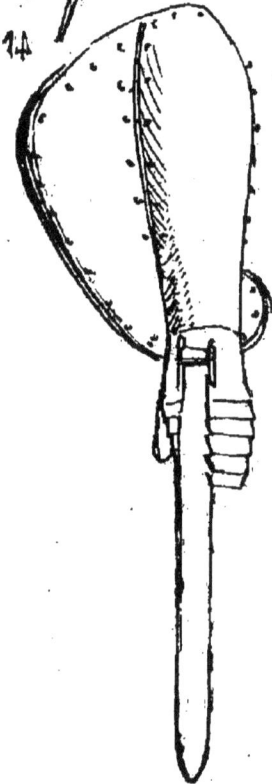

14. Gantelet allemand pour main
gauche, en fer, à targette ou
grande garde, et à longue épée.
Ce gantelet, du seizième siècle,
paraît également avoir été destiné pour la chasse à l'ours. —
Col. d'Ambras. Ces pièces sont
fort rares, elles doivent avoir
été très-peu répandues, et probablement dans le Nord seulement.

JAMBIÈRES ET CHAUSSURES

Grèves ou jambières. — Bas-de-chausses laniérés et maillés. — Chaussures en fer dites solerets et pédieux. — Bottes de guerre et housseaux.

Tous les manuscrits du huitième au dixième siècle montrent l'homme de guerre sans jambières ni grèves (*Beincshienen* et *Kettenstrümpfe* en allemand, *greves* en anglais), et, s'il n'est pas toujours représenté les jambes dépourvues d'aucune défense, il les a seulement enveloppées de lanières de cuir. Même dans les tapisseries de Bayeux, qui pourtant ne remontent pas au delà de la fin du onzième siècle, Guillaume le Conquérant seul a le bas des jambes armé, tandis qu'aucun de ses chevaliers ne porte de jambières maillées ou autrement armées. A partir du onzième siècle, haut et bas-de-chausses et chaussures qui paraissent adhérentes, ou ne formant qu'un seul vêtement, sont presque toujours en mailles de fer.

Vers la fin du treizième siècle apparaissent en France les premières jambières à plaques (*tumelières*, *grèves*, en allem. *Bienschienen*), les genouillères ou *boucles* (*Kniestücke* en allemand, *knee-caps* en anglais) et les cuissards (*Dieling* ou *Schenkelschienen* en allemand, *cuissards* en anglais), fabriqués d'abord en cuir bouilli et ensuite en fer et en acier. En Allemagne, les tumelières et les solerets ont déjà apparu à la fin du onzième, comme l'indique encore le monument de Mersebourg.

Ce n'est d'abord que le devant de la jambe qui est protégé par la plaque attachée au moyen de courroies sur le
bas-de-chausses en mailles. Le tombeau de sir Hugh Hastings, érigé en 1347, paraît démontrer qu'à cette époque
le chevalier anglais portait encore des chausses et grèves
en mailles, tandis que le monument de Mersebourg, du
onzième siècle, les miniatures du manuscrit du treizième
siècle à la bibliothèque de Berlin, et le *Lancelot du Lac*,
de 1360, représentent déjà l'armure à plates que l'Allemagne
et la Suisse paraissent avoir adopté les premières, puisque,
après le monument de Mersebourg et le manuscrit du treizième siècle, à Berlin, c'est le tombeau de Berthold, mort
en 1258, renfermant les plus anciens documents où l'on
voit représentée cette nouvelle armure.

Les solerets ou pédieux (du latin *pes*, *pedis*, pied ; *Ei-
senschuh* en allemand, *soleret* et *goad* en anglais), chaussures
articulées en fer ou lamées, ne paraissent remonter qu'au
commencement du quatorzième siècle. La chaussure don
est armé Rodolphe de Souabe dans le monument de 1080, à
la cathédrale de Mersebourg, ne montre pas de lames. Le
premier soleret connu est *pointu*, et s'approche du soleret *à
la poulaine* (de *poulaine*, bec de galère), que l'on croit à tort
appartenir seulement au quinzième siècle.

Une preuve incontestable que cette mode existait déjà
au douzième siècle, se trouve dans les mémoires de la
princesse byzantine Anna Comnena (1080-1148), où l'auteur
dit que : « Le Franc est terrible quand il est à cheval, mais
dès que sa monture s'abat, le cavalier ne paraît plus du tout
le même, alourdi qu'il est par son bouclier et *les longues
chaussures à becs* qui l'empêchent de marcher et le rendent
facilement prisonnier. » Le manuscrit allemand du treizième siècle, *Tristan et Isolde*, montre aussi déjà les chevaliers en chaussures *à la poulaine*, mode qui paraît être
venue de la Hongrie, où elle régnait universellement au
douzième siècle. On l'attribue cependant aussi à Falco IV,

comte d'Anjou (1087) et à Henri II roi d'Angleterre (1154-1189), qui l'adopta pour cacher une difformité, ce qui lui a valu le sobriquet de *Cornadu* ou *Cornatus*. A la bataille de Sempach (1386), les chevaliers autrichiens, après être descendus de cheval, coupèrent les longs bouts de leurs solerets. La chaussure à la poulaine, qui avait disparu vers le milieu du quatorzième siècle, pour faire place à la forme *demi-poulaine* ou *ogivale de lancette*, reparaît vers la fin de ce siècle, et se maintient de nouveau dans le courant du quatorzième, où, de 1440 à 1470, on adopta cependant aussi la forme *arc tiers point*, et, vers 1485, le *demi-sabot* ou *demi-pied d'ours*. Le *sabot* ou le *pied d'ours*, la chaussure propre aux armures cannelées, a régné de 1490 à 1560; il fut suivi du *bec de cane*. Ce dernier soleret fut remplacé par le housseau et la botte. La connaissance des formes de chaussures adoptées par les peuples chrétiens de l'Europe aux différentes époques du moyen âge et de la renaissance, est très-importante pour le classement des sculptures, des miniatures et des armes, car le vêtement militaire a toujours subi l'influence de la mode à laquelle était soumis le costume civil.

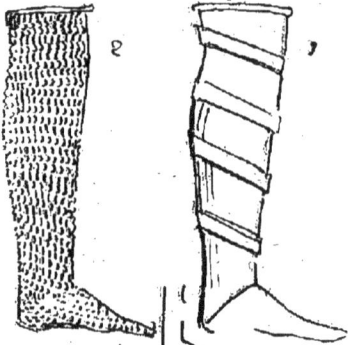

1. Bas-de-chausse laniéré en usage avant le onzième siècle.

2. Bas de chausse maillé de fer, qui apparaît au commencement du onzième siècle et disparaît en partie au commencement du treizième, où il est remplacé par les tumelières.

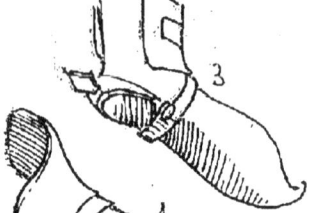

3. Premier soleret et première tumelière connus, d'après le tombeau de Rodolphe de Souabe, de 1080, à la cathédrale de Mersebourg.

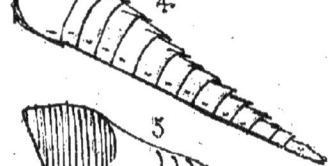

4. Pédieux ou soleret à la poulaine du douzième, du treizième et de la première moitié du quatorzième siècle.

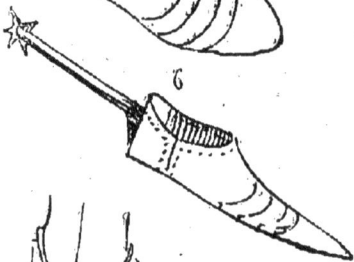

5. Pédieux ou soleret demi-poulaine ou ogivale-lancette, de la fin du quatorzième siècle.

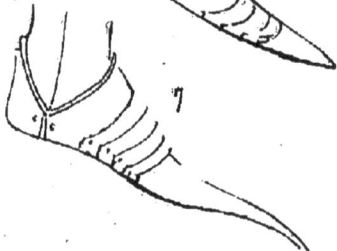

6 et 7. Pédieux ou solerets à la poulaine, du quinzième siècle.

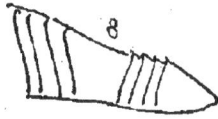

8. Soleret ou pédieux en arc tiers point, en usage de 1450 à 1485.

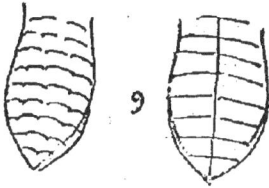

9. Soleret ou pédieux du milieu du quinzième siècle, d'après les bas-reliefs en marbre ayant fait partie de l'arc d'Alphonse V, roi d'Aragon, à Naples, à son entrée triomphale en 1443. Cette même forme de chaussures de fer se voit aussi sur une terre cuite de Nuremberg du quinzième siècle, qui fait partie de la collection de l'auteur, et dont le sujet représente Charlemagne.

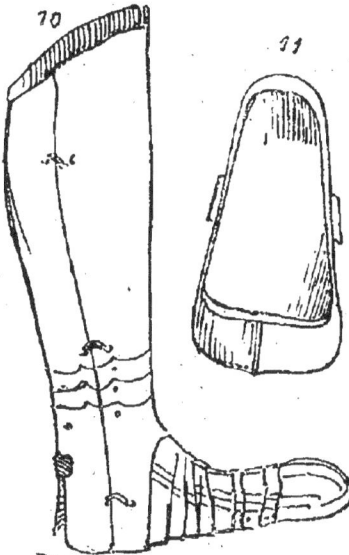

10. Grève avec soleret — demi-sabot, en usage vers 1480 et 1485; elle fait partie d'une armure allemande cannelée dite maximilienne, de la collection de l'auteur; les gantelets mitons ou moufles de cette armure, aussi bien que la forme du soleret, indiquent la fin du quinzième et un peu le commencement du seizième siècle.

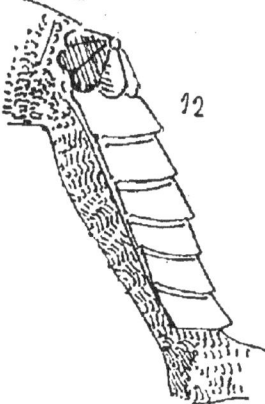

11. Soleret-sabot du seizième siècle (1490-1560). — Musée d'artillerie de Paris.

12. Grève persane, d'après un manuscrit du seizième siècle; copie du Schah-Nameh. — Bibliothèque de Munich.

13. Grève à soleret pied-d'ours, d'une armure allemande cannelée dite maximilienne et milanaise, en usage de 1490 à 1560.

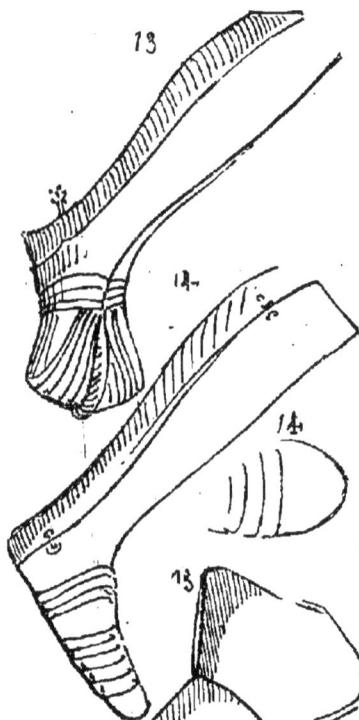

14. Grève à soleret bec-de-cane, d'une armure en usage vers 1560. Il ne faut pas confondre cette forme de solerets avec celle dite ogivale-tiers-point du quinzième siècle.

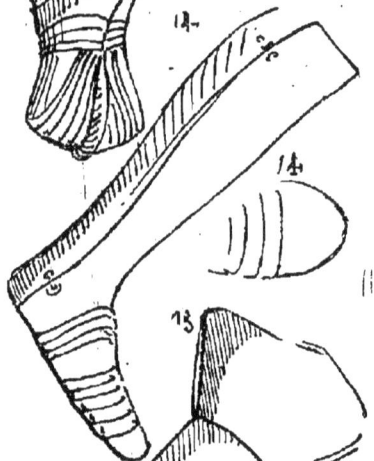

15. Bottes ou plutôt bottes-housseaux de carabinier, de 1680.

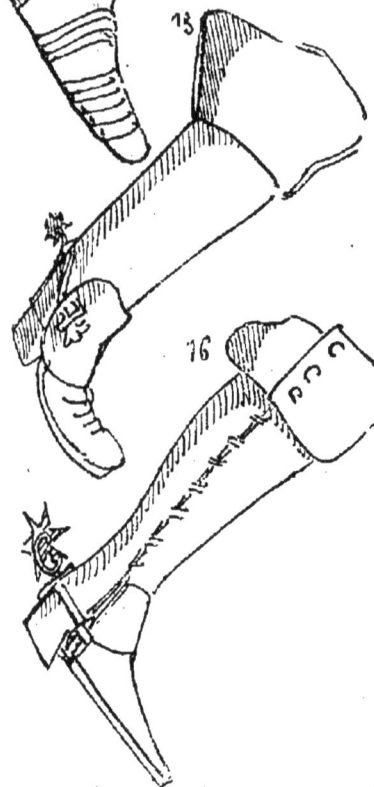

16. Housseaux français en cuir, du règne de Louis XV (1715-1774). Ils sont en forme de guêtre, les revers ont trois boutons, les jambières sont lacées, les bouts carrés et les talons de haute forme. Les éperons datent de la fin du règne de Louis XIV, et ressemblent grandement aux éperons mexicains. — A. 325. Musée d'artillerie de Paris.

L'ÉPERON.

L'éperon (de l'italien *sperone*) qui s'appelait, au moyen âge, *carcaire*, du *calcar* latin (en allemand *Sporn*, et en anglais *spur*), est composé de la branche (*Bügel* en allemand, *branch* ou *shank* en anglais), de la tige (*Hals* en allemand, *spurneck* en anglais) et de la pointe (*Stachel* en allemand, *prick* en anglais) ou de la molette (*Rad* en allemand, *rowel* en anglais).

L'éperon paraît avoir été employé d'abord par les Romains, qui en comuniquèrent probablement l'usage aux peuples du Nord. Les cavaliers des bas-reliefs assyriens n'ont point d'éperon, ni ceux des monuments persiques et égyptiens, et les Grecs des temps héroïques, qui n'avaient pas de cavalerie et manquaient même de verbe pour désigner l'action de monter à cheval, n'ont pas connu non plus cet instrument.

Les plus anciens éperons étaient à *un seul dard*, dont la forme ressemble à la pointe d'un pain de sucre, et qui était fort gros, sans tige et rivé directement sur la branche. Vers le dixième siècle, l'éperon montre déjà un *petit bout de tige* qui s'allonge vers le onzième, et se relève en biais au douzième siècle. La molette paraît vers la fin du treizième. Cette petite roue tournante indique par le nombre et la longueur de ses pointes aussi bien l'époque à laquelle appartient l'éperon, que la forme de la branche et de la tige. L'art héraldique en Angleterre fait dériver le *mullet* ou l'étoile héraldique de la molette de l'éperon à *cinq pointes*, quoique ces molettes appartiennent pour le plus grand nombre au dix-septième siècle, et qu'en Angleterre la molette à six pointes même fût inconnue avant le règne de Henri VI (1422), mais on en voit déjà dans les miniatures de l'histoire romaine, manuscrit bourguignon du commencement du quinzième siècle, conservé à la bibliothèque de l'Arsenal à Paris.

En Allemagne, on avait déjà des molettes à huit pointes au quatorzième siècle, comme le démontrent, au musée national de Munich, les éperons qui ont appartenu aux chevaliers de Heideck et au duc Albrecht II de Bavière. Ces éperons, où tout montre un fini de travail très-remarquable pour l'époque, se signalent encore plus par la forme et la disposition de leurs branches, qui indiquent que l'éperon était porté sur une grève en fer qui protégeait tout le pied, et dont la partie qui couvrait le tendon forme toujours un angle aigu. Avant l'adoption des grèves et plaques comme à l'époque où, vers la fin du dix-septième siècle, la botte avait remplacé la grève, les branches sont *arrondies*.

La tige qui, au temps du plus haut développement des armes de tournois, au quinzième siècle, s'était allongée outre mesure, se raccourcit de nouveau vers la fin du seizième siècle, où l'éperon a souvent des molettes à douze, quinze et dix-huit pointes.

L'éperon, du temps de Louis XIII, est petit et souvent enjolivé par des entailles, tandis que sous le règne de Louis XIV il affecte la forme mexicaine à larges tiges, découpées à jour, et à énormes molettes, souvent à neuf pointes. A partir du quinzième siècle, le nombre de pointes seul ne peut cependant plus servir de guide, puisqu'il y a continuellement confusion, et les pointes varient de six à vingt, selon les pays et les époques. De tout le harnais, l'éperon est la pièce qui offre le plus d'incertitude pour son classement chronologique.

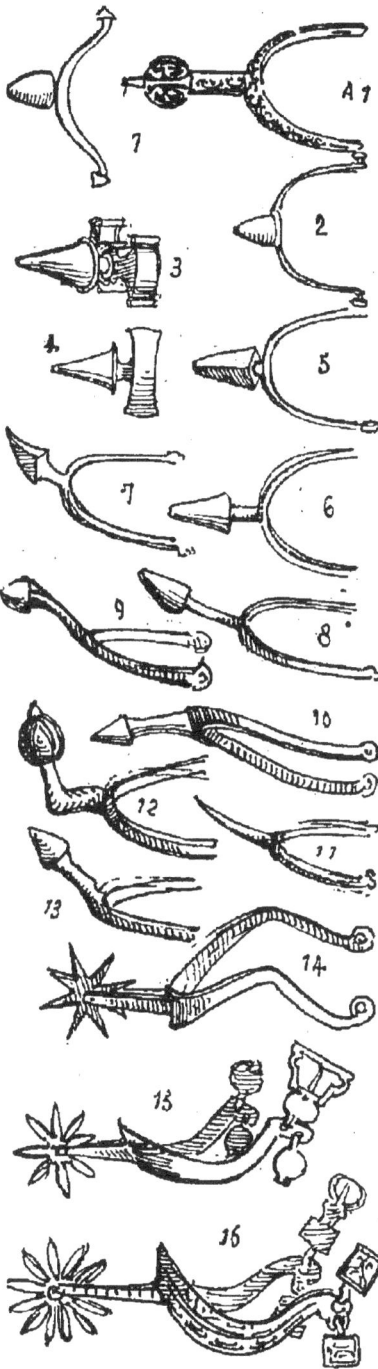

1 et 2. Eperons allemands en fer, du huitième siècle, trouvés à Groschnowitz, près Oppeln. — Musée de Berlin.

A 1. Éperon en or de Charlemagne. — Musée du Louvre.

3. Eperon danois en bronze, à pointe de fer, du huitième siècle. — Musée de Copenhague.

4. Eperon allemand en fer, du huitième siècle, trouvé à Gnevikon, à Ruppin. — Musée de Berlin.

5. Eperon allemand en fer, du dixième siècle, trouvé près Brandebourg.—Col. de l'auteur.

6. Eperon anglo-saxon ou normand, du dixième ou du onzième siècle. — Tour de Londres.

7. Eperon allemand, du dixième siècle, trouvé à Constance. — Musée de Sigmaringen.

8. Eperon allemand en fer, du onzième siècle. — Musée de Sigmaringen.

9. Eperon allemand en fer, du douzième siècle, d'après les peintures murales au dôme de Brunswick, exécutées sous Henri le Lion, mort en 1195.

10. Eperon anglais en fer, de la fin du douzième siècle, trouvé à Chesterford. — Musée Neville à Audley-End.

11. Eperon d'après un reliquaire du douzième siècle, de la collection du dernier roi de Hanovre.

12. Eperon en fer, du treizième siècle. — Musée de Hanovre.

13. Eperon suisse en fer, du treizième siècle, trouvé dans le lac de Morat. — Collection du gymnase, à Morat.

14. Eperon allemand en fer, du commencement du quatorzième

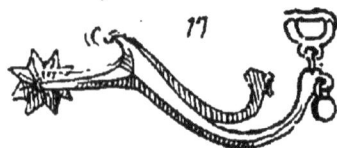

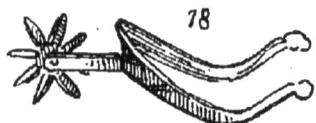

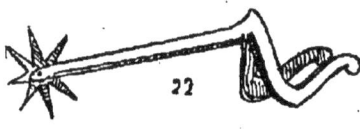

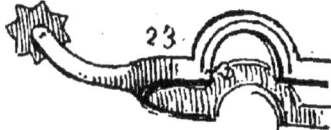

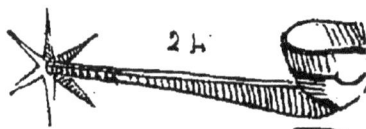

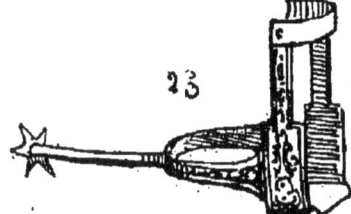

siècle, trouvé dans un tombeau près Brandebourg. — Col. de l'auteur.

15. Eperon allemand, de la fin du quatorzième siècle; il est à molettes à huit pointes, et a été trouvé dans le tombeau du chevalier de Heideck. — Musée de Munich.

16. Eperon allemand, de la fin du quatorzième siècle, dont la molette est à douze pointes. Il a appartenu au duc Albrecht II de Bavière. — Musée de Munich.

17. Eperon italien en fer, du quatorzième siècle. — Musée de Sigmaringen.

18. Eperon allemand en fer, du quatorzième siècle, trouvé à Constance. — Musée de Sigmaringen.

19. Eperon en cuivre, du quatorzième siècle. — Col. Llewelyn-Meyrink.

20. Eperon en fer à double tige, du quatorzième siècle, trouvé à Mayence. — Musée de Sigmaringen.

21. Eperon en fer à molette à six pointes, du quinzième siècle. — Col. Widter, à Vienne.

22. Eperon allemand en fer, du quinzième siècle, à molette à huit pointes, trouvé à l'île de Rügen. — Musée de Berlin.

23. Eperon en fer, de la fin du quinzième siècle. — Musée de Sigmaringen.

24. Eperon mauresque, du quinzième siècle. — Musée d'artillerie de Paris. De semblables éperons sont attribués, dans la collection d'Ambras, à la Pologne et au seizième siècle.

25. Eperon-étrier, cuivre doré,

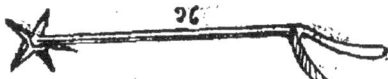

du quinzième siècle. Il a appartenu au duc Christophe de Bavière, et se trouve au musée de Munich.

26. Eperon allemand en cuivre, de 25 cent., de la fin du quinzième siècle. — Col. Soeter et col. d'Ambras.

27. Eperon anglais, en cuivre, 12 c., de la fin du quinzième siècle. — Col. Llewelyn-Meyrick.

28. Eperon en fer doré, du seizième siècle. — Musée d'artillerie de Paris.

29. Eperon en fer, du dix-septième siècle. — Musée de Sigmaringen. (Les branches sont déjà *arrondies*.)

30. Eperon anglais en acier, du seizième siècle. — Col. Llewelyn-Meyrick.

31. Eperon allemand en fer, du seizième siècle. — Musée de Sigmaringen.

32 A. Eperon anglais en fer doré. Il a appartenu à Ralph Sadler du règne d'Edouard VI (1547-1553). — Col. Llewelyn-Meyrick.

32 B. Eperon allemand, qui fait partie d'une armure pour homme et pour cheval.

33. Eperon allemand attribué au seizième siècle. Il est à trois molettes. Genre fort rare et qui me parait du dix-septième siècle à cause de sa branche *arrondie*.

34. Grand éperon en fer noirci, dont les branches sont creuses. Il servait de gourde ou pour cacher des dépêches. Le talon de la tige dévissé forme le goulot. — Col. Ambras à Vienne, et col. Francisco-Carolinum à Lintz.

35. Eperon allemand du seizième siècle. — Musée de Dresde.

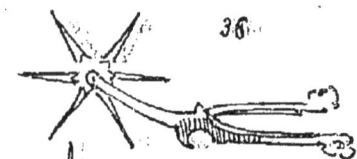

36. Eperon anglais de la fin du seizième ou du dix-septième siècle, de la collection Llewelyn-Meyrick, où il est attribué au quinzième siècle, ce à quoi s'oppose la courbure des branches.

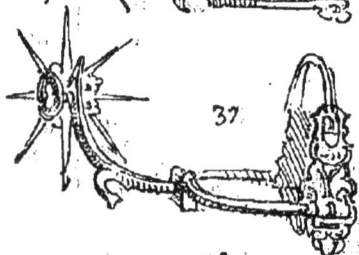

37. Eperon espagnol de la fin ou du milieu du dix-septième siècle, reproduit d'après un ouvrage espagnol qui l'attribue à Alphonse Perez de Guzman, né en 1278, mort en 1320, époque où la molette, bien plus petite, avait été à peine adoptée. On remarquera que les branches sont arrondies.

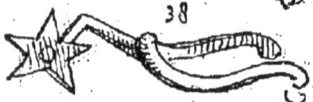

38. Eperon anglais, du seizième siècle. — Col. Llewelyn-Meyrick.

39. Eperon du seizième siècle, en cuivre doré, attribué à tort à Louis XIV (1643-1715). — Louvre.

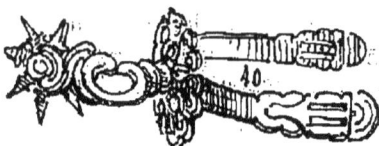

40. Eperon en fer du règne de Louis XIV (1643-1715). Il ressemble aux éperons mexicains. — Col. de l'auteur.

41. Eperon allemand en fer, du dix-septième siècle. — Musée de Sigmaringen.

42. Eperon anglais dit de guêtre. Fin du dix-septième siècle. — Col. Llewelyn-Meyrick.

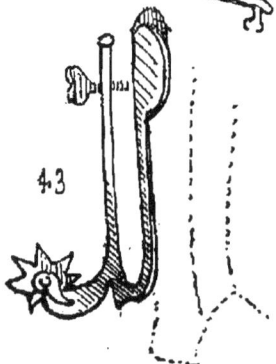

43. Eperon polonais du dix-septième siècle. — Musées de Prague et de Sigmaringen.

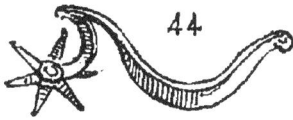

44. Eperon allemand du seizième siècle. — Musée de Berlin.

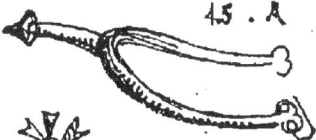

45 A. Eperon persan, du quinzième siècle. — Col. de l'auteur.

45 B. Eperon allemand, du dix-septième siècle. L'écartement des branches et leur courbure semi-circulaire ou ovale indiquent que cet éperon appartient à une époque où la grève n'existait plus. Les branches de l'éperon porté sur les grèves qui affectaient derrière le tibia la forme anguleuse du tendon, ne peuvent pas former de courbe.

46. Eperon africain ancien, en fer; cette même forme est encore en usage aujourd'hui.

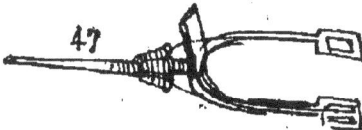

47. Eperon arabe;   Id.   Id.

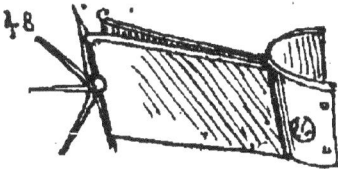

48. Eperon brésilien; Id.   Id.

L'ARMURE DU CHEVAL

L'armure du cheval de bataille et de tournois (*Panzer-decke* en allemand, *horse-armour* en anglais), est souvent nommée faussement *caparaçon* (de l'espagnol augmentatif de *cape*), mot qui désigne uniquement la riche couverture d'étoffe étendue par-dessus les bardes du destrier [1]. L'armure du cheval, au moyen âge chrétien, n'était arrivée à sa perfection, comme celle de l'homme, que vers le milieu du quinzième siècle, où elle se composait, dès lors, du *chanfrein* (de *camus,* le cou, et *framum,* frein, ou, plus simplement, de champ et de frein; en allemand *Rosstirne, chanfrin* en anglais), la partie qui couvrait le devant de la tête du cheval, et qui était *à vue* ou *aveugle* [2], de la *têtière* (*Kopfstück* en allemand, *head stall* en anglais), nom qui désigne la pièce de jointure du chanfrein et de la barde de crinière et les deux plaques de mâchoires, et aussi l'ensemble de l'armure de la tête du cheval; de la *barde de crinière* (*Mæhnenpanzer* ou *Kammkappe* en allemand, *crinet* en anglais); de la *barde du poitrail* (*Brustpanzer* ou *Vordergebüge* en allemand, *peytrel* en anglais), à charnière ou *à jupe* ou *tonnelle;* de la *croupière avec ses cuissards* (*Krupp und Lendenpanzer* ou *Hintergebüge* en allemand, *croupière* en anglais), soit complets et réunis en *jupe* ou *tonnelle,* soit en *armure coupée,* c'est-à-dire séparée sous la queue; du *garde-queue* (*Schwanzriempanzer* en allemand, *steel-*

---

[1]. Le destrier (du latin *dextra,* main droite) désignait le cheval de rechange que l'écuyer menait à *dextra,* ou en laisse, de la main droite.

[2]. Le chanfrein aveugle avait les oreillères fermées pour empêcher le cheval de se dérober.

reins en anglais ; des *flançois* (*Flanckenpanzer* ou *Seiten-blætter* en allemand, *flanchards* en anglais), qui reliaient la barde du poitrail à la croupière et aux cuissards ; de la *selle avec ses étriers*, de la *bride* avec son *mors* ou son *bridon* avec *bossettes*[1], pièces auxquelles il faut ajouter la *muse-rolle* (*Maulkorb* ou *Nasenband* en allemand, *noseband of a bridle* ou *horse-muzzle* en anglais), particulièrement en usage en Allemagne au seizième siècle, et dont, selon le *Diversarum gentium armatura equestris* de 1617, toute la cavalerie allemande était pourvue.

Ceci paraît contestable. La muserolle, qui se plaçait par dessus les naseaux du cheval, formait plutôt un ornement et ne pouvait être utile à la guerre ; on s'en servait proba-blement dans les fêtes pour ajouter à l'éclat du caparaçon-nement, comme l'a démontré Jobst Ammon dans la série de gravures de son traité d'équitation civile. L'armurier alle-mand avait poussé le perfectionnement de l'armure du cheval si loin, qu'un tableau de 1480, conservé à l'arsenal de Vienne, montre maître Albrecht, armurier de l'archiduc Maximilien, sur un cheval armé de *jambières articulées*.

Au commencement du quatorzième siècle, cette armure, comme dans bien des pays celle de l'homme, était encore en mailles, mais recouverte d'un caparaçon ou couverture d'étoffes. Le chanfrein proprement dit était déjà connu des Grecs, mais ne paraît avoir été adopté en Europe qu'à la fin du quatorzième siècle ou au commencement du quinzième, car avant cette époque la *têtière* du cheval est toujours représentée en mailles et à plaques en cuir bouilli.

---

1. L'ornement attaché aux côtés du mors. On appelle aussi bossette la pièce de cuir qui sert à couvrir l'œil du mulet.

1. Têtière (*Kopfstück* en allem., *head stall* en angl.), d'après un manuscrit du quatorzième siècle.

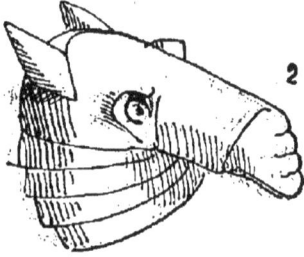

2. Id. Id. du quinzième siècle.

3. Chanfrein (*Rosstirne* en allem., *chanfrin* en angl.) à vue, du milieu du quinzième siècle.

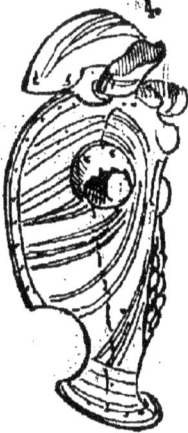

4. Têtière complète, dont le chanfrein est à vue.

5. Chanfrein aveugle, du seizième siècle.

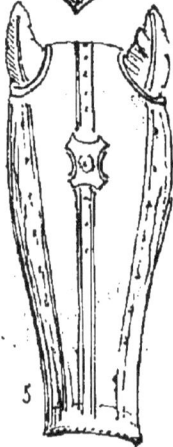

6. Chanfrein allemand à vue, du seizième siècle, richement repoussé; il fait partie d'une armure de l'arsenal impérial de Vienne. La collection Llewelyn-Meyrick, la col. d'Ambras, l'arsenal impérial de Vienne, l'armorial de Madrid, la col. de la Tour de Londres, la col. de M. le comte de Nieuwerkerke, le musée d'artillerie de Paris, etc., possèdent tous de bons exemplaires de ces pièces d'armures de cheval, sur lesquelles les armuriers de l'époque ont aimé à montrer leur savoir-faire.

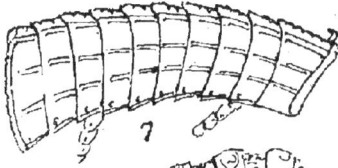

7. Barde de crinière (*Mæhnen-panzer* ou *Kammkappe* en allem., *crinet* en angl.), de la fin du quinzième et du commencement du seizième siècle.

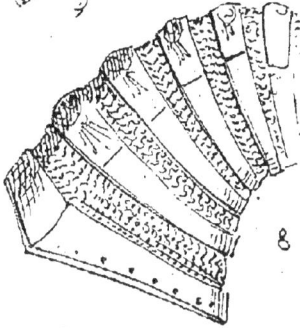

8. Barde de crinière à gorgeret en plaques et en mailles, d'une armure de la fin du quinzième siècle, attribuée à Maximilien Ier. — Col. d'Ambras. Une semblable armure dans la col. Nieuwerkerke.

9. Barde de poitrail (*Brustpanzer* ou *Vordergebüge* en allem., *peytrel* en angl.) du milieu du quinzième siècle.

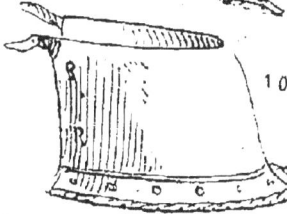

10. Barde de poitrail à jupe ou à tonnelle, du seizième siècle.

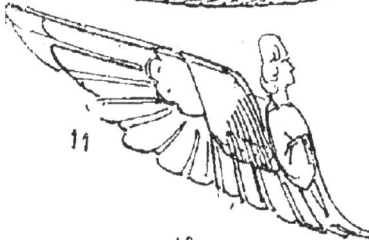

11. Barde de poitrail d'une armure de la fin du quinzième siècle, attribuée à Maximilien Ier. — Col. d'Ambras.

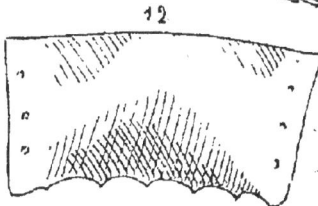

12. Flançois (*Flanckenpanzer* ou *Seitenblatt* en allem., *flanchard* en angl.), du milieu du quinzième siècle.

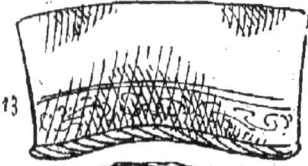

13. Flançois d'une armure de cheval dite à jupe ou à tonnelle.

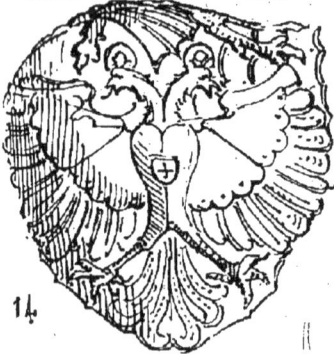

14. Croupière à cuissards (*Krupp* et *Lendenpanzer*, aussi appelée *Hintergebüge* en allem., *croupiere* en angl.), d'une armure de la fin du quinzième siècle, attribuée à Maximilien Ier. — Col. d'Ambras.

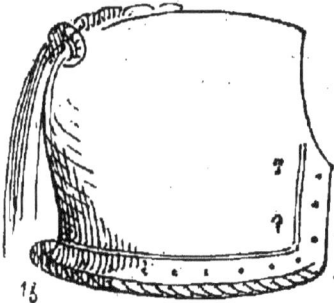

15. Croupière à jupe ou à tonnelle, du seizième siècle.

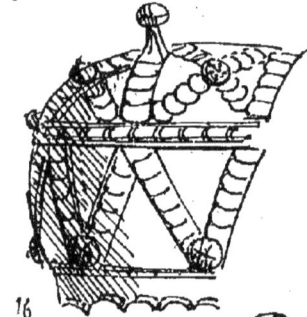

16. Croupière à jupe treillissée, de la seconde moitié du quinzième siècle, sinon du commencement du seizième. — Col. d'Ambras.

17. Garde-queue (*Schwanzriempanzer* en allem., *steel-reins* en angl.). — Col. Llewelyn-Meyrick.

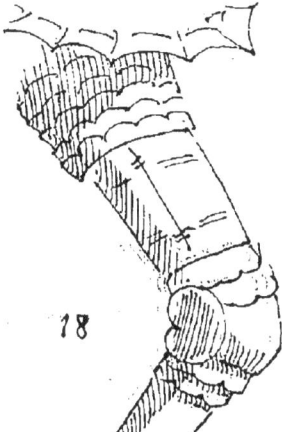

18

18. Jambière de cheval d'armure allemande, d'après une peinture de 1480 à l'arsenal de Vienne, qui représente à cheval maître Albrecht, l'armurier de l'archiduc Maximilien.

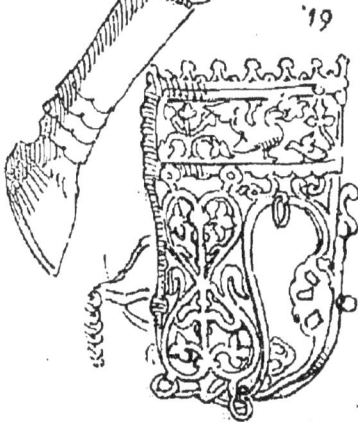

'19

19. Muserolle (*Maulkorb* ou *Nasenband* en allem., *noseband of a bridle* ou *horse-muzzle* en angl.). — Musées de Sigmaringen, de la Tour de Londres, arsenal de Turin, musée d'artillerie de Paris, col. d'Ambras et Llewelyn-Meyrick, etc., etc.

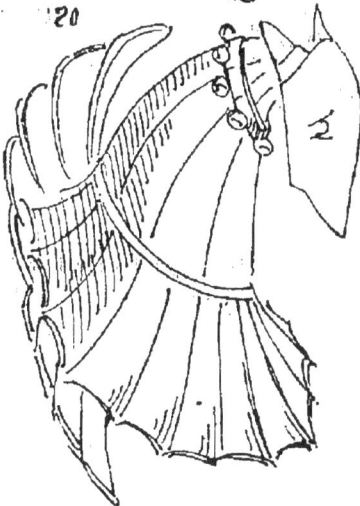

'20

20. Armure de cheval du devant (têtière, bardes de poitrail et crinière) avec la selle de tournois qui couvrait une partie de la poitrine et les jambes du cavalier. D'après la gravure d'un *Tournierbuch* (livre de tournois) du commencement du seizième siècle.

LA SELLE

La selle (du latin *sella*, siége ; *Sattel* en allemand, *saddle* en anglais) paraît avoir été inconnue dans l'antiquité avant notre ère. Les bas-reliefs assyriens ne montrent ni selles ni étriers, et sur les monuments égyptiens, le cheval est uniquement attelé au char. Les Grecs, privés d'abord de cavalerie, et manquant même de terme pour exprimer l'action de monter à cheval, ne devaient pas non plus avoir connu un ustensile que les Romains même ne paraissent avoir introduit chez eux que vers le quatrième siècle après J.-C. ; c'est Zonaras, auteur de cette époque, qui le premier a fait mention d'une selle proprement dite, en décrivant un combat livré en 340, par Constance à son frère Constantin.

L'usage de la selle paraît remonter, en Scandinavie, à l'âge du fer, à une période peut-être antérieure au sixième siècle, si on se rapporte aux pommeaux et aux étriers en bronze conservés au musée de Copenhague, et le *Codex aureus*, du huitième ou neuvième siècle, de Saint-Gall, représente déjà le coursier allemand avec selle et étriers. En France, on connaît un bas-relief attribué à cette même époque (?) à Saint-Julien de Brioude (Haute-Loire), et la tapisserie de Bayeux du onzième siècle, où selles et étriers figurent également. — La selle de guerre avait, presque déjà à son début, la même forme qu'à la fin du moyen âge, à l'exception de la dossière, qui était bien moins élevée. La selle de tournoi ou de joute était souvent, au treizième et au quatorzième siècle, en bois, et pourvue de deux *espèces de fourreaux* qui couvraient entièrement les jambes, les cuisses, et protégeaient même les hanches et une partie de la poitrine du cavalier, fourreaux qui furent remplacés plus tard par les cuissards en fer.

Les cinq exemplaires connus de ces curieuses selles, parvenues jusqu'à nous, se trouvent à Regensbourg, à Constance, à Schaffhouse, à la Tour de Londres et au musée germanique de Nuremberg.

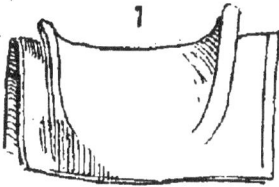

1. Selle d'armes allemande du huitième ou du neuvième siècle. — *Codex aureus* de Saint-Gall.

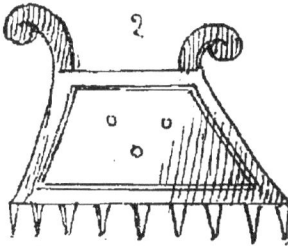

2. Selle d'armes normande du onzième siècle. — Tapisserie de Bayeux.

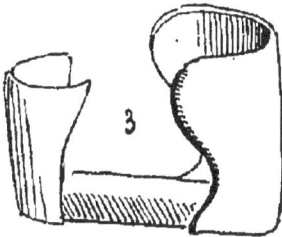

3. Selle d'armes bohémienne du treizième siècle. — Manuscrit de Boleslav, à la bibliothèque de Raudnitz.

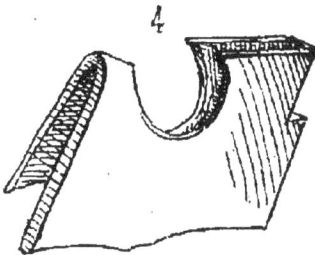

4. Selle d'armes allemande du treizième siècle. — Manuscrit *Tristan et Isolde*, à la bibliothèque de Munich.

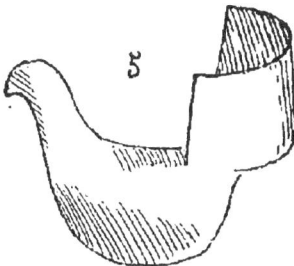

5. Selle d'armes allemande du treizième siècle. — Manuscrit de l'*Enéide allemande*. — Bibliothèque de Berlin.

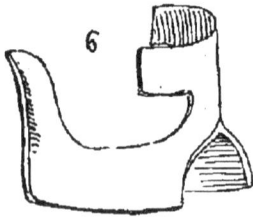

6. Selle d'armes, d'après un ivoire du quatorzième siècle.

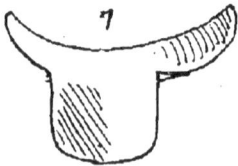

7. Selle d'armes italienne, d'après un drap imprimé du quatorzième siècle. — Col. Odet, à Sitten.

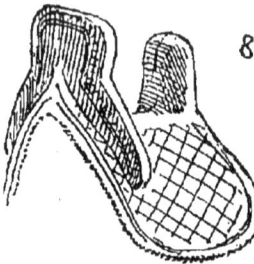

8. Selle d'armes italienne de la seconde moitié du quinzième siècle. Statue équestre de Bartolomeo Coleoni, à Venise.

9. Selle d'armes allemande de la moitié du quinzième siècle. — Musée d'artillerie de Paris.

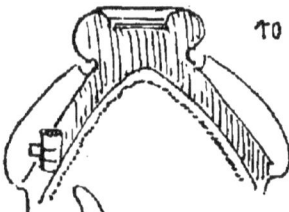

10. Selle d'armes allemande du commencement du seizième siècle, provenant de Strasbourg. — Musée d'artillerie de Paris.

11. Selle d'armes persane, d'après la copie du *Schah-Nameh*, exécutée vers 1600. — Musée de Munich.

32.

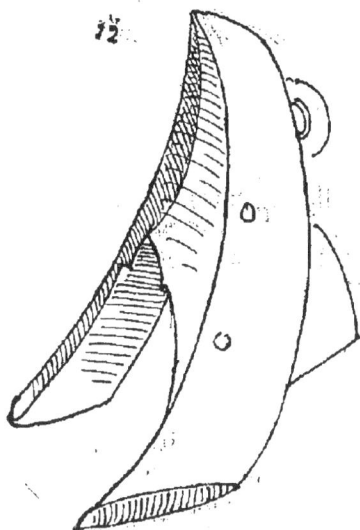

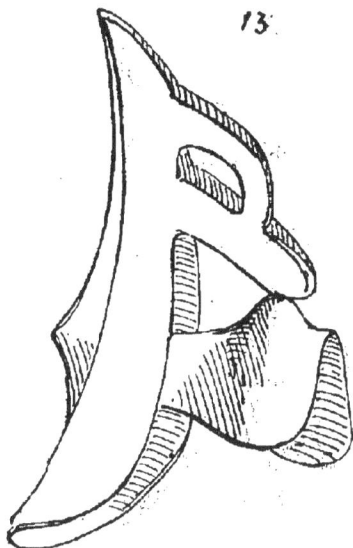

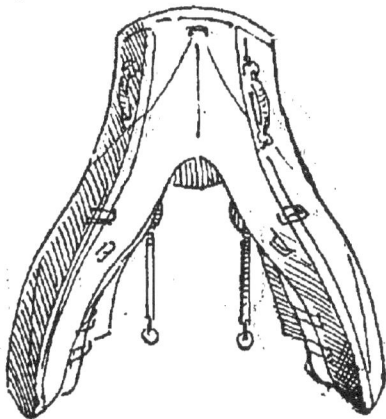

12. Selle de joute allemande ou suisse du quatorzième siècle, provenant de l'arsenal de Schaffhouze, où elle date du tournoi tenu dans cette ville en 1392. Elle est en bois recouvert de cuir de porc et ressemble aux selles conservées à la Tour de Londres et au musée de Ratisbonne, à l'exception de ce qu'elle servait à courir assis, tandis que le chevalier devait se tenir debout dans les selles susmentionnées. Elle a 1^m,07 de hauteur totale, mais la partie supérieure destinée à protéger le ventre et la poitrine ne mesure que 56 cent., tandis que cette même partie des deux autres selles a 75 cent. — Musée de la société historique de Schaffhouse et col. Rennö de Constance.

13. Selle de joute allemande de la fin du quatorzième ou du commencement du quinzième siècle, provenant de la collection Peuker à Berlin. Elle a 1^m,70 de hauteur et 1^m,14 de longueur et protégeait entièrement les jambes et la poitrine du cavalier qui était obligé de courir debout dans ses étriers. — Tour de Londres.

14. Selle semblable à la précédente provenant de la famille *Paulstorfer*, éteinte en 1622, et dont elle porte les couleurs, rouge et blanc. Cet exemplaire n'a qu'un mètre de hauteur et ne paraît remonter qu'à la seconde moitié du quinzième siècle; suspendu jadis dans la chapelle des Minorités à Ratisbonne où se trouvent les caveaux de la famille Paulstorfer, il fait actuellement partie du musée de Ratisbonne, ville où M. Hans Weiningen a bien voulu le dessiner pour moi. Le musée germanique possède une autre semblable selle provenant de la même famille.

Ces cinq exemplaires (Schaffhouse, Constance, Nuremberg et Londres) sont les seuls que l'auteur a trouvés dans les musées et les collections de l'Europe.

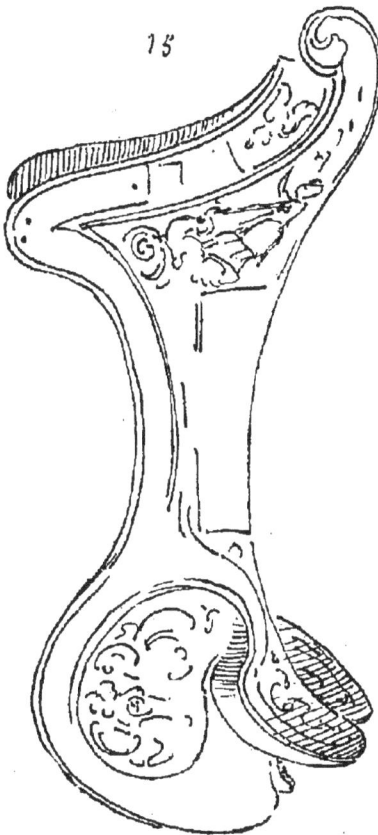

15. Selle allemande en ivoire de la fin du quinzième siècle. — Col. Nieuwerkerke, Meyrick, d'Ambras et musées de Montbijou à Berlin et de Brunswick; celle de ce dernier musée a appartenu au duc Magnus, mort à la bataille de Liefenhausen. La selle à la Tour de Londres porte l'inscription suivante :

« *Jch hoff des pesten*
« *Hilf Got wal auf Sand Jorgen*
Nam. »

(J'espère le mieux, si Dieu m'aide, au nom de saint George.)

16. Selle allemande de joute du seizième siècle, d'après le *Tournierbuch*. Elle ressemble aux nᵒˢ 12, 13 et 14, mais elle diffère de ces selles du quatorzième siècle, en ce qu'elle est bien moins haute et ne couvre entièrement ni les jambes ni la poitrine.

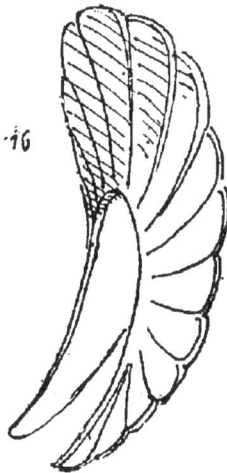

L'ÉTRIER

L'étrier (du bas latin *strivarium* ou *straparium; Steig-bügel* en allemand, *stirrup* en anglais) se compose de la *planche*, la partie où pose le pied, et de l'*œil*, l'ouverture où passe l'*étrière* ou l'*étrivière*, la courroie par laquelle l'étrier est suspendu à la selle.

Comme la selle était inconnue aux anciens avant l'ère chrétienne, l'usage de l'étrier aussi ne remonte probablement qu'au quatrième siècle, où Zonaras, auteur de l'époque, a fait le premier mention d'une selle proprement dite, en décrivant un combat livré en 340 par Constance à son frère Constantin.

La forme des étriers a grandement varié selon les temps et les peuples. Ils n'étaient d'abord qu'une simple courroie[1], à qui, plus tard, fut ajoutée la planche, soit en bois soit en métal, et enfin l'ensemble triangulaire tel qu'on le voit dans la peinture murale de Brunswich.

L'étrier *pyrophore* était un étrier à lanterne qui éclairait et chauffait en même temps les pieds du cavalier ; mais aucun exemplaire ne se trouve conservé dans les musées. Les étriers de femme, aussi bien que les quelques étriers d'armes du quinzième siècle qui remplaçaient le soleret, sont fermés par devant pour empêcher le pied de passer.

---

1. Voir le cavalier du bas-relief de Brioude.

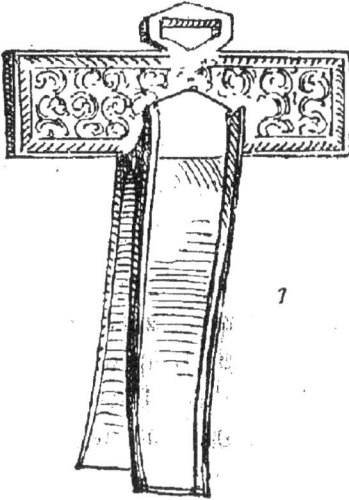

1. Étrier musulmano-espagnol du douzième siècle. L'exemplaire dont ci-contre le dessin a 45 cent. de hauteur et 30 cent. de largeur; il provient de la succession de l'empereur Maximilien qui l'avait envoyé, peu de temps avant sa mort, en Autriche, où il fait partie de la collection d'Ambras. Cette précieuse œuvre en fer, dont l'ornementation indique l'époque romane, a été probablement apportée en Amérique par des Espagnols dont les ancêtres l'avaient pris aux Maures. De semblables étriers se trouvent dans la collection de M. Culemann à Hanovre, au musée de Lyon et dans la possession d'un antiquaire de Genève.

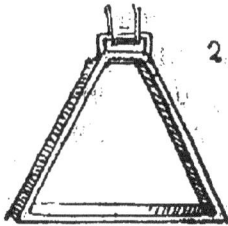

2. Étrier allemand du douzième siècle, d'après les peintures murales du dôme de Brunswick, exécutées sous Henri le Lion, mort en 1195.

3. Étrier allemand en fer, du treizième siècle. — Musée de Sigmaringen.

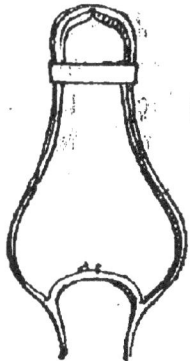

4. Étrier espagnol en fer, probablement de la fin du quatorzième siècle, mais attribué, à l'armeria de Madrid où il est conservé, au roi don Jacques I le Conquérant, mort en 1276.

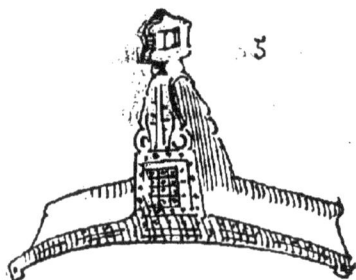

5. Étriers arabes en fer, du commencement du quinzième siècle. Ils sont richement niellés en or et argent. — Col. de l'auteur.

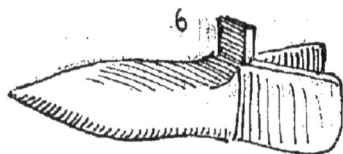

6. Étrier-soleret anglais en fer, du quinzième siècle. — Château de Warwick.

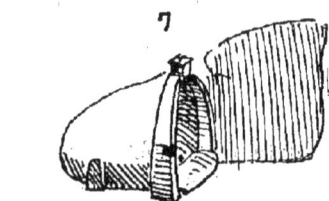

7. Étrier-soleret anglais en fer, du milieu du quinzième siècle, pour le pied droit (ou pour femme?). — Col. Llewelyn-Meyrick.

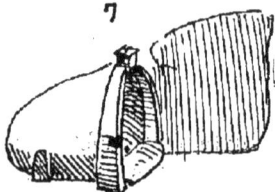

8. Étrier en fer de la fin du quinzième siècle qui fait partie d'une selle en ivoire sculpté, au musée historique de Montbijou de Berlin.

9. Étrier en fer de la fin du quinzième siècle. — Musée de Sigmaringen.

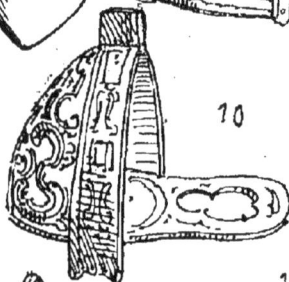

10. Étrier de tournois (ou pour femme?) du seizième siècle; il est découpé à jour et porte des armoiries. — G. 361, musée d'artillerie de Paris.

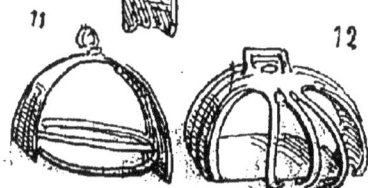

11. Étrier monstre, en fer, de 20 cent. de largeur et de 16 de hauteur, du seizième siècle. — Musée national de Prague.

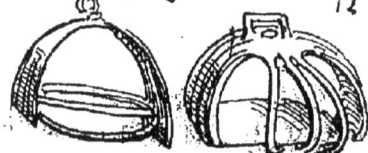

12. Étrier d'une armure d'homme et de cheval du seizième siècle. — Arsenal de Berlin.

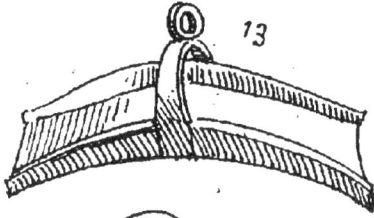

13. Grand étrier sarrasin en fer, du commencement du seizième siècle. — G. 130, musée d'artillerie de Paris.

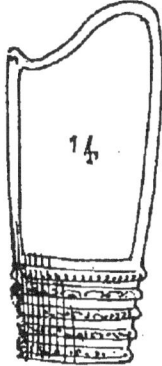

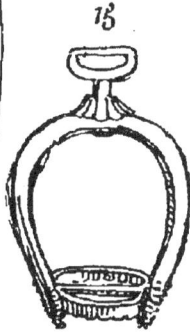

14. Étrier polonais en fer, percé à jour, du commencement du seizième siècle. — Col d'Ambras.

15. Étrier pour soleret en forme de bec-de-cane (1585).

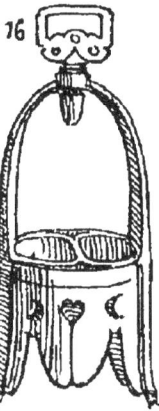

16. Étrier en fer ciselé, probablement pour mulet, du seizième siècle. — Col. de l'auteur.

17.   Id.   id.

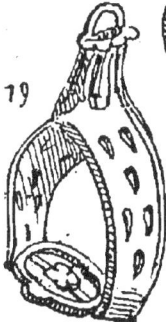

18.   Id.   id.

19. Étrier en fer repoussé et percé à jour, du seizième siècle. — Tour de Londres.

20

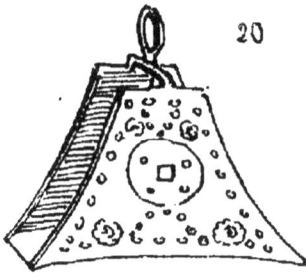

20. Étrier hongrois du seizième siècle, recouvert de filigranes d'argent, et orné de rosettes dorées et de pierres fines. — Col. d'Ambras.

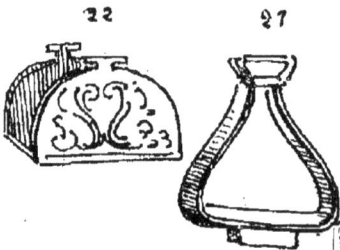

22   27

21. Étrier persan, d'après un manuscrit du seizième siècle.

22. Étrier arabe en fer, percé à jour. — Musée d'artillerie de Paris.

23

23. Étrier en cuivre jaune, de la fin du dix-septième siècle.

24. Étrier allemand en fer, du dix-septième siècle, trouvé à Dielfort. — Musée de Sigmaringen.

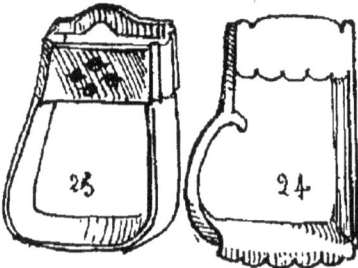

25   24

25. Étrier allemand en fer, du dix-septième siècle. — Musée de Cassel.

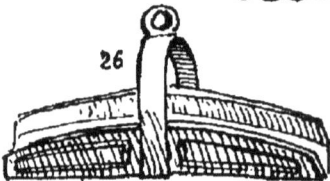

26

26. Étrier en fer, en usage dans l'Afrique du Nord.

LA BRIDE

La bride (du celtique *brid;* en allemand *Zaum*, en anglais *bridle*) est composée de la têtière à *frontal*, des rênes et du mors (*Gebiss* en allemand, *horse-bit* en anglais).

Le mors est ordinairement *sans brisure* ou *avec branches*.

Les mots *bridon* et *filet* (*Trense* en allemand, *snaffle* en anglais) désignent et le mors brisé sans branches, seul, et aussi la bride légère avec ses rênes et ses mors ou filet. Il y a des brides à doubles rênes avec mors et filet ou bridon.

L'emploi de la bride remonte à la plus haute antiquité, et se perd dans la nuit des temps, mais le *mors à branches* ne paraît remonter que vers la première partie du moyen âge, puisque les manuscrits du neuvième et du dixième siècle ne représentent que des bridons *sans branches* ou *traverses*. Les bridons ou mors *brisés* et *avec traverses*, du musée de Copenhague, attribués à l'âge du fer, ont tous l'apparence d'appartenir au moyen âge, et le mors romain sans brisure, de la collection Llewelyn-Meyrick, n'a point de branches ou traverses.

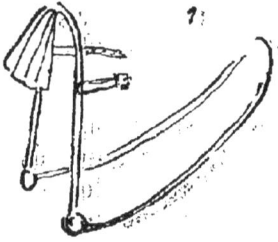

1. Bride danoise, d'après une porte d'église du dixième ou du onzième siècle, au musée de Copenhague.

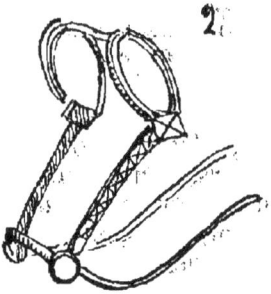

2. Bride danoise, d'après un aqua-manile du douzième siècle, au musée de Copenhague. Les têtières de ces deux brides n'ont point de frontal, et la seconde paraît être uniquement retenue par des oreillères à licornes. La première n'a pas même de nasal.

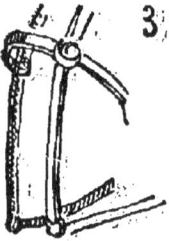

3. Bride, d'après un bas-relief de l'église de Brioude, du neuvième siècle (?).

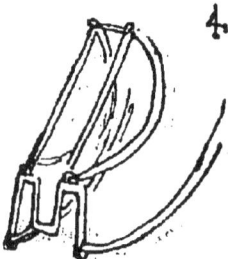

4. Bride normande du onzième ou du douzième siècle, d'après les tapisseries de Bayeux.

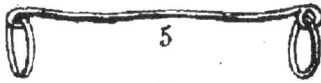

5. Mors romain sans brisure. — Col. Llewelyn-Meyrick.

6. Bridon aussi appelé filet ou mors brisé, sans traverses ou branches, d'après des manuscrits du neuvième au dixième siècle.

7. Mors normand sans brisure, de la fin du onzième siècle. — Tapisserie de Bayeux.

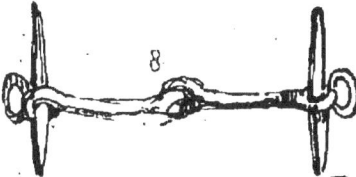

8. Bridon, filet ou mors brisé, avec traverses ou branches, de l'âge du fer ou du commencement du moyen âge. — Musée de Copenhague.

9. Mors allemand sans brisure et sans branches ou traverses, du seizième siècle, d'après un harnais du musée de Dresde.

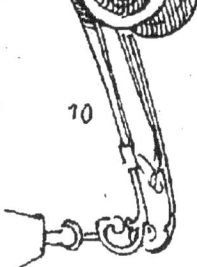

10. Mors allemand sans brisure et à longues branches ou traverses, de la première moitié du seizième siècle. — G. 62, musée d'artillerie de Paris.

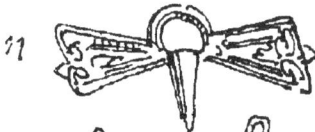

11. Branche ou traverse en fer percée à jour d'un mors ou bridon du seizième siècle. — Musée d'artillerie de Paris.

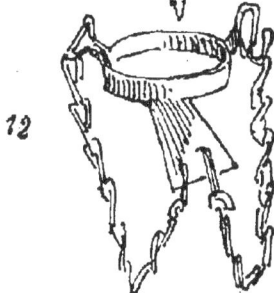

12. Mors à chaînettes d'une bride arabe. — Musée d'artillerie de Paris.

L'ÉPÉE[1].

L'épée (du latin *spatha*, de l'italien *spada* et l'espagnol *espada*, en allemand *Schwert* et *Degen*, en anglais *sword*) est une arme dont l'origine remonte à la plus haute antiquité et se retrouve chez toutes les nations. Les Grecs et les Romains ne la ceignaient qu'en temps de guerre, tandis que les Perses, les Germains, les Scandinaves et les Gaulois, la portaient en tout temps. Les Allemands ont conservé à l'épée le nom de glaive (*Schwert*) dès quelle appartient à l'époque de la chevalerie, ou dès qu'elle sert aux exécutions capitales.

L'épée est formée de deux parties principales : la *lame* (*Klinge* en allemand, *blade* en anglais), dont l'extrémité inférieure s'appelle *pointe* (*Spitze* et *Ort* en allemand, *point* en anglais), l'extrémité supérieure *soie* (*Angel* en allemand), c'est-à-dire la tringle qui entre dans la poignée, et *talon* (*Absatz* en allemand) partie saillante, où la soie commence ; — et de la poignée (*Griff* ou *Gefass* en allemand, *handle* en anglais). Celle-ci comprend le pommeau (*Knauf* en allemand, *knop* ou *pommel* en anglais), la *fusée* (*Hilse* en allemand, *spindle* en anglais), ordinairement en bois ou en corne, entortillée de fil de fer ou de cuivre, et qui recouvre la *soie*, les *gardes*, quelquefois doubles et triples (*Parierstangen* et *Stichblætter* en allemand, *hilts* en anglais), les *contre-gardes* (*Hinterparierstangen* en allemand, *arriere-hilts* en anglais), qui se trouvent placées du côté opposé des gardes et protégent le dessous de la main et du poignet, le *pas-d'âne*, garde inférieure qui avance au-dessous du talon, protége la main du côté de la lame, et dont l'usage s'est répandu seulement vers la seconde moitié du seizième siècle[2], les *quillons* (*Grosse*

1. Voir l'introduction du chapitre qui traite des armes de l'âge du fer pour les épées célèbres.

2. Voir cependant la gravure page 206, reproduction d'une peinture murale de la fin du quatorzième ou du commencement du quinzième siècle, où des hommes d'armes portent déjà des épées à *pas d'âne*.

33.

Gràde Quer Parierstangen en allemand, *right-hilts* en anglais), gardes qui traversent la lame horizontalement entre le talon et la soie, et font tous partie de la poignée. On appelle *écusson* (*Schild* en allemand) la plaque qui se trouve souvent sur la partie inférieure de la fusée, là où les quillons se joignent à la naissance de la soie; *corbeille* et *coquille* (*Korb* en allemand, *shell* ou *husk* en anglais), la garde de forme demi-sphérique des rapières et épées, la plupart espagnoles, qui couvre la main du côté de la lame, et *évidements*, les rainures pratiquées sur la lame (*Blutrinnen* en allemand, *sloping-cuts* en anglais) et destinées à en diminuer le poids.

L'*espadon* (de l'italien *spadone*) désignait d'abord plus particulièrement la longue épée à deux mains, mais, plus tard, toute grande et large épée à deux tranchants.

L'*estoc* (de l'allemand *Stock*, bâton, ou du celtique *stoc*, coup) était la longue et étroite épée plus propre à pointer qu'à tailler. L'expression *frapper d'estoc et de taille* n'est donc appliquable qu'à la large et longue épée, parce que la lame, mince, rigide, souvent triangulaire ou quadrangulaire, évidée et très-aiguë, de la rapière et de l'épée d'*estoc* en général, ne peut se prêter qu'aux *coups d'estoc*.

Les *rapières* qui appartiennent à cette espèce d'épée d'estoc, dont les lames fabriquées à Tolède, à Séville et à Solingue sont célèbres, ne remontent guère au delà du règne de Charles-Quint, sous lequel, en Espagne, l'*escrime* moderne (de l'allemand *Schirmen*) a pris naissance. La rapière a une garde en forme de coquille pleine ou percée à jour, et des quillons longs et droits. La rapière dite *colichemarde* ou épée à la *Koenigsmark* se reconnaît à son talon, très-large, et à sa lame taillée en carrelets. Elle ne fut en usage que sous Louis XIV, où on s'en servait dans les duels. Le mot colichemarde n'est qu'une corruption du nom de Koenigsmark.

Le *cimeterre* (du persan *Chimchir* ou *Chimichir*, le *Scymitar* en allemand, et le *scimitar* en anglais), l'*acinace* des

Romains, et qui a donné naissance au sabre, n'était guère en usage dans l'antiquité que chez les peuples orientaux dits barbares, et plus tard particulièrement chez les Maures d'Espagne, chez les Sarrasins en général et particulièrement chez les Turcs. La poignée de cette arme est sans garde, la lame d'un seul tranchant courbée, courte, convexe et à contre-pointe; elle s'élargit vers le bout.

Le *sabre* (de l'allemand *Sabel* ou *Saebel*, ou du slavon *sabla*; *sabre* en anglais) est l'arme qui descend en ligne directe du cimeterre. Il était inconnu aux Grecs et même pendant longtemps aux Romains, mais non pas aux Perses et aux habitants de l'Ibérie, probablement même avant la conquête de ce pays par les Visigoths et les Arabes. Le sabre était aussi l'arme principale des Daces du temps de Trajan (101 à 106 ap. J.-C.), comme le démontrent les bas-reliefs de la colonne qui représentait les épisodes des campagnes de cet empereur. La Dacie, qui avait pour bornes au sud le Danube, au nord-est les Alpes Bastarnes ou Karpathes, et au nord le Dniester, répondait à la Moldavie, à la Valachie, à la Transylvanie et à une partie de la Hongrie de nos jours. On voit le sabre apparaître en Allemagne vers la fin du quatrième siècle, et devenir d'un usage universel en Europe à partir de la première croisade. Cette arme, que Meyer, dans son livre d'escrime publié en 1570 appelle à tort *Dusæck*[1], et qui est souvent reproduite dans les gravures de Hans Burgmeier, était l'arme favorite des Musulmans, qui leur donnaient de petits noms comme à des animaux domestiques. Mohamed, le fondateur de l'islamisme, en avait neuf appelées : *Mabur, Al-Adhb, Daulfakar, Ali-Kola* (d'après la ville de Kola, où il existait alors beaucoup de fabriques d'armes), *Al-Ballar, Al-Hatif, Al-Medham, Al-Rosub* et *Al-Kadhib.*

La *véritable claymore* écossaise est à simples quillons et

---

1. Le dusæck est une espèce de sabre bohême d'une forme particulière et sans manche ni garde. On le maniait avec un gantelet de fer.

sans la garde grillée, qui recouvre toute la main; l'épée,
aussi bien que le sabre, pourvus de ces gardes, et faussement appelés claymores, servaient aux Vénitiens, et étaient
nommés *schiavona*, parce qu'ils étaient l'arme de la garde
esclavone des doges durant les seizième et dix-septième
siècles, comme le démontrent les tableaux de l'époque. En
Écosse, ils apparaissent seulement au dix-huitième siècle.

Le *yatagan*, le *khandjar*, le *flissa*, le *koukri*, le
kampak, etc., etc., sont presque tous des espèces de sabres-
hachettes, ordinairement sans gardes ni quillons. Ces
armes orientales se ressemblent tellement, et leurs formes
ont si peu varié durant des siècles, qu'elles n'offrent absolument rien pour l'étude qui concerne le classement chronologique si intéressant pour l'épée de guerre du moyen
âge chrétien dont l'étude nous occupe ici. Cette arme
était, dans les huitième, neuvième, dixième et onzième
siècles large, assez longue, à deux tranchants, à pointe
arrondie et propre seulement à frapper de taille, à simples
quillons droits, qui formaient avec la lame et la poignée
une croix latine. Le pommeau était ordinairement rond
ou aplati, et quelquefois *bilobé* et *tribobé* au onzième siècle
et au douzième. Les quillons, toujours droits et simples,
ont souvent, pendant le treizième siècle, les bouts légèrement recourbés vers la lame; cette épée est aiguë et a ordinairement 90 à 95 centimètres de longueur.

En Allemagne l'épée du treizième siècle était formidable.
Celle du chevalier Konrad Schenk de Winstetten (1209-
1240), conservée au musée de Dresde, est à quillons droits
sans aucune inclinaison, et mesure 1^m,40. Le pommeau a
10 centimètres de diamètre, la poignée 15, et les quillons
25. Ces dimensions sont cependant exceptionnelles.

L'épée du quatorzième siècle est plus longue encore que
celle des époques précédentes, ordinairement de 1^m,10 à
1^m,20. Les quillons sont toujours en simple croix.

L'épée du quinzième siècle a souvent la fusée plus

longue que les épées des époques précédentes; celle du seizième devient compliquée dans la forme de la garde et des quillons qui cessent de former une simple croix. A partir de cette époque l'épée a le *pas-d'âne*, des contre-gardes, etc.

Braquemart, malchus, coustil à croix, épée de passot, sont tous des noms qui désignent l'épée courte d'origine italienne, à lame très-large d'en haut et très-pointue, espèce de langue de bœuf dont la forme paraît dériver du *parazonium* antique. Cette épée appartient au quinzième siècle.

La *flamberge* ou l'épée flamboyante suisse, qu'il ne faut pas confondre avec l'épée flamboyante à deux mains, était une arme en usage durant le seizième siècle.

L'*épée à deux mains* (*Zweihaender* en allemand, *twonand-sword* en anglais) ou le véritable *espadon*, ne remonte pas au delà du quinzième siècle. Elle était, en Suisse, l'arme de l'homme de pied, et servait en Allemagne plus particulièrement à la défense des villes assiégées.

L'épée des lansquenets ou *lansquenette* du XVIe siècle était courte, large, à deux tranchants et aiguë. Sa fusée tronconique a le gros bout coupé à plat qui forme le pommeau.

Le *verdun* était une arme longue, étroite, dont le nom lui venait de la ville où elle était fabriquée.

La poignée de l'épée du dix-septième siècle est encore plus compliquée que celle du seizième. Il y a souvent profusion de gardes, contre-gardes et pas-d'âne. Les formes accusent le déclin par le manque de simplicité et de pureté de lignes. Quelques épées du seizième et du dix-septième siècle sont aussi pourvues, à la partie inférieure, de petites gardes, espèces d'anneaux pour y passer le pouce. Les Allemands les appellent *Degen mit Daumringe,* et les Anglais *swords with thumb-rings.*

Voir, pour l'épée de l'époque dite de l'âge du fer, le chapitre où les armes de ces périodes sont décrites. On y trouvera les noms des épées célèbres des temps héroïques et des sagas et poëmes.

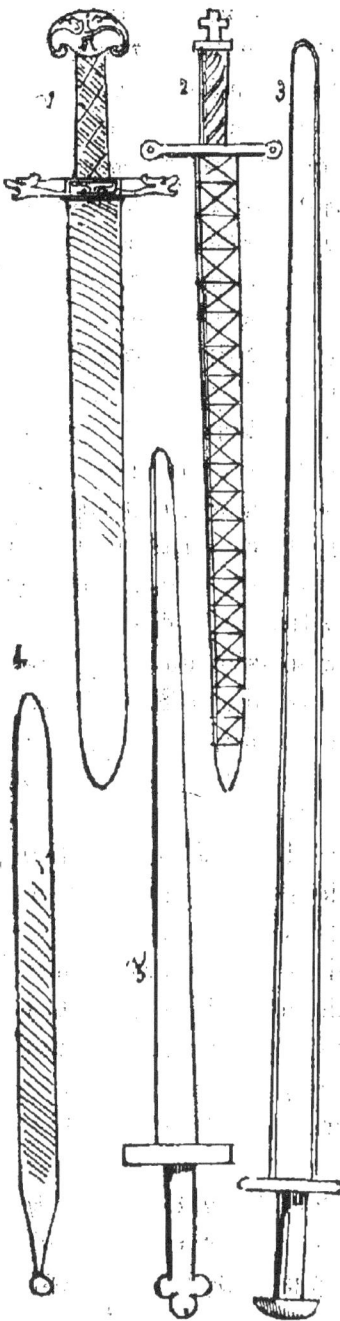

1. Épée de Charlemagne (771-814), de 90 cent. de longueur, conservée au Louvre. La poignée est en or repoussé, la lame très-large et non aiguë.

2. Épée dans son fourreau, du neuvième siècle, d'après la Bible de Charles II le Chauve (840 à 877), conservée au Louvre. On remarquera que le pommeau forme une croix.

3. Épée dans son fourreau, du huitième ou du neuvième siècle, d'après le *Codex aureus* de Saint-Gall. Elle mesure à peu près 1^m,20 à 1^m,25, et son bout est presque arrondi.

4. Épée anglo-saxonne du dixième siècle, de 60 cent. de longueur, trouvée dans le comté de Fairford et conservée au musée britannique.

5. Épée anglo-saxonne, du onzième siècle, d'après un manuscrit du musée britannique. Elle mesure à peu près 85 cent. et son pommeau est trilobé. On remarquera que les épées anglo-saxonnes sont plus courtes que les épées germaniques.

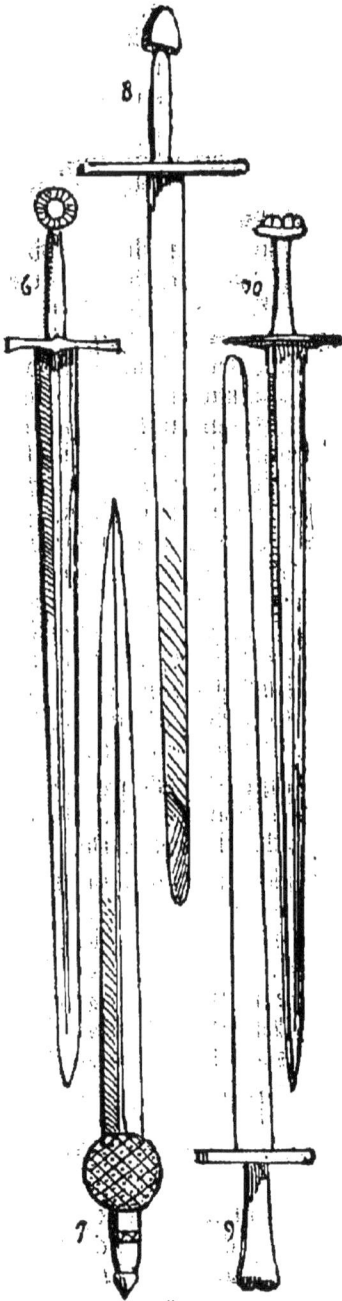

6. Épée de la fin du onzième siècle, de 95 cent. de longueur, en fer trempé, à l'exception du pommeau qui est en cuivre. — I. 1, musée d'artillerie de Paris. Cette épée à pointe aiguë est la même dont les chevaliers de la tapisserie de Bayeux sont armés.

7. Épée musulmane du onzième siècle. Elle mesure environ 85 cent.

8. Épée allemande ou française du onzième ou du douzième siècle, trouvée à Saint-Agatho di Gothi, dans le Napolitain. Elle mesure 90 cent. — Musée d'Erbach.

9. Épée allemande du douzième siècle, d'après les peintures murales du dôme de Brunswick, exécutées sous Henri le Lion, mort en 1195. Cette épée peu aiguë a le pommeau bilobé.

10. Épée allemande du onzième ou du douzième siècle, de 95 cent. de longueur et à pommeau avec cinq lobes. — Musée de Munich. M. le comte de Nieuwerkerke possède une épée pareille, mais à garde droite plus longue. Une autre épée semblable, mais à pommeau trilobé, est conservée au musée de Copenhague.

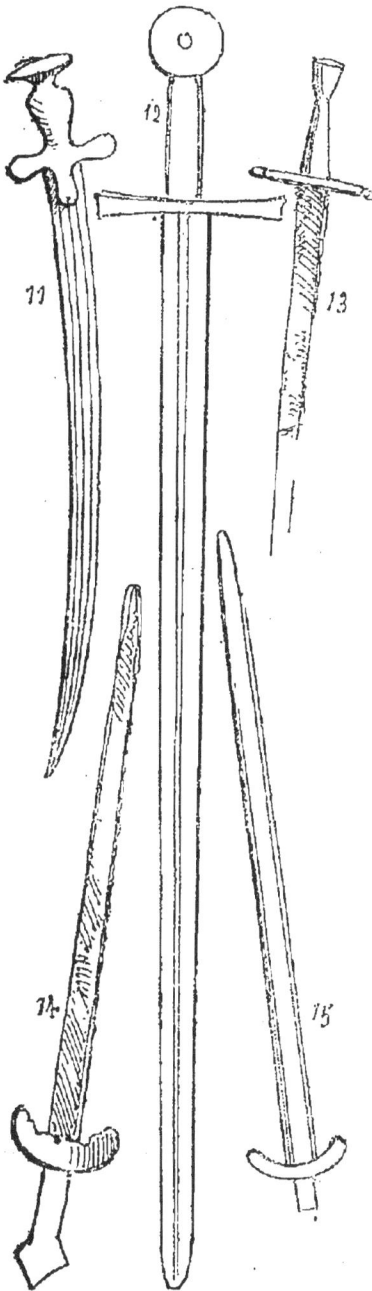

11. Sabre indien, probablement du douzième siècle. Cette arme, dont la poignée est richement incrustée d'argent, a été déterrée à Neumark en Bavière, et paraît provenir des croisades. — Musée national bavarois à Munich.

12. Épée allemande du treizième siècle, ayant appartenu au chevalier Konrad Schenk de Winterstetten (1209-1240). Elle est énorme, d'une longueur de 1 m. 40 cent., sur une largeur de 10 cent. Le pommeau a 10 cent. de diamètre, la poignée 15 et la garde 25 cent. de largeur. On lit sur la lame l'inscription suivante : « *Konrad viel werther Schenke Hierbei du mein gedenk Von Winterstetten hochgemuth lass ganz keinen Eisenhut.* » (Conrad, cher Schenck, souviens-toi de moi ; que Winterstetten le Brave ne laisse intact aucun chapeau de fer.)

13. Fragment d'épée du treizième siècle. — Col. de M. le comte de Nieuwerkerke.

14. Épée du treizième siècle, trouvée dans un tombeau en Livonie. — Musée britannique. Elle date de l'époque où l'ordre des chevaliers du Glaive (*Schwertritter*) réduit par les Lithuaniens s'est fondu dans l'ordre Teutonique. La garde, aux deux extrémités inclinées vers la pointe, indique bien le treizième siècle.

15. Épée britannique en fer, de 72 cent., du treizième siècle, comme l'indiquent les deux extrémités recourbées vers la pointe. Cette arme est appelée

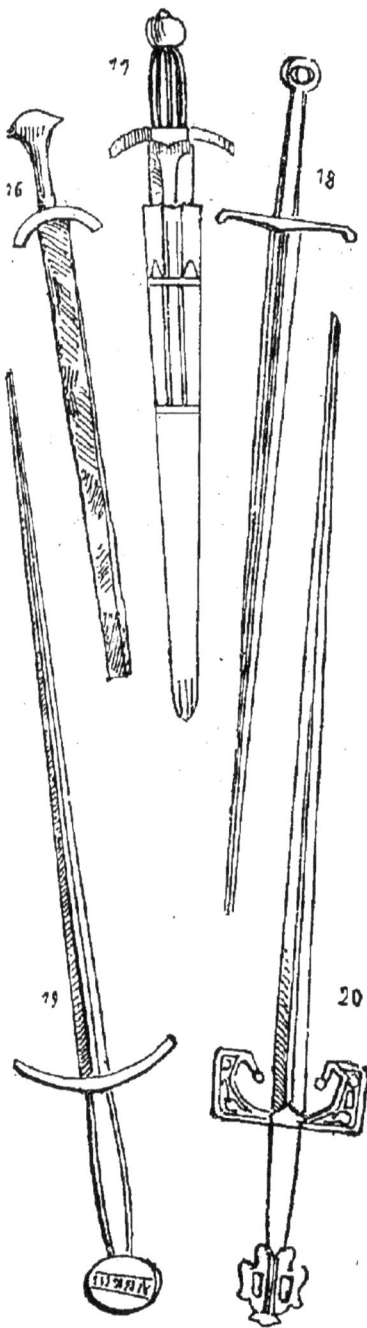

anglo-saxonne, à la Tour de Londres, où elle est conservée sous le n° $\frac{1}{176}$.

16. Épée britannique du treizième siècle; sa poignée ne mesure que 7 cent. Cette arme est attribuée à tort, comme la précédente, à l'époque anglo-saxonne. — N° $\frac{1}{174}$, Tour de Londres.

17. Épée dans son fourreau, probablement du treizième siècle, sinon d'une époque plus rapprochée encore. Cette arme, conservée à Jérusalem, y est attribuée à Godefroi de Bouillon (onzième siècle).

18. Épée du treizième siècle, de 95 cent. de longueur. La lame est à biseau au milieu et non évidée. L'inclinaison des extrémités des quillons vers la pointe indique l'époque.—J. 2, musée d'artillerie de Paris.

19. Épée de la fin du treizième siècle ou du commencement du quatorzième. Elle a 1 m. 10 cent. de longueur. L'inscription que porte le pommeau aplati, « MARIA, » en lettres gothiques majuscules, démontre qu'elle est antérieure à 1350 et non pas du quinzième siècle, comme le Catalogue du musée d'artillerie, où elle est conservée sous le n° I, 10, l'indique. Cette belle épée a été trouvée dans le bois de Satory.

20. Épée gothique en fer, de 90 cent., à pommeau de cuivre, de la fin du quatorzième siècle, trouvée près Brunnen dans le lac des Quatre-Cantons. — Col.

de M. Buchholzer, conservateur à l'arsenal de Luzerne.

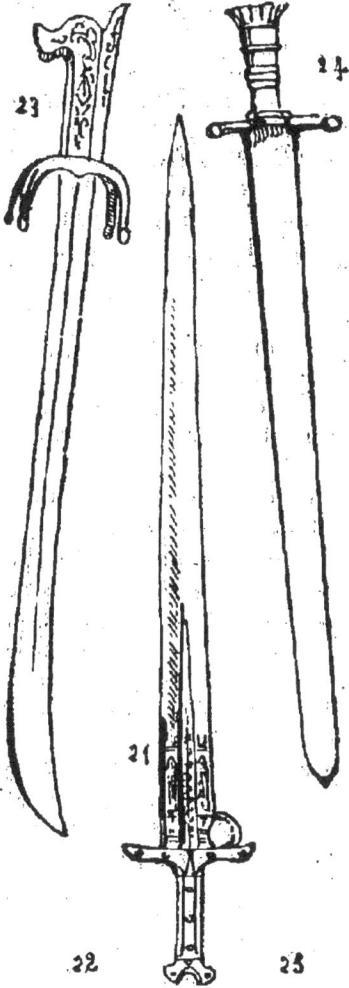

21. Épée allemande du quatorzième siècle. Elle a 83 cent. de longueur et un trou pour y placer le pouce. Si les ornements et les armoiries de la gravure n'indiquaient pas son origine, on pourrait croire cette arme de provenance orientale. — Musée national de Munich.

22 et **25.** Gravures de la lame de l'épée précédente.

23. Sabre arabe du quatorzième siècle, à poignée en argent doré et richement gravée. Elle est à doubles quillons recourbés vers la pointe. Cette arme montre le millésime de 1323 gravé en chiffres arabes, et elle ressemble par sa forme aux épées marocaines. — Col. Spengel, à Munich. Actuellement dans la collection Nieuwerkerke.

24. Épée d'exécution du quinzième siècle, de 68 cent. de longueur, et dont la poignée et le pommeau ressemblent à ceux des épées de lansquenets du seizième siècle. La lame montre une potence et le millésime de 1409.

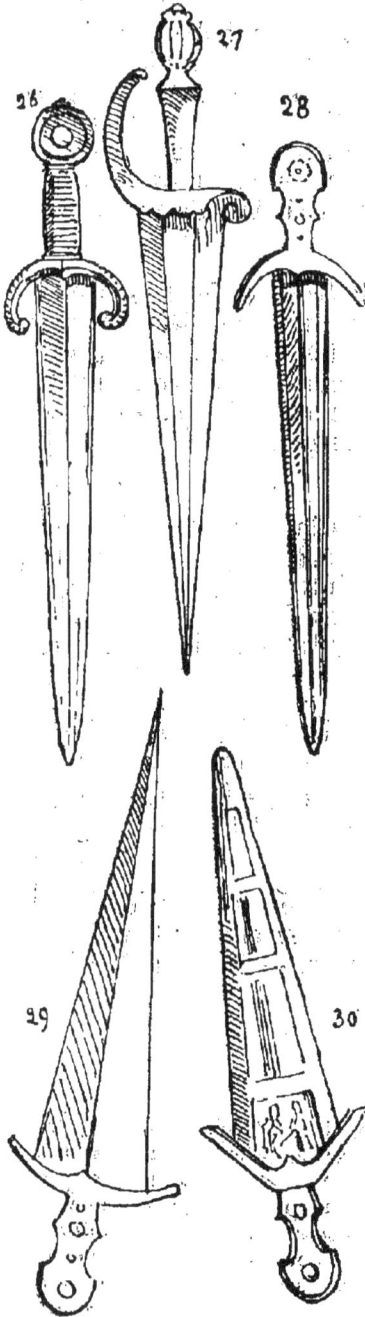

26. Épée du quinzième siècle, lame large[1] et courte de 65 cent., à deux tranchants, sans évidement et à biseau au milieu. Les quillons sont fortement recourbés vers la pointe de la lame. — J. 13, musée d'artillerie.

27. Épée italienne du quinzième siècle, lame large et courte, de 65 cent, à deux tranchants.

28. Épée italienne du quinzième siècle, à lame large de 11 cent. et longue de 65 cent., à deux tranchants, à rainures. Le manche est en ivoire. La garde porte le mot *Solla.* — Col. d'Ambras. Semblables épées à la collection de M. le comte de Nieuwerkerke, de M. Sœter, à Augsbourg et au musée de Munich.

29. Épée semblable à la précédente, de 60 cent. de longueur et plus large, appelée langue de bœuf[2]. — Arsenal du prince de Lobkowitz, à Raudnitz.

30. Épée semblable au numéro précédent, de 55 cent. de longueur. — J. 476, musée d'artillerie de Paris.

1. Ces sortes d'épées, nommées *pistos* et *anelaces* en Angleterre, représentent l'arme connue sous le nom de *braquemart, malchus, coustils à croc* et épées de *passot.*
2. C'est le *parazonium* ou la petite épée des anciens, qu'ils portaient au côté gauche.

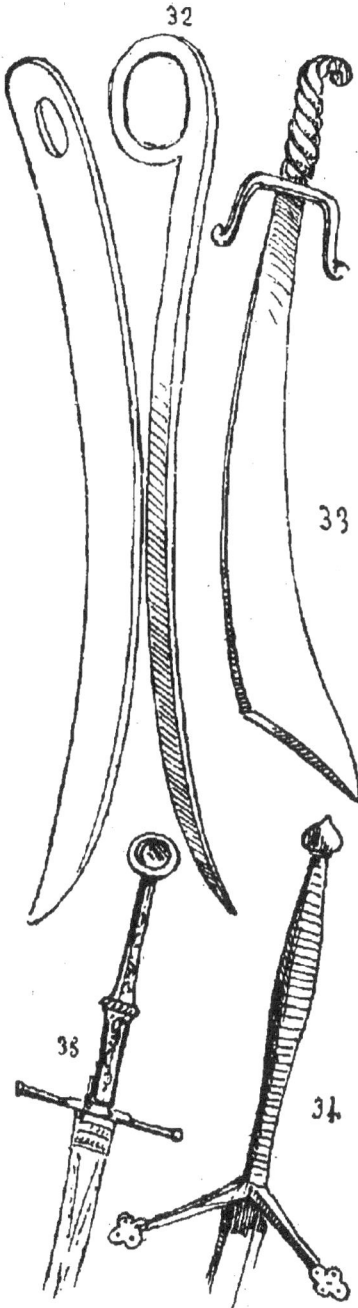

31. Sabre bohémien du quinzième siècle, nommé *Düsack* ou *Tesack*, de 95 cent. de longueur, entièrement en fer; on s'en servait la main couverte d'un gantelet en fer ou en daim qui remontait jusqu'au coude.

32. Sabre en fer d'une seule pièce du quinzième siècle. Cette arme, de 90, 95 cent. de longueur, usitée en Allemagne, ressemble au *Düsack* bohême. — Musée de Dresde.

33. Cimeterre d'une longueur de 85 à 80 cent., d'après un sujet peint, à Augsbourg, au quinzième siècle, sur une table. — Musée industriel, à Vienne.

34. La vraie *claymore* [1] ou épée écossaise du quinzième siècle, de 90 cent. de longueur. — Château de Warwick.

35. Épée allemande du quinzième siècle, de 98 cent. de longueur. — Musée de Munich.

1. Les épées du seizième siècle où la garde entoure toute la main d'un réseau de fer, et appelées faussement *claymores*, sont des épées vénitiennes dont le nom est *schiavona* (V. n° 69). Les épées et sabres à longues lames, pourvues de ces mêmes gardes, appartiennent à la fin du dix-septième siècle ou au commencement du dix-huitième, — armes de cavalerie de tous les pays.

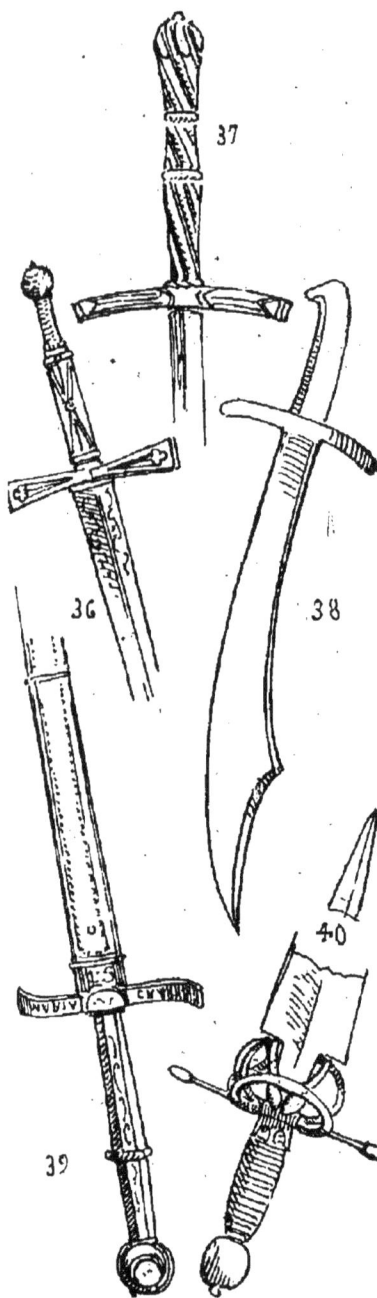

36. Épée allemande du quinzième siècle, de 96 cent. de longueur. Le pommeau est en cristal. — Musée de Munich.

37. Épée allemande du quinzième siècle, de 1ᵐ,20 de longueur. La fusée et le pommeau sont en cuivre. — Musée de Munich.

38. Coutelas-sabre du quinzième siècle, de très-grande dimension, 1ᵐ,10 à 1ᵐ,20 à peu près, d'après une gravure. — Cabinet d'estampes, à Munich.

39. Épée allemande d'un chevalier de Saint-George, de 1ᵐ,15 de longueur, du quinzième siècle. — Arsenal impérial de Vienne.

40. Épée suisse de la fin du quinzième siècle, à large lame et à poignée à quillons, à pas-d'âne[1] et à contre-garde. Longueur totale, 90 cent.—Col. de l'auteur.

1. C'est la plus ancienne épée à *pas-d'âne* que l'auteur a rencontrée. Des peintures murales de la fin du quatorzième siècle ou du commencement du quinzième, exécutées dans l'église de Mondonédo, montrent aussi des chevaliers armés d'épées déjà à *pas-d'âne*.

34.

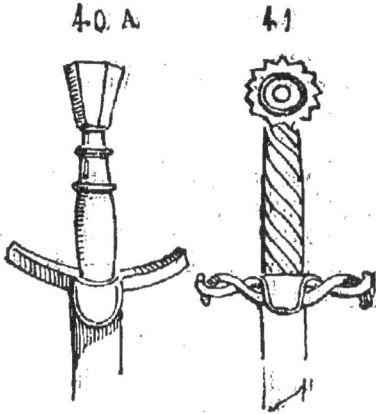

40 A. Épée du commencement du seizième siècle ou de la fin du quinzième, reproduite d'après les manuscrits : *Les Arsenaux de l'empereur Maximilien*, trois volumes d'aquarelles en polychromie exécutées, en 1505, sur les ordres de l'empereur d'Autriche par le peintre Nicolas Glockentohn; et qui contiennent toutes les armes remarquables conservées alors dans les trois arsenaux impériaux. — Col. d'Ambras.

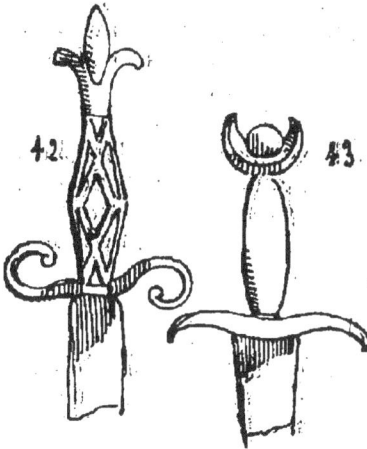

41. Même provenance et même époque.

42. Même provenance et même époque.

43. Même provenance et même époque.

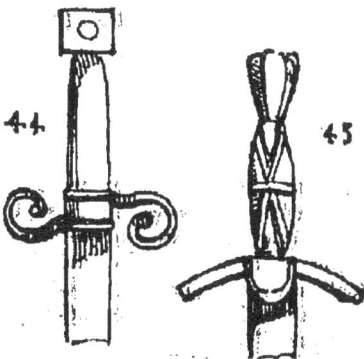

44. Même provenance et même époque.

45. Même provenance et même époque.

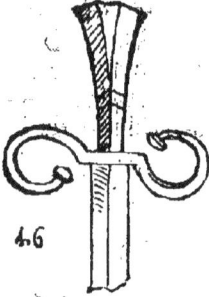

46. Épée du commencement du
seizième ou de la fin du quinzième siècle, même provenance
que les nᵒˢ 41 à 46.

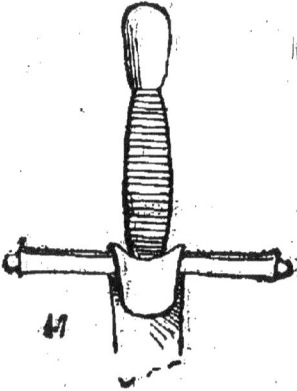

47. Épée de la fin du quinzième
et du commencement du seizième siècle, même provenance
que les nᵒˢ 40 à 46.

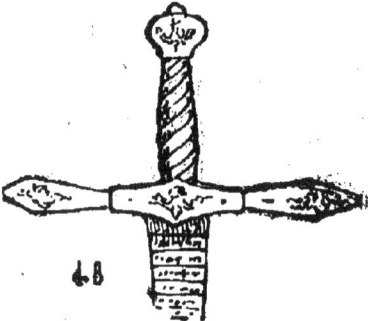

48. Épée à poignée et à garde
ornées de figures en cuivre doré.
La lame sur laquelle se trouve
reproduit, finement gravé, le
calendrier de l'année 1506 est
un morceau fort curieux. — Arsenal de Berlin.

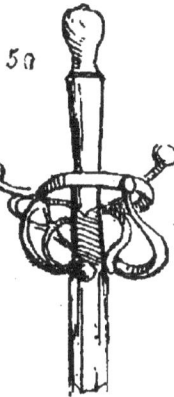

50. Épée allemande du seizième siècle, à quillons, à pas-d'âne et à garde à cinq branches. Elle a 1ᵐ,15 de longueur. — J. 52, musée d'artillerie de Paris.

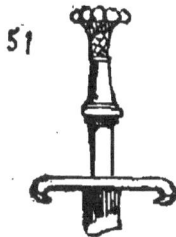

51. Épée suisse toute en fer; la lame a 80 cent. et la poignée 23 cent. de longueur (1ᵐ,05 en tout). Elle a appartenu au réformateur Zwingli, mort à la bataille de Cappel (1531). — Arsenal de Zurich.

52. Épée allemande du commencement du seizième siècle, de 1ᵐ,25 de longueur. La lame est ornée d'un crucifix en ronde-bosse, ce qui la rend impropre à entrer dans un fourreau. — Musée de Sigmaringen.

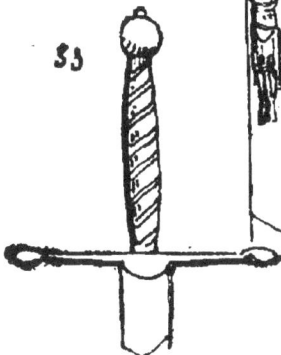

53. Épée hollandaise à lame longue et large, ayant appartenu à Guillaume le Taciturne, assassiné en 1584. — Arsenal de Berlin.

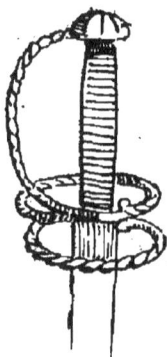

54. Épée allemande de lansquenet, du seizième siècle, modèle simple à contre-garde. Sa longueur totale est de 88 cent.; la lame mesure 73 cent. sur 5 cent. de largeur. — Musée de Sigmaringen.

55. Épée espagnole à ornement hispano-mauresque, du seizième siècle, appartenant à la collection de M. le marquis di Villaseca, où elle est attribuée à Boabdil, le dernier roi maure de Grenade, détrôné en 1492. Cette épée ressemble beaucoup à celle conservée à l'Armeria real à Madrid, et attribuée à don Juan d'Autriche, mort en 1578. Deux semblables épées se trouvent au cabinet de médailles à Paris et dans la possession de don Fernand Nuñez. L'épée du cabinet de médailles (n° 876) porte l'inscription : « Il n'y a de vainqueur que Dieu. »

56. Épée allemande du seizième siècle, fabriquée à Augsbourg. Elle a 1ᵐ,10 de longueur et le pommeau et les quillons ciselés. — Musée de Sigmaringen.

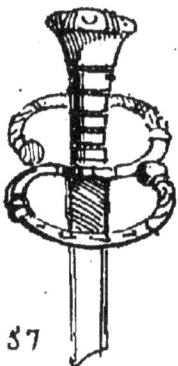

57. Épée allemande de lansquenet du seizième siècle, de 2 1/2 pieds de longueur. La double garde, la fusée et le pommeau sont en fer garni de cuivre. — Musée de Carlsruhe.

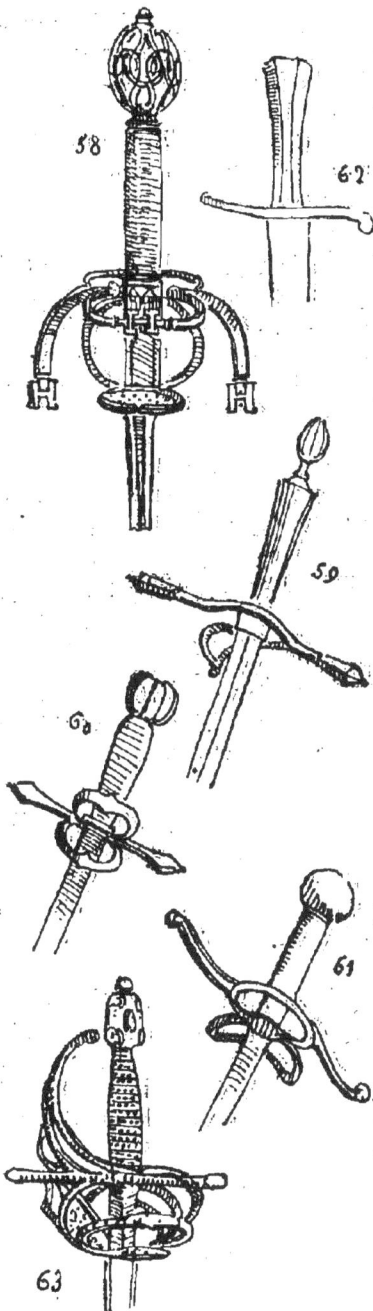

58. Épée française d'estoc, de 1ᵐ,22 de longueur, à lame effilée dans le genre des lames de fleurets ou rapières espagnoles. Les quillons recourbés et la garde portent les chiffres H; elle est à pas-d'âne et à pommeau à jour. Cette épée a appartenu au roi Henri II lui-même ou à un de ses gentils-hommes. Les ornements du pommeau montrent également des H entrelacés et les ornements de l'écusson sont formés par un H entrelacé dans un cœur. — Col. de l'auteur.

59. Épée allemande du seizième siècle. La lame est à double tranchant, étroite et à arête; la poignée en fer noirci. Les quillons sont courbés vers la pointe. Garde et pas-d'âne. — Nᵒ J. 27, au musée d'artillerie de Paris.

60. Épée allemande, estoc de guerre saxon, du commencement du seizième siècle. Lame à trois arêtes. Deux gardes et une contre-garde. Quillons droits. Fusée en peau de chagrin. Pas-d'âne. — Nᵒ J. 47, au musée d'artillerie de Paris.

61. Épée du milieu du seizième siècle à lame espagnole portant la marque de l'armurier Alenzo de Sahagon de Tolède. — Nᵒ J. 50, au musée d'artillerie de Paris.

62. Épée de tournois du seizième siècle, d'après un tableau de l'époque de la collection de M. le comte d'Engenberg.

63. Epée allemande du seizième siècle. Elle a 1ᵐ,15 de longueur,

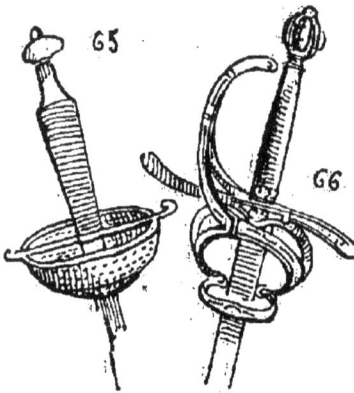

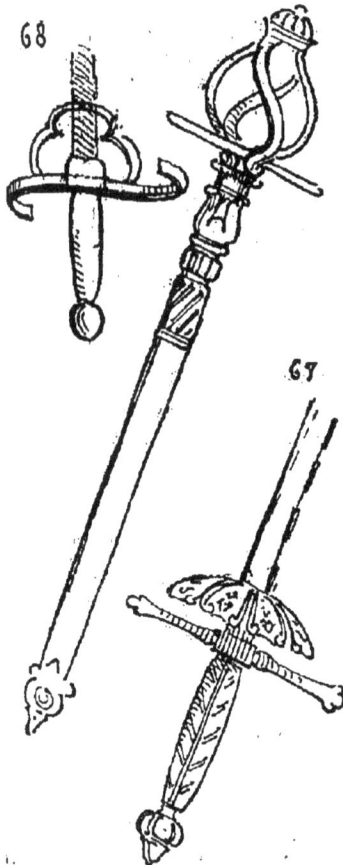

et la poignée à pas-d'âne[1] richement incrustée d'argent représente les figures allégoriques du Danube, du Rhin, etc. La lame est signée : PETER. MUNSTER. ME. FECIT. SOLINGEN. — Musée de Sigmaringen.

64. Épée allemande du seizième siècle, d'après les descriptions de noces princières, etc., par Wirzig. — Musée industriel de Vienne.

65. Épée dite rapière espagnole, de la fin du seizième siècle. Garde corbeille, quillons droits. — J. 85, musée d'artillerie de Paris.

66. Épée allemande, incrustée d'or et émaillée, du commencement du dix-septième siècle. Quillons et pas-d'âne. — Musée de Sigmaringen.

67. Épée dite rapière. — J. 102, musée de Paris.

68. Contours d'épée allemande du commencement du dix-septième siècle, à pas d'âne, et avec l'inscription allemande : « *Jch halte Jesus und Maria,* » qui est conservée à l'Armeria de Madrid, où on l'attribue à Saint-Ferdinand (1200-1252) ! De sorte qu'il n'y a que 400 ans de différence entre la date de la fa-

---

1. Rappelons de nouveau ici que l'on appelle ainsi la petite garde qui avance sur la lame. Ce n'est que vers la seconde moitié du seizième siècle que le pas-d'âne apparaît ordinairement, mais on a vu p. 401, n° 40, et par la note de cette page, que le pas-d'âne remonte jusqu'au quinzième siècle.

Voir aussi l'explication du mot *pas-d'âne* dans l'introduction de ce chapitre et au n° 63.

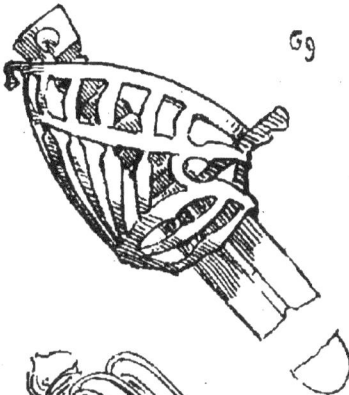

brication de cette épée et celle de l'époque à laquelle on l'attribue.

69. Épée vénitienne, de 84 cent. de longueur, du commencement du dix-septième siècle, appelée *schiavona*[1]. Cette épée et le fauchard étaient les armes offensives des Esclavons ou gardes des Doges. On la désigne presque dans toutes les collections sous la fausse désignation de claymore, arme écossaise à simple croix. — Musée de Sigmaringen et col. Failly. Dans cette dernière, une *schiavona* est estampillée du *Lion ailé* de Venise.

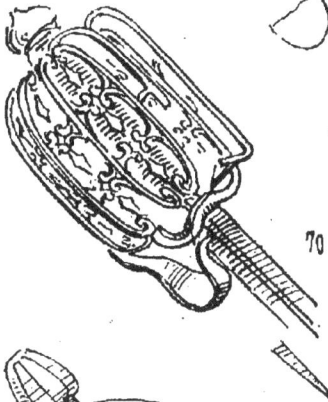

70.   Id.   id. — J. 119, musée d'artillerie de Paris, où elle figure sous la fausse désignation de claymore.

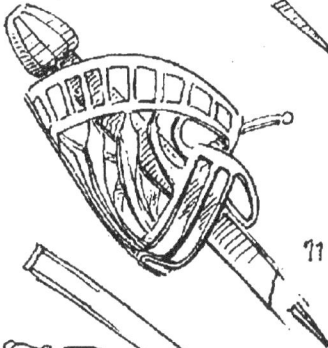

71. Épée de cavalerie de la fin du dix-septième siècle. — J. 96, musée d'artillerie de Paris.

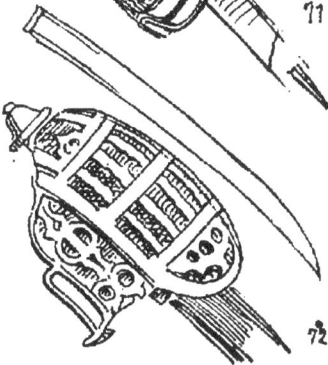

72. Sabre de cavalerie écossaise du dix-huitième siècle, faussement appelé claymore. — J. 118, musée d'artillerie de Paris.

1. Les tableaux de Pietro della Vecchia montrent souvent des personnages armés de cette épée.

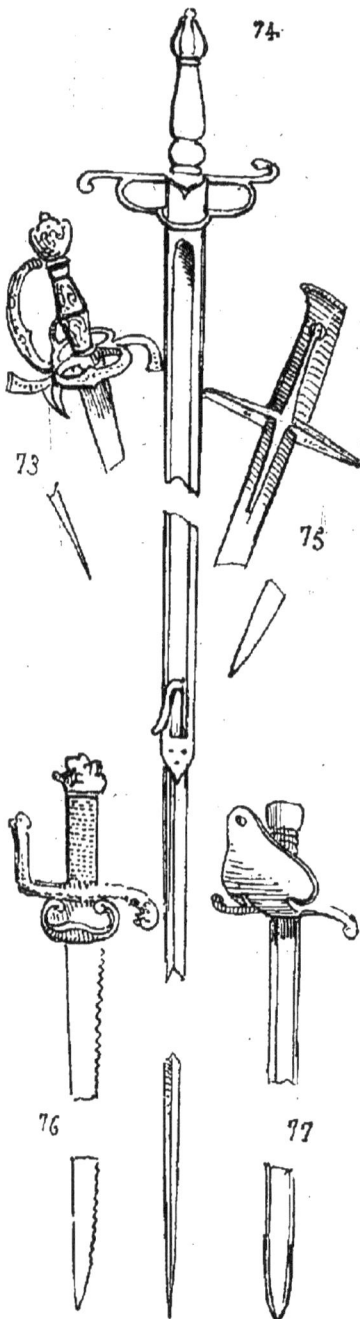

73. Épée savoisienne du commencement du dix-septième siècle. Elle a appartenu au capitaine Branaulieu-Chaffardin tué sous les murs de Genève, en 1602. — Arsenal de Genève.

74. Épée allemande du commencement du dix-septième siècle. Elle est à coulisse et mesure 2^m,18. Quillons et pas-d'âne. — Musée de Munich.

75. Épée des dernières années du dix-septième ou du commencement du dix-huitième siècle. Elle a 1^m,60 de longueur. — J. 135, musée d'artillerie de Paris et à l'arsenal impérial de Vienne.

76. Sabre de marin du dix-septième siècle, à quillons et contre-garde. — Musée d'Erbach.

77. Épée du dix-septième siècle, à garde pleine couvrant le dessus de la main et quillons dont les bouts sont courbés en sens inverse.

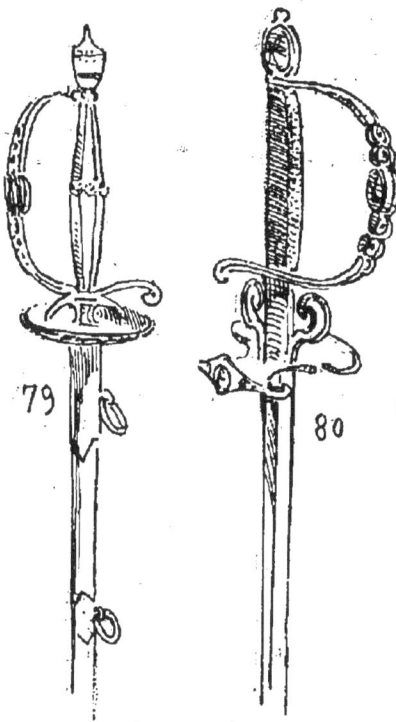

78. Épée de cour de l'époque de Louis XV (1715-1774), en fer ou acier poli, et taillé à facettes. — Col. Merville.

79. Épée de cour de l'époque de Louis XV (1715-1774), en acier doré; elle est à pas-d'âne, d'une forme rare. — Col. Merville.

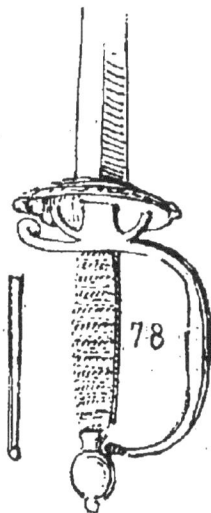

80. Épée de cour de l'époque de Louis XVI (1778-1793), en acier. — Col. Merville. On a fait une infinité de ces sortes d'épées dont les formes varient fort peu. Quelques-unes offrent à l'amateur un intérêt fort artistique, et où le cachet représente bien l'époque de la fabrication.

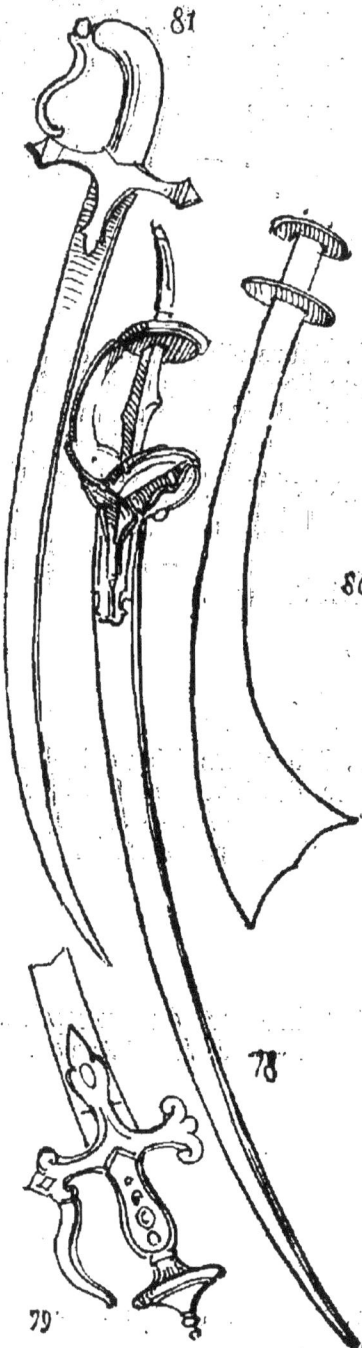

78 *bis*. Sabre indien dit *Kunda de rajah* [1], du seizième siècle, de 98 cent. de longueur et entièrement en fer. La lame est en damas; la poignée, la garde et le pommeau montrent de beaux ornements ciselés et repoussés. — Col. de l'auteur.

79 *bis*. Sabre indien dit *Johur de rajah* du commencement du dix-septième siècle. — Musée de Tsarskoe-Selo.

80 *bis*. Sabre de Népal ou Neypal (Népaul), appelé *Koukri kora*. — J. 453, musée d'artillerie de Paris.

81. Sabre indo-musulman en damas du Khoraçan. On remarque dans la forme de la poignée le goût indien qui fait distinguer cette épée des armes purement turques. La lame est jaunâtre dans le damas dit bileux, qui est le plus estimé. — J. 407, musée d'artillerie de Paris.

1. Au musée de Tsarskoe-Selo et au musée d'artillerie de Paris (J. 402) se trouvent de semblables épées.

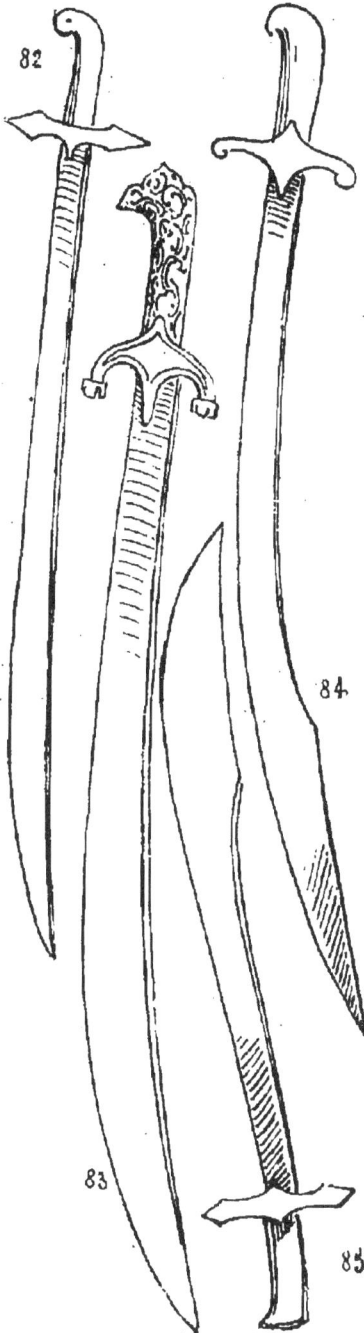

82. Sabre persan, d'après un manuscrit de 1600, copie illustrée du *Schah-Nameh*, poëme de Fidüsi, composé sous le règne de Mahmoud, vers 999, de notre ère. — Bibliothèque de Munich.

83. Sabre albanais ou arnaute[1] que l'on reconnaît à la forme particulière de la poignée, souvent garnie de chaînettes. Le manche et le fourreau sont plaqués d'argent blanc repoussé, et la lame en damas est de forme presque droite. — Musée d'artillerie de Paris.

84. Sabre turc, à lame de damas noir, de l'ancienne fabrique de Constantinople. — J. 390, musée d'artillerie de Paris.

85. Sabre turc du dix-septième siècle. — Musée de Dresde.

1. Les Turcs appellent les Albanais Arnautes.

87. B

87

87. A

86

83 E.

85 B. Cimeterre, d'après un manuscrit allemand du commencement du quinzième siècle.

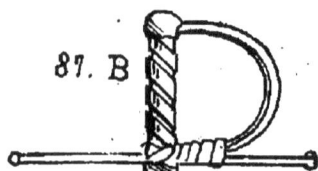

86. Cimeterre turc qui diffère particulièrement du cimeterre occidental par sa garde dont les bouts sont inclinés vers la pointe. Cette garde forme écusson comme celles de presque tous les sabres orientaux.

87. Cimeterre chinois, arme facilement reconnaissable comme presque tous les sabres chinois par l'absence de quillons, de contre-gardes, de pas-d'âne et de corbeille; par le ficelage de la poignée et par le pommeau qui rappellent la coiffure du Chinois.

87 A. Grand couteau marin. Lame, 60 cent. — Musée de Sigmaringen.

87 B. Épée de Matador avec laquelle le toréador combat à pied le taureau et le tue. La poignée de cette arme est entortillée d'un ruban de laine rouge. — Col. G. Arosa, à Paris.

35.

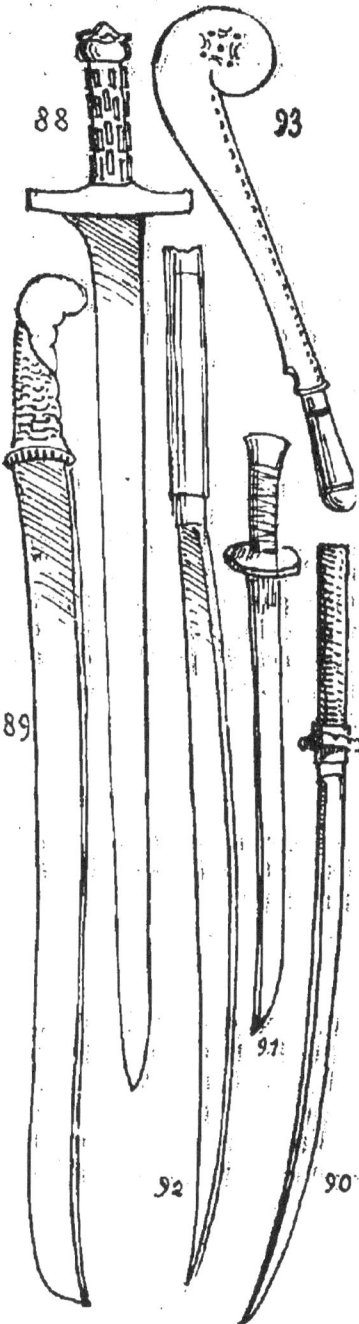

88. Yatagan japonais, à lame en damas et à poignée de corne de rhinocéros, à ornements posés en damier. — J. 439, musée d'artillerie de Paris.

89. Sabre japonais, à pointe taillée à contre-sens; la poignée est en bois sculpté et garnie d'argent. —J. 414, musée d'artillerie de Paris.

90. Sabre japonais appelé *Siobookatana.*

91. Sabre chinois. — Tour de Londres.

92. Sabre chinois moderne; manche en bois blanc. Il provient de la prise de Pékin et se trouve au musée d'artillerie de Paris.

93. Sabre-couteau chinois qui sert en Chine aux condamnés pour s'ouvrir eux-mêmes le ventre. — Musée de Berlin.

94. Yatagan turc à lame damas-quinée en or, pris aux Turcs devant Vienne en 1683.

95. Yatagan albanais. La poi-gnée comme le fourreau sont plaqués en argent blanc re-poussé et ciselé. La lame est en damas. — Musée d'artillerie de Paris.

96. Flissa-Kabyle à poignée gar-nie de cuivre. On remarquera que le flissa et le le yatagan se ressemblent.

97. Kandjar turc. Poignée en corne, ornée de pointillés de cuivre; lame en damas. — **J.** 427, musée d'artillerie de Paris. On remarquera que yatagans, flissas et kandjars se ressem-blent.

Toutes ces armes se ressem-blent et rendent le classement difficile. Le yatagan aussi bien que le flissa et le kandjar sont sans gardes et ordinairement à un seul tranchant; ce sont plu-tôt des sabres que des épées.

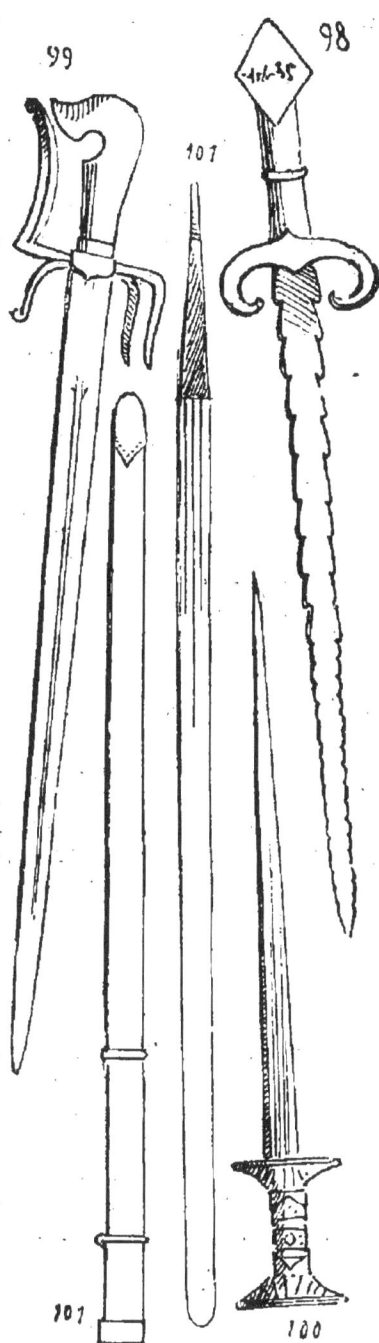

98. Épée arabe, conservée sous le n° G. 413, au musée d'artillerie de Paris où elle est désignée comme arme indienne. Les quillons sont recourbés vers la lame qui est dentelée.

99. Épée marocaine à poignée de rhinocéros. Elle a une garde de trois quillons recourbés vers la lame et une contre-garde.

100. Épée des Zanguebars (Africains orientaux), de 55 cent. La lame est d'un seul tranchant et a trois évidements. Le fourreau et la poignée sont en cuivre repoussé ou gravé et orné de pierreries. — Col. Cristy, à Londres.

101. Grande épée des Zanguebars à fourreau en cuir gaufré. La soie, fuyant au bout et entortillée, forme la poignée qui est sans garde ni quillons. Comme l'épée est très-longue, on s'explique difficilement le maniement de cette singulière arme. — Musée d'artillerie de Paris.

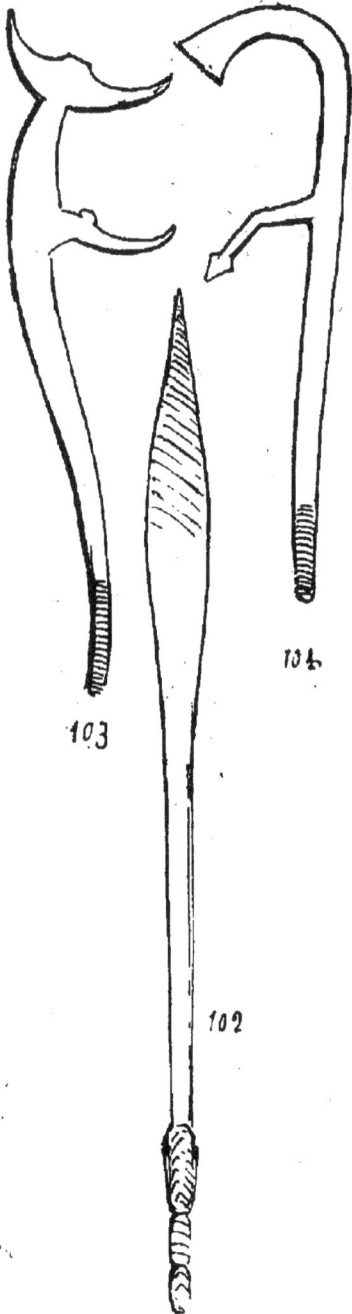

102. Épée des Zanguebars[1]. — Musée d'artillerie de Paris.

103. Yatagan faucheur touarik[2]. — Musée d'artillerie de Paris.

104. Yatagan-hachette touarik. — Musée d'artillerie de Paris.

103

104

102

1. La côte de Zanguebar est une vaste contrée de l'Afrique orientale qui s'étend sur la mer des Indes et se compose d'un grand nombre d'États parmi lesquels on peut nommer ceux de Magodocho, Meliade, Zanzibar et Quiloa.

Les habitants parlent cafre, et beaucoup d'entre eux sont Arabes.

2. Les Touariks, Touarchs ou Sourgous, habitent toute la partie moyenne du Sahara.

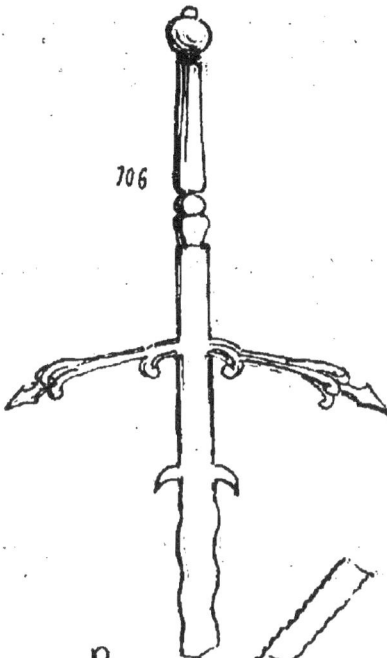

_106_

105. Épée allemande à deux
mains (*Zweihænder* en allem.,
two hand sword en angl.), du
quinzième siècle. — J. 148,
musée de Paris. Le musée britannique possède une arme semblable, qui mesure 1ᵐ,70.
C'était l'épée de parade (*State-
sword*) d'Édouard V (1475-1483).
Le fourreau et le pommeau sont
ornés d'émaux polychromes.

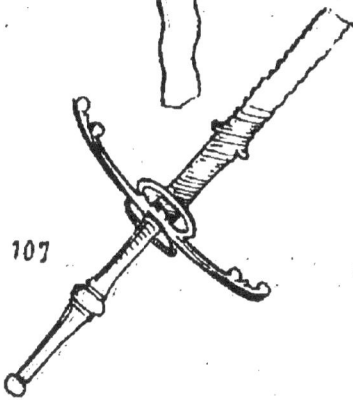

_107_

106. Épée allemande ou suisse
à deux mains, du seizième siècle; elle est à lame flamboyante
et à crochets. — J. 151, musée
d'artillerie de Paris. Une semblable épée à la collection Az,
à Lintz, porte le millésime de
1590, et l'inscription en allemand : *Weïch nit von mir o
treuer Got* (ne m'abandonne pas,
ô Dieu fidèle).

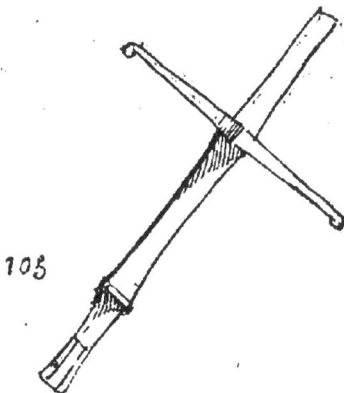

_105_

107. Épée suisse à deux mains,
du commencement du seizième
siècle.

108

109

110

111

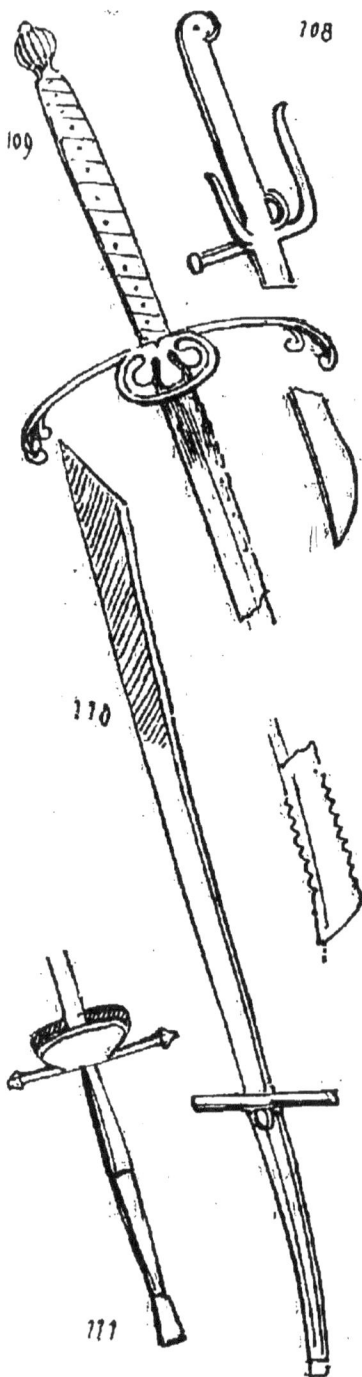

108. Sabre à deux mains de la fin du seizième ou du commencement du dix-septième siècle, comme paraissent l'indiquer la forme des quillons relevés vers le pommeau et l'anneau pour le pouce. — J. 169, musée d'artillerie de Paris.

109. Sabre suisse à deux mains et à lame courbe dentelée, de 1ᵐ,20 de longueur et à poignée de 45 cent. de longueur; les quillons sont recourbés vers la pointe; du quinzième siècle. Arsenal de Berne.

110. Sabre allemand à deux mains (*Zweihandiges-Hiebmesser*) de la fin du quinzième siècle. Cette singulière arme, qui a la forme d'un coutelas, n'est pas droite; lame et poignée sont en biais en sens opposés. — Arsenal de Vienne.

111. Épée allemande à deux mains avec ses coussins (*Faustkappen* en allem.), du seizième siècle. — Musée de Dresde.

LA DAGUE

LE POIGNARD, LE STYLET, LE KHOUTTAR, LE CRISS, ETC.

Cette espèce d'armes, le diminutif de l'épée, le couteau de guerre, était en usage chez tous les peuples et à toutes les époques. Les nuances qui indiquent la différence entre le poignard (du latin *pungere*, piquer, ou *pugnus*, point; *Dolch* en allemand, *poniard* en anglais) et la dague[1] (du celtique *dag*, pointe, *Grosser Dolch* ou *Dolchmesser* en allemand, *dagger* en anglais) sont souvent insaisissables, et ces deux armes sont continuellement confondues. Le poignard proprement dit est plus petit et plus court de lame que la dague, l'ancienne épée courte et large des peuples primitifs.

On a vu que le poignard a joué son rôle durant l'âge de la pierre brute ou taillée par éclat et de la pierre polie, époque à laquelle les armes danoises étaient les mieux finies et les plus artistiques.

Durant l'âge du bronze, le poignard régna également partout; — c'est le *parazonium* des Anciens porté du côté gauche, tandis que l'épée pendait du côté droit chez les Grecs et les Romains, mais du côté gauche chez les Égyptiens et les Assyriens.

La dague des Germains était le *scramasax* (v. ce nom), espèce de coutelas à un seul tranchant et à très-longue soie.

---

1. En terme de vénerie, on nomme *dague* le premier bois qui pousse à la tête du cerf vers la seconde année; d'où le nom de *daguet* donné au jeune cerf qui n'a pas trois ans.

Les gardes du poignard et de la dague, aussi bien que celles de l'épée, aident grandement à fixer les époques de leur fabrication, et on remarque particulièrement que, durant le treizième siècle, les bouts des quillons étaient légèrement inclinés vers la pointe de la lame.

La *miséricorde* est un poignard dont le nom provient de ce qu'elle servait à donner le coup de grâce à l'adversaire renversé ; ordinairement à lame triangulaire , elle était propre à être passée à travers les défauts de l'armure, ce qui la fit appeler en Allemagne *Panzerbrecher* (briseur de cuirasse). La miséricorde française du quatorzième et du quinzième siècle était cependant bien plus grande que le *Panzerbrecher* allemand, et elle servait aussi en Angleterre, sous le règne de Jacques Ier (1603), à être fichée dans le sol, pour y attacher le cheval.

La *dague simple à rouelle* (*Dolch mit Daumring* en allemand, *dagger with thumb-ring* en anglais), en usage à partir de 1410, est le long poignard espagnol dont la garde, au-dessous des quillons, offre un gros anneau pour pouvoir y placer le pouce. On la portait, vers la fin du quinzième siècle, au côté droit et aussi sur les reins. Elle était à *double rouelle* au seizième siècle, où on s'en servait pour la placer au bas des piques pour repousser la cavalerie.

La *langue-de-bœuf*, appelée en Angleterre *enelace*, probablement parce qu'on la portait jadis suspendue à un anneau, se distingue par la largeur considérable de sa lame, dont la forme, très-développée en haut et très-aiguë, ressemble à celle d'une langue pointue. Le petit couteau qui se trouve souvent sur le fourreau de cette arme, fabriquée en majeure partie à Vérone, s'appelait *bâtardeau*.

La *dague de lansquenet*, de la fin du quinzième et du commencement du seizième siècle, était assez longue, et se portait sur les reins, comme le montrent les gravures du temps. La dague du lansquenet suisse était plus courte, sorte de poignard à fourreau d'acier.

Les archers à pied, les francs archers, et en général presque tous les gens de pied du moyen âge étaient armés de dagues.

La *main-gauche* de la fin du quinzième et du seizième siècle, que l'on croit d'origine espagnole, et dont l'usage avait passé en Italie et en France, était surtout une arme de duel. On s'en servait pour parer avec la main gauche, tandis que la main droite était armée de la longue épée d'estoc. La main-gauche italienne, conservée au musée d'artillerie de Paris sous le n° J. 485, reproduite plus loin (v. n° 28), représente une de ces armes dont la lame se sépare en trois branches dès que l'on appuie sur un bouton placé au talon, et forme une avant-garde d'une très-grande étendue dans laquelle on tâchait de surprendre l'épée de l'adversaire.

Cette dague n'est cependant pas d'origine espagnole ni italienne, comme la compilation l'a toujours répété; elle était déjà connue en Allemagne au quinzième siècle, où elle servait aussi dans les séances occultes des Francs-Juges à la prononciation du serment qui était prêté au nom de la sainte Trinité, figurée par les trois branches de l'arme dont tous les *Schœffen* étaient pourvues.

Le *stylet* (*Spitzdolch* en allemand) est un petit poignard qui était en usage à partir du moyen âge, et dont on se sert encore aujourd'hui.

Le *criss*, que le Dictionnaire de l'Académie française écrit à tort *crid*, est une dague javanaise, le plus souvent à lame flamboyante, que les peuplades de la Malaisie rendent encore plus meurtrière en enduisant le fer d'une substance toxique.

Le *khouttar*, arme indoue, est formé d'une large lame de dague semblable à celle de la *langue-de-bœuf* italienne, montée sur un manche carré dans lequel la main entre tout à fait, et qui lui sert en quelque sorte de gantelet ou de garde jusqu'à la hauteur du poignet. Il y a des khouttars où la lame est divisée en deux pointes, mais ils sont plus rares et s'appellent lames *à langues-de-serpent.*

Le *wag-nuk* n'est pas un poignard proprement dit, mais une arme de hast avec laquelle on frappait comme le tigre frappe avec ses griffes. Il a été inventé, vers 1659, par Sevaja, le chef d'une société secrète, et servait aux assassinats de ces bandits; les blessures que l'arme faisait ressemblaient à celles des griffes du tigre et déroutaient les soupçons.

Les dagues italiennes sont réputées par leur beau travail en fer forgé, souvent incrusté ou damasquiné d'argent et à lames percées à jour. Il y a des dagues et poignards italiens et allemands anciens qui, dans les ventes publiques, à Paris, montent jusqu'à mille francs.

Dans les temps plus modernes, on appelle *couteaux-poignards*, *sabres-poignards*, *baïonnettes-poignards,* des couteaux, des sabres et des baïonnettes en forme de poignard, dont la lame est aiguë et tranchante des deux côtés.

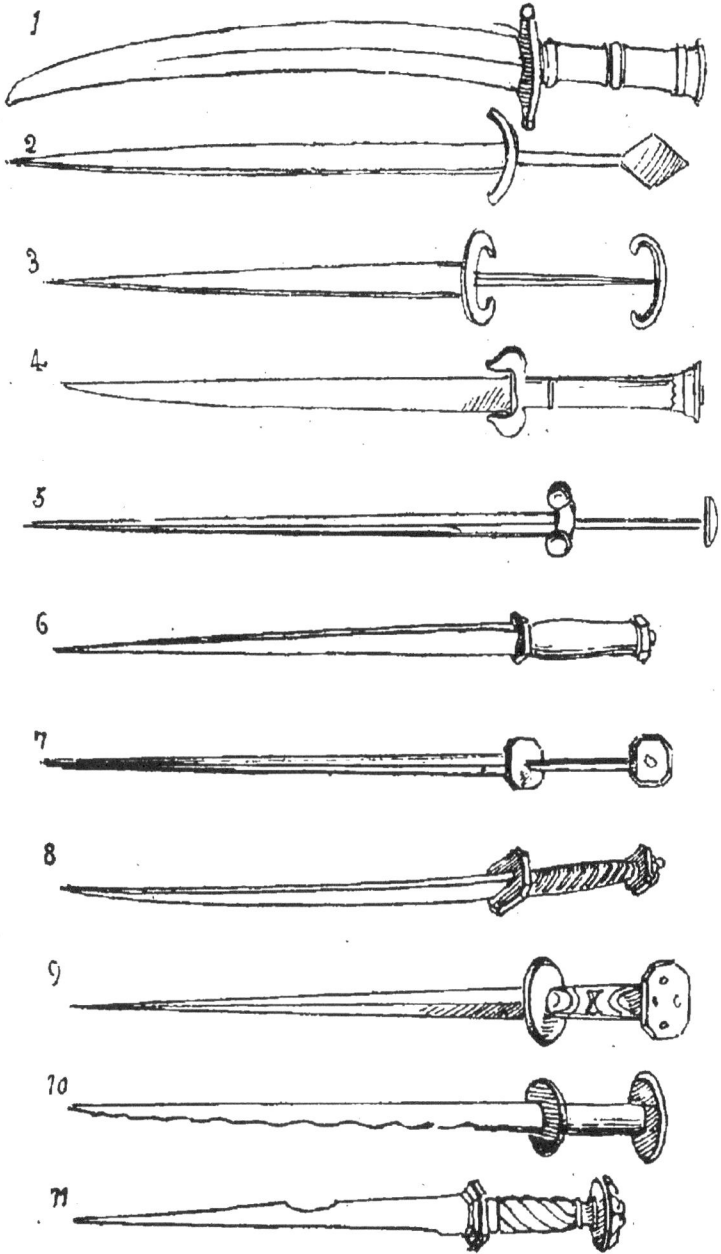

1. Coutelas britannique du dixième siècle. Il porte sur la lame les noms *Edwardus* et *prins agile*. On l'attribue à Edouard II. — Manuscrit de Machel.

2. Dague en fer, de 30 cent., du treizième siècle. — Musée cantonal de Lausanne.

3. Dague en fer du treizième siècle, dont la lame mesure 30 et la soie 12 cent. — Musée cantonal de Lausanne.

4. Poignard en fer probablement écossais, de $3^m,36$, du quatorzième siècle. — Col. du prince Charles de Prusse. (V. nº 13, à la page suivante.)

5. Id. id. id.

6. Poignard du commencement du quatorzième siècle.

7. Dague en fer, de 33 cent., du commencement du quatorzième siècle. La soie est très-longue. — Musée cantonal de Lausanne.

8. Dague en fer, de 48 cent., de la fin du quatorzième siècle. — Tour de Londres.

9. Dague en fer, de 36 cent., de la fin du quatorzième siècle. Elle a été trouvée dans le lac de Morat, son manche est en os sculpté. — Arsenal de Genève. Cette forme de poignard s'est continuée jusqu'au seizième siècle, car le *Feldbuch*, publié à cette époque à Francfort-sur-Mein chez Egge et conservé au cabinet d'estampes de Munich, en représente encore.

10. Dague en fer de la fin du quatorzième ou de la première moitié du quinzième siècle. — Col. de M. le comte de Nieuwerkerke. De semblables armes au musée britannique (trouvées dans la Tamise) et au musée de Sigmaringen (trouvées dans le Hohenzollern). Le manuscrit du quinzième siècle, que Zeilblom a illustré de dessins et qui appartient au prince de Waldbourg, montre également cette forme de poignards.

11. Poignard de la fin du quatorzième siècle.

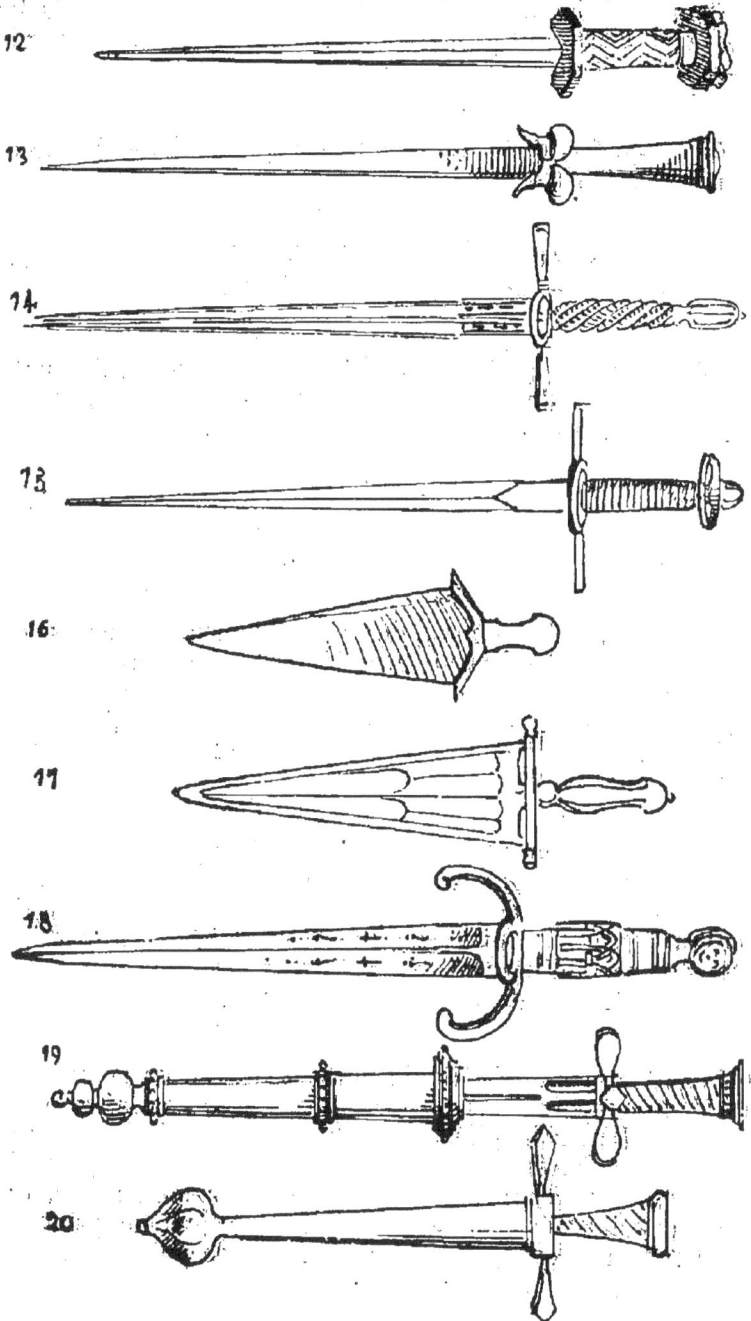

12

13

14

15

16

17

18

19

20

12. Dague du quinzième siècle, dont la forme se trouve déjà au quatorzième siècle. — Arsenal de Vienne.

13. Dague écossaise, de 36 cent. de longueur, manche en bois de bruyère, du quinzième siècle. Voir les observations aux épées dites claymores et la dague n° 4.—Col. de M. le comte de Nieuwerkerke.

14. Dague à simple rouelle, de 37 cent. de longueur, du quinzième siècle. — Col. de l'auteur.

15. Dague à double rouelle du seizième siècle. Les deux anneaux servaient aussi à fixer la dague sur des hampes et sur des lances pour repousser la cavalerie.

16. Dague dite langue-de-bœuf et dague de Vérone, du quinzième siècle. — Musée d'artillerie de Paris.

17. Dague dite langue-de-bœuf, nommée en anglais *enelace*, du quinzième siècle.

18. Dague du quinzième siècle. — Musée d'artillerie de Paris.

19. Dague de lansquenet allemand du seizième siècle. Elle a 35 cent. de longueur. Fourreau en acier poli. — Musée d'artillerie de Paris.

20. Dague allemande, du commencement du seizième siècle. — Col. Sœter, au musée Maximilien, à Augsbourg.

21

22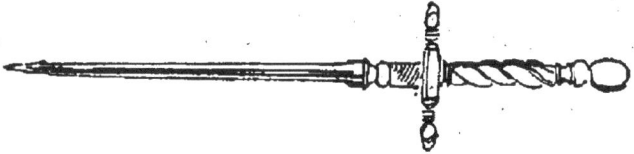

23

24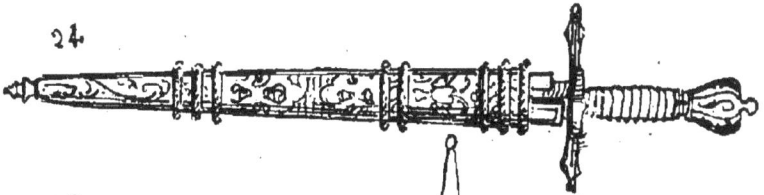

25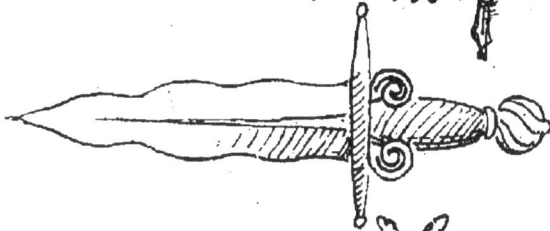

26

27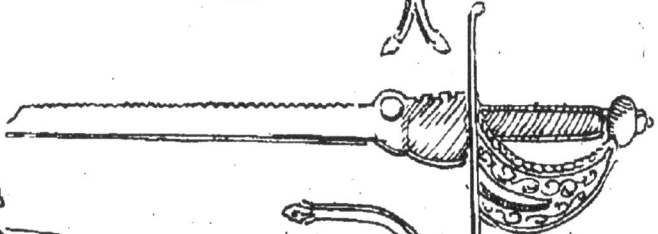

28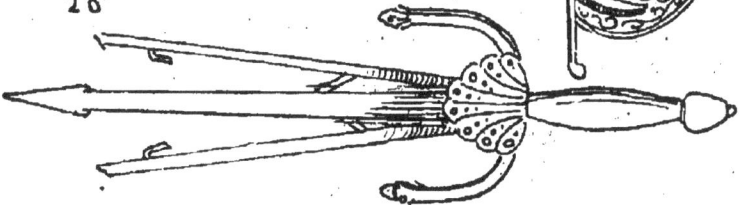

21. Poignard allemand du seizième siècle.

22. Stylet (*Spitzdolch*, en allem.), de 28 cent. de longueur, de la fin du seizième siècle. En Allemagne, on appelait aussi ces armes des *Panzerbrecher*, brise-cuirasse.

23. Dague suisse du seizième siècle, provenant de la collection Soltikoff. De semblables armes, appartenant à M. Buchholzer, à Luzerne et à M. le comte de Nieuwerkerke, à Paris, ont des fourreaux où à la place du sujet de chasse le repoussé représente la danse des morts. Ces dagues sont pourvues de leurs bâtardeaux ou petits couteaux qui servaient à couper les courroies des armures et aussi à percer des trous et à tout autre usage durant la campagne.

24. Dague allemande du seizième siècle. — Ancienne col. Soltikoff.

25. Poignard allemand à lame flamboyante, très-court et trèslarge. — Arsenal de la ville de Vienne.

26. Poignard allemand du seizième siècle. La garde est à quatre quillons. — Col. du roi de Suède Charles XV.

27. Main-gauche du seizième siècle. — Musée d'artillerie de Paris.

28. Main-gauche allemande du seizième siècle. — Musée d'artillerie de Paris et musées de Prague et de Sigmaringen. Voir aussi les armes des Francs-Juges.

29
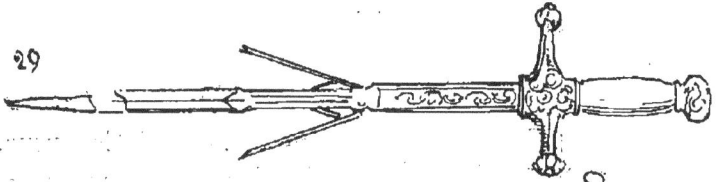

30
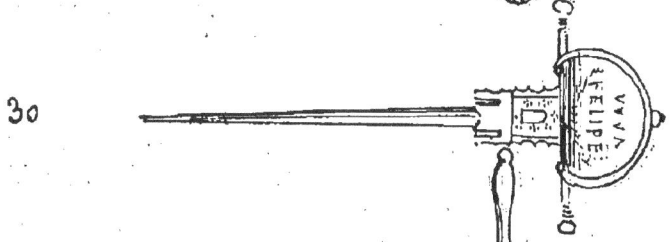

31

32
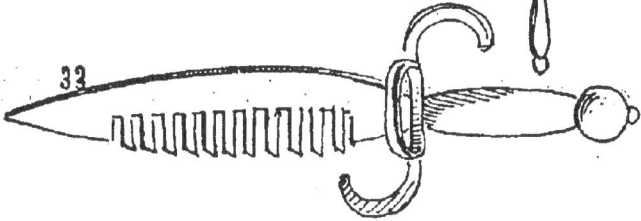

33

34
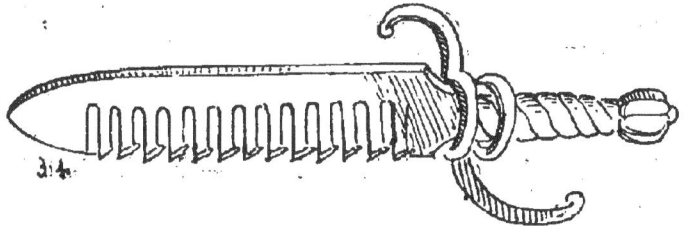

35

29. Dague allemande dite main-gauche, de 50 cent. de longueur, du seizième siècle. La poignée est richement ciselée. — Musée de Sigmaringen.

30. Dague espagnole, main-gauche avec inscription : VIVA. FELIPP. V. qui indique que cette arme était encore en usage en 1704. — Col. Llewelyn-Meyrick.

31. Dague allemande, main-gauche, lame brise-épée à dentelure, du seizième siècle. — Col. de M. le comte de Nieuwerkerke.

32. Dague allemande, main-gauche à lame brise-épée à dentelure; à rouelle et à quillons courbés, du seizième siècle — Col. Musée de Dresde.

33. La dentelure du n° 31.

34. Grand brise-épée allemand du seizième siècle. — Col. Llewelyn-Meyrick.

35. La dentelure du numéro précédent.

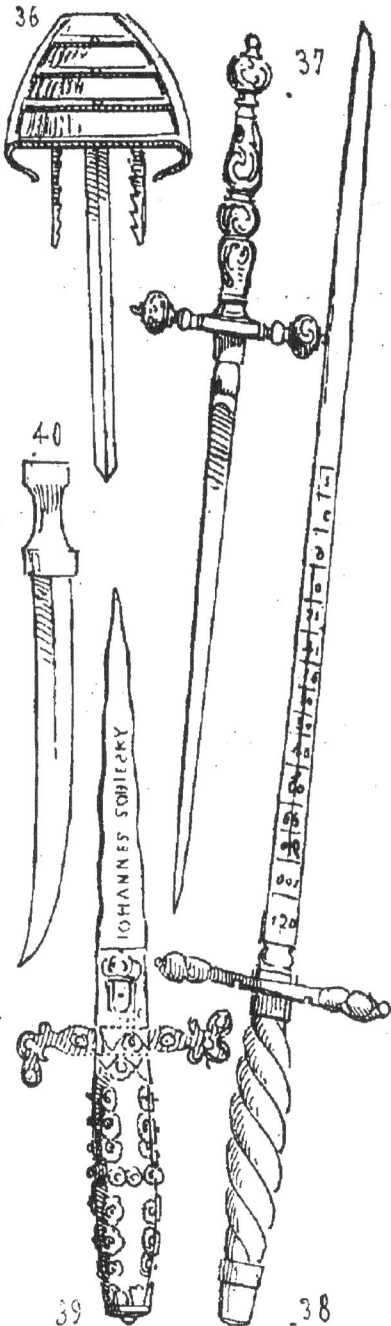

36. Dague allemande, grande main-gauche à quillons dentelés et grille brise-épée, du dix-septième siècle. Elle mesure 60 cent. sur 25. — Musée national de Munich.

37. Stylet allemand dit *Panzerbrecher*, brise-cuirasse, de 30 cent. de longueur, du seizième siècle. — Musée de Sigmaringen.

38. Poignard allemand dit *Panzerbrecher*, dont la lame numérotée servait probablement pour mesurer les calibres des canons. — Musée de Sigmaringen.

39. Poignard, de 23 cent. de longueur, richement orné de pierres fines. Cette arme a appartenu à Sobieski. — Musée de Sigmaringen.

40. Poignard persan. — J. 533, musée d'artillerie de Paris.

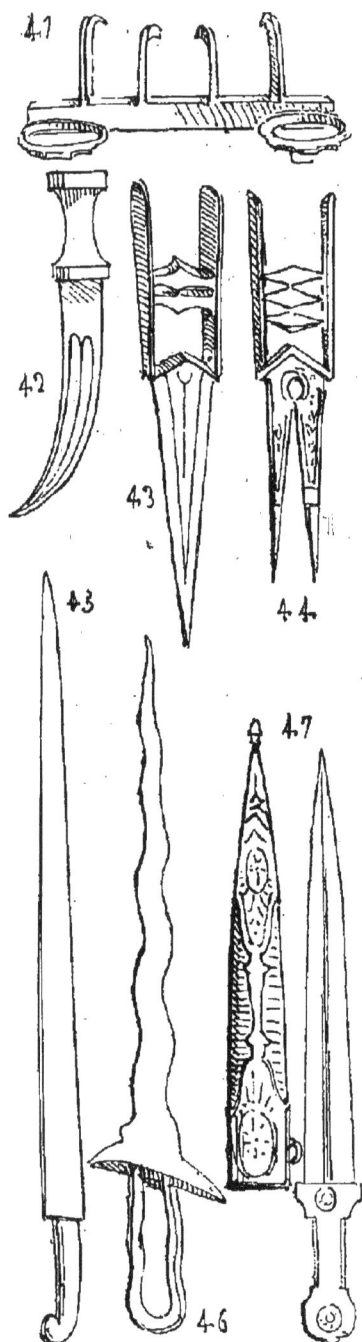

41. Wag-nuk ou griffe de tigre, de 2 pieds 1/2 de grandeur, arme indienne de société secrète, inventée vers 1659 par l'Hindou Sewaja. Elle servait aux assassinats, et en imitant les blessures faites par la griffe de la bête, déroutait les soupçons. — Col. Llewelyn-Meyrick.

42. Poignard persan. La lame est en damas et la poignée en ivoire.

43. Khouttar hindou à lame dite langue-de-bœuf. — Musée d'artillerie de Paris.

44. Khouttar hindou à lame dite langue-de-serpent. — Musée Tsarskoe-Selo.

45. Kandjar-dague, arme turque.

46. Criss javanais.

47. Dague javanaise de travail indien ou persan, de 43 cent. de longueur. La lame est à rainures, la poignée en ivoire massif et garnie de têtes de clous en fer damasquiné. Le fourreau, en chagrin, est orné de plaques niellées. — Col. de l'auteur.

LA LANCE, LA PIQUE ET L'ÉPIEU

La lance (du latin barbare *lancea*, *Speer* et aussi *Spies* en allemand, *lance* en anglais) existait déjà dans la plus haute antiquité; elle se trouve chez les Assyriens comme chez les Égyptiens. Du huitième au treizième siècle après J.-C., la lance avait conservé à peu près la même forme; c'était une simple hampe en bois lisse et cylindrique, de 12 pieds de longueur, et armée d'un fer à douille[1].

La lance de tournois, dont la première apparition ne remonte qu'au treizième siècle, et qui fut bientôt aussi utilisée à la guerre, était à poignée; elle était grosse à l'endroit où cette poignée était ménagée et pointue en haut et en bas. En France, la lance fut abolie sous le règne de Henri IV, en 1605. Les lances du dixième et du onzième siècle se signalent par la banderole attachée au-dessous de la douille de la pointe. Les lances des mercenaires, connus sous le nom de *lansquenets*, avaient ordinairement de petites lames dont les douilles étaient quelquefois à longues branches qui descendaient sur la hampe, où elles étaient fixées au moyen de vis; ces lances avaient de 7 à 8 mètres de longueur. Les lances des hommes de pied suisses n'étaient ordinairement que de 5 mètres, car la tactique suisse consistait ordinairement à former quatre rangs entièrement confondus et serrés étroitement.

L'épieu est une arme de chasse au sanglier.

---

1. Les tapisseries de Bayeux du onzième siècle, ainsi que plusieurs miniatures de la même époque, représentent des lances avec banderoles.

1. Lance germanique, d'après le *Codex aureus* de Saint-Gall du huitième ou du neuvième siècle.

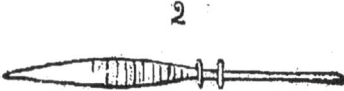

2. Lance germanique du commencement du neuvième siècle, appelée plus tard *Knebelspies*, reproduite d'après les miniatures du manuscrit *Wessobrunn* de 840, de la bibliothèque de Munich.

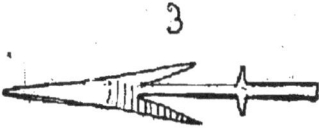

3. Lance normande[1] du onzième siècle, d'après les tapisseries de Bayeux.

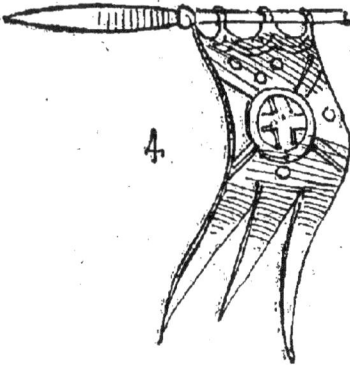

4. Id. avec banderole, id.

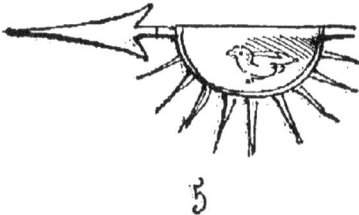

5. Id. avec enseigne, id.

1. La lance aussi bien que l'épée étaient chez les Normands les armes des *hommes libres*, puisqu'il est dit dans les lois de Guillaume le Conquérant au sujet de l'affranchissement d'un serf : *Tradidit illi arma libera, scilicet lanceam et gladium.*

6. Lance anglo-saxonne, d'après la miniature de l'*Aelfric*, manuscrit du onzième siècle, à la bibliothèque britannique.

7. Grand fer d'épieu de guerre (*Stecke* en angl.) du quinzième siècle, de 37 cent.; la lame mesure 26 et la douille 11 cent.; il est damasquiné d'or. — Col. Renné de Constance.

8. Grand fer d'épieu de guerre du quinzième siècle, sur longue hampe. — Arsenal de Zurich.

9. Lance de lansquenet (*Langspies* en allem.) de la fin du quinzième siècle. La hampe a 7 à 8 cent. de longueur et 4 c. de diamètre. Le musée de Salzbourg, possédant un certain nombre de ces lances, en a cédé à l'empereur Napoléon III qui les a données au musée d'artillerie de Paris. M. Az à Lintz en a également quelques exemplaires dans sa collection.

10 A et 10 B. Lances d'hommes de pied autrichiens de la fin du quinzième siècle. — Col. d'Ambras. On retrouve cette arme dans les dessins exécutés en 1505 par Nicolas Glockenthon, d'après les *Arsenaux de l'empereur Maximilien*.

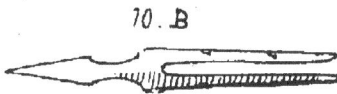

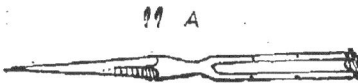

11 A. Lances d'hommes de pied suisses du quinzième et du seizième siècle. — Arsenaux de Soleure et de Lucerne.

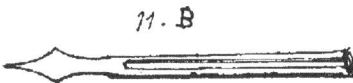

11 B. Id. id.

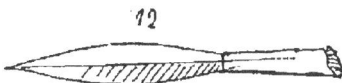

12. Lance légère nommée *Assagai*, provenant de l'arsenal de Rhodes et des chevaliers de Saint-Jean de Jérusalem (1522). — F. 43, musée d'artillerie de Paris.

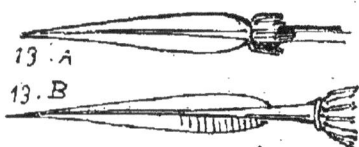

13 A. Longue lance légère du commencement du seizième siècle. Le fer a presque 1 pied 1/2 de longueur. — Dessins déjà mentionnés, qui furent exécutés vers 1505 par Glockenthon et se trouvent dans la collection d'Ambras.

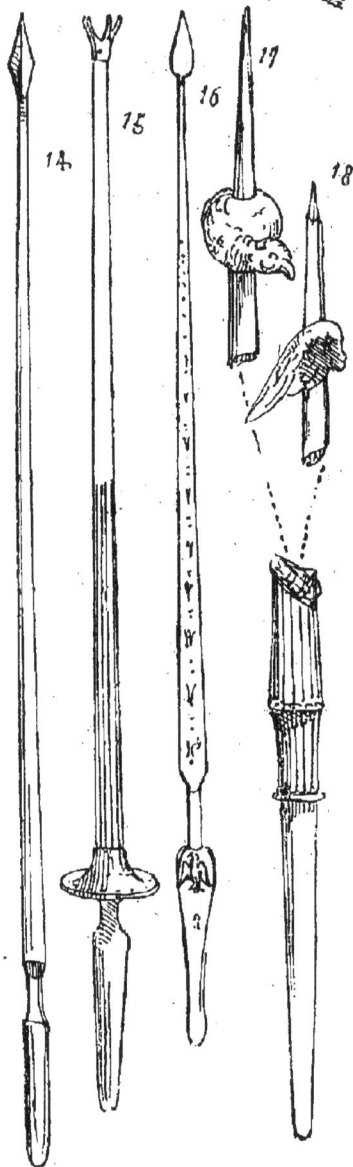

13 B. Id. id.

14. Lance de guerre du quinzième siècle, d'après une tapisserie provenant de la tente de Charles le Téméraire.

15. Lance de tournois avec sa rondelle en fer, du seizième siècle. — Col. Llewelyn-Meyrick.

16. Lance de guerre du seizième siècle; elle est partout ornée d'aigles rouges sur champ blanc, ce qui représente les armes d'Inspruck. — Col. Llewelyn-Meyrick.

17. Lance de guerre et de tournois, reproduite d'après le manuscrit déjà mentionné de Glockenthon, de 1505.

18. Id. id.

Toutes ces lances ont *la place de la poignée* qui ne date que de la fin du treizième siècle, où les tournois étaient déjà réguliers et réglés.

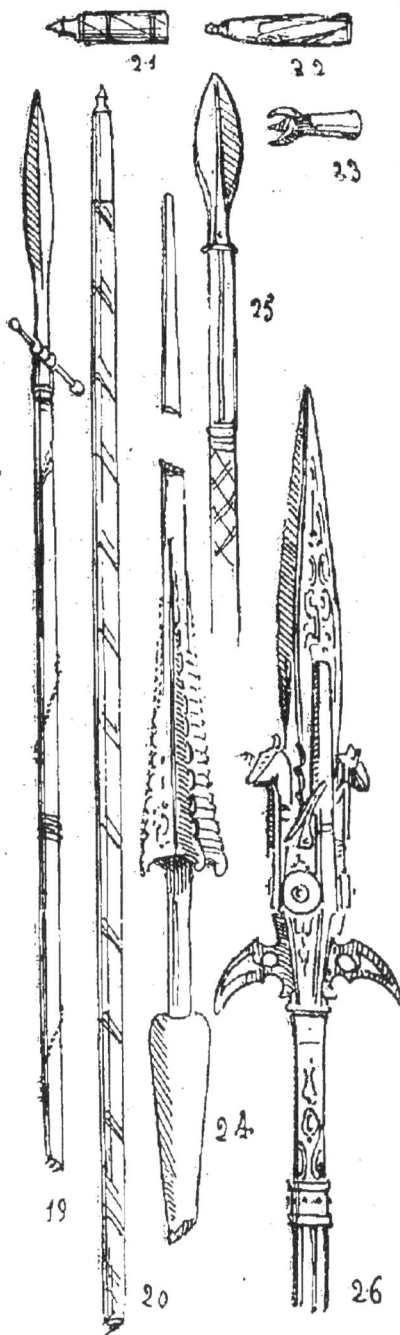

19. Lance allemande appelée *Knebelspies*, d'après le manuscrit de Glockenthon, de 1505, de la collection d'Ambras.

20. Javelot allemand de chasse du seizième siècle. — Musée de Dresde.

21. Pointe de lance allemande de guerre et de tournois du seizième siècle; elle a 18 cent. de longueur. — Musée de Dresde.

22. Id. de 20 cent. de longueur. — Arsenal de Berlin.

23. Id. de 14 cent. de longueur. — Arsenal de Berlin.

24. Lance de carrousel pour courir la bague. Règne de Louis XIII (1610-1643). — K. 262, musée d'artillerie de Paris. On trouve ce même modèle dans le traité d'équitation de Pluvinel.

25. Épieu allemand de chasse, du seizième siècle (*Sau* ou *Bœrenfanger*, aussi *Schweinsfeder*, en all.). Il servait particulièrement pour la chasse du sanglier.

26. Épieu de chasse à trois pistolets à rouet et à deux crochets de hallebarde; cette arme du seizième siècle a fait partie de la collection Saltikoff.

27. Lance du dix-septième siè-cle.

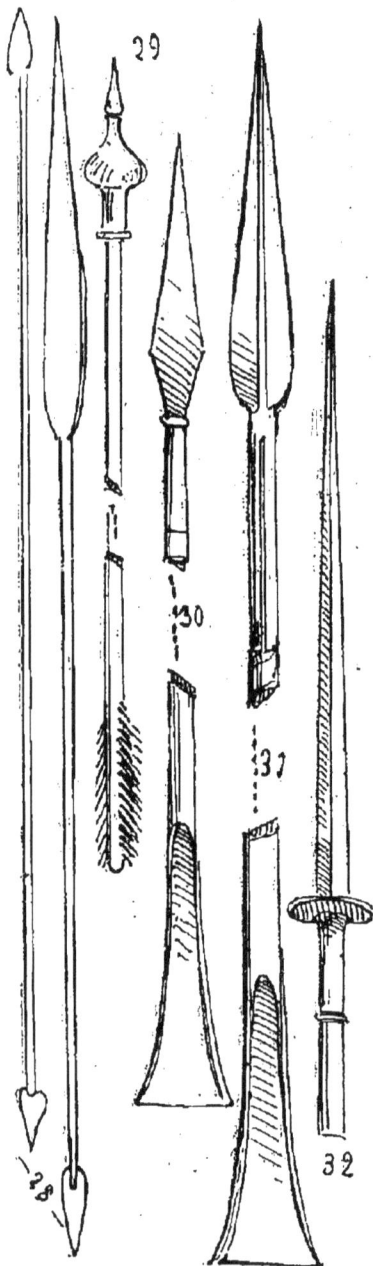

28. Lances persanes à double fer, d'après un manuscrit des dernières années du seizième siècle, copie du *Schah-Nameh* de Fisdusi de 999.

29. Lance-flèche à jet (*Wurffeil* en allem.) pour la chasse de l'ours. — Arsenal de Berlin.

30. Lance abyssinienne qui est facilement reconnaissable à son sabot en fer qui garnit la par-tie inférieure. Cette pointe large rappelle tout à fait les pointes en bronze et en fer des framées des âges du bronze et du fer, et dont une espèce, pourvue d'un anneau, est connue sous le nom de *celt*. — Musée d'artillerie de Paris.

31. Id. id.

32. Lance chinoise.

LA MASSE D'ARMES

La *masse d'armes* (du latin *massa*, massue, *Streitkolben* en allemand, *mace* en anglais), arme fort pesante d'un bout, impropre à percer et à trancher, et faite pour assommer, était fort répandue dans la cavalerie; on la voit déjà reproduite dans les tapisseries de Bayeux de la fin du onzième siècle.

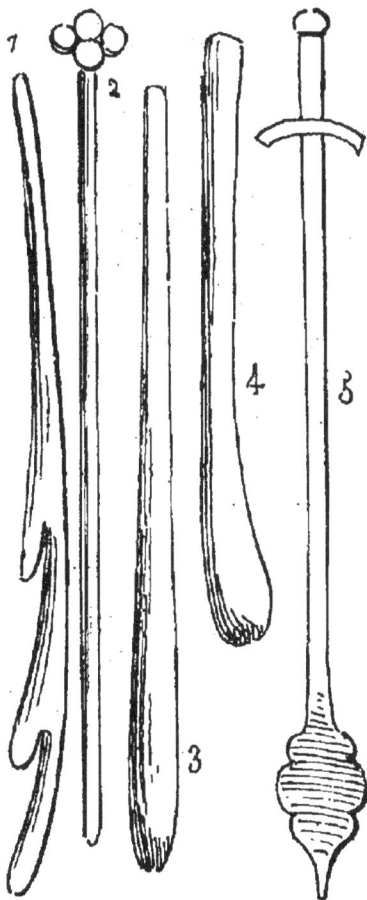

1. Masse d'armes en fer de la fin du onzième siècle. — Tapisse-series de Bayeux.

2. Id. id.

3. Id. id.

4. Masse d'armes, d'après l'*Énéide allemande* de Henri de Valdeck, du treizième siècle. — Bibliothèque de Berlin.

5. Masse d'armes bourguignonne du commencement du quinzième siècle, d'après un manuscrit, que l'on croit avoir appartenu au duc de Bourgogne. — Bibliothèque de l'arsenal de Paris.

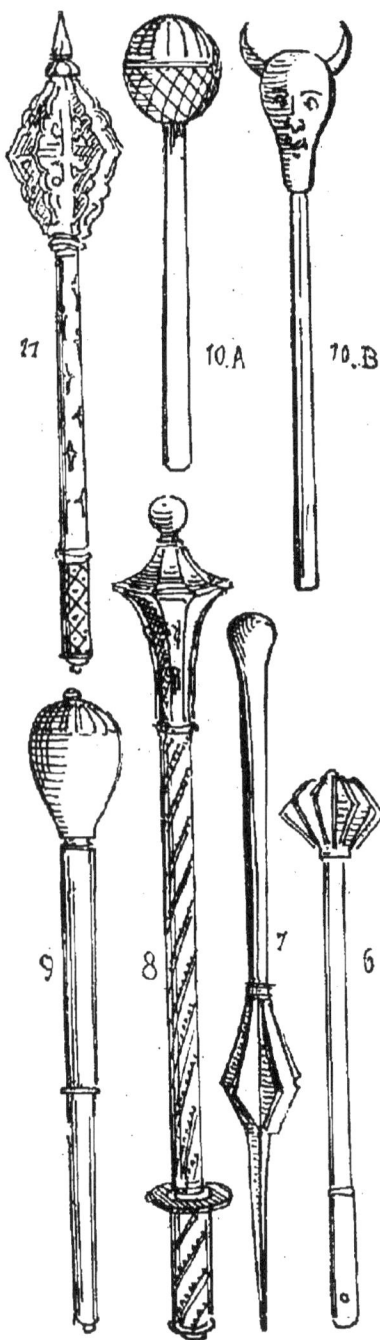

6. Masse d'armes anglaise en fer et en bois du règne de Henri V (1413-1422). — Col. Llewelyn-Meyrick.

7. Masse d'armes anglaise tout en fer du milieu du quinzième siècle.

8. Masse d'armes allemande du quinzième siècle. Elle est en fer ciselé, mesure 56 cent. et a la poignée ficelée. — Arsenal de Lucerne.

9. Masse d'armes turque en fer du quinzième siècle; le sommet forme une rosace damasquinée. — Musée d'artillerie de Paris.

10 A. Masse d'armes, d'après un manuscrit de la fin du seizième siècle, une copie illustrée de nombreuses miniatures, du *Schah-Nameh*, ou Livre royal composé par le poëte Fisdusi, sous le règne de Mahmoud (999). — Bibliothèque de Munich.

10 B.   Id.   id.

11. Masse d'armes française du seizième siècle.

LE MORGENSTERN

Cette masse d'armes, le plus souvent à longue hampe, hérissée de pointes en fer ou en bois, et dont les noms allemand *Morgenstern*, et anglais *morning-star* veulent dire *étoile du matin*, était déjà connue des anciens, puisque les musées en possèdent plusieurs fragments en métal de la période dite l'âge du bronze.

Le *Morgenstern* était très-répandu en Allemagne et en Suisse, où on lui avait appliqué son nom par un sinistre jeu de mots : c'est avec ses pointes que l'on souhaitait le bonjour à l'ennemi surpris dans son camp et dans sa ville.

Cette arme était devenue très-populaire à cause de la facilité et de la rapidité avec lesquelles elle pouvait être fabriquée. Le campagnard la créait aisément au moyen d'une poignée de gros clous et d'un tronc d'arbrisseau ; aussi, se retrouve-t-elle toujours grandement représentée dans les guerres des paysans qui ont désolé l'Allemagne à plusieurs reprises, et les arsenaux suisses en possèdent encore un grand nombre.

Il existe aussi des *Morgensterne* de cavaliers, qui sont courts de manche comme les marteaux, et ordinairement mieux fabriqués que les armes à longues hampes pour hommes de pied. Quelques-unes de ces petites masses d'armes, hérissées de pointes de fer, ont été même pourvues d'un canon à main. Ainsi construites, elles s'appellent en allemand *Schiesprügel*. (Voy. le n° 8.)

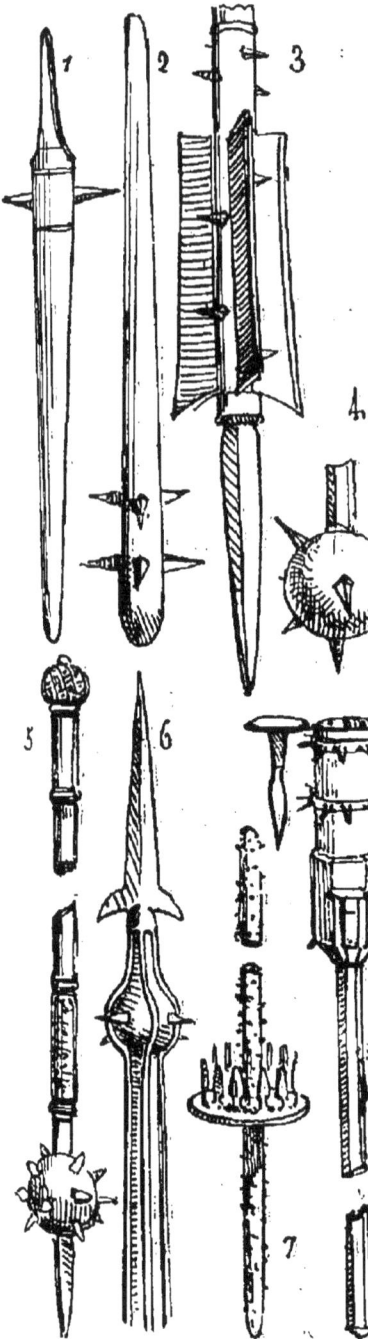

1 et 2. Masses d'armes qui devraient être classées parmi les armes de l'âge du fer, puisqu'elles ont été reproduites d'après la colonne de Théodose à Constantinople, qui date du quatrième siècle.

3. Morgenstern suisse du quinzième siècle, sur longue hampe. La longueur du fer, qui est garni de quatre lames et d'un dard, est de 45 cent. — Gymnase de Morat.

4. Morgenstern suisse du quinzième siècle, à boule de bois hérissée de pointes en fer, sur longue hampe.—Musée de Berne.

5. Morgenstern à main, probablement de cavalier. Il est tout en fer ciselé, a 65 cent. de longueur et un dard qui rentre dans le manche au moyen d'un ressort. — Musée de Sigmaringen.

6. Morgenstern - pertuisane sur longue hampe garnie de fer. — Col. Az, à Lintz.

7. Morgenstern de 3m 1/2 de longueur, à corbeille à lames, de la fin du quinzième siècle. — Arsenal de la ville de Vienne.

8. Morgenstern à canon à main, aussi appelé *Schiesprügel* en allem., de la fin du quatorzième ou du commencement du quinzième siècle. — Col. du prince Charles, à Berlin, col. d'Ambras et Meyrick et musée de Sigmaringen.

LE FLÉAU

Cette arme, dont le nom indique la forme (*fléau*, du latin *flagellum*, fouet, *Flegel* en allemand, et en anglais *military-flails* et aussi *holy water-sprinkler*[1], c'est à dire goupillon, par allusion à la forme et au sang qu'il peut faire jaillir), est composée de la hampe et de la *verge* ou du *battant*, avec ou sans pointes de fer; ou de la hampe et de la chaîne terminées par une boule en fer ou en bois hérissée de dards.

L'origine du fléau d'armes ne paraît pas remonter à l'antiquité.

La première mention de cette arme se trouve dans des manuscrits du commencement du onzième siècle.

Une statue de la même époque, et qui représente, au dôme de Naumbourg, en Allemagne, un des fondateurs de l'édifice, en est armée, ainsi que la statue du palatin Olivier au dôme de Vérone.

Le fléau, qui était très-répandu en Suisse et en Allemagne durant le quinzième siècle, était connu en Angleterre depuis la conquête normande (onzième siècle), et on le retrouve encore sous le règne de Henri VIII (1509-1547), mais il n'y servait guère, à cette époque, que dans les tranchées et sur les vaisseaux. Les fléaux d'armes à manches courts ont été particulièrement en usage en Russie et au Japon.

Le *fouet d'armes* ou le *scorpion* (*Scorpion* en allemand et en anglais) est une espèce de fléau à main, ou knout, à trois, quatre ou six chaînes.

---

1. Quelques auteurs donnent à tort ce nom au *morning-star.*

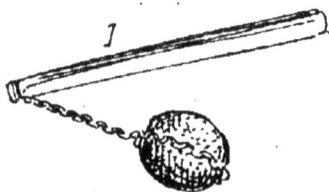

1. Fléau d'armes allemand (*Flegel* en allem., *holywater-sprinkler* en angl.) du onzième siècle, à chaîne et boule sans pointes, d'après la statue d'un des fondateurs du dôme de Naumbourg.

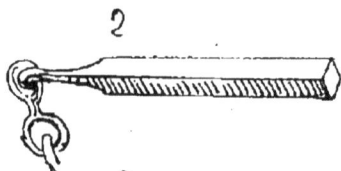

2. Battant ou verge de fléau d'armes en fer sans pointes, sur longue hampe, probablement du quatorzième siècle. — K. 83, musée d'artillerie de Paris.

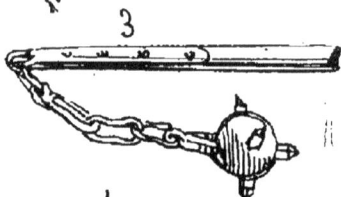

3. Fléau d'armes à chaîne et boule à pointes, sur longue hampe, probablement du quatorzième siècle. — K. 81, musée d'artillerie de Paris.

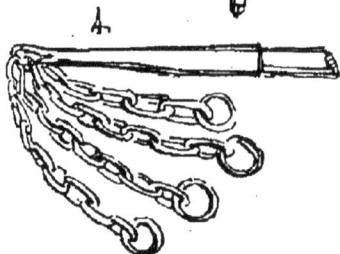

4. Fléau d'armes à quatre chaînes sans boules, appelé aussi fouet d'armes et scorpion (*Scorpion* en allem. et en angl.), armes hussites du quinzième siècle. — Musée national de Prague.

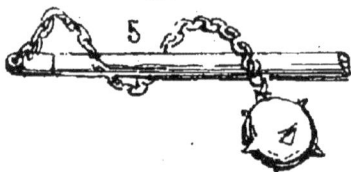

5. Fléau d'armes anglais à chaîne et boule à pointes, sur longue hampe, du règne de Henri VII (1485-1509). — Col. Llewelyn-Meyrick.

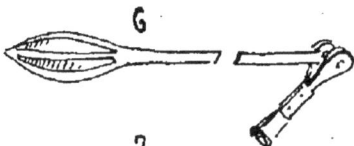

6. Fléau d'armes suisse à verge en fer, sur longue hampe. — Arsenal de Genève.

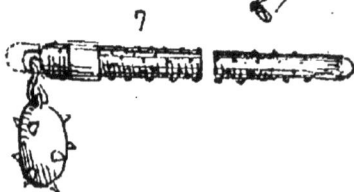

7. Fléau d'armes à manche court, de 78 cent. de longueur. — Musée national de Munich.

38

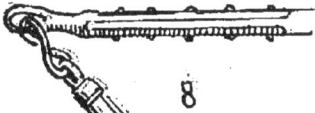

8. Fléau d'armes allemand du quinzième siècle, monté sur une très-longue hampe. Il est à verge hérissée de douze pointes.

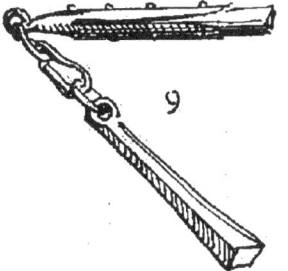

9. Fléau d'armes suisse du quinzième siècle, à verge en fer carrée et sans pointes. Il est sur longue hampe.

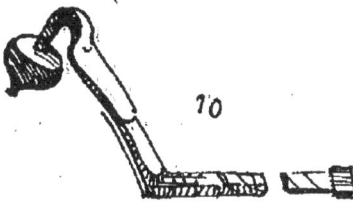

10. Ancien knout[1] russe, manche court. — Musée de Dresde.

11. Fléau d'armes japonais. Le manche n'a que 65 cent. de longueur et la boule qui se trouve au bout de la chaîne est hérissée de pointes très-aiguës.

1. Le knout dont on se sert actuellement en Russie pour les punitions diffère peu de l'ancien, et il répugne de croire à l'emploi d'un pareil instrument dans l'état actuel de la civilisation.

LA FAUX DE GUERRE

La *faux de guerre* (du latin *falx*, *Kriegssense* en allemand, *scythe of war* ou *bill* en anglais) est la faux aratoire redressée ; sa lame forme une ligne droite avec sa hampe[1]. *Elle n'a qu'un seul tranchant ; sa pointe est légèrement courbée vers le côté de ce tranchant,* tandis que le fauchard, qui est aussi à un seul tranchant, a la pointe fuyant vers le dos de la lame, et que le fer de la guisarme ou glaive-guisarme, est, comme le nom de glaive l'indique, à deux tranchants, comme l'épée d'estoc et de taille.

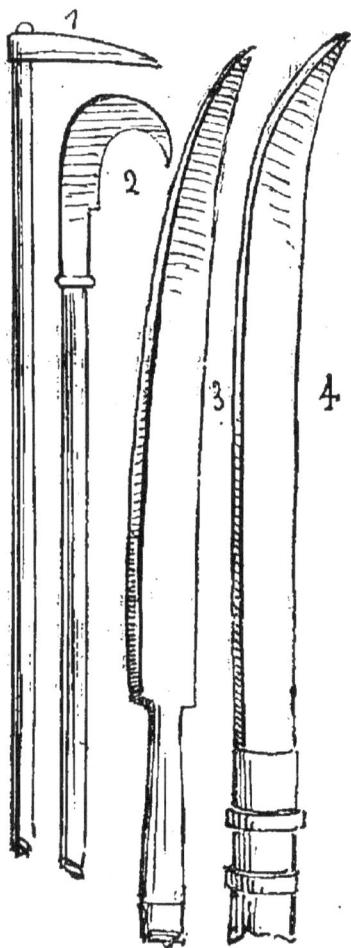

1. Faux de guerre non redressée du commencement du neuvième siècle. — Manuscrit de Wissobrunn de 810, à la bibliothèque de Munich.

2. Faux de guerre-croissant bohémien du treizième siècle. — Manuscrit de Valeslav, à la bibliothèque du prince de Lobkowitz, à Raudnitz.

3. Faux de guerre du quatorzième siècle. — K. 145, musée d'artillerie de Paris.

4. Faux de guerre suisse du quatorzième et du quinzième siècle. — Arsenaux de Soleure et de Zurich. Des faux de guerre d'une dimension colossale (1m,30 à 1m,40 de longueur de lame) servaient aux *Tschaïkists* autrichiens à faucher sur le Danube les équipages des bateaux ennemis. Les troupes autrichiennes ainsi nommées tiraient leur nom de la rivière *Tschaïke*. — Arsenal impérial de Vienne.

1. En Autriche, durant la Jacquerie ou guerre des paysans, les forgerons qui se prêtaient à transformer les instruments aratoires en armes étaient punis de mort.

Le *fauchard*, dont une espèce est aussi nommée *couteau de brèche*, et que l'on confond avec la guisarme, n'a qu'un seul tranchant, comme la faux de guerre dont il dérive; mais sa pointe fuit vers le dos de la lame, tandis que la pointe de la faux de guerre se courbe vers le tranchant. La partie supérieure du fer ou son piquant est quelquefois à double tranchant, et son talon à crochet. Le fauchard était surtout en usage en France au quatorzième siècle, comme le démontre la mention spéciale du poëme des *Trente*.

1. Fauchard bourguignon du quinzième siècle. — Manuscrit à la bibliothèque de l'arsenal de Paris.

2. Fauchard suisse avec hache de hallebarde du seizième siècle. — Musée de Sigmaringen.

3. Fauchard allemand du seizième siècle, avec pistolet à rouet. Il est richement damasquiné. — Musée national de Munich.

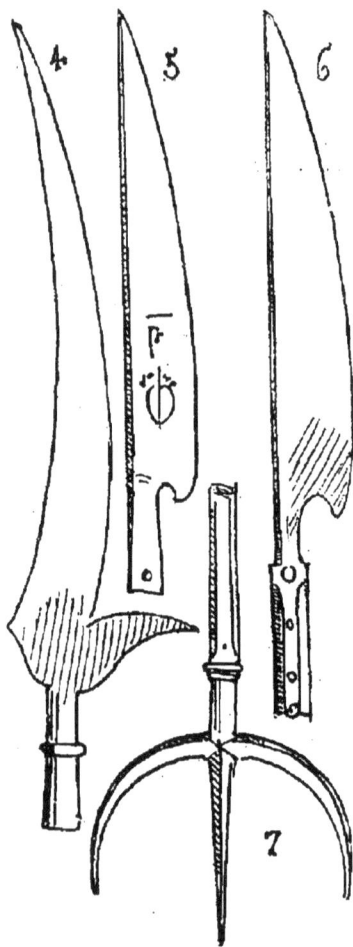

4. Fauchard appelé *Cracouse*, du dix-septième siècle. — Col. Klemm, à Dresde.

5. Fauchard [1] allemand, orné des armoiries du roi Ferdinand, de l'ordre de la Toison d'or et d'un *F*. — Col. Llewelyn-Meyrick.

6. Fauchard allemand, grand modèle, du seizième siècle. Il porte la date 1580 et les armes bavaroises. — K. 156, musée d'artillerie de Paris.

7. Fauchard trident pour la charge (*Sturmsense* en allem.), du dix-septième siècle. Arme allemande dont le fer, d'une dimension énorme, mesure 1^m,60 sur 1^m,30. — Arsenal impérial de Vienne.

1. Ce genre de fauchard est aussi appelé couteau de brèche (*Brechmesser* en allem.). Il fut particulièrement en usage en Autriche et dans d'autres parties de l'Allemagne, où il s'est continué jusqu'au dix-huitième siècle; mais ce n'est en définitive qu'un fauchard.

LA GUISARME

La *guisarme* ou glaive-guisarme (*Glæfe*, et aussi *Ross-chinder*[1] en allemand, *gisarme* en anglais), que les auteurs de la Grande-Bretagne confondent presque tous avec la hallebarde, est un *glaive monté sur une hampe*. La guisarme se distingue particulièrement de la faux de guerre et du fauchard en ce qu'elle est à double tranchant et à crochets. L'origine du glaive-guisarme remonte à l'époque celtique et germanique de l'âge du bronze, où plusieurs peuples avaient la coutume de porter des glaives ou épées de la forme des scramasax montés sur de longues hampes. Les habitants de Wales, en Angleterre, les appelaient *llawnawr*, nom qui dérive du *cleddyr* ou *gleddyr*. En quelques parties de l'Allemagne, le nom de *Glæfe* a fait place aujourd'hui à celui de *Sensener mit Spitzen*. Le nom français de guisarme paraît dériver de *guisard* ou partisan des Guise, qui en étaient armés. Cependant Olivier de la Marche, chroniqueur, né en 1426, attribue une haute antiquité au nom de guisarme, et croit que cette arme dérive de l'habitude que l'on avait jadis d'attacher une dague au bout d'une hache.

---

1. *Rosschinder*, — équarrisseur de cheval, — est une dénomination qui se rapporte aux coutumes des hommes de pied de couper avec cette arme les jarrets aux chevaux des chevaliers.

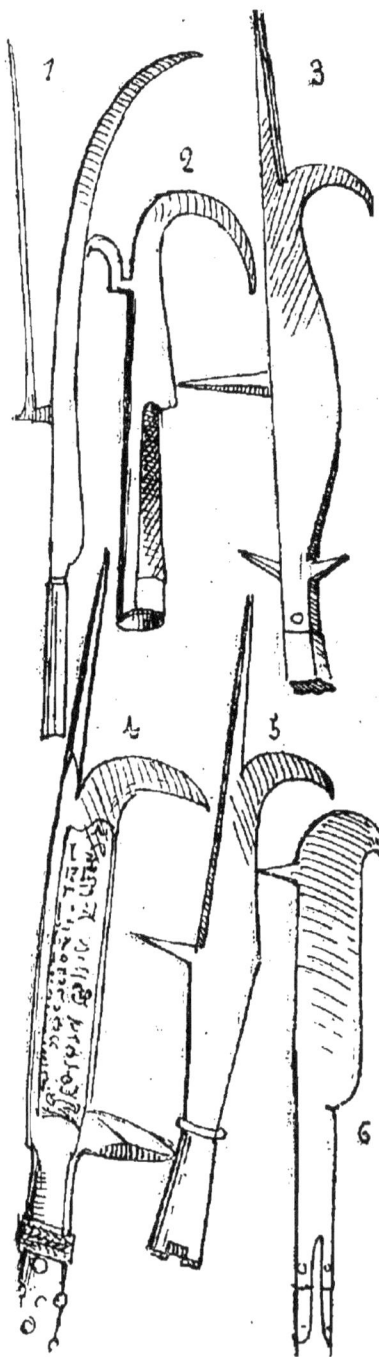

1. Guisarme anglaise (*Glœfe* et *Rosschinder* en allem., *gisarme* en angl.), dont les statuts de Westminster du douzième siècle font déjà mention. Les Chinois se servent encore aujourd'hui de cette arme comme on peut le voir au musée d'artillerie de Paris.

2. Guisarme suisse du treizième siècle. — Col. Troyon, au musée cantonal de Lausanne.

3. Guisarme suisse du quinzième siècle. — Arsenal de Soleure.

4. Guisarme suisse de la fin du quinzième siècle. — Musée de Sigmaringen.

5. Guisarme anglaise de la fin du quinzième siècle.

6. Guisarme suisse de la fin du quinzième siècle. — Arsenal de Zurich et col. Wittmann, à Geisenheim.

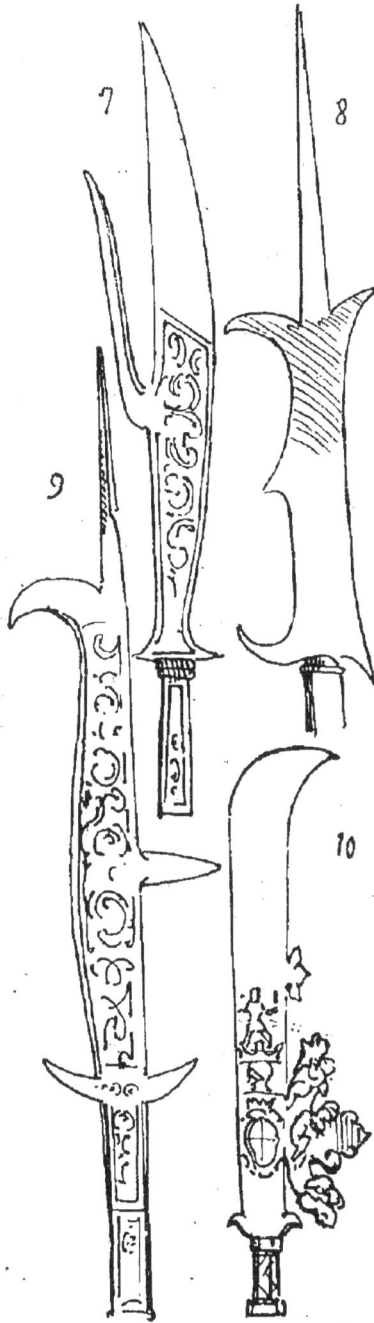

7. Guisarme italienne richement
gravée de la. fin du quinzième
siècle. — Col. Llewelyn-Meyrick.

8. Guisarme dont le fer a 75 c.
de longueur et qui est montée
sur une hampe garnie du fer.
La lame porte l'inscription X.
IVANI. X. — Col. Az, à Lintz.

9. Guisarme suisse du seizième
siècle ; elle est damasquinée. —
Musée de Sigmaringen.

10. Guisarme italienne de la
garde esclavone des doges de
Venise, qu'elle portait avec l'é-
pée à corbeille nommée *Schiavona* que dans presque toutes
les collections on a faussement
cataloguée sous le nom de *Claymore*, épée écossaise qui est à
poignée à simples quillons et
sans pas-d'âne ni corbeille.

LA VOUGE

Cette arme, appelée *voulje* en anglais, assez rare aujour-d'hui, et dont le fer est monté sur une longue hampe, a été une des plus anciennes armes suisses, et fort en usage en France au quinzième siècle, où y existait tout un corps d'infanterie nommé *voulgiers*. Beaucoup d'archers en étaient également dotés. Quelques auteurs donnent aussi à tort le nom de vouge à l'épieu de chasse des veneurs dont la forme n'a absolument rien de commun avec celle de l'arme de guerre ancienne.

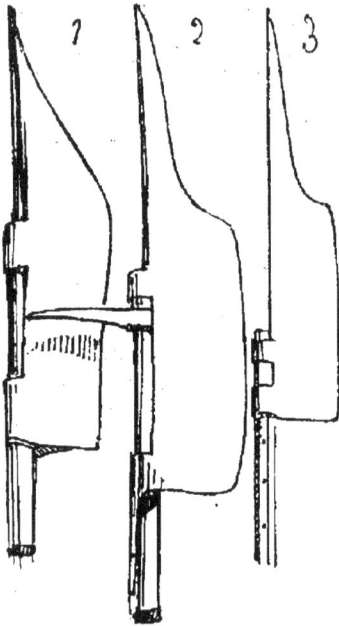

1. Vouge suisse, de 35 cent. de longueur, trouvée sur le champ de bataille de Morgarten (1319). — Arsenal de Lucerne.

2. Vouge suisse à crochet du quatorzième siècle.

3. Vouge suisse du quatorzième siècle. — Arsenal de Zurich. On retrouve cette même vouge dans les dessins d'un manuscrit du quinzième siècle de la collection Hauslaub.

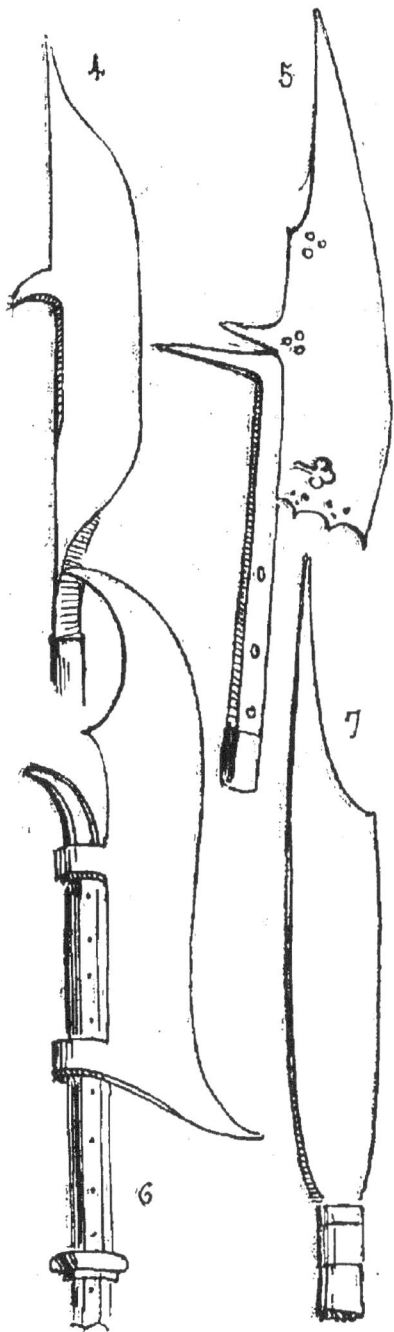

4. Vouge suisse de la fin du quatorzième siècle. — Col. Meyer-
Biermann, à Lucerne.

5. Vouge allemande de la fin du
quinzième siècle. — Col. Az, à
Lintz.

6. Vouge saxonne prise à la bataille de Mühlberg (1547). —
Arsenal impérial de Vienne.

7. Vouge autrichienne de 60 c.
de longueur. Elle provient de
la Jacquerie ou guerre des paysans (1620-1625), époque où
elle a été fabriquée avec un fer
de charrue. — Col. Az, à Lintz.

LE MARTEAU D'ARMES.

Monté sur une longue hampe, il est connu, en Allemagne et en Suisse sous la désignation du *Luzerner-Hammer*, marteau de Lucerne, puisqu'il était l'arme favorite des Lucernois. En anglais on peut le nommer *pole-hammer*, de *pole* perche. L'origine de ce marteau d'armes d'homme de pied remonte à la plus haute antiquité, comme le démontrent les marteaux des âges dits de la pierre et du bronze, et Charles Martel (715-741) doit son nom de guerre à cette arme, dont l'usage était devenu général au quatorzième siècle. Le poëme du *Combat des Trente* le mentionne :

> Cii combattait d'un mail qui pesoit bien le quart
> De cent livres d'acier, si Dieu en moi part.

Ce marteau de *vingt-cinq livres* était celui de Tommelin Belefort. On se servait aussi de cette arme dans les pas d'armes, comme le remarque Olivier de la Marche, né en 1426, dans ses Mémoires, là où il parle des pas d'armes du sire Hautbourdin et de Delalain.

Le marteau d'armes à manche court de cavalier (*Reiterhammer* en allemand, *horsemans hammer* en anglais), que les chevaliers portaient, comme la masse d'armes, suspendu à la selle, est d'une origine presque aussi ancienne que le marteau à hampe. Des bas-reliefs antiques au Louvre montrent des amazones attaquant leurs ennemis avec des maillets à manches courts et à double tranchant, dont l'un est formé par ce que l'on appelle, en terme d'armurier, le *bec-de-perroquet* et *bec-de-faucon*, quand le marteau était sur longue hampe.

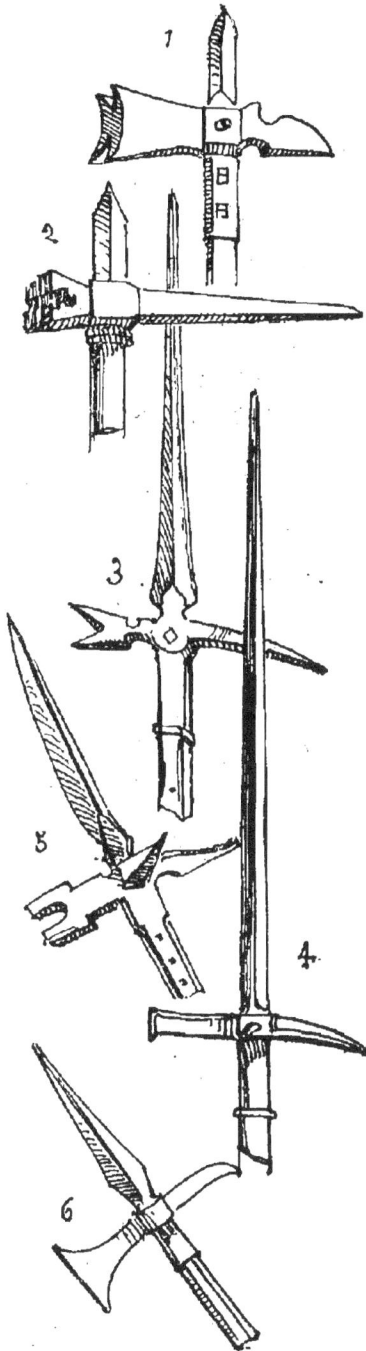

1. Marteau d'armes en acier du quatorzième siècle, monté sur longue hampe. (*Luzerner-Hammer* en allem., *pole-hammer* en angl.). — K. 84, musée d'artillerie.

2. Marteau d'armes en acier du quinzième siècle, monté sur longue hampe.

3. Marteau d'armes suisse en acier du quinzième siècle, monté sur longue hampe. Cette arme, dont l'arsenal de Lucerne possède un grand nombre, représente bien le type du *Luzerner-Hammer* ou marteau de Lucerne. — Col. Meyer-Biermann, à Lucerne, et musée de Sigmaringen.

4. Marteau d'armes en acier, monté sur longue hampe, de la fin du quinzième ou du commencement du seizième siècle. L'épée, qui le surmonte, a plus de 90 cent. de longueur. — K. 88, musée d'artillerie.

5. Marteau d'armes suisse en acier sur longue hampe, d'après un dessin de Jean Holbein (1445-1554) qui représente le *Combat de Thiebaud l'Arx*. — Musée industriel de Vienne.

6. Marteau d'armes-pique. Cette arme sur longue hampe était portée par des sous-officiers gardes-drapeau sous le premier Empire (1804-1814). — K. 275, musée d'artillerie de Paris.

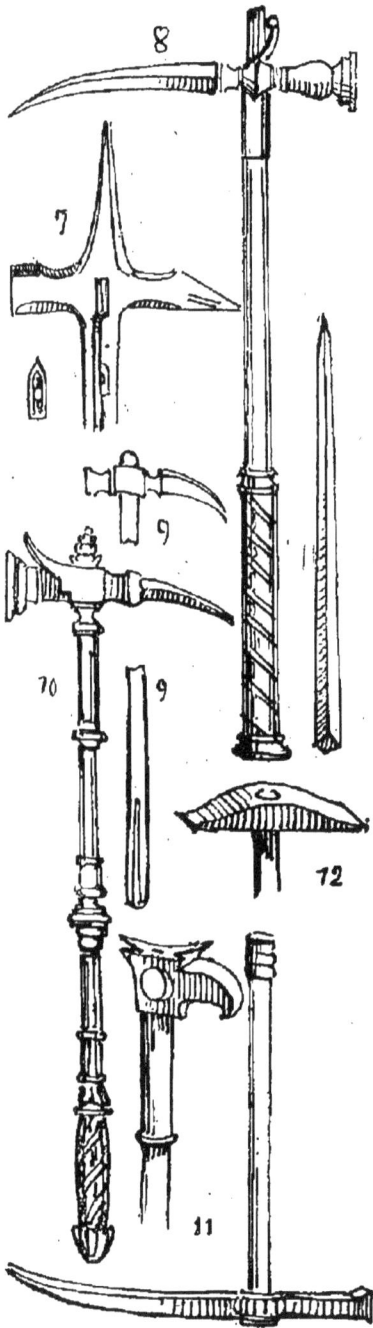

7. Marteau d'armes de cavalier (*Reiterhammer* en allem., *horsemans hammer* en angl.), de 60 cent. de longueur; il est en fer, à manche de bois incrusté d'ornements gothiques en cuivre, dont les ogives à dos-d'âne indiquent la fin du quinzième siècle. — Col. Renné de Constance.

8. Marteau d'armes, de 1 mètre de longueur, d'un chef hussite du quinzième siècle, qui servait à la fois d'arme et de bâton de commandement. La poignée, d'une longeur de 40 cent., est recouverte de velours rouge. Un dard, de 75 cent. de longueur, sort du marteau dès qu'on appuie sur le bouton de la douille. — Musée de Sigmaringen.

9. Marteau d'armes de cavalier dit perroquet, de la fin du quinzième siècle. — Col. Llewelyn-Meyrick.

10. Marteau d'armes de cavalier dit perroquet, du seizième siècle, tout en fer ciselé; il a 35 c. de longueur et des ornements fleurs de lis. — Arsenal de Berne.

11. Marteau d'armes de cavalier du seizième siècle, dit perroquet. — K. 69, musée d'artillerie de Paris.

12. Marteau d'armes d'escalade, pris aux Savoisiens commandés par Brenaulieu-Chaffardin, en 1602, sous les murs de Genève, ville qu'ils voulaient surpendre. — Arsenal de Genève.

13. Marteau d'armes de cavalier à verge très-longue, en fer et en cuivre et à manche de bois à poignée d'ivoire, du seizième siècle. — Musée de Dresde.

LA HACHE D'ARMES

La *hache d'armes* (hache, de l'allemand *Hacken*, et non pas du latin *ascia*) s'appelait en allemand *Streitaxt*, et en anglais *battle-axe*, en général, mais *Fuss-Streitaxt* en allemand, et *pole-axe* (de *pole*, perche) dès qu'elle était à longue hampe, et destinée aux hommes de pied. Cette arme cunéiforme, comme l'instrument domestique dont elle dérive, est une des plus anciennes ; elle était aussi une des plus répandues durant les âges dits de la pierre et du bronze, et l'arme favorite des races germaniques.

La hache des Francs, la célèbre *francisque*, était à manche court, tandis que celle des Saxons était montée sur une hampe tellement longue chez les Anglo-Saxons, qu'elle fut appelée *pole-axe* ou hache à perche, car le mot pole signifie aussi bien perche que crochet.

A la bataille de Hastings, en 1066, où Harold II fut défait par Guillaume le Conquérant, les Saxons repoussèrent d'abord avec succès les assauts répétés des Normands, qu'ils abattirent en grand nombre avec leurs *longues haches de guerre*, etc., arme qui était alors ordinairement chez eux d'un mètre et demi de longueur. On la trouve représentée dans les tapisseries de Bayeux, où elle ne montre *ni pointe ni croc*, et paraît aussi simple que la hache domestique et la francisque.

La hache d'armes d'homme de pied du quatorzième siècle n'est plus du tout la même que celle des siècles précédents. Hache d'un côté, elle offre du côté opposé ou le marteau à pointes de diamant ou la pointe aiguë du marteau d'armes, mais ordinairement plus recourbée et plus volumineuse, que l'on nommait *bec-de-faucon*, tandis qu'elle s'appelait *bec-de-perroquet* dès qu'elle faisait partie d'un marteau ou d'une hache à manche court à l'usage du cavalier.

Cette arme était aussi quelquefois pourvue d'un dard long, sorte d'épée plantée au bout supérieur.

La hache à manche court, qui était l'arme de la chevalerie (*Reiteraxt*, et aussi *Barthe* en allemand, *horsemans axe* en anglais), montre quelquefois, à partir de la fin du moyen âge, un canon encastré dans le manche, soit le canon à main primitif, soit le pistolet à rouet.

La hache d'armes à manche court était, comme le marteau, connue des anciens. C'était une de ces armes que l'on voit quelquefois sur les chars de guerre des Asssyriens et dans les sculptures qui représentent des Amazones.

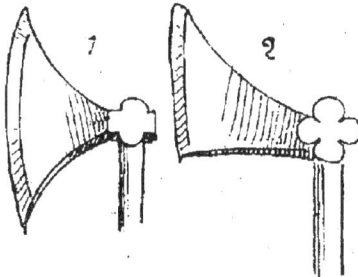

1 et 2. Haches d'armes à longue hampe, pour homme de pied (*Fuss-Streitaxt* en allem., *pole-axe* en angl.), de la fin du onzième siècle. — Tapisseries de Bayeux.

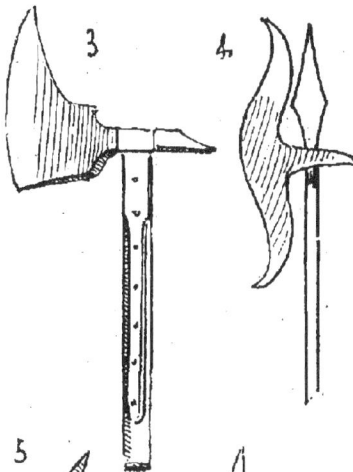

3. Hache d'armes allemande à longue hampe, pour homme de pied, de la fin du quatorzième siècle. — K. 93, musée d'artillerie de Paris.

4. Hache d'armes allemande à longue hampe, pour homme de pied, du quinzième siècle. — Gravure sur bois, au cabinet d'estampes de Munich.

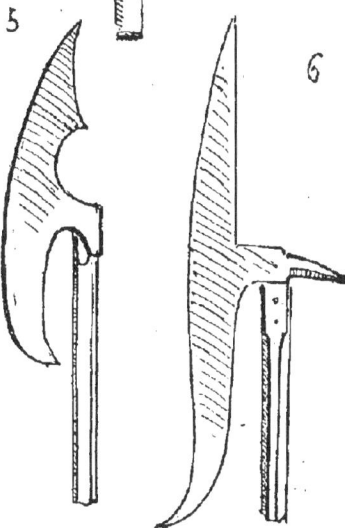

5. Hache d'armes allemande à longue hampe, pour homme de pied, du quinzième siècle. — Musée de Munich; collection du roi de Suède Charles XV et collection Llewelyn-Meyrick.

6. Hache d'armes suisse à longue hampe, pour homme de pied, du quinzième siècle. — Arsenal de Lucerne.

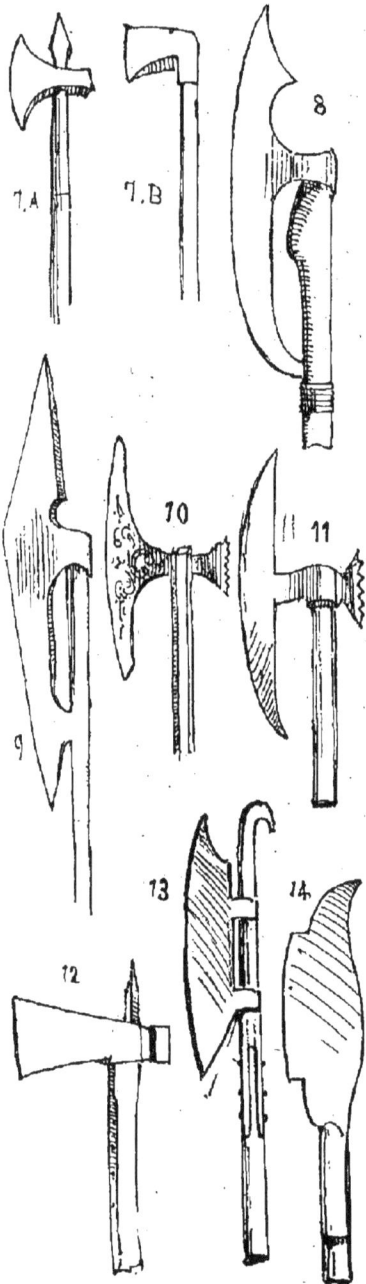

7 A. Hache d'armes allemande à longue hampe pour homme de pied, du quinzième siècle. — Incunable du cabinet d'estampes de Munich.

7 B. 　　　Id. 　　　id.

8. Hache d'armes russe à longue hampe pour homme de pied, appelée *Bardiche.* — K. 95, musée d'artillerie de Paris.

9. Hache d'armes russe[1] à longue hampe pour homme de pied, dont étaient armés les *Strélites* ou *Strelitzen.* — Musée de Tsarskoe-Selo.

10. Hache d'armes vénitienne à longue hampe et à marteau à pointes de diamant, du seizième siècle. — Col. Meyrick.

11. Hache d'armes suisse à longue hampe et à marteau à pointes de diamant, du seizième siècle. — Arsenal de Berne.

12. Hache d'armes suisse à longue hampe, à marteau et à dard. — Arsenal de Berne.

13. Hache d'armes à longue hampe, des *Lochaber*, arme nationale d'Ecosse. — Col. du prince Charles, à Berlin.

14. Id. allemande du quinzième siècle[2]. — Musée historique de Montbijou, à Berlin.

1. Les haches d'armes modernes des peuples qui habitent le Caucase ont encore aujourd'hui cette même forme, comme le démontre l'arme de Schamyl, conservée également au musée de Tsarkoe-Selo, et on les voit aussi sur des gravures allemandes du quinzième siècle au cabinet d'estampes à Munich.

2. Ces deux espèces de haches pourraient être rangées parmi les vouges.

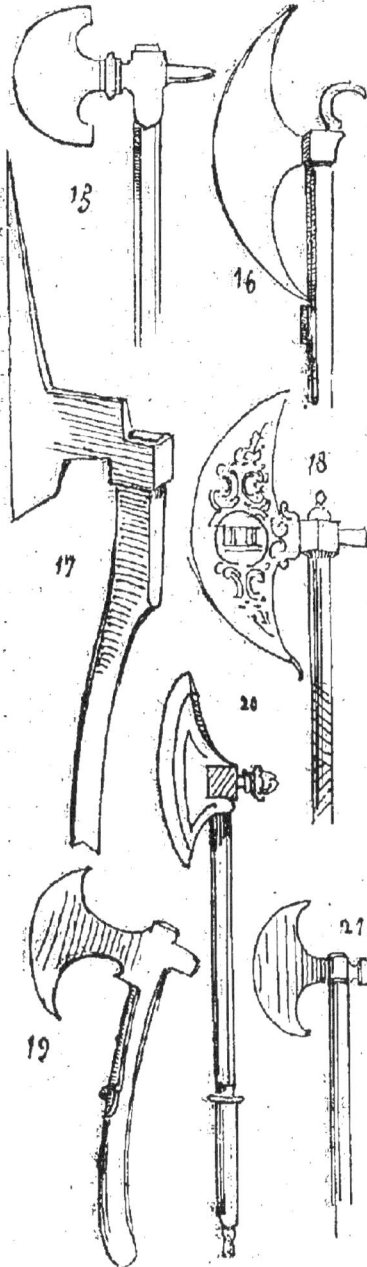

15. Hache d'armes anglaise de partisan à longue hampe pour homme de pied, appelée *Jedburg-axe*, du seizième siècle. — Col. Meyrick.

16. Hache d'armes probablement anglaise ou écossaise, à longue hampe, pour homme de pied. — K. 96, musée d'artillerie de Paris.

17. Hache d'armes allemande, à manche court, pour cavalier (*Reiteraxt* et aussi *Barthe* en allem., *horsemans axe* en angl.), de la fin du quinzième siècle. — Musée de Dresde.

18. Hache d'armes turque, à manche court, de cavalier, de la fin du quinzième siècle, ayant appartenu au sultan des Mamelucks Mahomed-Ben-Kaitbai, qui a régné de 1495 à 1499. Une inscription en lettres à jour dit : « *Le sultan, le roi victorieux, le père de la fortune, Mahomed Ben Kaitbai; que l'aide de Dieu soit glorifiée en lui!* » On y lit, en outre, en lettres kufiques, cinq fois le nom de Dieu. — Col. d'Ambras.

19. Hache d'armes sclave, à manche court, pour cavalier.— Dessin d'Albrecht Durer.

20. Hache d'armes à manche court pour cavalier, entièrement en fer, du commencement du seizième siècle.

21. Hache d'armes anglaise à manche court pour cavalier, du commencement du règne d'Elisabeth (1558).

22. Hache autrichienne, dont le manche mesure un mètre et qui porte la date de 1623 et la roue, signe de ralliement adopté par

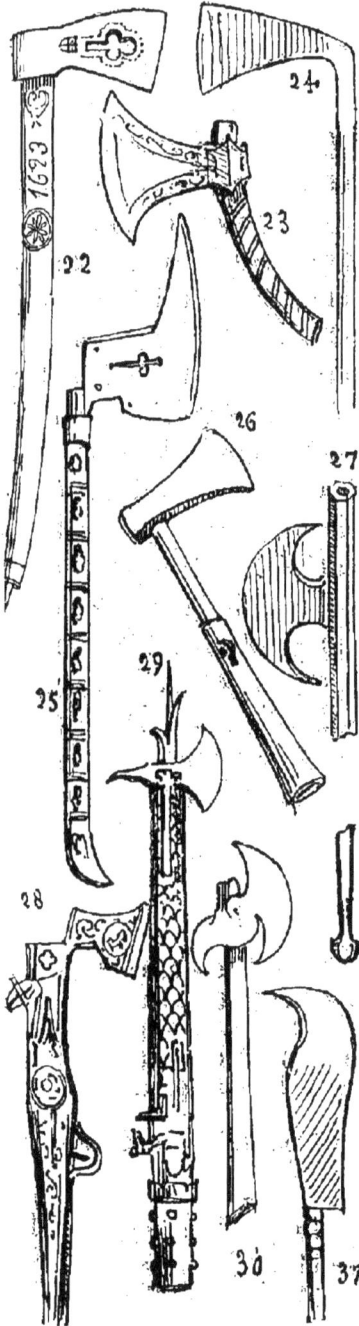

les paysans insurgés dans la Jacquerie, qui furent vaincus avec l'aide de la chevalerie bavaroise. — Col. Az, à Lintz.

23. Hache d'armes polonaise, à manche court entortillé de bandes de cuir, du commencement du dix-septième. — Col. Llewelyn-Meyrick.

24. Hache anglaise d'exécution, de la fin du seizième siècle, avec laquelle fut décapité le comte d'Essex sous le règne d'Elisabeth (1588-1608). — Tour de Londres.

25. Hache de parade de mineur saxon, appelée *Bergbarte*, datée de 1685; le manche est incrusté d'ivoire et la lame percée à jour. Ces armes, qui sont uniquement destinées aux cortéges de la corporation des mineurs, aux jours de fète, ne sont guère propres à un autre usage.

26. Hache d'armes de cavalier, à petit canon pour manche, du quinzième siècle.

27. Hache d'armes, à petit canon pour manche, du seizième siècle, de 85 cent. de longueur, ayant appartenu au réformateur Zwingli, mort à la bataille de Cappel, en 1531. — Arsenal de Zurich.

28. Hache d'armes allemande, à pistolet à rouet, de la fin du seizième siècle, incrustée d'ivoire et d'argent. — Musée Szokau (Hongrie) et musée de Sigmaringen.

29. — Hache d'armes, à pistolet à batterie à silex, de la fin du dix-septième siècle.

30. Hache d'armes chinoise. — Musée d'artillerie de Paris.

31.   Id.   id.

LA HALLEBARDE

La *hallebarde* (de l'allemand *Halbe-Barthe*, demi-hache d'armes, ou de *Helm*, casque, et *Barthe*, hache d'armes, ou de *alte Barthe*, ancienne hache d'armes, et nommée en anglais *halberd*) remonte, en Scandinavie et en Allemagne, aux premiers siècles de notre ère; elle fut introduite en France par les Suisses, vers 1420. Le président Fouchet, qui écrivait vers la fin du seizième siècle, en attribue l'introduction à Louis XI (1461-1483). « Ce prince, dit-il, fit faire à Angiers et autres bonnes villes de *nouvaulx ferremens de guerre appelés hallebardes*. » Ce dire est confirmé par des miniatures du commencement du quinzième siècle, où on voit déjà figurer la hallebarde dont la forme a grandement varié selon les temps et les pays.

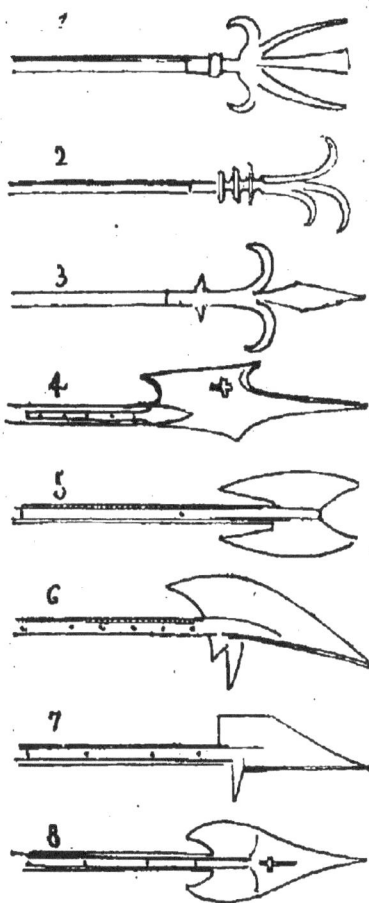

1, 2, et 3. Trois espèces de hallebarde, du genre des corsèques, — du onzième siècle. — Psalterum, manuscrit de la bibliothèque de Stuttgard.

4. Hallebarde suisse du quatorzième siècle.

5, 6, 7 et 8. Quatre hallebardes allemandes du quatorzième siècle. — Musée national de Munich.

9. Hallebarde suisse du commencement du quinzième siècle. — Col. de l'auteur.

10. Hallebarde suisse de la fin du quinzième siècle. — Arsenal de Berne.

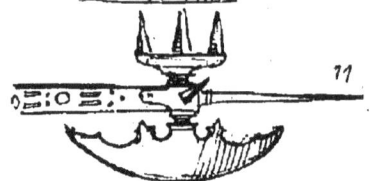

11. Hallebarde suisse à marteau-fourche de la fin du quinzième siècle. — Arsenal de Berne.

12. Hallebarde allemande à marteau-fourche du commencement du seizième siècle. — Arsenal impérial de Vienne.

13. Hallebarde suisse du milieu du seizième siècle. — Col. de l'auteur.

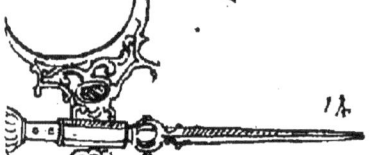

14. Hallebarde allemande du seizième siècle, dorée et ciselée, arme très-riche. — Musée de Sigmaringen.

15. Hallebarde allemande du seizième siècle. — Col. Sœter, au musée Maximilien, à Augsbourg.

16. Hallebarde vénitienne de la fin du seizième siècle. — Col. Llewelyn-Meyrick.

LA CORSÈQUE

La *corsèque*, espèce de pertuisane, originaire de la Corse, et qui paraît être la même arme que quelques auteurs appellent *ronçone*, arme des *ronseurs* (*Ranseurs* en allemand et en anglais), était très-répandue en Allemagne vers la fin du quinzième siècle. L'ancien *Cérémonial français* dit que c'était *une javeline ayant le fer long et large, à deux oreillons*.

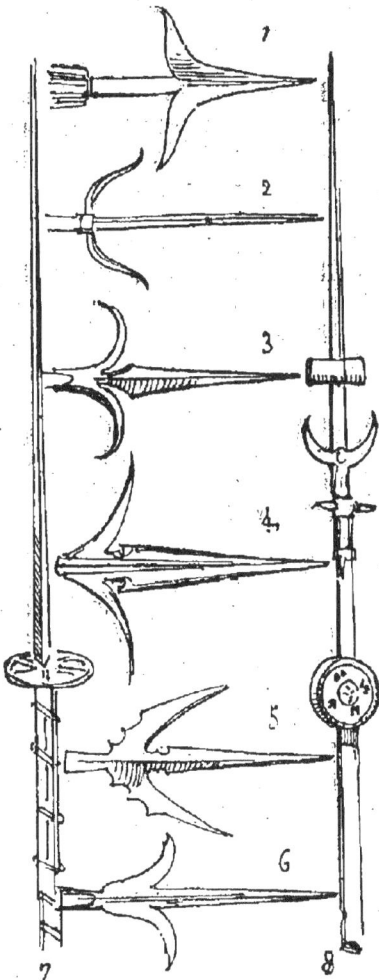

1. Corsèque ou ronçone bourguignonne, d'après les miniatures d'un manuscrit du quinzième siècle. — Bibliothèque de l'arsenal de Paris.

2. Corsèque de la fin du quinzième siècle. — K. 98, musée d'artillerie de Paris.

3. Corsèque allemande du commencement du seizième siècle. — Manuscrit de Glockenthon, à la collection d'Ambras.

4. Corsèque allemande du seizième siècle. — Col. Nieuwerkerke.

5. Corsèque italienne du seizième siècle.

6. Corsèque du dix-septième siècle. — Arsenal de Berlin.

7. Corsèque carrée à rouet du seizième siècle. La pointe a presque un mètre de longueur. — Arsenal de la ville de Vienne. Cette même corsèque se trouve aussi dans les dessins de 1505 de Glockenthon qui reproduisent les armes des arsenaux de Maximilien I.

8. Corsèque à rouet du commencement du dix-septième siècle. — Musée de Sigmaringen.

LA PERTUISANE

La *pertuisane* (de l'espagnol *partesana*, ou de *pertuis*, ouverture, parce qu'elle fait de larges blessures, ou peut-être simplement du français *partisan*; en allemand *Partisane*, et aussi *Bœhmischer Ohrloeffel*, et en anglais *partizan*) est une variété de la hallebarde. Son fer est long, large et tranchant; elle n'a point de hache, mais des ailerons dans le genre de ceux de la corsèque et de la roncone. Connue en France depuis Louis XI (1461) jusqu'à la fin du dix-septième siècle, son origine ne remonte pourtant pas au delà de 1400. Pietro Monti, dans son *Exercitiorum atque artis militaris collectanea*, Milan, 1509, qui a particulièrement voulu décrire cette arme, dont les gardes de François Ier et de ses successeurs étaient pourvus, l'a confondue avec les corsèques et les hallebardes, erreur qui a été encore commise de nos jours dans le catalogue de la célèbre collection Llewelyn-Meyrick à Goedrich-Court, où on a même classé des espontons et des baïonnettes langue-de-bœuf dans la catégorie des pertuisanes.

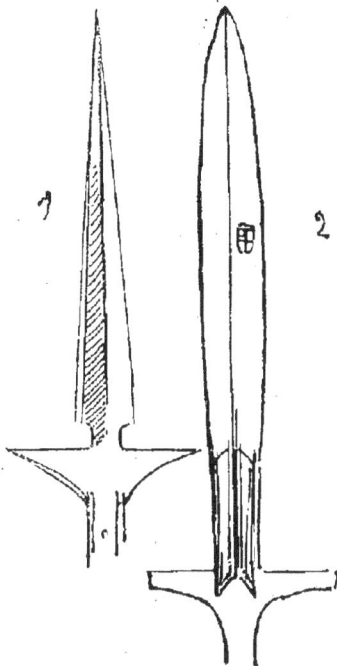

1. Pertuisane allemande (*Parti-sane* ou *Bœhmischer Ohrlœffel* en allem., *partizan* en angl.), dont le fer mesure 36 cent. Elle remonte probablement aux premières années du quinzième siècle. — Musée national de Munich.

2. Pertuisane suisse du quinzième siècle, avec marque d'armuriers. — Col. Meyer-Biermann, à Lucerne.

3. Pertuisane suisse du quinzième siècle, avec marque d'armurier. — Col. Meyer-Biermann, à Zurich.

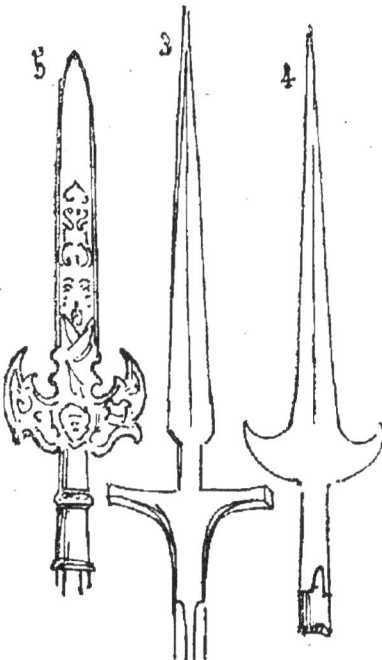

4. Pertuisane française du seizième siècle, du règne de François I. Elle est gravée. — K. 166, musée d'artillerie de Paris.

5. Pertuisane allemande, richement gravée et datée de 1615. Elle porte les insignes de la Toison d'or et provient des gardes du palatin du Rhin. — Col. Llewelyn-Meyrick.

LA BAIONNETTE

Presque tous les auteurs de dictionnaires et d'encyclopédies, en se copiant, comme d'habitude, les uns les autres, ont répété que la baïonnette (*Bajonnet* en allemand, *bajonet* en anglais) a été inventée et fabriquée à Bayonne par Puységur, mort en 1682. Cependant, cette sorte de dague ou d'épée n'a pas seulement été portée au bout du fusil proprement dit; elle avait été adaptée déjà à l'arquebuse, et peut-être même aux premières armes à feu portatives. On la trouve déjà mentionnée en France vers 1570, mais elle n'y fut universellement adoptée que vers 1640, où elle remplaça la pique dans une partie des troupes. La baïonnette, qui est composée aujourd'hui de la *lame* et de la *douille* à virole, dont l'invention est attribuée à tort en Angleterre à Mackay, en 1691, et en France à Vauban, était d'abord à *manche* en bois, fer ou corne, destiné à entrer dans le canon. Plus tard, la baïonnette fut fixée au bout du fusil au moyen de la douille dont l'échancrure pouvait tourner sur le tenon. C'était l'arme blanche réunie à l'arme à feu, appelée *fusil mousquet* ou *mousquet fusil*, attribuée à Vauban, que Couhorn, le rival de celui-ci, introduisit aussi dans l'infanterie hollandaise vers 1680.

Un mousquet à rouet de la fin du seizième siècle, conservé dans la collection Coulmann, à Hanovre, infirme cependant l'attribution qui a été faite à Vauban du premier emploi de la baïonnette à douille, car cette arme est pourvue d'une longue baïonnette à douille à virole, dont la lame sert en même temps de tire-bourre.

Il y a des baïonnettes *langue-de-bœuf*, des baïonnettes *espagnoles en forme de couteau*, des *baïonnettes triangulaires*, des *baïonnettes-fauchards* bohèmes, des *baïonnettes-sabres*, etc., etc.

40

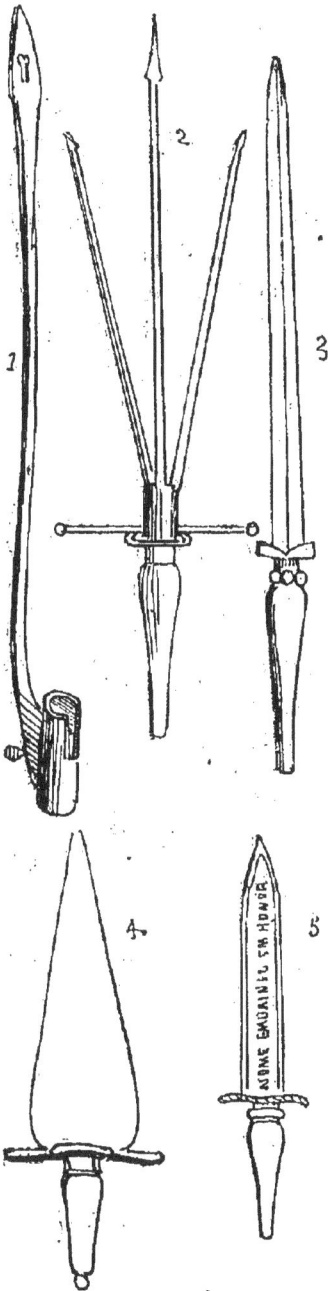

1. Baïonnette allemande, à douille à virole, du seizième siècle. — Coll. Coulmann, à Hanovre.

2. Baïonnette - poignard brise-épée à manche, de la fin du seizième siècle. Elle a 37 cent. de longueur. — Col. Sœter, à Augsbourg.

3. Baïonnette-poignard triangulaire à manche en bois, de 35 cent. de longueur totale, du dix-septième siècle. — Col. Sœter, à Augsbourg et arsenaux suisses.

4. Baïonnette anglaise, langue-de-bœuf (*Pflug - Bayonnet* en allem., *plug-bayonet* en angl.), de la fin du dix-septième siècle. — Tour de Londres. Une semblable, au même musée, porte l'inscription : « *God save king James the 2 d.* 1686. »

5. Baïonnette-couteau espagnole du dix-septième siècle, à manche en bois. Elle porte l'inscription :

« *No me saches sin razon*
« *Ne me embainez sin honor.* »

(Ne me dégaine sans raison et ne m'engaine sans honneur.)

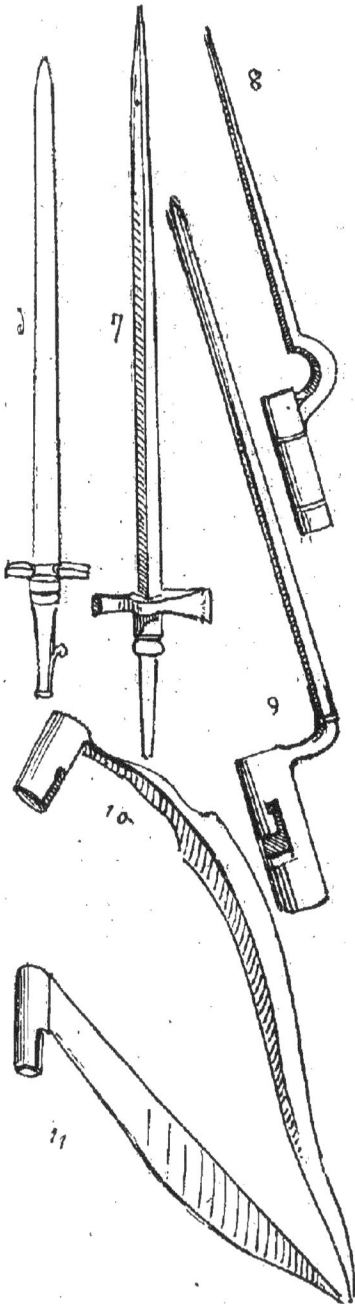

6. Baïonnette française, à manche avec ressort, du dix-septième siècle.

7. Baïonnette suisse, à manche, du dix-septième siècle.

8. Baïonnette française, à douille ordinaire, en usage en 1717.

9. Baïonnette française, à douille à entaille, en usage en 1768.

10. Baïonnette-fauchard bohème, à douille, du commencement du dix-huitième siècle. — Coll. du prince de Lobkowitz, à Raudnitz.

11.   Id.   id.

L'ESPONTON

L'*esponton* ou sponton (de l'italien *spuntone*, pointu, *Sponton* en allemand, *spontoon* et *half-pike* en anglais) était la demi-pique portée par les officiers d'infanterie à partir de la fin du dix-septième siècle jusqu'à la fin du dix-huitième. La forme disgracieuse et grotesque de cette arme indique parfaitement le temps de la perruque et des tricornes. Le dernier esponton en France est celui que portaient les gardes françaises en 1789, et dont on peut voir le modèle au musée d'artillerie de Paris.

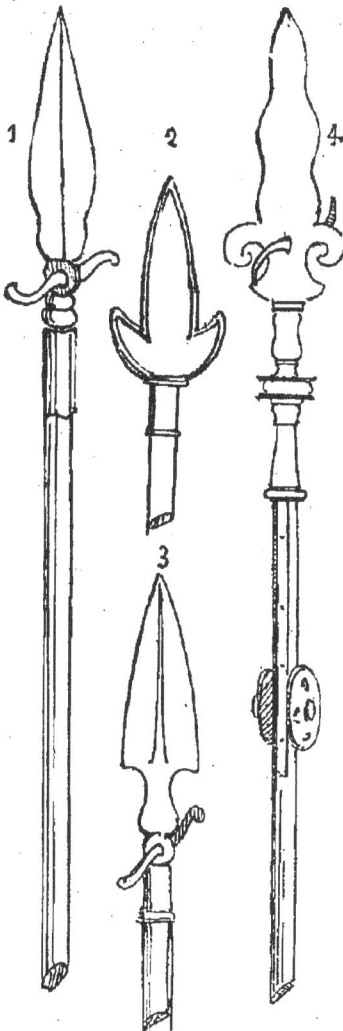

1. Esponton d'officier autrichien de la fin du dix-septième siècle.

2. Esponton d'officier d'une des petites principautés de l'Allemagne de la fin du dix-septième siècle.

3. Esponton prussien du règne de Frédéric II (1740-1786).

4. Esponton à rouet du dix-septième siècle. — Musée de Sigmaringen.

LA FOURCHE DE GUERRE

Cette arme (*military fork* en anglais, *Sturmgabel* en allemand) commence à apparaître vers la fin du quinzième siècle. On trouve à l'arsenal de Genève des *fourches d'échelles d'escalade* italiennes prises aux Savoisiens en 1602. La fourche de guerre est aussi mentionnée dans les récits du siège de Mons de 1691, où les grenadiers de l'ancien régiment Dauphin, commandés par Vauban, emportèrent d'assaut un ouvrage et saisirent les *fourches des Autrichiens*, etc. C'est pour récompenser cette action que Louis XIV accorda aux sergents de ces grenadiers le droit de porter une fourche à la place de la hallebarde.

40.

FOURCHES DE GUERRE.

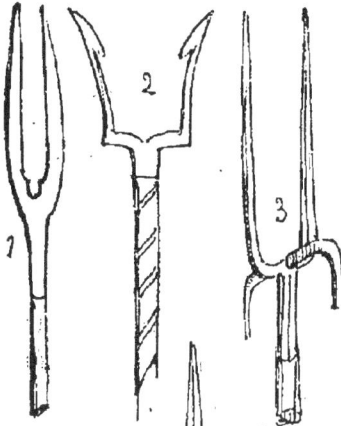

1. Fourche de guerre du quinzième siècle. — Incunable au cabinet d'estampes de Munich.

2. Fourche d'échelle allemande du commencement du seizième siècle. — Aquarelle de Glockenthon, exécutée en 1505, d'après les arsenaux de Maximilien I.

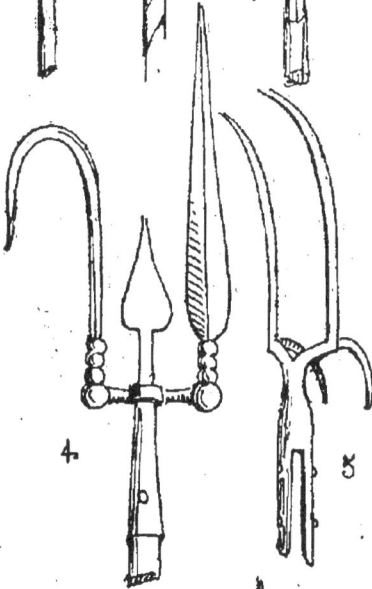

3. Fourche d'échelle italienne, prise aux troupes savoisiennes, sous les murs de Genève en 1602. — Arsenal de Genève.

4. Fourche d'échelle provenant du second siége de Vienne en 1683.

5. Fourche de guerre double du dix-septième siècle.

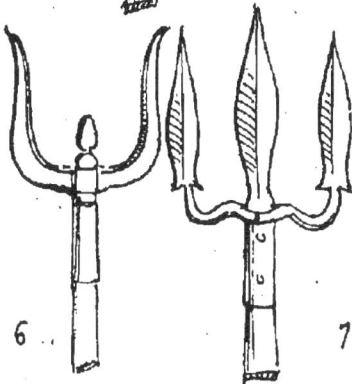

6. Fourche de guerre simple du dix-septième siècle. — Arsenal de Genève.

7. Fourche de guerre trident du dix-septième siècle. — Col. Az, à Lintz.

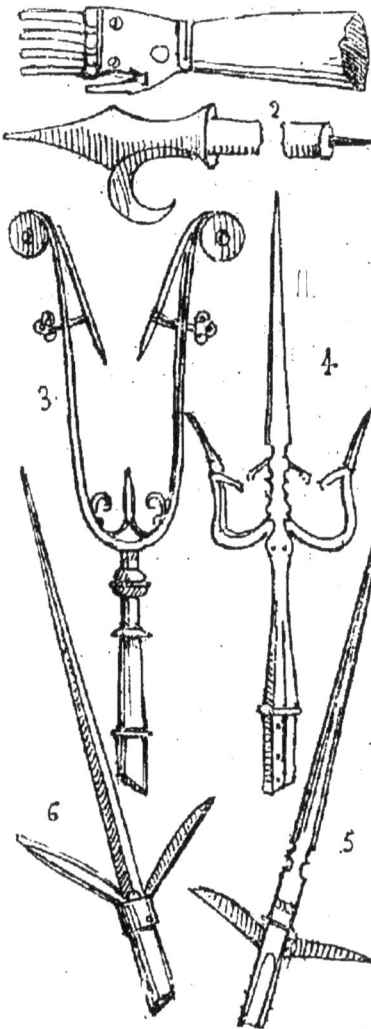

1. Main articulée en fer, du seizième siècle, attribuée à Gœtz de Berlichingen. — Musée de Sigmaringen. Une main pareille se trouve aussi au musée national de Munich.

2. Crochet de siége sur longue hampe pour arracher les phalariques ou flèches incendiaires; d'après le *Waltarius* de 1472 et un manuscrit du commencement du quinzième siècle de la bibliothèque Hauslaub, à Vienne. (Voir le chapitre où sont traitées les machines de guerre.)

3. Désarçonneur allemand (*Fangeisen* en allem., *catchpole* en angl.) du quinzième et du seizième siècle; il est monté sur une longue hampe et mesure 35 cent. Ce terrible engin, qui est à double ressort, servait à attraper le cou du chevalier et à le renverser de cheval. — Musées de Sigmaringen et de la Tour de Londres. Arsenal impérial de Vienne.

4. Désarçonneur allemand double du seizième siècle. — Musée de Dresde.

5. Arme de chasse à double couteau et ressort, damasquinée, du seizième siècle. Elle a 60 cent. de hauteur. — Musée de Dresde.

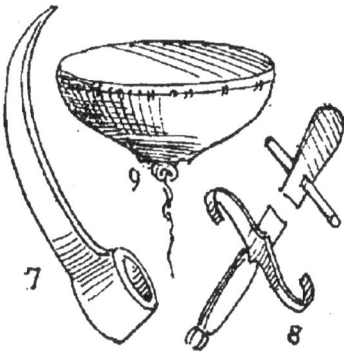

6. Arme de chasse à double couteau et ressort, du seizième siècle, signé *Bartolam Biella*. — Musée de Dresde.

7. Crochet d'armes du seizième siècle, trouvé sous les décombres du château fort d'Erperath, près Neus et de Dusseldorf, détruit par les Suédois. — Musée de Sigmaringen.

8. Épée de chasse, avec traverse au bout de la lame, du seizième siècle. — J. 171, musée d'artillerie de Paris.

9. Petits tambours turcs recouverts de peau humaine et pris par le général Rauchhaupt qui commandait, sous le règne du grand-électeur, la brigade brandebourgeoise à la bataille de Saint-Gothard, en Hongrie (1664). — Arsenal de Berlin et col. de l'auteur.

LES MACHINES DE GUERRE

Les machines de guerre (*Antwerc* en vieil allemand) dont on s'est servi durant le moyen âge et avant qu'elles n'eussent été remplacées par les armes à feu de gros calibre, ont été imitées d'après les machines des anciens. (Voy. p. 38, 39, 40, 67 et 68.) On retrouve la *baliste*, destinée à lancer de grosses flèches; la *catapulte* ou le *tormentum* des Latins, et l'*onagre*, en vieux français, qui lançaient des pierres et des blocs de rochers; le *bélier*, pour battre en brèche; le *trébuchet*, servant également à briser les murs; la *bascule*, l'ancien *tolleno* à deux paniers, qui versait les combattants dans les places assiégées. On se servait en Allemagne de *Manges*, de *Blindes*, de *Tribocs*, de *Patrarias*, de *Tanten*, de *Igel* (hérissons), de *Katzen* (chats) et d'une foule d'autres noms encore pour désigner tous ces genres de machines, modifiées et dénommées autrement dans les différents centres. Les miniatures du *Codex auræus* de Saint-Gall, du neuvième siècle, représentent des machines incendiaires en forme de poisson portées au bout des lances. Le musée d'artillerie de Paris possède deux arcs de baliste du château de Damas, et probablement de l'époque des croisades, et le cabinet des antiques de Zurich quantité de fers de flèches de baliste trouvés avec d'autres débris de ces machines sous les décombres du château de Russikon, détruit vers la fin du treizième siècle.

Les archives de Mons, de l'année 1406, parlent des machines de guerre dont on trouve toutes sortes de dessins dans les manuscrits de l'époque, particulièrement dans les dessins de Zeitblom du quinzième siècle, de la bibliothèque du prince de Waldburg-Wolfegg.

Ce qui préoccupait alors particulièrement les faiseurs de

projets pour machines de guerre, était de trouver des
moyens nouveaux pour incendier les places assiégées, et ils
allaient jusqu'à imaginer des appareils pour chiens et chats,
et même pour volailles, destinés à mettre le feu. Le pauvre
coq même, cette horloge chérie et vivante des lansquenets,
qui ne les quittait jamais dans leurs campagnes, était
transformé en phalariques par ces terribles chercheurs.

Deux phalariques ou plutôt torches incendiaires à main. — *Codex
aurœus* de Saint-Gall du neuvième siècle. La machine que le
cavalier porte au bout de sa lance, a la forme d'un poisson.
Le manuscrit le représente vomissant déjà du feu pendant que
la troupe n'est pas encore arrivée devant la place qu'elle veut
incendier; ce n'est donc pas de la poudre ni une autre matière
explosive. Ces torches paraissent simplement résineuses.

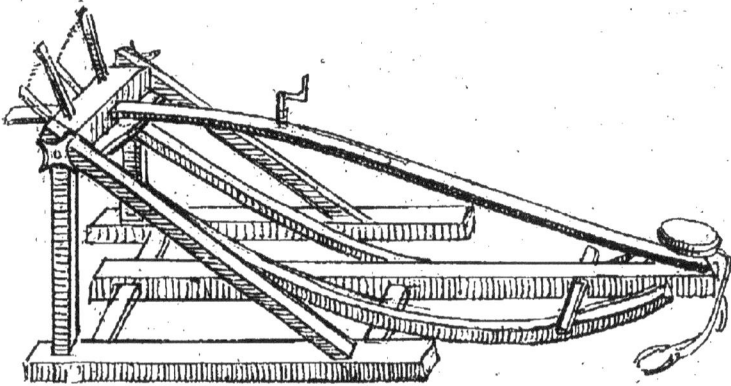

Machine de guerre à lancer de gros projectiles, tels que pierres, boules et blocs de rochers (la *catapulte* ou le *tormentum* des anciens, l'*onagre* français, le *Bleydenn* allemand),
reproduit d'après les dessins de Zeitblom, du quinzième siècle.
— Bibliothèque du prince de Waldburg-Wolfegg. Quelques
auteurs du quinzième et du seizième siècle ont donné un grand
nombre de ces machines, variant dans leur construction, et
dont la plupart sont plutôt des productions de fantaisie que des
copies d'après nature.

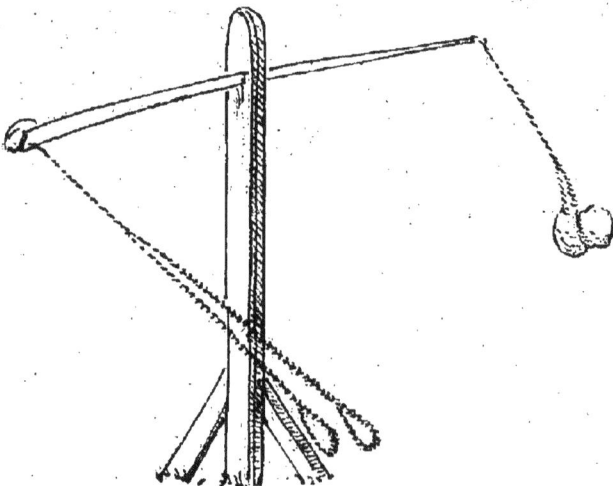

Machine de guerre à bascule, dite trébuchet simple, pour lancer
des pierres et battre en brèche, d'après les dessins de Zeitblom,
du quinzième siècle. — Bibliothèque du prince de Waldburg-
Wolfegg. Il existait aussi des trébuchets doubles qui lançaient

des projectiles sans interruption par le va-et-vient de l'arbrier appelé verge ou flèche, dont une extrémité était toujours chargée pendant que l'autre montait. Les trébuchets simples étaient mis en mouvement au moyen de cordes tirées par quatre hommes. Le trébuchet à fronde était à peu près construit de la même manière que le trébuchet simple ci-dessus; seulement, à un moment calculé, un crochet, attaché à l'extrémité de la pente longue de la verge, laissait échapper une des cordes de la fronde et la pierre s'élançait par la tangente du cercle décrit.

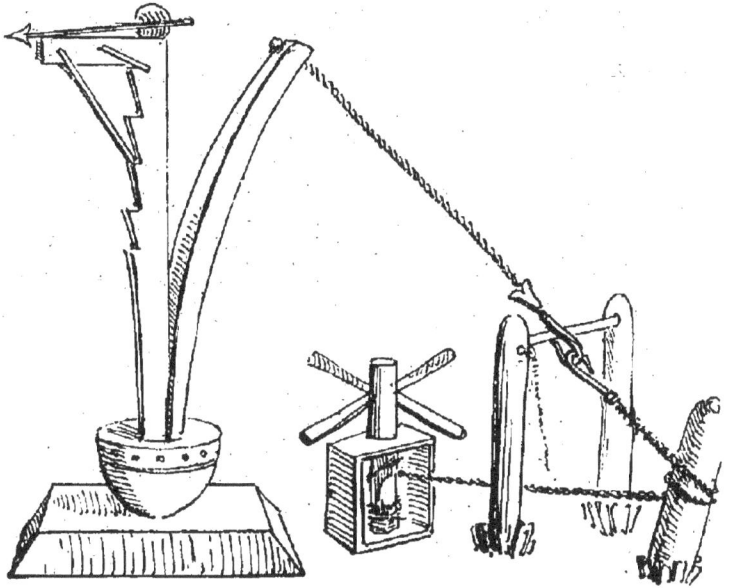

Machine de guerre à lancer des flèches (la *baliste* des anciens, le *Belagerungsbalester* allemand), reproduite d'après le *Walturius*, imprimé à Vérone, en 1472. — Bibliothèque Hauslaub à Vienne. Cette machine tire son impulsion de l'arc colossal qui, plié au moyen de cordes fixées sur des pilotis, rebondit vers l'arbrier, dès que les cordes sont lâchées, et lance la flèche.

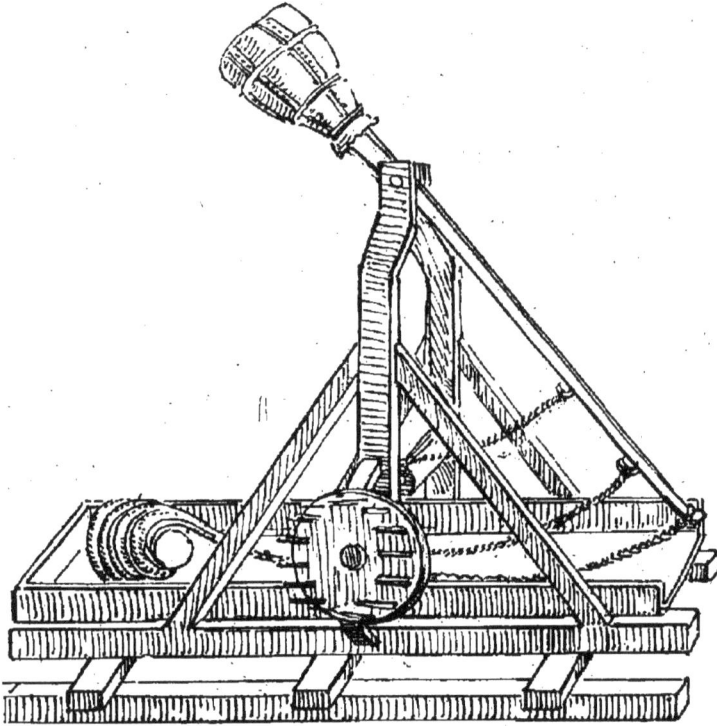

Machine de guerre à engrenage pour battre en brèche (de l'allemand *Brechen*, rompre, ou du celtique *brech, breca*, ouverture), dont l'emploi a dû être d'un effet bien plus grand que celui obtenu par le bélier dont les coups ne pouvaient produire que des trouées, tandis que la masse du battant devait renverser des pans de mur. Ce dessin est copié sur ceux de la *Pyrotechnie de l'Ancelot lorrain*; on trouve encore reproduite la même machine dans le *Walturius* de la bibliothèque Hauslaub, à Vienne.

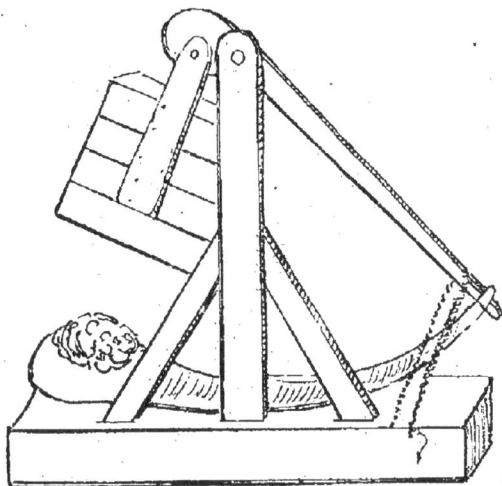

Machine de guerre à bascule et à fronde, d'après un manuscrit.
Recueil d'anciens poëtes, de la bibliothèque impériale de Paris.
C'est un des systèmes les plus simples; l'extrémité de la verge
affranchie de son attache remonte avec rapidité entraînée par
la lourde charge qui fait faire bascule et enlève la fronde avec
son projectile.

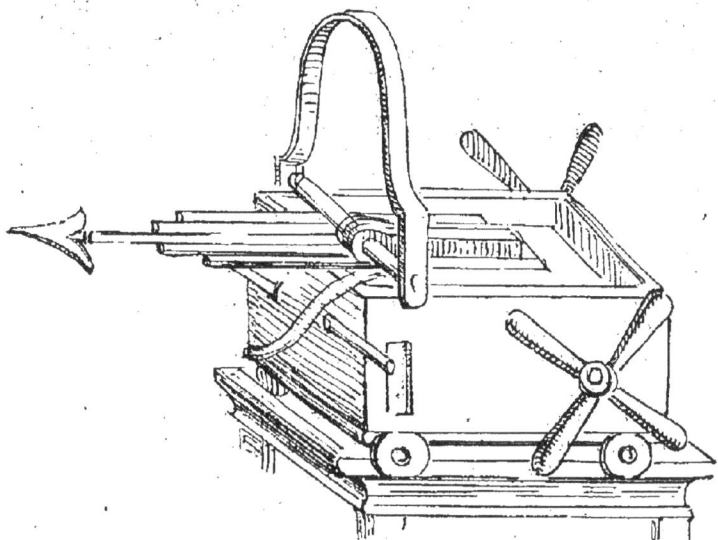

Baliste à quatre roues (*Balista quadrirota*), d'après la *Notitia
Utraque cum Orientis tum Occidentis,* etc. Bâle, 1552. L'auteur

de cette *Notitia*, qui reproduit des notes administratives des armées romaines de l'Orient et de l'Occident, du quinzième siècle, y a ajouté des dessins de balistes qu'il a copiés sur des machines ou des dessins de son époque.

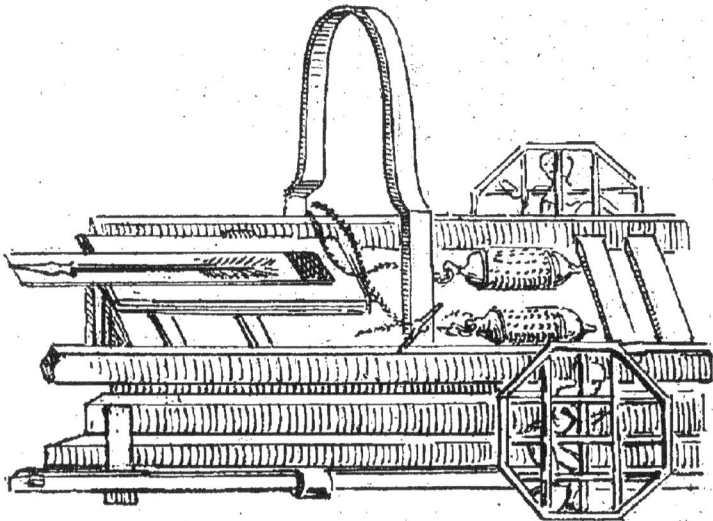

Machine de guerre, d'après la *Notitia Utraque cum Orientis tum Occidentis*, etc. Bâle, 1552, où elle est appelée *balista fulminatrix*. Cette machine est curieuse par son moteur qui consiste en hommes-écureuils. On trouve dans ce même ouvrage un bateau à roue appelé par l'auteur *Libourna*; les roues y sont mues par des bœufs.

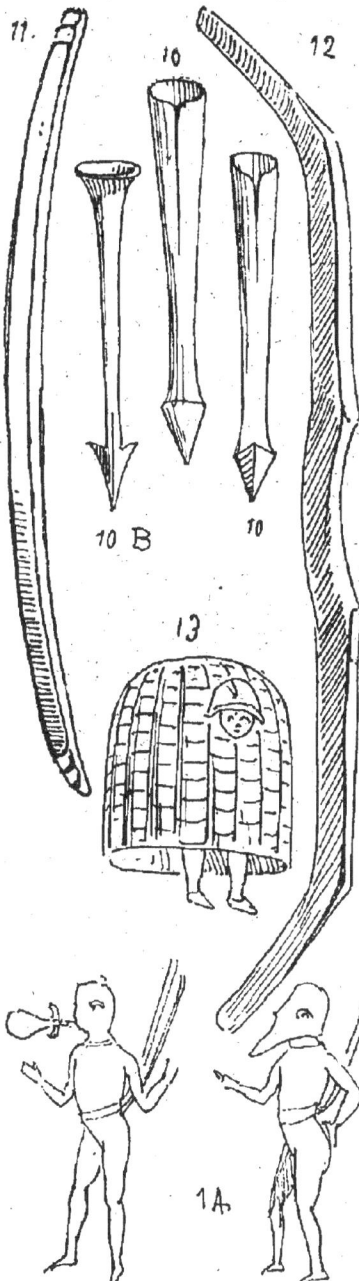

10. Fer de flèche de baliste, de 14 cent. de longueur, trouvé sous les décombres du château de Russikon, canton de Zurich, détruit vers la fin du treizième siècle.

10 bis. Fer de flèche de baliste, d'après le *Kriegsbuch* de 1573, par Fronsperger.

11. Arc de baliste provenant du château de Damas. Il est en bois de palmier et recouvert de tiges de corne. — Musée d'artillerie de Paris.

12.   Id.   id.

13. Corbeille de siége et de mineur, en osier, d'après un manuscrit du quinzième siècle, de la collection Hauslaub à Vienne.

14. Appareil de plongeur, d'après un manuscrit de la collection d'Ambras du quinzième siècle. Le dessin du manuscrit représente ces mannequins entièrement en noir, ce qui doit probablement imiter le cuir ou le caoutchouc.

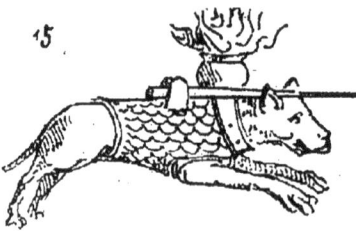

15. Chien cuirassé et armé avec phalarique pour incendier les camps. — Bibliothèque Hauslaub à Vienne.

16. Chat avec phalarique pour incendier les places assiégées, id.

17. Volatile, id.

18. Vase en terre cuite sans couverte, rempli de chaux vive, dont les assiégés se servaient contre les assiégeants. Il a été trouvé au Ketzerthurm. — Cabinet des antiques à Zurich. Voici comment Léonard Fronsperg explique l'emploi de ce projectile puéril dans son *Kriegsbuch* (livre de guerre), publié à Francfort, en 1573 : « Soll man fullen ein Theil mit Aschen und ungelæschten Kalch der Klein ist wie Mehl, derven unter die Feind geworfen mit Krafften dass die Hafen zerbrechen und unter sie streuen gleich wie man das Weihwasser giebt kommt dann in den Mundt, etc., etc. » (Il faut remplir ces pots avec des cendres et de la chaux vive pulvérisée, et les lancer avec force sur les assaillants où, brisés, ils répandent leur contenu et aspergent l'ennemi comme avec de l'eau bénite et lui entrent dans la bouche, etc., etc.)

18 bis. Baril incendiaire, dont se servaient les assiégeants, au moyen âge; reproduit d'après un manuscrit du commencement du quinzième siècle. — Bibliothèque Hauslaub à Vienne.

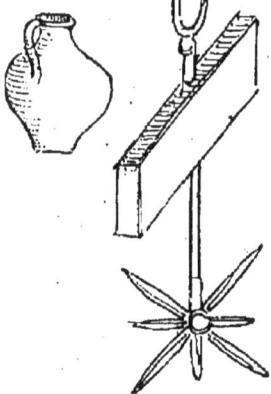

19. Chariot pour retranchement, encore en usage au dix-septième siècle dans la guerre contre les Turcs.

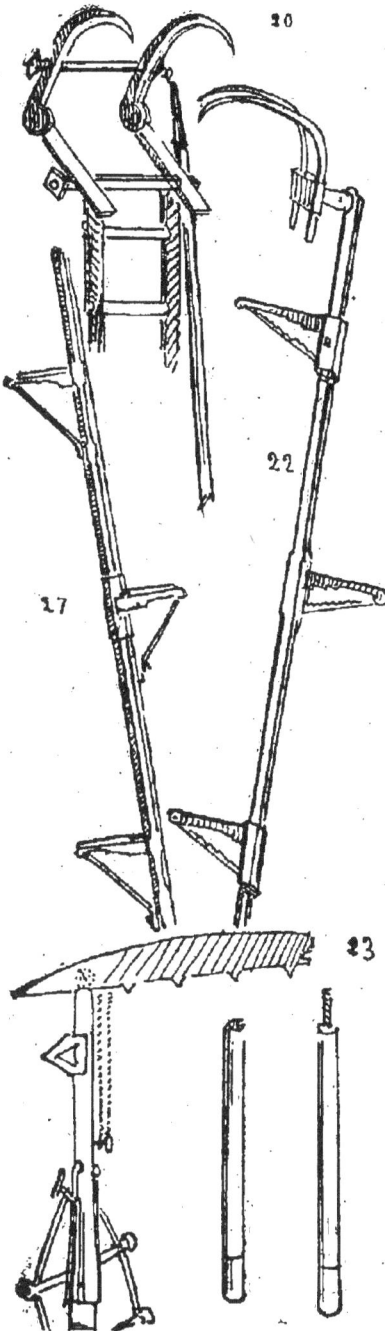

20. Échelle d'escalade allemande, en fer (*Sturmleiter* en allem., *storming* ou *scaling ladler* en angl.), d'après un manuscrit allemand du commencement du quinzième siècle. — Bibliothèque Hauslaub à Vienne.

21. Échelle d'escalade danoise, en fer, à articulations et pliante (*Stormstige* en danois.) — Musée de Copenhague.

22. Échelle d'escalade allemande, en fer, à articulations et pliante. Elle date du dix-septième siècle, de la guerre contre les Turcs. — Musée de Dresde.

23. Couteau d'escalade allemand, à bascule et à échelle (*Steugzeig* ou *Sturmleitersense* en allem., *storming-ladder with fauchard* en angl.), du commencement du dix-septième siècle. Cette ingénieuse arme, conservée au musée de Munich, est montée sur une longue hampe garnie à l'extrémité inférieure d'un pas de vis qui se visse sur d'autres hampes semblables, et l'allonge à volonté pour pouvoir atteindre les murs des places assiégées sur lesquels il s'accroche au moyen des dents du couteau à bascule. La longueur du fauchard à bascule est de 60 cent.

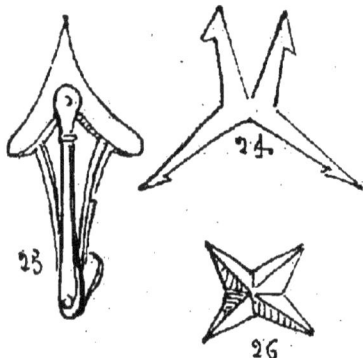

24. Chausse-trape (*Fussangel* en allem., *caltrop* en angl.), trouvée à Rosna. — Musée de Sigmaringen.

25. Chausse-trape, d'après les aquarelles que Glockenthon a faites, en 1505, d'après les armes accumulées dans les trois arsenaux de l'empereur Maximilien I. — Col. d'Ambras.

26. Chausse-trape, d'après un manuscrit du seizième siècle, de la bibliothèque Hauslaub à Vienne.

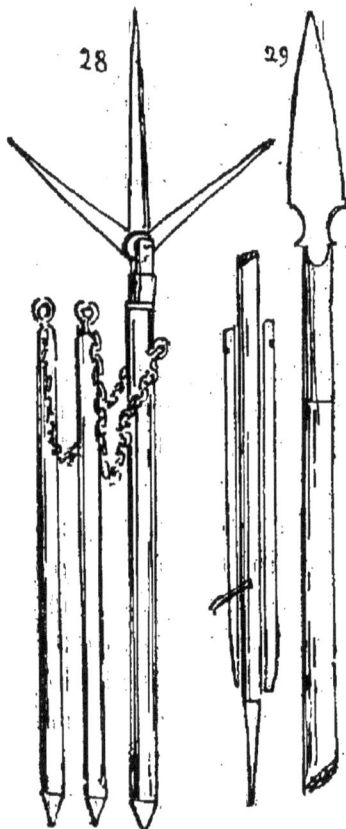

27. Couteau-chausse-trape (*Fussangel-Messer* en allem.), de 22 cent. de longueur, employé en Saxe durant la guerre de Sept ans (dix-huitième siècle). On le vissait sur des poutres avec lesquelles on garnissait le fond des fossés et qui étaient cachées sous l'eau. Le trou était destiné à l'introduction d'une traverse pour pouvoir plus facilement visser le couteau. — Col. Klemm à Dresde.

28. Cheval de frise (*Spanischer Reiter* en allem.) du dix-septième siècle, provenant de l'arsenal de Prague. Cet engin servait à se garantir contre les surprises de la cavalerie. — Arsenal de Berlin.

29. Cheval de frise du dix-huitième siècle, provenant des guerres de la République française. — Arsenal de Berlin.

LA FRONDE ET LA FUSTIBALE

La fronde (du latin *funda*, *Schlaeuder* en allemand, *schlinger* en anglais), qui s'écrivait autrefois fonde, et qui a donné son nom en France au parti qui prit les armes contre la cour sous la minorité de Louis XIV (1648-1652), est une arme de jet dont l'origine, comme celle de l'arc, remonte à la plus haute antiquité. Faite de corde ou de cuir, la fronde sert à lancer des pierres et même des balles. Après avoir placé le projectile dans le *creux* de la fronde, le frondeur fait tourner son arme en augmentant peu à peu la vitesse, et lorsque cette vitesse a atteint son dernier degré possible, il lâche une des deux *brides* en retenant l'autre.

La fronde, dont la portée dépassait ordinairement 500 pas, était l'arme de jet la plus connue dans l'antiquité et au moyen âge, où elle formait, avec l'arc, l'armement de la plus grande partie des gens de pied. Les habitants des îles Baléares étaient même réputés pour leur habileté dans le maniement de cette arme.

Les Grecs, les Romains et les Carthaginois, aussi bien que les Germains, avaient leurs corps de frondeurs.

L'usage de la fronde s'est même continué dans les armées européennes jusqu'au seizième siècle, où elle servait à lancer les grenades. Les peuplades sauvages l'ont toujours conservée, et il y en a qui réussissaient quelquefois à résister avec elle au feu de la carabine.

La *fustibale* ou le *fustibalus* (du latin *fustis*, bâton, et du grec *ballo*, lancer, *Stock-Schlœuder* en allemand, *staffsling* en anglais) était composée d'un bâton d'environ 1 mètre de longueur et d'une fronde en cuir attachée à son extrémité. On la prenait à deux mains, et on lançait ainsi des pierres avec une très-grande violence. Plus tard, elle servit à lancer des grenades.

On nommait aussi fustibales des machines plus grandes, sorte de catapultes, destinées à lancer de gros projectiles.

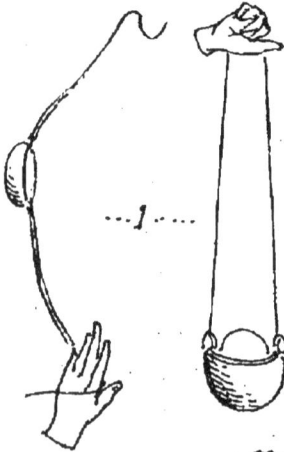

1. Frondes représentées, l'une la bride lâchée, l'autre les deux brides retenues, d'après un manuscrit du dixième siècle.

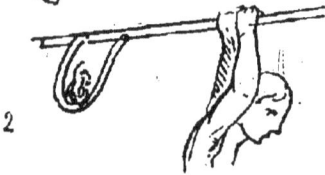

2. Homme maniant sa fustibale, d'après le manuscrit de Mathieu Paris, chroniqueur anglais, né à la fin du douzième siècle, mort en 1259, et de qui on a une *Historia major Angliæ* de 1066 à 1259.

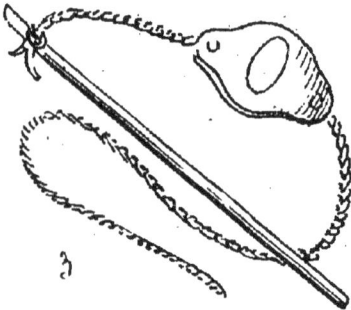

3. Fustibale-fronde, d'après un manuscrit du commencement du quinzième siècle. — Col. d'Ambras.

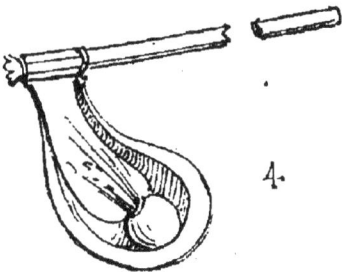

4. Fustibale à longue hampe, destinée à lancer des grenades. D'après un manuscrit du seizième siècle. — Bibliothèque du chevalier de Hauslaub à Vienne.

LA SARBACANE

De l'italien *cerbotana*, mot fait de *Carpi*, lieu où l'instrument était fabriqué, et du latin *canna*, roseau ; *Blasrohr* en allemand, *shovting-tube* ou le *lowpipe* en anglais. On s'en sert encore aujourd'hui pour chasser les petits oiseaux. Elle est faite d'un long tube par lequel on lance de petites balles en terre en soufflant par un des bouts. Comme arme de guerre, elle a servi à lancer des flèches empoisonnées, le feu grégeois qui s'en échappait en traits de fusées et de petites balles appelées dragées. Comme la sarbacane n'est qu'un simple tube qui varie seulement par la longueur et par l'épaisseur, il aurait été inutile d'en donner le dessin. Les sarbacanes modernes dont on se sert pour tuer les intéressants chanteurs emplumés sont souvent, comme les cannes à pêche, divisées en plusieurs pièces qui se vissent les unes sur les autres.

ARCS ET FLÈCHES

L'arc, du latin *arcus*, *Bogen* en allemand, *bow* en angl., désigne l'arme de trait formée par une *verge* élastique en bois ou en métal, renfoncée dans le milieu, et qui, pliée sous la *corde* fixée aux deux extrémités, lance le projectile, la *flèche* (*Pfeil* en allemand, *arrow* en anglais) dès que l'archer lâche la corde qu'il avait ramenée vers lui.

Les Scythes, les Crétois, les Parthes et les Thraces étaient aussi renommés dans l'antiquité pour le maniement de cette arme, que les Anglais durant le moyen âge chrétien. Plusieurs miniatures et les tapisseries de Bayeux démontrent que l'arc était, chez les Bretons et les Normands, comme chez les Celtes et les Gaulois, une arme de guerre, tandis que les Germains ne s'en servaient qu'à la chasse. Les Huns employaient cette arme, qui chez eux était entièrement en corne, aussi bien à la guerre qu'à la chasse.

Au douzième siècle, l'archer portait ordinairement deux étuis : l'un, le carquois ou *couir*, d'où dérive le *quiver* anglais, contenait les flèches (du vieil allemand *Flitz*) appelées alors, si l'on s'en rapporte aux chroniques de Saint-Denis, *pilles* et *sayettes*; l'autre, l'*archet*, destiné à l'arc.

Les fers des flèches ressemblaient ordinairement aux pointes des *carrels* ou *carreaux* de l'arbalète, qui a plus tard remplacé l'arc; ils étaient carrés, à deux, à trois et même à quatre pointes, et bien rarement barbelés comme celles de l'antiquité. La longueur de l'arc et des flèches variait selon les pays et la grandeur de l'homme. En Angleterre, où l'archer tirait au moins douze flèches dans une minute et manquait rarement son but à 220 mètres, le bois de l'arc était d'une longueur pareille à la distance qui se trouve entre les deux extrémités des doigts du milieu de l'archer quand il étend ses bras, mesure qui, chez un homme bien proportionné, équivaut à sa grandeur. Le bois une fois courbé, l'arc anglais mesurait à peu près la demi-longueur de l'homme. La flèche anglaise mesurait 90 cent. Le bois le plus employé en France pour la confection de l'arc était l'if, qui servait aussi à la fabrication des arbalètes.

Une ordonnance de Charles VII (1422-1463) enjoignit même de planter des ifs dans tous les cimetières de la Normandie, afin de ne pas manquer de bois pour les arbriers de la nouvelle arme, qui était alors en très-grande faveur en France, quoiqu'on n'y cessât cependant pas de garder aussi des corps d'archers à pied et à cheval, dont les compagnies d'ordonnance, sous Louis XII (1514), étaient les dernières.

La raison que l'arc s'est conservé jusqu'à l'apparition de l'arme à feu portative ou à main, et même au delà, à côté de l'arbalète, arme pourtant bien plus perfectionnée, réside dans sa simplicité et son usage facile et sûr. L'arbalète, plus difficile à bander, faisait perdre plus de temps. L'arbalétrier ne pouvait fournir que trois traits, pendant qu'un archer habile lançait dix à douze flèches. En outre, la pluie détendait la corde de l'arbalète et lui ôtait sa force, tandis que la corde de l'arc pouvait être facilement mise à l'abri de l'humidité. La perte de la bataille de Crécy (1346) fut en partie le résultat de cet inconvénient, puisque, aux traits des archers anglais, les arbalétriers français pouvaient à peine riposter, et lorsque, en 1356, après la défaite de Poitiers, l'infériorité de l'arbalète se fut de nouveau montrée sous ce rapport, on créa des archers français qui acquirent bientôt une telle habileté, que la jalousie de la noblesse en prit ombrage, et les fit dissoudre. L'Angleterre conserva plus longtemps l'usage de l'arc que les peuples du continent; habiles comme ils l'étaient, les archers anglais, devaient mépriser longtemps encore la lourde et grossière arme à feu portative des premières inventions. Sous le règne d'Élisabeth (1558-1603), l'organisation des corps d'archers avait même atteint son plus grand développement, et ils étaient tous pourvus de brigandines et de casques.

En 1627, au siége de La Rochelle, on trouve même encore des archers anglais mercenaires à la solde de Richelieu, ils y figuraient à l'attaque de l'île de Ré. (Voy., pour les arcs plus anciens, les chapitres où il est traité de toutes les armes de l'âge de la pierre, de l'âge du bronze et de l'âge du fer).

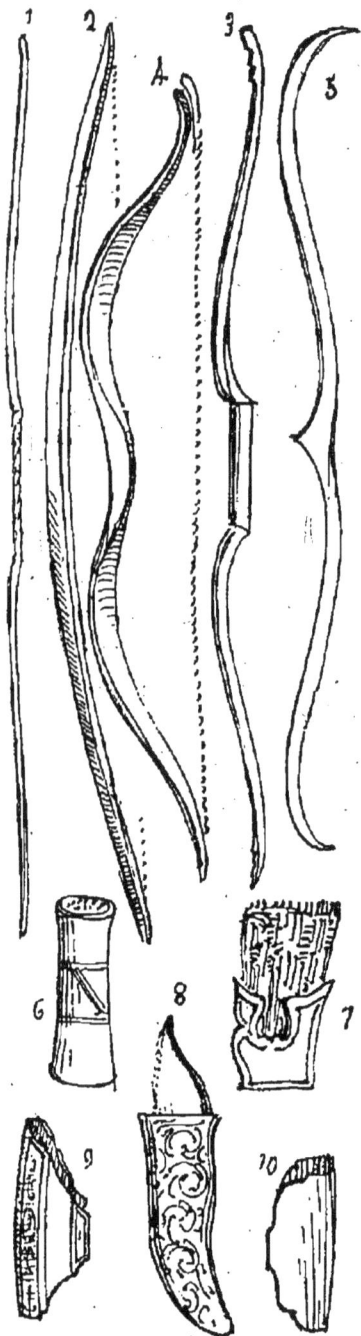

1. Arc allemand de la première partie du moyen âge. Il mesurait 1ᵐ,50 et était le plus souvent en orme ou en chêne.

2. Arc allemand de la fin du moyen âge, d'après les dessins de Glockenthon, de la collection d'Ambras.

3. Arc italien du moyen âge; il était ordinairement en acier et mesurait 1ᵐ,50.

4. Arc italien du quinzième siècle, d'après le *Walturius* illustré, imprimé, à Vérone, en 1472. — Bibliothèque Hauslaub à Vienne.

5. Arc oriental en acier, probablement de l'époque du moyen âge chrétien. — L. 89, musée d'artillerie de Paris.

6. Carquois allemand, d'après l'*Énéide* allemande de Henri de Valdeck, manuscrit du treizième siècle. — Bibliothèque de Berlin.

7. Carquois persan, d'après la copie du *Schah-Nameh*, manuscrit de la fin du seizième siècle. — Bibliothèque de Munich.

8. Archet persan, id.

9. Brassard d'archer en ivoire (*Spannarmband* en allem.; *brace* en angl.), qui servait à garantir le bras contre les chocs de la corde de l'arc.

10. Brassard, id. — L. 97, musée d'artillerie de Paris.

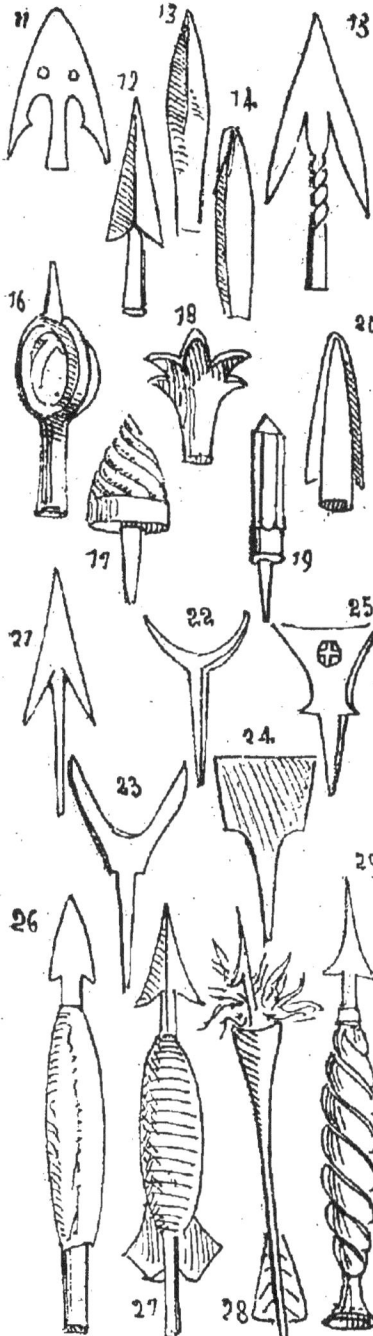

11. Pointe à barbe de flèche gothique, de 8 cent., du quatorzième siècle. — Col. Klemm à Dresde.

12. Pointe à barbe de flèche gothique, du quatorzième siècle. — Col. Sœter à Augsbourg.

13. Pointe de flèche hussite, du quinzième siècle.—Col. de l'auteur.

14.　　　Id.　　　　id.

15. Pointe de flèche italienne, du quinzième siècle. — Musée de Sigmaringen.

16. Pointe carcasse de flèche, id.

17. Pointe tire-bouchon pour flèche, fer et cuivre, id.

18. Pointe de flèche, forme pétale, du quinzième siècle, id.

19. Pointe de flèche octogone, en fer et cuivre, id.

20. Id., à barbette, id.

21.　　　Id.　　　　id.

22. Id., nommée *petite lune*, id.

23. Id., grande, id. Elle servait à couper les jarrets des hommes et des chevaux.

24. Pointe de flèche forme hache, du quinzième siècle. — Musée de Sigmaringen.

25.　　　Id.　　　　id.
Cette pointe porte l'aigle de l'empire germanique, en gravure et dorure.

26. Flèche incendiaire, allemande, trouvée à Vrach. — Musée de Sigmaringen.

27. Id. id., du quinzième siècle. Manuscrit de la bibliothèque Hauslaub.

28.　　　Id.　　　　id.
de Glockenthon. — Col. d'Ambras.

29.　　　Id.　　　id., du seizième siècle. — *Kriegsbuch*, par Fronsperger, de 1573.

L'ARBALÈTE

Du latin *arcus*, arc, et *balista*, baliste, arbaliste, arbalète; *Armbrust* en allemand, *cross-bow*, arc à crosse, et
arbaliste en anglais[1], que M. Rodios croit, à tort selon moi,
avoir existé déjà chez les Grecs, et qu'il appelle *gastrafète*, parce que l'arbalétrier ancien devait l'appuyer contre
le creux de l'estomac (V. les armes grecques, et aussi
p. 39 et 70 à 72), n'était connue de la princesse Anne Comnène (1083-1148) que pour l'avoir vue chez les hommes
d'armes de la première croisade venus du Nord. Il ne peut
y avoir de doute, puisqu'elle dit dans ses mémoires :
« Cette *tzagra, arc que nous ne connaissons pas*, etc. »

L'arbalète, composée de l'*arc*, de l'*arbrier* (*Rüstung* en
allemand) *à noix, à fronton de mire* et *à clef* ou *gâchette*,
et de la *corde*, est, selon toute probabilité, une invention
des soi-disant barbares.

Un manuscrit anglo-saxon du onzième siècle, de la bibliothèque britannique, et la peinture murale du dôme de
Brunswick, exécutée sous Henri le Lion, mort en 1195,
montrent déjà des arbalétriers, tandis que la tapisserie de
Bayeux, de la fin du onzième et du commencement du
douzième siècle, ne reproduit que des archers. Anne Comnène n'est pas le seul auteur de son époque qui ait parlé de
l'arbalète; Guillaume de Tyr l'a également mentionnée.

Cette arme, qui apparaît seulement en Chine sous le

1. Dès que l'arbalète était au-dessus de la grandeur ordinaire, les Allemands
l'appelaient *bellestre*, et les Anglais *latch* quand elle était à moufle. Le bellestre
allemand était le plus souvent une arbalète à galet.

règne de l'empereur Kien-Long (1736), était déjà très-répandue en France sous Louis le Gros (1108-1137). Un canon du second concile de Latran, tenu en 1139, en défend l'usage — entre chrétiens bien entendu, — mais permet d'en occire les infidèles et les mécréants.

En Angleterre, Richard Cœur de Lion (1157-1173) donna des arbalètes à un grand nombre de ses hommes de pied, ne tenant aucun compte du bref d'Innocent III, dans lequel fut renouvelée la défense du canon du second concile de Latran. Peu de temps après, Philippe-Auguste (1180-1223) aussi créa en France les premières compagnies régulières d'arbalétriers à pied et à cheval, qui prirent une très-grande importance. (Voy. aussi p. 491 et 492.)

Il est inutile de répéter ici ce qui a déjà été traité dans le chapitre historique, il suffit de bien désigner les différentes espèces d'arbalètes.

A. L'*arbalète à pied-de-biche,* dont le mécanisme destiné à bander la corde, appelé *pied-de-biche,* est détaché de l'arbrier ou y est adhérent, qui se reconnaît par l'emplacement des *deux goujons* (servant de point d'appui au pied-de-biche) *posés presque à côté de la noix.*

Cette arme a été fabriquée *avec* ou *sans étrier.*

B. L'*arbalète à cric à manivelle,* dont le cric, appelé *cranequin,* forme pièce à part. On distingue cette arbalète de l'arbalète à pied-de-biche, *en ce que les deux goujons* se trouvent ordinairement *placés à une distance de 15 cent. au-dessous de la noix,* parce que le cranequin a une prise bien plus longue que celle du pied-de-biche.

C. L'*arbalète à moufle*, aussi nommée arbalète *à tours, de passe* et de *passot.*

On l'appelle à tours, parce que la partie de la moufle destinée à être adaptée à l'arbrier, dès qu'on veut bander la corde, affecte souvent la forme d'une tour crénelée. L'arbrier de l'arbalète à moufle, où la mécanique détachée qui sert à bander est pourvue de deux manivelles et de deux roues à poulie dans laquelle passe une corde, n'a point de goujons; il est *toujours à étrier*. C'est de cette arbalète que les arbalétriers génois étaient armés à la bataille d'Azincourt (1420); elle était universellement répandue en Belgique, où elle servait particulièrement à la défense des remparts et au tir à la cible. En Allemagne, elle atteignait quelquefois une grandeur de 20 à 30 pieds.

D. *Arbalète à rouet d'engrenage*, espèce excessivement rare, que l'auteur n'a rencontrée dans aucune collection, et qu'il ne connaît que par des manuscrits du quinzième siècle. Le rouet d'engrenage, qui remplace le cranequin et le pied-e-biche, est fixé à l'arbrier dans une entaille, et se tourne au moyen d'une clef également fixe. Un *encliquetage*, tel qu'il en existe dans les crics, empêche le rouet de reculer dès qu'on lâche la clef. Les dessins représentent ces arbalètes avec l'*étrier*.

E. L'*arbalète à galet*, du seizième siècle, qui tire son nom des cailloux (galets) qu'il lançait aussi bien que des balles en plomb à la place des *carreaux* (flèches). L'arbrier, ordinairement courbé entre la noix et l'arc, est très-souvent en fer. Cette arbalète, d'une force médiocre, se bandait au moyen d'un levier adhérent à l'arbrier, ou simplement avec la main.

F. L'*arbalète à baguette*, qui serait mieux nommée *arbalète à demi-canon*, puisque son arbrier est surmonté d'un canon en bois ou en métal qui couvre la rainure où glisse le carreau, et dans laquelle passe la corde. Ce demi-canon donne quelquefois à l'arbrier l'aspect d'un fusil à canon. L'arbalète à baguette, qui était en usage au dix-septième siècle, a peu de force, se bande au moyen d'une *baguette* à poignée avec laquelle on refoule la corde, ou simplement avec la main, et a servi de modèle pour la fabrication des arbalètes modernes.

G. L'*arbalète chinoise* à tiroir à coulisse, qui fournit successivement vingt flèches, et que l'on pourrait nommer l'*arbalète à répétition* ou l'*arbalète revolver*.

Il y a des arbalètes gothiques où les extrémités de l'arc
en bois et en corne, dès que l'arme n'est pas bandée, se
redressent au lieu d'être inclinées vers la crosse, comme le
sont les arcs en acier. Ces arbalètes démontrent que la construction de l'arc était calculée pour produire cette courbe
en sens contraire, pour donner plus de force quand il était
bandé. Les arcs de ces arbalètes, qui étaient ordinairement
confectionnés en couches de bois et de corne combinées de
différentes manières, passèrent longtemps pour être des
phallus d'éléphants.

Les projectiles dont on se servait pour le tir de l'arbalète, à l'exception de l'arbalète à galets, s'appelaient *carrels* ou *carreaux* (*Bolzen* en allemand, *quarrel* ou *bolts* en
anglais).

Le *vireton* était un carreau empenné de plumes ou de
lames de bois ou de cuir inclinées vers l'arc pour imprimer
au trait un mouvement de rotation. Le *carreau assommeur*
ou le *matras* (*Fogelbolzen* en allemand), était terminé par
un disque rond ; il tuait en *assommant* sans répandre le
sang. Il servait à la chasse du gibier et particulièrement de
l'oiseau, dont on désirait conserver la dépouille intacte.

Arbalètes allemandes, d'après un manuscrit du commencemen t
du quinzième siècle. On y remarque l'arbalète à cranequin e t
des flèches incendiaires. L'un des hommes d'armes porte déjà
un canon à main. — Bibliothèque Hauslaub à Vienne.

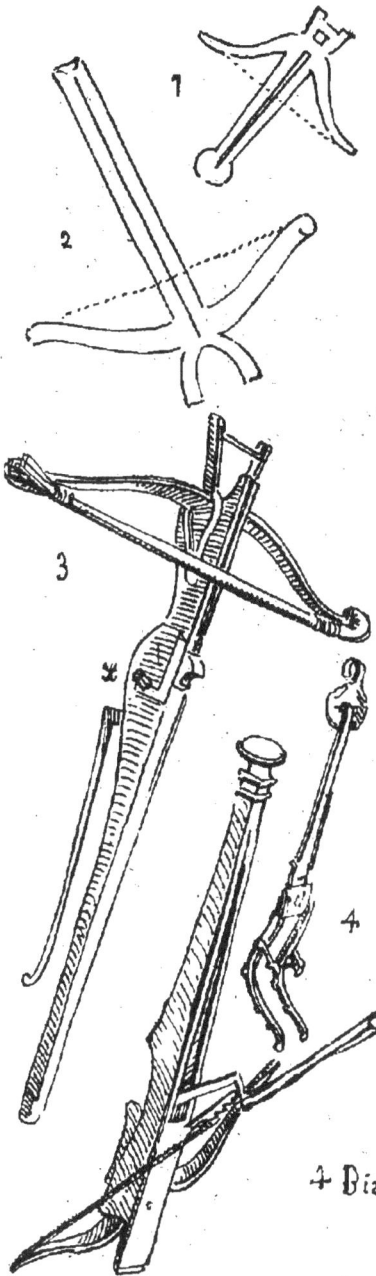

A. *Arbalètes à pied-de-biche* (*Armbrust mit Geisfuss* ou *Hebelarmbrust* en allem., *crossbow with goats-foot lever* en angl.)

1. Arbalète à pied-de-biche, d'après une miniature anglo-saxonne du onzième siècle. — Bibliothèque du musée britannique.

2. Arbalète à pied-de-biche, d'après les peintures murales du dôme de Brunswick, exécutées sous Henri le Lion, mort en 1195.

3. Arbalète à pied-de-biche. On observera que les goujons (*x*) se trouvent presque aux côtés de la noix. Le catalogue du musée de Copenhague où cette arbalète est conservée, la reproduit avec un cranequin qui n'en peut faire partie, puisque l'arbalète à cranequin a les goujons (*x*) placés au moins 15 c. au-dessous de la noix, à cause de la prise du cranequin qui est bien plus longue que celle du pied-de-biche.

4. Pied-de-biche (*Geisfuss* en allem., *goatsfoot-lever* en angl.), destiné à bander l'arbalète précédente.

4 *bis*. Arbalète avec son pied-de-biche, adhérente à l'arbrier [1].

1. Une arme semblable en bois de fer du seizième siècle, qui a appartenu à Ferdinand I, comme le prouve l'inscription gravée sur l'arc : *Dom Fernando rei de Romano*, àcôté de quatre toisons d'or estampillées, montre le nom de l'armurier espagnol *Juan Deneinas*. Cette précieuse arbalète, qui a appartenu à M. Spengel de Munich, se trouve actuellement dans la collection de M. le comte de Nieuwerkerke.

B. Arbalètes à cric à manivelle, appelées aussi à cranequin (Windenarmbrust en allem., cross-bow with windlass en angl.)

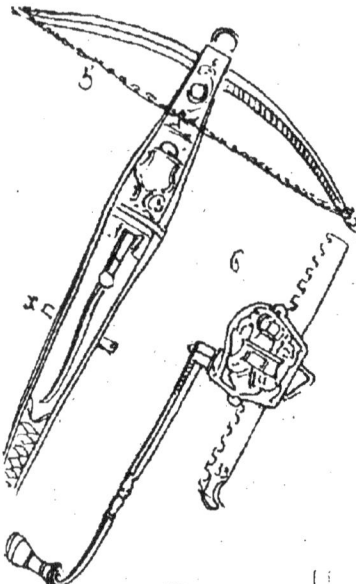

5. Arbalète allemande, à cranequin, du quinzième siècle. Les goujons (*x*) sont placés à une distance, de 15 cent. au-dessous de la noix. — Gewehrkammer impériale de Vienne.

6. Cranequin pour l'arbalète précédente. — Gewehrkammer impériale de Vienne.

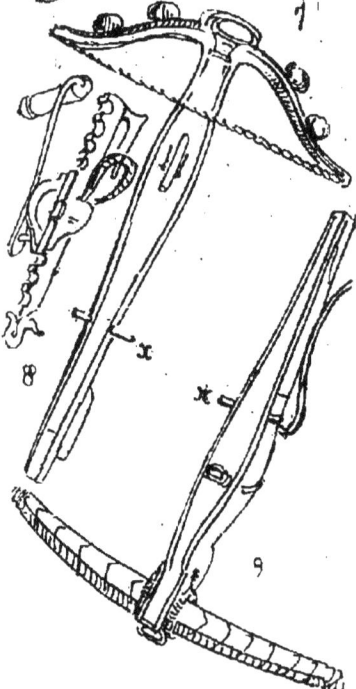

7. Arbalète à cranequin, suisse, du quinzième siècle. — Même observation que pour le n° 5.

8. Cranequin pour l'arbalète précédente.

9. Arbalète tyrolienne, à cranequin, de la fin du quinzième siècle. — Même observation que pour les n° 5 et 7.

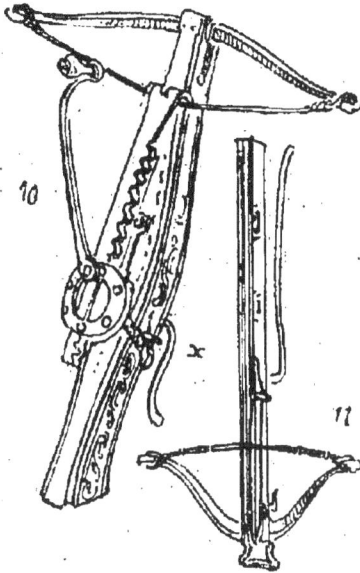

10. Arbalète avec son cranequin, posé sur l'arbrier. On remarque que les goujons (*x*) se
trouvent de 10 à 15 cent. de distance de la noix, puisque la prise
du cranequin demande un plus
grand espace que celle du pied
de biche.

C, Arbalètes à moufle, aussi nommées arbalètes à tours, de passe
ét de passot (*Flaschenzug-Arm-
brust* en allem., *cross-bow with
moulinet, catch* en angl.),
quand elle est très-grande.

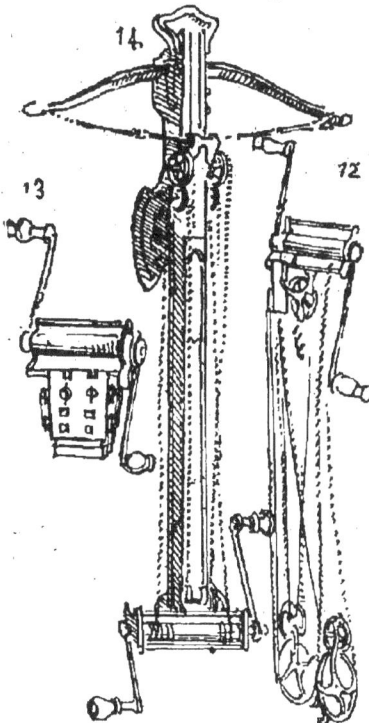

11. Arbalète à moufle. Elle n'a
point de goujons, puisque la
moufle s'adapte au pied de l'arbrier.

12. Moufle (*Flaschenzug* en allem., *windlass* en angl.), pour
l'arbalète précédente.

13. Partie de moufle, la pièce
qui sert à l'emboîture, en forme
de tour crènelée.—Musée d'artillerie de Paris.

14. Arbalète avec sa moufle appliquée.

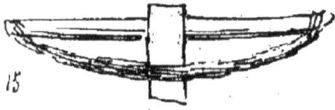

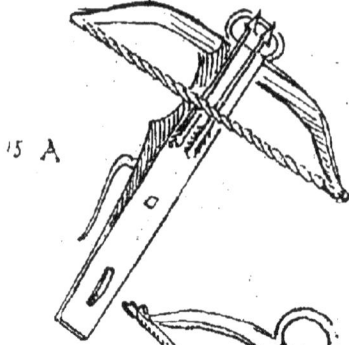

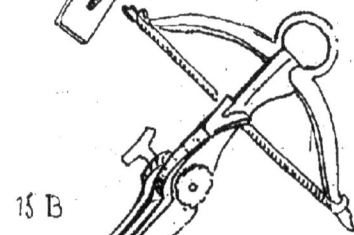

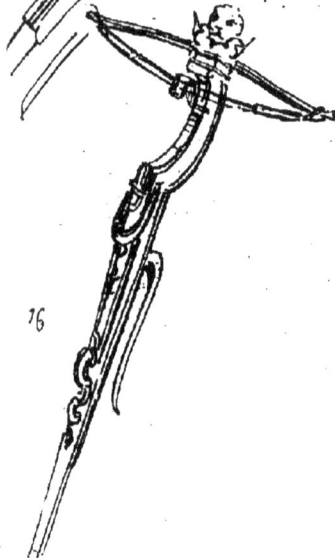

15. Arc d'une arbalète allemande, à moufle, de 1ᵐ,47, du commencement du quinzième siècle. Cette arme monstre dont l'arbrier mesure 1ᵐ,64 se trouve à l'arsenal de la ville de Munich. (Voir à l'introduction de ce chapitre.)

15 A. Arbalète pour tirer deux flèches à la fois, d'après le *Walturius* de 1472. — Bibliothèque Hauslaub à Vienne.

D. Arbalètes à rouet d'engrenage, à encliquetage (Zahnrad-Armbrust *en allem.,* wheel cross bow *en angl.*)

15 *b.* Arbalète à rouet d'engrenage du commencement du quinzième siècle, d'après un manuscrit. — Col. d'Ambras.

E. Arbalètes à galet, du seizième siècle (Stein ou Kugelarmbrust *aussi* Bellestre *en allem.,* prodd *en angl.*)

16. Arbalète à galet.

17. Chaîne en acier d'une arbalète à galet, espèce fort rare. — Col. Az, à Lintz.

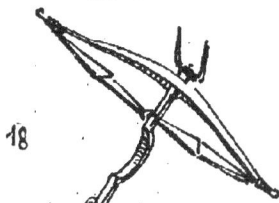

18. Arbalète à galet, en fer, de la fin du dix-septième siècle.

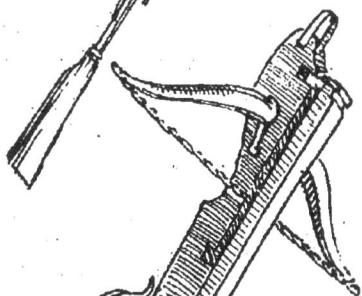

F. Arbalètes à baguétte, mieux nommées à demi-canon (Laut ou Rinnen - Armbrust en allem., growe cross-bow en angl.)

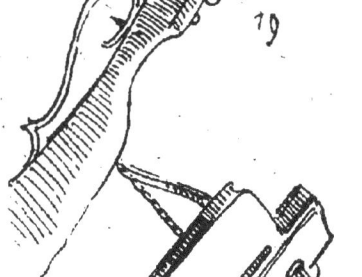

19. Arbalète à coulisse, du dix-septième siècle. — L. 72, musée d'artillerie de Paris.

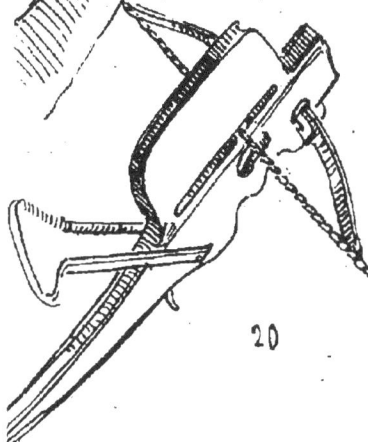

G. Arbalètes chinoises à répétition (Chinesische Repitilions- Armbrust en allem., chyna- repeating cross-bow en angl.)

20. Arbalète chinoise, à répétition. Elle est en ivoire et fournit successivement vingt flèches. — Musée d'artillerie de Paris.

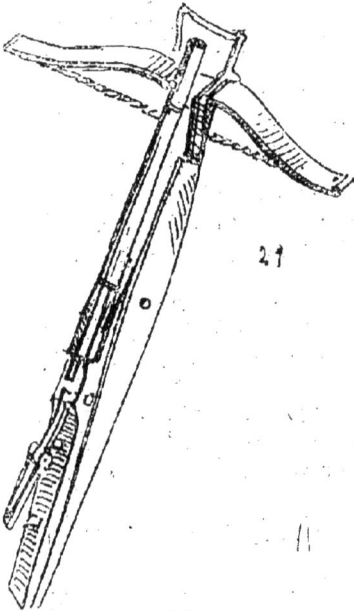

21. Arbalète à pistolet (*Pistolen-Armbrust* en allem., *gun-cross-bow* en angl.), du seizième siècle, ayant appartenu à Ferdinand I (1503-1564), comme le démontre le nom de *Ferdinandus*, ainsi que ses armoiries gravées sur le canon et sur l'arc qui est en acier. Cette arbalète, à double usage, mesure 76 c. sur 54. — Musée national de Munich.

22. Carreau d'arbalète de guerre (*Bolzen* en allem., *quarrel* ou *bolt* en angl.), provenant de la bataille de Sempach (1386). — Arsenal de Genève.

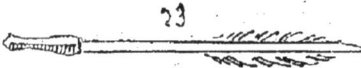

23. Carreau d'arbalète de guerre avec fer à une seule pointe et à ailettes en plumes.

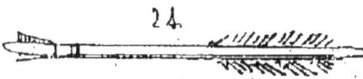

24. Carreau d'arbalète de guerre avec fer à trois pointes et à ailettes en plumes.

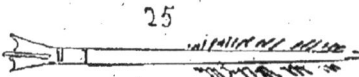

25. Carreau d'arbalète de guerre avec fer à quatre pointes et à ailettes en plumes.

43

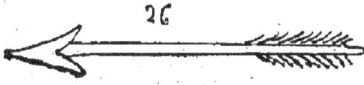

26. Carreau d'arbalète de chasse et de guerre à pointe barbelée (*Gewiderhackt*, en allem., *barbed* en angl.), et à ailettes en plumes.

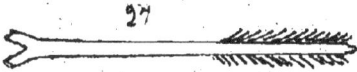

27. Carreau d'arbalète pour la chasse du chamois, à ailettes en plumes. Il était en usage dans le Tyrol.

28. Carreau d'arbalète pour la chasse du chamois, à ailettes en plumes. Tyrol.

29. Carreau d'arbalète dit vireton de guerre. La pointe en acier est taillée à trois pans et les ailettes sont en cuir, légèrement tordues en hélice pour imprimer au trait un mouvement de rotation.

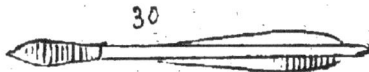

30.   Id.,   à une seule pointe.

31. Carreau d'arbalète assommeur nommé matras de chasse (*Fogelbolzen* en allem., *bird-bolt* en angl.); la tête ronde est plate et pourvue, au milieu, d'un filet d'acier carré légèrement saillant.

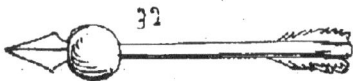

32. Carreau d'arbalète phalarique ou incendiaire. — Arsenal de Zurich.

33. Carreau, de 80 cent., d'une arbalète gothique de guerre à pointe barbelée (*Gewiderhackt* en allem., *barbed* en angl.), et à ailettes en plumes, qui mesure 1^m,64 sur 1^m,47, à l'arsenal de la ville de Munich.

34. Carquois pour carreaux d'arbalète (*Boltzen-Kœcher* en allem.,
boltsguiver en angl.), du douzième siècle, d'après les peintures murales du dôme de
Brunswick, exécutées sous
Henri le Lion, mort en 1195.

35. Carqnois pour carreaux d'arbalète en bois et en cuir. —
Col. du prince Charles, à Berlin.

36. Carquois pour carreaux d'ar-
balète en bois et en cuir. —
Musée historique au palais de
Montbijou, à Berlin.

37. Carquois pour petits carreaux
à chasser les oiseaux, en acier,
de la fin du seizième ou du
commencement du dix-septième
siècle. — Col. Llewelyn-Meyrick.

VII

L'ARME A FEU

L'histoire de l'arme à feu, à partir de son apparition en
Europe au commencement du quatorzième siècle, se trouve
développée p. 72 à 92, et chaque dessin des différentes
armes a été accompagné de détails qui n'ont pu figurer dans
le chapitre historique. Rappelons seulement que la poudre
à canon remonte à une antiquité indéterminée, et que la
première arme à feu était de gros calibre, — le *mortier*, —
le mortier domestique. En écrasant des mixtions de salpêtre, de soufre et de charbon, l'homme s'est vu rejeter, lui
et son pilon, par l'explosion amenée par le pilage. Profi-
tant de la leçon, il a pratiqué un petit trou à l'extrémité
inférieure de ce mortier de cuisine pour pouvoir y mettre
le feu sans danger pour lui-même, et la première arme à feu
fut inventée. Le mortier doit donc être regardé comme la
forme la plus ancienne de l'arme à feu de gros calibre; il fut
suivi successivement du *canon* (de *quennon*, nom qui dérive
de l'allemand *Kanne* ou *Canne*, pot, etc.) *se chargeant par
la culasse*; du canon où la charge s'effectuait au *moyen d'une*

boîte mobile (les veuglaires [1]); et du canon se *chargeant par la volée* (bouche).

D'abord en fer forgé, ces armes à feu furent fondues en bronze à partir du quinzième siècle, où apparaissent aussi les *tourillons* qui supportent le poids du canon, le tiennent en équilibre, empêchent le recul sur son affût, rendent le *heurtoir* superflu, et permettent de donner un pointage facile dans le sens vertical. Les affûts à roues avaient aussi remplacé les affûts immobiles, et bientôt après furent ajoutés les avant-trains.

Le petit canon à main ou la première arme à feu portative est contemporaine du canon se chargeant par la culasse, et remonte, comme celui-ci, à la première moitié du quatorzième siècle.

On a vu que les armes à feu de gros calibre ont pu être réduites à quatre espèces principales, malgré les nombreuses dénominations qui existaient chez les auteurs du seizième siècle, où souvent la même arme est désignée de dix manières différentes. Le classement de l'arme à feu portative aussi peut être simplifié dès qu'on réduit ses variétés uniquement à celles des mécanismes de la platine ou de la *batterie* (*Gewehrschloss* en allemand, *gun-lock* en anglais), et non pas aux variations de formes et de noms fantaisistes. On peut réduire toutes ces espèces d'armes à feu au nombre de douze, sans compter ni le fusil à vent, qui doit être placé à part, puisque sa force projective est créée par la pompe pneumatique et non pas par l'explosion d'une poudre, ni le *Stecher*, appelé improprement double détente en France, pouvant s'adapter à toute arme à feu destinée au tir de précision.

Ces espèces distinctes par le mécanisme de leurs platines sont :

1. Le système de la charge au moyen d'une chambre à feu mobile est encore actuellement en usage en Chine, puisque les pièces de rempart de trois mètres de longueur provenant de la campagne de 1860, et conservées au musée d'artillerie de Paris, sont presque toutes des veuglaires.

43.

Le *premier canon à main* du milieu du quatorzième siècle. En fer grossièrement forgé, attaché sur une pièce de bois presque brut, il ne pouvait être épaulé, et son trou de lumière (*Zündloch* en allemand, *touch-hole* en anglais), qui était *au-dessus* du tonnerre, avait quelquefois un petit couvre-platine à pivot destiné à préserver l'amorce de l'humidité. Plus court, il s'appelait *pétrinal* et servait à la cavalerie.

Le *canon à main à épauler*, de la fin du quatorzième siècle. Il se distingue du précédent en ce que son bois est plus façonné et souvent pourvu d'une crosse (*Kolbe* en allemand, *stock* en anglais) destinée à l'épaulement, et que le trou de lumière se trouve du côté droit du canon.

Le feu était mis à ces armes au moyen d'une *mèche détachée*.

Le *canon à main à serpentin, sans détente ni gâchette* (*mit Schlangenhahn-Lantentræger ohne Fehder noch Drücker* en allemand, *Guncock without trigger and spring* en anglais) inventé vers 1424. La mèche était dès lors portée par le serpentin.

Le *canon à main à serpentin à gâchette*, mais sans détente encore (*mit Schlangenhahn-Lantentræger and Drücker ohne Fêhder* en allemand, *Guncock for match with trigger but without spring* en anglais), qui permettait déjà de mieux viser [1].

La *haquebuse* (du vieil allemand *Hack-Busse*, *hackbus* en anglais), petit canon à main, à *serpentin*, à *détente* et à *gâchette*, (*Schlangenhahn-Lantentræger mit Drücker und Fehder* en allemand, *guncock for match with trigger and spring* en anglais), créé dans la seconde moitié du quinzième siècle. C'est la première arme qui permit de bien viser. Le canon avait ordinairement un mètre de longueur.

---

1. Aux Indes, chez les Mahrates, cette arme, introduite par des Européens du côté de l'Est vers la fin du seizième siècle, est toujours en usage. Le serpentin représente ordinairement la tête d'un dragon.

La *haquebuse double* (*Doppelhacken* en allemand, *double hakbus* en anglais). Elle se distingue de la haquebuse simple en ce qu'elle a deux serpentins qui s'abattent en sens opposé au moyen de deux détentes et de deux gâchettes. les canons de ces armes mesurent un mètre et demi à deux mètres ; ils étaient ou supportés par un pied souvent à pointes de fer ou garnis de roues, ou posés sur le mur d'enceinte. Elles avaient à cet effet des *crochets* (*Hacken*) d'où peut aussi bien venir le nom de *Hack-Busse* que du *serpentin*. Toutes ces armes, qui n'avaient ni visière (*Visir* en allemand, *visoer* en anglais) ni point de mire (*Kern* en allemand, *point de visoer* en anglais) tiraient des balles de fer, de plomb ou de fer recouvert de plomb.

L'*arquebuse à mèche* qui ne diffère presque en rien, dans sa construction, de la haquebuse.

L'*arquebuse à rouet* ou l'*arquebuse allemande* (*Deutsche Radschlosbüchse* en allemand, *arckbus with wheel-lock* en anglais), inventée à Nuremberg en 1545. Elle se signale par sa platine à rouet qui est déjà composée de dix pièces et n'a plus rien de commun avec les armes à mèche, remplacée par la *pyrite sulfureuse* ou *pyrite jaune,* dite aussi *martiale* et *marcassite* (*Schwefelkies* en allemand, *sulphurous pyrite* en anglais).

Le *Stecher,* piqueur, inventé à Munich en 1543, et improprement nommé en français *double détente* (*trigger* en anglais), mécanisme ingénieux destiné à rendre presque insensible le mouvement produit en lâchant la détente ordinaire, ne peut pas donner lieu à la formation d'une catégorie d'armes, puisqu'il peut être adapté à toutes les platines d'arquebuses.

L'*arquebuse à canon rayé* (*Büchse* en allemand, *arckbus with rifflet barrel* en anglais). La rayure du canon a été inventée en Allemagne, selon les uns à Leipzig en 1498, selon d'autres à Vienne ou à Nuremberg, par Gaspard Zollner ou Kullner.

Quant au *mousquet* à rouet (*Muskete* en allemand, *mousket* en anglais), il ne diffère de l'arquebuse que par son plus gros calibre.

L'*arquebuse ou le fusil à chenapan* (*snaphance* en anglais), dont le nom corrompu de l'allemand *Schnapphahn*, coq qui happe, indique l'origine de son invention. Elle remonte au seizième siècle. (V. p. 86).

La batterie à chenapan, qui fonctionnait encore au moyen de la pyrite sulfureuse, était le précurseur de la batterie à silex.

Le *fusil à batterie à silex, dite française*[1] (de l'italien *focile*, dérivé du latin *focus*, feu, *Flinte* en allemand, *fusil* ou *mousquet with french lock with silex* en anglais), probablement inventé en France entre 1630-1640. (V. p. 86 et 87.)

La *carabine* (de l'arabe *karab*, arme), qui est une arme à canon rayé, et dont le nom est donné aussi bien à la petite arme de la cavalerie qu'en Allemagne à l'arme de chasse, ne peut former une catégorie à part. C'est l'arquebuse et le fusil à canon rayé.

Le *fusil à percussion* ou *à piston* inventé par l'armurier écossais Forsilh en 1807. (V. p. 88 et 89.)

Le *fusil à aiguille* inventé en 1827 par l'Allemand Nicolas Dreyse. (V. p. 91.)

---

1. Cette arme, qui était arrivée à une grande perfection, se composait du *canon* (*Lauf* en allem., *barrel* en angl.), dont la partie postérieure s'appelle *tonnerre*, la partie antérieure *volée*, le vide intérieur *âme* et son diamètre *calibre*; de la *platine* (*Schloss* en allem., *lock* en angl.) et du *bois* (*Schafst* en allem., *stock* en angl.). On appelle *queue* le morceau de fer du canon qui dépasse la culasse du tonnerre, *lumière* l'ouverture où passe le feu pour enflammer l'amorce (*Zündloch* en allem., *touche hol* en angl.), *gâchette* (*Drücker* en allem., *trigger* en angl.) la clef par laquelle on fait jouer la *détente* (*Feder* en allem., *spring* en angl.) pour faire tomber le *chien* (*Hahn* en allem., *cock* en angl.)

LE MORTIER

Le *mortier* (du latin *mortarium*, *Moerser* ou *Boehler* en allemand, *mortar* en anglais), la plus ancienne arme à feu européenne, dont le nom et même l'existence dérivent du vase hémisphérique qui sert à piler des substances solides, était d'abord, à son apparition, vers la fin de la première moitié du quatorzième siècle, en fer forgé et sans *tourillons* (*Zapfen* en allemand, *trunnions* en anglais), c'est-à-dire sans la paire de pivots ou l'axe, placée au milieu du corps des bouches à feu, destinée à empêcher leur recul sur l'affût et à faciliter le pointage.

Cette amélioration fort importante remonte au quinzième siècle ; elle fut accompagnée de la *fonte* des pièces qui étaient confectionnées jusque-là avec des barres de fer réunies entre elles par des cercles, comme les douves d'un tonneau par ses cerceaux. (V. p. 72 à 82.)

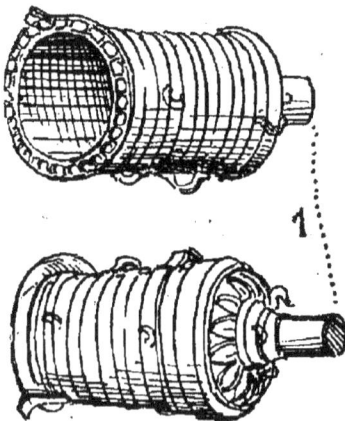

1. Mortier allemand monstre, fabriqué de barres de fer forgées, qui, placées en long dans l'âme, sont réunies extérieurement au moyen de cercles. Cette pièce, qui a 1^m,10 de calibre et 2^m,50 de longueur, et où la forme de l'écusson, placé entre les anses, indique la première moitié du quatorzième siècle, a été forgée à Stier, en Autriche, et prise par les Turcs à qui les Autrichiens l'ont reprise en 1529. — Arsenal impérial de Vienne.

2. Mortier en fer forgé, à anneaux et sans tourillons, du milieu du quatorzième siècle. —
Musée d'Épinal.

3. Mortier-pierrier (*Stein-Bœhler*
ou *Stein Morser* en allem., *ston-
mortar* en angl.), du siége de
Waldshut (1468).

4. Mortier en fer forgé, de 80 c.
de longueur, calibre 29 cent.
Cette arme est déjà à tourillons
(*Zapfen* en allem., *trunnions* en
angl.), et ne peut remonter au
delà du commencement du quinzième siècle. — Arsenal de
Berlin.

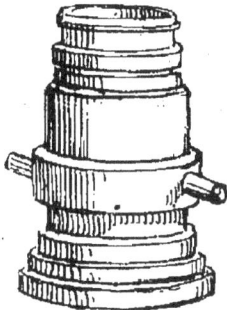

5. Mortier en bronze, sans tourillons et à anneau, de la fin du
quinzième siècle. Il se trouve
dans les dessins que Glockenthon a exécutés vers 1505, d'a-
près les pièces contenues dans
les arsenaux de l'empereur
Maximilien I. — Col. d'Ambras.

LE CANON

La partie antérieure de cette bouche à feu, ordinairement conique, dont le nom dérive de l'allemand *Kanne*, mais non pas du grec Χαννα, roseau (*Kanone* en allemand, *cannon* et *great gun* en anglais), et qui a été précédée par le mortier, se nomme *volée ; bourrelet*, la moulure annulaire extérieure de la volée ; *tourillons*, l'axe ou la paire de gros pivots placée au milieu et destinée à empêcher le recul sur l'affût, et à faciliter le pointage. Les pièces à jour souvent en forme de dauphins qui surmontent le canon s'appellent *anses ; âme*, sa cavité intérieure, dont le diamètre est le *calibre*, et la partie postérieure, la *culasse*, souvent terminée par le *bouton*.

Les premiers canons se chargeant par la culasse et appelés *bombardes* et *pierriers* furent bientôt suivis du canon se chargeant au moyen de la boîte mobile et appelé *veuglaire*, et du canon qui se chargeait *par la volée*. (V. p. 72 à 82.)

Serpentines, coulevrines, demi-coulevrines, faucons, fauconneaux, passe-volants, basilics, spirales, bombardes, son des noms plus ou moins vagues par lesquels on désigne souvent les mêmes espèces de canons selon les différentes localités.

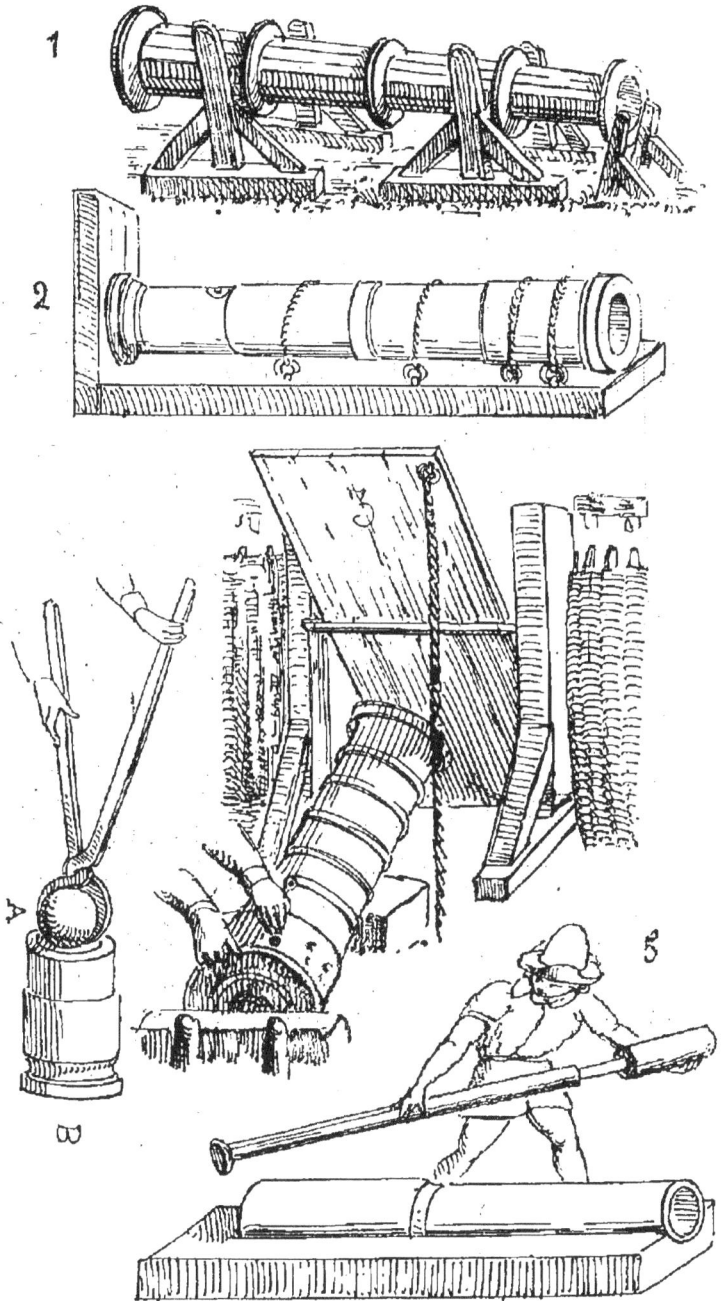

1. Canon ou bombarde en fer forgé, ouvert aux deux extrémités et se chargeant par la culasse, arme anglaise de la bataille de Crécy (1346).

2. Canon ou bombarde ouvert aux deux extrémités et se chargeant par la culasse, le heurtoir s'abaisse pendant la charge. — Manuscrit du quatorzième siècle.

3. Canon ou bombarde se chargeant par la culasse avec son mantelet ou sa blinde (*Schirmdach* en allem.), de la seconde moitié du quatorzième siècle.

4. Canon ou bombarde qu'un artilleur charge par la culasse de boulets rougis au feu. — Manuscrit[1] du commencement du quinzième siècle, de la collection d'Ambras.

5. Canon ou bombarde se chargeant par la culasse, manuscrit du quinzième siècle. — Col. d'Ambras.

---

1. Le dessin de ce manuscrit prouve que ni Franz de Sickingen, en 1525, ni Étienne Bathory, roi de Pologne, ne se sont servis les premiers de boulets rouges. On sait, du reste, que des boulets rouges ou des morceaux de fer enveloppés de linges mouillés furent déjà lancés au quinzième siècle pour incendier les places assiégées. C'est au dix-septième siècle que l'usage des boulets rouges devint seulement général.

La partie A représente la culasse, et celle marquée d'un B la volée (bouche).

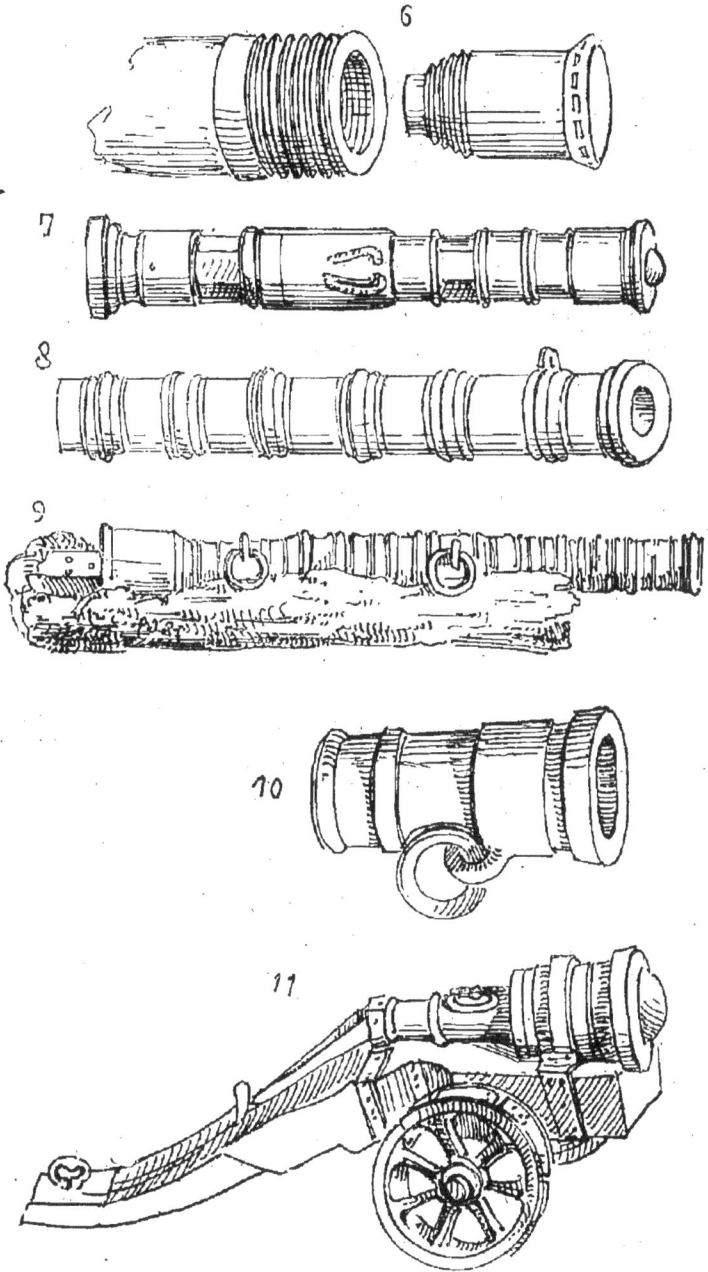

6. Bombarde flamande se chargeant par la culasse. Cette curieuse pièce, représentée avec sa chambre à feu à vis, est en fer forgé et a été fabriquée à Gand entre 1404 et 1419.

7. Bombarde allemande en bronze fondu, au commencement du quinzième siècle. Elle a 4 mètres de longueur et 60 cent. de diamètre. On y lit l'inscription (en allemand) : *Je me nomme Catherine, méfie-toi de mon contenu. Je punis l'injustice. George Endorfer me fondit.* Et : *Sigismond, archiduc d'Autriche, anno 1404.* Cette pièce, qui a déjà des anses, et montre des traces d'un couvre-platine, provient de Rhodes ; elle fait partie du musée d'artillerie de Paris (nº 18).

8. Canon en fer forgé, provenant de la bataille de Grandson (1476). Il a 1ᵐ,50 de longueur, 5 cent. de diamètre, et point de tourillons. — Musée de Lausanne.

9. Bombarde en fer forgé, du quinzième siècle ; elle se charge par la culasse et provient d'un vaisseau coulé au commencement du seizième siècle. — Tour de Londres.

10. Bombarde en fer forgé provenant de la bataille de Grandson (1476). Elle a 1ᵐ,50 de longueur et 56 cent. de diamètre. — Musée de Lausanne.

11. Canon ou bombarde en fer forgé, sur affût à roues, provenant de la bataille de Morat (1476). Il a 75 cent. de longueur et 18 cent. de diamètre ; l'affût est long de 2 mètres ; le boulet en granit a 24 cent. de diamètre. Ce canon bourguignon n'a point de tourillons. — Gymnase de Morat.

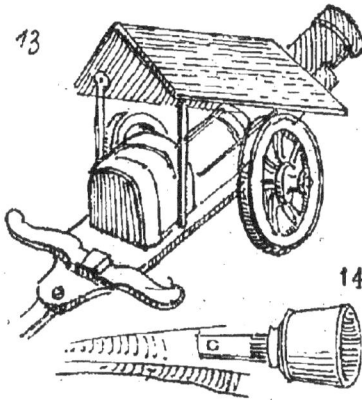

13. Canon ou bombarde se char- geant par la culasse avec toi- ture et affût à roues, de la fin du quinzième siècle. Il est tou- jours encore sans tourillons.

14. Canon ou bombarde en fer forgé, sans tourillons, se char- geant par la culasse, provenant du château de Sainte-Ursane en Suisse, où il fut placé après la bataille de Morat (1476). — Musée d'artillerie de Paris. Mar- tinus Jacobus (*De machinis libri decem.* 1449[1]) donne le dessin d'une bombarde semblable.

15.   Id.   id.

16. Bombarde ou canon coudé allemand, du quinzième siecle, à chambre à feu et se chargeant par la culasse, d'après les gra- vures de l'*Institutionum repu- blicœ militaris*, etc., par Nicolai Marescalci, imprimées à Ros- tock, en 1515. — Bibliothèque Hauslaub, à Vienne.

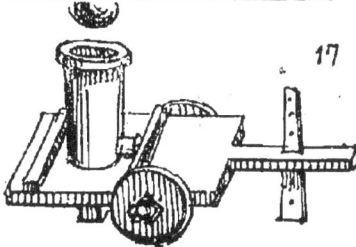

17. Bombarde ou canon coudé italien, du quinzième siècle, à chambre à feu et se chargeant par la culasse, d'après Martinus Jacobus (*De machinis libri de- cem.* 1449).

1. Manuscrits de la bibliothèque de Saint-Marc, à Venise.

18. Bombarde ou canon du quinzième siècle, se chargeant par la culasse. — Manuscrit de la bibliothèque Hauslaub, à Vienne.

19. Veuglaire (de l'allemand *Vogler* et *Vogelfanger* et du flamand *vogheler*), canon en fer forgé, du quinzième siècle, se chargeant au moyen d'une boîte mobile qui s'appelle chambre à feu. La volée est à point de mire. — Musée de Bruxelles et manuscrit de la bibliothèque Hauslaub, à Vienne.

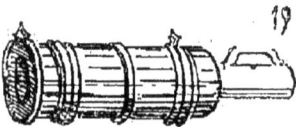

20. Veuglaire en fer forgé, du quinzième siècle. Il est à chambre à feu ou boîte mobile. — Tour de Londres.

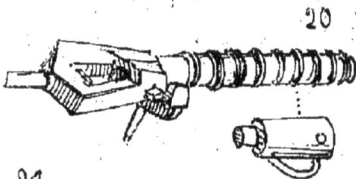

21. Veuglaire allemand du quinzième siècle, d'après un manuscrit de la collection d'Ambras, à Vienne.

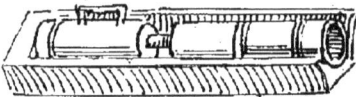

22. Veuglaire anglais du quinzième siècle. A. Chambre à feu ou boîte mobile.

23. Veuglaire en fer forgé, du quinzième siècle, déjà à tourillons[1]. La boîte mobile ou chambre à feu manque. — N° 1, musée d'artillerie de Paris.

1. Voir l'explication de cette dénomination au commencement de ce chapitre. Voir aussi plus loin le veuglaire n° 34.

44.

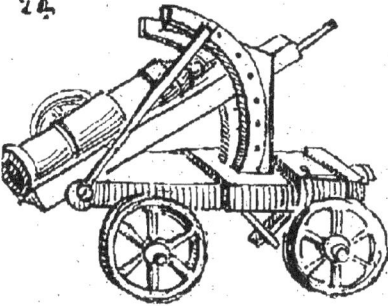

24. Canon allemand nommé coulevrine (en allemand *Feld-schlange*), se chargeant par la volée, sans tourillons, mais sur affût mobile à crémaillères, d'après un manuscrit du quinzième siècle, de Zeitblom. — Bibliothèque du prince de Waldburg-Wolfegg.

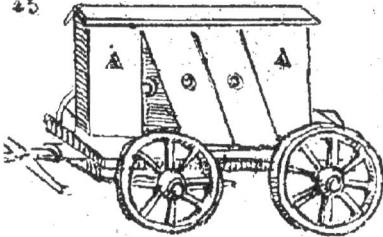

25. Chariot de guerre allemand, garni de petits canons.
Id.   id.   id.

26. Canon allemand, se chargeant par la volée. Il est encore sans tourillons, mais à affût mobile à crémaillères.

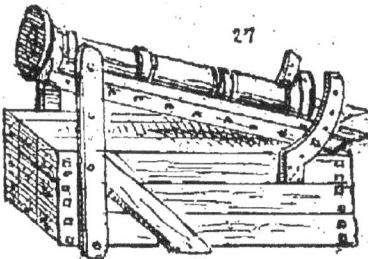

27.   Id.   id.

28. Canon allemand nommé coulevrine (en allemand *Feld-schlange*), se chargeant par la volée, de la seconde moitié du quinzième siècle. Il est toujours sans tourillons, mais sur affût mobile à crémaillères.

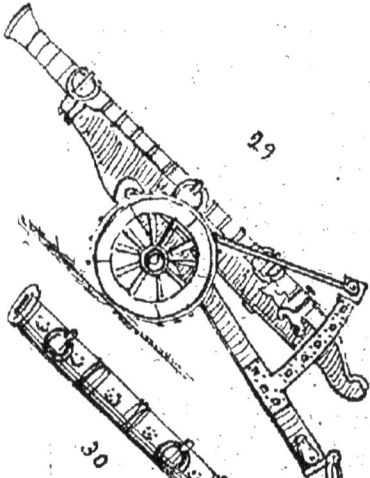

29. Canon bourguignon, se chargeant par la volée, sans tourillons, mais sur affût à crémaillères; cette arme provient de la bataille de Nancy (1477) et se trouve à Neuveville.

30. Canon anglais, sans tourillons et se chargeant par la volée, de la fin du quinzième siècle. — Tour de Londres.

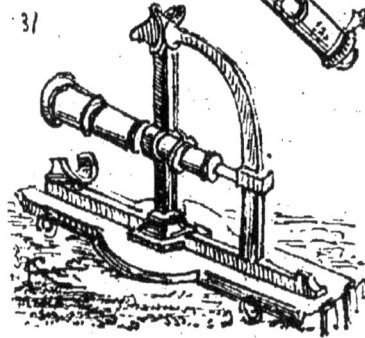

31. Canon anglais, se chargeant par la volée, sans tourillons et sur affût à coulisse.

32. Canon allemand, se chargeant par la volée et sans tourillons, du quinzième siècle. — Bibliothèque Hauslaub, à Vienne.

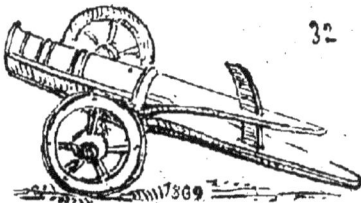

33. Chargette de canon suisse, aussi appelée lanterne, du quinzième siècle. Elle est en cuivre et montée sur une longue hampe dont l'extrémité inférieure est armée d'un tire-bourre. — Arsenal de Soleure. Voir aussi plus loin ce même genre de chargette, d'après le livre de Fronsperger, du seizième siècle.

34 A et B. Orgue à serpentins, allemand (*Orgelgeschütz* en allem.; voir aussi, page 80, le *Todtenorgel* ou orgue de mort!), en fer forgé, à cinq canons se chargeant par la volée, du milieu du quinzième siècle. — Musée de Sigmaringen.

35. Orgue à serpentins, allemand, de quarante canons, d'après les *Reproductions des armes de l'empereur Maximilien I*, exécutées en 1505 par Nicolas Glockenthon. — Col. d'Ambras. Voir, plus loin, les orgues du dix-septième siècle.

36. Canons à tourillons qui ont fait leur première apparition vers le milieu du quinzième siècle; on appelle tourillons la paire de goujons placée au milieu du corps du canon et destinée à empêcher le recul de la pièce. Ils rendent le heurtoir inutile et permettent de diriger la volée dans le sens vertical; ils supportent le poids du canon et le tiennent en équilibre.

37. Veuglaire allemand, à tourillons, d'après les dessins déjà mentionnés de Glockenthon, de 1505. Voir aussi le veuglaire n° 23. — Col. d'Ambras.

Char de guerre allemand appelé en français *Ribaudequin*, armé de flèches et de quatre falconets en bronze. Dessins d'après les arsenaux de l'empereur Maximilien I, exécutés en 1505 par Glockenthon. — Col. d'Ambras.

39

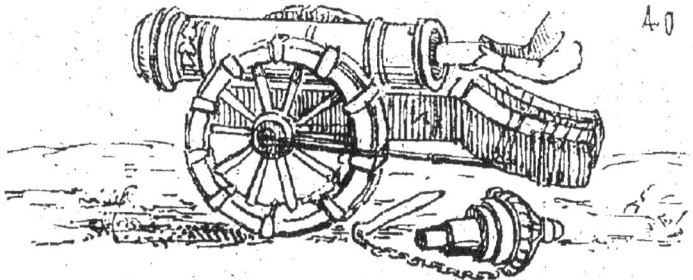

40

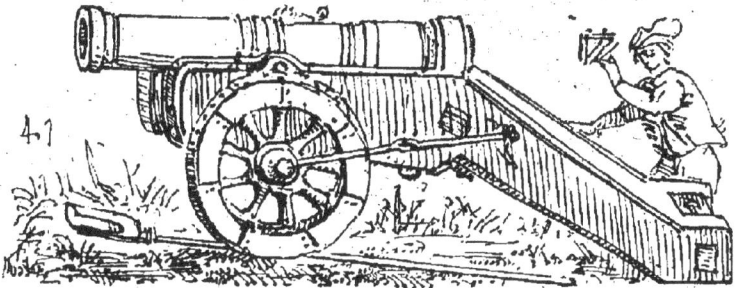

41

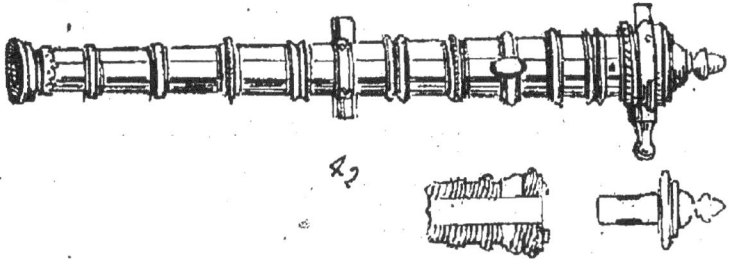

42

39. Falconets jumeaux en fer et à tourillons, d'après les dessins que Glockenthon a exécutés en 1505 d'après les arsenaux de l'empereur Maximilien I. — Col. d'Ambras.

40. Canon à tourillons et se chargeant par la culasse, d'après un manuscrit de *Senftenberg* qui commandait l'artillerie de Dantzig, au seizième siècle.

41. Canon à tourillons et se chargeant par la volée, appelé par Fronsperger *Basilium* (dans le *Kriegsbuch*, que cet auteur a publié en 1573 à Francfort), et pesant 75 quintaux ; il portait 70 livres de fer et était traîné par 25 chevaux. On remarquera à côté du canon la chargette en cuivre, appelée lanterne, déjà mentionnée sous le n° 33. L'artilleur vise au moyen d'une équerre. L'armée autrichienne se servait encore de cette chargette à la bataille de Mollwitz, en 1741, tandis que l'armée prussienne avait déjà adopté depuis longtemps les charges préparées d'avance. Le refouloir et son écouvillon (brosse) sont toujours en usage.

42. Canon rayé à tourillons et se chargeant par la culasse, de la fin du seizième siècle. Il a 2^m,10 de longueur, 18 cent. de diamètre et 8 cent. de calibre. La boîte de la culasse est à coulisse et sert à fermer le canon ; la coupe du tonnerre se trouve représentée à côté. — Arsenal de Zurich.

43. Orgue à serpentins, à quarante-deux canons se tirant par
sept décharges. Du dix-septième
siècle. — Arsenal de Soleure.

44. Petits canons suédois, à tourillons et se chargeant par la
volée, — du dix-septième siècle.
Ils sont de $1^m,20$ de longueur,
sur 8 cent. de diamètre. Le
tuyau intérieur en cuivre mince
est extérieurement ficelé et le
tout recouvert de cuir. — Arsenaux de Berlin et de Hambourg, musée d'artillerie de Paris et col. du roi de Suède. On
trouve aussi à l'arsenal impérial
de Vienne un canon en cuir
garni d'un tuyau de bronze, que
la ville d'Augsbourg fit offrir à
l'empereur Joseph I (1705-1711).

45. Canon à tourillons et se chargeant par la volée, fait d'un tube
de cuivre matelassé tout autour
d'une épaisse couche de chaux
et le tout recouvert de cuir;
arme fort légère et facile à transporter dans les montagnes. Elle
mesure $2^m,30$ et appartient au
dix-septième siècle. — Arsenal
de Zurich.

46. Serpentin suisse (*Doppelhacken*) se chargeant par la culasse, du dix-septième siècle. —
Arsenal de Soleure.

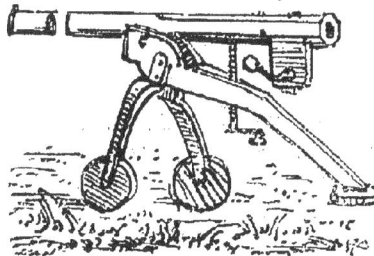

47. Serpentin suisse se chargeant par la culasse, signé : *Zell
Blasi*, 1614. — Arsenal de Bâle.

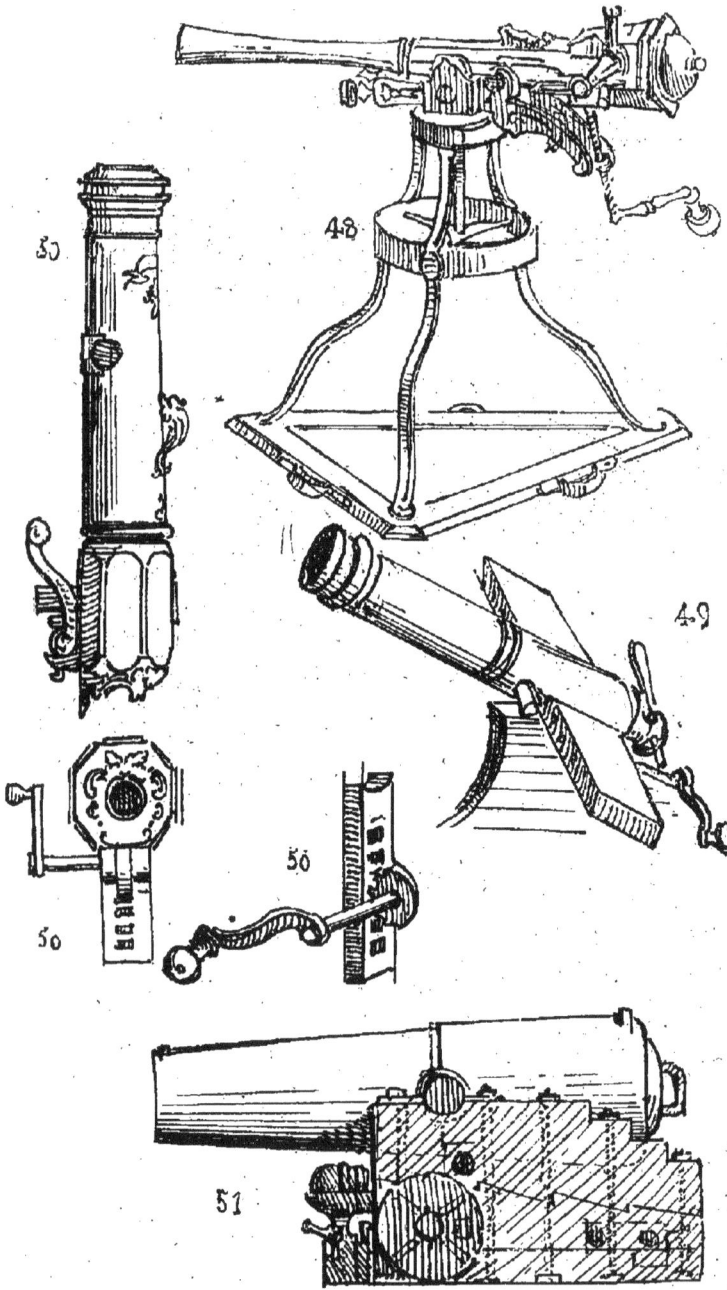

48

50

49

50

56

51

45

52

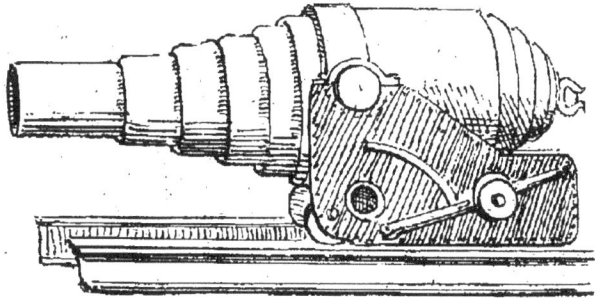

33

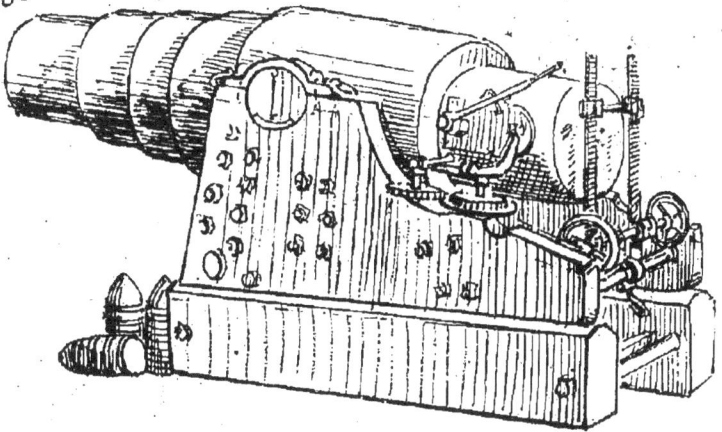

34

55

48. Petit canon en fer se chargeant par la culasse èt sur affût tournant appelé en allemand *Drehbasse*. Cette pièce a été abandonnée à Munich, par Gustave-Adolphe, en 1632.

49. Petit canon suisse, à répétition, en cuivre, se chargeant par la culasse et tirant successivement dix coups. Il a 67/56 c. et porte la signature de *Welten. Inventor.* 1742. — Arsenal de Zurich.

50. Canon du dix-huitième siècle, se chargeant par la culasse, d'après les mémoires du colonel Wurstemberger.

51. Canon-obusier à la Paixhans, inventé en 1822 par le chef de bataillon du corps royal de l'artillerie anglaise H. C. Paixhans.

52. Canon Armstrong, calibre de 600, imaginé par Sir William Armstrong.

53. Canon monstre, prussien, se chargeant par la culasse, en acier, fondu dans l'usine de M. Krupp et exposé à Paris en 1867. Il pèse 50,000 kilogr. et ses projectiles, également en acier fondu, 550 kilogr. chaque.

54. Canon de campagne rayé, prussien, se chargeant par la culasse, en acier fondu, inventé par M. Krupp. Ce canon, qui est du même calibre que le canon français pièce de douze, est chargé avec des projectiles pleins recouverts d'une enveloppe de plomb pour être forcée dans les rayures de la pièce.

55. Fermeture Krupp des canons précédents. Cette fermeture est adaptée au moyen d'une targette latérale. Un tour de clef pousse la targette et ferme la culasse au moment du tir.

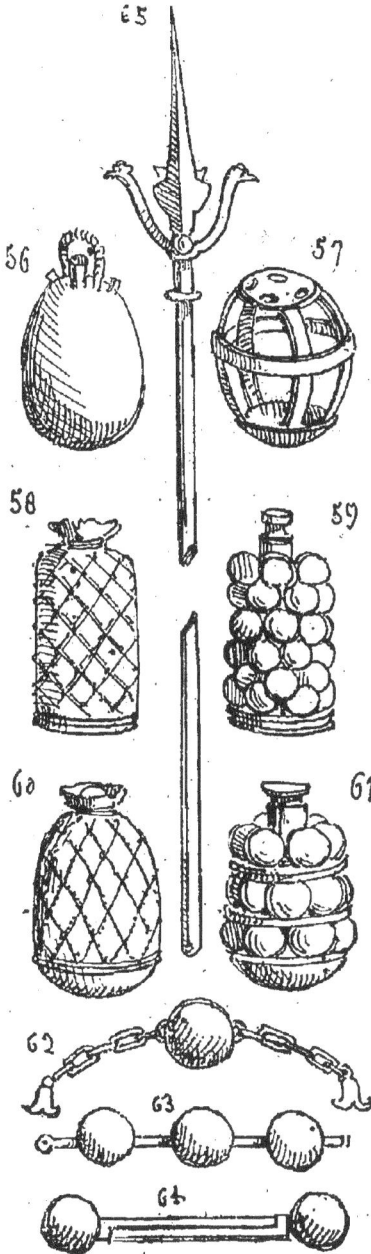

56. Grenade-carcasse en sac de toile, du seizième siècle; elle était lancée par des mortiers.

57. Carcasse intérieure de la grenade précédente.

58. Grappe de raisin (*Trauben-hagel* en allem.), du seizième siècle. Elle consistait en seize balles réunies autour d'une carcasse en bois et renfermées dans un sac.

59. Vue intérieure de la grappe précédente.

60. Grappe de raisin de dix-huit balles.

61. Vue intérieure de la grappe précédente.

62. Boulet armé dit chaîne ramée.

63. Boulets conjugués.

64. Boulets à essieux.

65. Porte-mèche pour canon (*Luntenstock* en allem., *linkstok* en angl.) — Arsenal de Woolwich.

L'ARME A FEU PORTATIVE OU A MAIN

L'histoire de l'arme à feu portative a été présenté p. 82 à 92, et résumée de nouveau au commencement de ce chapitre.

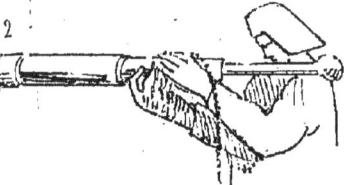

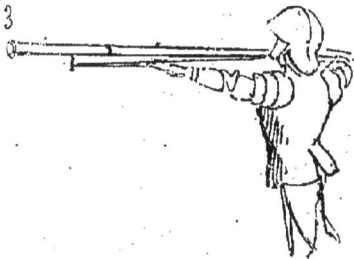

1. Canon à main d'homme de pied, en fer forgé, de la première moitié du quatorzième siècle. Le trou de lumière (*Zundloch* en allem., *touch-hole* en angl.) se trouve au-dessus du canon. — Arsenal de Berne et musée national de Prague.

2. Canon à main d'homme de pied, d'après un manuscrit de la fin du quatorzième siècle. Le trou se trouve au-dessus du canon.

3. Canon à main d'homme de pied, d'après un manuscrit de 1472, de la bibliothèque Hauslaub, à Vienne.

4. Canon à main de cavalier, du quinzième siècle, appelé *pétrinal* (V. chap. historique), d'après un manuscrit de l'ancienne bibliothèque de Bourgogne. L'armure déjà à plates et articulée, malgré l'espèce de bacinet à visière mobile, indique la seconde moitié du quinzième siècle. L'usage de ces canons à main s'est conservé à côté des haquebuses à serpentins et même des arquebuses et mousquets à rouet, jusqu'au commencement du seizième siècle, comme le démontrent les dessins de Glockenthon qui reproduisent les armes de l'empereur Maximilien I (1505).

45.

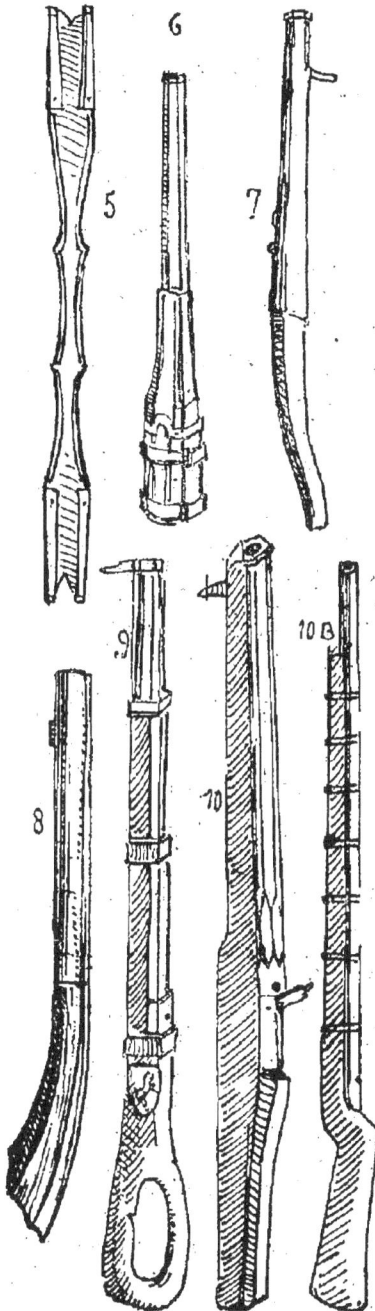

5. Canons à mains allemands sur planchette, du commencement du seizième siècle. Les trous de lumière se trouvent encore au-dessus du canon. Dessins de Glockenthon de 1505. — Col. d'Ambras.

6. Canon à main allemand, en fer cannelé, de la fin du quinzième ou du commencement du seizième siècle. Il n'a que 23 c. de longueur sur 5 de diamètre et est attaché sur un bois de chêne de 1m,44 de longueur. — Musée germanique où il est attribué à tort au quatorzième siècle.

7. Canon à main de cavalier, en fer forgé, dit pétrinal, de la fin du quinzième siècle. — Musée d'artillerie de Paris.

8. Canon à main à crosse (*Kolbe* en allem., *butt-end* en angl.), de la fin du quatorzième siècle. Le trou de lumière se trouve au-dessus du canon.

9. Canon à main en fer anguleux et à crosse, pour la défense des remparts. Il a 1m,80 de longueur et le trou de la lumière est placé au-dessus du canon. Cette pièce a servi à défendre Morat contre le Téméraire (1479). — Gymnase de Morat.

10. Canon à main en fer, à huit pans et à crosse. Le trou de lumière placé au-dessus du canon est pourvu d'un couvre-lumière pivotant. Cette pièce, d'une longueur totale de 1m,35, et qui tirait des balles de 3 c. de diamètre, appartient au commencement du quinzième siècle. — Musée de Dresde.

10 bis. Canon à mèche persan, de la fin du seizième siècle,

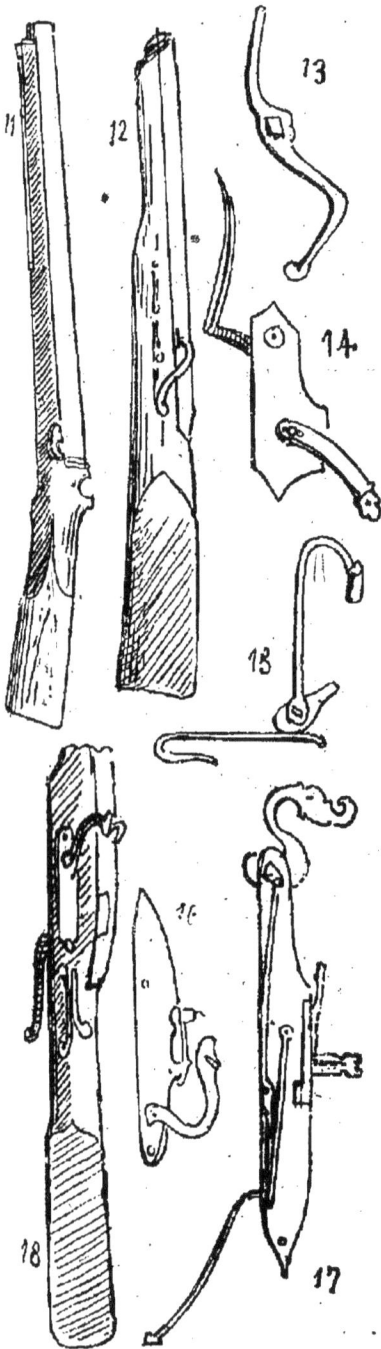

d'après le *Schah-Nameh*, de la bibliothèque de Munich.

11. Canon à main à crosse, de la fin du quatorzième ou du commencement du quinzième siècle. Ici le trou de lumière est déjà placé au côté droit du canon.

12. Canon à main à serpentin, sans détente ni gâchette (*Schlangenhahn-Luntentræger ohne Fehder und Drücker* en allem.; *guncock without trigger and spring* en angl.), inventé vers 1424.

13. Serpentin (*Schlangenhahn-Lantentræger* en allem.; *guncock fer match* en angl.), sans détente ni gâchette.

14. Serpentin sans détente, mais à gâchette.

15. Serpentin à détente (ressort), mais sans gâchette.

16. Platine à serpentin, sans détente et sans ressort.

17. Platine ou mécanisme d'haquebuse à mèche, qui est à détente et à gâchette (*Hackbüchsen Schloss mit Fehder und Drücker; Hack-buss-cock with spring and trigger*.)

18. Haquebuse (de l'allemand *Hackenbüchse*, du vieil allemand *Hack-buss*, en anglais *hack-buss*) ou canon à main, à crosse perfectionnée et à platine à serpentin, de la seconde moitié du quinzième siècle. La mèche n'est plus détachée mais portée par le serpentin qui est à détente et s'abat au moyen de la gâchette. Le canon a ordinairement un mètre de longueur et un crochet (*hacken*) qui empêche son recul, posé sur le mur ou sur le support; c'est de

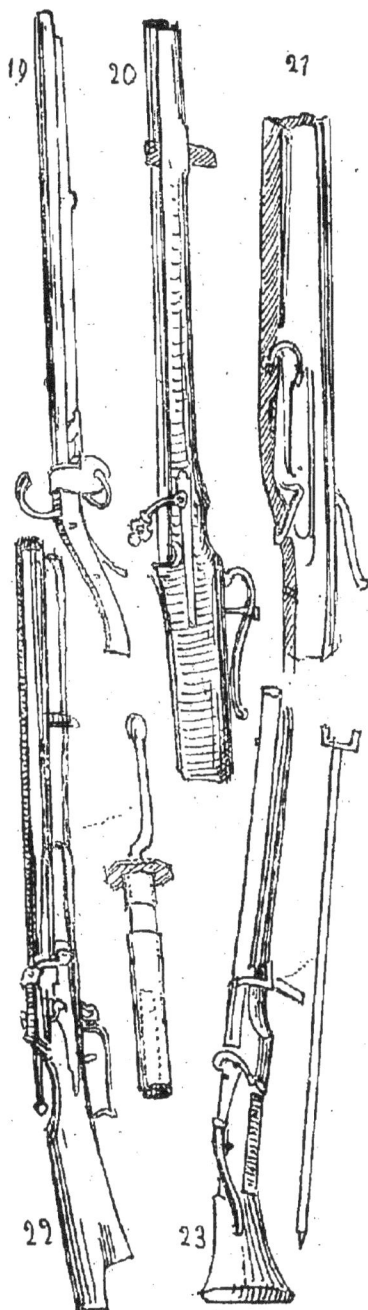

là que dérive peut-être son nom.
La haquebuse sans crochet
et mieux confectionnée prit
bientôt le nom d'arquebuse à
mèche. Elle avait alors déjà une
visière (*Visir* en allem., *visoer*
en angl.) et un point de mire
(*Kern* en allem., *point de visoer*
en angl.)

19. Haquebuse chinoise. — Tour
de Londres.

20. Haquebuse suisse, de la seconde moitié du quinzième siècle. — Arsenal de Schaffhouse.

21. Haquebuse double ou à deux
serpentins (*Doppelhacken* en allem., *double hack-buss* en angl.)
qui s'abattent en sens opposé.
Cette arme servait ordinairement à la défense des remparts
et son canon mesurait 1ᵐ1/2
à 2 mètres.

22. Haquebuse se chargeant par
la culasse au moyen d'une boîte
mobile dite chambre à feu, arme
appartenant au commencement
du seizième siècle. — Arsenal
de Berne. Une arquebuse double de rempart, de 3 mètres de
longueur et se chargeant également par la culasse, mais pourvue d'un rouet et d'un serpentin,
arme de la fin du seizième siècle,
se trouve au musée de Zurich.

23. Haquebuse avec sa fourche
(*Gabel* en allem., *gun-forck* en
angl.), d'après les dessins que
Glockenthon a exécutés en 1505
dans les arsenaux de l'empereur
Maximilien I, et qui se trouve
aussi sur la gravure, *le Triomphe de l'empereur Maximilien I*.
On voit par cela que la haquebuse ou l'arquebuse à mèche
s'est conservée fort longtemps à
côté de l'arquebuse à rouet.

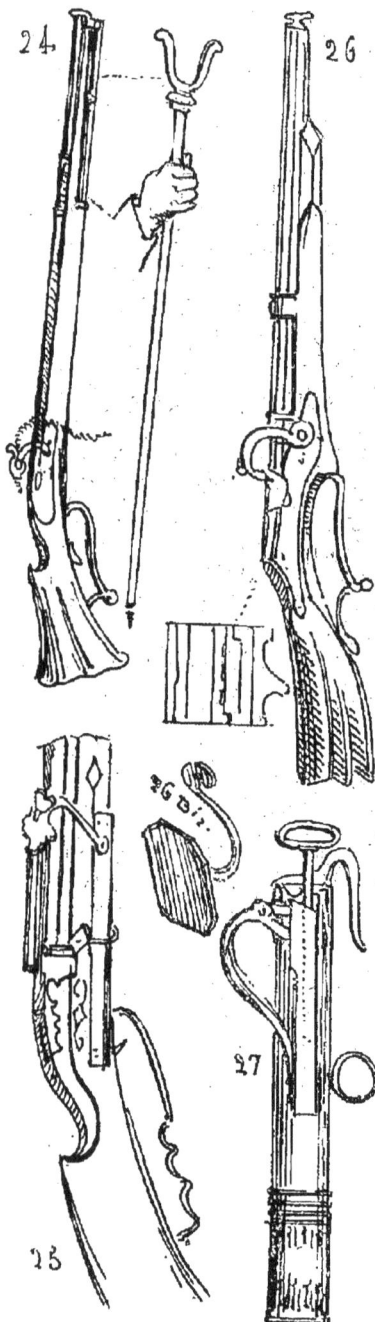

24. Haquebuse à serpentin à mèche, appelée aussi mousquet[1], avec sa fourche nommée *four--quine*.

25. Haquebuse à mèche, appelée mousquet[1]. — Tour de Londres.

26. Haquebuse à serpentin à mèche, aussi appelée arquebuse, se chargeant par la culasse au moyen d'une boîte mobile, nommée chambre à feu. Elle date de 1537 et porte la marque W. H. à côté d'une fleur de lis. — $\frac{12}{1}$, Tour de Londres.

26 *bis*. Cache-l'œil d'un mousquet, à l'arsenal de Genève.

27. Canon à main avec râpe, du commencement du seizième siècle; il est tout en fer et nommé *Monchsbüchse* (arquebuse de moine). Pendant longtemps, l'ignorance y a voulu voir la première arme à feu due à un moine, Berthold Schwarz (1290-1320), à qui on avait aussi attribué l'invention de la poudre à canon. Cette petite arme, de 28 cent. de longueur et d'un calibre de 12 cent., paraît avoir précédé l'invention du rouet et en avoir donné la première idée. Une râpe fait jaillir des étincelles par son frottement contre de la pyrite sulfureuse dès qu'on la retire. — Musée de Dresde.

1. On aura remarqué que l'auteur a rangé toutes les armes à feu *à serpentin*, *à mèche*, sous le nom de *haquebuses*, quoiqu'on les appelle encore *arquebuses* et *mousquets* à mèche. Le mousquet se distingue de l'arquebuse par son plus gros calibre.

Canon à main sur affût et haquebusiers allemands, d'après les
Reproductions des trois arsenaux de l'empereur Maximilien I,
exécutées en 1505, par Glockenthon. — Col. d'Ambras.

Ce dessin est intéressant pour l'étude des costumes, et prouve
que le simple canon à mains de gros calibre était encore en usage
à côté des haquebuses à mèches et des arquebuses à rouet même.

Canon à main à serpentin et haquebusier allemands, d'après les dessins de Glockenthon, mentionnés à la page précédente.

L'arme paraît être à trois canons. Comme on ne voit qu'un seul serpentin, deux canons étaient probablement déchargés au moyen de la mèche détachée.

Haquebusier allemand, d'après les dessins de Glockenthon, de 1505, mentionnés aux pages précédentes.

Le sac à munitions se trouve suspendu au côté gauche et au-dessus de la lansquenette. La haquebuse est à serpentin.

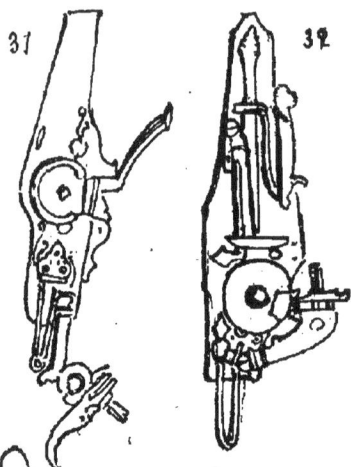

31. Platine à rouet (*Deutsches Schloss* ou *Radschloss* en allem., *wheel-lock* en angl.), inventée en 1515 [1], à Nuremberg. Elle est composée de dix pièces et n'a plus rien de commun avec les platines à serpentin, puisque la mèche est remplacée par la pyrite sulfureuse (*Schwefelkies* en allem., *sulphurus pyrite* en angl.)

32. Id. id., vue à l'intérieur.

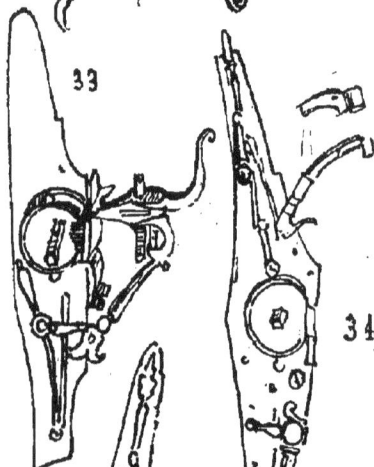

33. Id. id., vue à l'extérieur.

34. Platine à serpentin et à rouet.

35. Platine riche à serpentin et à rouet.

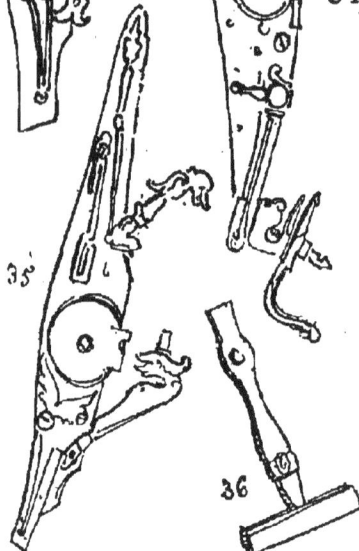

36. Clef pour platine à rouet.

1. Un collectionneur en Angleterre, M. Pritchett, possède une platine à rouet qu'il croit remonter à 1509.

46

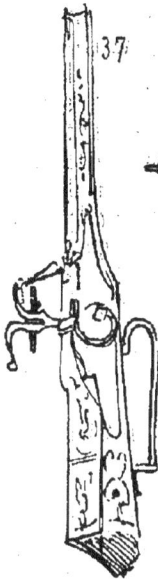

37. Arquebuse à rouet, du seizième siècle. — Musée d'artillerie de Paris.

38. Mousquet à rouet, du seizième siècle. — Musée d'artillerie de Paris.

39. Mousquet à rouet, du seizième siècle, se chargeant par
la culasse au moyen d'une boîte
mobile dite chambre à feu. —
Musée de Sigmaringen. Le musée de Dresde possède une semblable arme.

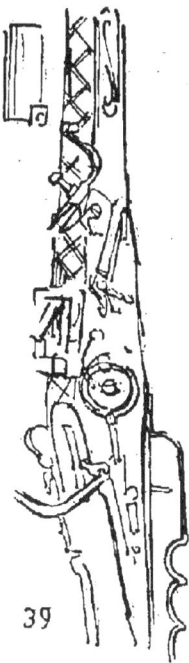
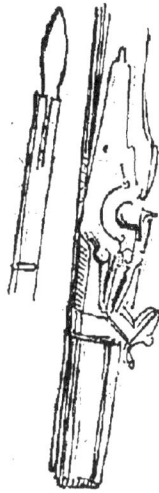

40. Fourche ou *fourquine* de
mousquet à mousqueton à rouet
(*Mousketen Gabel* en allem., *forck
of rest for mousket* en angl.), du
commencement du dix-septième
siècle. Elle a 1^m,70 de longueur.—Musée de Sigmaringen.

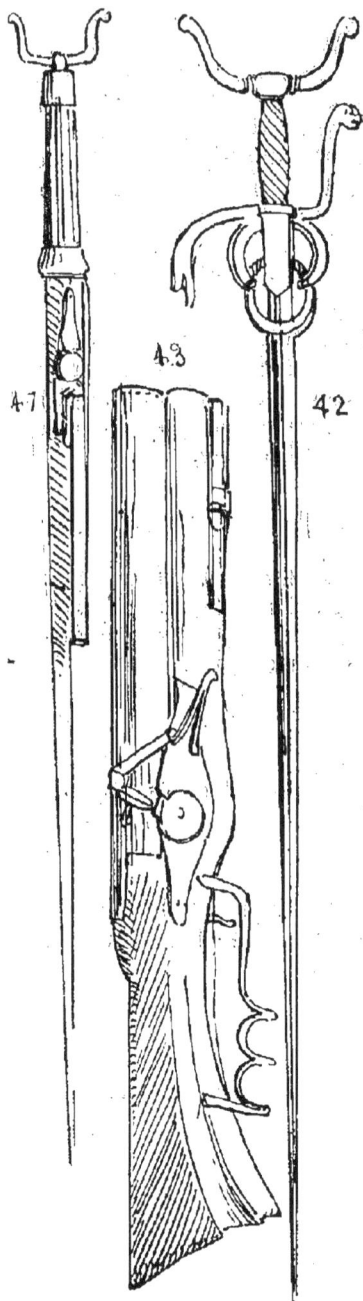

41. Fourche ou *fourquine* de mousquet, de 1m,50 de longueur. Elle consiste en un dard triangulaire en acier, damasquiné d'or et garni d'un pistolet à rouet. Cette arme, qui date de la fin du seizième siècle, ressemble à l'arme précédente. — Musée historique du palais de Montbijou, à Berlin.

42. Fourche ou *fourquine*-épée de mousquet (*Mousketen Gabeldegen* en allem.), du commencement du dix-septième siècle. — Col. du prince Charles, à Berlin.

43. Tromblon à rouet et à canon en cuivre, recouvert de gros cuir, dans le genre des canons suédois; le tromblon a 65 cent. de longueur et le canon 4 c. 1/2 de diamètre. — Musée de Sigmaringen.

44.

44. Double ou seconde détente, appelée avec plus de logique en allemand *Stecher*, pointeur (*trigger of precision* en angl.), inventée à Munich en 1543. Elle a été adaptée à toutes sortes de platines à rouet d'armes de précision.

45.

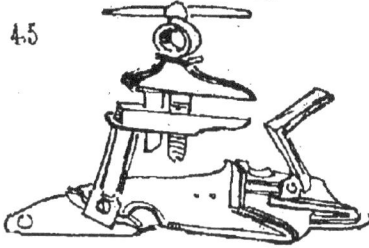

45. Batterie à chenapan (de l'allemand *Schnaphahn*, chien qui happe, *snaphance* en angl.) Elle fonctionne au moyen de la pyrite sulfureuse.

46.

46. Batterie à silex, probablement inventée en France de 1630 à 1640. Ancien modèle, vue extérieure.

47.

47. Id. id., vue intérieure.

48.

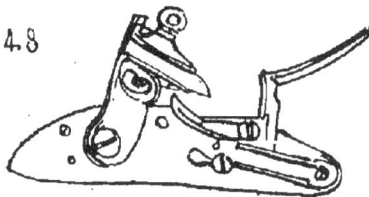

48. Batterie à silex d'un fusil français de 1670. Vue extérieure.

49. Id. id., vue intérieure.

49.

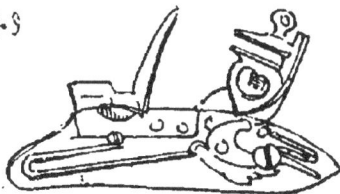

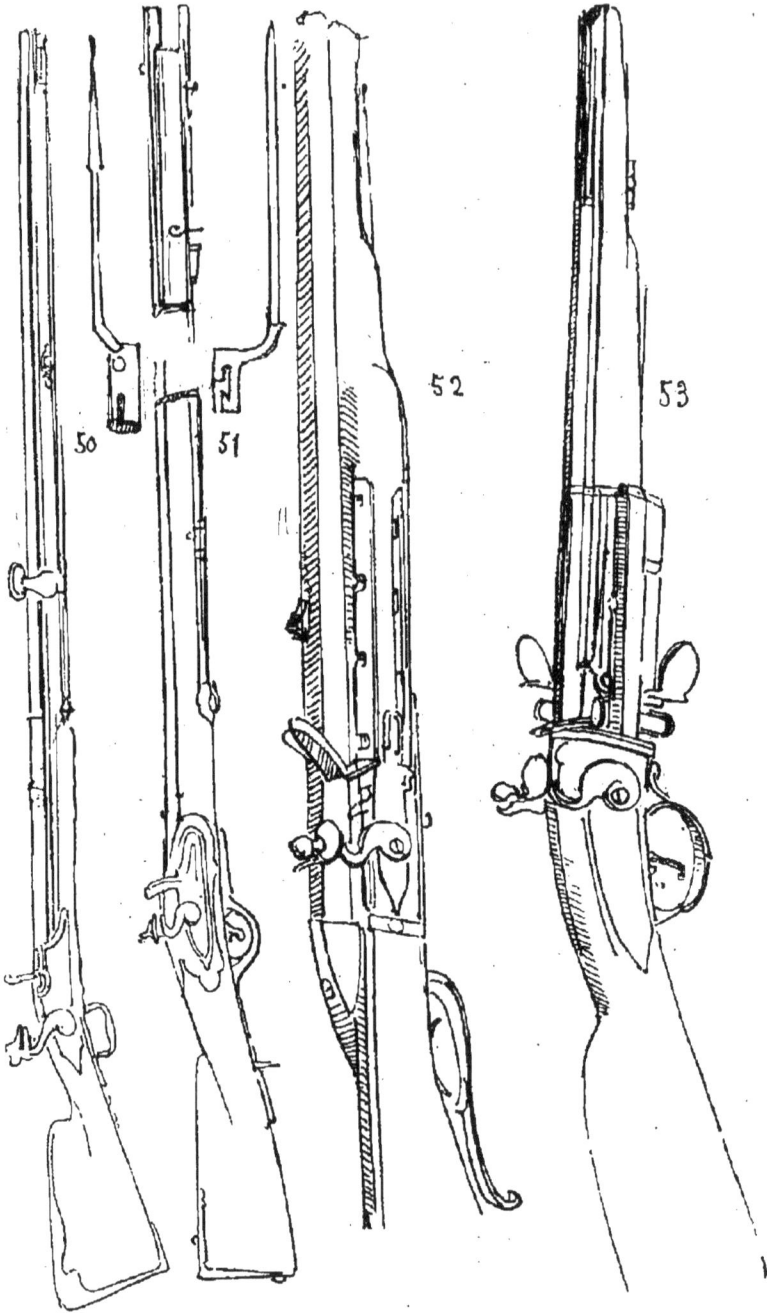

50   51   52   53

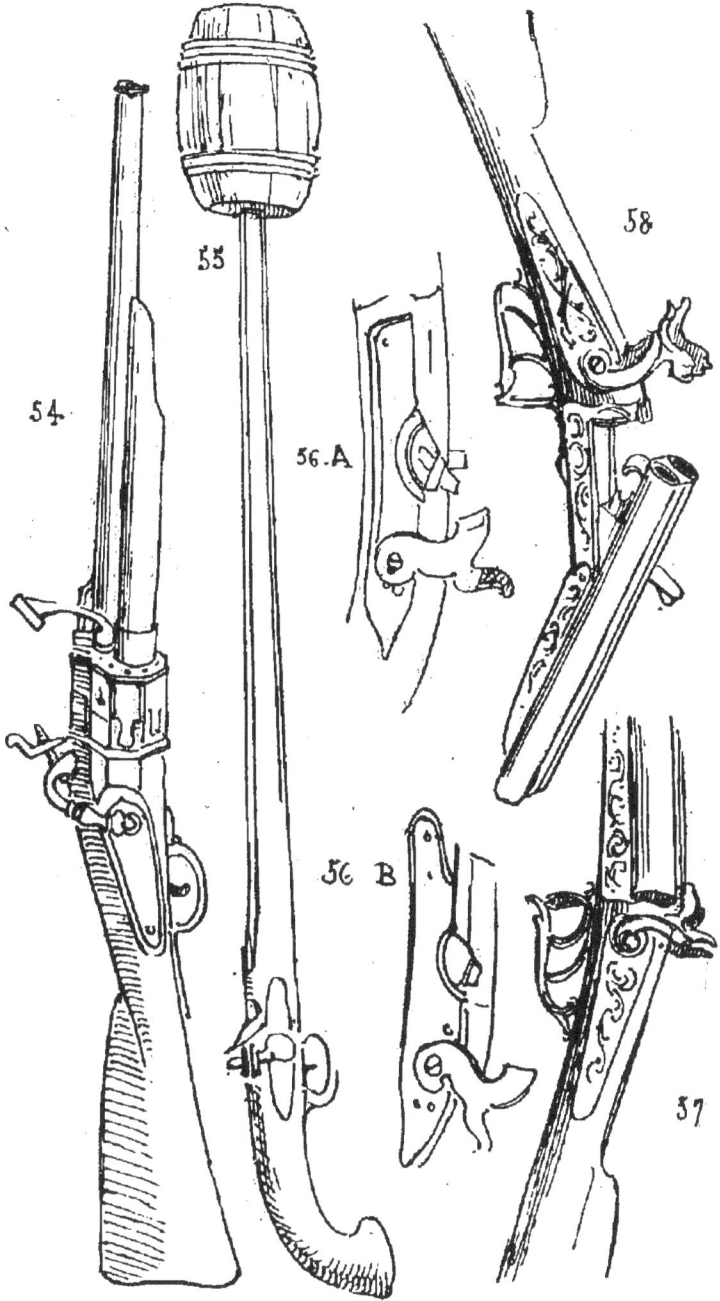

54

55

56.A

56 B

58

57

50. Fusil français, à silex et à baïonnette, de la fin du dix-septième siècle.

51. Fusil prussien, à silex et à baïonnette, du temps de Frédéric le Grand. Cette arme fut pourvue, en 1730, de la baguette en fer, innovation qui contribua au gain de la bataille de Mollwitz. Le prince Léopold I d'Anhalt-Dessau, l'organisateur de l'infanterie prussienne, l'avait déjà introduite dans sa garde en 1698.

52. Fusil allemand, à répétition, à coulisse, à six coups successifs, du dix-septième siècle. — Musée de Sigmaringen.

53. Fusil allemand, à revolver, à cylindre tournant, à quatre coups. Fin du dix-huitième siècle. — Musée de Sigmaringen.

54. Carabine revolver de huit coups, à cylindre tournant, pour cavalerie.

55. Fusil à raquette, du dix-huitième siècle. — Arsenal de Berlin.

56 A et B. Batteries à percussion et à piston, inventées en 1807 par l'Ecossais Forsith.

57. Fusil double à percussion et se chargeant par la culasse (*Breach loading* en angl.), système Lefaucheux.

58.   Id.   id.   id.

Ce dernier dessin montre le tonnerre ouvert pour recevoir la charge.

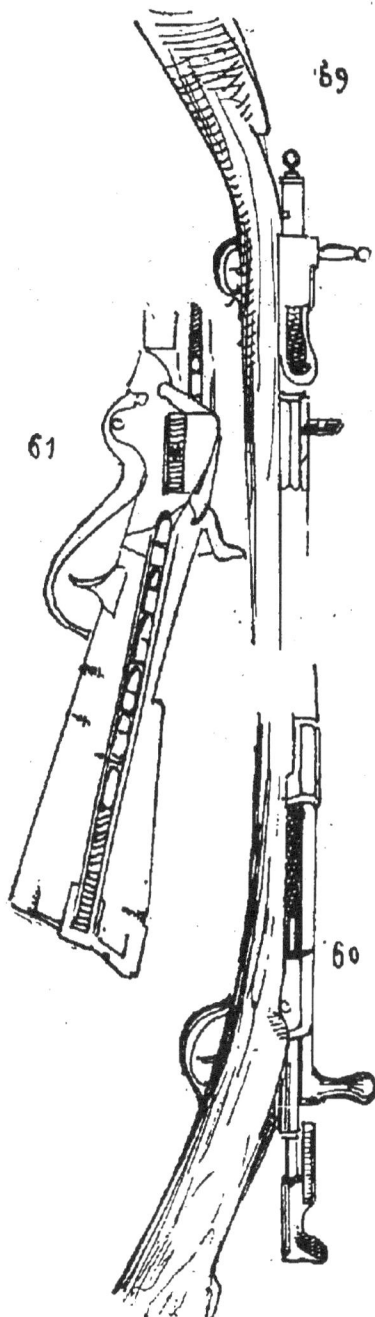

59. Fusil à aiguille prussien (*Zündnadelgewehr* en allem., *needle-gun* en angl.), inventé en 1827, par l'Allemand Nicolas Dreyse, né en 1787, mort en 1868.

L'arme est représentée ouverte et prête à recevoir la charge.

60. Fusil à aiguille français, inventé par M. Chassepot, en 1866, d'après le modèle Dreyse. Le fusil est représenté ouvert, prêt à recevoir la charge.

61. Fusil à répétition Spencer, du milieu du dix-neuvième siècle, imaginé par MM. Spencer et Winchester. Ce fusil à répétition est une ancienne invention allemande, comme le démontre l'arme conservée au musée de Sigmaringen. (V. p. 545, n° 52.) Feu Dreyse avait aussi fait plusieurs essais déjà, en 1828, avec un fusil à répétition de son invention, mais le trouvant inférieur à son fusil à aiguille, il l'abandonna. Son fils a cependant repris actuellement ce projet et continue à faire faire des essais.

LE PISTOLET

Cette arme, dont le nom dérive probablement de *pis-tallo*, pommeau, garniture, et non pas de *Pistoja*, ville, paraît originaire de Perouge, où, en 1364 déjà, on a fabriqué des *petits canons à main* qui avaient la longueur d'un palme [1].

Aucun musée ne possède, que je sache, un pistolet à mèche, et la *Moenchsbüchse* au musée de Dresde, le petit canon à main, à *rape*, dont il a été question dans le chapitre historique et dans l'introduction de celui-ci, paraît avoir précédé les fusils à rouet, les plus anciennes armes de ce genre encore existantes.

Le *coup de poing*, petit pistolet, que les Allemands appellent *Tercerol*, n'est pas d'invention moderne, car l'auteur possède une telle arme du seizième siècle à rouet, entièrement en fer, et dont le canon ne mesure pas 15 cent. Les pistolets à revolver aussi, comme les fusils à revolver, ont déjà existé au dix-septième et au dix-huitième, et ceux fabriqués de nos jours, parmi lesquels le revolver Colt est le plus réputé, ne peuvent pas être regardés comme le résultat d'une invention, mais comme le produit d'une reprise.

1. Le palme romain équivaut à peu près à 17 cent. 1/2.

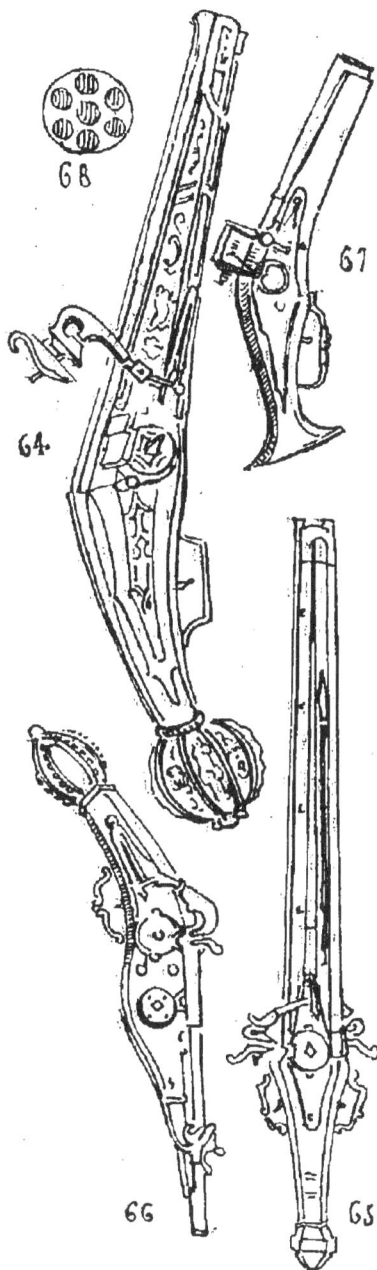

64. Pistolet à rouet du seizième siècle. C'est ce genre de pistolet dont était armée la cavalerie allemande et qui était l'arme des *Reîtres*.

65. Pistolet double à rouet, de la fin du seizième siècle. — Arsenal de Zurich. Le musée de Dresde possède de tels pistolets à rouet-double et à triple canon.

66. Pistolet à rouet et à double canon, du commencement du dix-septième siècle. — Tour de Londres.

67. Pistolet à rouet à sept coups, du seizième siècle. — Musée de Sigmaringen.

68. Volée du canon du pistolet précédent.

69

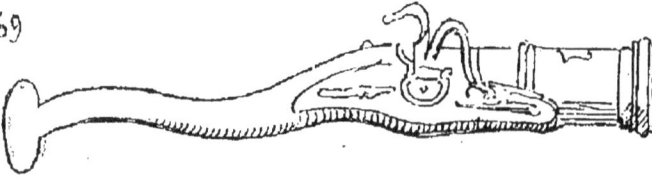

70

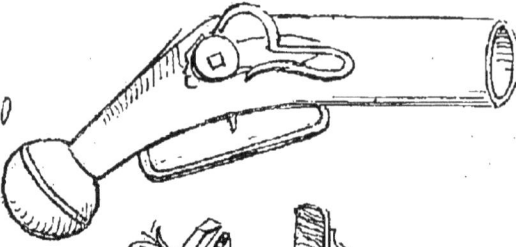

71

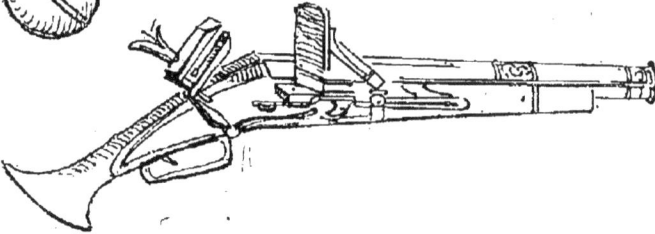

72

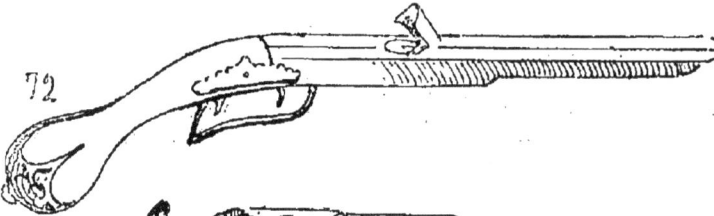

73

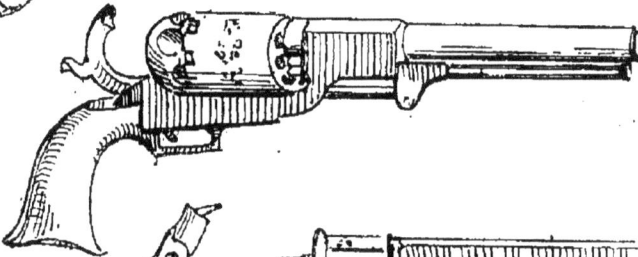

14.

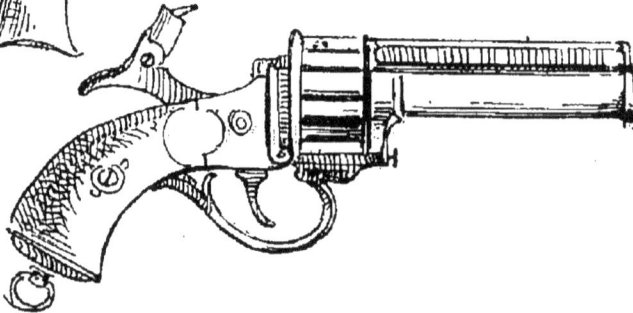

69. Pistolet-mortier à rouet, nommé en allemand *Katzenkopf*, (tête de chat), du dix-septième siècle.— Arsenaux de Woolwich et de Berlin.

70. Pistolet-mortier à rouet entièrement en fer, du dix-septième siècle. — Château de Lœwenburg sur le Wilhelmshöhe près Cassel.

71. Pistolet à batterie à silex, de la fin du dix-septième siècle. — Tour de Londres.

72. Pistolet à repoussoir, à silex, du commencement du dix-huitième siècle. — Musée de Prague et Gewehrkammer de Dresde.

73. Pistolet revolver Colt, imaginé par Samuel Colt des États-Unis, en 1835.

74. Pistolet revolver Mat, imaginé par M. Le Mat, il y a peu d'années.

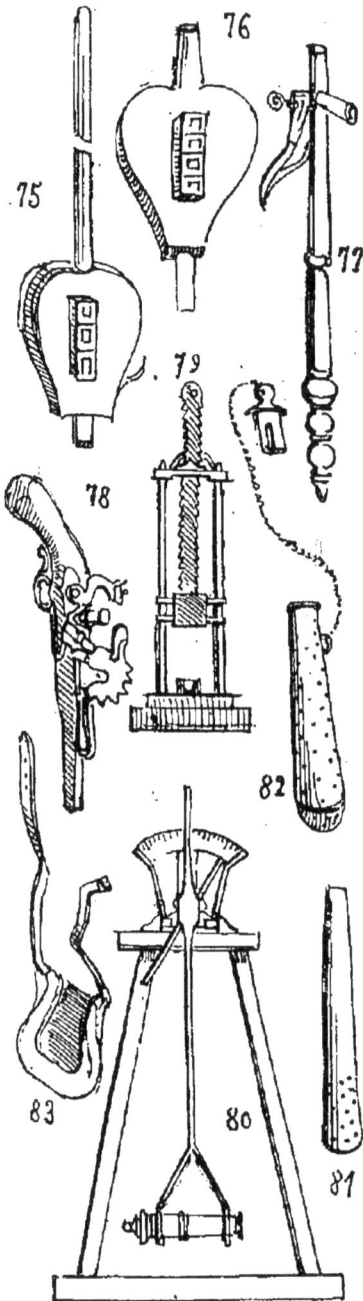

75. Tournevis - amorçoir pour fusils à rouet. — Arsenal de Berlin.

76.   Id.   id.
— Col. Ternow, à Berlin.

77. Tournevis - amorçoir pour fusils à rouet. — Musée de Prague et col. Spengel, à Munich.

78. Éprouvette de poudre à silex et à rouet.

79. Éprouvette de poudre, à engrenage.

80. Éprouvette de poudre, à pendule.

81. Couvre-mèche de mousquetaire, inventé par les Hollandais.

82. Couvre-mèche de grenadier bohémien. — Col. de l'auteur. On voit de pareilles pièces au musée historique du palais de Montbijou à Berlin, et à la collection d'armes du prince de Lobkowitz, à Raudnitz, en Bohême.

83. Sac de munition pour arquebusier, de la fin du quinzième siècle, d'après les dessins de Glockenthon. — Col. d'Ambras.

47

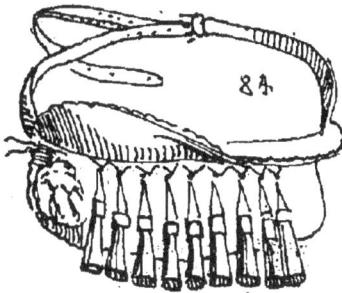

84. Baudrier dit buffleterie de mousquetaire[1], garni de capsules en bois (*Patronen Gürtel* en allem., angl.)

85.   Id.   id.

Cette buffleterie est garnie en plus du pulvérin, du sac à balles et de mèches.

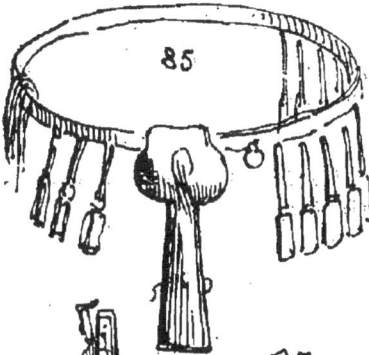

86. Amorçoir allemand de la fin du seizième siècle, en chêne incrusté d'ivoire et de cuivre doré. — Col. Llewelyn-Meyrick.

87. Amorçoir italien (*Zündpulverflasche* en allem., *primer* ou *tousch-boxe* en angl.), de la fin du seizième siècle. Il est en or. — Col. Llewelyn-Meyrick.

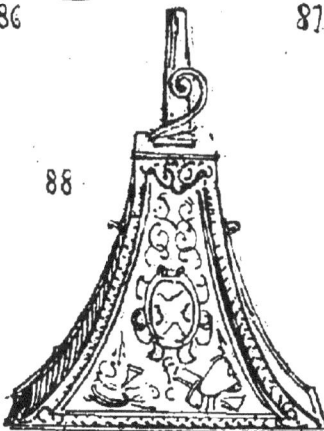

88. Poire à poudre allemande pour arquebusier, de la seconde moitié du seizième siècle.

1. Pour charger l'arquebuse on se servait de la poire à poudre. — On reconnaît donc facilement le mousquetaire à la buffleterie garnie de *capsules* appelées par les Allemands *Pulvermassen*.

89. Corbin à poudre (*Pulfer-horn* en allem., *powder-horn* en angl.) allemand, dit saxon, de 30 cent. de longueur, de la fin du seizième siècle. La corne blonde est ornée de belles gravures. La garniture est en fer. — Col. de l'auteur.

90. Poire à poudre (*Pulferflasche* en allem., *powder-flasks* en angl.), cuir bouilli et garni de fer.

91. Corbin à poudre, allemand, du seizième siècle, en corne de cerf, de 22 cent. de longueur. — Musée de Sigmaringen.

92. Poire à poudre, allemande, en ivoire, du dix-septième siècle; elle mesure 17 cent. — Musée de Sigmaringen.

93. Corbin à poudre, allemand, en ivoire, du seizième siècle, de 28 cent. de longueur. — Musée de Sigmaringen.

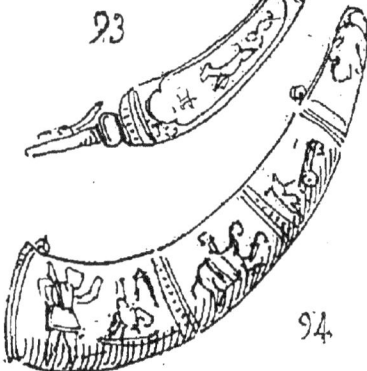

94. Corbin à poudre, allemand, du commencement du dix-septième siècle; il a 40 cent. de longueur. — Musée de Sigmaringen.

VIII

LE FUSIL A VENT

Le *fusil à vent* (*Vindbüchse* en allemand, *air-gun* en anglais) inventé par Guter de Nuremberg en 1560, et perfectionné successivement par Gerlach et par Sars à Berlin, Contriner à Vienne, Fachter à Liége, Martin Fischer à Suhl, Futter à Dresde, Schreiber à Halle (1760-1769), C. G. Werner à Leipzig (1750-1780), Gottsche à Mersebourg, Muller à Varsovie, Valentin Siegling à Francfort-sur-Mein, Vrel à Coblentz, Jean et Nicolas Bouillet à Saint-Étienne, Bate en Angleterre, Facka Speyer en Hollande, et autres, est une arme où l'explosion est produite par la dilatation subite de l'air comprimé au moyen d'une pompe pneumatique. On connaît deux espèces de fusils à vent : l'une, où le récipient se trouve dans la crosse; l'autre, où l'air est enfermé dans une boule de cuivre placée soit au-dessus, soit au-dessous du tonnerre. Ce fusil, dont l'usage est prohibé en France, doit être classé parmi les armes à répétition, puisque son canon peut recevoir jusqu'à vingt balles qui permettent de tirer autant de coups sans recharger. Il a servi à la guerre en Autriche, à la fin du dix-huitième siècle où il était l'arme spéciale de quelques compagnies.

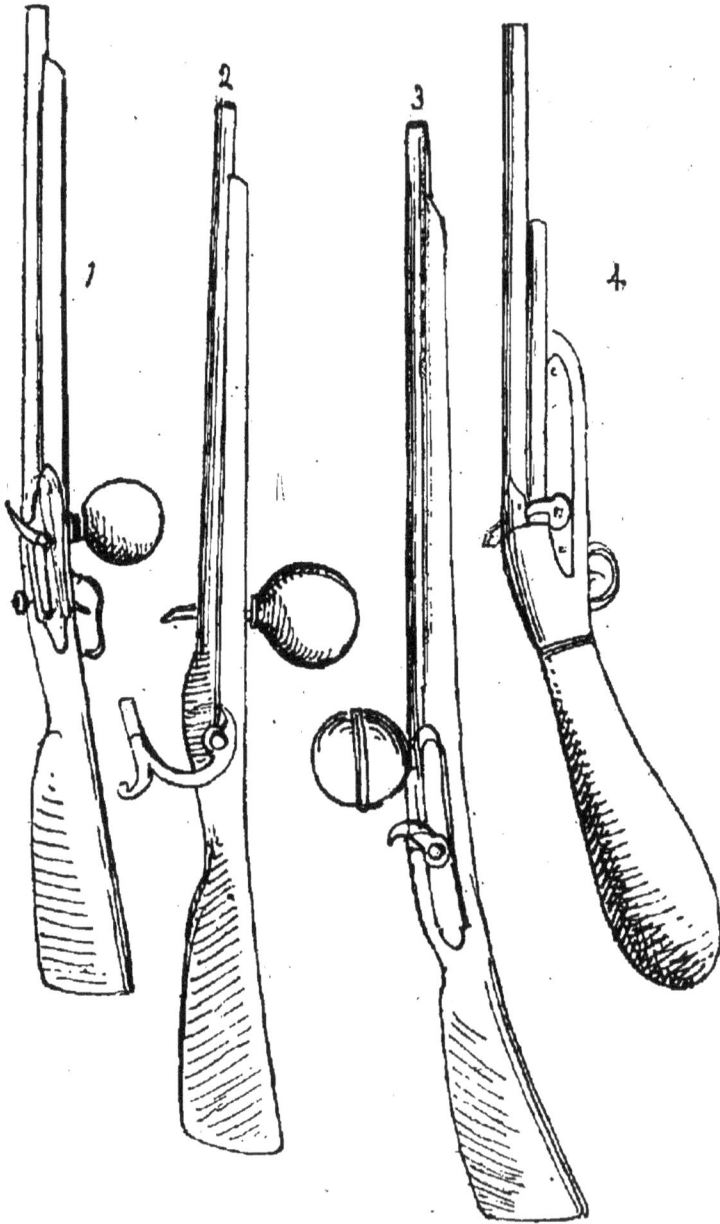

1. Fusil à vent, canon et récipient en cuivre. Ce dernier est placé au-dessous du canon. — Arsenal du prince de Lebkowitz, à Raudnitz en Bohême.

2.　　　　　　Id.　　　　　id.　　　　　id.

Un fusil à vent de la même construction, n° 1348, au musée d'artillerie de Paris, porte la signature : *T. C. Sars, à Berlin.*

3. Fusil à vent, où le récipient est placé au-dessus du canon œuvre de *G. Gerlach,* de Berlin. — Arsenal de Berlin. N° 1349, au musée d'artillerie de Paris, est construit dans ce même système.

4. Fusil à vent avec récipient ménagé dans la crosse; œuvre de *Contriner*, de Vienne. — Arsenal de Berlin. Le musée d'artillerie de Paris possède des fusils à vent où le récipient est également ménagé dans la crosse.

L'ART DE L'ARMURIER

ET DE L'ARQUEBUSIER[1]

MONOGRAMMES, INITIALES, ET NOMS D'ARMURIERS

———

En Orient, la fabrication des armes de luxe avait déjà atteint une très-grande perfection pour la *niellure* (2) et l'*incrustation* (*Tauschierarbeit* en allemand, *inlaid work* en anglais), aussi nommées *damasquinage*, et pour la *fabrication du damas* (3), particulièrement dans l'Hindoustan, en Perse

1. Aujourd'hui armurier désigne aussi bien le fabricant de l'armure défensive que celui des armes blanches et à feu. Primitivement le fabricant d'armures, seul, s'appelait *armurier*, et *arquebusier* celui qui fabriquait l'arme à feu portative et de gros calibre.

2. La *niellure* (*Email* ou *Schmelz tauschierarbeit* en allemand, *inlaid enamel work* en anglais), est l'incrustation de petits filets et d'ornements en émail noir (*galène*) dans des métaux précieux et autres; la galène est un minerai composé de plomb, de soufre et de matières terreuses. Il y a de la galène antimoniale, dite galène argentifère, de la galène de bismuth, de fer, et de la galène fausse.
Le *damasquinage* est l'incrustation de petits filets d'or ou d'argent dans le fer et dans l'acier.

3. Le *damas* dit aussi *acier de l'Inde* et *acier Wootz*, dont la fabrication ne doit pas être désignée par le verbe damasquiner, mais par celui de *damasser*, désigne l'*acier moiré* de différentes nuances. On confond continuellement les mots *nieller*, damasquiner et incruster, qui signifient tous, en définitive, *incruster en métal*, car l'incrustatation en bois et autres matières végétales s'appelle *marqueter*.
Le *damas* est de l'acier fondu dans lequel beaucoup de dessins moirés sont

au *Khoraçan*, et même à Java, lorsque la majeure partie de l'Europe se servait encore d'armes grossièrement forgées;

uniquement dus à la présence d'un carbure de fer cristallisé et mis à découvert par l'emploi des acides. D'autres de ces dessins proviennent de petites quantités de métaux tels que le platine, l'argent, le palladium. Il y a des damas noirs, gris, bruns, etc., qui, alliés à l'acier, le *damassent*.

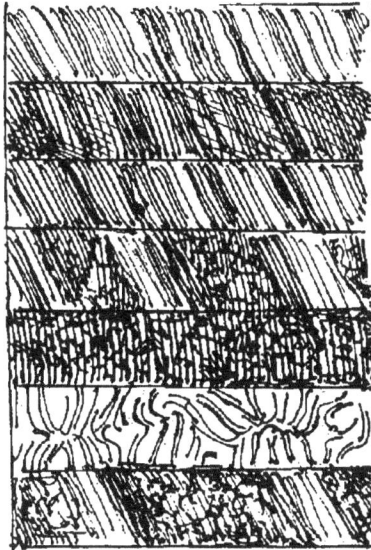

Clouet, en 1804, est le premier en France qui imita le damas, dont la fabrication a été grandement améliorée depuis par Degrand, Gurgey, Couleaux, et particulièrement par Stodart et Faraday en 1822. Les manufactures des Bouches-du-Rhône envoyèrent même leurs lames en damas platiné en Orient. Liége emploie depuis longtemps le damas rubanné et autres à la fabrication de ses canons de fusils et carabines de chasse, même pour les plus communs, qu'elle fournit à des prix d'un bon marché incroyable.

Le *damasquinage*, qui est donc un travail tout à fait différent de celui de la production du *damas*, et n'est autre chose que l'*incrustation*, s'opère de la manière suivante : après que le damasquineur a fait bleuir sur le feu la lame ou la plaque, il grave au burin le sujet qu'il veut figurer ; dans les creux il incruste un fil de métal qu'il achève de refouler à l'aide d'un *matoir* (outil qui sert à *mater* ou rendre mat, petit ciseau en acier non aigu). Quand le dessin a fait corps, il égalise le tout au moyen d'une lime fine et polit après. Le damasquinage était connu et pratiqué vers la fin du moyen âge et durant l'époque de la renaissance en Italie, en Espagne et en Allemagne. Il n'a été introduit en France que sous le règne de Henri IV.

mais l'art de repousser (4) le fer (*Treiben des Eisens* en allemand, *enbossment* en anglais) et celui de combiner des armures articulées complètes appartient bien plus au moyen âge chrétien et aux peuples du Nord de la plus récente civilisation, qu'à l'antiquité et aux Orientaux.

A la fin du quinzième siècle, le repousseur de l'Europe centrale, qui avait grandement dépassé pour son dessin l'armurier persan et grec, était arrivé au dernier degré artistique en même temps qu'à la plus grande solidité.

La renaissance, dont l'influence se fait sentir dans l'armurerie par ses ornements de détails et ses admirables ciselures (*Ausgestochene Arbeiten* en allemand, *chasings* en anglais) ne pouvait, dès lors, être qu'une cause de décadence; elle apportait des réminiscences d'une antiquité enjolivée, et dont les tendances et le goût de tradition n'étaient guère en harmonie avec la conception nouvelle et originale qui, après avoir créé le style gothique dans l'art et l'individualisme dans l'homme, avait produit la réforme et le droit nouveau.

L'armurier qui était arrivé à marteler le timbre du casque d'une seule pièce sans aide mécanique, avait cependant imaginé des armures dont l'ingénieuse conception et l'admirable travail feront toujours le désespoir du contrefacteur.

Peu de documents concernant l'armurerie du moyen âge sont parvenus jusqu'à nous. On a vu au chapitre qui traite des armures complètes de cette période la reproduction d'une miniature du treizième siècle, (p. 194), qui montre un armurier forgeant un heaume; outre cela, le *Weiss Kunig*, rédigé entièrement par l'empereur Maximilien Ier lui-même, vers la fin du quinzième siècle, montre l'atelier complet d'un de ces célèbres artisans.

---

4. On confond souvent le *repoussage* (*Treiben* en allemand, *enbossment* en anglais), la *ciselure* (*das Ausstechen* en allemand, *the chasing* en anglais), et la *gravure* (*das Stechen* en allemand, *the ingraving* en anglais), dont la différence est pourtant grande.

Ce sont particulièrement l'Italie et l'Allemagne qui ont joui d'une grande renommée pour la fabrication des armes défensives, tandis que l'Espagne était connue pour ses armes blanches, parmi lesquelles les lames de Tolède sont restées réputées.

En Italie, cette fabrication se faisait même souvent sur une si grande échelle, que les armuriers de la seule ville de Milan purent fournir en peu de jours, après la bataille de Macalo (1427), des armes et des armures pour 4,000 cavaliers et 2,000 hommes de pied. *Pilippo, Nigroli et ses frères*, qui travaillaient pour Charles-Quint et pour François Ier, *Jean Ambrogio l'aîné, Bernardo Civo* et le Milanais *Hieronimo Spacini*, l'auteur du célèbre bouclier de Charles-Quint, de cette époque, sont les armuriers italiens les plus connus auxquels il faut joindre les *Figino*, les *Ghinello*, les *Pellizoni* et les *Piatti*. On voit que c'est particulièrement durant l'époque de la renaissance que l'armurerie italienne a brillé de son plus grand éclat; ses produits du moyen âge ne peuvent pas soutenir autant la concurrence des produits allemands, hispano-musulmans, français et anglais.

Quant à l'arme à feu portative, l'Italie, où le pistolet peut aussi avoir été inventé, occupe une des premières places. *Antonio Picinino, Andrea de Ferrare*, du dix-septième siècle, pour les armes blanches; *Ventura Cani, Lazarino Cominazzi, Colombo* et *Badile*, ainsi que *Francino, Mutto, Berselli, Bonisolo, Giocatane* et *Cotel*, du dix-huitième siècle, pour les armes à feu, sont des noms qui n'ont pas passé dans l'oubli, car ce sont des signatures qui ont été recueillies sur des armes d'un travail supérieur.

En Espagne, c'est Madrid, Cordoue, Cuença, Catugel, Saint-Clément, Cuella, Badajoz, Valence, Séville, Valladolid, Saragosse, Orgoz, Bilbao et particulièrement Tolède qui sont les villes réputées pour leurs armureries d'armes blanches dont on trouvera plus loin près de deux cents monogrammes qui ne remontent cependant pas au delà de la seconde moitié du seizième siècle ; mais on peut admettre que la fabrication date, dans plusieurs de ces localités, du treizième siècle, et qu'elle est due, comme toute l'industrie espagnole, aux Arabes. L'acier dont se servaient ces fabriques était tiré des mines de Biscaye et de Guipuscoa.

L'Allemagne, où le moine Schwartz, de Fribourg, en Brisgau, avait, au commencement du quatorzième siècle, fait faire les premiers pas à l'artillerie européenne, brille déjà durant toute la seconde partie du moyen âge et autant à l'époque de la renaissance par ses magnifiques armes défensives, dont beaucoup passent dans les musées et collections privées pour des produits italiens et espagnols.

Après que Rodolphe de Nuremberg eut trouvé, en 1306, l'art de tréfiler le fer (*Drahtziehn*), qui mettait dorénavant la cotte de mailles rivée ou à points d'orge à la portée de presque tous les hommes d'armes, l'armure articulée dite à plates, dont toutes les améliorations concernant la défense et peut-être même l'invention sont dues aux armuriers d'outre-Rhin, sortait vers la fin du moyen âge et à l'époque de la renaissance, en objets d'art, des mains d'un *Desiderius Kollmann* d'Augsbourg, d'un *Lorenz Plattner* (l'armoirie de l'empereur Maximilien Ier), d'un *Wilhelm Seussenhofer* d'Inspruck (l'armoirie de Charles-Quint et de Ferdinand Ier), et d'autres qui ont laissé ces magnifiques armures, dont le goût se ressent malheureusement déjà de l'influence étrangère. Seussenhofer est mort en 1547, et Kollmann vivait vers 1532, époque où il a fourni, entre autres à Philippe d'Espagne, les belles armures qui existent encore.

L'admirable harnais complet pour homme et pour cheval, au musée de Dresde, est sorti probablement du même atelier ; l'artiste y a représenté les *Travaux d'Hercule*. Kollmann, à qui il fut payé 14000 écus, somme énorme relativement à l'époque, pour une seule armure, occupait alors

une des premières places parmi les armuriers allemands.

M. de Hefner-Alteneck a publié chez l'éditeur Brukmann à Munich ' les photographies de 86 des 170 dessins originaux à l'encre de Chine, projets destinés à plus de 25 armures complètes pour hommes et pour chevaux, qui furent

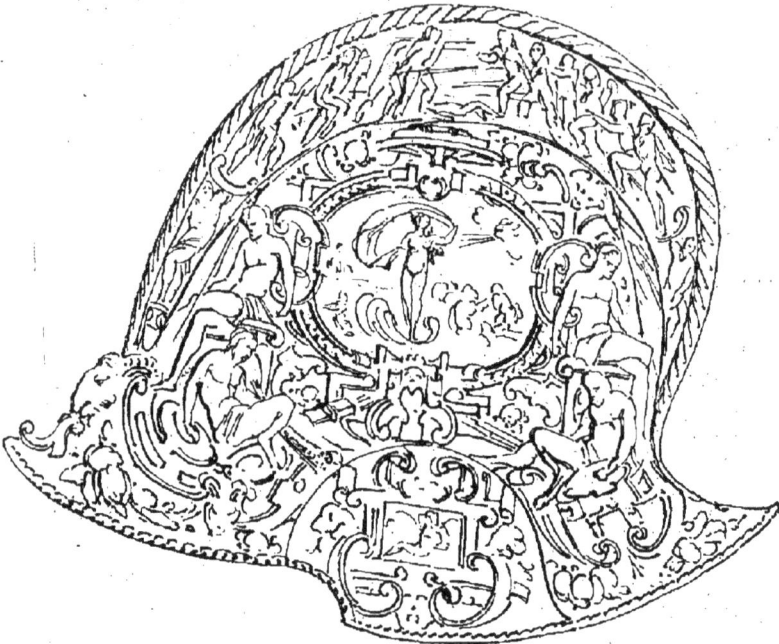

composés et exécutés en demi-grandeur par les peintres *Schwarz* (mort en 1597), *Van Achen*, *Brockberger* et *Jean Milich* (né à Munich en 1517, mort en 1572), pour les ateliers des armuriers de Munich et d'Augsbourg. Ces dessins qui portent les traces de leur emploi, et où tout indique la composition des peintres susnommés d'après des réminis-

1. *Dessins originaux de maîtres allemands pour armures de luxe destinées à des rois de France*, publiés par J. H. de Hefner-Alteneck, photographiés à l'institut photographique de Frédéric Brukmann, à Munich, in-folio.

Quelques autres de ces dessins sont la propriété du général chevalier de Hauslaub, à Vienne, et de M. Destailleur, architecte du gouvernement, à Paris, tous acquis en 1840 à la vente de la collection du conseiller d'État Kirschbaum.

cences de graveurs allemands (V. les reproductions aux pages précédentes de deux de ces dessins, pris au hasard), sont les projets de toutes les pièces des armures de François Ier, de Henri II et de l'empereur Rodolphe II, attribuées faussement jusque-là aux armureries italiennes et espagnoles.

L'Espagne aussi a tiré d'Augsbourg et de Munich les plus riches armures qui figurent encore à l'Armeria real de Madrid sous le nom d'armes italiennes et espagnoles. Grâce aux recherches que l'ambassadeur prussien, M. le baron G. de Werthern, a bien voulu faire faire dans les archives, le doute n'est plus permis.

Voici la copie textuelle de la lettre de M. le baron de Werthern :

« Nous avons eu ici l'hiver passé deux compatriotes, M. Bergenroth et M. Friedmann, qui étaient venus faire des recherches dans les archives de Madrid et de Simancas pour le compte du gouvernement anglais.

« Une observation jetée dans la conversation par M. Bergenroth, concernant l'influence de l'art allemand en Espagne, m'a donné l'idée d'engager M. Friedmann à rechercher dans les comptes rendus des règnes de Charles V et de Philippe II, s'il ne s'y trouvait pas des noms d'armuriers allemands auteurs de la plupart de ces belles armures conservées à l'arsenal de Madrid, et où le caractère de l'exécution paraît indiquer la main de l'artiste allemand.

« Je vous envoie le résultat de ces recherches qui ont pleinement confirmé mes prévisions. » Et plus loin : « M. Bergenroth aussi se souvient parfaitement d'avoir vu aux archives plusieurs comptes rendus du règne de Charles V, qui montrent encore d'autres noms de nos célèbres armuriers allemands.

« Il m'a promis d'en prendre copie à son retour, qui aura lieu l'hiver prochain, etc., etc.

« Madrid, 13 avril 1866.

« *Signé* : Baron G. DE WERTHERN,

« *ambassadeur prussien.* »

Extrait textuel et légalisé des archives :

Simancas Estado. Leg. 1565. Fol. 33.

Anuentas de la capa de don Philipe de Austria principe
de España.

Augsburg. — 755 1/4 escudos de oro por diez copas de plata
donado warpradoc aqui a razon de 17 1/2 y 16 flonucel marco.
— *Aug*. 25 hebr. 1549.

Augsbourg. — Por pagas compradas an Aqueta, 1720, due. —
Bruss. 30 may 1549.

Munich. — Por 8 arcabuzes à *Peter Pah von Minichen*, 100 escudos de oro. — *Antwerp*, 19 sept. 1549.

Augsbourg. — Por ciertas armur que ha de hacer maestre
Bulff, veino de Lanuete (*mousquet à rouet*), 100 escudos de
22 baçor. — *Aug*., 18 julio 1550.

Augsbourg. — A Camargo por 5 sacabuches (Passauer
Schwerter?) por il 80 escudos. — *Augusta*, 20 ag. 1550.

Augsbourg. — A *Colman* (Kollmann), *armero de Augusta*, 2,000
escudos de oro en cuenta de 3,000 que ha de aver por unas armur
que haze pasa mi sevoais. — *Augusta*, 22 oct. 1550.

Munich. — A *Peter Pah de Munich*, 52 escudos por ciertos
ascabuzer. — *Aug*. 10 oct. 1550.

Augsbourg. — A *Desiderio Colman* armero de Augusta, 400 duc.
en cuenta de loque a de aver por unas armas negras que haze
para mi. — *Augusta*, 27 febr. 1551.

Munich. — A *Peter Pah* por quatro carabuzes 41 escudo. —
19 marco 1551.

Munich. — A maestro *Bolfe* (Bulff) 250 escudos por unas armas
que hace por mi persona 24 mace y 150 mas por ciertas armas
que hace por don Antonio de Toledo.

Augsbourg. — A maestro *Haur* (*Staur*?) de Augusta, 50 du-
cados por ciertas armas que muado hacer y quedavon con il.
— *Augusta*, 10 de abril 1551.

Munich. — A M. *Pedro Mallero*, de Minich, 114 escudos por
ciertas pieças de malla. — *Aug*., 7 abr. 1551.

Munich. — A *Pedro*, arquebuzes de Munich, 40 escudos por
ciertos arquebuzes. — 28 abr. 1551.

Munich. — A maestro *Vulff* (Bolfe? Bulf?), 225 escudos, 200 por
unas armas doradas que ha de hacer y 25 por unas pillar que
hiro por un harneo blanco que havia hecho para mi personio. —
Aug., 2 mayo 1551.

Augsbourg. — A *Colman*, 650 escudos por una armas. —
12 mayo 1551.

Munich. — A *Pedro* de Minich, 30 escudos por un arcabuz y
20 escudos por los moços de Colman de merced.

Une autre importante découverte pour l'histoire des origines d'œuvres d'art et pour la gloire des armuriers allemands de cette époque, est celle de l'archiviste d'Inspruck.

M. Schoenherr a trouvé dans les archives de la capitale du Tyrol la preuve que :

« *Joerg Seusenhofer*, d'Inspruck, maître *armurier* et *armoirier* (*sic*) de Ferdinand Ier, avait été chargé de l'exécution d'un harnais magnifique que son maître destinait à François Ier, roi de France. Le cadeau terminé ne fut cependant point expédié, et c'est ce même harnais que Napoléon Ier fit enlever à la collection d'Ambras, à Vienne, pour l'envoyer à Paris, où il fut reçu en séance solennelle comme *armure de François Ier*[1]. Deux autres harnais du même maître furent cependant expédiés aux fils de François Ier ; le fond de ces harnais, qui devait être d'abord en or, ne put être terminé à temps, de sorte que les ornements furent exécutés sur un fond noir.

« Seusenhofer fabriqua aussi six autres harnais pour la cour de France, et un bon nombre d'armures pour les rois d'Angleterre et de Portugal. »

Passau et Solinge se sont signalés de bonne heure pour la fabrication des armes blanches, dont la qualité était aussi appréciée que celle des lames de Tolède.

Georg Springenklee, armurier célèbre de Passau, localité dont la renommée pour les armes remonte à la fin du treizième siècle, obtint au commencement du quatorzième de l'empereur Charles IV des armoiries (*deux épées croisées*) pour sa corporation. Une autre marque très-ré-

---

1. C'est cette armure qui se trouve au Louvre, où elle passe pour une œuvre italienne.

pandue, le *loup*[1], que l'on croit avoir été accordée à la corporation des armuriers de Passau par l'archiduc Albert, en 1349, se trouve aussi sur d'anciennes armes de Solinge, où *Clément Horn* et *Johann Hopp* sont des armuriers qui florissaient au commencement du seizième siècle. La fabrication d'armes de cette dernière ville remonte également vers la fin du douzième siècle, où elle y fut introduite par des armuriers styriens. Pendant lontemps Solinge avait son *contrôle de fabrique* établi sur la grande place du marché, où tont armurier était obligé de faire vérifier et estampiller ses produits, contrôle qui fut supprimé sous la domination française.

Le damasquinage ou l'incrustation, dont il a été déjà question au commencement de ce chapitre, a été pratiqué en Allemagne dès la fin du moyen âge avec une solidité qui dépasse celle des armuriers espagnols, comme le démontrent les magnifiques armures de l'arsenal impérial de Vienne.

Pour l'arme à feu portative, l'Allemagne n'a presque pas eu de rivale.

Les belles armes de précision du seizième et du dix-septième siècle conservées dans les musées et collections, sont toutes allemandes, — à l'exception de quelques pièces italiennes et françaises de parade, remarquables par leur ciselure et leur sculpture.

Dès le seizième siècle, la fabrication des armes à feu s'était tellement répandue dans ce pays, qu'il n'y avait pas de petite ville privée d'un armurier capable de confectionner une arquebuse sans aide mécanique. *Valentin*, *Stephan Klett* et *Clauss Reitz* à Suhla (Suhl), dans le comté de Henneberg, avait déjà, en 1586, deux fabriques si importantes, qu'ils ont pu fournir à la Suisse 2,000 armes à feu diverses et 500 mousquets de précision. On a vu que la

---

1. Les épées ainsi estampillées sont très-recherchées par les habitants du Caucase.

rayure du canon avait été inventée en Allemagne à la fin
du quinzième siècle, et la platine à rouet et la batterie du
chenapan au seizième siècle, ainsi que le fusil à vent et le
fusil à aiguille.

La France, qui doit avoir eu certainement des armuriers
habiles, a laissé tomber les noms des artistes dans l'oubli,
car, nonobstant de longues recherches, je n'ai pu trouver
ni de noms ni de monogrammes d'armuriers français
remontant au delà du commencement du dix-septième
siècle.

Chamblay (Oise) était pourtant réputé au moyen âge par sa
fabrication de cottes de mailles que d'anciens auteurs désignent à tort sous le nom de *doubles mailles*, car il n'existe
de cette provenance qu'une seule espèce de mailles *plus ou
moins serrées*. On peut admettre que la *batterie à silex* qui
remplaça la batterie chenapan à la pyrite sulfureuse été
inventée en France dans la première moitié du dix-septième, siècle mais on ignore où et par qui.

Parmi les armuriers français modernes, il faut citer les
Delvigne, les Minié, les Lepage, les Gastine-Renette, les
Lefaucheux et les Chassepot.

L'armurerie anglaise ancienne a laissé de beaux casques
de joute et de guerre dits *heaumes*, qui sont particulièrement remarquables par leur solidité et l'épaisseur de leur
acier. Malheureusement, aucun nom de ces habiles artisans n'a été conservé, et les monogrammes aussi sont
très-rares.

Mêmes observations pour la Suisse et les Flandres,
quoique ce dernier pays ait joué un rôle important dans
la fabrication des armes à feu de gros calibre dès l'apparition du canon, et qu'il est aujourd'hui si réputé pour ses
armes de chasse et de guerre fabriquées à Liége. Quant à la
Russie, c'est la ville de Toula qui s'est signalée par des fabriques d'armes fondées en 1712.

L'art de l'armurerie hindoue, célèbre déjà dans l'antiquité, particulièrement pour les boucliers forgés à froid à Delhi, où on les confectionna en deux pièces, celle du milieu et celle qui forme la bordure a conservé sa réputation jusqu'à ce jour. Chose remarquable! plus le bouclier hindou était couvert d'ornements, moins il avait de prix, car les fleurs damasquinées ou incrustées ne servaient qu'à cacher les défauts du travail.

Gwalior et *Lushkur* étaient renommés pour les armes blanches, *Nurwur* et *Lahor* pour les armes à feu, et *Nurwur* et *Shahjehanabad* célèbres par les armures damasquinées et les cottes de mailles, ont été aussi réputés par les beaux produits de leurs armes blanches.

La Perse, comme l'Hindoustan, continuent à fabriquer ces armures damasquinées (casques, brassards, petits boucliers ronds, plastrons et cottes de mailles, dont beaucoup sont rivés, dits à *grains d'orge*), où les formes sont aussi belles qu'elles étaient au quinzième et au seizième siècle.

Les fabriques d'armes à feu portatives les plus importantes de l'Europe vers la fin du dix-huitième siècle, étaient :

En Allemagne, celles de Saint-Blasien, dans la Forêt-Noire ; Dantzig (établie en 1720), Chemnitz, Essen, Harzberg, dans le Hanovre, Klosterdorf, Linz, Olbernhau, Prague, Remscheid, Solinge, Spandau (établie en 1720), Suhl, Teschen et Wiener-Neustadt ;

En Italie, celles de Brescia, Florence, Milan et Turin ;

En Espagne, celles d'Esqualada, Oviedo, Plascencia, Sililos et Tolède ;

En France, celles d'Abbeville, Charleville, Saint-Étienne, Maubeuge et Versailles ;

En Angleterre, celles de Birmingham, Scheffield et Londres ;

En Belgique, celle de Liége ;

En Russie, celle de Toula.

MONOGRAMMES, INITIALES & NOMS D'ARMURIERS

MONOGRAMMES, INITIALES ET NOMS D'ARMURIERS ALLEMANDS.

Trébuchet est un nom d'armurier qui figure dans le poëme épique *le Percival*.

Schöyt, le fils du précédent (Willehalm, 356-16).

Kinn de Munleun, autre armurier, mentionné dans Willehalm (429-28).

Monogramme recueilli sur deux lames d'épée du quatorzième siècle, conservées à l'arsenal de Zurich. C'est probablement la marque du loup que Passau et Solinge ont employée simultanément à partir du treizième siècle.

Monogramme d'un armurier allemand recueilli sur une armure de la collection d'Ambras, le n° 37, attribuée à l'année 1476.

Marque des repousseurs (*Tauchirer*) d'Augsbourg.

M. Marque du commencement du seizième siècle.

Clément Horn, de Solingue, signature recueillie sur des épées du seizième siècle aux musées d'artillerie de Paris et de Dresde.

Clemens Horum est la marque en latin de ce même armurier recueillie sur une épée à deux mains au musée d'artillerie de Paris.

H. K. Initiales relevées sur une arquebuse à rouet, à canon rayé, du commencement du seizième siècle. — Musée d'artillerie de Paris.

I. et W. Initiales relevées sur une arquebuse à canon rayé à rouet, du milieu du seizième siècle, au musée d'artillerie de Paris.

M. W.   Id.   Id.

F. L. F. H. V. ZZ.   Id.   Id.

Boest der Junge, nom recueilli sur un pistolet à rouet, daté de 1569, conservé à la Tour de Londres.

P. O. V. G. Initiales relevées sur une arquebuse à rouet, à canon rayé, et datées de 1590. — Musée d'artillerie de Paris.

Peter Munster, recueillie sur une lame d'épée qui porte en outre la marque du *loup*. Le nom de cet armurier, du seizième siècle, ainsi que celui de son frère **Andreas Munster**, se trouvent aussi sur des épées au musée de Dresde. Peter Munster a signé également une magnifique épée conservée au musée de Sigmaringen. (V. n° 63.)

H couronnée est la marque de l'armurier d'armures (Plattner) qui a confectionné l'armure de tournoi de l'empereur Maximilien Ier (1459-1519), ainsi que l'épée de ce monarque, conservées à la collection d'Ambras.

Ce monogramme n'est pas celui d'un armurier; il est composé de l'initiale de Maximilien II, et a été recueilli sur une hallebarde datée de 1566. — Musée d'artillerie de Paris.

Monogramme recueilli sur une hallebarde allemande de la fin du seizième siècle, qui montre les armes d'Autriche. — Musée d'artillerie de Paris.

Schönberg (J. A. V.) est le nom d'un célèbre armurier de Munich du seizième siècle, dont plusieurs ouvrages se trouvent à l'arsenal de cette ville.

Ambrosius Gemlich et **Wilhelm Seusenhofer**, tous les deux de Munich, étaient des armuriers de Charles-Quint (1516-1558) et de Ferdinand Ier.

Jörg Seusenhofer et **Kollmann Helmschmitd** [1], Plattner (armuriers d'armures) d'Augsbourg, travaillaient au seizième siècle, et expédiaient beaucoup d'armes en Espagne.

Franz Grosschedl, à Landshut, qui a travaillé vers 1568, et à qui le duc de Bavière a payé 1325 flor. pour une seule cuirasse.

1. « Forgeur de casques. »

Martin Hofer, de Munich, a travaillé vers 1578.

Anton Pfeffenhauser, d'Augsbourg, vers 1580.

Paul Schaller, vers 1606.

Antonin Miller, d'Augsbourg, vers 1592.

Paul Vischer, de Landshut, vers 1600.

Johann Allich.

Meves Berns, de Solingue.

Peter Brock.

Clemens Koller.

Johann Kirschbaum.

Clemens Meizen.

Johann Moum.

Heinrich et **Peter Pather.**

Hans Prum de Mesene.

C. Pols.

Peter Wersberg.

Ces quinze noms d'armuriers se trouvent sur des armes, la plupart du seizième siècle, au musée de Dresde.

Bartholomes Hachner est la signature d'un armurier recueillie sur une arquebuse à rouet à canon rayé, et dont le bois est incrusté de plaques dessinées et gravées.

T. est une marque recueillie sur une arquebuse de chasse allemande à rouet, de la fin du seizième siècle.— Musée d'artillerie de Paris.

Johann Broch, signature recueillie sur une épée du seizième siècle au musée d'artillerie de Paris.

Monogramme et initiales recueillies sur une petite arquebuse allemande de la fin du seizième siècle. — Musée d'artillerie de Paris.

Monogramme d'armurier allemand du seizième siècle recueilli sur un cranequin d'arbalète.

Id.   Id.

Johannes Hopp, signature recueillie sur un glaive de justice du seizième siècle. — Musée d'artillerie de Paris.

J. P. 1595. Arme à feu allemande, magnifique, de la collection Erbach.

H. C. R.   Initiales relevées sur une arquebuse à rouet à canon rayé, et datées de 1600. — Musée d'artillerie de Paris.

H. V. K.   Initiales dont est marquée une arquebuse à rouet et à canon rayé au musée d'artillerie de Paris.

 Monogramme d'une arquebuse à rouet et à canon rayé. (Allemand. ?)

   Id.   Id.

Ces deux armures, au musée d'artillerie de Paris, pourraient bien ne pas être allemandes.

Johann Georg Hoffmann, signature recueillie sur une arquebuse à rouet et à canon rayé au musée d'artillerie de Paris.

Andreas M. Sigl.

Georg et **André Seidel.**   Id.   Id.

H. et **S.**   Id.   Id.

Johann Hauer, 1612. Signature d'armurier de Nuremberg, avec millésime, recueillie sur une armure patricienne gravée, qui se signale à l'arsenal impérial de Vienne par sa dossière, où l'armurier a repoussé la place des bosses dont le patricien était doté.

M. H. I. B.   Initiales recueillies sur une hallebarde allemande, datées de 1613. — Musée d'artillerie de Paris.

J. K.   1620. Initiales et date recueillies sur un fusil à silex[1] de la collection Erbach.

---

1. La date me paraît douteuse, puisque le fusil à silex n'a été introduit en France que vers 1640.

Monogramme d'une pertuisane allemande qui montre en outre les armes du prince Palatin, duc des Deux-Ponts, et le millésime de 1613. — Musée d'artillerie de Paris.

Angustinus Kolter, signature recueillie sur une arquebuse à rouet à canon rayé, et datée de 1616. La même signature sur une semblable arquebuse, datée de 1621. — Musée d'artillerie de Paris.

H. F. 1638. Recueillies sur des armes à feu.

Johannes Keindt, de Solingue, signature recueillie sur une épée d'homme d'armes de la première moitié du dix-septième siècle, conservée au musée d'artillerie de Paris.

Mierovimus Léger, signature recueillie sur une arquebuse allemande à rouet à canon rayé, et datée de 1632. — (Musée d'artillerie de Paris.

T. A. M. 1630. Arme à feu de la collection Erbach.

H. V. Initiales recueillies sur une arquebuse allemande à rouet, et qui servait à la chasse. Elle est datée de 1656. — Musée d'artillerie de Paris.

Jottan Gsel Artzberg est la signature d'un armurier allemand[1] sur une arquebuse à rouet. — Musée d'artillerie de Paris.

Matheus matl, signature d'une arquebuse à canon rayé, et datée de 1661. — Musée d'artillerie de Paris.

Hans Heinrich Deiler, à Frankfurt, 1663. Arme à feu à canon rayé, de la collection Erbach.

Georg Hoch, 1654. Arme à feu, de la collection Erbach.

L Initiale, probablement celle de l'empereur Léopold (1660-1705), recueillie sur un couteau de brèche allemand. — Musée d'artillerie de Paris.

Killian Zollner, de Salzbourg. Arquebuse de chasse à rouet, à l'arsenal de Berlin.

Ich. Sommer, à Barnberg, 1685, réputé pour ses arquebuses.

Hans Breiten, signature d'arquebuse à canon rayé, et datée de 1666. — Musée d'artillerie de Paris.

1. Ce *Gzel* pourrait bien être Suisse.

Breitenfelder, arme à feu de la collection Erbach.

Georg Alt. F. A., signature d'une arquebuse à canon rayé, et datée de 1666, au musée d'artillerie de Paris.

Dietrich Veban, signature d'une arquebuse à canon rayé, et datée de 1668. — Musée d'artillerie de Paris.

Ioh. Ulrich Tilemann, de Marpurg (Marburg), 1676, signature recueillie sur un fusil à silex, de la collection Erbach.

Marius Linck, à Prague, de la seconde moitié du dix-septième siècle. — Tour de Londres.

H. Nic. Markloff, à Hanau, 1680, fusil à silex de la collection Erbach.

Wilhelm Eïch, du dix-septième siècle, au musée d'artillerie de Paris.

Ian Sander, de Hanovre, signature recueillie sur une arbalète (hanovrienne) datée de 1669. — Musée d'artillerie de Paris.

Johann Gutzinger, 1677, signature recueillie sur un gros fusil de rempart et sur un fusil de rempart, daté de 1677.

Clément Poëter, de Solinge, signature recueillie sur une épée du dix-septième siècle, au musée d'artillerie de Paris.

Hans Jacob Stumpf, de Mossbrunn, armurier et graveur à l'eau forte, en 1682.

Johann Martin, signature sur une arquebuse à canon rayé et datée de 1684. — Musée d'artillerie de Paris.

Leonhardies Bieslinger, de Vienne, signature sur une arquebuse à canon rayé, à mèche, à serpentin, qui est datée de 1687. — Musée d'artillerie de Paris.

Daniel Eck, de Nordlinger, signature sur une arquebuse à rouet et à canon rayé, datée de 1688. — Musée d'artillerie de Paris.

H. Martin Müler est la signature recueillie sur un mousquet à canon rayé de la fin du dix-septième siècle.

Andreas Prantner a signé une carabine qui est datée de 1675, et conservée à la Tour de Londres.

P. V. 1678, recueillis sur une haquebuse à la Tour de Londres.

49

Simon Ruef ou **Rvef**, in Filwang (?), est la signature que porte une arquebuse à rouet à canon rayé, et daté de 1689.

H. P. réunis en monogramme, est une autre marque qui se trouve sur cette même arquebuse.

A. Wasungen, 1690. Fusil à silex de la collection Erbach.

Heinrich Keimer, nom d'armurier qui a signé une arquebuse à rouet à canon rayé, et datée de 1691. — Musée d'artillerie de Paris.

Léon Georg Dax, nom qui a été recueilli sur une arquebuse à rouet et à canon rayé au musée d'artillerie de Paris; elle date de la fin du dix-septième siècle.

Baissellmans Schachner, à Inspruck, arquebuse à rouet et à canon rayé, au musée d'artillerie de Paris.

Johann Adam Alter, nom d'armurier recueilli sur une arquebuse à rouet à canon rayé.

Andreas Zaruba, de Salzbourg, est le nom d'un armurier recueilli sur une arquebuse à rouet et à canon rayé.

Johann Seitel, avec la date de 1704, se trouve sur une arquebuse à rouet à canon rayé, au musée d'artillerie de Paris.

Georg Dinckl, du Haut-Tyrol, signature gravée sur une arquebuse à rouet et à canon rayé. — Musée d'artillerie de Paris.

Joseph Hamerl, de Vienne, a signé une arquebuse à rouet et à canon rayé, conservé au musée d'artillerie de Paris.

T. P. C. D. G. E. B. 1702, initiales recueillies sur un fusil à silex de la collection Erbach.

Wilhelm Brabender est une signature d'armure allemande N° $\frac{10}{35}$, à la Tour de Londres.

Stanislaus Paczelt, nom d'armurier gravé sur un fusil de chasse, daté de 1738. — Tour de Londres.

W. est l'initiale qui se trouve sur un esponton allemand du règne de Charles VI (1711-1740) au musée d'artillerie de Paris.

Chiffre de Charles VI (1711-1740).

Ces deux monogrammes, recueillis sur un esponton allemand, sont formés des initiales de Marie-Thérèse et François de Lorraine, qui avait épousé l'impératrice en 1738. — Musée d'artillerie de Paris. Le dernier est cependant aussi pareil à celui du palatin Charles-Théodore.

Écusson recueilli sur un épieu allemand de chasse, du dix-septième siècle. — Musée d'artillerie de Paris.

Wilfing, signature sur une arquebuse à rouet, du commencement du dix-huitième siècle. — Musée d'artillerie de Paris.

Daniel Anthoine, de Berlin, signature recueillie sur un petit épieu allemand, d'officier prussien, du règne de Frédéric II (1740-1786).

Utter, établi à Varsovie, a signé une arquebuse à rouet à canon rayé, et datée de 1759. — Musée d'artillerie de Paris.

Joseph Graf et ⎰ sont la signature et les initiales d'un armurier allemand recueillies sur une carabine.

I. A.

Turschen-Reith, inscription recueillie sur une carabine.

Ulrich Wagner, d'Eychstett,   Id.

Hartmann est le nom d'un armurier allemand qui a travaillé à Amsterdam, et de qui le musée d'artillerie de Paris possède un mousqueton à batterie (silex).

Rewer, à Dresde, nom d'armurier dont est signée une carabine à rouet, datée de 1797. — Tour de Londres.

Daniel Heishaupe, à Ulm, est l'armurier du milieu du dix-huitième siècle qui a signé la carabine à batterie (silex) conservée au musée d'artillerie de Paris sous le n° M. 343.

Zwalter, signature d'une carabine à batterie (silex).

Eckart, de Prague,   Id.

Pgerttel, de Dresde,   Id.

Johann Hereiter, de Salzbourg, est la signature recueillie sur une carabine rayée, conservée au musée d'artillerie de Paris.

Riegel, à Zweibrücken, armurier du dix-huitième siècle, qui a signé un fusil à batterie (silex), conservé au musée d'artillerie de Paris.

Andréas Gans, à Augsbourg, a signé le fusil de chasse allemand, conservé sous le n° M. 1288, au musée d'artillerie de Paris.

Spazierer, à Prague,   Id.,   M. 1289.

Picart Ohringen,   Id.,   M. 1291.

T. W. Peter, in Ottingen,   Id.,   M. 1292.

Ertel, à Dresde,   Id.,   M. 1294.
et dans la collection Erbach.

Christian, à Vienne,   Id.,   M. 1297.

F. L. L. I. G.   sont les initiales d'un armurier de Bayreuth, qui a signé un fusil de chasse allemand, conservé au musée d'artillerie de Paris.

Georg Keiser, de Vienne, signature recueillie au musée d'artillerie de Paris.

Christoph Joseph Frey, à Munich.

Adam Kulnic,   Id.

Heinrich Kapel,   Id.

Valentin Siegling, à Francfort-sur-Mein, auteur d'un fusil à vent du dix-huitième siècle, au musée d'artillerie de Paris.

Fi. Bosier, à Darmstadt,   Id.

Vrel, à Coblentz,   Id.

S. Gerlach, à Berlin,   Id.

S. Gerlach, à Meerholz. Fusil à vent. — Collection Erbach.

Müller, à Varsovie. — Musée d'artillerie de Paris.

Contriner, à Vienne.   Id.

Stephan Stockmar, à Postdam, mort en 1782, réputé pour ses fusils.

J. C. Sars, à Berlin, réputé pour ses fusils à vent.

C. Z. *avec la moitié d'une roue de voiture*, est la marque de la fabrique de **Ziegler**, de Dresde, du dix-huitième siècle, réputé pour ses lames d'épées.

Valentin Makl, armurier allemand, établi à Copenhague, a signé un pistolet à batterie (silex), au musée d'artillerie de Paris.

J. A. Kuchenreiter, de Regensburg, signature d'un pistolet à batterie (silex), au musée d'artillerie de Paris. Cet armurier est très-réputé en Allemagne.

Joh. Andreas Kuchenreiter, signature du même armurier recueillie sur un fusil à silex, du commencement du dix-neuvième siècle, au musée de Sigmaringen.

I. I. Behr, signature recueillie sur un fusil de rempart du dix-huitième siècle. (Voir p. 582.)

May, à Manheim,   Id.

Georg Koint,   Id.

Nock a signé un fusil de rempart daté 1793.

Stirlets a signé un fusil de rempart.

G. Nuterisch, à Vienne, est un armurier de la seconde moitié du dix-huitième siècle, qui a signé une carabine conservée à la Tour de Londres.

C. E. F. sont des initiales d'armurier recueillies sur un fusil à silex de la collection Erbach.

H. T. à Heubach,   Id.   Id.

J. Belen, Auguste Hortiz, F. G. Gurz, Isidore Soler, N. O. et **F. R. Bis**, sont des armuriers allemands dont les marques et monogrammes ont été donnés d'après les armes conservées dans l'Armeria real de Madrid, par don José Maria Marchesi, dans la table de monogrammes des armuriers qui ont habité Madrid de 1684 à 1849.

Manuel Soler, Martin Manuel, Samuel Til et **Ferdinand Dez**, sont des noms d'armuriers allemands recueillis sur le tableau des monogrammes d'armuriers en passage à Madrid et recueillis par le même auteur dans la même Armeria real.

ARMURIERS ALLEMANDS DES DERNIÈRES ANNÉES DU XVIIIᵉ SIÈCLE ET DU COMMENCEMENT DU XIXᵉ, RÉPUTÉS POUR LES ARMES A FEU ET A VENT.

Heinrich Albrecht, à Darmstadt. — Collection Erbach.
Anschütz, à Suhl.
D'Argens, à Stuttgard.
David Arnth, à Mergentheim.
V. Bartholomae, à Potsdam.
Baumann, à Villingen.
Behr, à Wallenstein. — Collection Erbach.
Brenneck.   Id.
Bergsträsser.   Id.
Bergh.   Id.
Calvis, à Spandau.
Claus, à Halberstadt. — Collection Erbach.
Cornelinus Coster.   Id.
Dinkel, à Hall.   Id.
S. Dison.   Id.
Ebert, à Sondershausen.
Echl aîné, jeune et puîné, à Berlin.
Echl (von der), à Berlin.
Léopold Eckhard, à Prague.
J. M. Felber, à Ravensberg.
Martin Fischer, à Suhl.
Christoph Wilhelm Freund, à Furstenau. — Collection Erbach.
Carl Freund, à Furstenau. — Collection Erbach.
Fremmery, à Berlin.
Friedler, à Ulm.
J. Georg, à Stuttgard.
Jean Grenet, à Perleberg. — Collection Erbach.
Gottschalck, à Ballenstædt.
J. C. Gorgas, à Ballenstædt.

Stack, — Collection Erbach.

Starck, à Vienne. **Id.**

Tanner, à Coethen. — Collection Erbach et musée de Dresde.

Töll, à Sahl.

Ulrich, à Eberndorf. — Collection Erbach.

Christian Voigt, à Altbourg.

J. Jos. Vett. — Collection Erbach.

Waas, à Bamberg.

Walster, à Saarbruck. — Collection Erbach.

M. Wertschgen, à Willingen.

Jean Zergh. — Collection Erbach.

Zurich, à Vienne.

Pfaff, à Cassel.

Pfaff, à Posen.

Pistor, à Schmalkalden. — Collection Erbach.

A. Pötzi, à Carlsbad.

Polz, à Carlsbad.

Presselmeyer, à Vienne.

Quade, à Vienne.

Rasch, à Brunsvick.

David Reme. — Collection Erbach.

Ioh. Rischer, à Spandau.

C. Rener. — Collection Erbach.

J. Roscher, à Carlsbad.

Manfried Reichert. — Collection Erbach.

J. And. Rechold, à Dolp. **Id.**

Peter Saeter, à Lemgo, en Lippe-Detmold. — Coll. Erbach.

Georg Reck (1782-1769). — Collection Erbach.

Schackau, à Bamberg.

Schedel, à Stuttgard.

Schirrmann, à Basewalck.

Schramm, à Zelle.

Fr. Schulze, à Breslau.

Spaldeck, à Vienne.

Harz, à Cranach.

Hauser, à Wurzbourg.

Heber, à Carlsbad.

Christ. Hirsch. — Collection Erbach.

Jach, à Spier, fusil double, canon damassé, de la collection Erbach.

F. Jaiedtel, à Vienne.   Id.   Id.

Junker, à Grambach. — Collection Erbach.

Jung, armurier allemand, établi à Varsovie.

Kaufmann. — Collection Erbach.

George Kayser, à Vienne. — Musée d'artillerie de Paris.

Kemmerer, à Thorn.

G. Kalb. — Collection Erbach.

H. H. Kappe.   Id.

J. C. Klett, à Potsdam.

Knopf, à Salzthal.

Krawinsky, à Posen.

Kruger, à Ratibor.

Kleinschmdt, à Wisterburg. — Collection Erbach.

J. Lammerer, à Cranach.

Lichtenfels, à Carlsruhe.

Lippe (Van der), à Stettin.

Lippert, à Coethen.

Marter, à Cologne.

Damien Marter, à Bonn.

Mathe, à Manheim. — Collection Erbach.

Muller, à Bernburg.

Muller, à Steinau.

Naumann, à Cassel.

Ioh. Neureuter, à Salzbourg. Très-réputé.

Nordmann, à Berlin.

Oertel, de Dresde, établi à Amsterdam.

M. Oït, a Wisbade.

Otto, à Brandebourg.

MONOGRAMMES, INITIALES ET NOMS D'ARMURIERS ITALIENS.

Danielo de Castelo Milano, de 1475, nom d'armurier recueilli au musée de Dresde, où, selon l'auteur de ce traité, on le croit à tort Espagnol.

A. B. en monogramme, vers 1480.

BAB Id.

S. Id.

Antonio Romero, célèbre armurier du seizième siècle.

Philippi Nigroli, de Milan, vers 1522.

S. P. Q. R. Initiales recueillies sur une rondache italienne du milieu du seizième siècle, au musée d'artillerie de Paris. Ce sont les initiales des mots *Senatus Populus que Romanus*.

Bartolam Biella, signature recueillie sur une arme de chasse damasquinée, au musée de Dresde.

Johannes de la Orta, signature recueillie sur une épée du milieu du seizième siècle, et qui porte les armes des Montmorency. — Musée d'artillerie de Paris.

Johannes de l'Orta, est une variété de la signature précédente qui se trouve sur une arme du musée de Dresde, rangée à tort dans l'école espagnole.

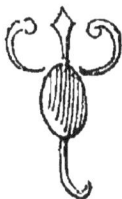

Monogramme d'armurier italien du commencement du seizième siècle, dit *le Scorpion*, recueilli sur une guisarme italienne de la collection Soeter, à Augsbourg.

Antonio Piccinino, signature recueillie sur N° $\frac{9}{60}$, rapière du commencement du dix-septième siècle, conservée à la Tour de Londres.

Monogramme d'armurier, recueilli sur une épée vénitienne[1], genre claymore, conservée au musée de
Sigmaringen.

Lazaro Lazaroni, à Venise, vers 1640, réputé pour ses armes
à feu.

Andrea, de Ferrare, a marqué une soi-disant claymore du
dix-septième siècle.—N° J. 118, au musée d'artillerie de Paris.

Ventura Cani, signature recueillie sur une arquebuse italienne, à rouet, du commencement du dix-septième siècle. —
Musée d'artillerie de Paris.

Lazarino Cominazzi (aussi **Commazzo**), signature d'un célèbre armurier, recueillie sur des pistolets, au musée de
Sigmaringen.

Lazarino Cominaco, signature du même armurier recueillie
sur une arquebuse à rouet, de la seconde moitié du dix-
septième siècle, et sur un fusil du dix-huitième siècle, n° M.
113 et 1285, au musée d'artillerie de Paris, ainsi que sur un
fusil à silex de la collection Erbach.

Colombo, nom recueilli sur un mousquet italien du dix-septième siècle. — Musée d'artillerie de Paris.

Matteo Badile, signature recueillie sur un pistolet, un mousqueton et une arquebuse à rouet, de la seconde moitié du dix-
septième siècle, au musée d'artillerie de Paris.

Geo. Bat. Francino, signature sur une arquebuse à rouet et
sur un pistolet, de la seconde moitié du dix-septième siècle,
au musée d'artillerie de Paris ; un pistolet avec la même signature se trouve à la Tour de Londres.

Geronimo Mutto ou **Motto**, du milieu du dix-huitième siècle.

Borselli, à Rome, a signé un fusil à rouet.

Laro Zarino ou **Lazaro Lazarino**, signature d'un pistolet à
batterie, du commencement du dix-huitième siècle.

Antonio Bonisolo,   Id.

---

1. Ces sortes d'épées étaient des armes à l'usage de la garde des doges et
s'appelaient *chiavona*.

Giocatane, signature recueillie sur un pistolet à batterie, du dix-huitième siècle.

Bartolomeo Cotel, armurier qui travaillait vers 1740, selon la signature recueillie sur un fusil, à la Tour de Londres.

Johandy, à Brescia, et **Postindol**, à Specia, des dernières années du dix-huitième siècle, sont réputés pour leurs armes à feu.

Carlo Contino, nom d'armurier, recueilli sur un fusil à silex, de la collection Erbach.

MONOGRAMMES ET NOMS D'ARMURIERS ESPAGNOLS ET PORTUGAIS.

C. A. Mora, vers 1586, recueillie au musée de Dresde.

Sébastien Hernandez, vers 1599, recueillie au musée de Dresde.

Johannes Rucoca,	Id.	Id.
Martinez Deivan,	Id.	Id.

Juan Vencinas est le nom de l'armurier qui a signé l'arbalète de Ferdinand Ier, de la collection Spengel, à Munich, et qui l'a faite vers 1533.

Thomas di Ajala est le nom d'un armurier du seizième siècle relevé sur des armes au musée de Dresde.

Quant aux armuriers de Tolède, on connaît les noms des plus renommés et leurs coins depuis la seconde moitié du seizième siècle jusqu'au dix-huitième, grâce à la publication de Don Manuel Rodriguez Palomino, qui en a fait un relevé exact dans les archives de l'Ayuntamiento. On y voit que plusieurs de ces maîtres ont aussi travaillé à Madrid, Cordova, Cuença, Catugel, Saint-Clément, Cuella, Badajoz, Séville, Valladolid, Saragosse, Lisbonne, Orgoz et Bilbao; mais les principaux centres renommés pour la fabrication des armes espagnoles étaient Tolède, Saragosse, Séville et Saint-Clément.

Des 99 monogrammes, les plus recherchés sont les *ciseaux* (n° 21), le *loup* ou la *chèvre* (n° 59), et celui du n° 76, dont se servit Lupus Aguado. Souvent, les armuriers espagnols ont fait accompagner le monogramme de leurs noms gravés soit sur la lame même, soit sur la soie (le bout de la lame qui entre dans la fusée du manche).

Voici la reproduction de ces monogrammes :

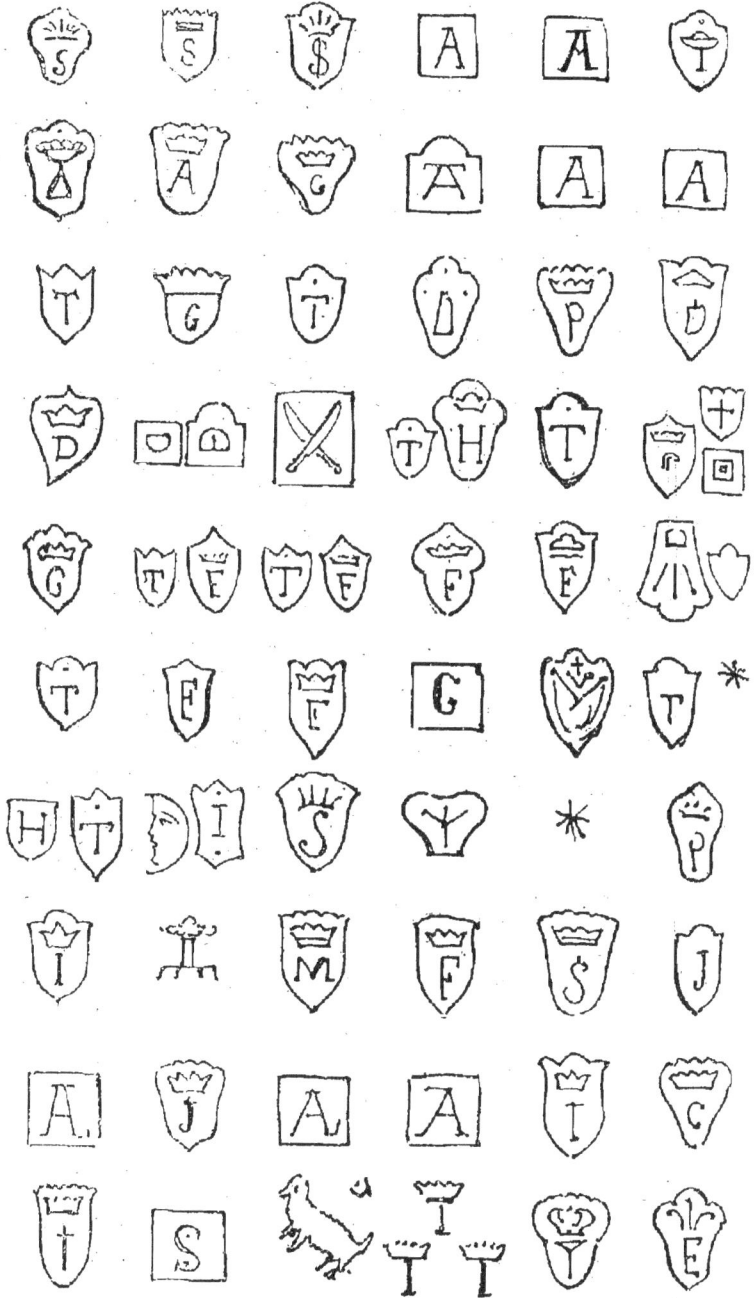

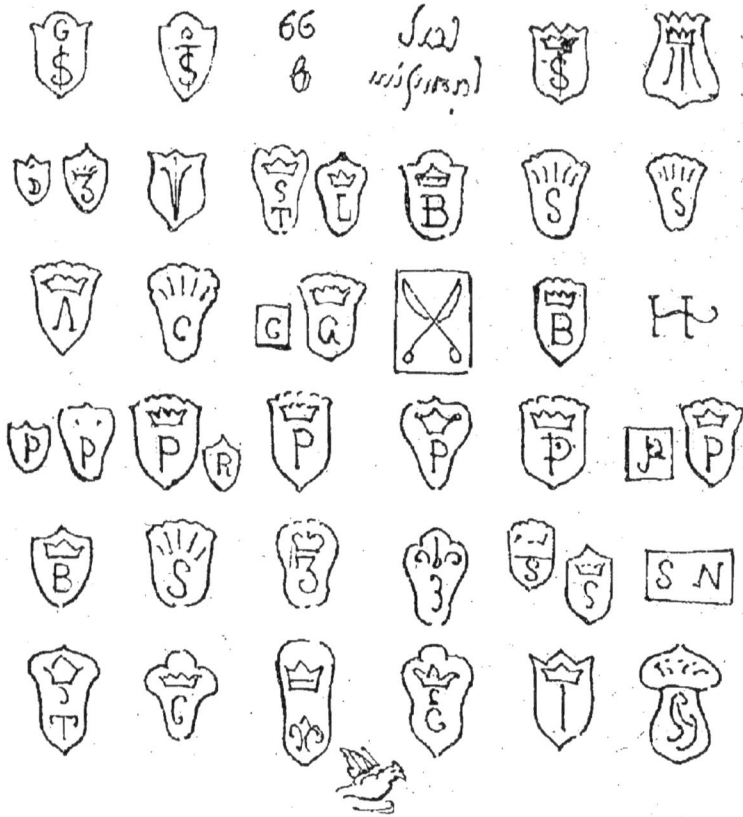

Tous ces monogrammes appartenant aux armuriers de Tolède, Madrid, Cordova, Cuença, Catugel, Saint-Clément, Cuella,
Badajoz, Séville, Valladolid, Saragosse, Orgoz et Bilbao ont été
placés dans l'ordre de la liste suivante :

1. Alonzo de Sahagun, le vieux, vers 1570.
2. Alonzo de Sahagun, le jeune, vers 1570.
3. Alonzo Perez.
4. Alonzo de los Rios, qui travailla à Tolède et à Cordova.
5. Alonzo de Caba.
6. Andres Martinez, fils de Zabala.
7. Andres Herraez, qui travailla à Tolède et à Cuença.
8. Andres Munesten, qui travailla à Tolède et à Catugel.
9. Andres Garcia.
10. Antonio de Buena.

11. Anton. Guttierrez.
12. Id.   Id.
13. Anton. Ruy, qui travailla à Tolède et à Madrid.
14. Adrien de Lafra, qui travailla à Tolède et à Saint-Clément.
15. Bartholome, de Nieva.
16. C. Alcado, de Nieva, qui travailla à Cuella et à Badajoz.
17. Domingo de Orosco:
18. Domingo Maestre, le vieux.
19. Domingo Maestre, le jeune.
20. Domingo Rodriguez.
21. Domingo Sanchez Clamade.
22. Domingo de Aquirre, fils de Hortuno.
23. Domingo de Lama.
24. Domingo Corrientez, qui travailla à Tolède et à Madrid.
25. Favian de Zafia.
26. Francisco Ruiz, le vieux.
27. Francisco Ruiz, le jeune, frère d'Antonio.
28. Francisco Gomez.
29. Francisco de Zamora, qui travaillait à Tolède et à Séville.
30. Francisco de Alcoces, qui travaillait à Tolède et à Madrid.
31. Francisco Lourdi.
32. Francisco Cordoi.
33. Francisco Perrez.
34. Giraldo Reliz.
35. Gonzalo Simon.
36. Gil de Alman.
37. Id.
38. Hortuno de Aquirre, le vieux.
39. Juan Martin.
40. Juan de Leizade, qui travailla à Tolède et à Séville.
41. Juan Martinez, le vieux,   Id.
42. Juan Martinez, le jeune,   Id.
43. Juan de Alman.
44. Juan de Toro, fils de Pierre Toro.
45. Juan Ruiz.
46. Juan Martus de Garata Zabala, le vieux.
47. Juan Martinez Menchaca, qui travailla à Tolède et à Lisbonne.
48. Juan Ros, qui travailla à Tolède et à Lisbonne.
49. Juan de Salcedo, qui travailla à Tolède et à Valladolid.
50.
51. Juan de Maladocia.
52. Juan de Vergos.
53. Joannez de la Horta, qui vivait vers 1545.
54. Joannez de Toledo.
55. Joannez de Alquiviva.

56. Joannez Maleto.
57. Joannez le vieux.
58. Joannez Uriza.
59. Julian del Rey, qui travailla à Tolède et à Saragosse.
60. Julian Garcia, qui travailla à Tolède et à Cuença.
61. Julian Zamora.
62. Joseph Gomez.
63. Josepe de la Hera, le vieux.
64. Josepe de la Hera, le jeune.
65. Josepe de la Hera, le petit-fils.
66. Josepe de la Hera, fils du petit-fils.
67. Josepe de la Hera, fils de Sylvestre.
68. Ygnacio Fernandez, le vieux.
69. Ygnacio Fernandez, le jeune.
70. Louis de Rivez.
71. Louis de Ayala.
72. Louis de Velmonte.
73. Louis de Sahagun Ier.
74. Louis de Sahagun II.
75. Louis de Nieva.
76. Lupus Aguado, qui travaillait à Tolède et à Saint-Clément.
77. Miguel Cantero.
78. Miguel Suarez, qui travaillait à Tolède et à Lisbonne.
79.
80. Nicolas Hortuno de Aquirre.
81. Petro de Toro.
82. Petro de Arechiga.
83. Petro de Lopez, qui travailla à Tolède et à Urgos.
84. Petro de Lopez, qui travailla à Tolède et à Séville.
85. Petro de Lazaretta, qui travailla à Tolède et à Bilbao.
86. Petro de Orezco.
87. Petro de Vilmonte.
88. Rogue Hernandez.
89. Sebastian Hernandez le vieux, vers 1637.
90. Sebastian Hernandez le jeune, qui travailla à Tolède et à
    Séville.
91. Silvestre Nieto.
92. Silvestre Nieto fils.
93. Thomas Ayala, vers 1625. (Une belle épée de cet armurier
    se trouve à l'arsenal de Munich.)
94. Zamorano, surnommé el Toledano.
95 à 99. Cinq monogrammes appartiennent à des fabricants de
    Tolède dont on ignore les noms.

Marques et monogrammes d'armuriers qui ont *habité* Madrid
de 1684 à 1849. Ils ont été publiés en 1849 par don José Maria
Marchesi dans son *Catálogo de la Real Armeria*, et apparte-
naient aux armuriers espagnols et allemands suivants :

Albarez (Dieg.).

Algora.

Baeza (M. A.).

Cano (I. P.).

Dorcenarro (S. V.).

Fernandez (I. U.).

Gomez (A.).

Lopez (F. R. C.).

Lopez (G. R. E.).

Santos (S. E. V.).

Soto (Juan de).

Targarona.

Zegarra.

Zuloaga et quelques autres, ainsi qu'à **Auguste Hortez, Isidore Soler, J. Belen, N. O.** et **F. R. N. Bis,** armuriers allemands établis à Madrid.

Matheo (sur une épée).

Daniel de. Com. (sur une dague).

Léon id.

Joan de Oipe *me fecit* (sur une arbalète).

Johan id.

Salado (sur une arme à feu), sont les noms de six armuriers donnés par le même auteur et recueillis sur des armes de la même Armeria, sans indication d'époque ni de nationalité.

Aporioio (A.).

Barzina (J.).

Cantero (Manuel).

Dez (Ferdinand), Allemand.

Esculante (Basilio).

Fernandez (P.).

Lopez (Balens).

— **(Francisco).**

— **(Jose).**

— **(Juan).**

Martin, Allemand.

Martinez.

Mâtheo (Hilario).

Montokeis (Carlos).

Navarro (Antonio).

Ramirez (P.).

Rodrigue (Carl.).

Santos (Z).

— **(L).**

Soler (Mânuel), Allemand.

Til (M. S.), id. sont vingt et un noms d'armuriers qui se trouvent sur des tables de monogrammes du même ouvrage, où ils sont désignés comme noms d'armuriers *ayant travaillé passagèrement à Madrid,* — sans fixation d'époque, mais tous recueillis également sur des armes conservées au musée de Madrid.

Quant aux marques et monogrammes recueillis pêle-mêle sur des épées, dagues, lances, hallebardes, boucliers, etc., à l'Armerial real, et donnés par M. Marchesi sans aucune critique ni indication d'époque et de nationalité, je n'ai pas jugé utile de m'en occuper ici, puisque ces reproductions ne pouvaient servir à rien.

Bartolam Biella, est le nom d'un armurier recueilli sur une arme de chasse du seizième siècle, au musée de Dresde.

Bastian Armando.

De Pedro de Belmonte, armurier du roi.

Hispango.

C. A. Mora (1586).

Francisco et **Antonio** et **Frederico Picino** sont des armuriers de Tolède, du seizième siècle, recueillis au musée de Dresde, et qui ne se trouvent pas sur le relevé des archives de l'Ayuntamiento, publié par don Manuel Rodriguez Palamino, ni dans le catalogue de M. Marchesi.

Marque d'armurier recueillie sur une armure espagnole richement incrustée d'or, du seizième siècle, à l'arsenal impérial de Vienne.

Alonzo de Schagon, de la fin du seizième siècle, était aussi, selon Jæger, un des plus célèbres armuriers de Tolède ; il a été omis sur la liste des archives.

Juan et **Clément Pedronsteva.**

Eudal Pons et **Martin Marchal** étaient réputés à Tolède vers les dernières années du dix-huitième siècle.

Camo, nom d'armurier recueilli sur une épée du dix-septième siècle, au musée d'artillerie de Paris.

Thomas Haïala,   Id.

Sahagom,   Id.

et V. Monogramme et initiale d'une pertuisane espagnole, du commencement du dix-septième siècle. — Musée d'artillerie de Paris.

Lasinto Laumandreu, de Manresa, travaillait vers 1739, selon sa signature sur un revolver, conservé à la Tour de Londres.

G. Morino, armurier espagnol, qui a signé et daté de 1745 un fusil, à la Tour de Londres.

MONOGRAMMES ET NOMS D'ARMURIERS FRANÇAIS.

Monogramme recueilli sur une armure française (?) du règne de Louis XIII (1610-1643) au musée d'artillerie de Paris, sur laquelle il est répété trois fois.

Monogramme recueilli sur une hache à marteau d'armes, à longue hampe, et qui paraît bourguignonne. — Collection de M. le colonel Meyer-Biermann, à Lucerne.

Monogramme recueilli sur une épée du règne de Louis XIV (1643-1715), n° J. 133, au musée d'artillerie de Paris.

Claude Thomas, à Épinal, 1623. — Pistolets de la collection Erbach.

D. Jumeau, signature recueillie sur une arquebuse à rouet de la première moitié du dix-septième siècle. — Musée d'artillerie de Paris.

Arbois, probablement le nom de la ville d'*Arbois*, recueilli sur une cuirasse du seizième siècle.

Jean Simonin, de Lunéville, nom recueilli sur une arquebuse à rouet, datée de 1627.

Gabriel, nom d'armurier du dix-septième siècle, recueilli sur un pistolet, au musée d'artillerie de Paris.

Pierre Baroy, mort à Paris en 1780, est l'auteur d'un ingénieux fusil à quatre canons et à silex, conservé à l'arsenal de Berlin.

Pierre Bevier, horloger-ingénieur et armurier à Grenoble au commencement du dix-septième siècle, est auteur d'un système particulier de platine d'un pistolet à double feu, au musée d'artillerie de Paris.

Bouillet frères, de Saint-Étienne, étaient des armuriers du temps de Louis XV (1715-1774), réputés pour les fusils à vent.

De Thuraine, de Paris, a signé une carabine à batterie (silex) de l'époque de Louis XV (1715-1774).

Brezol-Laine, à Charleville, nom d'armurier recueilli sur un tromblon, au musée d'artillerie de Paris.

Marchan, à Grenoble, armurier du dix-huitième siècle, qui a signé un fusil à batterie (silex), au musée d'artillerie de Paris.

Philippe de Selier, armurier du dix-huitième siècle, qui a signé deux fusils à batterie (silex) conservés au musée d'artillerie de Paris, et un de la même espèce, de la collection Erbach.

H. Renier, de Paris, a signé des pistolets à batterie (silex) du dix-huitième siècle.

Liouville, à Paris,　　　　　　Id.

Lame, à Mézières, fusil à silex, de la collection Erbach.

Chateau, à Paris,　　　　　　Id.

Boutet, armurier à Marseille, vers la fin du dix-huitième siècle.

Frappier, à Paris, pistolet au musée d'artillerie de Paris.

Acquis-Grain.

Lamarre, nom d'armurier recueilli sur un pistolet à silex au musée d'artillerie de Paris.

Jean Dubois, à Sedan, signature (d'un armurier) sur un pistolet.

Hubert, à Bordeaux, est la signature d'un armurier recueillie sur un grand fusil de rempart, provenant de la citadelle de Blaye. — Musée d'artillerie de Paris.

Giverde, Hilpert et **Rubersburg,** à Strasbourg, étaient des armuriers réputés pour leurs armes à feu dans les dernières années du dix-huitième siècle.

Vincent, fusil à silex, de la collection Erbach.

Jean Griottier, fusil à double canon, de la collection Erbach.

Jean Renier, armurier du milieu du dix-huitième siècle, dont le nom se trouve gravé sur un pistolet conservé au musée d'artillerie de Paris.

Gustave Delvigne, qui depuis 1826 a constamment amélioré le tir à canon rayé dont la balle n'avait plus besoin d'être forcée à coups de maillet.

Julien Leroy, Gastine Renette et **Lefaucheux** sont d'autres armuriers français réputés pour leurs armes se chargeant par la culasse.

Depuis, ce sont MM. **Robert, Manceaux** et **Vieillard**; et, en dernier lieu, M. **Chassepot,** dont les noms sont connus dans l'armée pour l'amélioration qu'ils ont apportée aux fusils.

MONOGRAMMES, INITIALES ET NOMS D'ARMURIERS ANGLAIS.

Radoc, armurier de la fin du seizième siècle, connu par la mention d'un payement à lui fait en 1588, de la part du chambellan de Norwich, en rétribution d'un changement de platine à rouet de pistolet, qu'il avait remplacée par une batterie de chenapan.

H. Martin Muler est le nom d'un armurier recueilli sur un mousquet à canon rayé, dont le bois est enrichi des armes d'Angleterre et d'autres incrustations, probablement du règne de Jacques II (1685-1689). — Musée d'artillerie de Paris.

A. couronné était la marque de la compagnie des armuriers de Londres sous le règne de Georges 1er (1714-1727).

A. R. sont des initiales recueillies sur deux fusils de rempart marqués **Tower**, 1739 et 1740, conservés au musée d'artillerie deParis.

Stephean, à Londres, armurier de la fin du dix-huitième siècle, a signé un fusil à rouet, ainsi qu'un fusil à vent conservé au musée d'artillerie de Paris.

N. Thomson, né en Angleterre et établi à Rotterdam, était réputé, vers la fin du dix-huitième siècle, pour ses armes à feu.

Bate, armurier anglais, dont le nom est gravé sur la fausse platine d'un fusil à vent, conservé au musée d'artillerie de Paris.

Forsith, armurier écossais, qui inventa, en 1807, le fusil à percussion ou piston.

Joseph Eggs, armurier anglais, inventeur de la capsule fulminante.

MONOGRAMMES ET NOMS D'ARMURIERS SUISSES.

Marque recueillie sur une hallebarde suisse, du quinzième siècle, de la collection de l'auteur.

Marque recueillie sur une hallebarde suisse, du seizième siècle, de la collection de l'auteur.

Marque recueillie sur une pertuisane (probablement du commencement du seizième siècle), de la collection de M. le colonel Meyer-Biermann, à Lucerne.

Id.   Id.

Zell Blasi, 1614, signature recueillie sur un serpentin, à l'arsenal de Bâle.

Wys, à Zurich, mort en 1788, réputé pour ses armes à feu.

Stranglé et **Michel** père et fils, de Zurich, des dernières années du dix-huitième siècle, réputés pour leurs armes à feu.

Frorrer, à Winterthur, et **Husbaum**, à Berne, étaient réputés, aux dernières années du dix-huitième siècle, pour leurs armes à feu.

Vitt, à Schaffhausen, arme à feu à canon rayé, de la collection Erbach.

Pauly, de Genève, qui imagina, vers 1808, un fusil à percussion qui différait de celui de l'inventeur de cette arme, Forsith, et qui se chargeait par la culasse.

MONOGRAMMES ET NOMS D'ARMURIERS FLAMANDS
ET HOLLANDAIS.

Jacobus van Oppy, à Anvers, signature recueillie sur un fusil de rempart du milieu du dix-septième siècle, conservé à la Tour de Londres.

Johannes Wyndd, recueillie sur une épée d'infanterie du dix-septième siècle, qui porte en outre la marque de la *levrette*, n° J. 103. — Musée d'artillerie de Paris.

Clœde Hiquet, de Liége, signature qui se trouve sur un fusil à batterie (silex) et sur un pistolet, de la fin du dix-septième siècle, conservé au musée d'artillerie de Paris.

Gathy, à Liége, signature recueillie sur un pistolet à batterie (silex) du dix-huitième siècle, au musée d'artillerie de Paris.

L. Gosuni, a Liége, a signé un fusil à magasin.

Le Clerk, à Maestricht. — Collection Erbach.

Van Walsen, à Maestricht. Id.

Micharius, à Bréda, fusil à silex. Id.

Tendermann, à Utrecht, fusil à silex. — Collection Erbach.

Mercier, à Liége, fusil à double canon damassé, de la collection Erbach.

Fachter, à Liége, réputé pour ses fusils à vent.

Facka Speger est le nom d'un armurier hollandais qui se lit sur un fusil à vent du dix-huitième siècle, dont le récipient est dans la crosse, et qui fait partie du musée d'artillerie de Paris.

MONOGRAMMES, INITIALES, MARQUES ET NOMS D'ARMURIERS ET DE LOCALITÉS RECUEILLIS SUR DES ARMES ORIENTALES.

Sur un grand nombre d'armes chrétiennes et turques, provenant de l'ancienne église de Saint-Irène, à Constantinople, où était l'arsenal de Mahomet II, armes qui pourraient remonter à la fin du quinzième ou au commencement du seizième siècle; on y trouve cette marque, qui n'est pas celle d'un armurier, mais probablement l'estampille de l'arsenal, et exprime en cufic : *Allah*. Ce monogramme se trouve aussi sur une cuirasse de janissaire, au musée d'artillerie de Paris, G. 134.

Hussein, vers 1094 de l'hégire (1680).

Cette marque est attribuée aux lames d'épée que les croisés avaient fait faire ou estampiller à Jérusalem. Je l'ai cependant recueillie sur une épée de l'arsenal de Berlin, où le manche indique le seizième siècle.

Nurwur est le nom d'une localité dans les Indes centrales anglaises, où existait une manufacture d'armes à feu au dix-huitième siècle. Ce nom a été recueilli avec les initiales

A. D.	de l'armurier, et le millésime	1649	de l'ère hindoue

(1786 de l'ère chrétienne), sur un fusil à mèche, de la Tour de Londres.

Shahjehanabad, nom de localité indienne où a existé une fabrique d'armes, inscrit sur des brassards damasquinés, conservés à la Tour de Londres.

Gwalior et **Lushkur** sont des noms de villes de fabriques d'armes que l'on trouve sur des armes blanches ; et

Lahore, sur des armes à feu.

MONOGRAMMES ET SIGNATURES DONT L'ORIGINE EST INDÉTERMINÉE.

A. F. 1605 — Initiales et date recueillies sur une hallebarde de la Tour de Londres.

Tayras, signature recueillie sur une cuirasse de la fin du dix-septième siècle, de la Tour de Londres.

H. K. — à côté d'un poinçon de fabrique, représentant un *cygne*, recueillies sur un pistolet avec belle sculpture, conservé au musée d'artillerie de Paris.

Jean-Paul Cleft, signature recueillie sur un pistolet à rouet, du dix-septième siècle, conservé au musée d'artillerie de Paris.

Rudolstadt (ville)   Id.   Id.

A. C. — Marque recueillie sur une baïonnette de l'époque de Louis XIII.

X

ARMES, CROIX ET SIGNES

DE TRIBUNAUX DE FRANCS-JUGES

Les tribunaux francs (*Fehmgerichte*), dont la création s'explique par le désordre et l'état de morcellement excessif dans lesquels les institutions féodales, poussées jusqu'aux dernières limites, avaient précipité l'empire, ne remontent pas jusqu'à Charlemagne, comme on l'a cru longtemps ; mais elles sont, certes, le développement de sa législation peu homogène.

Malgré l'application partielle du droit romain, le souvenir d'un droit tout national appliqué au grand jour et en plein air par tous les hommes libres (l'origine de nos jurys), et le sentiment de l'individualisme, inné à la race germanique, devaient donner naissance, dès que le droit manuel avait fini par rendre la justice régulière illusoire, à cette justice prompte et terrible, à la fois occulte et autorisée, que le romantisme a entouré de tant d'horreurs et de mystères.

Si, comme il est prouvé aujourd'hui, beaucoup de lieux où des tribunaux francs siégeaient, étaient publiquement connus, les recherches historiques n'ont pu infirmer leur procédure occulte et leurs exécutions sommaires et terribles. La *terre rouge*, par laquelle on désignait dans le langage symbolique des initiés, la Westphalie, où l'institution des tribunaux francs avait été créée, et où tout *Freischoeffe* (échevin indépendant, franc-juge) devait être *reçu* ou initié, était bien alors une terre rougie par le sang humain.

Il est aussi certain qu'un grand nombre de cours constituées en dehors des cours autorisées siégeaient dans des lieux connus seulement des *Wissenden* (initiés qui *connaissaient*), où la haine, l'envie et la vengeance se donnaient pleine carrière sous le masque de la justice.

Les armes attribuées aux tribunaux des francs-juges sont plus rares dans les collections que les instruments de tortures dont ils firent usage pour obtenir des aveux, et on ne doit admettre l'authenticité de ces armes, aussi bien que celle des alphabets et des signes, qu'avec grande réserve.

La dague à trois branches du musée de Sigmaringen, attribuée à ces *Fehmrichter* ou francs-juges, est, en tout point, pareille aux *mains-gauches* à ressorts, en usage du quinzième au dix-septième siècle.

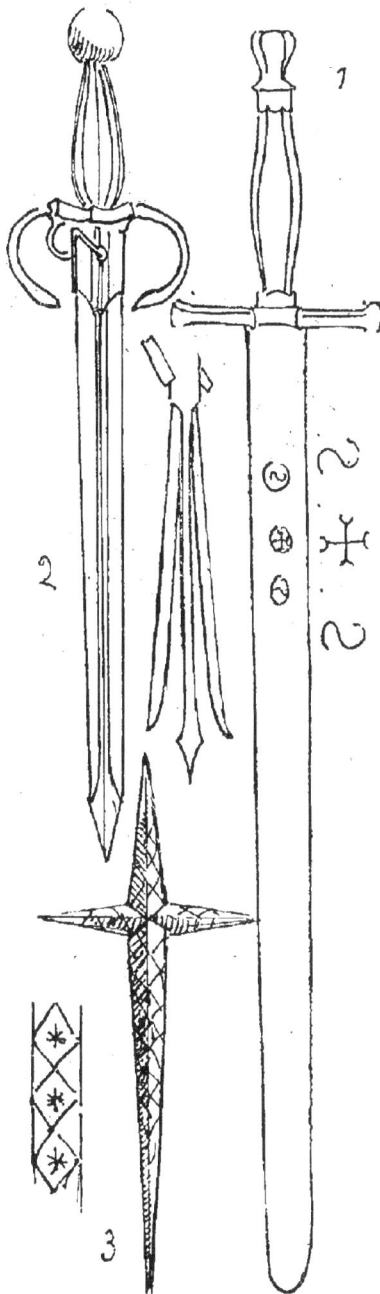

1. Epée d'exécution de franc-juge. La lame montre trois cercles ciselés en croix, où celui du milieu contient la croix grecque à quatre croissants, signe symbolique dans ces tribunaux occultes, et les deux autres chacun un S (*Sacrificium Sanctum*). — Musée de Sigmaringen.

2. Dague de franc-juge avec inscription effacée. La lame se divise en trois parties, au moyen d'un ressort, et la poignée est pourvue, du côté opposé au ressort, d'une rouelle pour pouvoir y passer le pouce. On croit que cette arme servait à faire prêter le serment *au nom de la Trinité*. Longueur, 43 centimètres. — Musée de Sigmaringen.

3. Croix en fer de 24 cent. sur 38, de tribunal de francs-juges. Elle fut employée par les exécuteurs pour désigner la *justice du tribunal*. Ils l'enfonçaient dans l'arbre au-dessus du supplicié; elle servait aussi pour accompagner la *citation*. Dans ce dernier cas, la croix était enfoncée à la porte de la demeure ou du château fort, au-dessus de la citation (*Ladung*) affichée. — Musée de Sigmaringen.

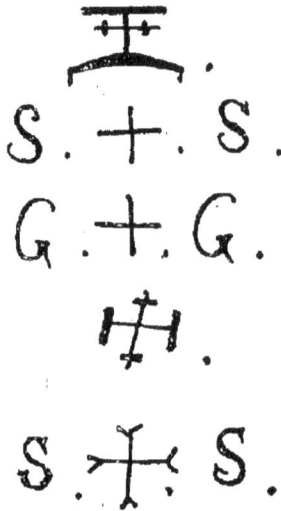

Les S séparés par des croix représentaient, selon quelques archéologues, les mots *Sacrificium Sanctum.*

On attribue aussi les trois alphabets reproduits à la page suivante, à trois de ces tribunaux occultes (*Freistühle* en allem.), de la Westphalie.

51.

A	B	C	D	E	F

G	H	I	K	L	M

n	o	p	q	r	s

t	u	w	x	y	z

XI

CONSEILS ET RECETTES

POUR LES AMATEURS D'ARMES

Pour éviter le nettoyage répété d'une arme en fer ou en acier, on peut la couvrir d'une légère couche de vernis copal incolore et délayé dans de l'essence, sous laquelle toutes les finesses du travail restent visibles.

On dérouille le fer le plus facilement et le plus promptement en le frottant avec de l'émeri en poudre ou avec du papier ou de la toile émerisés et arrosés d'une composition de pétrole ou benzine, d'essence et d'esprit de vin. Les armes finement damasquinées, polies, ciselées ou niellées, sur lesquelles le frottement avec de l'émeri enlèverait la finesse, doivent être trempées huit à trente jours dans un bain de benzine et frottées après avec des chiffons de laine. Toute pièce nettoyée doit être séchée au feu et légèrement humectée d'huile.

Pour rouiller promptement les pièces refaites et pour produire sur ces parties les concavités de vétusté, on peut se servir de l'acide muriatique coupé avec de l'eau. Le fer, humecté par ce liquide corrosif, doit être exposé à l'air un ou plusieurs jours, et humecté à plusieurs reprises jusqu'à ce qu'il ait atteint le degré d'oxydation voulu; lavé après avec de l'eau fraiche, il faut le graisser pour arrêter l'oxydation.

Pour obtenir des concavités, on asperge le fer avec de l'encre lithographique; tous les endroits qu'elle couvre restent préservés de la rouille, tandis que l'acide creuse et ronge à côté.

On distingue l'acier du fer en versant sur la surface polie du métal une goutte d'acide sulfurique coupée avec de l'eau : si ce liquide produit une tache noire due au charbon mis à nu, c'est de l'acier; si la tache est verdâtre et que l'eau l'enlève facilement, c'est du fer.

La *fonte*, que la contrefaçon a rendue très-difficile à distinguer du fer martelé, et qu'elle sait même rendre malléable, met souvent l'amateur dans l'embarras. Il faut avoir recours à la lime pour observer le *grain*, qui, sous la loupe, paraît *plus gros* et en même temps *plus luisant*.

FIN

TABLE DES CHAPITRES

INTRODUCTION. 1

I. — HISTOIRE ABRÉGÉE DES ARMES ANCIENNES. 23

II. — ARMES DES ÉPOQUES ANTÉHISTORIQUES, DE L'AGE DE LA
PIERRE. 92

    Armes en pierres taillées par éclats. 92
    Armes en pierres polies. 97

III. — ARMES ANTIQUES DES AGES DU BRONZE ET DU FER. . . 102

    Armes hindoues en bronze et fer. 103
    Armes américaines. 105
    Armes assyriennes, etc., etc. 109
    Armes égyptiennes 117
    Armes grecques et étrusques. 122
    Armes romaines, samnites et daces. 133

IV. — ARMES DE L'AGE DU BRONZE, DES PEUPLES DITS BARBARES
DE L'OCCIDENT. 142

    Armes germaniques en bronze. 144
    Armes celtico-gauloises, gauloises, bas-bretonnes, etc.,
      en bronze. 148
    Armes britanniques en bronze. 151
    Armes scandinaves en bronze. 154
    Armes en bronze de pays divers. 159

V. — ARMES DE L'AGE DU FER DES PEUPLES DU NORD. . . . 160

    Armes germaniques de l'âge du fer. 166
    Armes scandinaves de l'âge du fer. 175
    Armes diverses de l'âge du fer. 176

VI. — Armes du moyen age chrétien, de la renaissance et
des xvii⁰ et xviii⁰ siècles.. 177

Armements complets du moyen âge 178
Armements complets de la Renaissance.. 213
Armements complets des xvii⁰ et xviii⁰ siècles. 234
L'armure dans ses détails, hors le casque. 239
Le casque.. 257
Le bouclier. 306
Cottes et cuirasses.. 320
Le brassard. 347
Le gantelet. 351
Jambières et chaussures. 356
L'éperon. 362
L'armure de cheval. 369
La selle 374
L'étrier 381
La bride. 386
L'épée. 389
La dague, le poignard, etc., etc. 420
La lance, la pique et l'épieu.. 434
La masse d'armes.. 440
Le morgenstern.. 442
Le fléau 444
La faux de guerre.. 447
Le fauchard. 448
La guisarme. 450
La vouge. 453
Le marteau d'armes. 455
La hache d'armes 458
La hallebarde. 464
La corsèque. 466
La pertuisane. 467
La baionnette. 469
L'esponton.. 472
La fourche de guerre. 473
Armes et ustensiles divers de guerre et de chasse. . . . 475
Les machines de guerre et les armes de siége.. 477
La fronde et la fustibale. 488
La sarbacane 490
Arcs et flèches. 490
L'arbalète... 495

VII. — L'ARME A FEU. 508
   L'arme à feu de gros calibre. 513
   Le mortier. 513
   Le canon. 515
   L'arme à feu portative ou à main. 533
   Le canon à main, la haquebuse, l'arquebuse, le fusil, etc. 533
   Le pistolet. 549
   Accessoires pour armes à feu. 553

VIII. — LE FUSIL À VENT. 556

IX. — L'ART DE L'ARMURIER ET DE L'ARQUEBUSIER ; MONOGRAMMES,
  INITIALES ET NOMS D'ARMURIERS. 559

   Monogrammes et noms d'armuriers allemands. 575
   Armuriers allemands des dernières années du XVIIIe et du
     commencement du XIXe siècle, réputés pour les armes à
     feu et à vent. 582
   Monogrammes et noms d'armuriers italiens. 585
   Monogrammes et noms d'armuriers espagnols et portugais. 587
   Monogrammes et noms d'armuriers français. 595
   Monogrammes, initiales et noms d'armuriers anglais. . . 597
   Monogrammes et noms d'armuriers suisses. 595
   Monogrammes et noms d'armuriers flamands et hollandais. 590
   Monogrammes, initiales, marques et noms d'armuriers et
     de localités, recueillis sur des armes orientales. . . . 600
   Monogrammes et signatures dont l'origine est indéterminée. 601

X. — ARMES, CROIX ET SIGNES DES TRIBUNAUX DE FRANCS-JUGES. 602

XI. — CONSEILS ET RECETTES POUR LES AMATEURS D'ARMES. . . 607

ERRATA

—

Page ligne

8   3 lisez : *patricien* à la place de : pratieien.
10 3 » 1501 à la place de : 1551.
11 5 » *Lincy* à la place de Lancy.
11 11 » *et renfermant* à la place de : renferment.
38 34 » *de guerre ; outre le char...* à la place de : de guerre outre le char.
38 35 » *assyrienne et beaucoup d'autres machines.*
39 1 » *ils avaient les béliers,* à la place de : les béliers.
39 6 supprimez : *mentionnés.*
49 32 lisez : *Naumbourg,* à la place de : Haumbourg.
51 4 » *banderole,* à la place de : petits pavois.
70 35 » *dont l'usage,* à la place de : son usage.
72 10 supprimez la virgule après *lançait.*
82 22 lisez : *que dans la première moitié du XIV⁰ siècle,* à la place de : vers le milieu, etc.
88 8 » *un palme,* à la place d'une palme.
88 31 » *muriate oxygéné ou chlorate de potasse.*
91 5 » *dont la construction,* à la place de : dans le système.
98 20 » *angon,* à la place : d'ajonc.
120 21 » *ombilic,* à la place de : rombelic.
132 12 » *cuivre,* à la place de : cuir.
134 9 » *un palme,* à la place : d'une palme.
142 2 » *barbares, de l'Occident.*
306 11 » *Schildnabel,* à la place de Schildnahel.
357 13 » *qui fournissent,* à la place de : qui renferment.
358 8 » *ogival-lancette,* à la place de : ogival de lancette.
380 8 » *une telle selle,* à la place de : la selle.
386 4 » *sans brisure et avec branches,* à la place de : sans brisure ou avec branches.
389 1 » (du latin *spatha,* en italien *spada,* en espagnol *espada,* en allemand *Schwert et Deger,* en anglais *sword*).
434 22 » *d'habitude,* à la place de : ordinairement.
436 17 » *mètres,* à la place de : centimètres
446 8 » *est tel que,* au lieu de : comme.
456 30 » *Thiebaud d'Arc,* à la place de : Thiébaud l'Arx.
463 26-29 » *canon à main,* à la place de : canon pour manche.
469 23 » *Culmann,* à la place de : Coulmann.
463 6 » Foucher, à la place de : Fouchet.
477 26 » *rencontre,* à la place de : trouve.
485 21 » *ungeloeschten Kalk,* à la place de : ungelaeschten Kalch.
490 3 » *blowpipe,* à la place de : lowpipe.
503 23 » *balestre,* à la place de : belestre.
504 7 » *Coulissen ou Rinnen,* au lieu de : Laut ou Rinnen.
504 18 » *à tiroir,* au lieu de : en ivoire.
566 22 et 30 lisez : *comptes* à la place de comptes rendus.

TABLE GÉNÉRALE

La liste générale de tous les amateurs et collectionneurs se trouve rangée par ordre alphabétique sous COLLECTIONS, et celle des musées publics et arsenaux, dans le même ordre, à la suite du mot MUSÉE.

A

Abbeville (fabrique d'armes à), 571.
Abyssiniennes (armes), 439.
Achen, peintre. V. Van Achen.
Acinace, 33, 111.
Affûts fixes, 79.
— mobiles, 79.
— sur roues, 79.
Ailettes, 54, 256.
Ajala, armurier, 587.
Akinace. V. Acinace.
Albanaises (armes), 412.
Albrecht, armurier du seizième siècle, 370.
Albrecht, armurier du dix-huitième siècle, 582.
Alhambra (sculpture de l'), 204.
Allemandes (armes), 186, 187, 191, 192, 194, 197, 202, 210, 211, 212, 213, 214, 215, 216, 217, 218, 219, 220, 221, 222, 224, 225, 226, 227, 228, 229, 232, 235, 238, et depuis cette page, presque sur toutes les pages suivantes.
Allich, armurier, 574.
Alt, armurier, 577.
Alter, armurier, 578.
Amalzen, moine, 73.
Ambras (collections d'), 12, 210, 211, 212, 214, 220, 221, 222, 227, 230, 232, 235, 256, 260, 284, 289, 292, 302, 316, 322, 323, 324, 325, 326,

337, 341, 342, 344, 355, 365, 366, 371, 372, 373, 380, 384, 385, 399, 402, 436, 438, 443, 462, 466, 484, 487, 493, 494, 503, 517, 524, 525, 527, 534, 538, 539, 540, 553, 573.
Ambrogio, armurier, 562.
Amentum, 123.
Ame (du canon), 515.
Américaines (armes), 101, 105.
Amoniures fulminants, 88.
Amorce. V. Capsule.
Amorçoirs, 554.
Amsterdam (antiquités à l'hôtel de ville d'), 209.
Amsterdam (collection de la Société archéologique d'), 21.
Amusette du maréchal de Saxe (l'), 90.
Andrea de Ferrare, armurier, 562.
Angers (sculptures à), 185.
Anglaises et britanniques (armes), 95, 151, 183, 196, 245, 269, 270, 272, 273, 274, 277, 278, 281, 286, 293, 297, 319, 354, 364, 366, 367, 383, 396, 397, 400, 408, 418, 425, 427, 451, 461, 462, 463, 470, 571.
Anglo-saxonnes (armes), 184, 185, 436. V. aussi anglaises et britanniques.
Angon, 45, 98.
Annelée (cotte), 332.
Anschütz, armurier, 582.
Anses (du canon), 515.
Antenne, 125.
Antoine, armurier, 579.

Antwerc, 477.
Arabes (armes), 368, 385, 382, 398, 416.
Arbalète, 68, 70, 495.
— allemande, 72, 497, 503.
— chinoise, 72, 498, 504.
— à cranequin. V. à cric.
— à cric, 71, 496, 501.
— à baguette, 72, 497, 504.
— à galet, 72, 497, 503, 504.
— à moufle, 72, 496, 502.
— à passot. V. Arbalète à moufle.
— à pied-de-biche, 72, 496, 500.
— à pistolet, 505.
— à rouet d'engrenage. V. Arbalète allemande.
— à tour. V. Arbalète à moufle.
Arbois, armurier, 595.
Arbrier d'arbalète, 494.
Arcs, 69, 490, 493.
Archet, 491, 493.
Aretin, directeur, 18.
Argens, armurier, 582.
Armes à feu, 72, 82, 508.
— à feu de gros calibre, 513.
— à feu portatives, 533.
— antiques (bronze et fer), 102.
— de l'âge de la pierre, 92.
— de l'âge du bronze des peuples de l'Occident, 142.
— de l'âge du fer, 160.
— de la renaissance, 213.
— des différents peuples. V. leurs noms.
— du dix-septième et dix-huitième siècle, 234.
— du moyen âge chrétien, 177.
— de siége, 476.
— et ustensiles divers de guerre et de chasse, 475.
Armets (casques), 297.
Armoiries (origine des), 59.
Armstrong, 82, 531.
Armure détaillée (l'), 239.
Armures de cheval, 61, 369.
Armuriers espagnols du seizième au dix-huitième siècle. V. la liste par ordre alphabétique, 589, 590, 591, 592, 593, 594, 595.
Arnautes. V. Albanais.
Arnth, armurier, 582.
Arosa (Gustave) collection, 413.
Arquebuse, 84, 511.

Arquebuse à chenapan, 85.
— à mèche, 511.
— à rouet, 511, 542.
— du moine. V. Moenchsbüchse.
— rayée, 85, 511.
Art (l') de l'armurier, etc., 560.
Arizberg, armurier, 576.
Assagai (lance), 436.
Assyriens et babyloniens (armements), 30.
Assyriennes et babyloniennes (armes), 94, 109.
Augsbourg (musée d'), 125, 126, 144, 173, 269, 465.
Avant-trains, 79.
Avenches (musée d'), 38, 137, 140, 167.
Aventicum. V. Avenches.
Az (collection), 145, 166, 286, 289, 313, 413, 436, 443, 452, 454, 463, 474, 504.

B

Babyloniennes (armes). V. Assyriennes.
Babyloniens (armements). V. Assyriens.
Bacinet (grand) casque, 276, 277, 278.
Bacinet (petit) casque, 54, 268.
Badajoz (fabriques d'armes à), 562.
Badile, armurier, 562, 585.
Baïonnette, 86, 87, 469.
Bâle (arsenal de), 20, 528.
— (sculptures de la cathédrale de), 256.
Baliste, 19, 477.
Balles de plomb, 82.
— forcées, 85.
Banderoles, 435.
Bardes de l'armure du cheval, 61, 130, 372, 373.
Bardiche, 461.
Baroy, armurier, 506.
Bartholomæ, armurier, 582.
Bas-bretonnes (armes), 148.
Bascule (machine de guerre), 477.
Bas-de-chausses, 356, 359.
Basilics, 80, 515.
Bassinet de fusil, 87.
Bâtardeau (couteau), 421, 429.
Bate, armurier, 557, 598.
Battant de fléau, 444.

Batteries d'armes à feu, 85, 86, 87, 514, 546.

Baudrier de mousquetaire, 554.

Baumann, armurier, 582.

Bavarois (musée). V. Munich.

Bayeux (tapisserie de), 49, 69, 188, 189, 265, 309, 334, 376, 387, 395, 435, 440, 460.

Bayon, chimiste, 88.

Beaumont (de), auteur, 20.

Bec-de-faucon et de perroquet de marteaux d'armes, 455, 456, 457, 459.

Beenjanuggur (monuments de), 34.

Behr, armurier, 581, 582.

Belen, armurier, 581.

Belges (armes), 519, 571.

Béliers, 39, 132, 477.

Berg, armurier, 582.

Bergbarte. V. Hache de mineur.

Bergstraesser, armurier, 582.

Berlin (arsenal de), 15, 82, 287, 312, 383, 404, 438, 439, 466, 476, 487, 558.

Berlin (bibliothèque de), 194, 197, 272, 282, 440, 493.

Berlin (musée de), 94, 101, 104, 111, 121, 124, 126, 131, 174, 276, 280, 364, 367, 368, 414.

Berlin (musée de Montbijou à), 280, 288, 312, 320, 321, 380, 383, 401, 507, 543, 553

Berne (arsenal de), 20, 275, 313, 410, 443, 457, 461, 465, 533, 546.

Berns, armurier, 574.

Berselli, armurier, 562.

Bertholet, chimiste, 88.

Bevier, armurier, 596.

Biella (Bartholam), armurier, 476, 585.

Bieslinger, armurier, 577.

Bilbao (fabriques d'armes à), 562.

Birmingham (fabriques d'armes à), 571.

Bis, armurier, 581.

Blanc-haubert, 53.

Blasi, armurier, 599.

Blinde, 77.

Boest, armurier, 573.

Bogaert (collection), 21.

Bohèmes (armes), 95, 193, 400, 471.

Boîte mobile (charge à la), 76.

Bombardes, 75, 80, 515, 520, 521.

Bonisolo, armurier, 562, 585.

Bonstetten (collection), 128.

Bosier, armurier, 580.

Bossette (de la bride), 370.

Bottes militaires ou de guerre, 61, 356.

Boucles (jambières), 356.

Boucliers, 53, 145, 307.

Bouillet, armurier, 556, 596.

Bouldure, chimiste, 88.

— à essieux, 532.

Boulet de canon armé de chaînes, dit ramé, 532.

Boulets de canon conjugués, 532.

— coniques, 78.

— en fer, 78.

— en pierre, 78.

— en plomb, 78.

— rouges, 78.

Bourguignonnes (armes), 205.

Bourguignotes (casques), 260, 289.

Bourrelet (du canon), 515.

Boutet, armurier, 596.

Bouton (du canon), 515.

Brabender, armurier, 578.

Braconnières, 246.

Braquemart (épée), 393.

Brassards, 248, 347, 348, 349.

Brassards d'archer, 493.

Braun, auteur, 19.

Brayette, 247.

Breitenfelder, armurier, 577.

Brenneck, armurier, 582.

Brescia (fabriques d'armes à), 571.

Brésiliennes (armes), 368.

Bretonnes (armes), 40.

Brezol-Laine, armurier, 596.

Brides, 386, 387, 388.

Bridon, 386.

Brigantine, 55, 327, 336, 337.

Brioude (sculpture à), 179.

Britanniques (armes). V. Anglaises.

Britannique (musée), 30, 32, 94, 95, 99, 109, 110, 111, 112, 113, 114, 115, 116, 121, 125, 129, 152, 153, 183, 184, 185, 264, 265, 280, 394, 396, 418, 425.

Broch, armurier, 574.

Brock, armurier, 574.

Brockberger, peintre, 565.

Brunswick (musée de), 295.

— (peintures murales à la cathédrale de), 194, 380.

Bruxelles (musée de), 21.

Buchhalzer (collection), 398, 429.

Buffleterie de mousquetaire. V. Baudrier.

Buffletins, 327, 345.

Bulff, armurier, 567.
Burgondes (armes), 170.

C

Cabassets (casques), 295.
Calibres, 79, 515.
Calottes d'armes, 286, 287, 288.
Calvis, armurier, 582.
Camail, 49.
Campenhouten, auteur, 13.
Cané, armurier, 562, 585.
Cannelées (armures), 57, 218.
Canons, 75, 78, 515, 516, 517, 518, 519, 520, 522, 523, 524, 525, 528, 530.
Canons en cuir suédois, 528.
Canons à main, 510, 533.
Canons prussiens, 531.
Caparaçon, 369.
Capsules pour mousquets, 554.
— (petites), 89, 90.
Carabine, 85, 87, 512.
— de Versailles, 85.
— revolver, 446.
Carcaire. V. Eperon.
Carlsruhe (musée de), 130, 405.
Carquois, 507.
Carreaux (flèches), 72, 505, 506.
— barbelés, 506.
— tyroliens, 506.
Carrels (flèches), 72, 505, 506.
Cartouches, 87.
Cartouchière. V. Giberne.
Casques (chapitre où sont traités les), 257 à 288.
Casques à l'antique, 299.
Cassel (musée de), 5, 146, 147, 385. V. aussi Lœwenburg.
Catapultes diverses, 39, 477.
Catugel (fabriques d'armes à), 552.
Caucasiennes (armes), 461.
Celt (arme nommée), 40.
Celtiques (armes), 40, 95, 99, 100, 148.
Chaldéen (armement). V. Assyrien.
Chambly (armes de), 55, 329, 570.
Chambre à feu, 76.
Chanfrein, 61, 371.
Chapeaux d'armes, 282, 283, 284, 285, 286, 288.
Charles XV (collection du roi de Suède), 19, 81, 278, 429.

Charles de Prusse (collection du prince) 425, 443, 461, 507, 543.
Charles le Chauve (armes de), 46.
Charlemagne (armes de), 46.
Charleville (fabrique d'armes à), 571.
Chassepot, armurier, 91, 548, 570.
Chateau, armurier, 596.
Chausse (V. bas et haut-de-).
Chausses-trape, 140, 487.
Chaussures du moyen âge, 356.
— grecques, 122.
— romaines, 134.
Chemnitz (fabriques d'armes à), 571.
Chenapan, 85, 512, 544.
Chevaux de frise, 487.
Chiavona (épée), 392, 408.
Chien de batterie, 87.
Childéric (armes de), 45, 169, 173.
Chimchi et Chimichir. V. Cimeterre.
Chinoises (armes), 67, 305, 413, 414, 439, 463, 509, 536.
Cimeterres, 33, 390, 413.
Civo, armurier, 562.
Claymore (épée), 391, 400.
Claus, armurier, 582.
Cleft, armurier, 601.
Clerc, armurier, 600.
Clouet, fabriquant de damas, 560.
Cluny (musée de), 335, 337.
Cnemides, 130.
Cochet (l'abbé), archéologue, 173.
Coiffette en mailles, 268.
Colombo, armurier, 562.

COLLECTIONS qui se trouvent ici par ordre alphabétique, et qu'il faut rechercher sous chaque lettre respective :

Collection Ambras.
— Arosa (Gustave).
— Az.
— Bogaert.
— Bonstetten.
— Buchhalzer.
— Charles XV (du roi de Suède).
— Charles (du prince de Prusse).
— Cristy.
— Cruseman.
— Culemann.
— Demmin.
— Destailleur.
— Erbach.
— Failly.

Collection à Godrich-Court. V. Llewe-lyn-Meyrick.
— Guillaume III (du roi de Prusse).
— Hauslaub.
— Hefner-Alteneck.
— Klemm.
— Llewelyn-Meyrick.
— Lobkowitz. V. Raudnitz.
— au Loewenburg.
— Mazis.
— Merville.
— Meyer-Biermann.
— Napoléon III (de l'empereur).
— Nieuwerkerke (du comte de).
— Odet.
— Parham.
— Portales.
— Renné.
— Romano (du collége).
— Six.
— Soeter.
— Soltikof.
— Spengel.
— Ternow.
— Troyon.
— Villaseca.
— Waldburg-Wolfegg.
— Warwick (au château de).
— Widter.
— Wittmann.
— Zu Rhein.
Colichemarde (épée), 390.
Colletin, 244, 345.
Colman. V. Kollmann.
Colombo, armurier, 585.
Colt, armurier, 91, 552.
Cominazzi, armurier, 562, 585.
Comnene (Anna) (Mémoires d'), 68, 357.
Coniques (boulets), 78.
Constable, 77.
Contino, armurier, 587.
Contriner, armurier, 556, 558, 580.
Copenhague (musée de), 20, 95, 96, 100, 155, 156, 157, 174, 175, 190, 200, 364, 387, 388, 395, 486, 500.
Coquille d'épée, 390, 407.
Corbeille d'épée. V. Coquille.
— de siége, 484.
Corbins à poudre, 555.
Cordoue (fabriques d'armes à), 552.
Corne (armes en), 44.
Cosse de pois (forme et tabule), 57, 344.

Corsèques, 466.
Coster, armurier, 582.
Cotel, armurier, 562, 587.
Cottes d'armes, 51, 52, 55, 327.
Couteaux, fabricant de damas, 560.
Couleuvrine, 80, 515.
Coulisse (fusil à). V. Fusils.
Coup-de-poing (tercerol), 88, 549.
Coussins pour les épées à deux mains, 419.
Coustil à croix (épée), 393.
Couteaux de brèche, 448.
— d'escalade, 486.
— chausse-trape, 487.
Couvre-mèches, 89, 553.
Couvre-lumière, 83.
Cracouse, 449.
Crémation, 29, 148.
Crête-échelle, 255.
Criss (dague), 420, 422, 433.
Cristy (collection), 20, 95, 99, 100, 101, 416.
Crochet de siége, 475.
Croupière de l'armure du cheval, 61, 378.
Crusman (collection), 21.
Cubitière, 250, 347, 348.
Cuella (fabrique d'armes à), 562.
Cuirasses, 327, 341, 342, 343, 344, 345, 346.
Cuissard, 249, 252, 253, 356.
Culasse (du canon), 515.
— (charge par la), 77, 89, 90.
Culemann (collection), 87, 382, 470.

D

Daces (armes), 137, 139.
Dagues, 419.
Damas, 559, 560.
Damasquinage (définition du), 559.
Danielo, armurier, 585.
Danoises (armes). V. Scandinaves.
Dantzig (fabrique d'armes à), 571.
Darmstadt (bibliothèque de), 196, 285, 336.
Dassière, 244.
Dax, armurier, 577.
Degrand, fabricant de damas, 560.
Deiler, armurier, 576.
Deivan, armurier, 587.
Delvigne, armurier, 89, 570, 597.
Demmin (collection), 95, 99, 150, 218,

234, 244, 294, 303, 354, 360, 364,
365, 367, 368, 383, 384, 401, 406,
411, 427, 433, 465, 476, 494, 553,
555.
Denon, savant, 35, 117, 119, 120.
Désarçonneur, 475.
Dessau (prince de), 87.
Destailleur (collection), 565.
Destrier, 369.
Détente, 87, 510, 535.
— double, 89, 511, 544.
Devisme, armurier, 91.
Dez, armurier, 581.
Dijon (musée de), 382.
Dinckl, armurier, 578, 582.
Dison, armurier, 582.
Double détente (Stecher), 89, 511, 544.
Douille de baïonnette, 86.
Dresde (musée de), 11, 85, 90, 254,
255, 286, 287, 292, 293, 318, 335,
336, 337, 339, 366, 388, 400, 412,
419, 431, 438, 446, 457, 461, 475,
476, 486, 534, 587, 553, 572, 574.
Dreyse (Nicolas), armurier, 91, 548.
Dubois, armurier, 596.
Dusaek (sabre), 391, 400.

E

Ebert, armurier, 582.
Ecaillée (cotte), 333.
Echelles d'escalade, 486.
Echl, armurier, 582.
— (Von der), id., 582.
Eck, armurier, 577.
Eckart, armurier, 580.
Ecossaises (armes), 400, 408, 461.
Ecu (petit) bouclier, 183, 194, 198,
205, 308, 310.
Ecusson de l'épée, 390.
Eggs, armurier, 88, 598.
Egyptiennes (armes), 94, 117.
Egyptiens (armements), 35.
Eich, armurier, 577.
Enarmes, 129, 134, 307.
Enseignes, 141, 435.
Epaulière, 244, 250.
Epaulière-garde-bras, 249.
— à passe-gardes, 250.
Epées, 62, 388 à 419.
— à deux mains. V. Espadons.
— (noms d') célèbres, 163.
Eperons, 61, 362 à 368.

Epieux, 434.
Epinal (musée d'), 514.
Eprouvettes de poudre, 553.
Erbach (musée), 16, 137, 139, 146,
310, 320, 321, 338, 395, 409, 575,
576.
Errata, 612.
Ertel, armurier, 580.
Escopette, 82.
Escrime, l'étymologie du mot, 62, 390.
Escualada (fabriques d'armes à), 571.
Espadons, 390, 393, 418.
Espagnoles (armes), 190, 204, 206,
230, 311, 367, 405, 413, 470, 571.
Espontons, 472.
Essen (fabriques d'armes à), 571.
Estocs, 390.
Etoile du matin. V. Morgenstern.
Etriers, 381 à 385.
Etrusque (armement), 37.
Etrusques (armes), 122.
Evidements de l'âme de l'épée, 90.

F

Fachter, armurier, 556, 600.
Failly (collection), 408.
Faraday, fabricant de damas, 560.
Fauchards, 448, 449.
Faucon, 80, 515.
Fauconneau, 80, 515.
Faucre, 254.
Faux de guerre, 447.
Felber, armurier, 582.
Fer à cheval romain, 140.
Fergusson ou Fergessen, capitaine, 88.
Feu grégeois, 73.
Figino, armurier, 562.
Filets (bridons), 88, 386, 387, 388.
Fischer, Martin, 556, 582.
Flamandes (armes), 519, 571.
Flamberge (épée), 393.
Flançois (de l'armure du cheval), 61,
372, 373.
Fléaux, 444, 445, 446.
Flèches, 69, 490 494.
Flissa (épée), 392, 415.
Florence (fabriques d'armes à), 571.
Forsith, armurier, 88, 547, 598.
Foucher, auteur, 260, 464.
Fouet d'armes, 444.
Fourche (de mousquet). V. Fourquine.
Fourches de guerre, 473.

Fourcroy, chimiste, 88.

Fourquine (de mousquet), 85, 536, 542, 543.

Francs (armements), 44, 167, 168, 172, 173.

Françaises (armes), 185, 198, 406, 438, 441, 468, 470, 571.

Francino, armurier, 562, 586.

Francisque, 44.

Francs-juges (armes des), 602.

Frappier, armurier, 596.

Fremmery, armurier, 582.

Freund, armurier, 582.

Frey, armurier, 580.

Fribourg (musée de), en Suisse, 95.

Friedler, armurier, 582.

Fronde, 68, 135, 488, 489.

Fronton de mire de l'arbalète, 495.

Frorrer, armurier, 599.

Fulminates, 88.

— de mercure, 88.

Fusée (de l'épée), 389.

Fusil à aiguille, 91, 512, 548.

Fusil à batterie française. V. Fusil à batterie à silex.

Fusil à batterie à silex, 86, 512, 545, 546.

Fusil à chenapan. V. Arquebuse à chenapan.

Fusil à coulisse. V. Fusil à répétition.

Fusil à percussion, 88, 512, 546.

Fusil à piston. V. Fusil à percussion.

Fusil à raquettes, 546.

Fusil à répétition, 90, 545, 548.

Fusil à vent, 555.

Fusil-mousquet, 469, 512.

Fusil Spencer. V. Fusil à répétition.

Fusil Vauban. V. Fusil-mousquet.

Fustibale, 68, 488, 489.

Futter, armurier, 556.

G

Gabriel, armurier, 596.

Gachette, 84, 87.

Gambeson. V. Gamboison.

Gamboison, 53, 327, 335.

Gans, armurier, 580.

Gantelet, 60, 249, 350 à 355.

Gantelet articulé, 353, 354.

— miton ou moufle, 353, 354.

Garde-bras, 250.

Garde-queue, 373.

Gay-Lussac, chimiste, 88.

Garde-reins, 247, 248.

Gardes et contre-gardes de l'épée, 389.

Gastine-Renette, armurier, 90, 570, 597.

Gastrafète, 68, 132.

Gathy, armurier, 600.

Gauloises (armes), 148.

Geisenheim. V. Wittmann.

Gemlich, armurier, 573.

Genève (arsenal de), 20, 291, 297, 300, 303, 409, 425, 445, 457, 474, 505, 537.

— (musée de), 159, 167.

Georg, armurier, 582.

Gerlach de Berlin, armurier, 556, 558, 580.

— de Meerholz, id., 580.

Germanique (musée), à Nuremberg, 534.

Germaniques (armes), 41, 94, 99, 144, 145, 166, 167, 168, 169, 170, 171, 172, 173, 174, 180, 181, 182.

Ghinello, armurier, 562.

Giacatane, armurier, 562, 587.

Giberne, 87.

Giverde, armurier, 597.

Goloises (armes), 40, 95, 99.

Goodrich-Court (collection de). V. Llewelyn-Meyrick.

Gorgas, armurier, 582.

Gosuni, armurier, 600.

Gottschalk, armurier, 582.

Gottsche, armurier, 556.

Goupillons (fléaux), 444.

Graf, armurier, 579.

Grains d'orge, 54, 329.

Grappes de raisin, 532.

Grec (armement), 36.

Grecques (armes), 122.

Grenade, 81, 532.

Grenades-carcasses, 532.

Grevelot, fabricant, 90.

Grèves, 249, 356, 361.

Griffe de tigre. V. Wag-Nuk.

Griottier, armurier, 597.

Grosschedl, armurier, 573.

Grue d'Archimède. V. Polyspaste.

Guige, 129, 307.

Guillaume III (collection du roi de Prusse), 137.

Guillaume le Conquérant (armes de), 49.

Guisarmes, 450, 451, 452.

Gurggey, fabricant de damas, 560.

Gurz, armurier, 581.

Guter, armurier, 555.
Gutzinger, armurier, 577.
Gwalior (fabriques d'armes à), 571, 601.

H

Hache de mineurs, 463.
Haches d'armes, 458 à 463.
Hachner, armurier, 574.
Hall (musée de la porte de), 21.
Hallebardes, 464, 465.
Hallstadt (cimetière de), 41.
Hamata, 38, 135.
Hamerl, armurier, 578.
Hamus ferreus. V. Chausse-trape.
Hanovre (musée de la ville de), 94, 147, 166, 174, 364.
Hanovre (musée Welf ou Guelfe), 291, 320.
Haquebuse, 510, 535.
— double, 511, 536.
Harpé, 139.
Hartmann, armurier, 579.
Harz, armurier, 584.
Harzberg (fabriques d'armes à), 571.
Hast, 123.
Hastaire, 37, 134.
Haubergeon, 54.
Haubert, 49, 53, 321.
— (blanc), 334.
Hauer, armurier, 575.
Haur. V. Stauer.
Hauslaub (collection), 283, 284, 453, 475, 480, 481, 484, 485, 486, 487, 493, 494, 503, 520, 521, 523, 533, 565.
Hauser, armurier, 584.
Hausse-col, 244, 245.
Haute-pièce, 255, 256.
Heaume, 54, 269, 270, 271, 272, 273, 274, 275.
Heber, armurier, 584.
Hefner-Alteneck, auteur, 18, 565.
— (collection), 276, 277, 283.
Helvétiques et suisses (armes), 95, 100, 121, 122, 174, 184, 203, 418, 451, 460, 462, 465, 468, 471, 536.
Héraldique, origine du mot, 59.
Heranandez, armurier, 587.
Hermann, armurier, 91.
Heubach, 584.
Heurtoir, 78.
Hewitt, archéologue, 15.

Heimbourg (sculpture à), 187.
Heishaupe, armurier, 579.
Hindou (armement), 34.
— (armes), 103, 304, 340, 396, 411, 571.
Hildesheinn (sculpture à la cathédrale de), 265.
Hilpert, armurier, 597.
Hiquet, armurier, 599.
Hirsch, armurier, 584.
Histoire abrégée des armes anciennes, 23.
Hoch, armurier, 576.
Hofer, armurier, 573.
Hoffmann, armurier, 575.
Hollandaises (armes), 21, 197, 209, 234.
Hongroises (armes), 101, 159, 236, 237, 292, 385.
Hoplite, 126.
Hopp, armurier, 568, 575.
Horn, armurier, 568, 577.
Hortiz, armurier, 581.
Horum, armurier. V. Horn.
Housseaux, 61, 356, 361.
Howard, chimiste, 88.
Hubert, armurier, 597.
Hunguls (les pierres), 34.
Hussein, armurier, 600.

I

Ibériques (armes), 95, 100.
Imbriquées (cottes), 333.
Incrustations; définition de ce terme, 559.
Indiennes (armes). V. Hindous.
Introduction, 1.
Iohandy, armurier, 587.
Italiennes (armes), 199, 200, 208, 223, 231, 452, 461, 465, 466, 493, 554, 571.
Iumeau, armurier, 595.
Iunkers, armurier, 584.
Ivani, armurier, 452.

J

Jach, armurier, 584.
Jaiedtel, armurier, 584.
Jambières d'hommes d'armes, 356.
— de cheval, id., 374.
Janissaires, 346.

Japonaises (armes), 138, 305, 414.
Jaque d'armes, 327, 334, 338.
Javanaises (armes), 104, 433.
Javelot, 123.
Joute, 65.

K

Kabyle (arme), 415.
Kalb, armurier, 584.
Kampak (épée), 302.
Kandjar (épée), 415.
Kapel, armurier, 580.
Kappe, armurier, 584.
Kaufmann, armurier, 584.
Kayser, armurier, 584.
Keimer, armurier, 577.
Keint, armurier, 576.
Keiser, armurier, 530.
Keller, archéologue, 73, 167, 199.
Kemmerer, armurier, 584.
Kensington (musée de), 104.
Khandjar (épée), 392.
Khoraçan, 560.
Khouttar (dague), 420, 422, 433.
Kinn, armurier, 572.
Kirschbaum, armurier, 574.
Kleinschmidt, armurier, 584.
Klemm (collection), 144, 146, 159, 172, 449, 484, 494.
Klett, armurier, 569, 584.
Klosterdorf (fabriques d'armes à), 571.
Knopf, armurier, 584.
Knout, 444, 446.
Kœnigsmark (l'épée de), 390.
Koiut, armurier, 581.
Koller, armurier, 574.
Kolter, armurier, 576.
Kollmann, armurier, 563, 567, 568, 573.
Koukri (épée), 392.
Krawinsky, armurier, 584.
Kruger, armurier, 584.
Krupp, fabricant, 82, 531.
Kuchenreiter, armurier, 581.
Kulnic, armurier, 580.

L

Lamarre, armurier, 596.
Lamé, armurier, 596.
Lammerer, armurier, 584.
Lahaye (musée de), 82.

Lahore, 601.
Lances, 434 à 439.
Lance-flèche, 439.
Langue-de-bœuf (épée), 399.
— (poignard), 421, 427.
Lansquenette (épée), 393, 405.
— (dague), 421.
Lauzanne (musée de), 159, 167, 425, 451, 519.
Lazarino, armurier, 585.
Lefaucheux, armurier, 90, 570, 597.
Léger, armurier, 576.
Lehner, conservateur, 17.
Leitner, auteur, 14.
Lemery, chimiste, 88.
Lenormand, armurier, 91.
Lepage, armurier, 90, 570.
Leroy, armurier, 90, 597.
Leuwenburg près Cassel (collection à), 318, 552.
Lichtenfels, armurier, 584.
Liebig, chimiste, 88.
Liége (fabriques d'armes à), 560, 570 571.
Liesthal (arsenal de), 20.
Linck, armurier, 577.
Lintz (fabriques d'armes à), 571.
Lintz (musée de), 99, 144, 271, 366.
Liouville, armurier, 596.
Lippe (Van der), armurier, 584.
Lippert, id., 584.
Llewelyn-Meyrick (collection), 15, 95, 100, 126, 152, 153, 173, 253, 256, 281, 293, 300, 301, 304, 317, 319, 321, 340, 343, 344, 346, 366, 367, 371, 380, 383, 388, 431, 433, 437, 441, 444, 445, 449, 452, 457, 460, 461, 463, 467, 468, 507, 554.
Lobkowitz (collection). V. Raudnitz.
Lochaber, 461.
Lofler (Georges), armurier, 79.
Londres (fabriques d'armes à), 571.
Londres (musée de la Tour de), 14, 90, 124, 189, 153, 167, 172, 173, 269, 272, 274, 278, 279, 281, 291, 294, 296, 297, 303, 305, 314, 364, 371, 379, 380, 384, 397, 425, 463, 470, 519, 521, 523, 537, 550, 552, 573.
Lorenz, armurier. V. Plattner.
Loup (marque du), 569.
Louvre (musée du), 30, 32, 109, 112, 113, 114, 115, 116, 121, 124, 125,

149, 150, 169, 171, 173, 263, 294, 364, 367, 394.
Lucerne (arsenal de), 20, 316, 436, 441, 453, 460.
Lumière de fusil, 87.
Lund (musée de), 171, 172.
Lushkur (fabriques d'armes à), 571, 601.
Lyon (musée de), 382.

M

Machines de guerre, 62, 67, 141, 477.
Mackay (général), 84, 469.
Maclée (cotte), 332.
Madrid (fabriques d'armes à), 562.
— (musée d'armes de), 20, 299, 315, 371, 382, 405, 407.
Mahrates (armes), 304.
Mains-gauches, 422, 429, 431, 432.
Mains en fer, 475.
Mailles, 333.
— doubles, 54, 329.
Makl, armurier, 581.
Malchus (épée), 393.
Malero, armurier, 567, 568.
Malte (musée de), 20.
Manceaux, armurier, 597.
Manteaux d'armes, 250, 251, 252.
Manteaux d'évêques en mailles, 327, 335.
Manuel, armurier, 584.
Marchan, armurier, 596.
Marckloff, armurier, 577.
Marinette, armurier, 91.
Marocaines (armes), 416.
Marteaux d'armes, 455, 456, 457.
Marter, armurier, 584.
Martin (Johann), armurier, 577.
Masses d'armes, 440, 441.
Massettes (tournois aux), 66, 275.
Mat, armurier, 552.
Matl, armurier, 576.
Matoir (outil), 560.
Matras (flèche), 72, 506.
Maubeuge (fabriques d'armes à), 571.
Maximiliennes (armures), 57, 218.
May, armurier, 581.
Mayence (musée de), 20, 124, 125, 126, 128, 129, 130, 131, 137, 139, 140, 172, 173.
Mayenfisch (baron de), conservateur, 17.

Mazis (collection), 16.
Médiques (armements). V. Assyriens.
Meiningen (musée de), 321.
Meizen, armurier, 574.
Mentonnières, 250, 251, 252, 255, 256.
Mercier, armurier, 600.
Merville (collection), 410.
Mexicaines (armes), 101, 106, 107.
Meyer-Biermann (collection), 454, 456.
Meyrick, archéologue, 4.
— (collection). V. Llewelyn.
Micharius, armurier, 600.
Michel, armurier, 599.
Milan (fabriques d'armes de), 571.
Milich, peintre, 565.
Miller, armurier, 574.
Mines à brûlots, 79.
— à poudre, 79.
Minié, armurier, 570.
Mire d'arbalète. V. Fronton de mire.
Miséricorde (dague), 421.
Mœnchsbüchse, 85, 537.
Mongoles (armes), 304, 339.
Molettes d'éperon, 61, 362, 363, 364 à 368.
Mondonedo (peinture à), 206.
Monogrammes d'armuriers, 572.
Monti, auteur, 467.
Mora, armurier, 587.
Morat (arsenal à), 20, 364, 443, 519, 534.
Morgenstern, 442, 443.
Morions (casques), 294.
Mors de bride, 386.
Mortiers, 75, 80, 513, 514.
Motto, armurier, 585.
Moum, armurier, 574.
Mousquet, 85, 611.
— fusil, 469.
— tonnerre, 88, 543.
— tromblon. V. Mousquet-tonnerre.
Mudavien (fabriques d'armes à), 340.
Müler, armurier, 577, 597.
Müller, armurier, 580, 584.
Müller, armurier, 556.
Munich (arsenal de la ville de), 18, 295, 319, 503, 506, 573.
Munich (bibliothèque de), 33, 180, 233, 267, 270, 441, 447, 493, 535.
Munich (cabinet d'estampes à), 460, 461, 474.
Munich (musée national à), 18, 30, 99, 145, 146, 149, 166, 170, 172, 173,

187, 335, 337, 341, 365, 366, 377, 395, 396, 398, 399, 400, 401, 409, 432.
Munster (Andrieux), armurier, 573.
Munster (Peter), armurier, 407, 573.

MUSÉES ET ARSENAUX, mentionnés dans cet ouvrage et qui ont été classés dans la table selon les initiales des *villes* où ces musées se trouvent :

Musée d'Amsterdam.
— d'artillerie à Paris.
— impérial à Vienne.
— de la ville de Vienne.
— d'antiquités, à Vienne.
— industriel, à Vienne.
— d'Augsbourg.
— d'Avenches.
— royal de Berlin.
— du palais Montbijou à Berlin.
— du prince Charles à Berlin.
— Britannique à Londres.
— de Brunswick.
— au Belvédère. V. Vienne.
— à Bruxelles, à la porte de Hall.
— de Carlsruhe.
— de Cassel.
— de Cluny.
— de Copenhague.
— de Dresde.
— d'Epinal.
— d'Erbach.
— de Fribourg en Suisse.
— de Genève.
— Germanique. V. Nuremberg.
— Guelfe. V. Hanovre.
— de Hanovre.
— de Kensington à Londres.
— de Lahaye.
— de Lauzanne.
— de Lintz.
— du Louvre.
— de Lucerne.
— de Lund.
— de Lyon.
— de Madrid.
— de Malte.
— de Mayence.
— de Meiningen.
— de médailles à Paris.
— de Munich.
— de Naples.
— de Neville.

Musée de Nuremberg.
— de Prague.
— de Raudnitz.
— de Ratisbonne.
— de Rouen.
— de Saint-Germain.
— de Salzbourg.
— de Schaffhouse.
— de Schwerin.
— de Sigmaringen.
— de Soleure.
— de Stockholm. V. Suède.
— de Szokau (Hongrie).
— de Turin.
— Tzarskoë-Selo. V. Pétersbourg.
— de la Tour de Londres.
— de Vannes.
— de Venise.
— de Vienne.
— de Woolwich.
— Welfes. V. Hanovre.
— de Zurich.
Muserolles, 374.
Mutto, armurier, 562.

N

Naples (musée de), 116.
Napoléon III (collection d'armes de l'empereur), 19, 30, 213.
Naumann, armurier, 585.
Naumbourg (sculpture à), 186.
Neufchâtel (sculpture à), 203.
Neureuter, armurier, 585.
Neville (musée), 364.
Neuville (musée de), 523.
Niellure (définition de la), 560.
Nieuwerkerke (collection d'armes du comte de), 20, 39, 48, 182, 198, 212, 213, 253, 255, 256, 264, 271, 276, 277, 281, 295, 296, 321, 342, 344, 371, 372, 380, 395, 396, 398, 399, 425, 427, 429, 431, 466, 500.
Nigroli, armurier, 562, 585.
Nock, armurier, 581.
Noix d'arbalète, 405.
Nordmann, armurier, 585.
Normands (armes et armements), 50, 188, 189, 309.
Nuremberg (arsenal de), 80, 82.
— (musée Germanique à), 375, 379.
Nurwur, 601.
Nuterisch, armurier, 581.

O

Obsidienne, 101.
Ocræ, 38, 134.
Odet (collection), 199, 200, 377,
Oertel, armurier, 585.
Oit, armurier, 585.
Olbernhau (fabriques d'armes à), 571.
Olivier de la Marche, chroniqueur, 450.
Ombilic, 129, 306.
Ombriens, 125.
Onagre, 68, 479.
Oppy (Van), armurier, 599.
Orange (arc d'), 41.
Orges à serpentins, 80, 528.
Orgoz (fabriques d'armes à), 562.
Oringen, armurier, 580.
Orla (Johannes de la), armurier, 585.
Ossine, 93.
Otto, armurier, 585.
Oviedo (fabriques d'armes à), 571.
Oziersky (collection), 159.

P

Paczelt, armurier, 578.
Padoue, 82.
Pah (Peter), armurier, 567.
Paixhans, 82, 531.
Palme (le) (mesure), 549.
Parazonium, 36, 137, 139.
Parham (collection), 270.
Paris (musée d'artillerie de), 15, 90, 112,
124, 125, 126, 127, 128, 129, 130,
131, 137, 138, 339, 140, 141, 150,
167, 169, 170, 171, 172, 173, 214,
219, 245, 246, 247, 248, 253, 256,
267, 270, 272, 273, 274, 278, 280,
285, 287, 288, 289, 291, 293, 295,
297, 299, 300, 301, 302, 303, 305,
312, 314, 315, 316, 317, 319, 320,
337, 339, 341, 346, 353, 360, 361,
365, 366, 371, 377, 383, 384, 385,
388, 395, 397, 399, 404, 406, 407,
408, 411, 412, 414, 415, 416, 417,
418, 419, 427, 432, 433, 436, 438,
439, 441, 445, 447, 448, 449, 451,
456, 457, 460, 462, 463, 466, 468,
476, 484, 493, 502, 504, 521, 534,
542, 558, 572, 573, 574, 575, 576.
Paris (bibliothèque impériale de), 183,
263, 271, 3?

Paris (Id. de l'arsenal), 205, 440, 446.
— (cabinet de médailles à), 195, 405.
— (cabinet de médailles à), 125, 169.
Parma, 38, 132.
Pas-d'âne (de l'épée), 383, 401, 407.
Passau (fabriques d'armes à), 568.
Passes d'armes, 63.
Passe-volant, 80, 515.
Passot (épée de), 393.
Pather, armurier, 574.
Pauly, armurier, 88, 90, 599.
Pavois (boucliers), 312, 313.
Peabody, armurier, 91.
Pédieux. V. Solerets.
Pedro. V. Mallero, armurier.
Penguilly-l'Haridon, conservateur, 16,
19, 45.
Pèlerines en mailles, 327, 335.
Percussion (fusil à), 88, 546.
Pérouse, 82, 88.
Persanes (armes), 301, 339, 368, 385,
412, 433, 493, 571.
Perses (armes), 233.
Perses (anciens armements). V. Assy-
riens.
Persiques (armements). V. Assyriens.
Pertuisanes, 467.
Perugia. V. Pérouse.
Pétard, 81.
Peter, armurier, 580.
Pétersbourg (musée de). V. Tzárskoc-
Selo.
Pétrinal, 83.
Pfaff, armurier, 583.
Pfeffenhauser, armurier, 574.
Pgerttel, armurier, 580.
Phalariques, 478, 506.
Piatti, armurier, 562.
Picinio, armurier, 562, 585.
Pierre (boulets en), 77.
Pierriers, 80, 515.
Pilum, 38.
Pilles, 69, 491.
Pillizoni, armurier, 562.
Piques, 434.
Piqueur (de fusil). V. Double détente.
Pistoia, 88.
Pistolet, 88, 549.
— revolver, 90, 91.
Piston. V. Percussion.
Pistor, armurier, 583.
Plascencia (fabriques d'armes à), 571.
Plastron, 57, 244, 256.

Platine à chenapan, 544.
Platines à mèche, 535.
— à rouet, 541.
— à silex, 544.
Plattner (Lorenz), armurier, 563.
Plongeur (appareils de), 484.
Poëter, armurier, 577.
Pœtzi, armurier, 583.
Poignards, 420.
Poires à poudre, 554, 555.
Polonaises (armes), 292, 303, 367, 463.
Polz, armurier, 374, 583.
Polygares (armes), 304, 340.
Polyspatse, 39.
Portalès (collection), 138.
Porte-mèche pour canon, 532.
Postindol, armurier, 587.
Pots-en-tête, 283, 285.
Poudre à canon, 72.
Poulaine (chaussures dites à la), 61.
Prague (fabriques d'armes à), 571.
Prague (musée de), 41, 95, 150, 159,
264, 271, 279, 287, 367, 383, 429,
445, 533, 552, 554.
— (bibliothèque), 283.
Prantner, armurier, 577.
Presselmeyer, armurier, 583.
Prisse d'Avesnes, archéologue, 35, 119,
121.
Prum, armurier, 574.
Pulverin, 89, 554.
Pulvermassen, 554.
Puyséjour, lieutenant général, 469.
Pyrite jaune. V. Pyrite sulfureuse.
Pyrite sulfureuse, 84.
Pyrite marcassite. V. Pyrite sulfureuse.
Pyrite martiale. V. Pyrite sulfureuse.

Q

Quade (armement), 44.
— armurier, 583.
Quillons (de l'épée), 389.

R

Radoc (Henri), arquebusier, 86, 597.
Rainures sur les lames d'épée, 167.
Rapière, 390, 407.
Rasch, armurier, 583.
Raudnitz (bibliothèque à), 193, 447.
— (collection d'armes à), 399, 471,
553, 558.

Rayure, 82, 85.
Ratisbonne (musée de), 379.
Recettes pour les amateurs, 607.
Rechold, armurier, 583.
Reck, armurier, 583.
Reichert, armurier, 583.
Reitz, armurier, 569.
Reme, armurier, 583.
Remscheid (fabriques d'armes à), 571.
Rener, armurier, 583.
Renier, armurier, 596.
Renné (collection), 255, 278, 281, 335,
379, 436, 457.
Repoussé (définition du), 561.
Reyer, armurier, 579.
Revolvers, 89, 90, 91, 546, 551, 552.
Ribaud, 79.
Ribaudequins, 79, 525.
Riegel, armurier, 580.
Rischer, armurier, 583.
Robert, armurier, 597.
Rodios, auteur, 39, 68, 132.
Rodolphe de Nuremberg, tréfileur, 52,
563.
Romaines (armes), 133.
Romano (collection du collége), 139.
Romero, armurier, 585.
Romington, armurier, 91.
Roncones, 466.
Rondaches (boucliers), 316, 317.
Rondelles (boucliers), 318, 319, 320.
— de lance, 253.
— de plastron, 245, 254.
Ronseurs, 466.
Roscher, armurier, 583.
Rouen (musée de), 149.
Rouet (de platine), 84.
Rubens (Benjamin), savant, 82.
Rubersburg, armurier, 597.
Rucoca, armurier, 587.
Rudolstadt, 601.
Ruef, armurier, 577.
Russes (armes), 101, 159, 300, 461,
571.
Russikon (les antiquités du château de),
67.
Rustrée (cotte), 332.

S

Sabini, armurier, 140.
Sabre, 33, 391.
Sabres de Mahomed, 391.

Sac de munition pour arquebusier, 553.
Sucken (baron de), auteur, 13, 143.
Saeter, armurier, 583.
Saint-Blasien (fabriques d'armes à), 571.
Saint-Clément, id., 562.
Saint-Etienne, id., 571.
Saint-Gall (bibliothèque de), 178, 181, 186, 263.
Saint-Germain (musée de), 20, 101, 131, 138, 149, 159, 170, 172.
Saint-Maurice (trésors de), 182, 264.
Saint-Remi, auteur, 85.
Salades (casques), 278.
Salzbourg (musée de), 436.
Samnites (armes), 138.
Sander, armurier, 577.
Saragosse (fabriques d'armes à), 562.
Sarbacane, 490.
Sarrasines (armes), 341.
Sars, armurier, 556, 558, 580.
Savoisiennes (armes), 409.
Sayettes, 69, 491.
Scala librorum, 79.
Scandinaves (armes), 95, 96, 100, 155, 175, 190, 201, 387.
Schachner, armurier, 577.
Schackau, armurier, 583.
Schaffhouse (musée de), 370.
Schaller, armurier, 574.
Schedel, armurier, 584.
Scheffield (fabrique d'armes à), 571.
Schiavona, 452.
Schiesprügel, 443.
Schoenberg, armurier, 573.
Schoyt, armurier, 572.
Schram, armurier, 584.
Schreiber, armurier, 556.
Schrenck, auteur, 13.
Schulze, armurier, 584.
Schwarz, moine, 73, 563.
— peintre, 565.
Schwerin (musée de), 20.
Sclaves (armes), 169, 462.
Sclopeto. V. Escopette.
Scorpion (fouet d'armes), 444, 445.
Scrama-sax, 44, 167, 167, 168, 169, 420.
Sedan (musée d'armes de), 16.
Seitel, armuriers, 578.
Selier, armurier, 596.
Selles, 62, 375 à 380.
— (canon), 80, 515, 528.
Serpentin (platine), 84, 535.

Serpentin-revolver, 80.
Servant, 77.
Seussenhofer (Wilhelm), armurier, 563, 568, 573.
— (Joerg), armurier, 573.
Séville (fabriques d'armes à), 562.
Shahjehanabad, 601.
Sigl, armurier, 575.
Siegling, armurier, 556, 580.
Sigmaringen (musée de), 17, 19, 45, 80, 90, 94, 144, 145, 146, 147, 166, 168, 170, 171, 172, 173, 174, 211, 275, 287, 312, 313, 337, 364, 365, 366, 367, 382, 383, 385, 404, 405, 407, 408, 413, 425, 429, 431, 432, 443, 448, 451, 452, 456, 457, 463, 465, 466, 472, 475, 476, 487, 494, 524, 542, 543, 546, 550, 555, 573, 604.
Signum, 141.
Sililos (fabriques d'armes à), 571.
Simonin, armurier, 596.
Six (collection), 197.
Snider, armurier, 91.
Soeter (collection), 275, 344, 366, 399, 427, 470, 494.
Soie (de l'épée), 389.
Soler, armurier, 581.
Solerets (chaussures de fer), 60, 61, 249, 356, 359, 360.
Soleure (arsenal de), 20, 81, 289, 292, 345, 302, 447, 451, 528.
Solinge (fabrique d'armes à), 568, 571.
Sollen (collection), 140.
Soltikoff (collection), 429, 438.
Spacierer, armurier, 579.
Spacini, armurier, 562.
Spaldeck, armurier, 584.
Spandeau (fabriques d'armes à), 571.
Spencer, armurier, 90, 548.
Spengel (collection), 279, 285, 349, 398, 553.
Speyer (Facka), armurier, 557.
Spirales, 80, 513.
Springenklee, armurier, 568.
Squamata, 38, 135.
Stack, armurier, 583.
Starck, armurier, 583.
Stauer, armurier, 567.
Stecher. V. Double détente.
Stephan, armurier, 598.
Stirlets, armurier, 581.
Stockmar, armurier, 580.

Stodart, fabricant de damas, 560.

Stranglé, armurier, 599.

Strasbourg (arsenal de), 16.

Stumpf, armurier, 577.

Stuttgard (bibliothèque de), 180, 182, 184, 263, 464.

Stylets, 420, 422, 429, 432.

Suède. V. la coll. de Charles XV, roi de Suède.

Suhl. V. Suhla.

Suhla (fabriques d'armes à), 569, 571.

Suisse (arsenaux), 20.

— (armes). V. Helvétiques.

Szokau (musée de), 463.

T

Table des chapitres, 609.

Taille des hommes anciens, 56.

Talon (de l'épée), 389.

Tambour turc, 476.

Tanner, armurier, 583.

Targes (boucliers), 309, 310, 311, 314, 315.

Targettes (boucliers), 321.

Tassette, 246, 247.

Tendermann, armurier, 600.

Tercerol. V. Coup-de-poing.

Ternow (collection), 553.

Tesack. V. Dusack.

Teschen (fabriques d'armes à), 571.

Tétière, 371.

Théodose (colonne), 138, 176, 449.

Thomas, armurier, 595.

Thomson, armurier, 598.

Thuraine, armurier, 596.

Til, armurier, 584, 594.

Tilemann, armurier, 577.

Toel, armurier, 583.

Tolède (fabriques d'armes à), 562, 571.

Tombeaux (construction des), 29, 148.

Tormentum, 68, 477.

Tortue, 30, 132.

Touariques (armes), 417.

Toula (fabriques d'armes à), 571.

Tour de Londres (collections à la). V. Londres.

Tourillons, 78, 513, 515.

Tournevis-amorçoir, 553.

Tournois, 63.

Trajane (Colonne), 137, 138, 139.

Trébuchet, armurier, 572.

Trébuchets (machines de guerre), 477.

Tréfiler (l'art de), 563.

Treillissée (cotte), 333.

Tromblon, 543.

Trou de lumière de fusil. V. Lumière.

Troyon, archéologue, 170.

Troyon (collection), 451.

Tumelières, 356.

Turin (l'Armeria à), 17, 124, 126, 292, 317, 321.

Turin (fabriques d'armes à), 571.

Turques (armes), 340, 412, 413, 415, 462.

Turschen-Reith (nom d'armurier ou de localité), 579.

Tzagara (arbalète), 68.

Tzarskoe-Selo (musée de), 20, 300, 302, 303, 304, 411, 433, 461.

U

Ulrich, armurier, 583.

Umbo. V. Ombilic.

Utter, armurier, 579.

V

Valadolid (fabriques d'armes à), 562.

Valence, id., 562.

Valentin, armurier, 569.

Van Achen, peintre, 565.

Vannes (musée de), 99.

Vauban, 87, 469.

Vauquelin, chimiste, 88.

Veban, armurier, 577.

Vélite, 37, 134.

Vencinas, armurier, 587.

Venise (musée de), 20.

— (sculptures à), 209.

Verdeur (épée), 393.

Verge (de fléau), 444.

Versailles (carabine de), 85.

— (fabriques d'armes à), 571.

Vett, armurier, 583.

Veuglaires, 76, 80, 515, 521.

Vieillard, armurier, 597.

Vienne (arsenal impérial à), 13, 75, 90, 215, 217, 218, 222, 223, 224, 225, 226, 228, 229, 231, 236, 237, 238, 246, 253, 274, 287, 288, 289, 294, 298, 317, 342, 343, 345, 353, 371, 401, 409, 419, 427, 443, 447, 449, 454, 465, 475, 513, 521.

Vienne (arsenal de la ville de), 14, 288, 429, 466.
Vienne (musée des antiquités à), 99, 125, 141, 144, 146, 147, 166, 170.
Vienne (Bibliothèque impériale à), 202.
— (Musée industriel à), 289, 290, 294, 400, 407, 456.
Vienne (Gewehrkammer), 501.
Vienne (Musée au belvédère de), 36, 119.
Villaseca (collection à), 405.
Vincent, armurier, 597.
Vireton, 72, 506.
Vischer, armurier, 574.
Vis-porte-lance, 255.
Vitt, armurier, 599.
Voigt, armurier, 583.
Volée, 76, 515.
Vouges, 453.
Voulgiers, 453.
Vrel, armurier, 556, 580.
Vulff, V, Bulff, armurier, 567.

W

Waas, armurier, 583.
Waenzel, armurier, 91.
Waerndl, armurier, 91.
Wagner, armurier, 579.
Wag-Nuk (arme), 423, 433.
Waldburg-Wolfegg (bibliothèque du prince de), 470, 522, 681.
Walster, armurier, 583.
Walzen, armurier, 600.
Warwick (collection au château de), 277, 286, 383, 400.
Wazungen, armurier, 577.
Weigel, auteur, 80.
Werner, armurier, 556.

Wersberg, armurier, 574.
Wertschgen, armurier, 583.
Widter (collection), 365.
Wiener-Neustadt (fabrique d'armes à), 571.
Wiifing, armurier, 579.
Winchester, armurier, 90, 91, 548.
Wittmann (collection), 454.
Woolwich (arsenal de), 532, 552.
Worsaae, archéologue, 154.
Wyndd, armurier, 599.
Wys, armurier, 599.

Y

Yatagan (épée), 392, 414, 415.

Z

Zanguebars (armes des), 16, 417.
Zaruba, armurier, 578.
Zend (la langue), 32.
Zergh, armurier, 583.
Zollner (Caspar), arquebusier, 85.
— (Rilian), arquebusier, 576.
Zu-Rhein (collection), 266.
Zurich armurier, 583.
Zurich (arsenal de), 20, 81, 285, 341, 404, 436, 447, 451, 453, 463, 506, 527.
Zurich (musée de), 30, 44, 45, 67, 100, 159, 168, 172, 174, 485, 531.
Zwalter, armurier, 579.

P. S. Voir pour les armuriers espagnols du seizième au dix-huitième siècle, la liste alphabétique, pages 589 à 594 et 595.

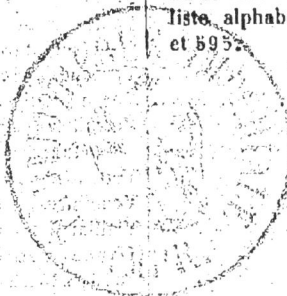

Paris. — Imp. P.-A. BOURDIER, CAPIOMONT fils et Cie, rue des Poitevins, 6.

www.ingramcontent.com/pod-product-compliance
Lightning Source LLC
Chambersburg PA
CBHW060831220326
41599CB00017B/2305